Fourth Edition

photo/IMAGING

Formerly PHOTOCOMMUNICATION

How to communicate with camera and computer

David H. Curl
Adjunct Professor of Art
Kalamazoo College

A text designed for
first-semester college courses
in art, communication
and photojournalism,
and for adult independent study

"The real function of a formal education is to teach you how to educate yourself when you're done with your formal education."

— Edward Albee, playwright

Oak Woods Media

Library of Congress Cataloging-in-Publication Data

Curl, David.
Photo/IMAGING : how to communicate with camera and computer / David H. Curl. — 4th ed.
p. cm.
Rev. ed. of: Photocommunication. 3rd ed. c1991.
"A text designed for first-semester college courses in art, communication and photojournalism, and for adult self-study."
Includes bibliographical references and index.
ISBN 0-88196-009-8
1. Photography. I. Curl, David. Photocommunication. II. Title.
TR145.C976 1997
770--dc21 97-4064
CIP

Printed in the United States of America
with soy-based ink on recycled paper

PRINTED WITH SOY INK

Published by Oak Woods Media
PO Box 19127
Kalamazoo MI 49019
(616) 375-5621

ISBN 0-88196-009-8

Notes:

- ***When specific products are mentioned in the text, it should be assumed that the name is a registered trademark owned by the manufacturer.***

- ***Masculine pronouns occuring within quotations or elsewhere should be interpreted as gender neutral.***

On Vision

So
you've come
to ask me
to teach you photography.

By means of the tools
I shall oblige;
for son,
the mechanics
may be easy.

But once you have
mastered these,
                    please,
do not return
to ask me
                    for vision.

For
you must first
learn of yourself
and life in others,
before
you learn
to see.

Judith Baker Martin

KENNETH ZELNIS

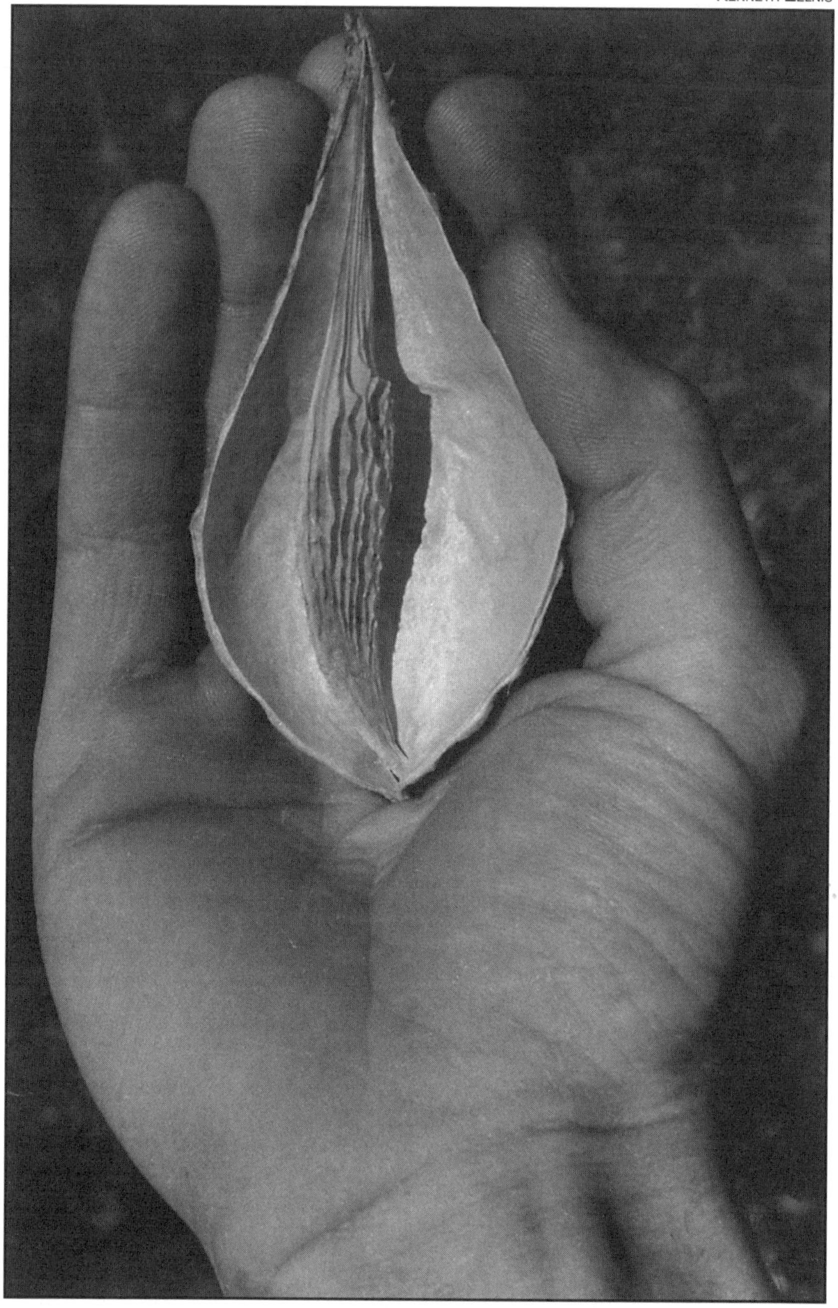

"When simple forms are repeated they bring to the eye the kind of pleasure that music brings to the ear."

— Victor B. Scheffer, educator

Preface to the Fourth Edition

"As you grow older, art and life become the same thing."

— Georges Braque, artist

Many people must share the credit for any success this book may have as a teaching tool. I am proud that my teachers have included such giants of photography as Ansel Adams, Eliot Porter, Henry Holmes Smith, Jerry N. Uelsmann, and Clarence White Jr. Many others have shared with me both insight and information

Those who have taught me the most over the years, however, have been my own students who have shown me that the best way to learn something is to attempt to teach it to others.

"'What is the use of a book,' thought Alice, 'without pictures ...'"

— Lewis Carroll, author

Most of the photographs in this book are typical of the excellent work that can be expected from college students. These fine images were created in response to class assignments and I have given credit to each photographer in the appropriate caption. The spot-news photo by Brian Lanker on page 25 is reproduced by courtesy of the Topeka *Capital-Journal*. Steve Curl and Rich Zesiger created many of the line drawings throughout the book, while most of those in Chapter Seven were originated by James A. Nemsik.

"The eternal struggle of art is to leave out all but the essential."

— Oliver Wendell Holmes, poet

The numerous quotations punctuating and illuminating the text came from various sources — many of which, unfortunately, must remain undocumented. Scholastic Magazines Inc. and the International Fund for Concerned Photography generously gave permission to quote frequently the words of great photographers as spoken in the *Images of Man* audiovisual series. *The Daybooks of Edward Weston,* published by Horizon Press and George Eastman House, provided many significant short quotations, as did Ansel Adams' *Basic Photo Series,* published by Morgan & Morgan.

"No work is ever finished. It is merely abandoned."

Joseph Conrad, author

Lloyd Chilton and Dave Novack of Macmillan Publishing Co. made possible the 1978 first edition of this book. Completion of the latest revision was encouraged and expedited by Tom Thinnes, Diane Worden and Ardyce Czuchna-Curl. To them, to my students who contributed images and advice, and to all the other people who helped in so many ways, I offer a humble and sincere thank you!

Your suggestions for improving the next edition will be welcome.

"Much madness is divinest sense To a discerning eye; Much sense the starkest madness."

— Emily Dickinson, poet

Jorg Jasper

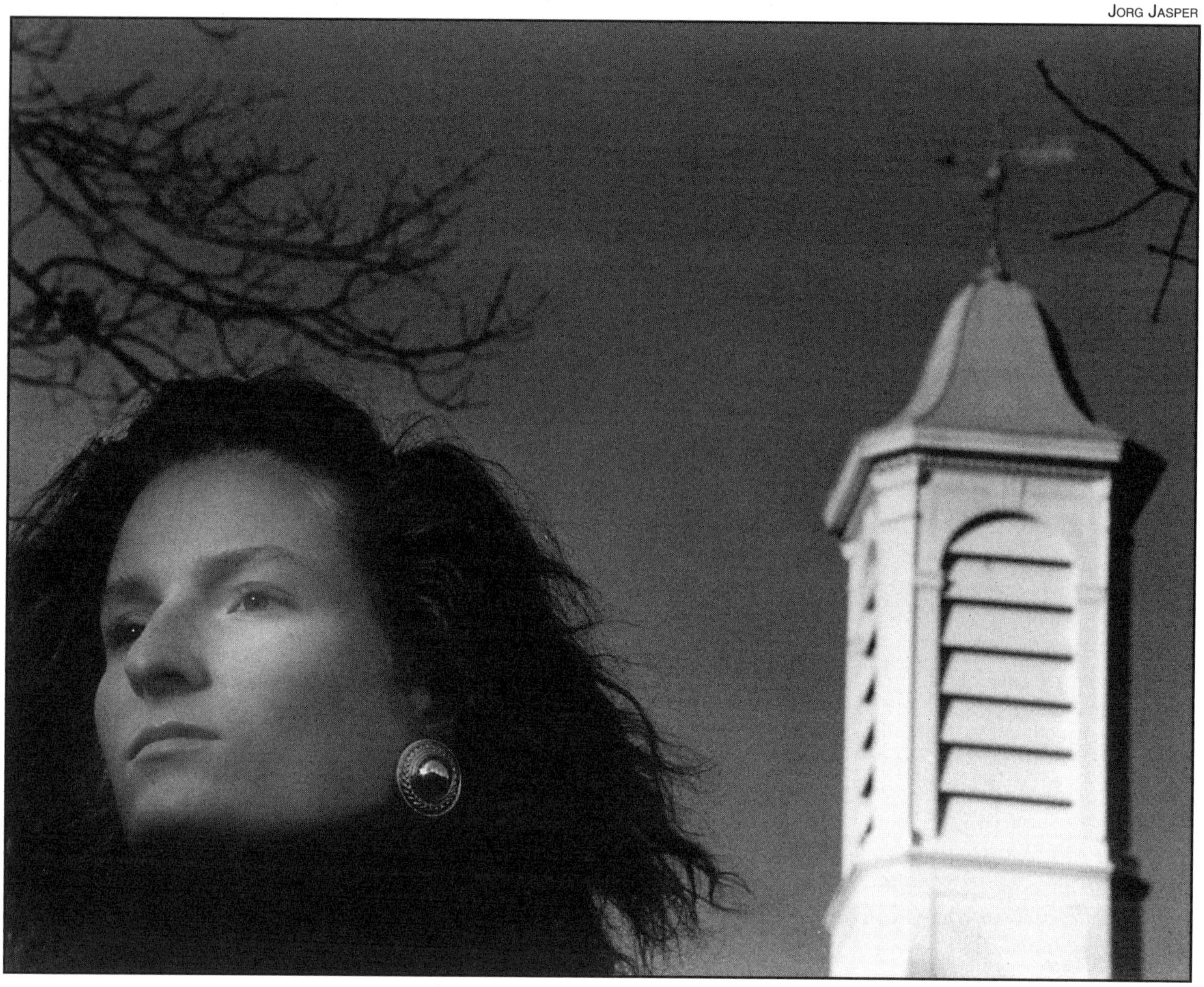

"The seasons have changed
And the light
And the weather
And the hour.
But it is the same land.
And I begin to know the map
And to get my bearings."

— Dag Hammarskjold, statesman

Table of Contents

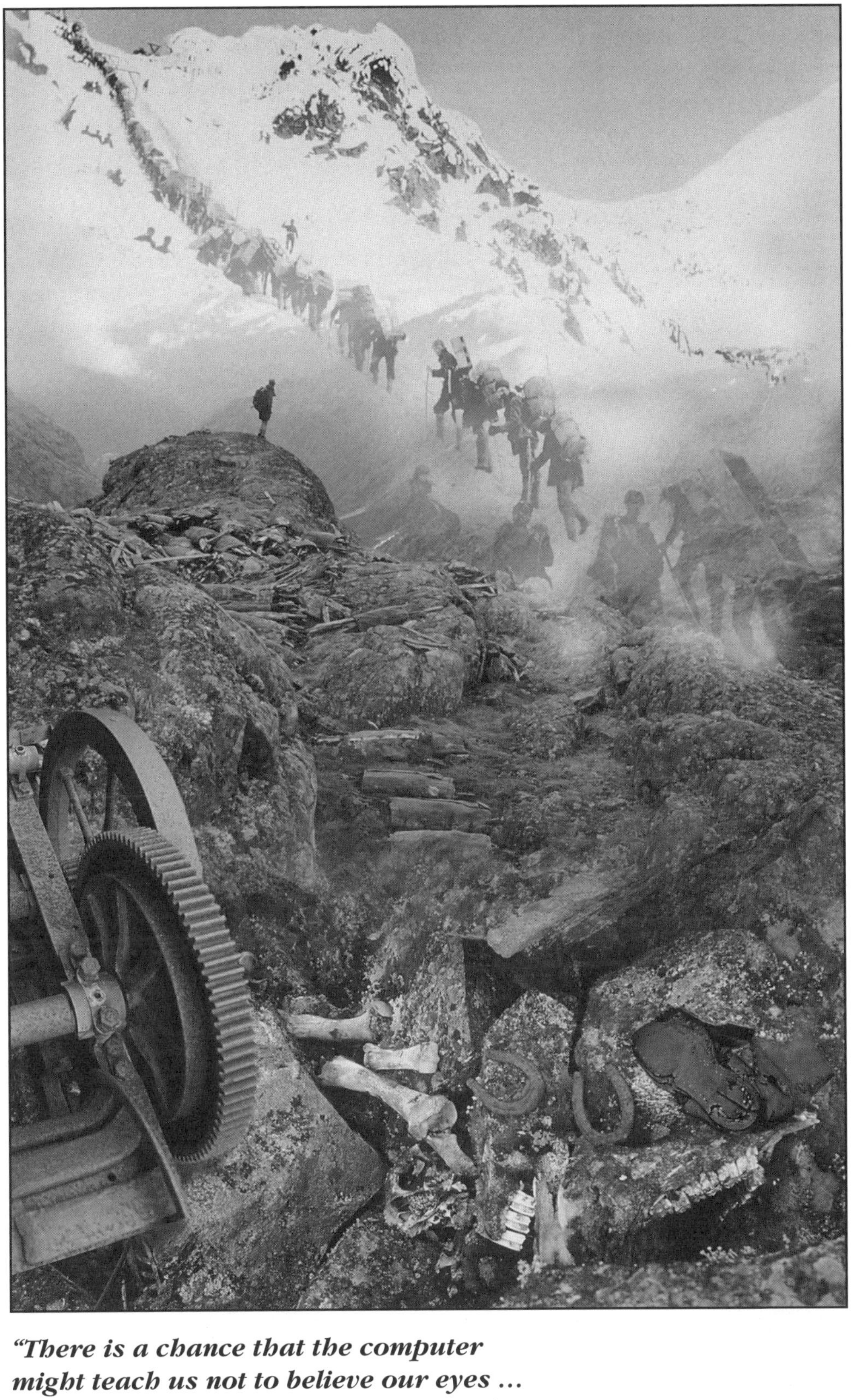

"There is a chance that the computer might teach us not to believe our eyes ... The question is what will we believe if we no longer believe what we see!"

— Vicki Goldberg, critic and author

David H. Curl

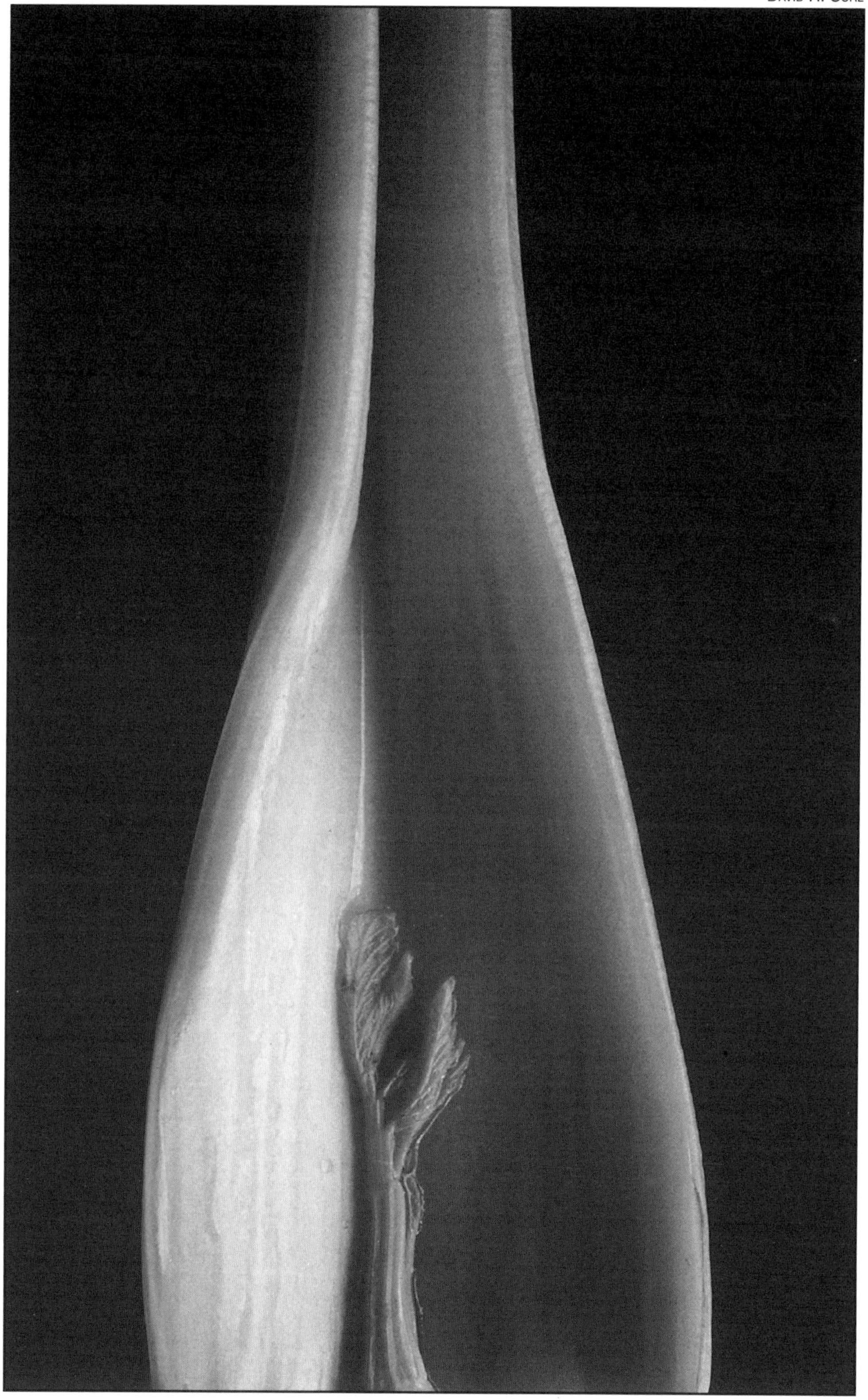

"... That split second when the familiar suddenly is transformed into the profoundly new ..."

— Larry West, photographer

Introduction

The "Aha!" Phenomenon

It happened again this morning. The "aha!" phenomenon when ideas begin to click into place in students' minds.Their eyes light up. Sometimes grins flash across their faces. A teacher lives for this kind of moment.

I began the discussion by showing the class a large black-and-white photograph of a stalk of celery with a new sprout growing inside it. This image always stimulates perception and comment. After asking, "What is it?" I received the following response:

"A stalk of celery," Mark responded immediately. Then Marlene added, "With a sprout inside."

"OK, that's what it *is.* Now, *what else* is it?" I asked. "Let's try word association. Give me single words ... short phrases."

"Growth," Jerrie exclaimed. Other students offered such words as fresh, crisp, moist, green, rejuvenation, protection and spring.

I turned the photo upside down.

"Birth," Mary said. "A stream of milk being poured from a pitcher," Kevin observed.

Upside down, the growing sprout became also the dangling tail of a horse or a donkey. Held sideways, the image became a landscape of snow-covered hills; then a canoe.

Then I asked, "Where did these ideas come from? Why did we get reactions like these from looking at a picture of a vegetable?"

Most of these young women and men are first-year students and they are quick learners.

Kate, an English major, explained: "It's like *simile* in language. Visual simile is when something *looks like* something else ..." Deanna interrupted: "You mean like when we saw that the celery looked like a landscape when we looked at it one way and, upside down, it reminded someone of the rear end of a horse?"

"Yes," Kate continued. "And visual *metaphor* is when an object in a picture represents something abstract or completely different. As when people mentioned spring and birth and growth. A metaphor is a symbol that only has meaning people bring to it from their personal experience."

How could I have said it better myself?

The best part is that I didn't have to explain anything. The students discovered — spontaneously — a connection between verbal and visual language — between literature and art. Because they observed it themselves, they'll retain the concept and use it. Many of the photographs they make in future weeks will reveal new vision. They will perceive before their eyes and lenses familiar subject matter enriched by what Ansel Adams described as *endless horizons of meaning.*

Art and Science

Far from enjoying photography as art, many people are more intrigued with the technical aspects of the medium. Some enjoy testing the latest cameras and lenses and comparing films and developers. In science departments, photography courses often are organized around physics and chemistry. Journalism programs emphasize communication. Technical schools teach technique and processes. Many courses are based on the history of the medium. Frequently, instructors teach *about* photography in the hope that students somehow will be able to apply this basic knowledge creatively within their vocational goals.

"Photography is at once a science and an art ... inseparably linked throughout its astonishing rise from a substitute for skill of hand to an independent art form."

— Beaumont Newhall, historian

At first I taught photography as if it were *not* an art form but a scientific, academic subject. To my surprise, I discovered that some students were becoming effective imagemakers not so much because of the facts I had been teaching them, but because of an internal urge to express their own observations and feelings. My students taught me that no one can be taught to be a artist or a communicator — that one must learn by doing.

"To help persons learn ... don't give them a lecture full of directions ... Get them started doing the very thing they want to learn."

— Kenneth Macrorie, educator

Another mistake I made was to assume that one had to master the fundamentals of technique before being able to communicate. But now I realize that was a very old-fashioned idea. It's like saying that before a young child can write an exciting story about something of interest, the child must first memorize all the rules of perfect punctuation, spelling, and grammar.

"It is more important to generate enthusiasm than to convey knowlege. Knowledge is easily forgotten, while enthusiasm makes anything possible."

— Harold Allen, educator

Now I think I've learned the secret: first you should become excited about photography — or about writing — by photographing or by writing. Once you get to doing a thing, you'll discover "how to" soon enough. This book will be a handy resource to look up stuff when you're ready for it.

"I am excited by the need to render what I personally experience."

— Claude Monet, painter

Communication Comes First

"Art is the affirmation of life."

— Alfred Stieglitz, photographer

"Life, or its eternal evidence, is everywhere."

— Ansel Adams, photographer

"Technique is simply the means of conveying to the printing paper what the photographer has seen so that someone else might see it, too."

— Margery Mann, educator

Technical processes merely are means to an end — means to creating an image that communicates something to someone else or expresses the image maker's feelings or impressions of a situation or subject. Although technique — the essential *craft* of photography — is important enough to be stressed in this book and in my course, I believe it is a mistake to treat technique as if it were an end in itself.

"You can have craft without art; but not art without craft."

— Ansel Adams, photographer

For most people, technique is easiest to learn. The hardest part is learning to see and to visualize.

"Seeing means perceiving the visual relationships that exist in the world. Visualizing means perceiving visual relationships ... as they will exist as translated into a photographic print."

— Phil Davis, educator

Let's take technical details in small doses and invest most of our time in opening up eyes and stimulating imagination. Would it surprise you to learn that many top professional photographers don't do any of their own darkroom work? (But at some point most of them learned how). Paradoxically, there are thousands of competent technicians who rarely produce any photographs that, from an artistic point of view, are worth viewing.

MICKEY HOWELL

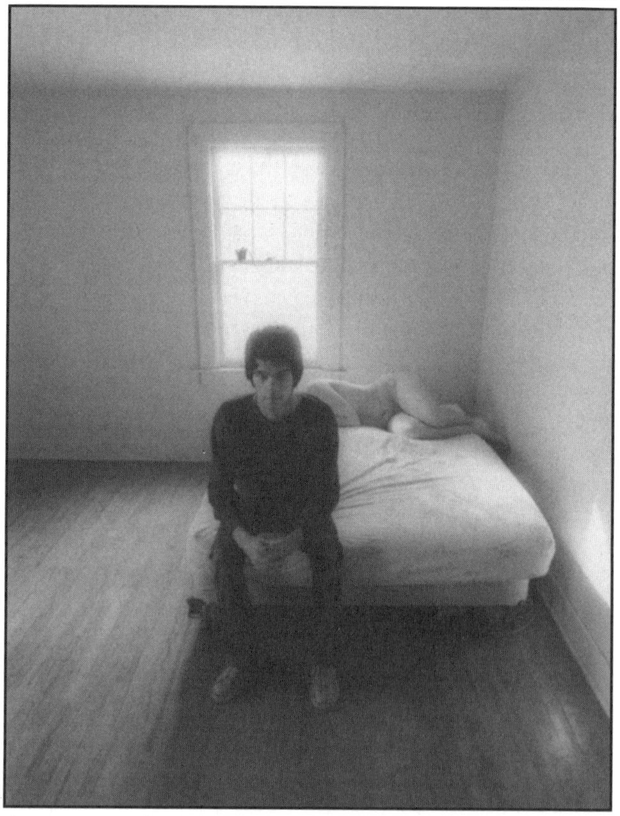

Are you puzzled and intrigued by the bizarre lack of information in this photograph? Why is the room empty except for the bed and the tiny plant in the window? Why are the man and woman juxtaposed in this manner?

"I believe in making the best pictures you can, even if nobody likes them."

— David Vestal, photographer

You should start by making photographs that mean something to you, despite technical flaws, and then see how other people react. To my surprise, I have found that this simple system works especially well with beginning photogaphers — those who are not yet aware of what they cannot do because of "limitations" of the medium. Students blossom rapidly within a nonthreatening, nontechnical environment in which they are competing only with themselves. They see more, they see it much sooner, and they are more able to talk with conviction about what they have seen and why they felt is was worth photographing.

"Knowledge is power."

— Francis Bacon, philosopher

"Imagination is more important than knowledge."

— Albert Einstein, physicist

Technique is important in photography, but motivation and self-confidence come first. I have found that nearly all of the technical problems that I would have "covered" in lectures will come out in print critiques. These problems usually appear in the form of questions that are asked when the learner is ready and eager for the answers.

"The greatest gift we can give is to help those who want to learn, find out what they love to do."

— Richard Bach, writer

Criticism Is Important

"One should challenge accepted thinking, particularly one's own."

— Edward Weston, photographer

Most people crave response to their work, and most artists will readily admit their dependence on constructive criticism.

Raimonds Ziemelis

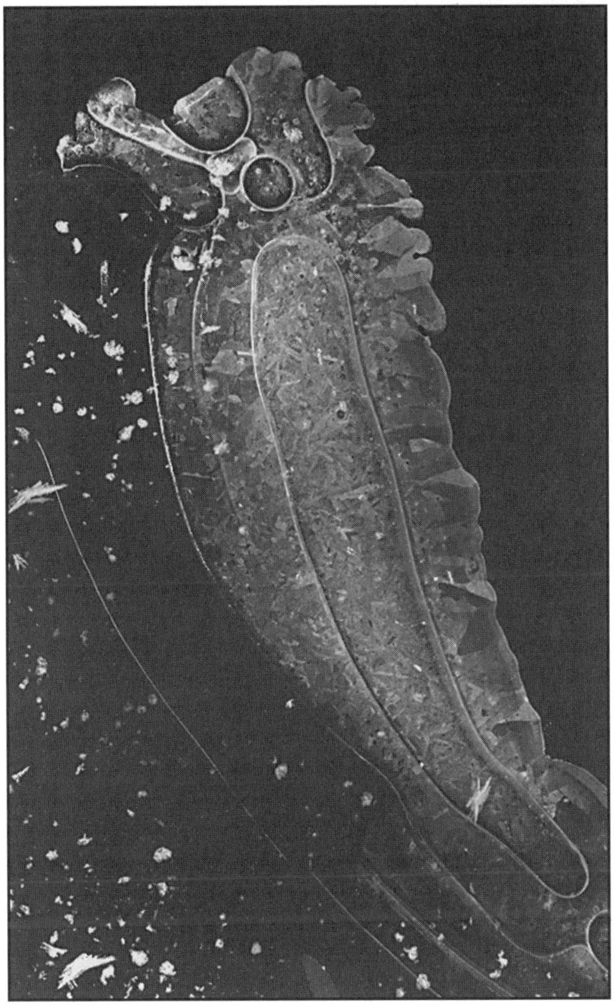

What is it? a seahorse? Or is it a photomicrograph of an amoeba or an aerial view of a glacier? Actually, it's a few inches of ice along the edge of a puddle, but ambiguity of scale creates a provocative puzzle.

"Criticism ... is the analysis of a product or performance for the purpose of identifying and correcting its faults or reinforcing its excellences ... Criticism lies at the very heart of education. To learn is to submit oneself to the discipline of a standard, even if the standard is self-created and self-imposed."

— Robert Paul Wolff, educator

Jim Nixon

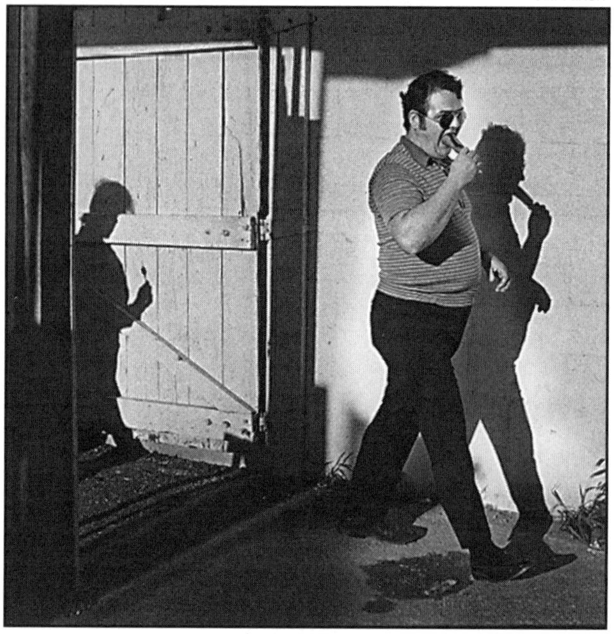

Was your first impulse to laugh when you saw this photogaph? But upon second examination, are there sinister elements? Notice the graphic impact of repetition with variation, and contrast of both form and value.

Not only is it intriguing to discover what other people see in your pictures, but it's important to find out whether what you're trying to say with your images is getting across. Praise is pleasurable and ego-satisfying, but sometimes you can't be objective about the picture when memories of a scene, event or personality remain vividly in your mind. It's important also to be aware of unforeseen communication barriers in your work, such as extraneous elements, distracting backgrounds, and careless lab work.

"There is a certain exchange going on between a good photograph and the person looking at it."

— William Albert Allard, photojournalist

It's fun sometimes to learn what friends and family members see in your photographs. Also, when your work is on display, it can be instructive to overhear comments from strangers. But the most constructive critiques will come from colleagues and classmates — knowledgeable and sensitive people with an interest as keen as your own in communicating through photographic images. Usually it's helpful to have your instructor or another sympathatic expert at critique sessions as catalyst and moderator, to keep the comments flowing and to help unravel technical mysteries as they appear.

"If a picture is worth a thousand words as the saying goes, then one should be able to say something besides, 'I like it.'"

— Richard Zakia, educator

Why Black-and-White?

Color photography is everywhere — in movies, TV, catalogs, books, magazines, newspapers, on the internet, and on billboards and packaging. If color illustrations can have such stunning impact, why bother making black-and-white photographs? I'll tell you why — because viewing the world in monochrome will teach you to "see." Have you wondered why some of the classic motion pictures were shot in black-and-white, decades after color film was available? Have you noticed that black-and-white photos often are used effectively in advertising and in photojournalistic essays?

"With color you see the subject; with black-and-white you see the form of the subject."

— Ruth Bernhard, photographer

To make excellent black-and-white images, you must perceive and reproduce the esssential graphic elements of the subject. Color alone may capture the eye in an otherwise uninteresting image. If you study *National Geographic* magazine, for example, you'll discover that some of the strongest color photographs consist of a limited palette. They are composed and lighted so that color often is incidental, and not the dominant feature of each photograph.

"I do not believe any tuition is a better bargain than $100 worth of film put to work in an attempt to make each picture, each roll, better than the last."

— Wallace Hanson, editor

By removing the element of color you increase the importance of graphic elements; thus a black-and-white photograph is an abstraction. When compelling subject matter is supported by strong graphic design, then that image will command attention. Color often makes a strong image stronger still.

> ***"One always has to begin with something. One can then remove all appearance of reality: one can run no risk, for the idea of the abstract has left an ineffaceable imprint. It is the thing that aroused the artist, stimulated his or her ideas, stirred his or her emotions."***
>
> — Pablo Picasso, artist

Picasso, of course, was a master of abstraction. Simplicity of line and form was the essence of his mature work, and among the strongest are his black-and-white line drawings.

> ***"When you go out to paint, try to forget what objects you have before you — a tree, a house, a field, or whatever. Merely think, here is a little square of blue, here an oblong of pink, here a streak of yellow, and paint it just as it looks to you ... until it gives your own ... impression of the scene before you."***
>
> — Claude Monet, painter

Monet painted with a palette of selected hues — pigments of limited color value and muted intensity. Black-and-white reproductions of his paintings reveal Monet's strong sense of limited positive and negative space related by atmospheric perspective — very much like fine photographs of the natural landscape. Viewing the originals, especially the series paintings, one sees how Monet applied color as a subtle transition for the viewer back from abstract form to the reality of subdued color.

You might not choose to become a professional imager. But as an "appreciator" of the arts, I hope you will use this book as a stimulus to heighten your awareness and sensitivity to the shapes, textures and colors of the visual world. Use it as a guide to some of the fundamental facts, and as a source of comparison, so that you can criticize intelligently and constructively your own work and that of other imagemakers.

> ***"Photography can be an extra sense, or a reservoir for the senses ... Photography can teach people to look, to feel, to remember in a way that they didn't know they could."***
>
> — Edwin H. Land, inventor

> ***"An artist is not a special kind of person; every person is a special kind of artist."***
>
> — Eric Gill, sculptor and typographer

GARY CIALDELLA

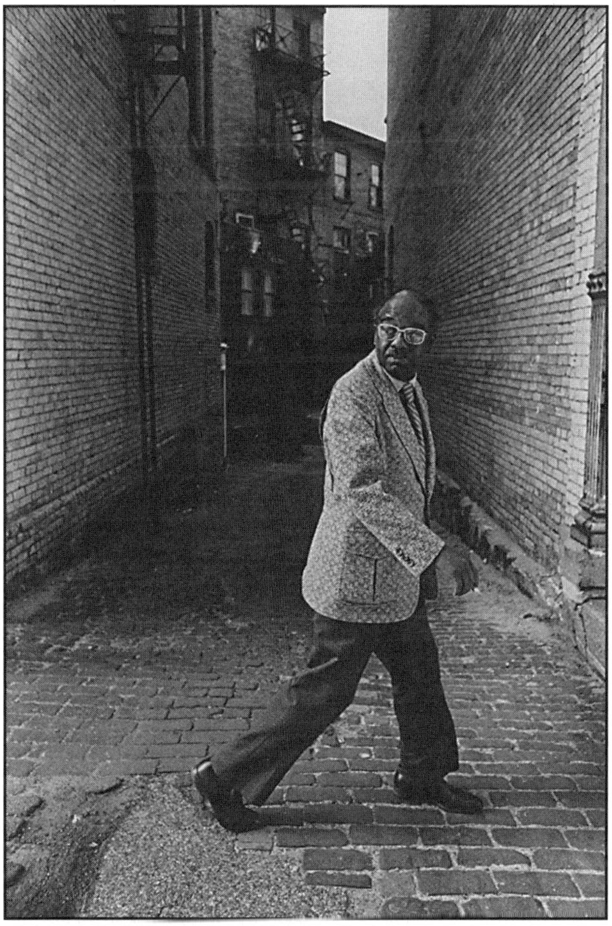

Do you wonder why this man is looking over his shoulder? What is the effect of the converging walls on your interpretation of this photograph?

Looking Back: Roots in the Past

For more than a century-and-a-half, photographers have preserved images that show us what people looked like, the way they lived, and the things and places that were important to them. Even beyond their subject matter, some historic images *suggest* more than they *show.* The best of these old photographs communicate the thoughts and feelings of the artists who produced them long ago, at a time when documentary photography was evolving into art.

Looking Ahead: Cameras & Computers

For the first 150 years, the basic principals of photography remained much the same; but now the industry is going through major change. Electronic images already rival the quality of chemically produced photographs. And costs are coming down fast.

But computers are dumb until interfaced with human intelligence and imagination. They can only process images that are fed into them. A camera and lens still are needed to gather and focus rays of light, and the principals of camera use remain unchanged.

Digital cameras linked to computers provide convenient and versatile ways of producing what we have already learned to do with light and chemistry. But in the electronic "darkroom," we can save time, be much friendlier to the environment, and produce work of infinitely greater variety.

Prepare for the Future

There is no substitute for still imaging. Video is a motion picture medium. Although the rules of conceptualizing and framing are similar to still imaging, film and video exist in the dimension of time. Still photography abstracts time in a way that even a still video or film frame cannot. Effective still pictures must suggest for the viewer what came *before* and what might come *after* the "decisive moment" of exposure, or must tantalyze us by withholding this information.

To prepare for the 21st century, think of yourself not only as a photographer, but as an imagemaker. Master the skills of visual communication now. Human imagination and creativity never will become outdated. Brains and sensitivity always will be needed to select and conceive images, and some kinds of cameras will be required to capture them.

CARMEN ANDERSON

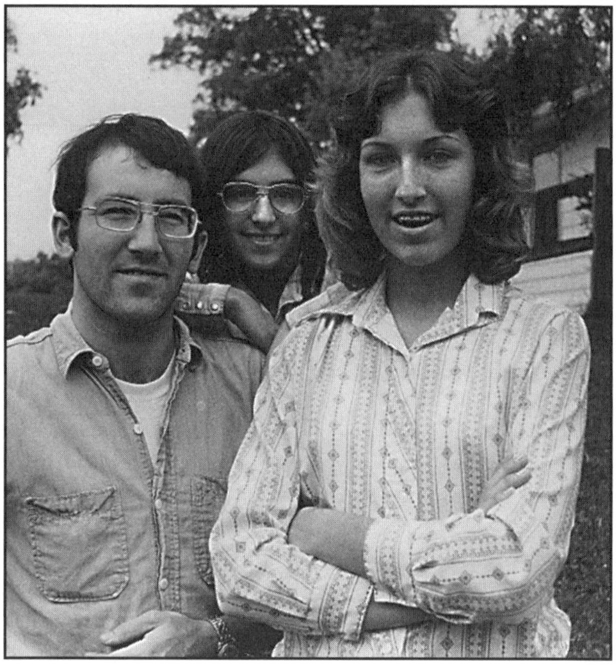

Snapshot or portrait? How does one decide? Can one traditional photograph be both a personal recall picture and an image with broader significance?

CATHERINE NOBLE

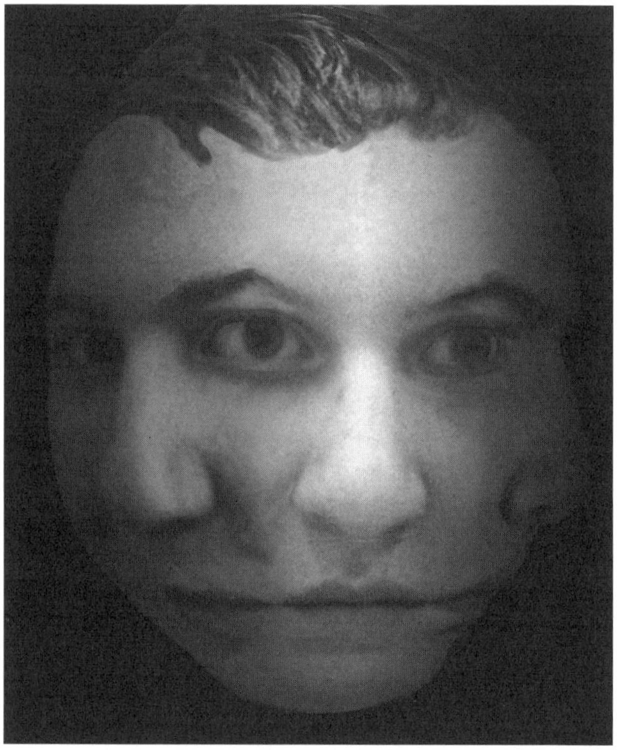

As technology advances, how will our ideas change about how pictures should look? Could this computer-manipulated self-portrait convey more meaning than the straight photograph we might have expected?

The Language of Images 1

> ***"Photography is a language with which a knowledgeable photographer can produce records, reports, essays, diary entries — even poetry!"***
>
> — Ansel Adams, photographer

Communicating with Camera and Computer

Photography is the closest thing we have to a universal medium of communication. Although there are some cultural variations in the way people respond to them, photographs transcend most traditional social and literary boundaries.

> ***"I believe that photography can be one of the most powerful means of sharpening human awareness — one of today's most faithful, permanent, and universal means of communication. Through it we can provide an accurate and believable mirror of the human condition — a mirror that mankind must finally face."***
>
> — Cornell Capa, photographer

Photography reaches people on many levels — most of which cannot be classified as art. Photography informs and educates. Much of what we know about the world we have observed in the photographic images presented to us on television and movie screens, computer monitors, and on the pages of newspapers, magazines and books. Photography tempts us and persuades us. It sells us food, furniture, clothes, cars, cosmetics and candidates. It entertains us. Photography works for us behind the scenes in countless unapparent ways as an extension of the human eye and the human mind in scientific research, engineering and medicine. Photography for millions of people is a diary for preserving fleeting moments of time. And photography for many of us is becoming, in the words of Alfred Stieglitz to define art, "an outer expression of inner growth."

> ***"The mission of photography is to explain man to man and each man to himself."***
>
> — Edward Steichen, photographer

Photography is rooted in reality, that's why the ethics of imaging are so important. In the transfer of ideas from one person to another, which we call communication, lies the potential for governments and for individuals to overcome ignorance and misunderstanding. Because they are realistic and therefore believable, photographic images can be potent means of communication.

> ***"There were two things I wanted to do. I wanted to show the things that had to be corrected. I wanted to show the things that had to be appreciated."***
>
> — Lewis W. Hine, photojournalist

Photographs preserve the present and immortalize the past. They take us to distant places or to places that have never existed. Photographs provide information and add life and excitement to the words of the teacher and the journalist. Photographs answer questions and stimulate curiosity. They often arouse deep feelings and intense emotions.

> ***"A good photograph says something so well that it cannot be said better in any other way. It may be factual or poetic; but always it will be so true that from it we can learn of life."***
>
> — Beaumont Newhall, historian

Photographs often help to correct mistaken ideas people have. But because photography is so believable, a careless or unscrupulous imagemaker or publisher can misrepresent events or situations, or even use photography to tell deliberate lies. This possibility is made more acute because the very presence of press and TV cameras can make an event appear a thousand times more important than other events not covered by the visual media. And digital technology makes possible undetectable manipulations.

"Television cannot present the trivial. By being presented, even trivia becomes of enormous importance."

— Jay Chidsey, philosopher

"The camera doesn't lie, but photographers often do!"

— Fred Tonne, photojournalist

Because photographs are so believable, we must learn to react to the language of visual stimuli as we should react to written and spoken words. We must learn to ascertain the imagemaker's or editor's intentions and to recognize the impact of each medium. We must be able to tell when someone is presenting us with facts, appealing to our need to "belong," or challenging our wits with visual simile or metaphor.

"I always wanted to take the best picture I could, one that would satisfy me. But at the same time I wanted to take pictures that would influence people. I wanted to show people that the natural world was valuable for them. This was in a sense propaganda. But I don't think there is anything wrong with certain kinds of propaganda."

— Eliot Porter, photographer

Visual Literacy

"The knowledge of photography is just as important as that of the alphabet. The illiterate of the future will be a person ignorant of the use of the camera as well as the pen."

— László Moholy-Nagy, artist

The grammar of imaging is very closely related to that of verbal language, and visual literacy has become as important as the ability to use and understand words. Today's educated person both comprehends visual messages and composes clear, even eloquent, visual statements. The most visually literate understand the grammatical parallels of visual and verbal language and have some experience with the tools of visual communication. Perhaps most important, familiarity with visual communication leads to appreciation, as well as healthy, critical skepticism of the visual arts and mass media.

ABIGAIL PICKETT

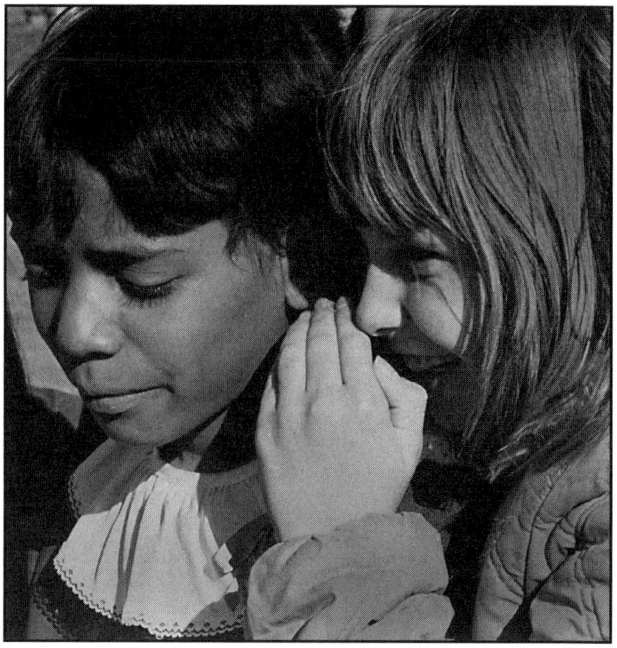

Who are these children? What secret is being whispered? Can you describe an experience that you are reminded of by this picture?

"If these 'mass media' should serve only to weaken or corrupt previously achieved levels of verbal and pictorial culture, it won't be because there's anything inherently wrong with them. It will be because we've failed to master them as new languages in time to assimilate them to our total cultural heritage."

— Marshall McLuhan, philosopher

Commercial television and film have, as Marshall McLuhan has suggested, pushed written language toward the spontaneity and freedom of the spoken idiom. At the same time, the media have made us intensely aware that words often cannot communicate true feelings as effectively as facial expression, tone of voice and body gesture. Also there has been widespread — and unfounded — fear that literate culture will somehow be "cheapened" by the visual media.

"One picture is not necessarily worth a thousand words. But pictures, plus related facts, plus visual presentation, do constitute the language of photography."

— John R. Whiting, editor

"Don't merely record what you saw, but tell others how you felt about what you saw."

— Susan Wood, photographer

The Meaning of Images

The purpose of photography may be to portray objects and events realistically or to elicit an emotional response. But the ultimate meaning of a photograph may be altered by differences in the way the picture is made.

"Facts are not interesting. It's a point of view on facts which is important."

— Henri Cartier-Bresson, photojournalist

Robert Rowan

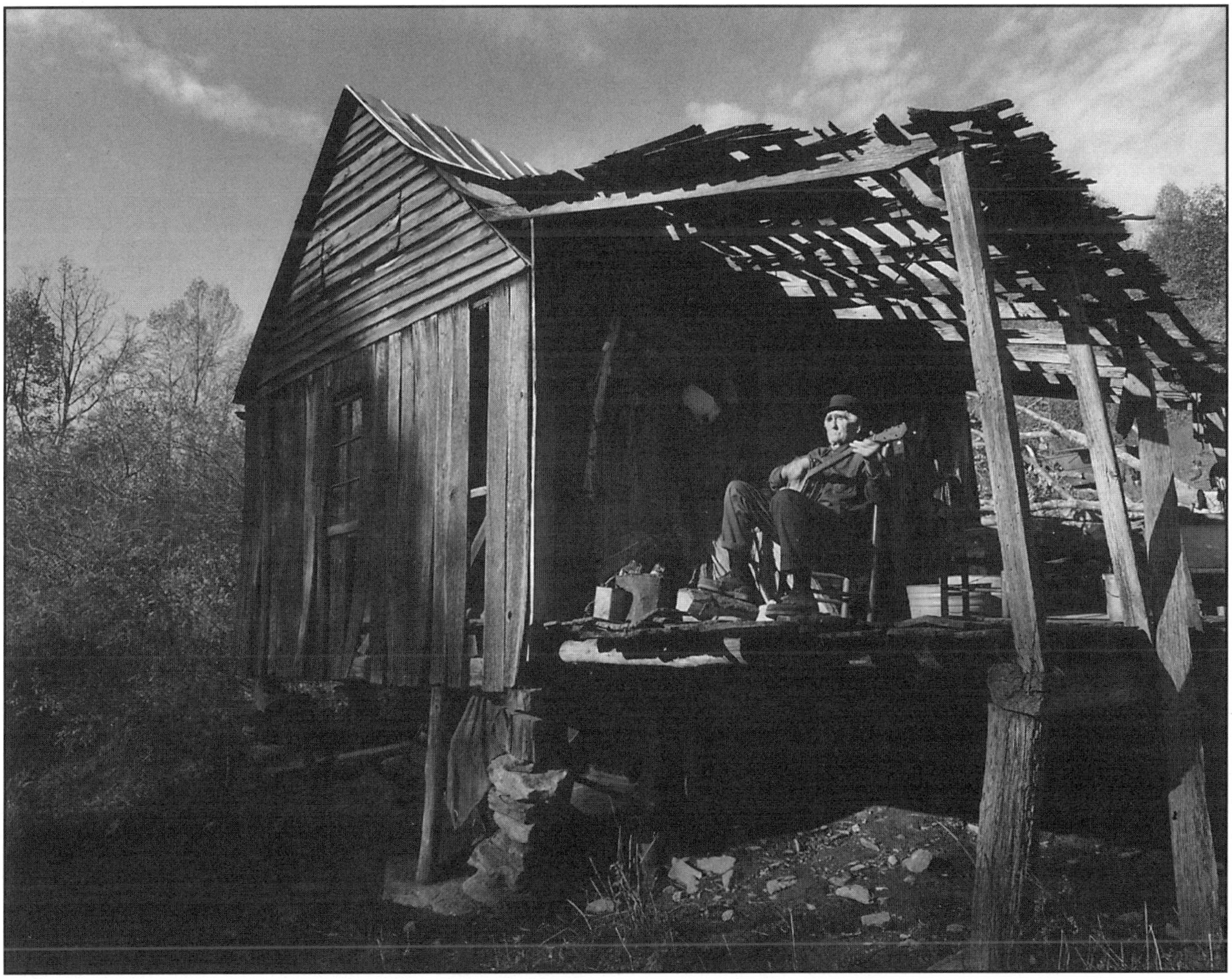

What can we know from looking at this picture? How much must we infer?

The weather, for instance, or time day can affect the appearance of the subject being photographed. The point of view or type of lens chosen by the photographer can make one object seem larger or smaller in relation to other objects. The photographer directs or diverts the viewer's attention by choosing what is to be included or excluded from within the camera's field of view.

"Writing about a visual medium tends to make the simple complex. ... If you want to judge a good photograph, ask yourself: Is life like that? The answer must be yes and no, but mostly yes."

— Charles Harbutt, photojournalist

The photographer's use of light may mean the difference between a natural-looking picture or one that appears contrived. Light can make the scene appear bright and happy; its absence can make it appear dark and sad or mysterious. When more light is allowed to fall on one part of a subject, people tend to pay more attention to that part of the photograph.

Our responsibility as photographers is to use our technical knowledge and creativity to make images that will be of the greatest interest and significance to people who see them. In doing so we can satisfy ourselves because creating images that communicate to others can be an active, satisfying experience.

Lowell McCoy

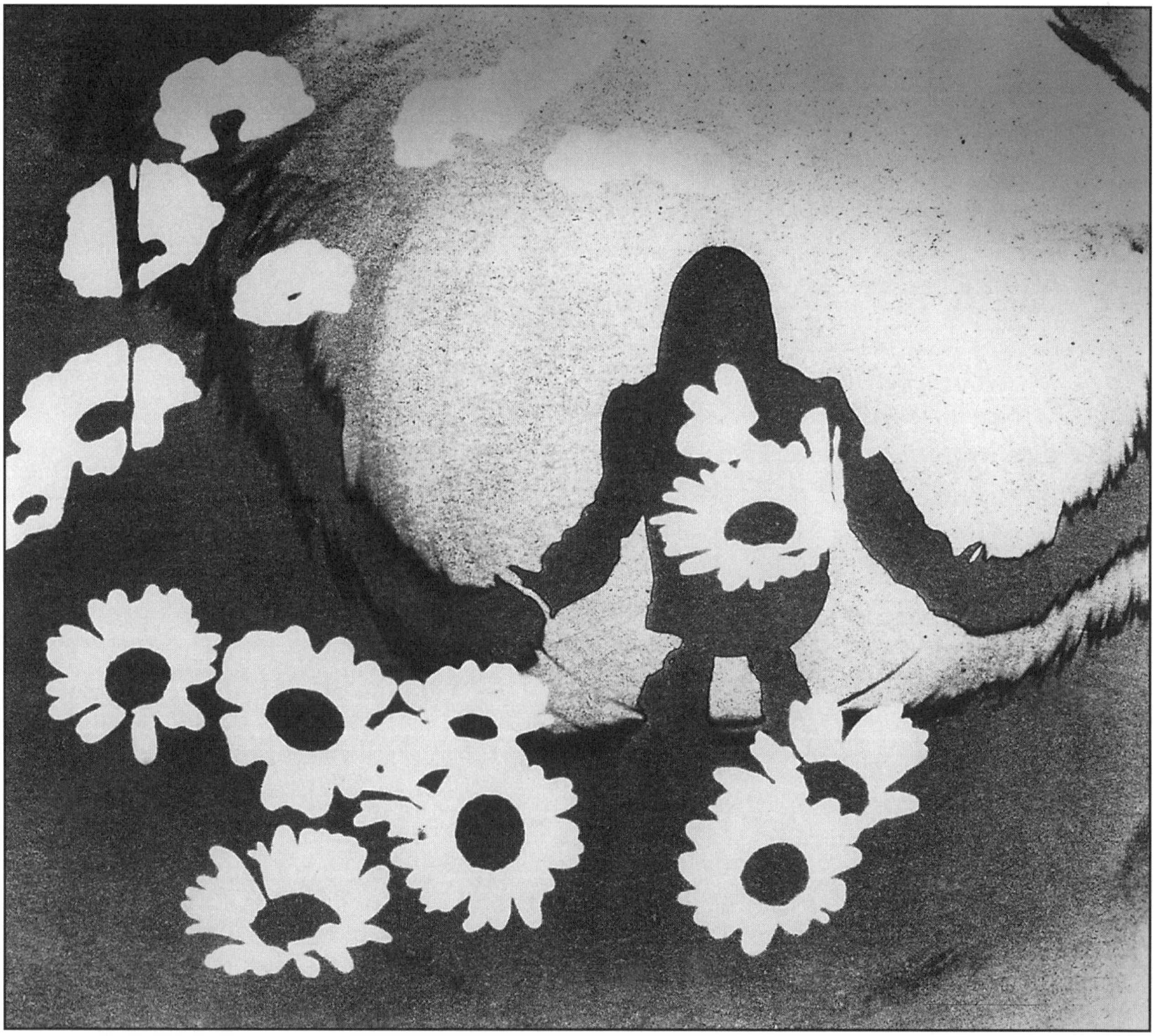

Which is object and which is reflection? What effect is created by the high-contrast treatment of this image?

Gary Cialdella

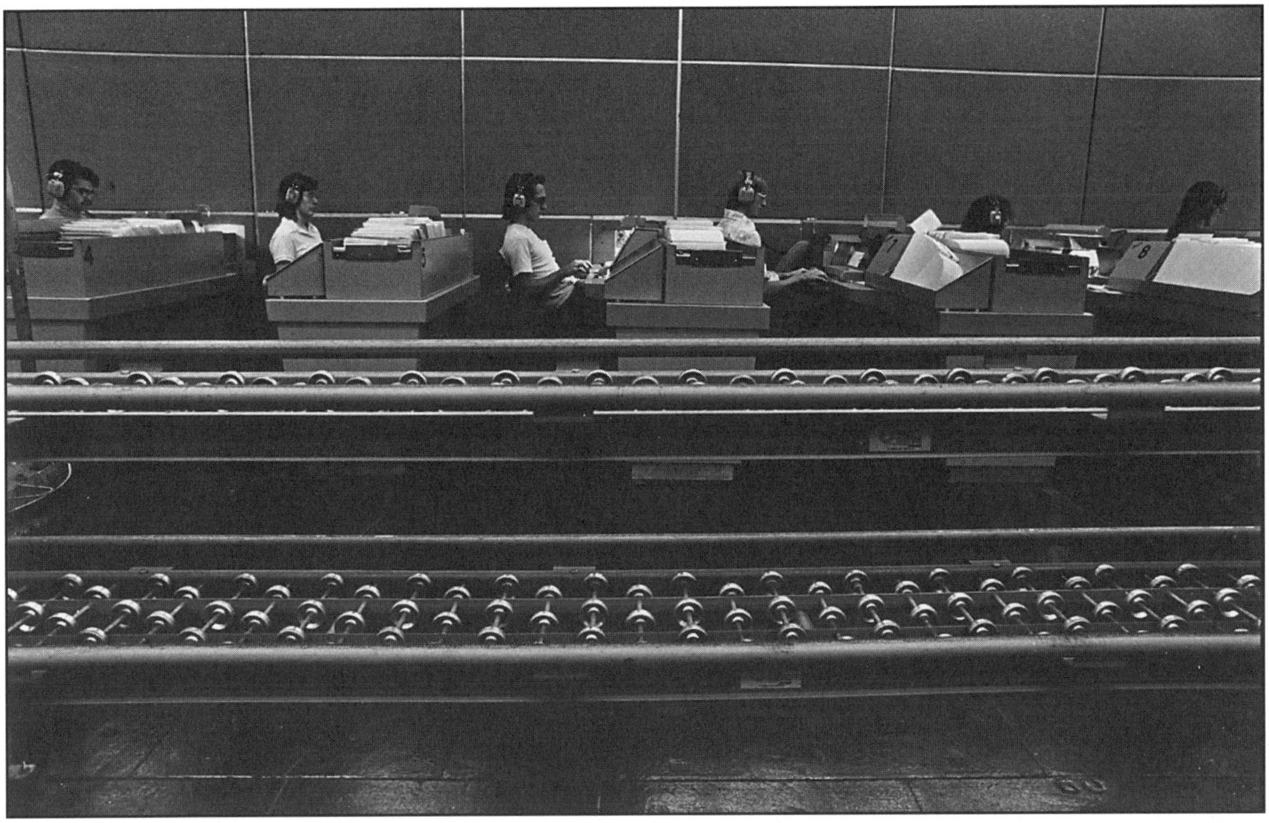

Does this photograph seem humorous to you, or is it frightening? Are these postal workers on the conveyor or have they become part of the machines they operate?

"The best pictures are made by those ... who feel some excitement about life and use the camera to share their enthusiasm with others. The camera in such hands is a medium for communicating vital experience."

— Roy Stryker, editor

Looking at Photographs

"Photography, to me, is simply a way of showing to someone else someone or something that has excited me."

— William Albert Allard, photojournalist

"By revealing my own fantasies, I'm also exposing yours!"

— Kurt Oldenbrook, artist

Looking at pictures can be an active and satisfying experience. When a photograph appeals most strongly to you, it may reveal not only an accurate visual record, but it may also excite your imagination. Perhaps it will stimulate your thinking by reminding you of personal experiences or desires, or by challenging you to think new thoughts.

"There is no greater esthetic power than the conversion of the familiar into the unbelievably new."

— Edwin H. Land, inventor

Many strong photographs stand by themselves as visual experiences without benefit of caption, context, or title. These successful photographs need no words at all. The images appeal to nearly everyone.

At other times, words and pictures work together most effectively to communicate ideas. Photographs can provide information or stimulate interest when words alone might fail. Written captions, however, often are required to clarify facts, to place an image or series of images into context, and to call attention to details that the casual viewer might overlook.

"You're always looking for the picture that sums it up, the picture that makes a point."

— Brian Lanker, photojournalist

Think Before You Shoot!

"Discovery consists of seeing what everybody has seen and thinking what nobody has thought."

— Albert Szent-Györgyi, philosopher

A photograph is only as good as the thinking that goes into it. As an artist working independently, you cannot communicate your ideas if you have nothing to say, nor, as a professional, can you report an event or communicate a client's ideas if you have no feelings about the subject or about the audience.

"By seeing things I could be seen. And by feeling things and capturing my feelings on film I could be felt."

— Bruce Davidson, photojournalist

Sometimes artists who claim not to be trying to communicate any message at all, say a lot about themselves. Those of us who consciously attempt to communicate with others should think about ways to be more articulate. I urge you to consider the following advice:

1. Decide first what you are trying to say or convey to others. Do you want to present information or facts, create emotional impact, or provide esthetic satisfaction? Although a "good" photograph can fulfill any one of these functions, most truly great images work on all three, or at least two of the three levels simultaneously. Study great pictures and try to figure out why they are effective.

"A photograph that fails to move the viewer and to leave him different than he was before has failed as art because it has failed as communication."

— Harold Allen, educator

2. Previsualize the essentials of the image. A photograph communicates via subject matter, lighting, perspective, composition and technical quality. All of these elements make up your imagemaker's vocabulary; how well you communicate depends on how well you use your vocabulary. Practice frequently. Seldom do these factors combine themselves by accident into an effective image.

JORG JASPER

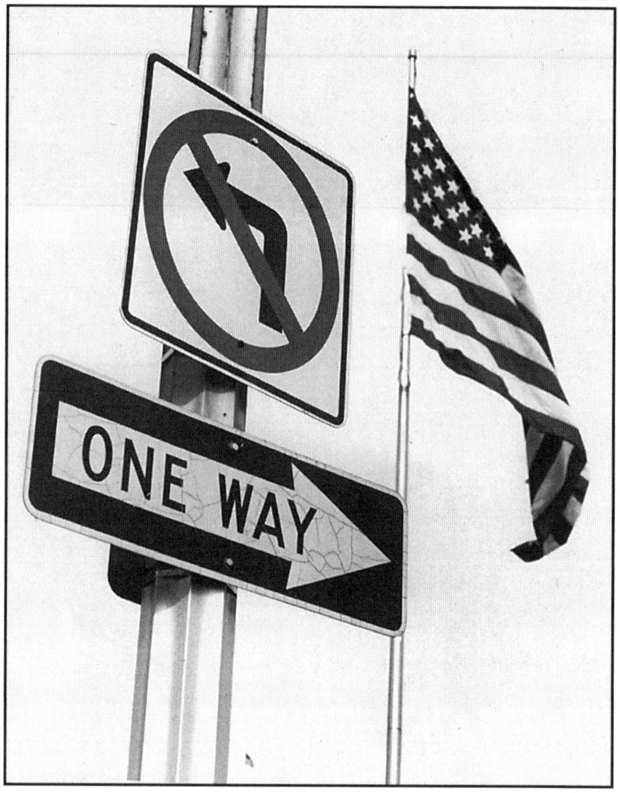

Seen together, what message do these three common symbols convey to you? How would you describe the composition?

"I think once you get interested in photographing it makes you very alert to the environment around you. You see much more."

— Eliot Porter, photographer

3. Study every image you see. Look at photographs, paintings, films, and more photographs. When you react strongly to a still photo or a movie or TV shot that has real impact, try to analyze the treatment of subject matter in terms of lighting, perspective, composition and technique to learn why it succeeded. Study your own pictures to determine just how each one could be improved. Seek advice from others who are knowledgeable, but most of all be your own severest critic. Look at every newspaper, magazine and photographic book you can. Study the pictures and the page layout. See how the images hold your attention (or fail to). Don't copy the work of others exactly, but never hesitate to adopt good techniques nor to adapt good ideas that have meaning for you. Improve on other imagemakers' successful pictures, but don't repeat their mistakes.

"I am the adventurer on a voyage of discovery, ready to receive fresh impressions, eager for fresh horizons ..."

— Edward Weston, photographer

4. Discover the world around you. Try to see things the way a camera does. Jacques Henri Lartigue wrote that, as a child learning to take pictures, when he ran out of film he would aim his head at a subject he wanted to preserve, close his eyes for a few moments, and then blink his eyelids open and then quickly close them again. Then he would go home and draw with pencil and crayon the "photographic" image he had retained in his mind.

"I don't take pictures, pictures take me. I can do nothing except have film in the camera and be alert."

— Charles Harbutt, photojournalist

"The first impression is essential. The first glance, the shock, the surprise."

— Henri Cartier-Bresson, photojournalist

Like Lartigue, you can teach yourself to "see" by pretending to be a camera. The lens records things in a circumscribed way, and the shutter determines the impression of movement that is to be retained. When you try to *see* like a camera, notice how every familiar thing changes its appearance under varied lighting conditions and when seen from different points of view. Challenge yourself to notice new things in your everyday environment and to examine familiar things in new ways. Enjoy the different textures, forms and relationships you discover, but don't limit yourself to studying inanimate objects. Most of all, even if you are attracted strongly by the natural landscape, don't be shy about observing people and interacting with them.

Gary Cialdella

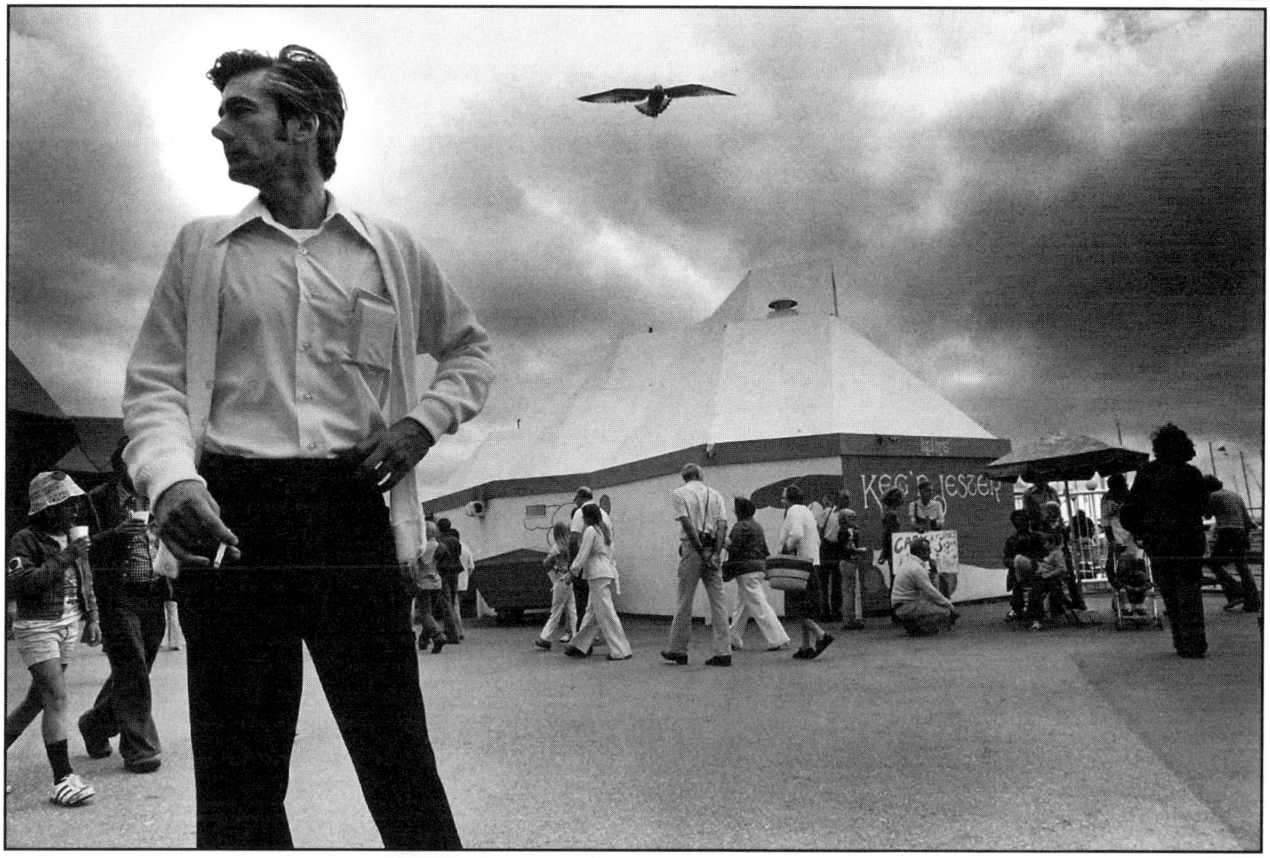

Does this photograph portend that something terrible is about to happen?
If so, is it the subject matter or because of the experience that you bring to the photograph?
Have you seen the Alfred Hitchcock movie, "The Birds," or read the short story by Daphne Du Maurier upon which the film is based?

"Talk to people, but listen to them more. Cultivate a genuine interest in everyone's problems, troubles, successes and achievements, no matter how small. Learn to take everyone for what he or she is worth. Learn to meet every type of person on their own level. In other words, learn to like people!"

— Ed Farber, photojournalist

5. Develop your interest in people. Go to shopping malls and supermarkets, parks and playgrounds. Attend concerts, plays, picnics, meetings and social and sporting events. Watch people at these places and activities, and observe them at their work or in school. Watch how they sit, lean, laugh, or cry. Watch how they argue, walk, or run. Most of us are interested in pictures of other people, especially when others are shown to be somewhat like ourselves. But it's not easy to photograph people in meaningful and insightful ways. It takes insight, empathy, patience and persistence.

"I try to reveal but not to interpret. I observe but do not intrude."

— Henri Cartier-Bresson, photojournalist

"The photographer establishes an intimate relationship between himself and whatever he is photographing."

— Edward Steichen, photographer

"The camera simply becomes a tool to introduce a person to you ... to record the kinds of things that surround him. The kind of country he lives in. The way he lives. The way he works. Hopefully, if the photograph is good, it might even tell you a little bit about the way he thinks. And what he likes to do."

— William Albert Allard, photojournalist

Communication as Participation

"To communicate is to take part ... to partake in a joint effort which transforms those so engaged, reconstructs their lives a little and sometimes a lot."

— Edgar Dale, educator

Communication is often described as a one-way process originating with a sender (speaker, writer, or visualizer) through a medium (speech, written word, photograph, or painting) to a receiver (listener, reader, or viewer). Communication is thus sometimes seen as a linear process rather than a circular or continuous one. Edgar Dale explained that in *one-way* communication, the sender assumes that the receiver is a target to be aimed at, but gives the "target" little or no opportunity to shoot back.

"Irresistibly, you share a photograph with someone ... and he or she gets a deeper insight into you as well as what you discerned."

— Edwin H. Land, inventor

GRETCHEN POKORSKI

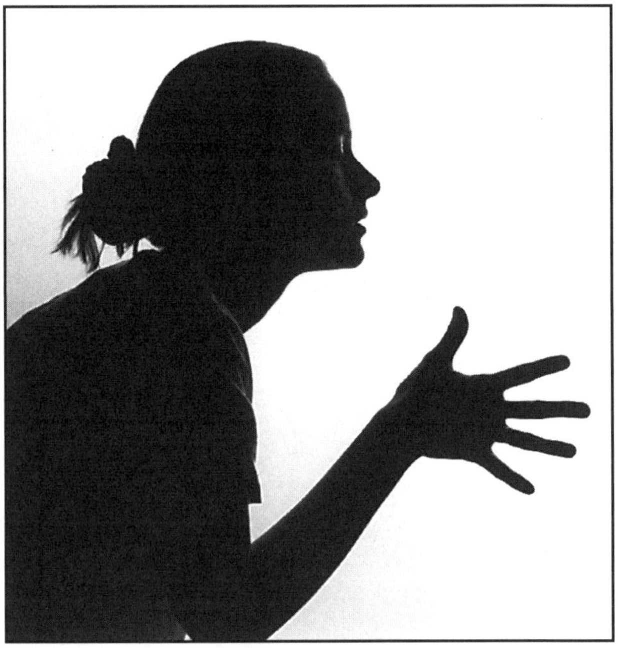

Did this self-portrait silhouette grab your eye? Both figure and background form interesting shapes, and the image is strengthened by high contrast.

Roger Hansen

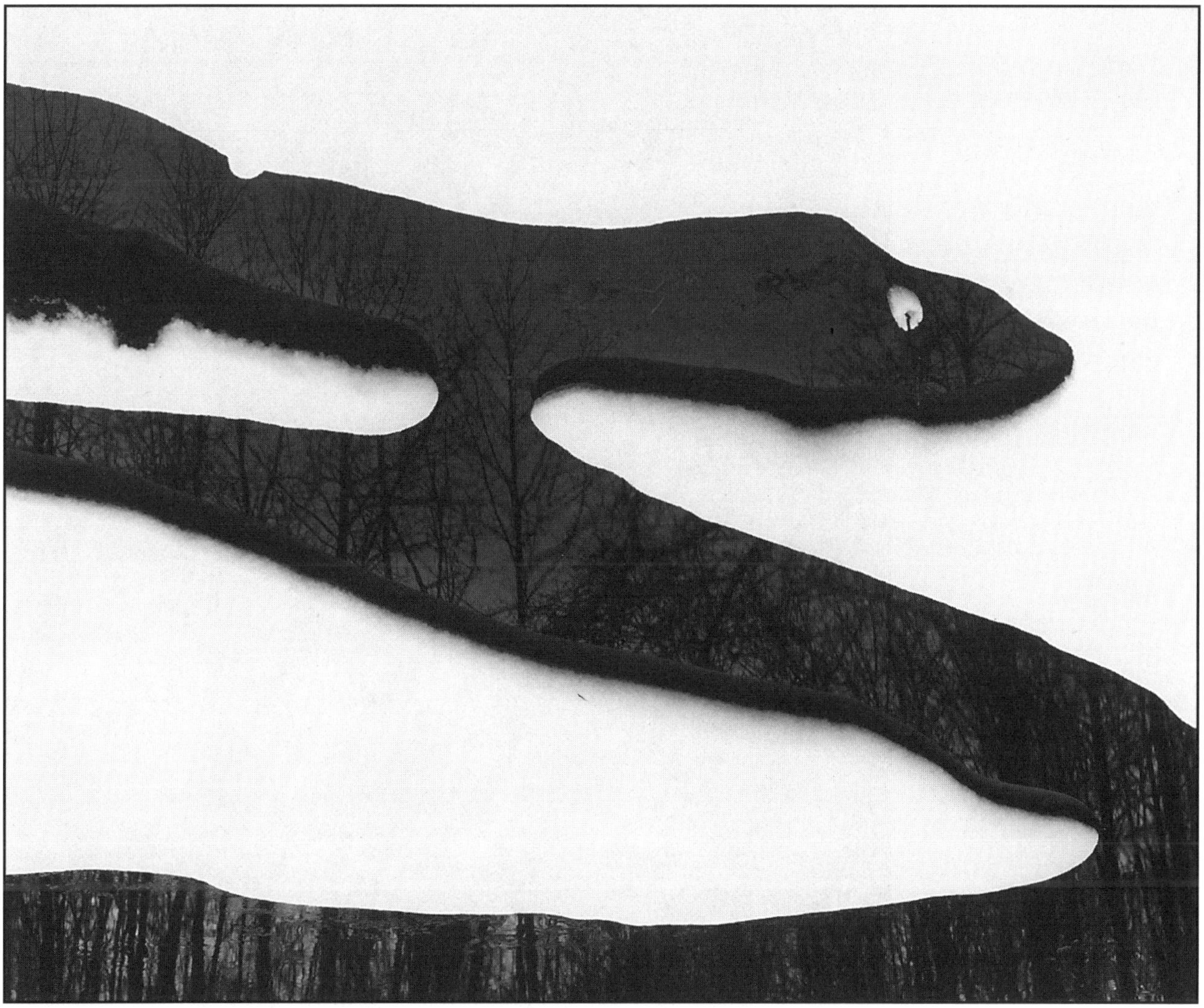

When viewed from a distance, this winter landscape becomes an interaction between abstract forms of white on black — or is it black on white? Is this image upside down? Which form is foreground and which is background?

Communication can be defined in a broader sense to mean "to share in common, to participate in." An effective image can be a bridge for people to share common experiences. A photograph makes a literal statement: "This is how this object or person appeared at a certain moment in time;" or "these were the participants and this is the setting for an event that once took place." Or the photograph can say, "Share the excitement (or pain or joy or togetherness or solitude) of these human beings." Or the photograph may speak eloquently of texture, line, mass, balance, light and shade or color. "I was moved by this beauty," the photographer might confide to you through an image, "and I wanted you to share my pleasure." Or the photographer might be saying, "I was horrified and repulsed by what I saw. Maybe if you, too, are horrified, together we can begin to change things." Or the photographer could say, "I felt strangely elated (or terrified) when I realized what this image seems to contain. Can you help me sort out its meaning?"

To communicate effectively with others, first we must understand ourselves. We must recognize our own strengths and frailties, our hopes and fears, our envies and prejudices. I know of no better means than creative imagemaking to aid us in the better understanding of our world — and of ourselves.

"To look at a thing is very different from seeing a thing."

— Oscar Wilde, playwright

DAVID M. POSTHER

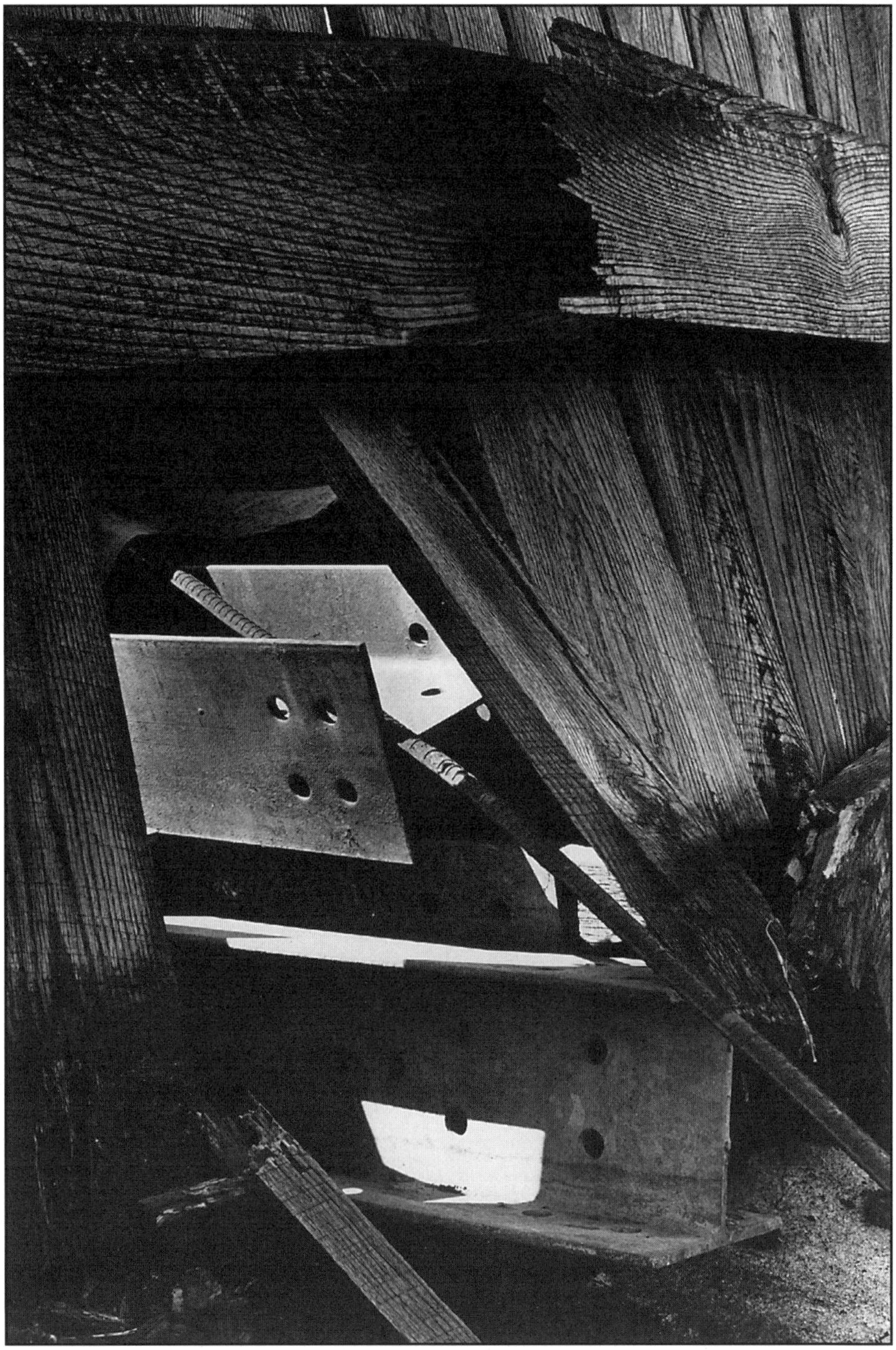

What kinds of contrasts are evident in this photograph? Can you imagine an audible effect from this image, in addition to its visual impact?

"Much is missed if we have eyes only for the bright colors."

— Eliot Porter, photographer

Selecting Subject Matter 2

"Two may do the same thing, and it is not the same thing."

— Publilius Syrus, philosopher

"I've been in places where the photographers were literally elbow to elbow. And yet everyone comes up with a different picture."

— William Albert Allard, photojournalist

What Are You Saying?

"A thought is not a thought unless it is one's own. There is all the difference between having something to say and having to say something."

— John Dewey, educator

Deciding what to photograph isn't much of a problem if you've developed the habit of seeing. Finding subject matter is not hard if you already have a lot to say in the way of social comment, or if there is specific information you want to communicate. As we summarized earlier, you have to decide what you are trying to say — present information or facts, create emotional impact, share esthetic pleasure, or stimulate the viewer's imagination. When you've decided what you want to do with images and why, then you can begin to study how.

"I can read in any photo book what the temperature of my developer is supposed to be ... I want to know what makes a good photograph and the books fail me ... what good is a perfect print of a rotten picture?"

— A student

The anonymous student asks a very good question. Later on in this book, I'll discuss plenty of routine details, such as the temperature of your developer and the way you can control image contrast. But before we get into technique, I want you to be creating images in your mind as well as with your camera and computer. I want you to become so excited about what you're seeing that you can't wait to see it printed.

"Let us first say what photography is not. A photograph is not a painting, a poem, a symphony, a dance. It is not just a pretty picture, not an exercise in ... technique ... It is, or should be, a significant document, a penetrating statement, which can be described in a very simple term — selectivity."

— Berenice Abbott, photographer

Selectivity means choosing what to include in your pictures and what to omit. The choice, ultimately intuitive, is at first conscious and deliberate, and you can learn much about selectivity by studying other people's pictures. In doing so you'll find yourself going through three states of awareness: first, noticing; then analyzing; and finally, reacting. When you become interested in photography, you begin to notice things to which you might not have paid any attention before.

"Learn from the mistakes of others — you can never live long enough to make them all yourself!"

— Fred Tonne, photojournalist

We can also learn from other people's successes as well as from failures — consciously observing and adapting to our own work effective compositional arrangements, lighting techniques and camera angles. As you learn more about visual language, you will begin to analyze every aspect of each image, from concept to quality, in the objective way that a juror should judge images in competition. You will experience real gut reactions, and you will start trying to figure out why you (and others) feel the way you do about certain images and why you react differently to others.

"There are no new ideas in the world. There is only new arrangement of things."

— Henri Cartier-Bresson, photojournalist

"If there is something to see and everybody sees it, that is observation. If there is nothing to see, yet you see it, that is poetry. But if you can make something out of nothing and make everybody see it — that is poetry in photography."

— Ernst Haas, photographer

If you study the work of great imagemakers, you can ask yourself, "How would so-and-so have looked at this subject? What portions of the scene would probably have been included? At what time of day would the picture have been made? Or where would he or she have placed the lights? Don't hesitate to "borrow" ideas and styles until you evolve a style of your own. *Emulation* need not be the same as *imitation.*

"The seeing process is primarily a purposive searching of the visual environment for instances of order."

Norman F. Carver Jr., photographer

ROBERT D. HAVIRA

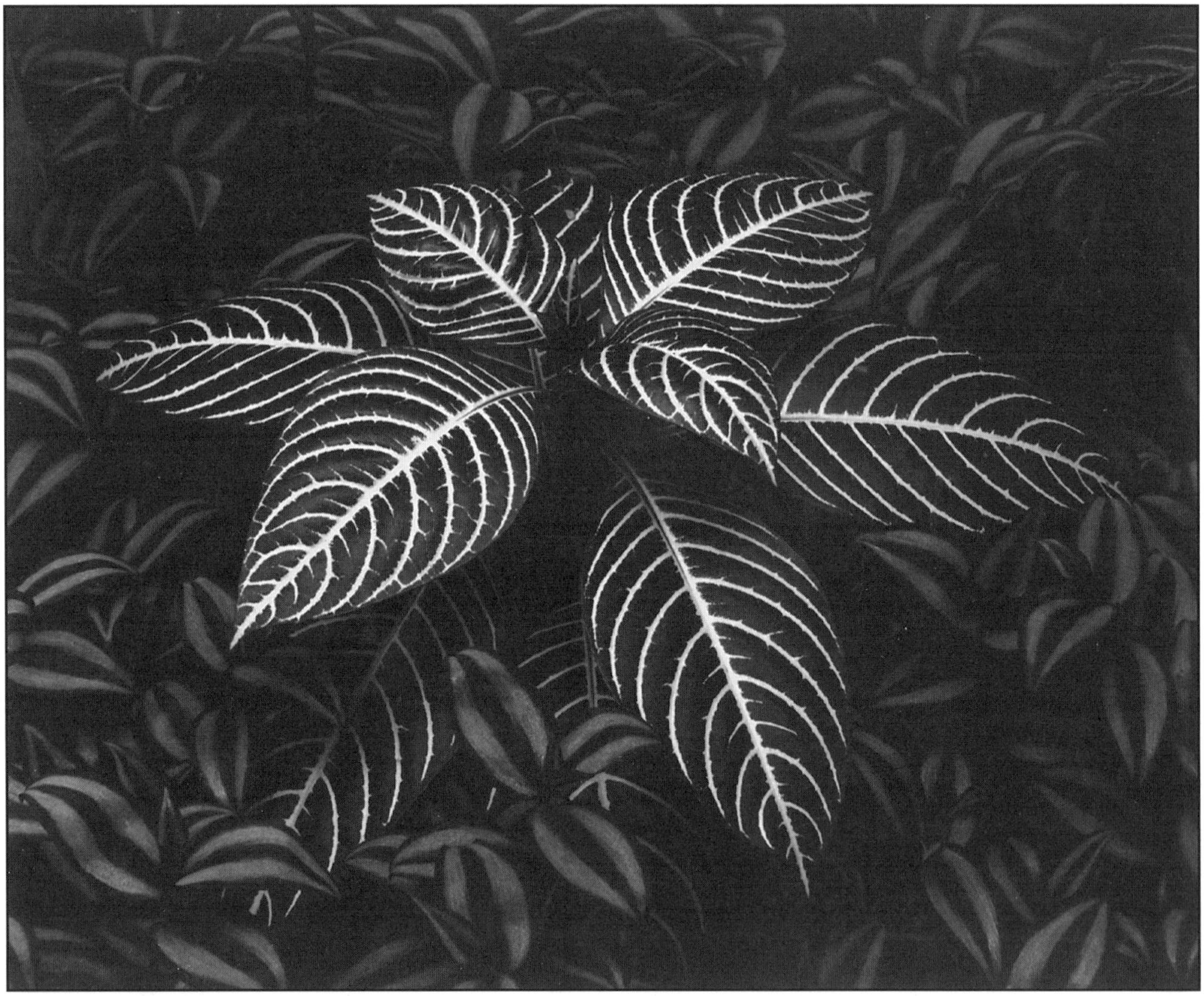

Images of beauty attract attention whether the subject matter is majestic mountains, pretty plants, or attractive people. Repetition is the keynote in this delicately balanced composition. Notice the subtle variations as lines, forms and values are repeated.

JAMES M. RHOADS

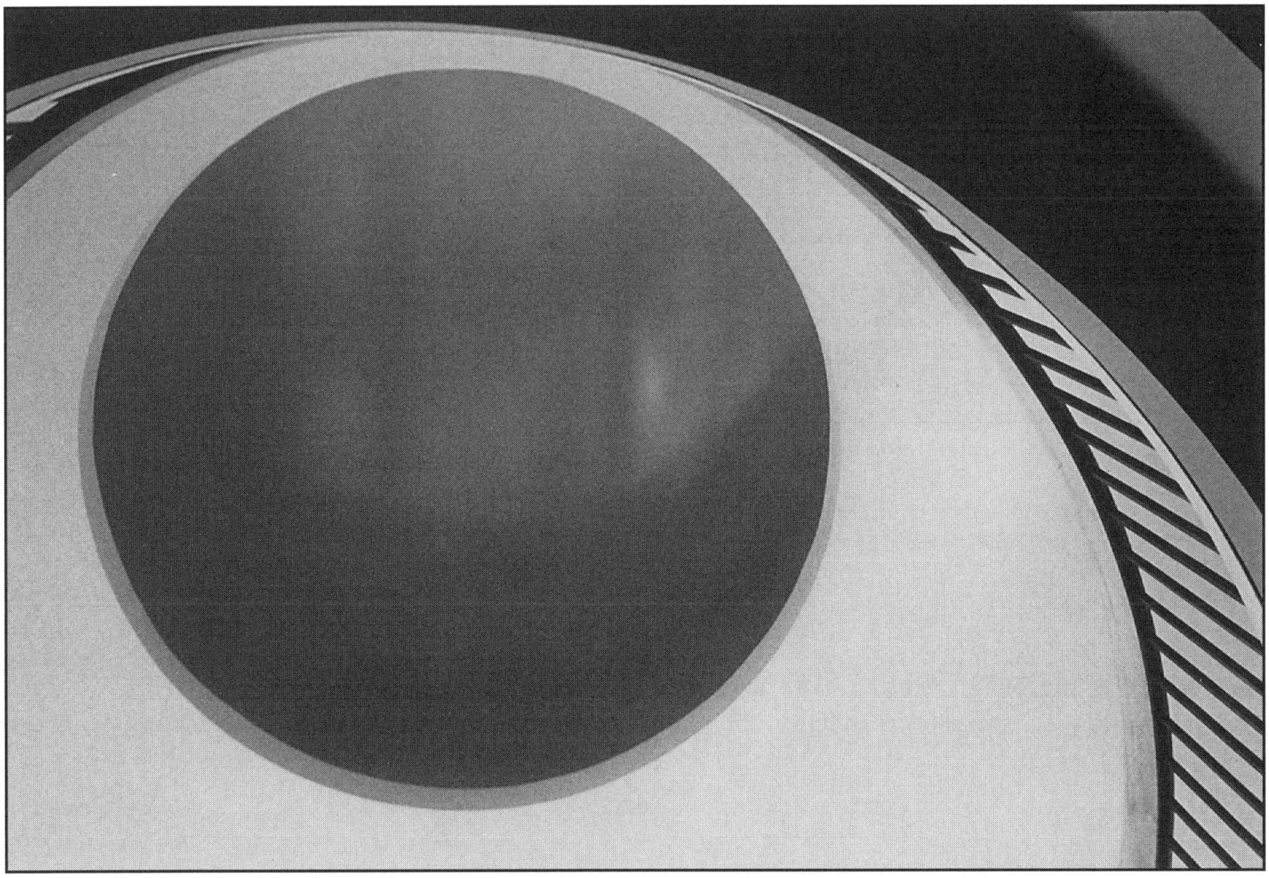

A simple, yet dynamic visual statement can attract a viewer's attention from across a room. Whether the image succeeds or not may depend on whether attention, once captured, can be held and rewarded by rhythms and detailed elements within the image. Notice in this photograph how converging, rotating lines seem to set the large sphere spinning.

A Visual Vocabulary

"The photographic image is different in form and meaning from any other image. It has its own grammar, vocabulary, and interpretation. When and if the student learns this language, he will be able to photographically translate his own thoughts."

— WALTER CIVARDI, EDUCATOR

"Photography is about going back and looking again and discovering something you didn't see before."

— Stephen Wilkes, photographer

"Let other people see the world through your eyes."

— Richard Shirk, photographer

At your disposal are all of the fundamental elements: subject matter, tone, contrast, perspective, composition and technique. Let's see some examples, and study in detail these tools of visual vocabulary.

The Natural Landscape

"I believe in photography as one means of ... affirming the enormous beauty of the world."

— Ansel Adams, photographer

Some of us never tire of discovering, photographing, rediscovering and rephotographing the endless beauty of the world. Often we expose more film when we travel to new and exotic places, but I think that is because we have discarded for a time the blindfold of daily preoccupation and we simply notice more. Often there is as much visual excitement at home, but seeing requires looking.

"I'm discovering to my delight that there's as much to see and photograph in my own backyard as I have found in any exotic place."

— George Herben, photographer

Our attention is captured by dramatic vistas of grand scale, but don't overlook microcosms of beauty and natural order found on the forest floor or in the streets of your city. Respond to the shouts, of course, but listen for the whispers.

NORMAN F. CARVER JR.

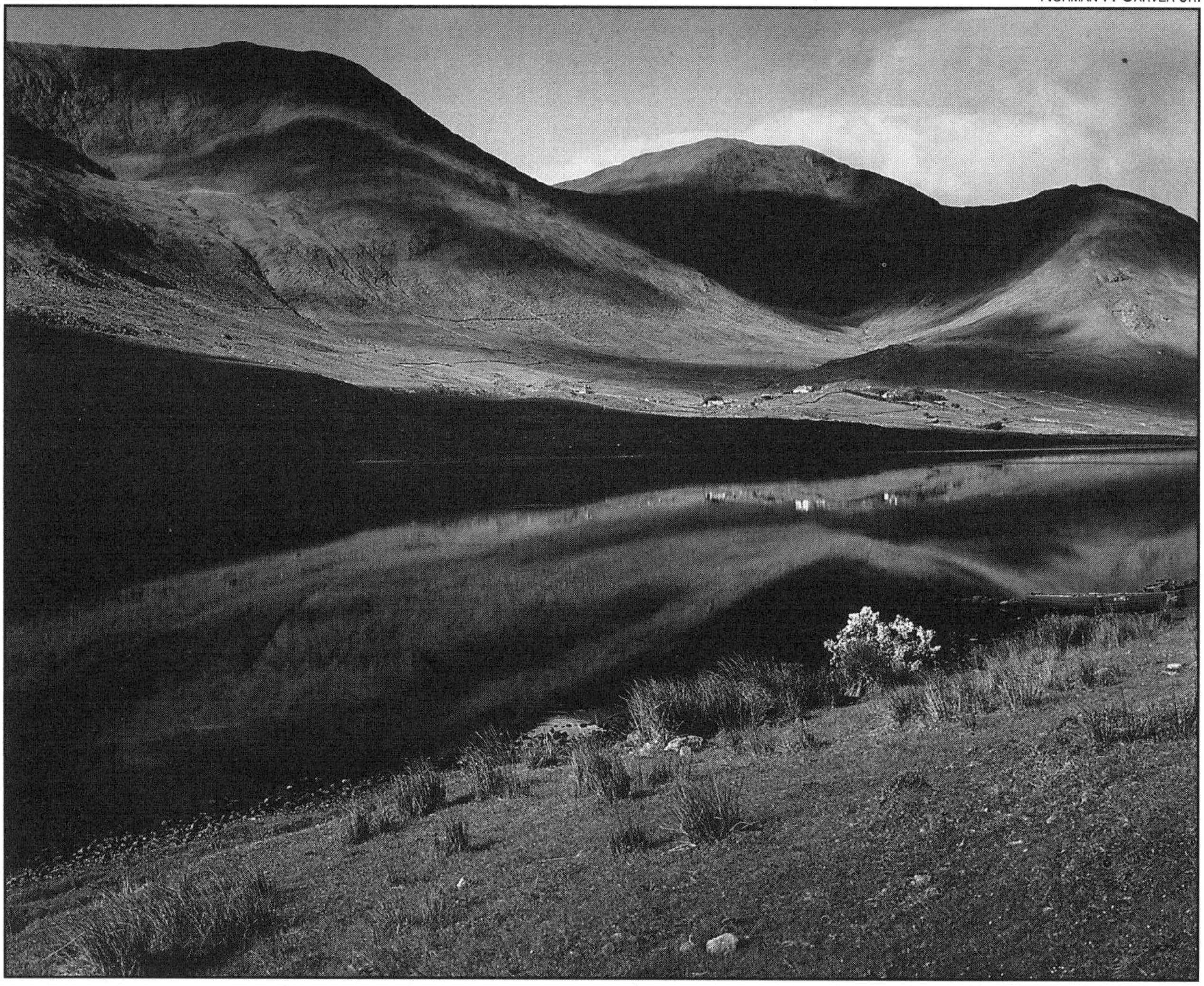

Notice the contrast here betweeen repose and motion as these sensuous lines and forms are repeated and reflected. What compositional role is played by the white flowering bush in the right foreground?

MICHAEL SARNACKI

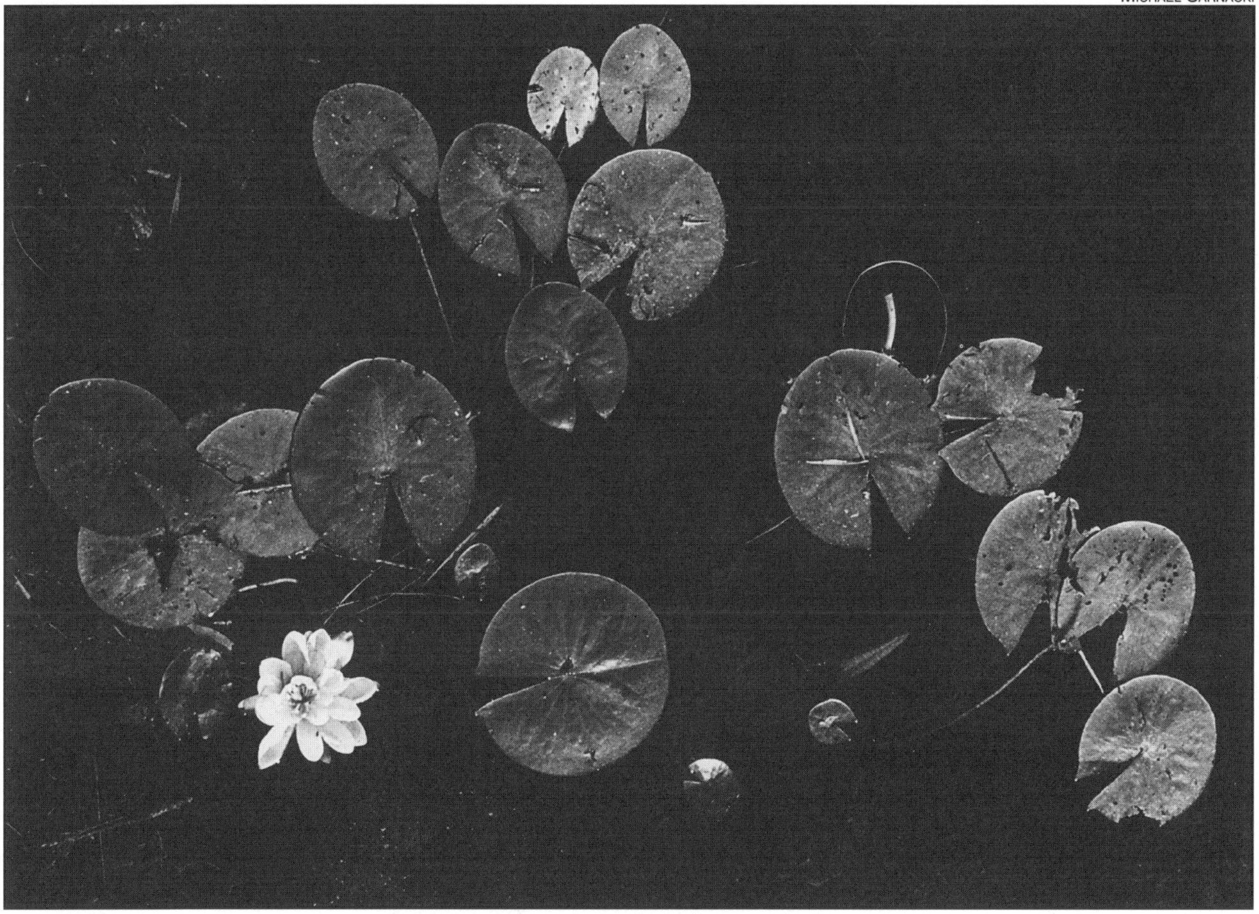

Although the scale is very different from the landscape on the facing page, how are these two images similar in design?

"I photograph nature ... because I believe nature is terribly important."

— Ansel Adams, photographer

Traditional views of dramatic and colorful landscapes are popular for calendars and posters because they remind people of idyllic experiences. However, many people who claim not to like any kind of abstract art will be attracted subconsciously to a fine image of recognizable subject matter that is built upon strong elements of graphic design. Some people will be attracted to such an image without really knowing why. Those who do understand visual vocabulary well enough to recognize the underlying order and balance may receive distinct aesthetic pleasure from the simple act of viewing such a work.

"I try now to pay more attention to the earth, to always note such easily taken-for-granted miracles as sunrises and moonsets."

— Stephen Trimble, photographer

"Only in fragments of the whole is nature's order apparent."

— Eliot Porter, photographer

"Less is more."

— Ludwig Mies van der Rohe, architect

Gary Cialdella

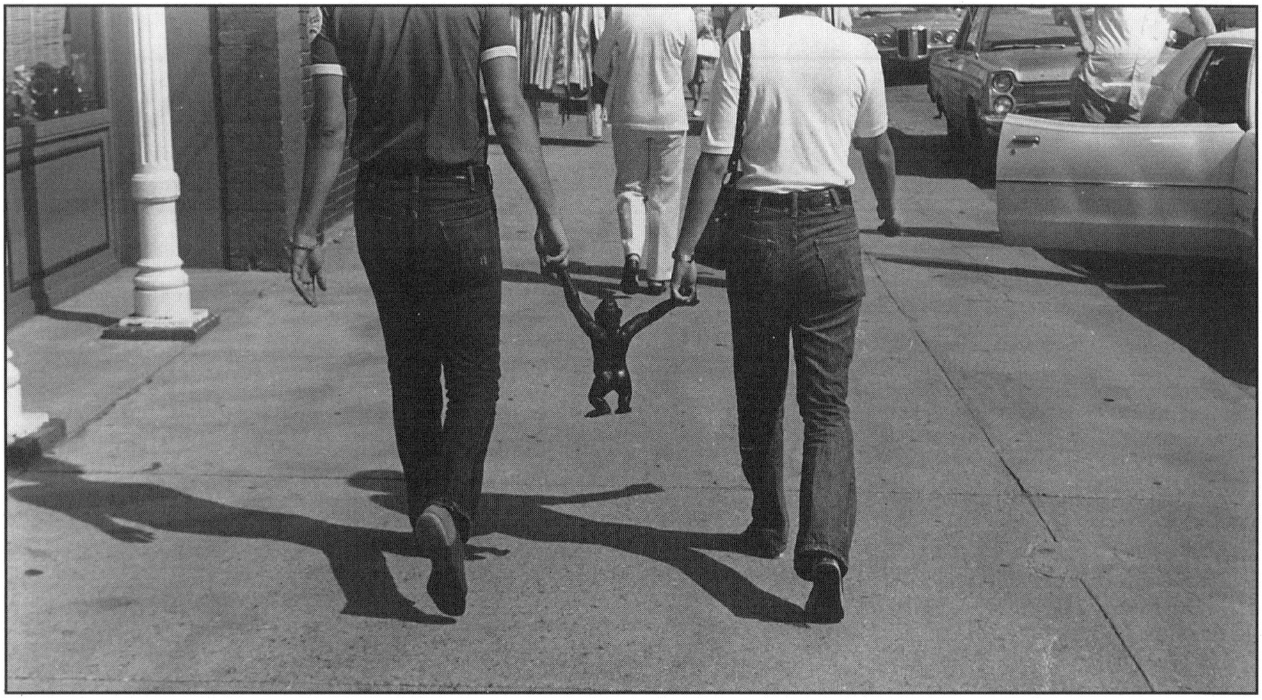

Did you chuckle with the sheer absurdity of this picture? It is an instant in time — an image that could only be photographic — that succeeds, despite breaking all the "rules" of composition and previsualization

Gretchen Pokorski

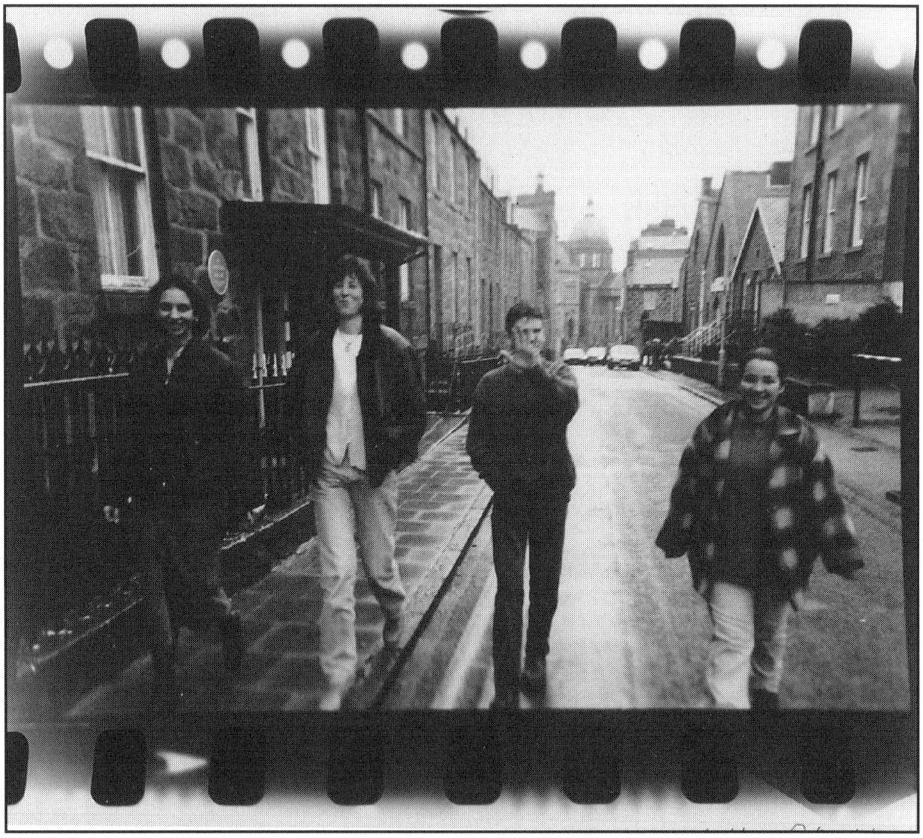

Street photography takes courage, especially when snapping strangers. When friends are your subject, the result can be an image that brings back memories, yet will be much more interesting to other people than the usual posed snapshot. This photographer wanted a "photographic" look, so she printed with an oversized negative carrier that showed the film sprockets.

The Social Landscape

"I like to take people in their environment ... the animal in its habitat."

— Henri Cartier-Bresson, photojournalist

Many contemporary photographers have been turning away from pictorial subjects and toward recording moments of everyday reality — catching people unaware as they interact with one another and with the environment people have created. Bearing a superficial resemblance to the uninspired snapshot, such a photographically immortalized instant sometimes makes a significant comment.

"I work with a hand camera, invisibly and quickly ... Interacting with the subject changes the nature of the image and its meaning."

— Gary Monroe, photographer

Another kind of selective "snapshot" is the documentation of humanity. Humorous, tragic, or merely "the way it was," history demands honest recordings in every decade of the way people live, look, dress and act.

"Cameras are a lifesaver for shy people who have nowhere else to hide. Behind a lens they can disguise the fact that they have nothing to say to strangers."

— Pat Conroy, novelist

JOHN A. LACKO

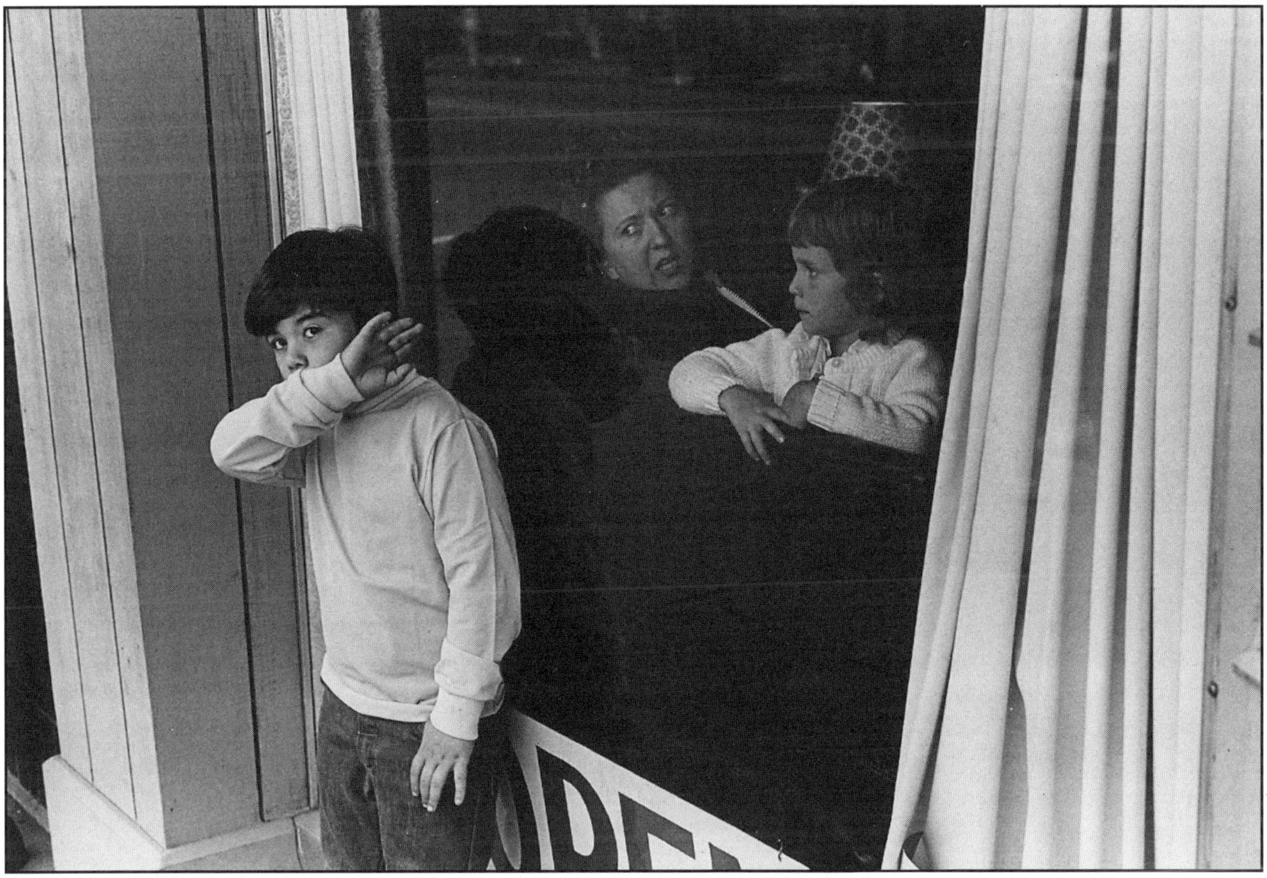

Has this boy been sent from the restaurant for some obscene infraction of table manners? What has he done (if anything at all)? We'll never know, but the photograph poses a provocative puzzle for us as it records a moment of human drama.

John A. Lacko

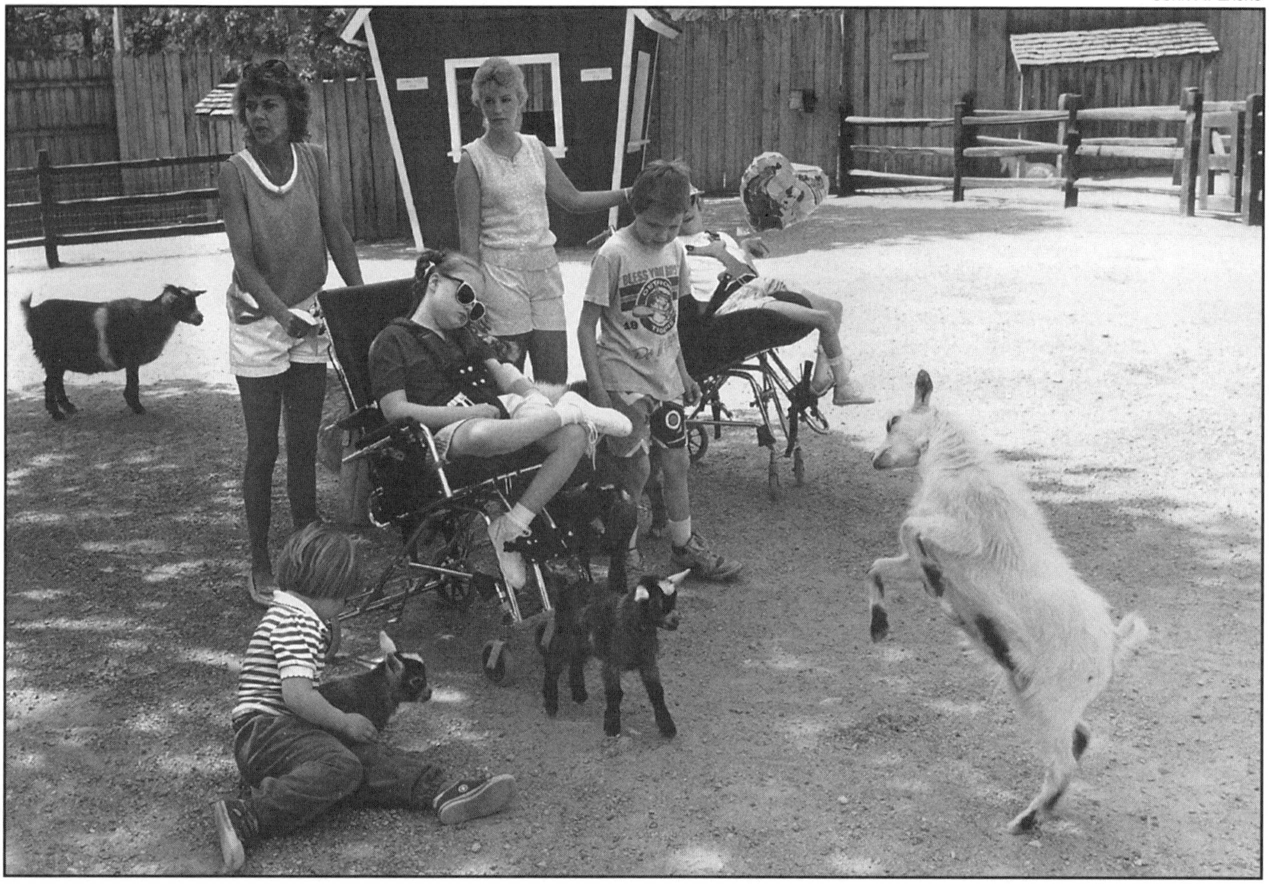

Who's paying attention to what? Can you describe the interactions between people and animals? Besides social interest, what is the significance here of graphic design?

Jim Nixon

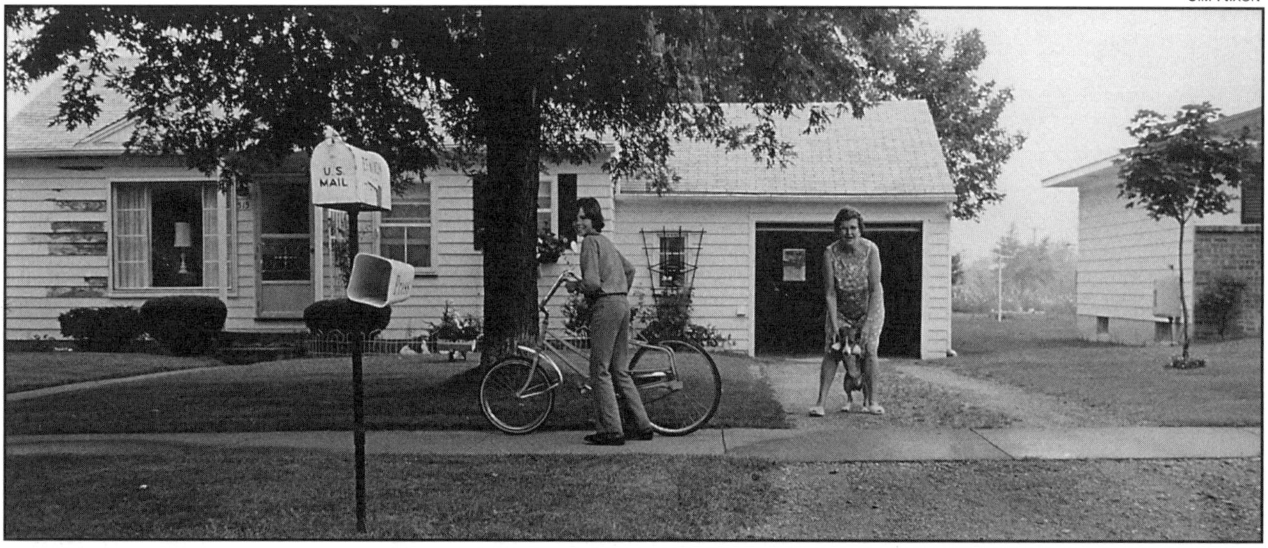

Is this a snapshot or a serious photograph? Can it be both? Does it make a statement about suburban life in America while presenting some interesting elements of design?

BRIAN LANKER, TOPEKA CAPITOL-JOURNAL

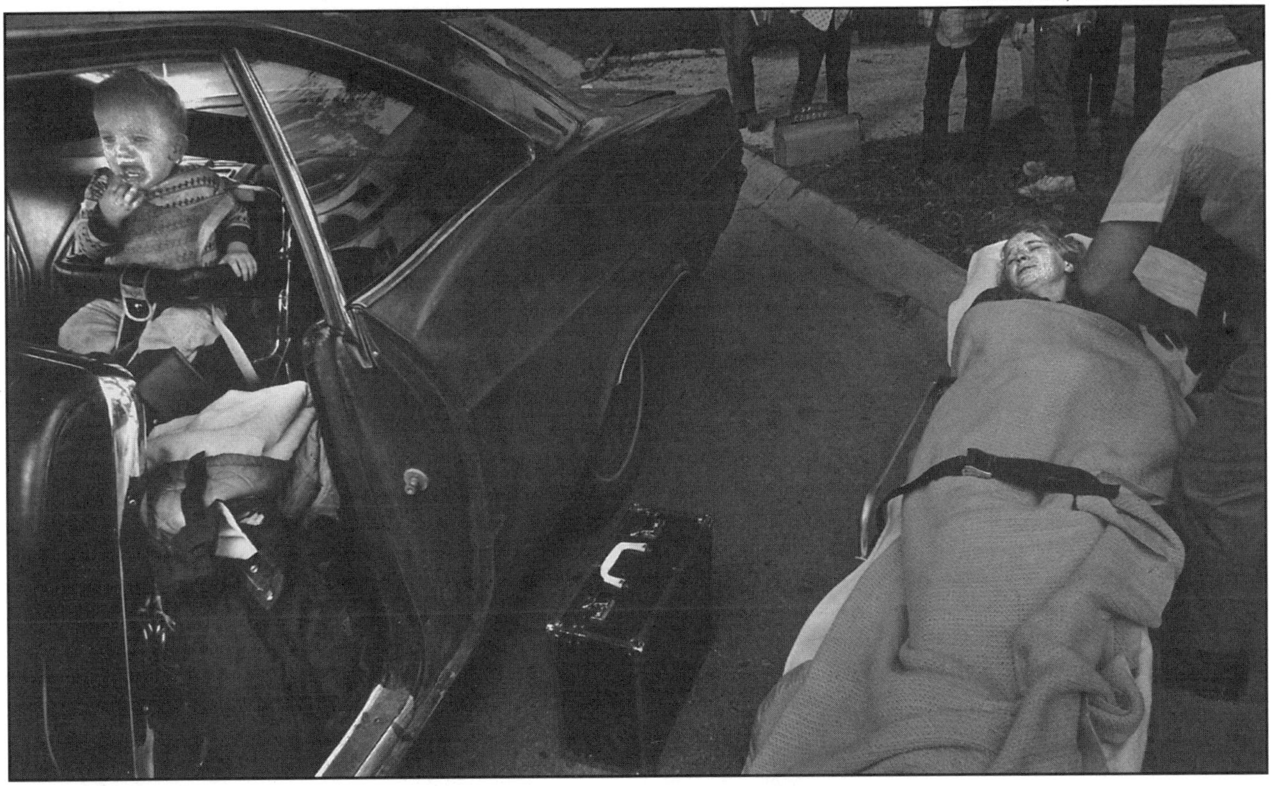

What is there about injury and death that appeals to morbid curiosity? Why are people fascinated by the misfortunes of others? Could it be that we are secretly relieved that it didn't happen to us? Brian Lanker says, "People seem to have something for tragedies. When they go on in my town, I've got to photograph them."

"There is nothing more artistic than to love people."

— Vincent van Gogh, painter

Why, in the world of popular culture, are pictures of babies, attractive young men and women, and animals so appealing? Perhaps because the subjects and their cute poses are familiar to everyone and evoke sentimental ideals of life. Although personal snapshots fulfill this purpose for millions of people, many thousands will happily purchase "professional snapshots" to display on their walls and coffee tables. The fine artist probably won't be concerned as much with cuteness and salability, but the skillful professional might surprise and educate a client by incorporating quality and design into an otherwise ordinary image.

"I feel you have to strongly like or dislike a subject. You have to care one way or the other. You can't be indifferent."

— William Albert Allard, photojournalist

If you enjoy a natural sense of humor, let it show in your photographs. People respond to a touch of whimsy in an otherwise somber scene, and a naturally comic situation always gets a spontaneous reaction. On the other hand, strong images of tragedy can stir up emotions of sympathy, empathy, indignation, and anger. They can stimulate reactions of commitment or they can result in distrust and disgust. War photographs, for example, and photographs of starving children or accident victims often shake us to our emotional roots as we identify with the plight of the people.

"If ... my photographs could cause compassionate horror within the viewer, they might also prod the conscience of that viewer into taking action."

— W. Eugene Smith, photojournalist

DIANE OSBORNE

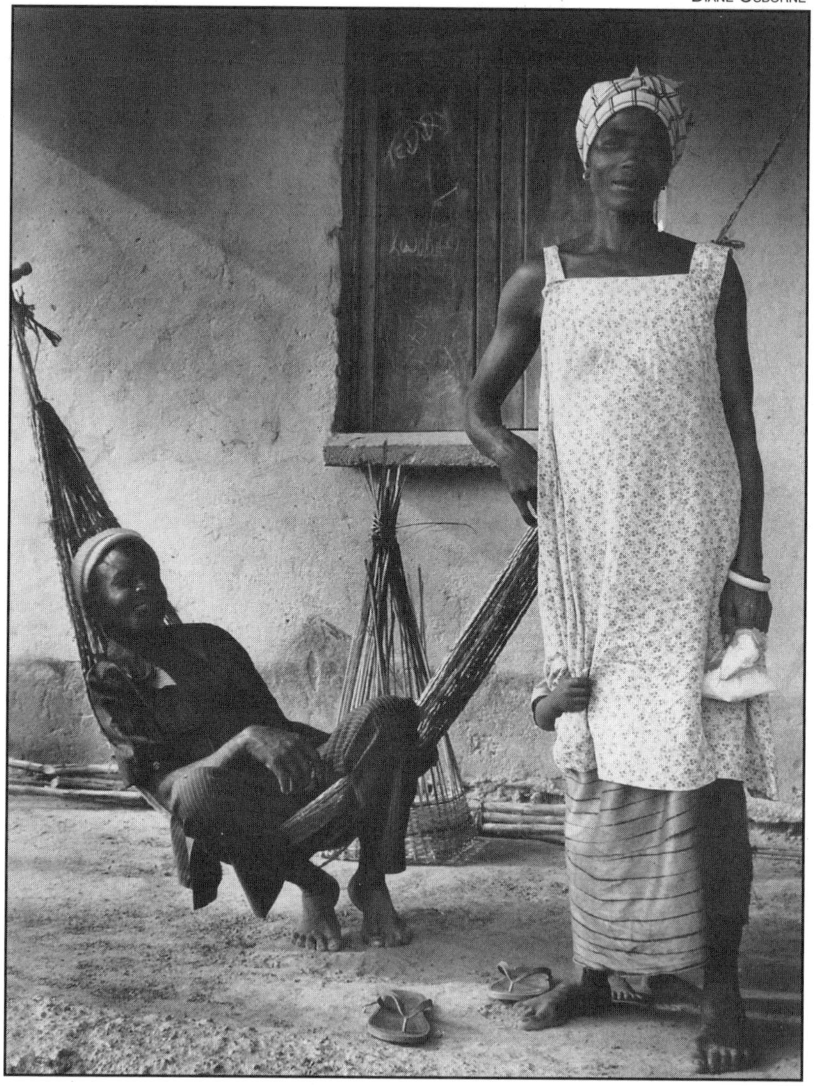

By visiting and photographing people whose lives are different from ours, what can we learn about our own culture? (Look carefully for the surprise in this photo. Also describe the design elements in the composition.)

JOHN A. LACKO

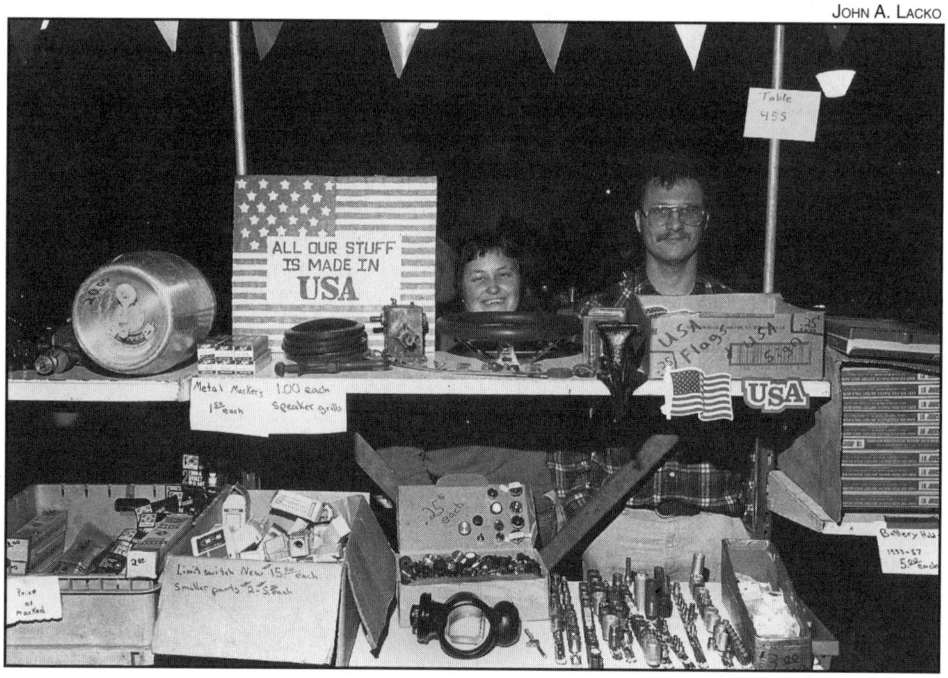

What has the photographer documented about the culture of America in the last years of the 20th century? Of what future interest might be such an image?

TODD WICKERSHAM

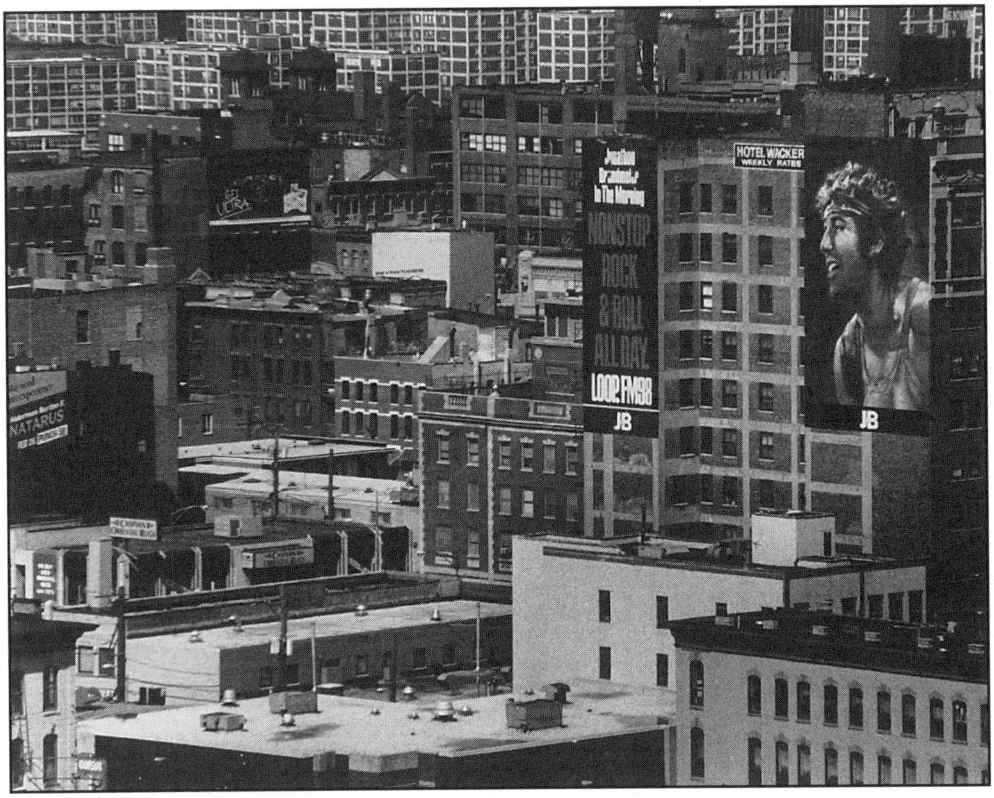

In viewing this urban/cultural landscape, what feelings do you have about city life? In addition to the subject matter and the mental images it stimulates, are you aware of geometric relationships?

The Cultural Landscape

"The visual soul of America is the highway, a hamburger joint, and a dime store. I love the loneliness and power and craziness of America. It is me."

— Burk Uzzle, photojournalist

Architectural landmarks were among the first subjects toward which early photographers pointed their primitive cameras. And photographic documentation of today's evidence of humanity's presence — beautiful, ugly, dramatic or mundane — will continue to be valuable to future historians.

"This mysterious quality of believability or implied truthfulness ... raises to the level of art the simplest, most direct snapshot, when the process of selection is in the hands of a creative person."

— J. H. Troup Jr., educator

How is *cultural* different from *social?* As I define it, *social* landscape emphasizes interaction between people while *cultural* landscape emphasizes people interacting with the artifacts of human civilization. And then urban landscape deals with city life, etc. Of course, the categories overlap broadly, but the idea simply is to help us recognize what we are doing. Whatever the subject matter, *the important thing is to take an interest in what is going on around us.*

"Any photographer who takes the time to react to what he is photographing, as well as to aim the lens and push the button ... will never feel the same about his subject."

— Margery Mann, photographer

"Photography is the simultaneous recognition, in a fraction of a second, of the significance of an event, as well as the precise organization of forms which gives that event its proper expression."

— Henri Cartier-Bresson, photojournalist.

Jeff Keyes

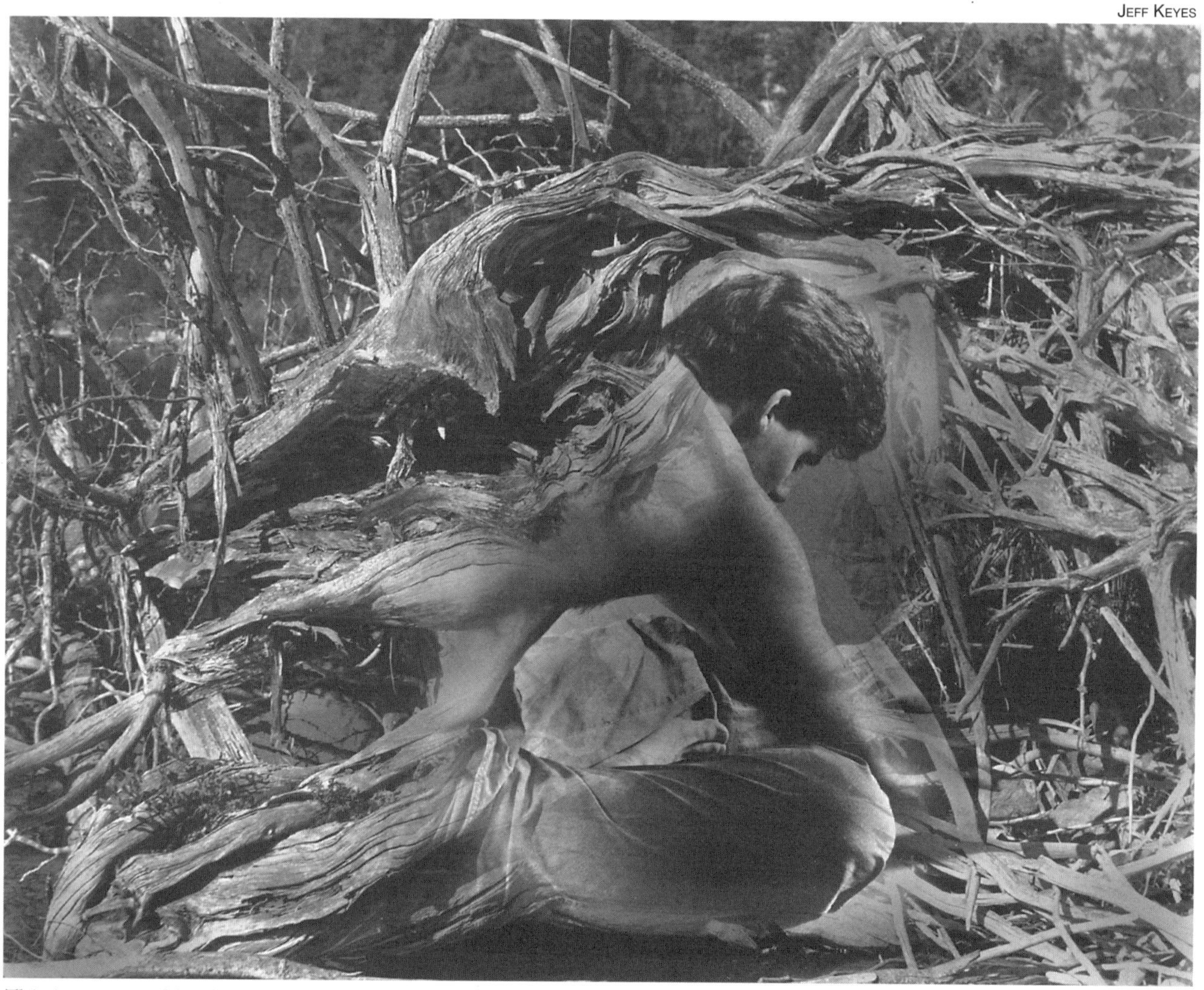

This image was blended in the darkroom from two negatives, although it might have been easier to create with a computer. What does it mean to you? What do you think the photographer had in mind?

The Personal (Inner) Landscape

"I like to present a problematic situation and let the viewer in his inventive way come to grips with it on personal terms."

— Jerry N. Uelsmann, imagemaker

A "stopper" image may not always be easy to understand. The secret is in trapping the viewer into studying it long enough to become committed to decoding the visual puzzle or metaphor that the imagemaker hid within it. To establish rapport, you have to offer viewers an intellectual and emotional challenge so personal and so tempting that they are compelled to accept it.

Such a compelling image could be a straight, unmanipulated photograph, but often our ideas call for the enhancement or surreal treatment enabled by advanced darkroom effects or computer work.

"Nothing is ever the same as they said it was. It's what I've never seen before that I recognize."

— Diane Arbus, photographer

People love to be surprised and amused by the bizarre. As a movement in art, surrealism involves deliberate distortion of the ordinary, or incongruous juxtaposition of objects. If you can shock viewers into spending enough time with your image, you can also reward them with serendipitous discoveries within it.

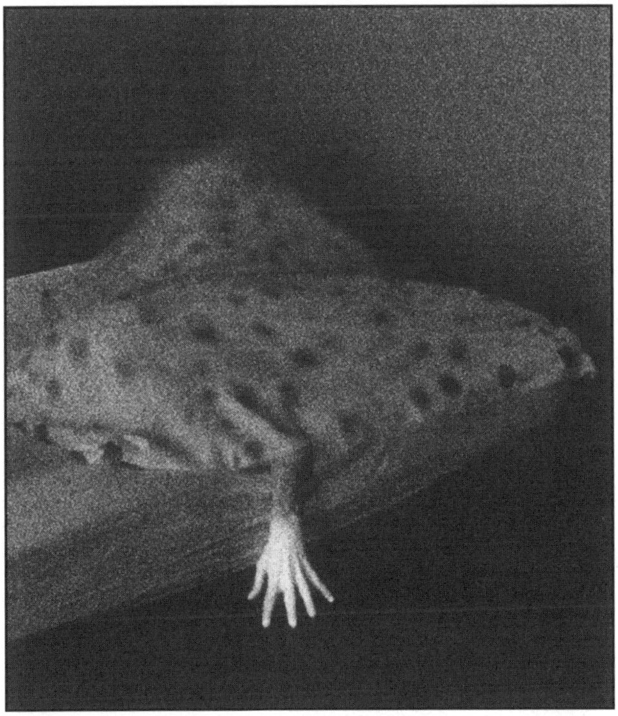

This photograph sends a chill up my spine. Does it have a similar effect on you? Does the murky, grainy tonality of the image affect its psychological impact?

WILLIAM BEVERLY
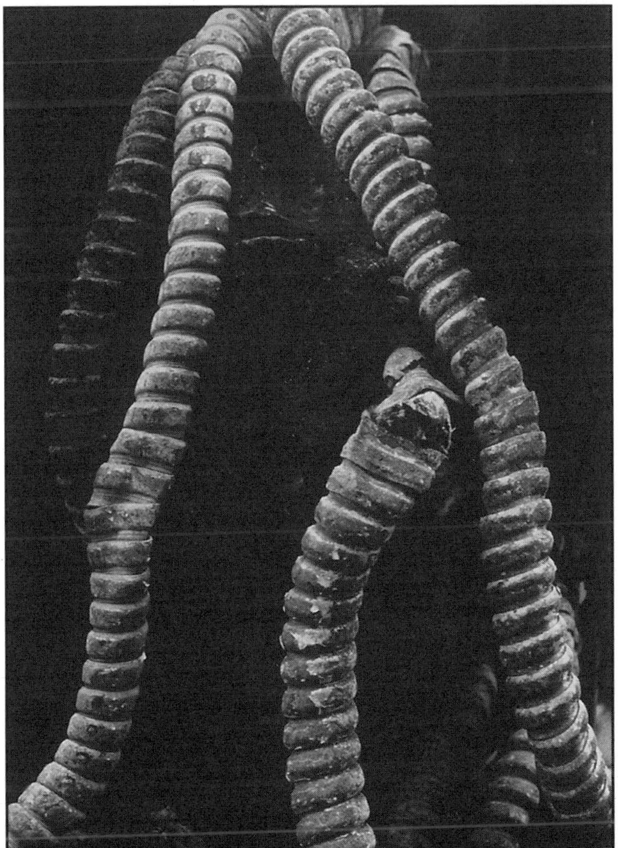

Besides being what it is ... what else is it?

The meaning of an image does not have to be limited to identifying its subject matter. Try photographing things, as photographer-teacher Minor White suggested, not so much for what they *are,* but for *what else* they are.

> ***"To the man who knows nothing, mountains are mountains, waters are waters, and trees are trees. But when he has studied, and knows a little, mountains are no longer mountains, water is no longer water, and trees are no longer trees. Finally, when he has thoroughly understood, mountains are once again mountains, waters are waters, and trees are trees."***
>
> — Zen philosophy quoted by
> Edward Weston, photographer

Of course, many photographs succeed on strength of subject matter alone. Pulitzer prizes have been awarded to journalists whose instincts and luck brought them to exactly the right place at the right time, and who had the nerve and the presence of mind to release the shutter at the climactic instant of a newsworthy event. But others can carry cameras around their necks for a lifetime — everywhere they go — and never get a single notable news picture.

(But having a camera with you might remind you to look for strong images of other kinds).

> ***"Without the influence of the subject matter, there is little reason to find form."***
>
> — Gary Monroe, photographer

> ***"A photograph should sometimes be more of an intriguing suggestion than an obvious statement."***
>
> — John A. Lacko, photographer

Most good pictures require conscious awareness of the potential of a situation, and the skill and patience to make the photograph happen. Good images also depend generally on the skillful and fortuitous combination of interesting subject matter with some of the elements of lighting, perspective, composition, and technique.

DARREN HATHAWAY

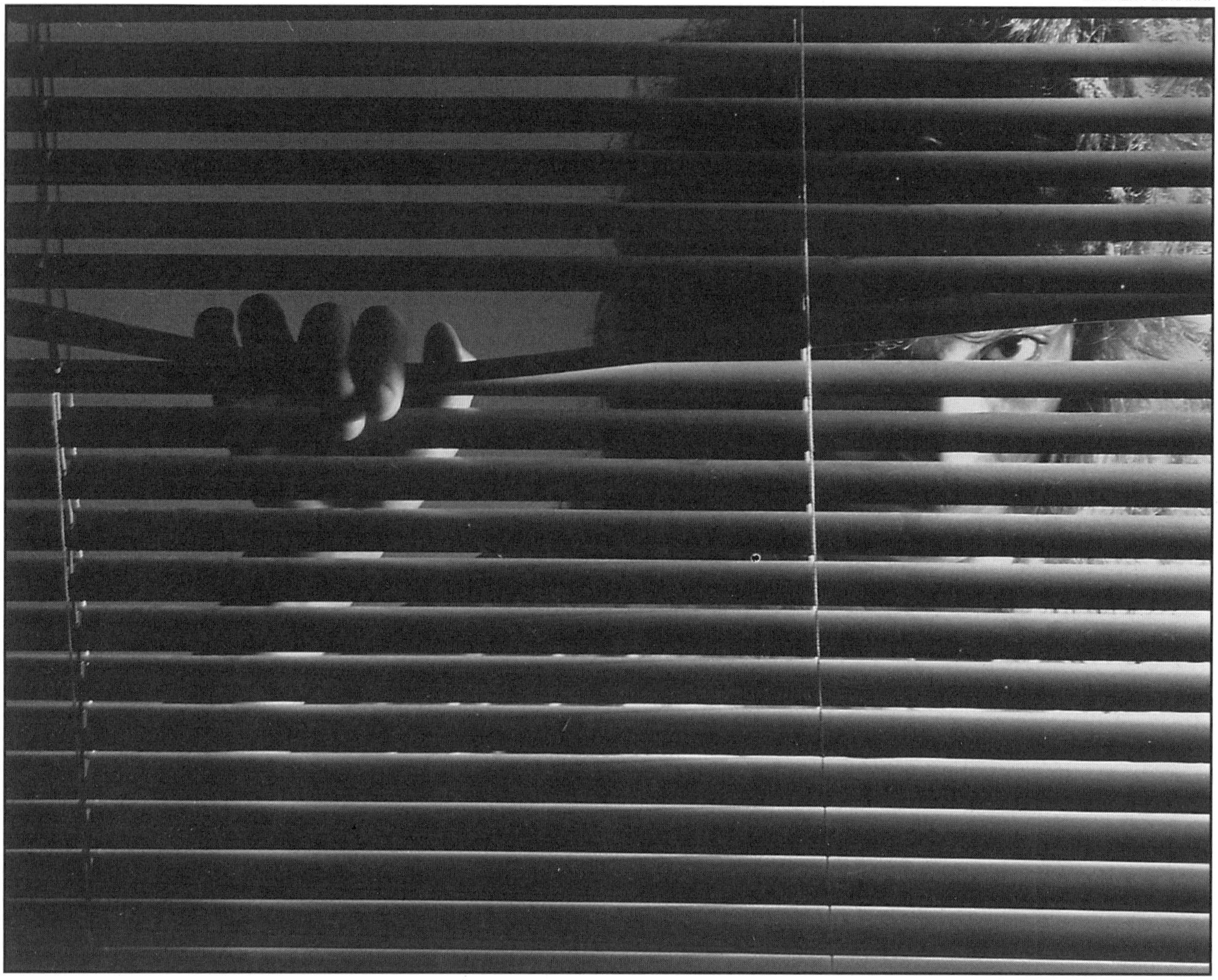

How do the elements of line, tone and contrast affect your reaction to this image?

"Photography combines those elements of spontaneity and immediacy that say, 'this is happening, this is real,' and creates an image through a curious alchemy ..."

— Dan Weiner, photographer

Although some photographs can be successful because of their subject matter alone, there has never been such an image that couldn't have had additional impact. Great pictures demand a blending of all the elements of the imagemaker's visual vocabulary, most prominent of which is light.

"Wherever there is light, one can photograph."

— Ansel Adams, photographer

Consider light in terms of tone and contrast — in other words, what light does to and for subject matter.

Tone

We live among cultural clichés about color meanings, and stereotypes about tonality. In the North American/ European tradition, for example, lightness and brightness imply cleanliness, goodness, hope and inspiration; darkness is often taken to mean the opposite: *blacklist, blackmail, black market, black sheep, "in the dark."*

The ancient oriental symbol of the eternal struggle between good and evil depicts good as white and evil as black or red. In Western movies, we all know who wears the white hat and who wears the black hat. Black, in the culture of the Western world, is the traditional symbol of death and mourning. Perhaps some of the roots of racial prejudice are traceable to ancient myths and taboos about darkness and blackness. Most people instinctively associate dark photographs with sadness, mystery or something ominous. Lightness usually suggests happiness, openness, innocence and hope.

Colors are stereotyped, too. Red, orange and yellow are traditionally warm, active, and advancing. Green and blue are considered to be cool, passive, and retreating. Although these conventions generally are accepted, some interesting paradoxes have been created by imagemakers bold enough to violate them.

"[When looking at a photograph] we experience a swift, intuitive response to the photograph as a whole — an emotional reaction that cannot be precisely verbalized — resulting from the interplay of shapes, forms, textures, lights, and darks. More or less simultaneously we try to find a rational meaning to the event or situation portrayed.

Why is the photographer showing us this particular fragment of time and space? What meaning, if any, did it have for him and may it have for us?"

— Arthur Goldsmith, educator

ALLEN BRAGDON

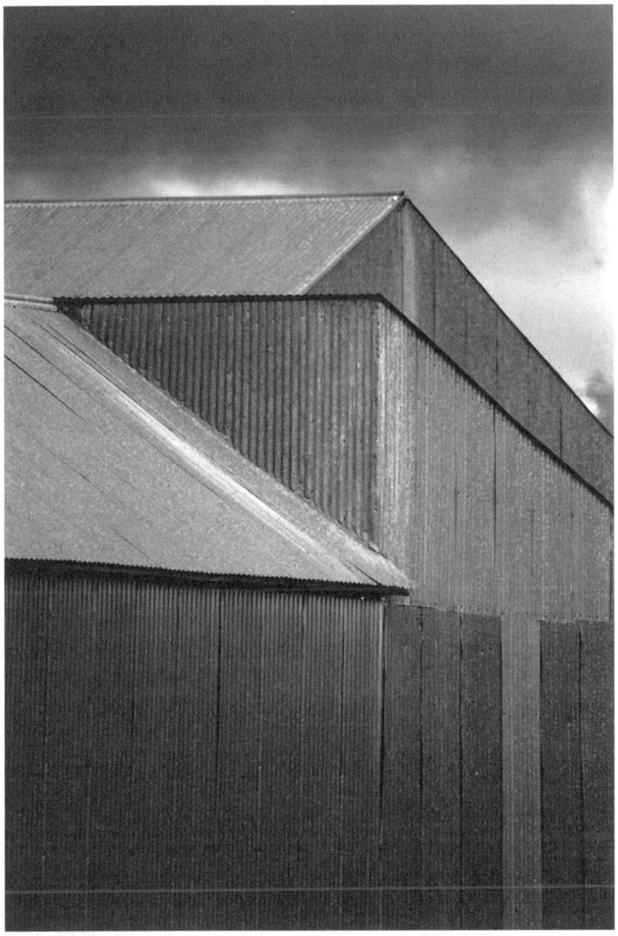

What design element dominates this image? Has the composition been strengthened by eliminating much of the building and most of the background?

Contrast

"It is two elements which are suddenly in conflict. There is a spark between two elements. There are always two pulls and one cannot exist without the other one. It's these tensions I'm always moved by."

— Henri Cartier-Bresson, photojournalist

Cartier-Bresson, one of the world's most respected photojournalists, was referring to conflict and contrast between forms and objects, as well as between elements of light and dark and conflicting colors. Contrast (conflict) is a basic element of visual composition.

Photography is possible because some objects and portions of objects reflect more light than others. Shadows, to put it most simply, are crucial. The term *contrast* refers to the relative brightness, or reflectivity, of various portions of the subject or of the photograph as a whole.

"We are ... utterly captivated by the problems of light; the, dangerous, dreamlike, living, dead, clear, misty, hot, violent, bare, sudden, dark, spring-like, falling, straight, slanting, sensual, subdued, limited, poisonous, calming, pale light. Light."

— Ingmar Bergman, film director

CHAD BENNETT

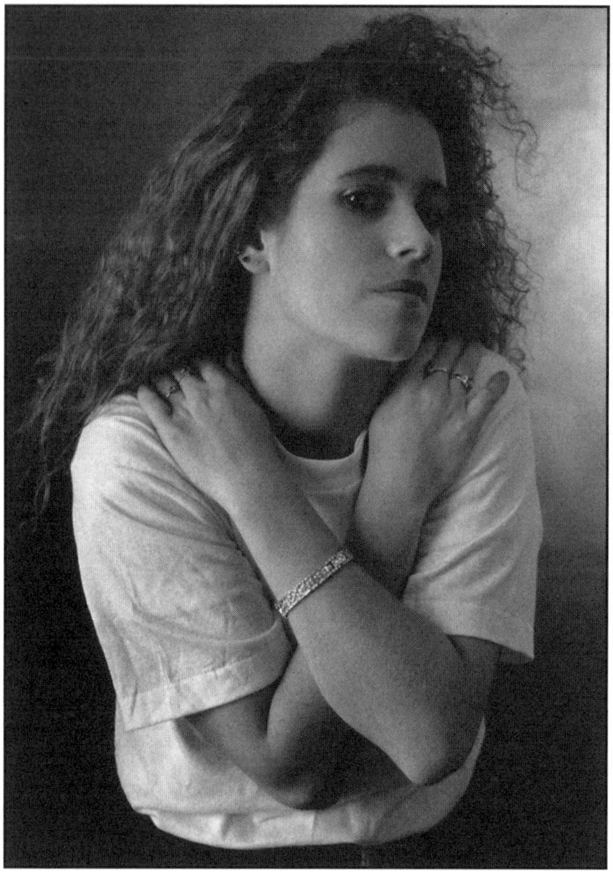

Compare this portrait with the one on the right. What differences in mood and effect have been created by posing, lighting and composition?

JORG JASPER

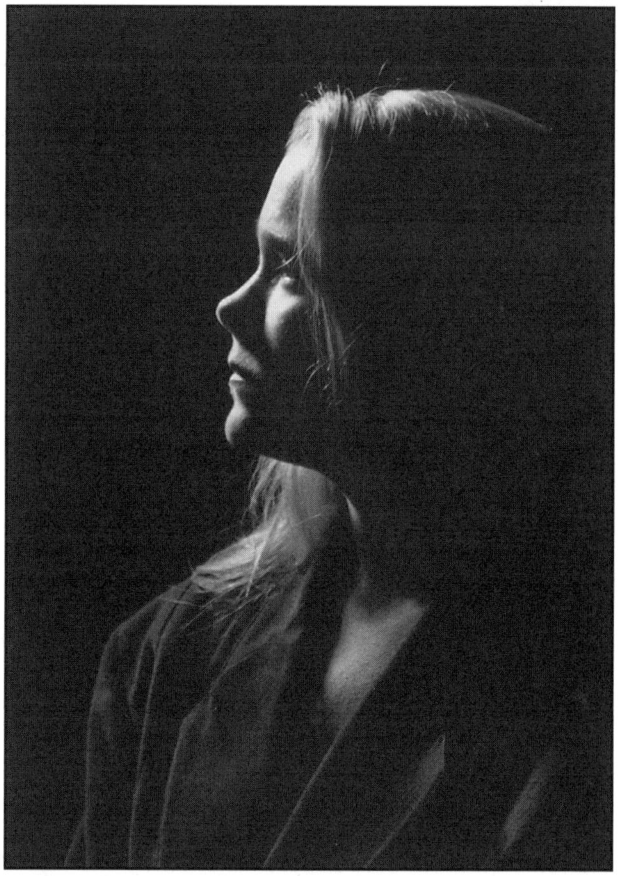

Analyze the pose and lighting of this portrait. Where has the key light been placed? What do you think this picture suggests about the personality of the subject?

Soft, low-contrast lighting, in which shadows are diffuse and luminous, often creates a mood of delicacy and softness, even femininity, especially when the image is predominantly light in tone, or *high key.* Contrasts in lighting, on the other hand, tend to form harsh, dark shadows on and around the subject, emphasizing texture and roughness. And remember what darkness may imply! If the predominant mood is extremely dark, there may be mystery (what evil lurks in those sinister shadows?) An image that consists mostly of dark areas is said to be *low key.*

"One of the most beautiful things to do is to paint darkness which, nevertheless, has light within it."

— Vincent van Gogh, painter

Extreme lighting contrast is often thought to be appropriate for enhancing the rugged appearance of masculine character subjects and simulating the dramatic effect of stage lighting. As a spotlight singles out the principal performer on stage, so the *main* or *key* light draws the viewer's attention to the lightest portion of a picture.

As you study photographs, prints and paintings, notice whether your eye is drawn to the lightest area, and then whether this area is the most significant point, or the center of interest. It's often distracting, for example, to allow a print to have very large white areas in the corners or bright areas in the background that compete for attention. Irresistibly, the eye is drawn away from the primary center of interest. The skilled imagemaker tries to control the direction and relative contrast of light and chooses which portions of a picture to illuminate.

Chiaroscuro is a term used by artists to describe the placing of light against dark, and dark against light. Extraneous detail sometimes is suppressed by placing it in the shadows. Balance is as important between light and dark tones as it is between various hues and intensities of color. Look for the chiaroscuro effect in nature and in works of art. Try to employ it in your images.

Perspective

"The snapshot is a picture made with the eye only. The creative photograph, on the other hand, is made with the mind."

— Wilson Hicks, editor

In the broadest sense, *perspective* means point of view. The term refers to the rendering of lines and surfaces and three-dimensional forms on the flat film plane inside the camera. It refers also to the effect of size relationships and camera angle to the viewer's interpretation of the photograph.

Should you correct a distorted rendering of perspective? Although our eyes see parallel lines as converging, and straight lines as curved, an accepted convention in architectural and most product photography is that parallels should be rendered parallel and that straight and perpendicular lines should be shown as being straight and perpendicular. With the right kind of equipment, we can either "correct" or deliberately distort perspective, depending on the effect we have in mind.

Allen Bragdon

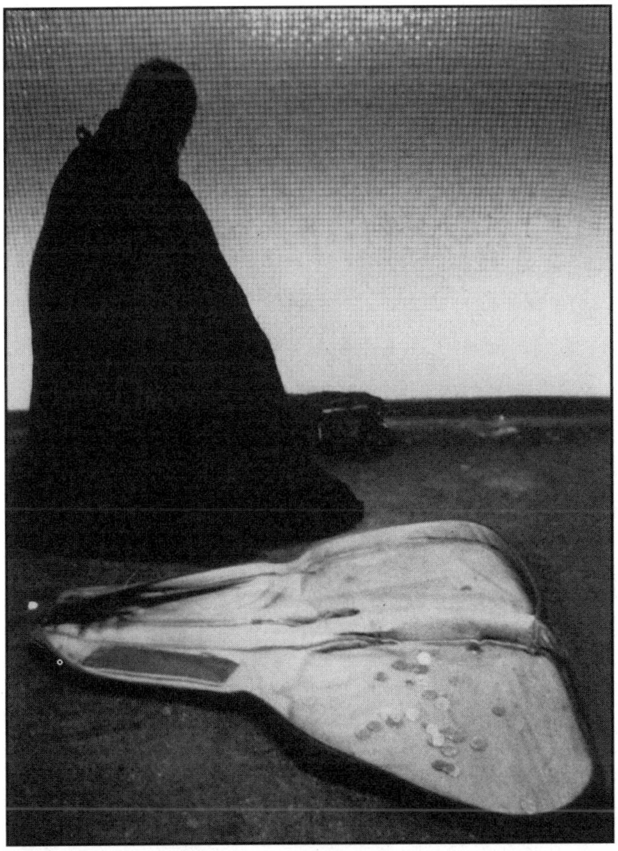

Notice how the chiaroscuro effect reinforces this simple composition of strong, repeated graphic forms?

In size relationships, *Biggest=Most Important.* That's the general rule, with exceptions made by skillful use of lighting and compositional balance to emphasize areas or objects that are smaller in size.

"… it is the relationship between things [that is] important."

— Henri Cartier-Bresson, photojournalist

When we look up at someone or something, that subject seems to increase in stature and significance, as a child's-eye view of an adult. Conversely, looking down tends by association to diminish or to de-emphasize. Notice the altered feeling of identification when you confront a child or a pet eye-to-eye. Sometimes a change in camera angle adds interest or drama to an ordinary scene.

Composition

"The contemplation of things as they are, without error or confusion, without substitution or imposture, is in itself a nobler thing than a whole harvest of invention."

— Francis Bacon, philosopher

"To photograph a rock, to have it look like a rock, yet more than a rock …"

— Edward Weston, photographer

"The camera allows the photographer to select and save rectangular bits and pieces of the all-encompassing, ever-changing reality in which we exist … The photographer … applies the camera's frame to nature to include, to exclude, to associate, to disassociate, to isolate designs, and to show significance."

— J. H. Troup Jr., educator

SALLY PUTNEY

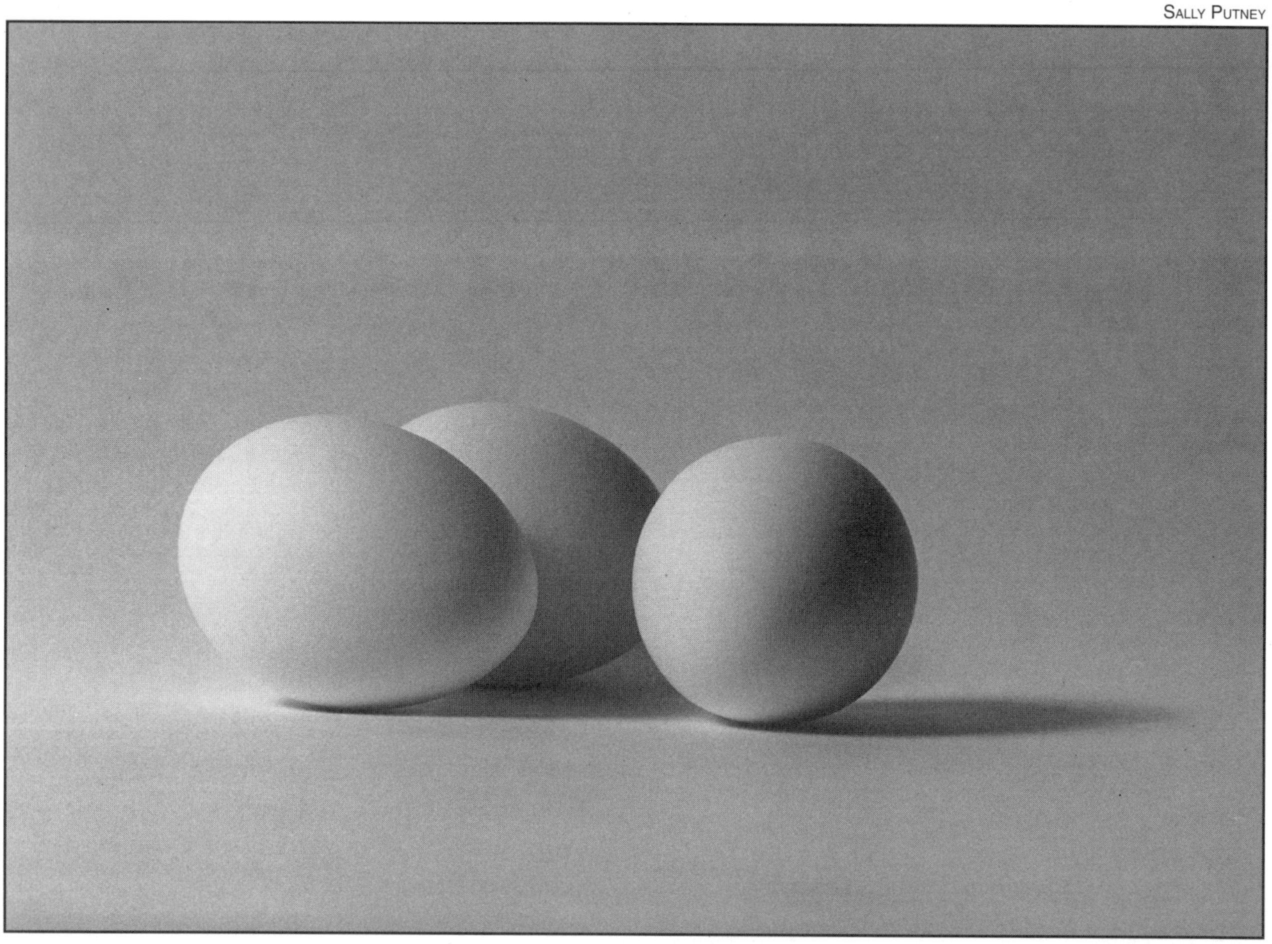

In this high-key photograph, notice that roundness and texture are retained in the eggs, although only relatively small shadow areas have a value below Zone VI.

WALLACE KIRK

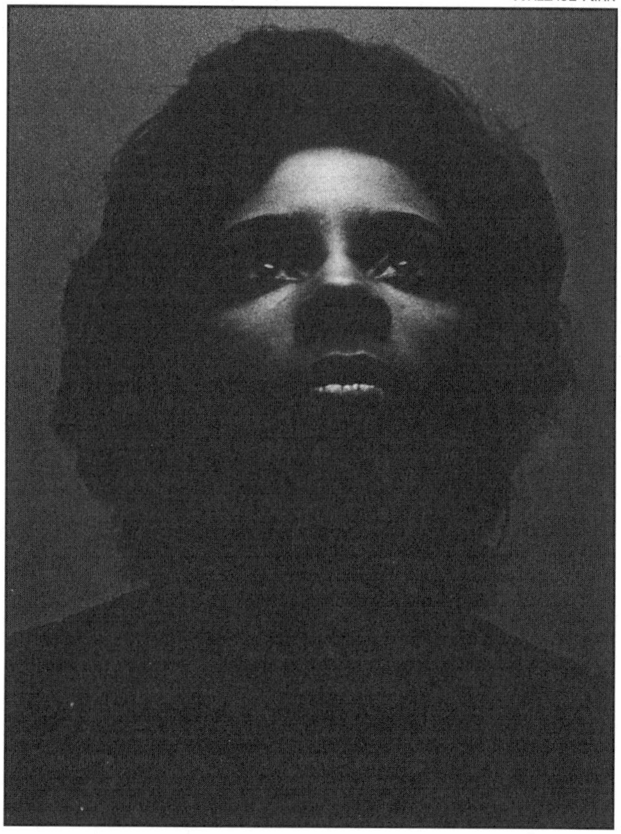

This low-key portrait retains a sparkle and feeling of quality although composed mostly of values below Zone V. Loss of separation between the darker zones seems relatively unimportant because attention is diverted to highlights in the eyes and onto the major planes of the face.

Jim Nixon (2)

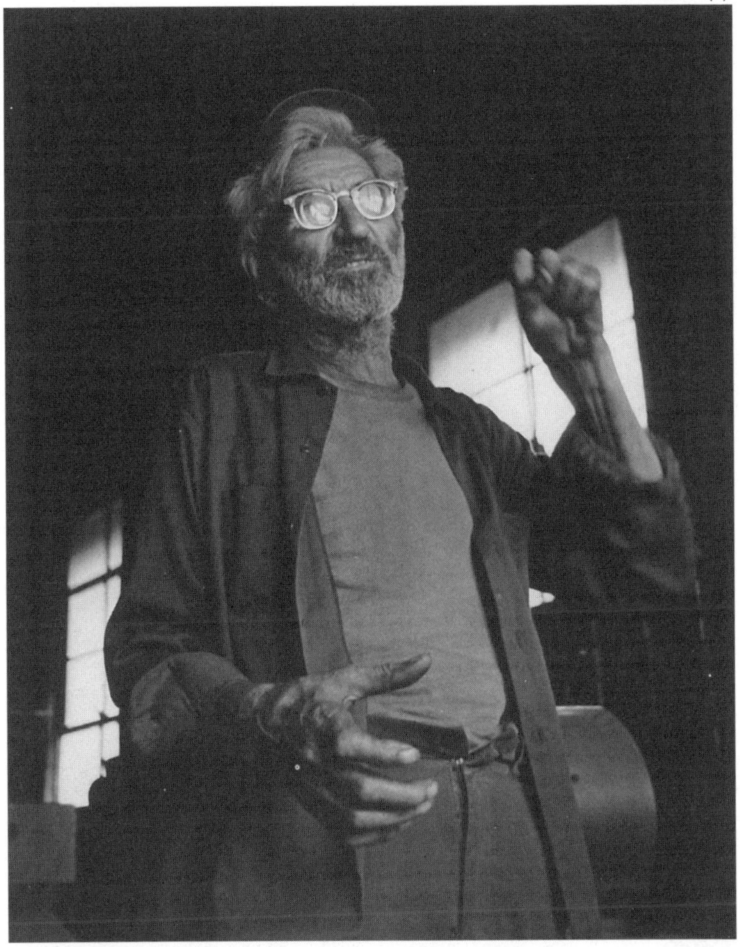

Does looking up at a subject increase its apparent stature? Do the hand and arm gestures in this example and the one below contribute to the effects of enhancement and diminution?

What effect does viewpoint have on psychological interpretation? Are feelings of diminution and vulnerability the result of looking down on a subject, as we are accustomed to looking down on a child?

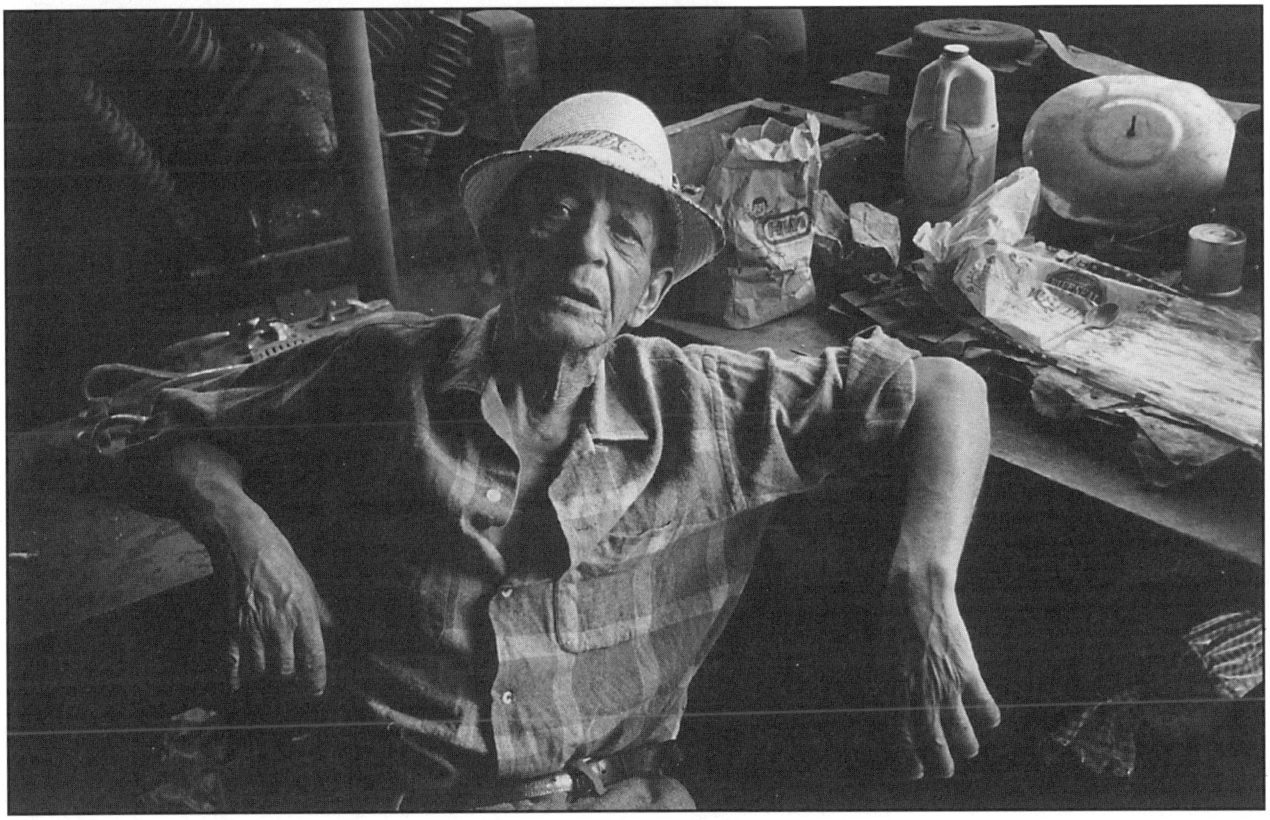

James M. Rhoads

Does this combination of vertical format and jagged diagonals imply both height and action? Besides strong line and texture, this image contains unusual spatial relationships.

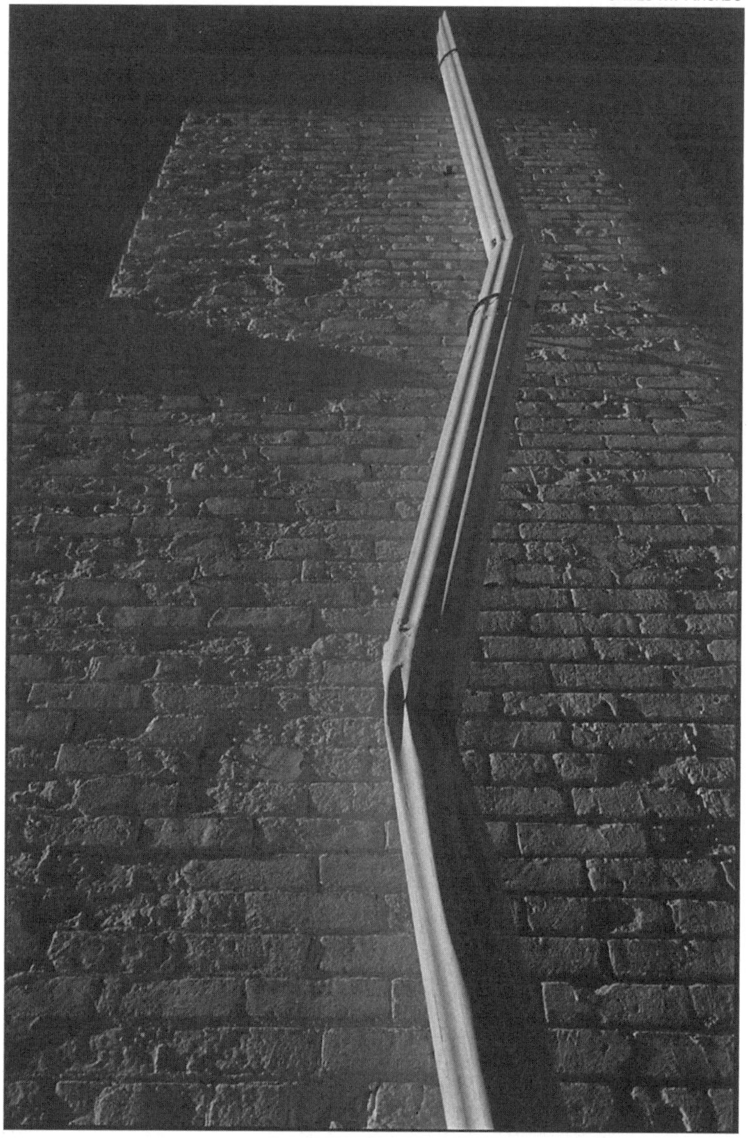

The sensuous S-curve, peaceful horizontal format, and restful tonal values of the quiet landscape below, contrast strongly with the violent jaggedness of the photo to the right. Do both of these compositions apply the Rule of Thirds? (See page 40.)

Jim Nixon

In the quotation on page 33, Troup distills the essence of the difference between the work of the painter and that of the photographer.

While the painter starts with simple space (a blank canvas), and then adds basic lines and forms, concluding finally with the complex elements of texture and color, the photographer must do exactly the reverse. Photographers work from the complex to the simple. From the bewildering array of visual stimuli confronting him or her, the photographer must isolate and select, including the significant elements within the space bounded by the edges of the ground glass or viewfinder, and excluding the extraneous.

"It's just as important to decide what not to include in the frame as it is to decide what to include."

— Gary Monroe, photographer

A camera, correctly adjusted, will record an image of everything within its field of view. The camera's eye merely records facts. It is the eye and brain behind the instrument that must determine which facts are worth recording and in what way.

MEL TEAGUE

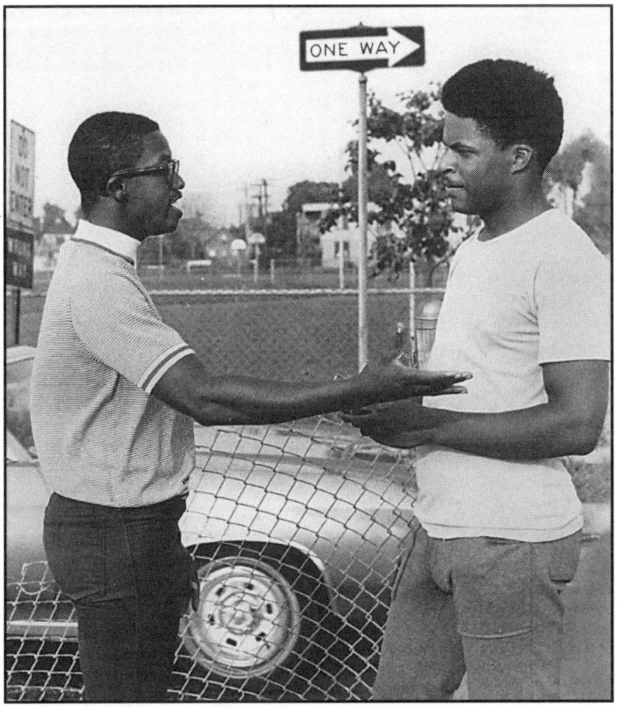

Do the signs, poles, wheel, fence texture, and other details provide essential supporting information in this photograph or are they distractions?

"The camera is dumb!"

— Gary Winogrand, photographer

"Abstraction releases everyday forms from their everyday associations — allows them to take on new and symbolic meanings."

— Norman F. Carver Jr., photographer

One assignment often recommended to student photographers is to get permission from the owner of a junkyard to come in with camera and tripod on a weekend or holiday when dangerous equipment is not in action. Obviously, the biggest challenge in taking pictures in a junkyard is the discipline of searching for pleasing designs and patterns among unrecognizable subject matter. Unburdened by concern about "What is it?," viewers of the resulting images can share the imagemaker's joy of discovery.

"The junkyard proved to me that there are things to photograph everywhere. Until I shot that assignment I didn't believe it."

— A student

Some painters try to produce abstract images by leaving out all identifiable objects. Interestingly, these are the kinds of expressionist images that a perceptive photographer can discover anywhere!

"More has been written about composition than should have been."

— John R. Whiting, editor

What Whiting means is that iron-clad rules have been set down through the years by art critics, professors, and jurors of competitions. They have used these rules as inflexible criteria for measuring the value of photographs as art. Many of these so-called rules have become such a part of traditional criticism that many people accept them, dismissing good pictures that fail to follow the formulas. But in the same way that photographs should not be rejected or ridiculed solely because they don't meet certain accepted compositional criteria, neither should empty and meaningless images be accepted and praised solely because they do.

David Knoblauch (2)

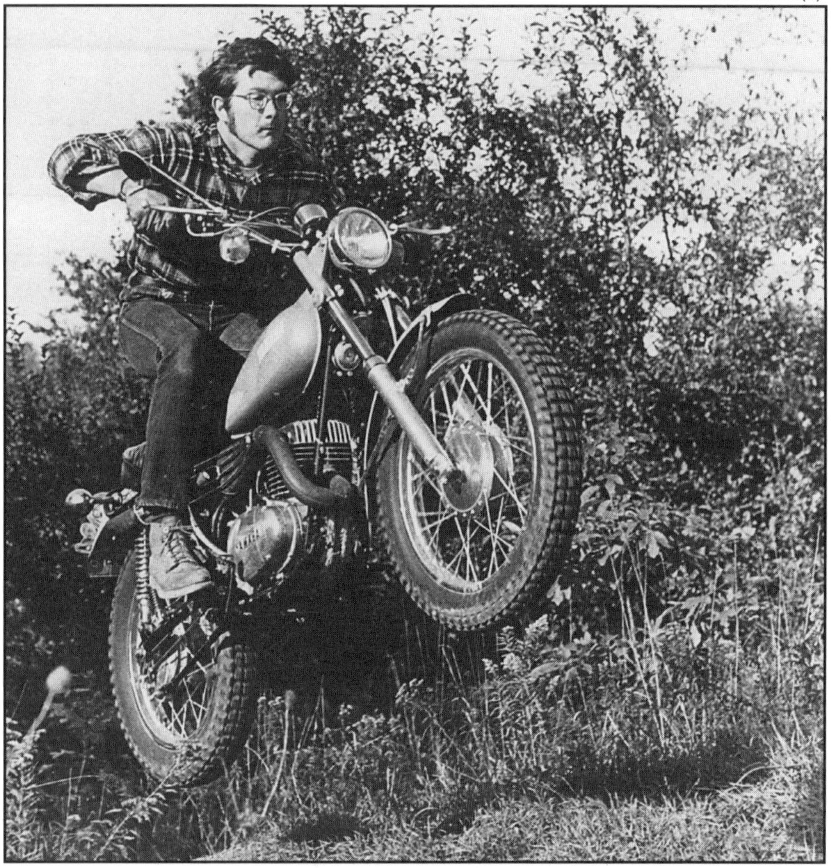

Does it make any difference to you whether the cyclist appears to be moving into the frame or out of it? In the photograph below, does he seem to be coming to a screeching halt? (If you try photos like this, remind the biker to wear a helmet!)

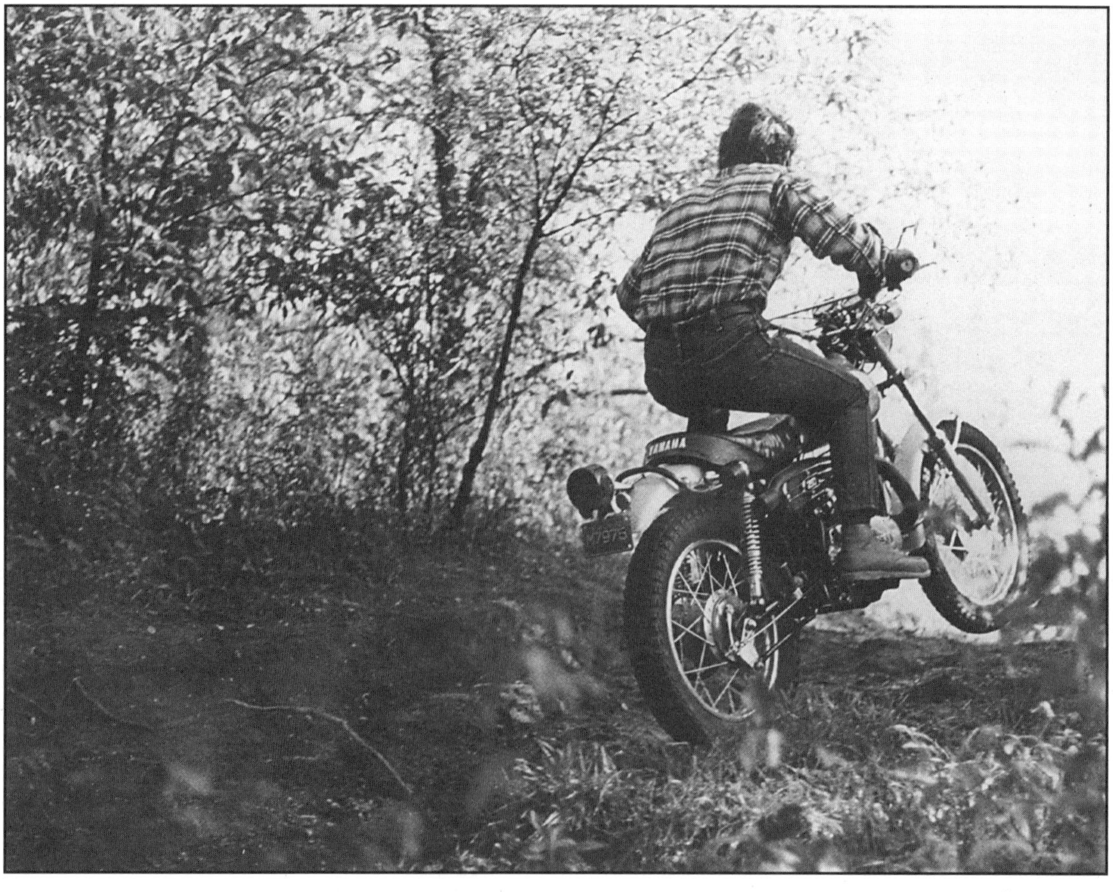

"Compositional rules are nothing more than the experience of others that has become accepted. To accept and follow the rules uncritically means to accept other people's experience and not to allow yourself to experiment."

— Gerhard Bakker, educator

The "rules" are worth studying, however, because they will help you to produce stronger and more successful images. Once you've become familiar with the "rules," you can feel free to break them when you want to — but never because of ignorance. Break a rule only when breaking it makes your statement stronger.

"Photography is about responding to things."

— Sam Abell, photojournalist

"When I make what I think is going to be a fine photograph, I feel it. I can feel it in my stomach."

— William Albert Allard, photojournalist

Part of what Allard means is that he has an innate feeling for design, order and balance — intuition deep inside that says, "Move the camera a few inches to the left ..." And, "This is it ... shoot!"

"The 'world' out 'there' is as much a projection from inside our heads as it is a perception ... [because of this] it is a miracle that we communicate at all."

— Robert Fulghum, philosopher

JAMES M. RHOADS

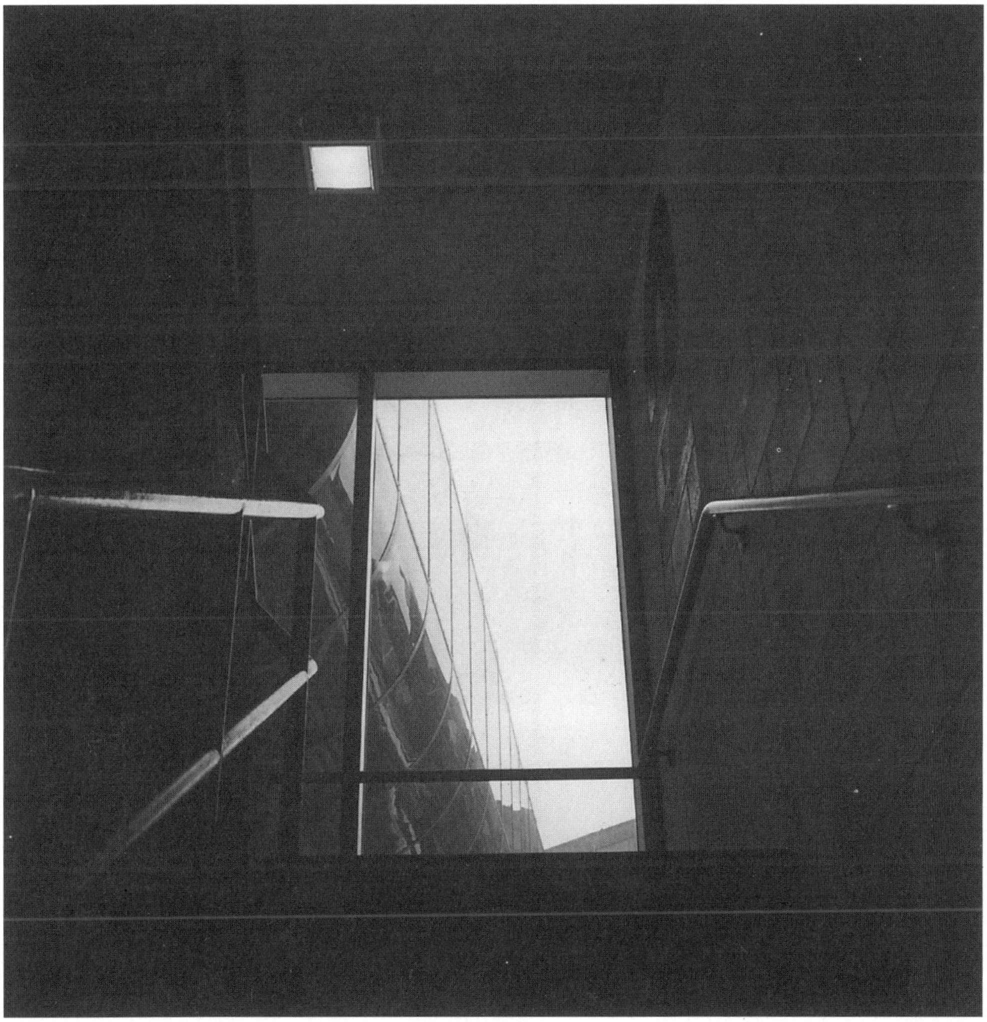

Dark on light, or light on dark? Which is foreground and which is background? If the large white rectangle is a window or a doorway, where does it lead — in or out? The mystery and drama seem heightened by visual contrast and by delicate balance of positive and negative space.

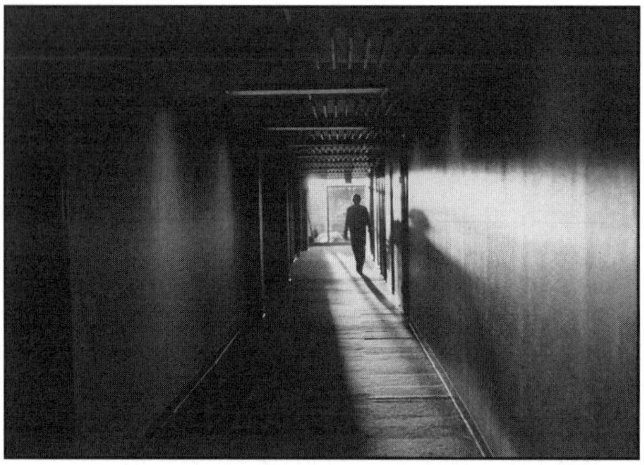

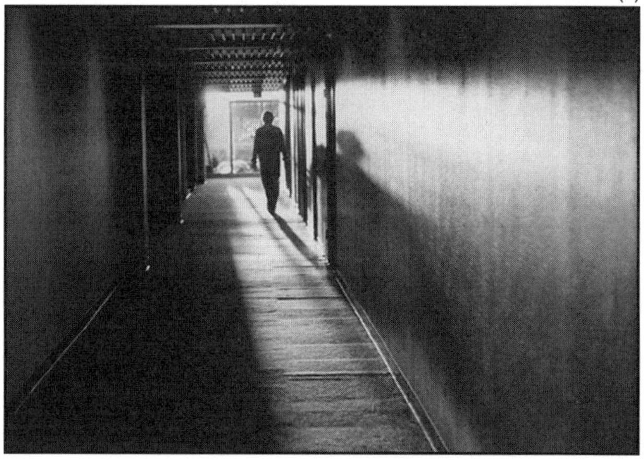

Which cropping do you prefer? The version on the right illustrates the widely stated rule that the center of interest should be placed approximately one third of the distance from either top or bottom of the frame and also about one third the distance from either left or right. This "Rule of Thirds" makes the compositon more dynamic, but sometimes centering the subject is appropriate. You decide!

The "Rule of Thirds" (right) suggests that dominant horizontal or vertical lines and principal subjects should be spaced at a ratio of about one-third to two-thirds within the space outlined by the image frame.

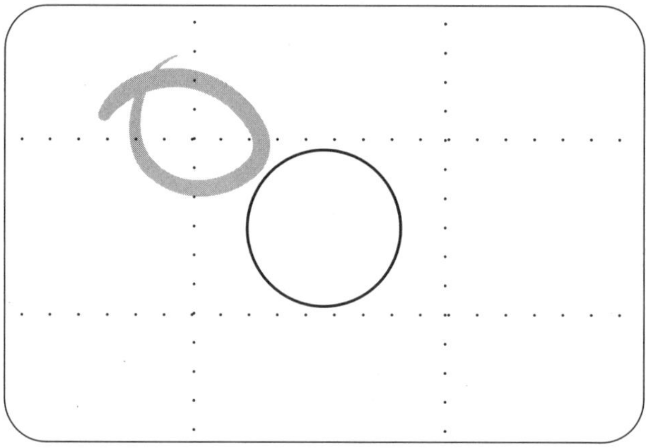

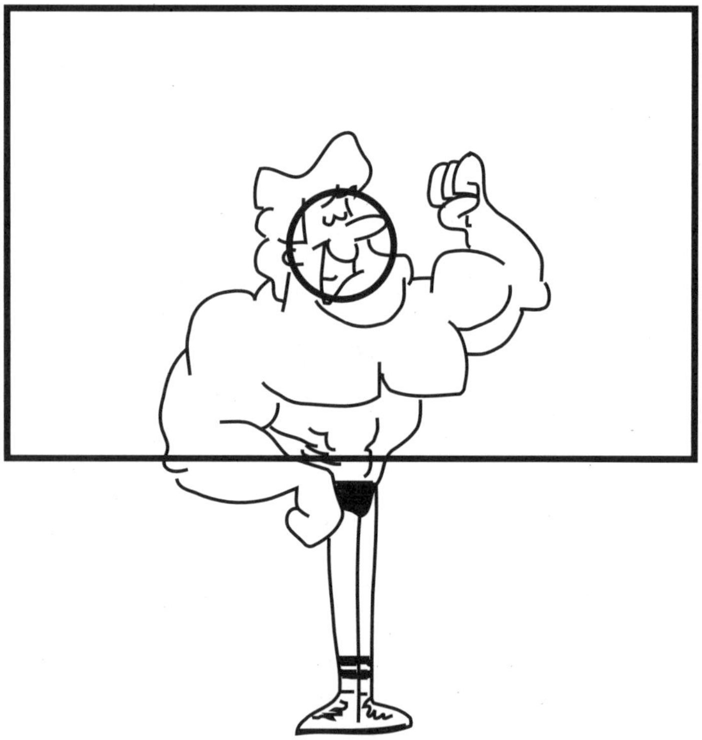

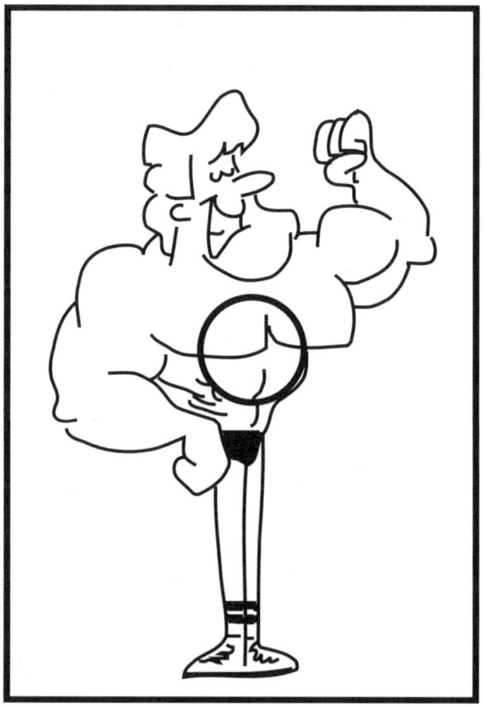

The "Center Circle Syndrome" describes the tendency of beginners to place the center of the picture (often a person's head) in the center of the camera viewfinder. Experience teaches us to fill the entire frame, balancing the essential parts of the scene and eliminating everything else. At this point, decide whether to compose horizontally or vertically.

By studying other people's photographs, and comparing them to your own, you'll see when the following "rules" have strengthened a picture and when the imagemaker was right in daring to break them.

Some "Rules" of Composition:

1. Select a single, dominant center of interest.

2. Place the center of interest away from the center of the picture. Follow the "Rule of Thirds."

3. Keep the horizon level, placing it according to the "Rule of Thirds." Don't divide a picture into two equal parts either horizontally or vertically.

4. Keep vertical lines such as buildings and trees parallel with the edges of the frame.

5. Select a contrasting background so that important tones and textures in your main subject don't merge with the background.

6. Fill the frame. Do most of your cropping in the camera viewfinder before taking the picture.

7. Crop or remove extraneous objects.

8. Don't amputate parts of your main subject at awkward places.

9. Avoid distracting shapes at the edges of the image. Light or bright colored areas at edges and corners tend to draw a viewer's eye out of the frame and away from the center of interest.

10. Have the main subject facing or moving into the frame, instead of out of the frame.

11. Frame the principal subject with a complementary foreground object. (Especially in natural landscapes).

12. Attract the viewer's attention with leading lines, such as converging diagonals or an S curve that direct the eye into the composition.

13. Employ strong diagonal lines to imply action or conflict.

14. Compose in vertical format to emphasize height and dignity, or to imply potential motion. A horizontal format may suggest peace and stability.

15. Remember these "rules," but violate them freely when doing so will create a stronger or more meaningful image!

"I don't know any formal rules of composition ... Composition is simply the strongest way of seeing."

— Edward Weston, photographer

Megan Salyers

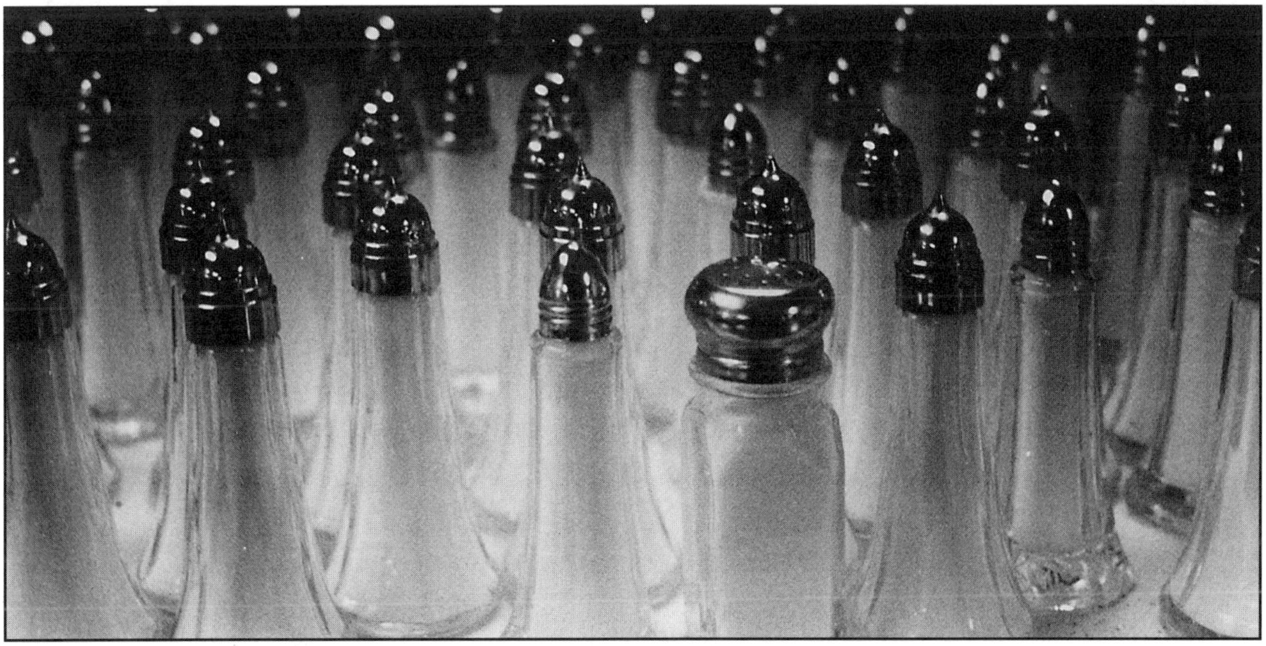

Repetition is an excellent compositional idea, but without variation, repetition can be boring. Sometimes all you need is just one object different from the rest

Weston's wisdom is right on target. But while you're strengthening your personal vision, by observing the "rules" you'll be able to make pictures that will sell, get good grades, and achieve other kinds of recognition. By totally ignoring them you risk failure. Sometimes, by deliberately violating the "rules," you may audaciously achieve a fantastically successful image. It depends on what else besides composition you've managed to put into your picture.

Elements of Composition

Fundamental to effective composition are the artist's elements of form, space, line, tone, texture, rhythm, and contrast.

Form is the shape of objects that dominate the design within the image. When repeated with variation in size, tone, color or texture, these echoes of the basic form can create a harmonious composition.

> ***"When simple forms are repeated they bring to the eye the kind of pleasure that music brings to the ear."***
>
> — Victor B. Scheffer, educator

F. L. Feick

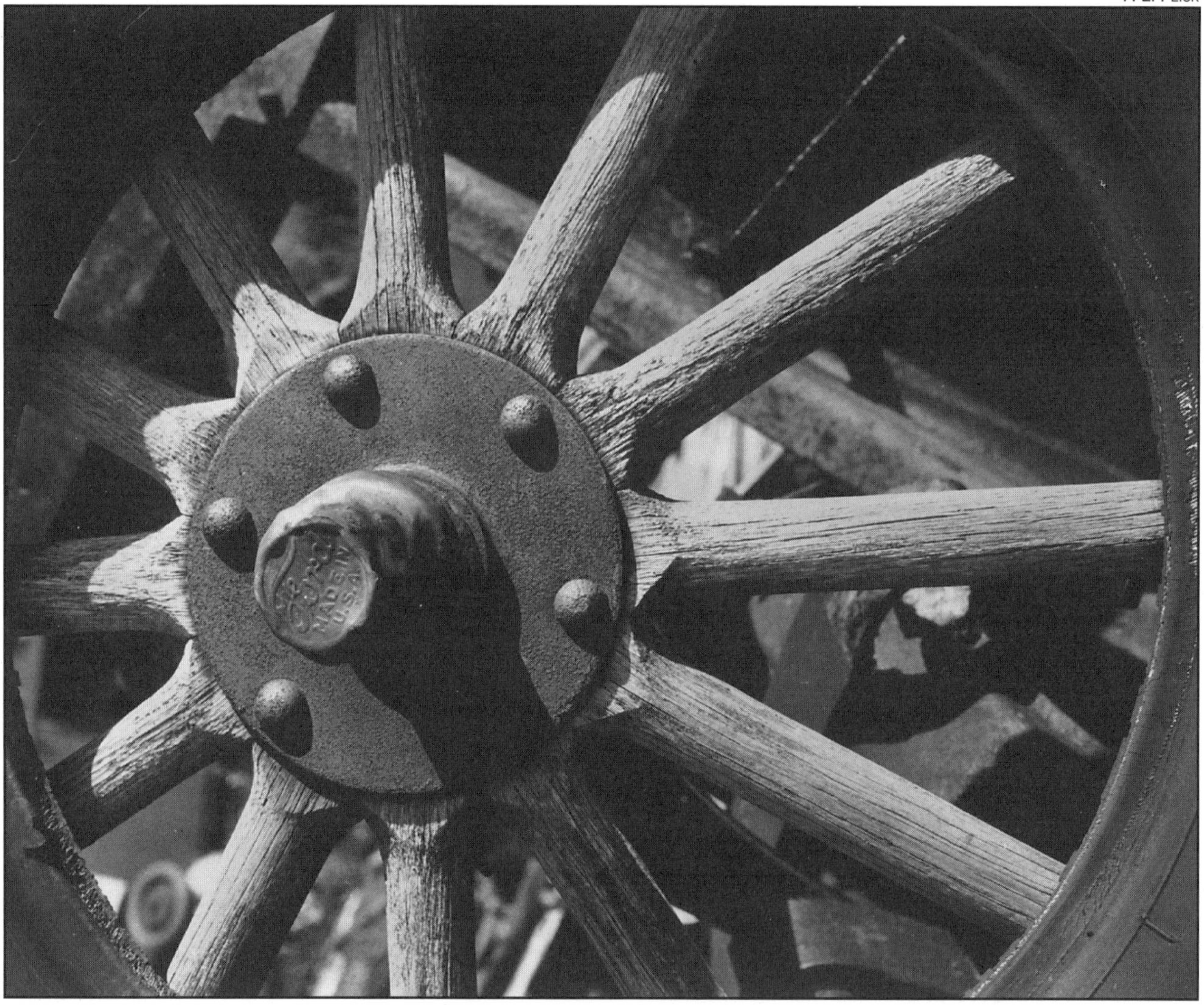

Although other elements are important in this photograph, we expect to be able to "feel" the textures of rusty iron and weathered wood. Oblique sunlight, a small lens opening, and a steady tripod yield a sharp image that, when examined up close, does not dissappoint us.

Beth Shirk

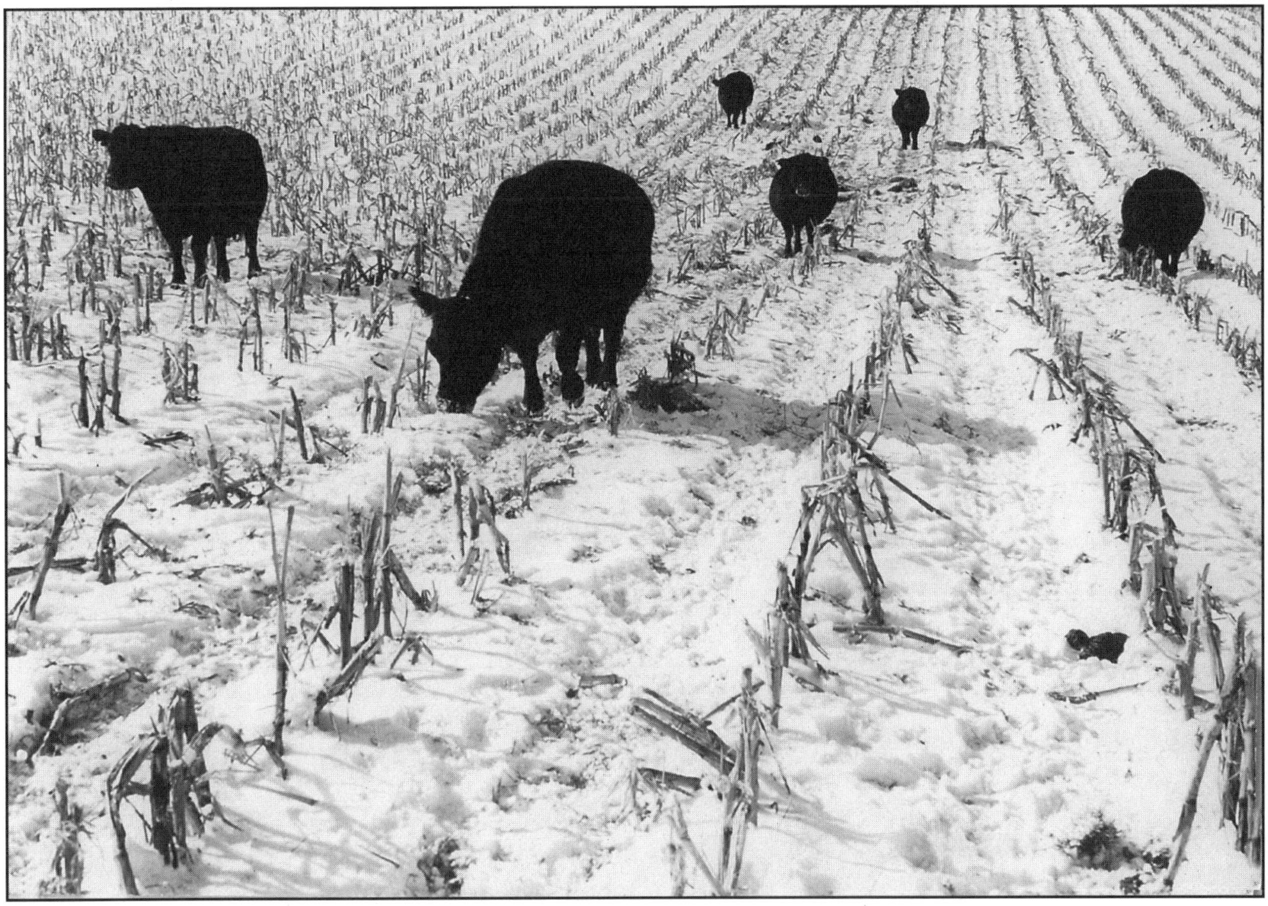

Squint at this photograph. Do the cattle appear to be floating in space? Do their diminishing sizes give an illusion of depth and distance? Notice that the three-dimensional effect is enhanced by the converging perspective of the rows of corn stubble.

Space is simply the area of the image that is not form. Space is the field or background surrounding objects within the frame.

Line defines itself as linear emphasis, whether outlining form and separating it from space, or leading the viewer's eye as it moves around within the image.

Tone is the relative value or brightness of an object or an area. The term also can describe the overall lightness or darkness of the entire image. Whether in shades of gray or color values, tones can be contrasted, harmonized, or merged, depending on the effect you want to achieve. Whether the background remains in the background, in what is sometimes referred to as negative space, depends on the relative tonal values in the image. If the main subject merges with the background, both form and space may be poorly defined.

Texture is another element of beauty and interest. Texture in a visual image is roughness or smoothness that you can "feel" with your eyes: tree bark, sand or skin that your mind vicariously can caress and explore.

"You can think of [texture] as form on a smaller scale. It describes the finer parts of a pattern. When you see a spider web at a distance you think of its texture, but when you look closely at one you think of its form ... As you bring your eye closer to the bark of a tree you gradually lose the feeling of texture and begin to see bold lines and curves. Now you see how form and texture are related by scale."

— Victor B. Scheffer, educator

William Beverly (3)

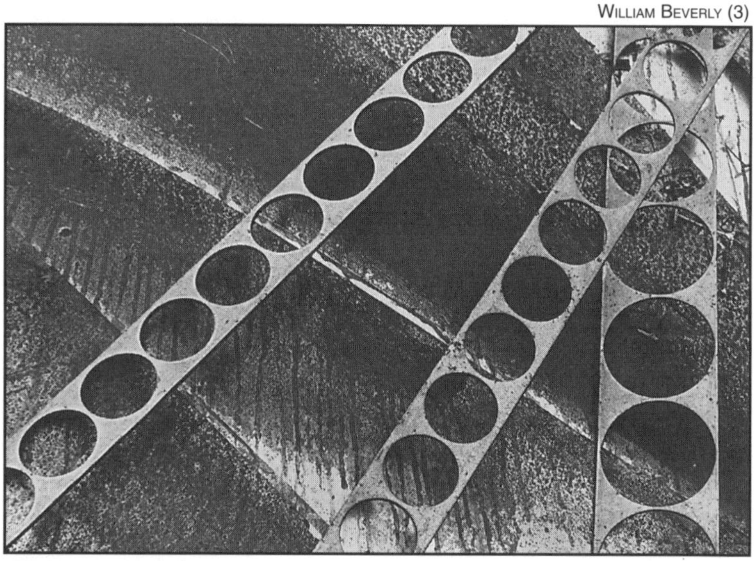

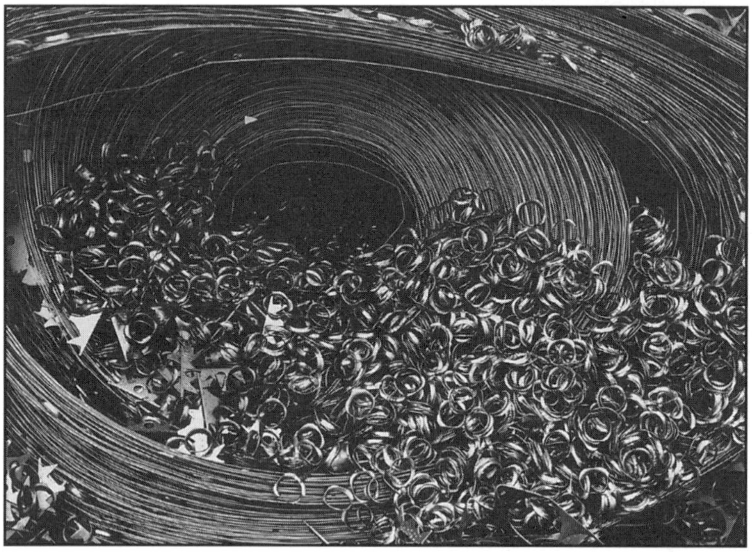

I hear music when I examine these three photographs. Do you? With one I can hear a strident march, with another a waltz, and looking at the third I hear jazz.

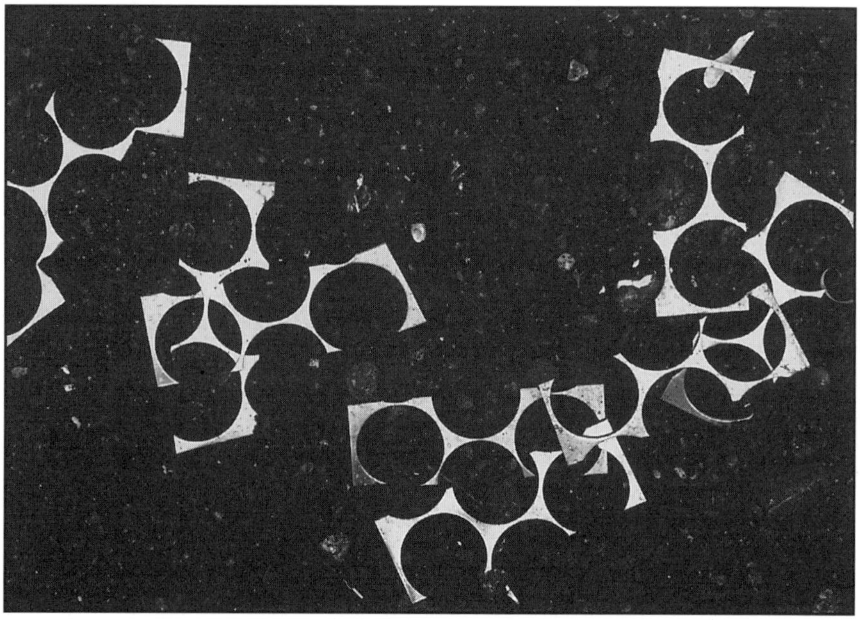

Elaine Logie

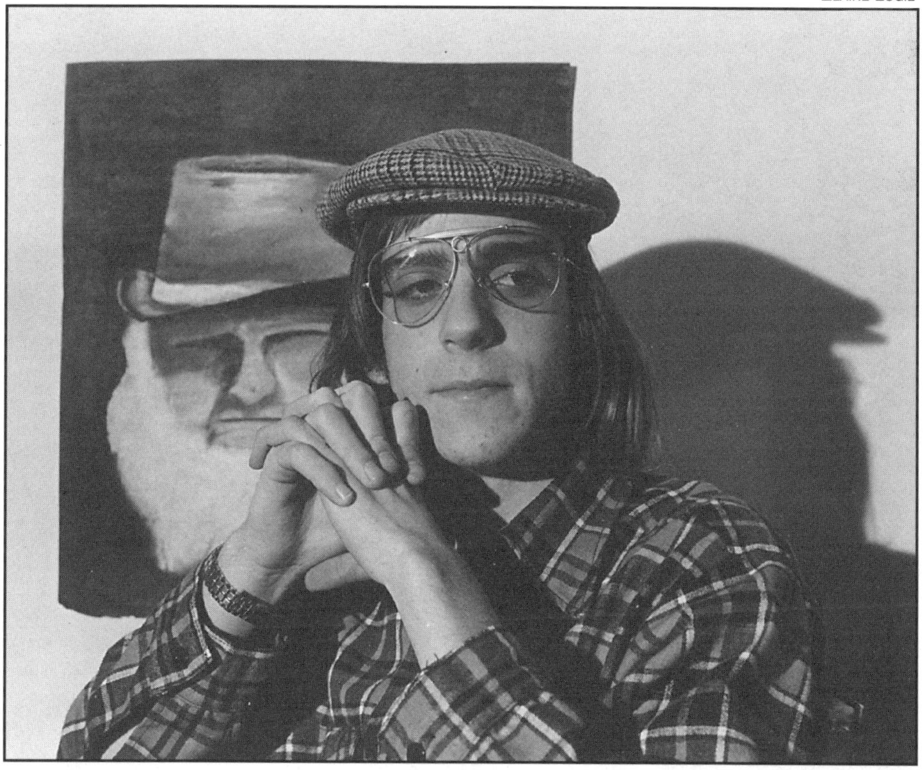

Notice in this portrait that the subject's face and cap are repeated, with variation, both in the painting and in the shadow on the wall.

Jack Urban

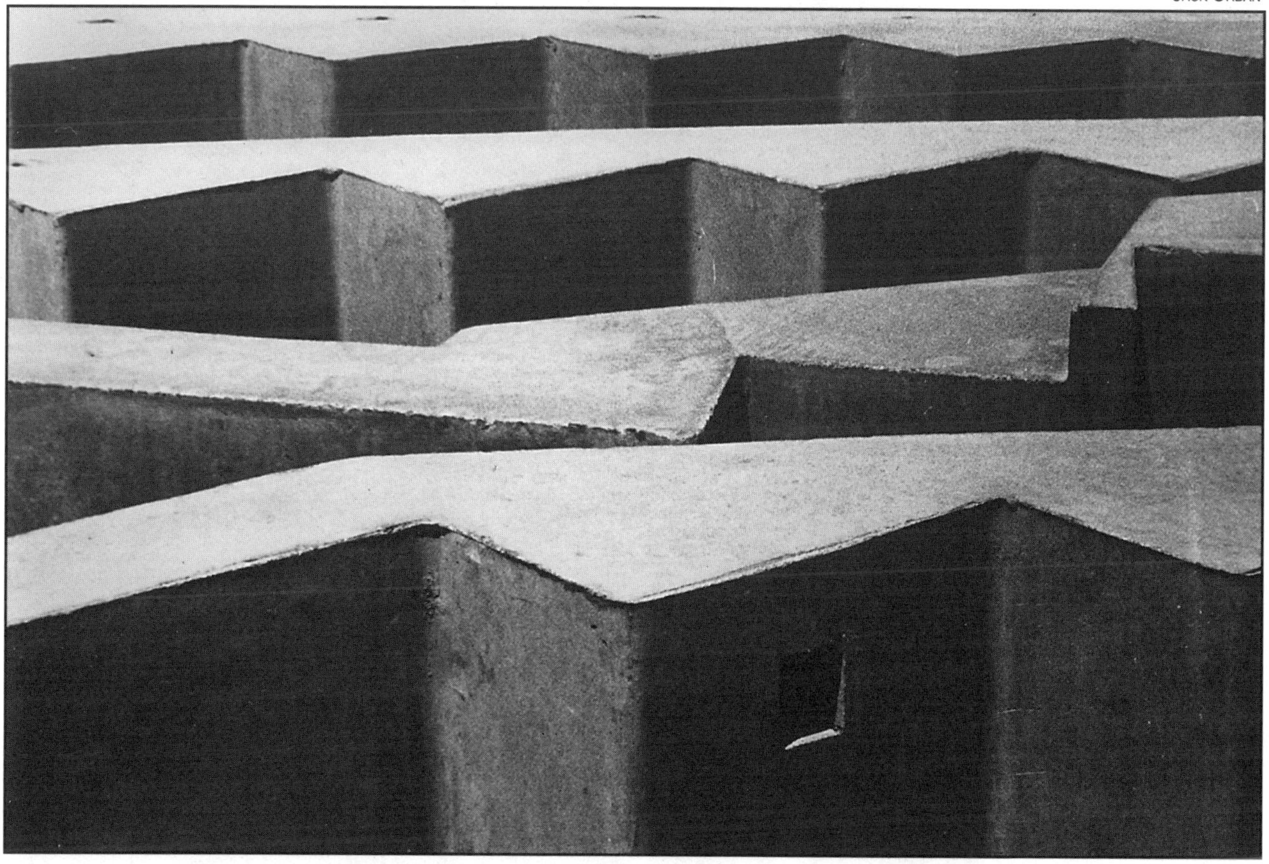

The photograph above contains all the compositional elements of form, space, line, rhythm, tone, texture and contrast. Do you find it graphically interesting? Is it also a bit mysterious, as a visual puzzle of unknown scale? Does it surprise you to learn that these are edges of precast concrete steps lying on their sides?

Jack Sizer

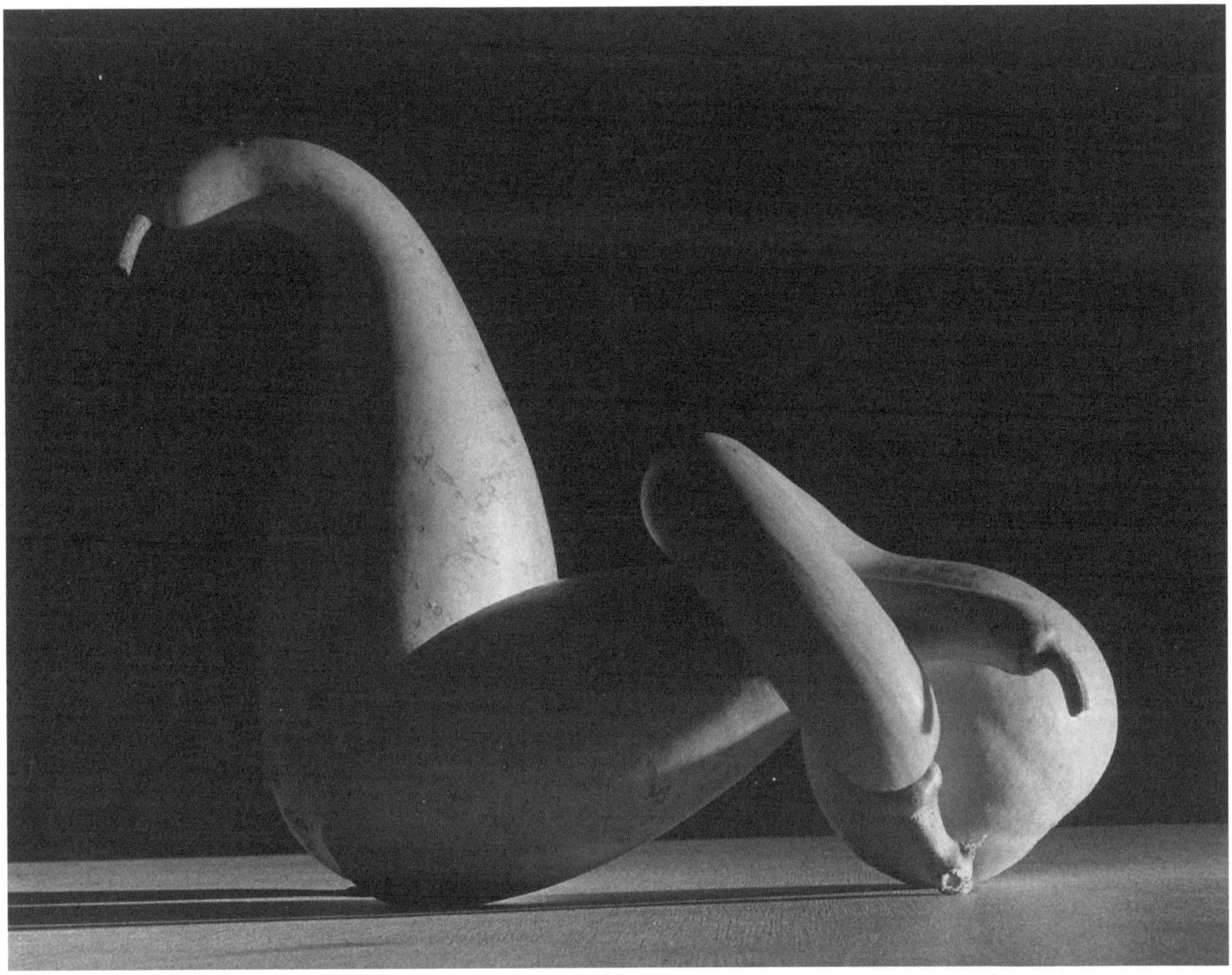

John Stites

Although the objects in these two photographs are far from identical in form, texture and size, are they not visually very similar?

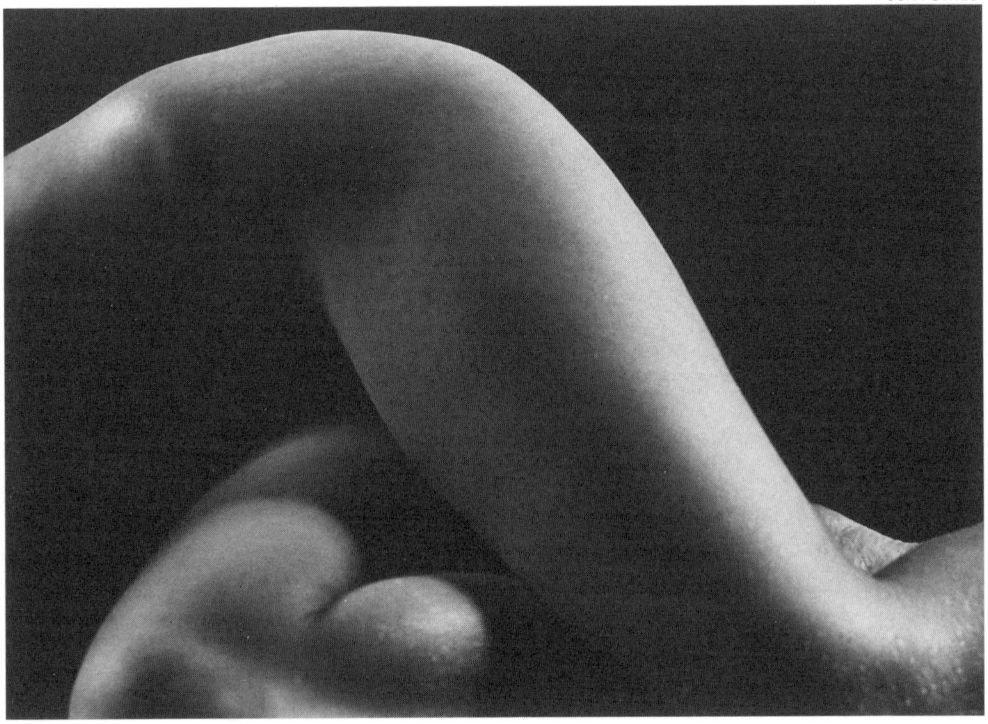

MEGAN DANFORTH

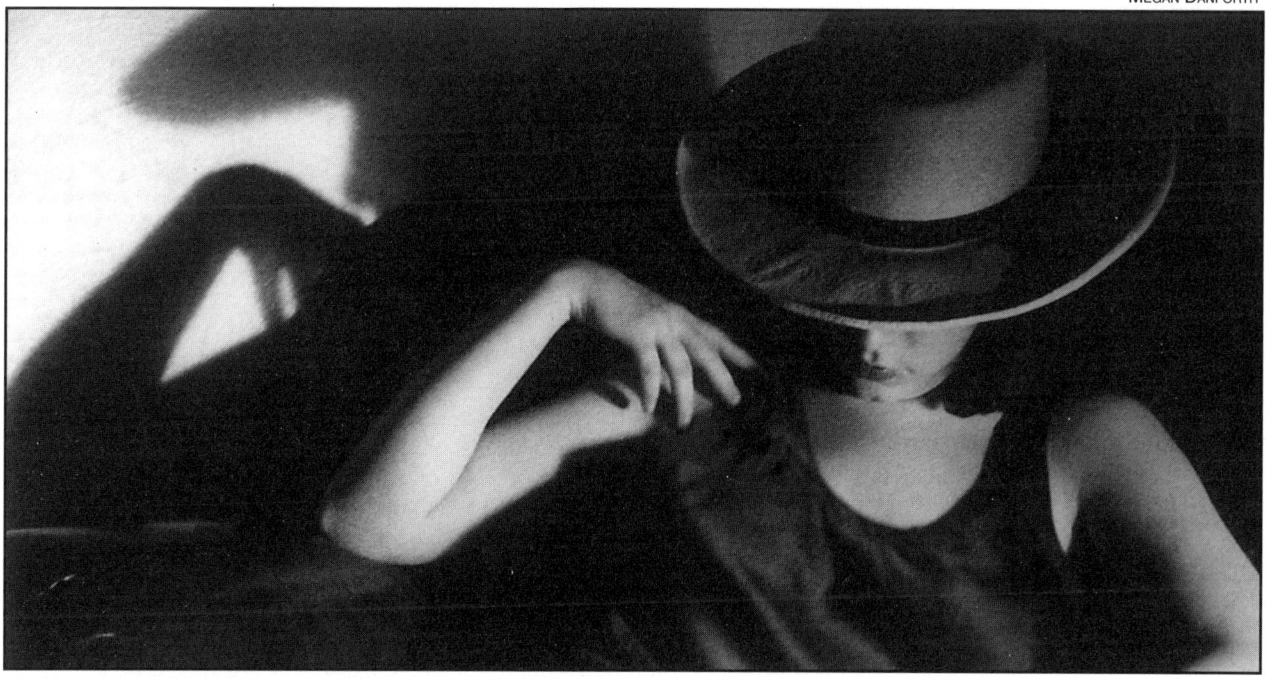

In this portrait, how many visual elements can you identify?

Rhythm and ***repetition*** are everywhere — in music, in architecture, in the natural landscape, in the human figure. *Form* is the basic thematic statement — the basic plan — of the composition. Everything else is either support, repetition, or embellishment.

In music, syncopation is the term used to describe unexpected interruptions in rhythm. The principle of syncopation applies also to the visual arts.

"Whenever I can feel a Bach fugue in my work I know I have arrived."

— Edward Weston, photographer

Rhythmic, repeated patterns of *line* and *form* can be interesting in themselves. But even more exciting images can be created if the pattern is varied by one single item being different from the rest — contrasting in size, shape, value, texture or direction. As in musical composition, *repetition with variation* usually is a strong basis for an interesting visual composition. When you repeat *form* and *line* with *variation*, the variation can be a slight irregularity or a gross distortion, depending on how subtle you want it to be.

"Social landscape is like jazz — improvisational and spontaneous. There is tension between form and content."

— John A. Lacko, photographer

"Architecture is frozen music."

— J. W. von Goethe, poet

Contrast means the visual difference between light and dark tonal values. The term *contrast* also can describe conflict or contradiction between opposites.

"Opposites will always be present ... but [in an ineffective image] they will be at war with each other and not working as a team. For example, background objects will interfere with the foreground, highlights will blast while shadows are impenetrable."

— Nat Herz, photographer

Dynamic balance is a compositional way of placing unlike elements into equilibrium. Strong images often are filled with opposites — not only light versus dark, large versus small, rough versus smooth — but opposing and contradictory elements: flesh and steel, high and low, youth and age, birth and death, growth and decay, joy versus sadness, moving versus still, sun versus ice, rectangle versus circle, straight versus curved. Visualize in terms of contrasts and contradictions. Deliberately build your images around them.

JOHN BARTOCCI

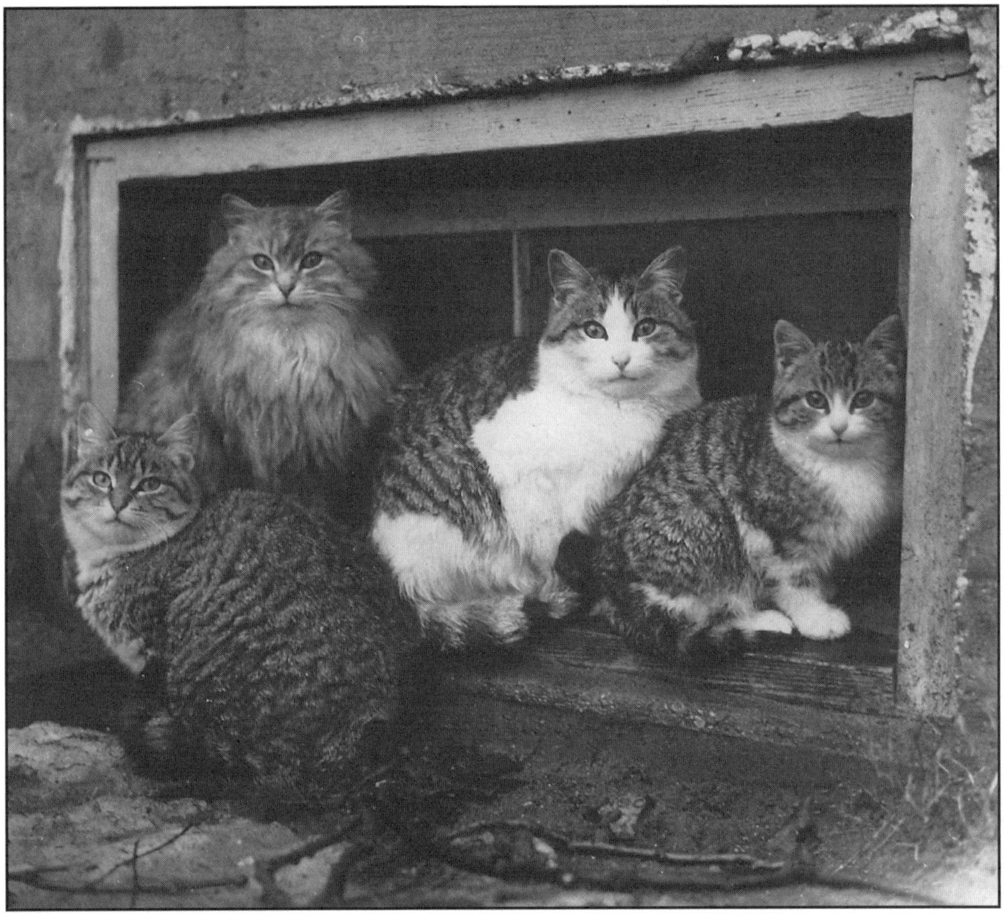

In this simple photograph the main compositional device is repetition with variation. Analyze also the elements of form, space, line, tone, texture, rhythm and contrast.

Think in terms of contrasts in size, shape, tone, texture, direction, mood, color and content. Composition is the sum total of all the elements we've described, put together with a feeling for the effect you want to achieve.

"I get a greater joy from finding things in nature, already composed, than I do from my finest personal arrangements."

— Edward Weston, photographer

Many imagemakers look consciously for compositional elements, and many abstract photographs depend solely on these elements as their reason for existence. Photojournalist Henri Cartier-Bresson said he was always intuitively aware of geometric structure, but "you can't go shooting for shapes, for patterns ..." However, in order to make successful images like Cartier-Bresson made of people and events, you must always be subconsciously aware of compositional elements and ready release the shutter at "the decisive moment" when the subject matter and the compositional elements are in appropriate harmony or conflict.

"Photographs come from the moment in the process of cognition before the mind has analyzed meaning or the eyes design ... Photographic design is ... spontaneous, instinctive, even subconscious."

— Charles Harbutt, photojournalist

There may be an element of luck involved in making a excellent image, but mostly it will be the result of hard work and determination. Therein lies the greatest element of skill in photography and the one aspect that it is most difficult to teach. Only by studying thousands of images and by making countless photographs yourself, both on film and in your mind's eye, will you teach yourself to be a really superb visual communicator.

"I photograph something to see what it will look like photographed."

— Garry Winogrand, photographer

Cameras and Lenses 3

"The camera is an instrument that teaches people how to see without a camera."

— Dorothea Lange, photojournalist

The camera is at once an expedient to communication and a barrier to expression. This paradox is explained by the fact that while many people recognize the camera (and now the computer) as indispensable tools for recording and preserving impressions of the world, others have considered these devices to be intruders — obstacles — contraptions that mechanize and de-humanize the act of "creating" pictures. This contradiction illustrates one of the most charming characteristics of humanity, however; that people are pleased and satisfied by different things, methods, approaches, and results. Because cameras have certain characteristics that make photography unique among media, I can assume that you have more than a casual interest in what can be done with imaging technology, or you wouldn't have read this far.

"The camera need not be a cold mechanical device. Like the pen, it is as good as the [person] who uses it. It can be the extension of mind and heart."

— John Steinbeck, writer

The Basic Camera

All types of cameras have the same basic parts:

1. Light-tight box.
2. Holder and transport system for light-sensitive film.
3. Lens to form an image on the film.
4. Diaphragm, or aperture, to control the amount of light passing through the lens.
5. Shutter to control how long the film is exposed to light.
6. Viewfinder for aiming the camera and composing the image.

All cameras, except the very least expensive, have a means for moving the lens forward or backward to adjust for the sharpest focus, variable shutter speeds, and a diaphragm with an adjustable aperture to allow more or less light through the lens.

The question, "Which is the best camera for me?" can only be answered by asking further: "What kinds of pictures are you going to take?" and "How will your pictures be used?"

No one camera can do all photographic jobs equally well. Although one of the popular pocket-sized "point and shoot" automatic cameras may suffice for family snapshots, to do "serious" imagemaking you'll need to know about the various styles and formats of advanced or "professional" cameras and the kinds of work each does best.

"Technology doesn't mean. It is means."

— Robert Rauschenberg, artist

"... [computers] are another important tool for me, just like lenses or different formats of cameras or film. Even with these tools ... you still have to start off with excellent photography."

— Gerald Bybee, imagemaker

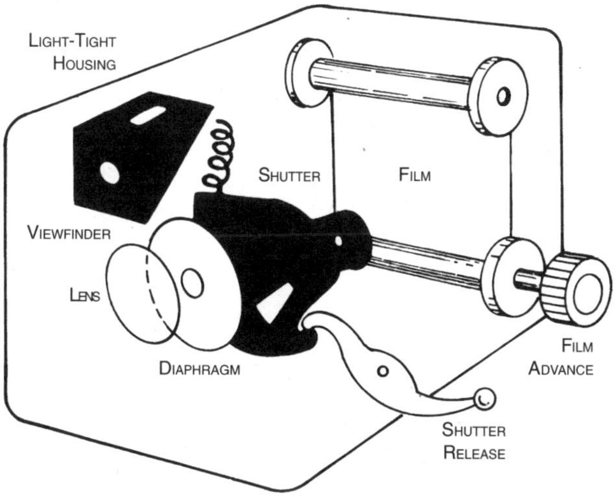

Modern cameras include all the features of this basic "box" camera, which was invented in the 19th century.

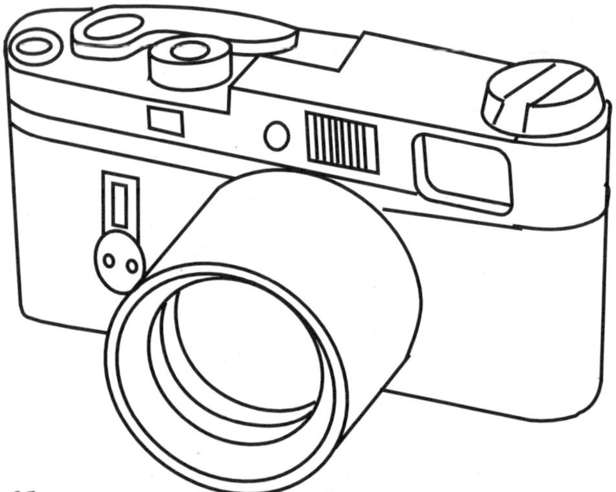

35mm
Rangefinder

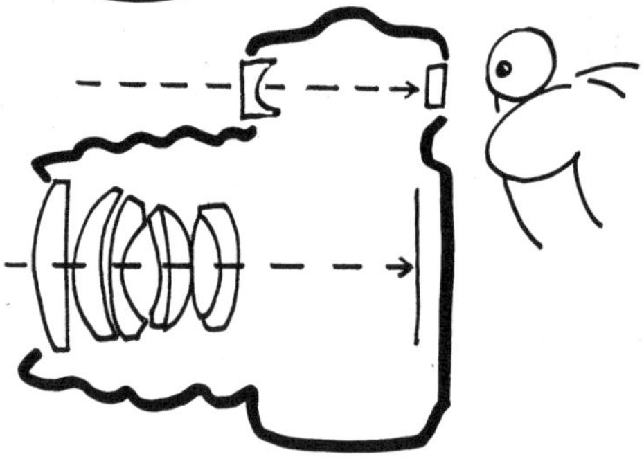

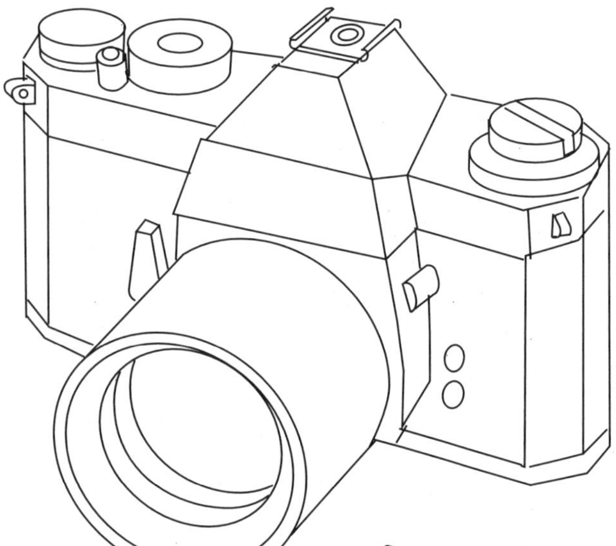

35mm SLR

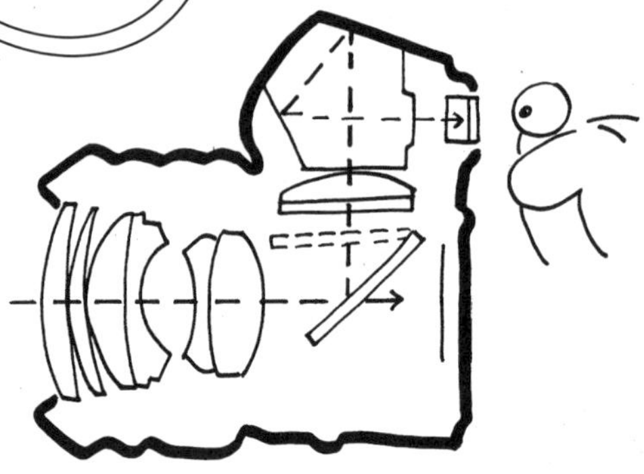

Camera Formats

Rangefinder, 35mm

Advantages: Very light and portable, cameras such as the legendary Leicas and their compact, lower-priced descendents are easy to handle rapidly and easy to focus in dim light. 35mm film magazines contain up to 36 exposures, reducing the cost per frame to a minimum. Interchangeable "fast" lenses of excellent quality allow shooting by existing light in many situations. A relatively quiet shutter simplifies unobtrusive "candid" shooting and many recent models feature automatic control of shutter speed, aperture, focusing and flash for quick, "no-think" shooting. The new APS (Advanced Photo System) cameras accept only special film magazines which simplify processing and printing by automated laboratory equipment.

Disadvantages: As with all 35mm cameras, the tiny negatives or transparencies scratch easily and attract dust and fingerprints, so they must be handled with special care (the APS system bypasses these problems). Extreme enlargement tends to make the grain of the film visible, and to make more objectionable the blur resulting from camera movement. Different viewpoints of lens and viewfinder (parallax) make it difficult to frame and focus accurately when working closer than two or three feet from the subject. Forgetful photographers have been known to leave the lens cap on while shooting.

Single-Lens Reflex (SLR), 35mm

Advantages: These are very popular, convenient and versatile cameras. SLRs such as Canon, Minolta, Nikon, Olympus, and Pentax are similar in operation to rangefinder cameras, but the large, bright, prism viewing screen simplifies focusing and accurate framing, especially when shooting extreme close-ups and when using telephoto and zoom lenses. The ability to view the subject and focus the image through the lens is the most important advantage of the SLR. This feature allows predetermination of depth of field and selective focus effects, and makes possible the use of extensive systems of lenses of various focal lengths and many special-purpose accessories. The latest models offer programmed electronic automation of exposure and focus, rapid film advance for action sequences, and synchronized fill-in flash. Some APS and many digital cameras are SLRs. Instead of using film, digital cameras record images on a removeable magnetic card. They are somewhat bulkier than conventional cameras, but their operation is very similar.

Disadvantages: As with all 35mm films, SLR negatives must be handled very carefully. Most SLRs are somewhat heavier and bulkier than most rangefinder cameras. Certain models are hard to focus with some lenses in dim light and when following action. Momentary image-blackout is a problem when shooting rapid action and with flash, because you can't see through the viewfinder at the instant of exposure. A relatively noisy mirror and shutter tend to call attention to the photographer at quiet events such as concerts and weddings, and movement of the mirror may shake the camera during long exposures. Older-type lenses without an automatic diaphragm are troublesome because it's easy to forget to set the lens opening each time before shooting. Electronic animation can become a liability in case something goes wrong with the mechanism or if the battery fails. Autofocus lenses used carelessly can result in out-of-focus pictures.

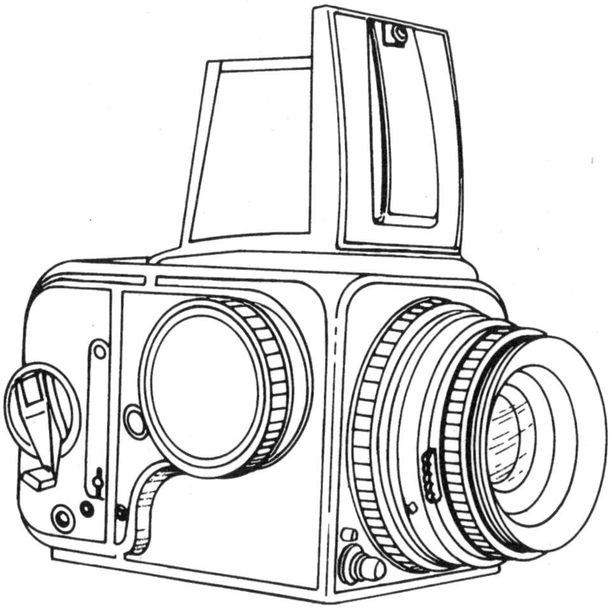

Medium-Format SLR

Single-Lens Reflex, Medium-Format (6x7, 6x6, or 6x4.5 cm)

Advantages: 120-size roll film yields images two to four times larger than 35mm, lessening problems of grain, dust, scratches, and camera movement. The larger ground-glass viewing area of medium-format cameras such as Bronica, Hasselblad, Mamiya, Pentax and Rollei simplifies composition and focusing and allows predetermination of depth of field and selective focus effects. Extensive accessory systems are available, including interchangeable backs that permit switching film type in mid-roll and use of Polaroid instant film or a digital back.

Disadvantages: Medium-format cameras are noisier, heavier, and bulkier than 35mm SLRs. 120 film is economical, although more expensive per frame than 35mm. Cameras and accessories are very expensive.

Twin-Lens Reflex, Medium-Format (6x6 cm)

Advantages: Convenient and rapid in operation, TLRs have the advantage of 120-size roll film negatives. This so-called 2 1/4-square format was once very popular. Today, the larger camera stores may have several models of used Mamiya, Rollei and Yashica cameras available at bargain prices.

Disadvantages: Somewhat bulky, most models do not accept interchangeable lenses, and few accessories are available. Unless an auxiliary prism is attached, focusing below eye level is required and this point of view may be inconvenient. The image is also reversed — left-to-right. Parallax between the two lenses prevents accurate framing close to the subject.

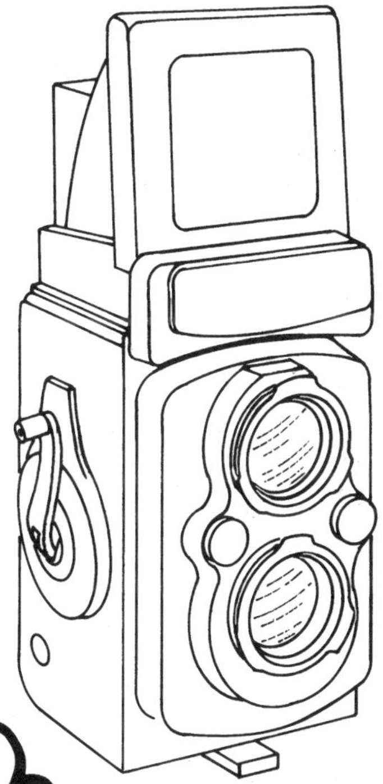

Twin-Lens Reflex

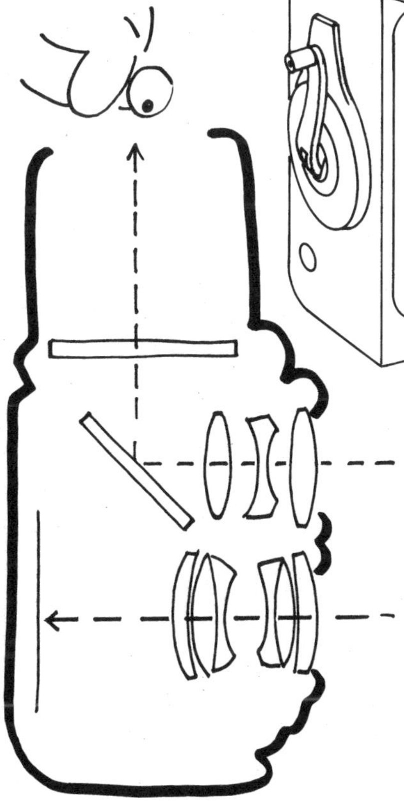

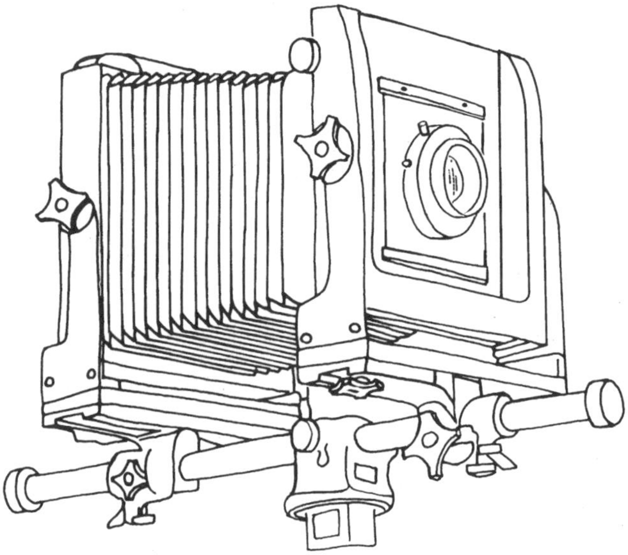

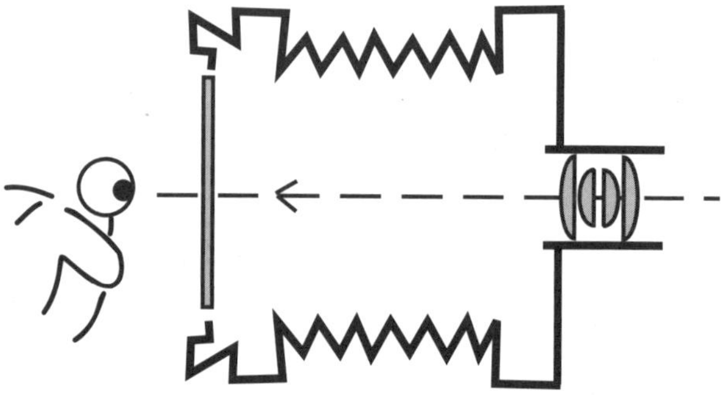

Jim Nixon

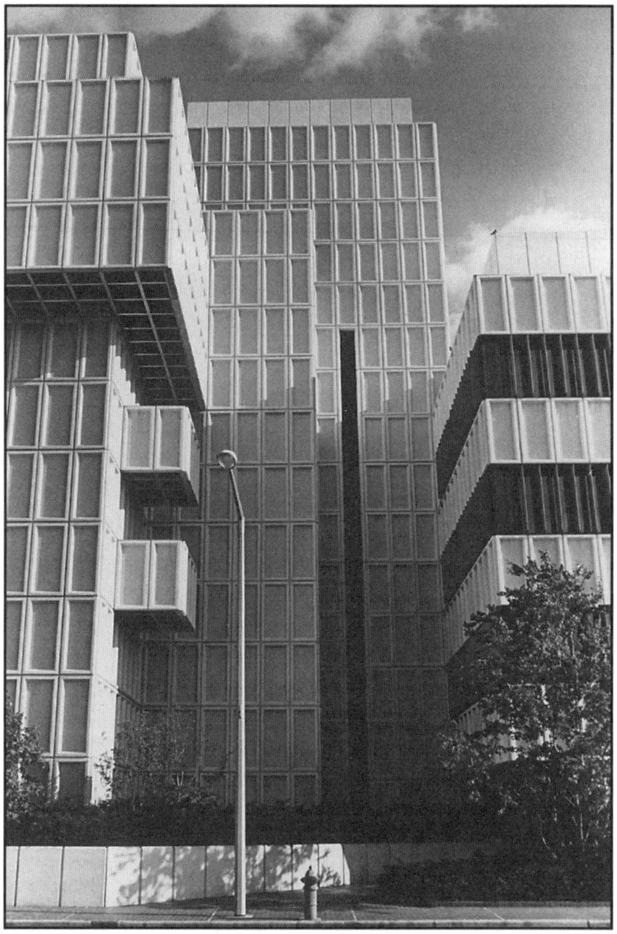

The walls of this building converge because the camera was tilted upward. Architectural photographers, frequently preferring to keep walls parallel, tilt the lens and the back of the camera to the same plane as the building (see illustration on Page 53).

View Camera, Large-Format (4"x5" and larger)

Advantages: The enormous negatives and transparencies reproduce with such sparkling quality that large-format cameras often are the first choice in commercial studios and by many photographers who concentrate on the natural landscape. They are a favorite for photographing building exteriors and interiors, furniture, food, packaged products, etc., because the swing, tilt, rise, and shift adjustments of both front and back can correct perspective distortion and maximize depth of field. View cameras are good for copying and for graphic-arts work because of the large negative size (up to 8"x10" and even much larger!) and the wide variety of specialized types of film available. Large sheet-film negatives allow retouching, if desired, and permit great enlargement or fine-quality contact prints. The large ground-glass screen in the camera back encourages careful composition and focusing. Polaroid instant film can easily be used and a high-resolution digital back may be attached.

Disadvantages: A view camera must always be set up on a tripod or heavy studio stand. The large lenses are slower, so at equivalent lens openings they have less depth of field than comparable shorter focal-length lenses on smaller cameras. It takes a while to get used to the upside-down image on the ground glass. Rapid shooting is difficult because several things must be done by hand before and after making each exposure. Sheet film is expensive, and the film holders are awkward to handle. The holders usually must be loaded individually in a darkroom or light-tight changing bag, and kept protected from bright light. Although many of the world's most respected photographers have used view cameras extensively, this bulky instrument is not suitable when the photographer is in a hurry or has to travel light.

David Harrison (2)

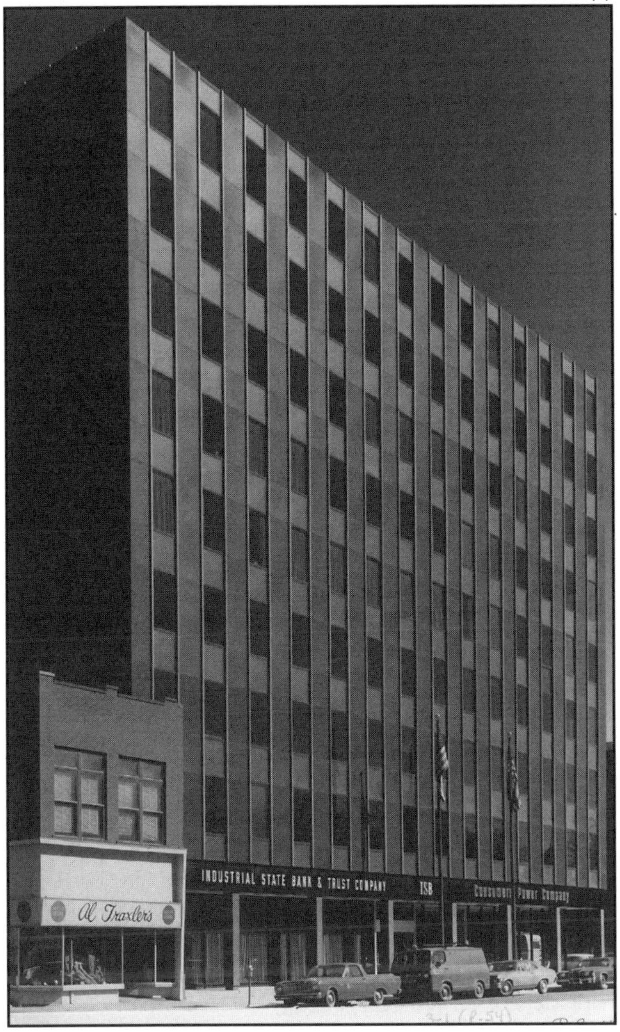

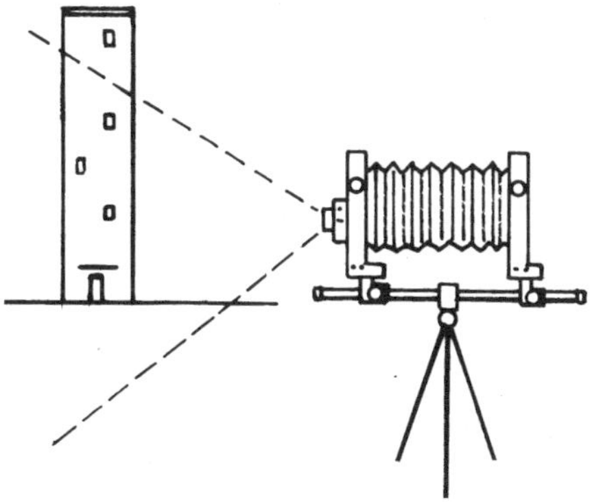

To include the top of a tall building, the camera usually must be tilted upward. But aiming the camera upward causes convergence. The solution either is to raise the lens or to tilt both the front and the back of the camera.

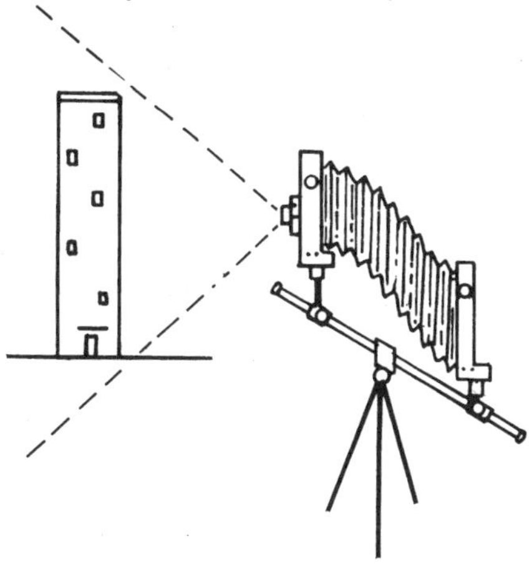

The building at left was photographed with the camera adjusted as shown in the drawing above. The lens, the film plane, and the building are parallel with one another..

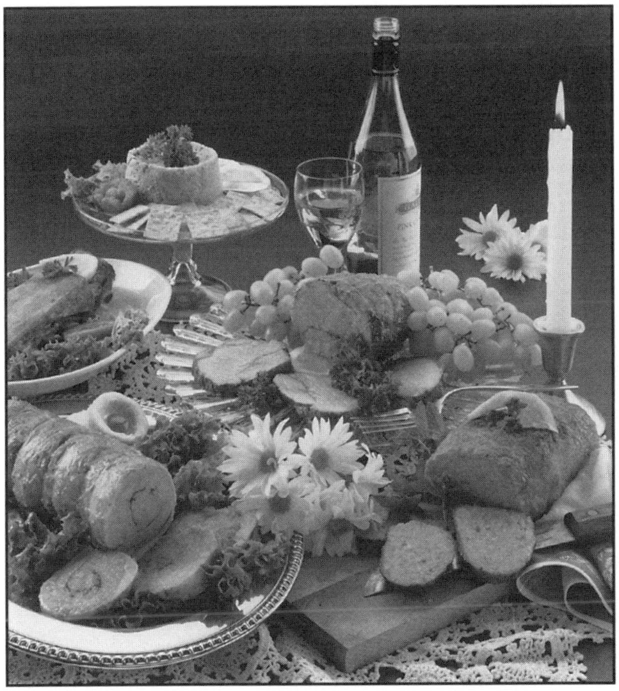

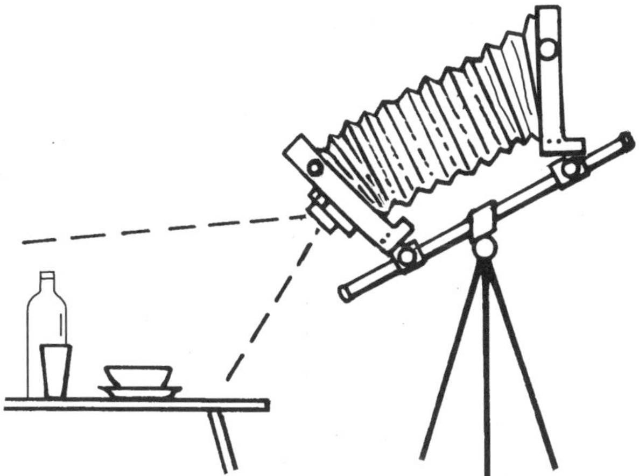

Commercial illustration frequently requires that tall objects, such as this wine bottle and candle, be parallel with the camera back. To frame the image and maximize depth of field, the lens has been aimed downward and tilted toward the plane of the table top.

Specialized Cameras

In addition to your regular equipment, you might want to own one or more special-purpose cameras. A Polaroid "instant" camera, for example, or an accessory Polaroid back can be very useful for checking lighting arrangements or composition before exposing conventional color or black-and-white film.

Instant photography offers unusual spontaneity in portraiture because the photographer and the sitter can immediately critique the expression, pose, and lighting. Digital equipment now makes this process even more rapid.

Large-format panoramic cameras were popular for group portraits early in the 20th century, and a few types are available today that use 120 roll film. Producing an extremely long, narrow image, this format appeals to imaginative landscape and experiment-minded imagemakers. A "panoramic" format is one of the cropping options in APS cameras.

Although waterproof housings can be bought or built for many cameras, the popularity of scuba diving and other water-related sports such as rafting, canoeing and water skiing has created a market for water-tight, 35mm cameras such as the Nikonos. It simplifies taking pictures in wet places and reduces the risk of dunking a conventional camera.

Some people enjoy owning and using unusual cameras, or actively collecting antique, classic, or unique equipment. Organizations catering to camera collectors publish newsletters and sponsor exhibits and sales.

"... I would like my cameras to be a complete and true extension of myself."

— William Albert Allard, photojournalist

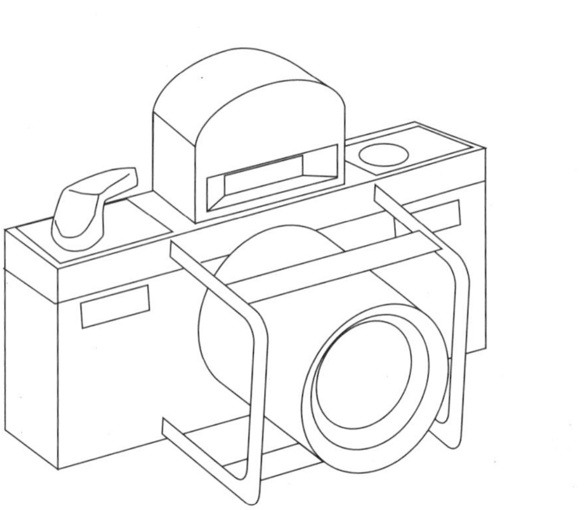

The ultra-wide-angle lens of a professional panorama camera forms a larger image over two or more standard film frames instead of merely cropping a standard frame.

Choosing a Camera

After becoming familiar with the various types of cameras and deciding on the format you prefer, you have to face the dilemma of choosing a particular make and model from the many quality cameras available. That's not so easy, because investing in a camera is a lot like buying a car — the dependability of the dealer may be more important in the long run than the brand you purchase or the price you pay. Any kind of car will get you where you want to go, and there are literally dozens of quality cameras, each of which will make excellent photographs if intelligently used.

Because personal preference is so important in choosing a camera, it's important that you work with a knowledgeable salesperson who will help you select the best equipment for your needs, preferences, and budget. If you encounter impatience or ignorance, I suggest you take your business elsewhere.

You'll want to try the "feel" of various cameras, because different models employ different focusing systems and viewfinder images vary significantly in brightness, relative size of the image, and ease of focusing. Placement of the controls may seem more convenient for you on one camera than on another, as will reading the numbers on the lens and body or on the display panel. If you handle several cameras, you'll probably find that you prefer the feel of one model over another.

If you're thing of going into photography seriously, your dealer can advise you on which camera manufacturers offer systems of quality lenses and accessories that are likely to be available as your interests, needs, and financial resources grow. And your dealer should be the kind who will see to it that you receive prompt and proper service when you need it — and perhaps even loan you a camera in an emergency!

Although price isn't everything, many local camera stores will meet the advertised prices of mail-order and discount competitors. They know that if you're satisfied you'll come back to buy accessories, supplies, and services. If you're considering the purchase of a used camera, be sure to study "How to Test Your Equipment" in Chapter 4.

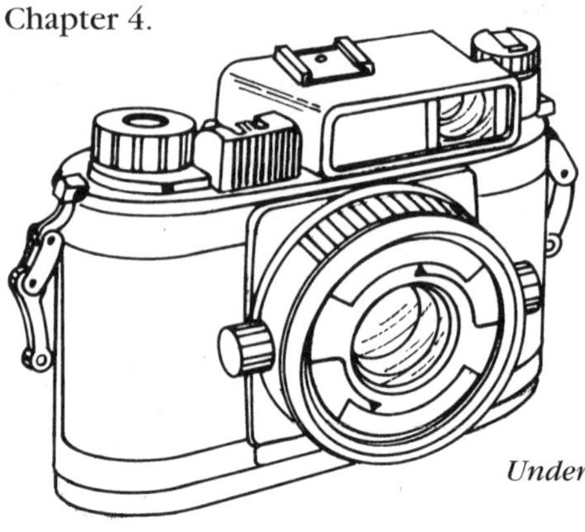

Underwater Camera

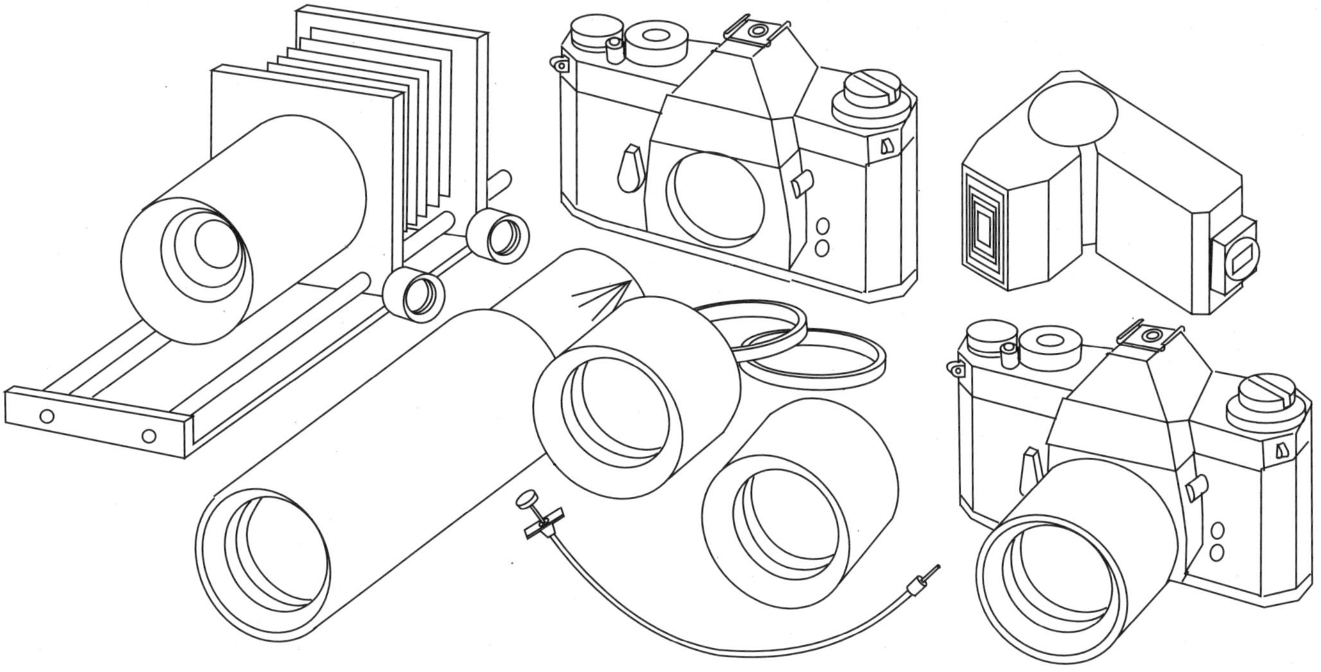

Each major camera manufacturer offers a series of lenses of various focal lengths. Also available are close-up focusing devices, filters, and dedicated flash equipment that extend the versatility of that particular camera, but may not be compatible with cameras made by competitors. Choose your camera system carefully because it can represent a sizable investment.

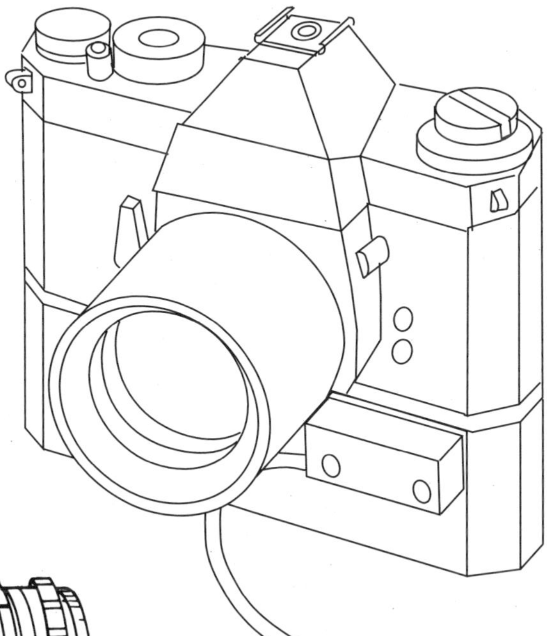

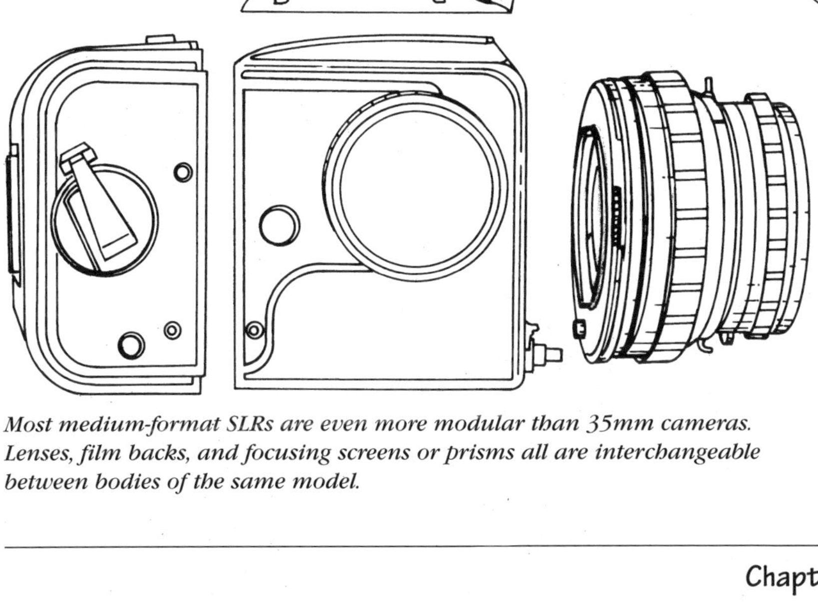

Most medium-format SLRs are even more modular than 35mm cameras. Lenses, film backs, and focusing screens or prisms all are interchangeable between bodies of the same model.

Digital cameras frequently look like conventional cameras modified with some electronics underneath, or in an attaching back. A cable connects camera and computer for downloading files, or images may be transferred using a special magnetic storage card.

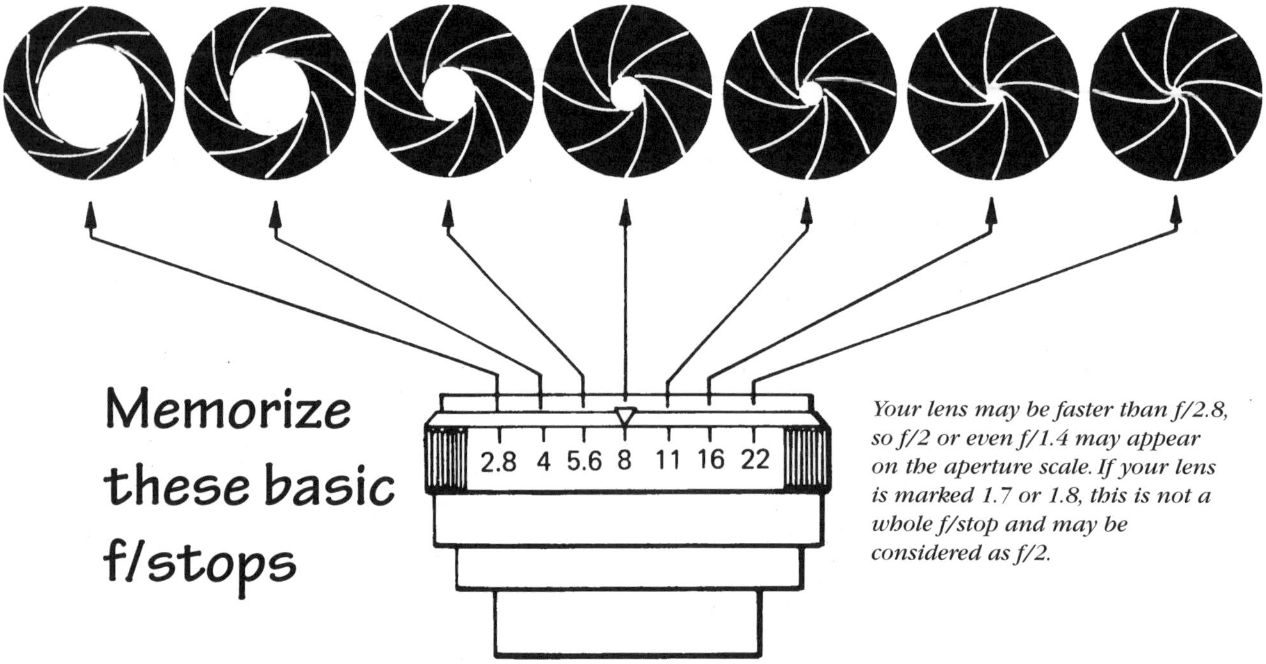

Memorize these basic f/stops

Your lens may be faster than f/2.8, so f/2 or even f/1.4 may appear on the aperture scale. If your lens is marked 1.7 or 1.8, this is not a whole f/stop and may be considered as f/2.

Exposure Controls

"A photographer needs a short-circuit between his brain and his fingertips."

— Alfred Eisenstaedt, photojournalist

"In photography you've got to be quick, quick, quick, quick. Like an animal and a prey."

— Henri Cartier-Bresson, photojournalist.

People who earn a living with their cameras or who use photography as a creative or scientific tool know that there isn't time to make calculations every time they want to take a picture. Like driving a car, playing a musical instrument or riding a bicycle, the technical processes have to become second nature so you can concentrate all your psychic and emotional energy on perceiving and selecting the perfect arrangement and the decisive moment. For many beginners, the most difficult and confusing aspect of photography is exposure. Fortunately, there are only a few simple principles to learn.

"The camera should become an extension of your eye ..."

— Ernst Haas, photographer

E = I x T

Yes, it looks like algebra, but don't panic! This little equation tells it all: Exposure = Intensity of light x Time. That's it. Exposure means the total amount of light reaching the film. That quantity of light is very important because it has a lot to do with the quality of your negatives and color transparencies. *Underexposure* is the result of not enough light affecting the emulsion of the film; *overexposure* is from too much light.

The amount of light reaching the film is controlled both by the size of the lens aperture (f/stop) and the length of time the shutter is allowed to remain open (shutter speed). You should be in control of both factors.

Lens openings (f/stops)

The larger the lens opening, the more light gets through at any given shutter speed. The numbered apertures (f/stops) on most lenses are spaced so that moving from one full f/stop to the next will result in either doubling or halving the amount of light passing through. "Opening up" the lens (larger aperture opening) increases the light, while "stopping down" the lens (smaller aperture opening) reduces the light. So far, so good? The confusing part is that the f/stop numbers engraved on lenses are the opposite of logic: ***the larger the f/number, the smaller the aperture.*** Remember that!

Although the entire range of numbers from f/1 to f/64 will never appear on any one lens, you should memorize at least the basic scale of f/stop numbers shown in

The speed of a lens (maximum f/number) is determined by dividing the focal length (F) of the lens by the diameter (D) of the maximum aperture. Focal length is the distance from the optical center of the lens to the focal plane (film surface) when the lens is focused on infinity (far away).

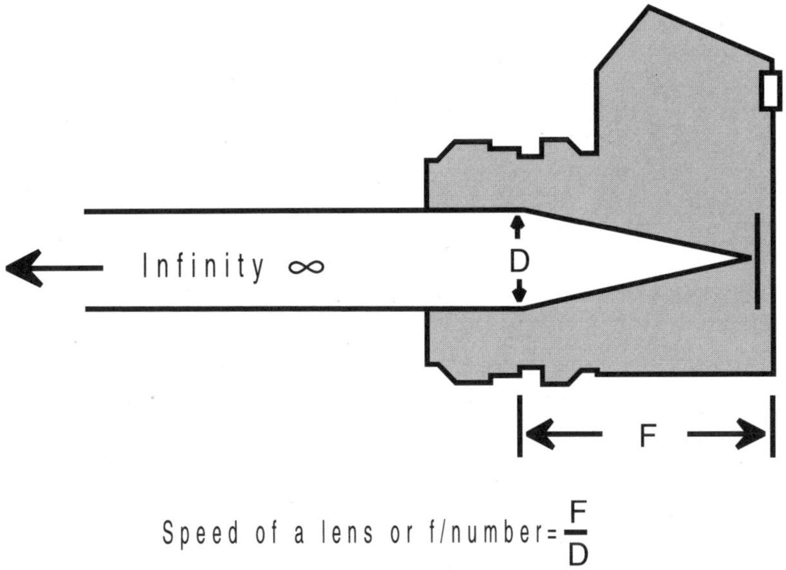

the illustration on page 56. Don't be misled by half-stop "click" indentations on your lens — these make it easier for you to make in-between settings. The half-stops are not part of the regular scale for calculating exposure.

An easy way to remember the stops is that the numbers are cut in half (or doubled) every other number. But don't try to use the same arithmetic in calculating exposure. The amount of exposure increases or decreases by a factor of *two times* between every adjacent pair of full f/stops on the scale. Very few lenses stop down to f/45 or f/64, although many go as far as f/22 or f/32. Many lenses for small cameras do not stop down smaller than f/16.

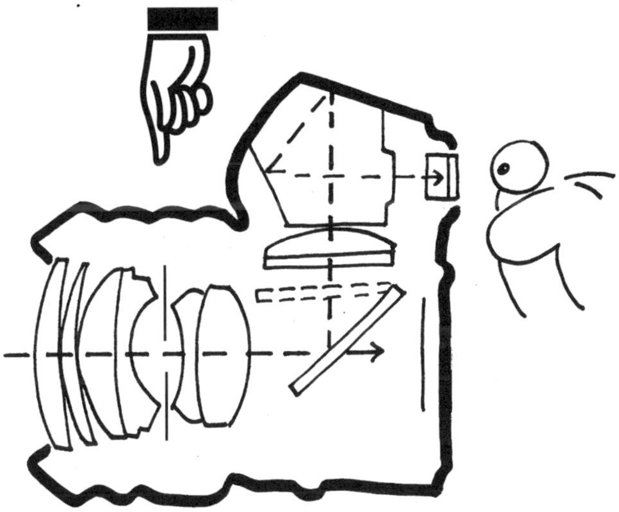

The aperture is located between lens elements

The larger the f/number, the smaller the lens opening. Smaller f/numbers mean larger apertures.

If the maximum aperture on your lens shows an odd number such as f/1.8, f/3.5, or f/4.5, this number will not be a full stop larger than the next smaller f/stop. Because the speed of a lens is expressed in terms of its largest f/stop ***(largest opening=smallest number),*** manufacturers like to impress people with a slightly lower f/number (larger aperture). These irregular apertures, however, are only slightly larger than the next whole f/stop, and for practical purposes you can ignore the difference. An f/1.8 lens, for example, is only negligibly faster than f/2. An f/2 lens is considered *fast,* whereas a lens with a maximum aperture of only f/4.5 would be comparatively *slow.* Don't be misled into thinking that an f/1.2 or f/1.4 lens is significantly *better* than an f/2 lens. Although the f/1.4 will be a full stop faster than the f/2 (and may be a little easier to focus in dim light), you will be paying for extra glass that you may seldom use, and also will be sacrificing some sharpness at the wider aperture.

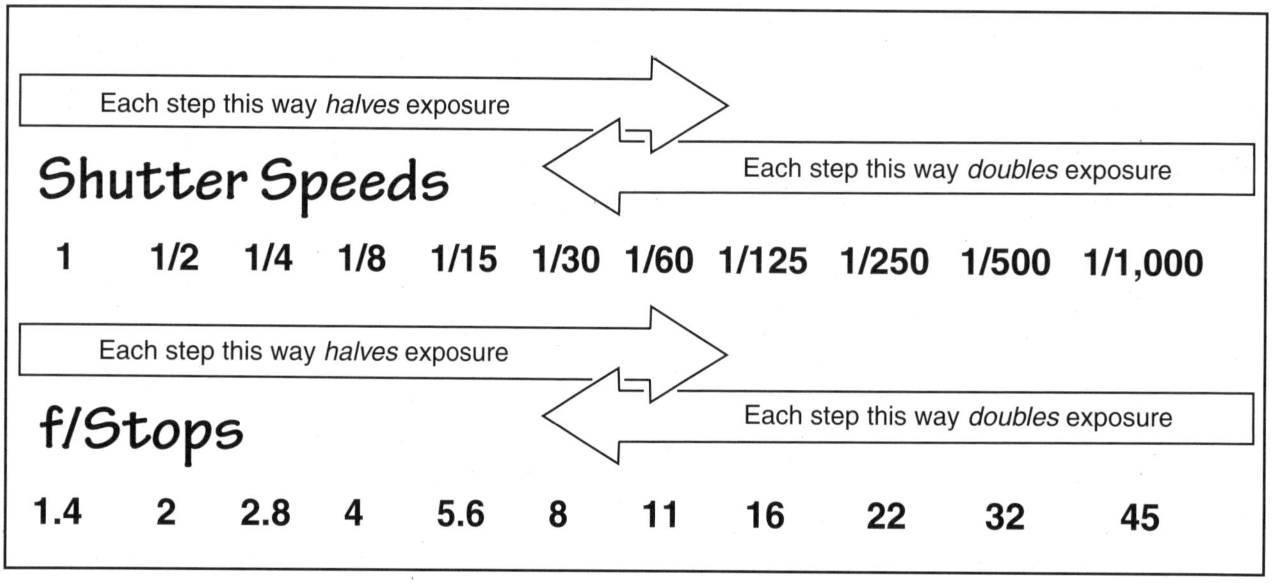

Shutter speeds

The other important variable in controlling exposure is the shutter speed. The speeds in the table above are the standard markings found on most modern cameras. Each speed is expressed in terms of a fraction of a second, down to one full second. Some electronic cameras include shutter speeds as slow as 2, 4 and 8 full seconds and at the other end of the scale go as fast as 1/8,000. Nearly all cameras have a setting marked "B," which allows the shutter to be held open as long as the release button is depressed. Some cameras also have a "T" setting that opens the shutter when the release is depressed, then closes the shutter or drops the mirror when the release is depressed a second time. The shutter speeds (except B and T) affect exposure in the same way as the f/stops — that is, each change from any speed to the adjacent speed effectively doubles or halves the amount of light reaching the film at a given f/stop.

Sometimes a symbol will appear next to one shutter speed, usually 1/60 or 1/125 second, or one of those speeds will be marked in red. That should be the setting for flash. (Learn more about flash in Chapter 9).

Shutter speed and lens opening work together.

Many combinations of f/stop and shutter speed will admit the same amount of light, resulting in identical total exposure. Using the next slower speed, such as 1/60 of a second instead of 1/125, admits light for twice as long. This gives the same effect on exposure as opening up the lens aperture one full f/stop, such as f/8 instead of f/11, which doubles the amount of light passing through. Thus an exposure of 1/30 at f/16 will produce the same exposure on the film as 1/60 at f/11, 1/125 at f/8, 1/250 at f/5.6, 1/500 at f/4, or 1/1,000 at f/2.8.

Do you see how the lens opening and the shutter speed are interconnected? Once you have determined the correct amount of light your film needs for a particular photograph, then you have a choice of camera settings. You could choose a small aperture (f/16) to keep objects in focus both near and far (depth of field) or select a fast shutter speed (1/1,000) to "freeze" a moving subject. In either case, you would then adjust the other control to admit the correct amount of light to expose the film properly.

One shutter-speed change = one f/stop-change in exposure.

Practice setting your camera until you can compensate easily for changes of several stops of speed or aperture in either direction. You can set the lens between f/stops to make minor exposure adjustments (for example, halfway between f/5.6 and f/8)). But don't set the shutter between marked speeds.

"Before trying to use any camera, especially an electronic automatic camera, please read the instruction book!"

— Roger Cook, camera salesman

Controlling an Automatic Camera

When locked into *aperture priority, shutter priority,* or *programmed* mode, cameras with automatic exposure control do all the calculating and compensating for you. But because cameras differ in how they should be set, be sure to study your owner's manual.

In shutter priority, whenever you set the shutter speed, the camera will choose the appropriate lens opening. In aperture priority mode, when you select an f/stop to control depth of field, the camera will adjust the shutter speed. Usually these settings can be read either in the viewfinder window, or from a liquid crystal display on top of the camera.

Many newer cameras have one or more *program* settings that will select both aperture and shutter speed. If you buy one of these cameras, be sure it also can be set manually. The owner's manual will explain your choices of programmed modes and tell you how to override the automatic features. Chapter 5 in this book describes how to determine correct exposure and how to suspect when the exposure meter in your camera may be giving you wrong settings. Please read that chapter now if you're going out right away to take pictures before reading more about cameras and accessories.

"Automatic simply means that you can't repair it yourself."

— Mary H. Waldrip, photographer

The Lens

"A camera has but one eye — the lens. It can record only a fragment of the visual world.
The photographer provides a second eye. This is the eye of selection.
The artist has a Third Eye, the eye of creative imagination."

— Author unknown

Most camera lenses consist of three or more separate glass elements instead of a single piece. The sharpest and fastest lenses have many elements. A lens should never be taken apart except by an experienced camera-repair technician.

How to keep <u>autofocus</u> lenses from giving you <u>out-of-focus</u> pictures!

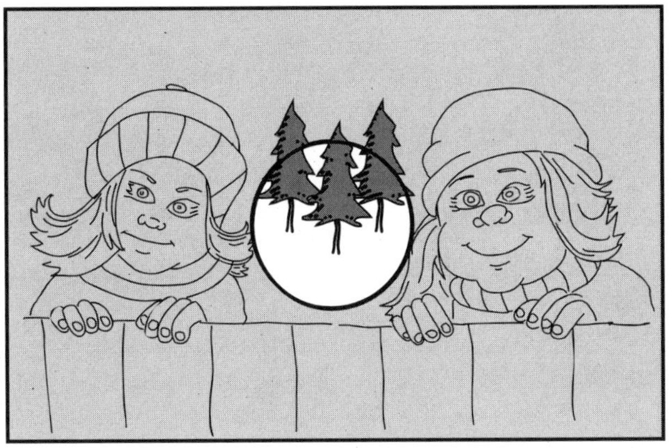

(1) Most cameras, when in "automatic" or "programmed" mode, will read the exposure and focus the image in the center of the picture. If the main subject is not in the center, the lens may focus on the background. If the background is much lighter or darker the exposure may be incorrect.

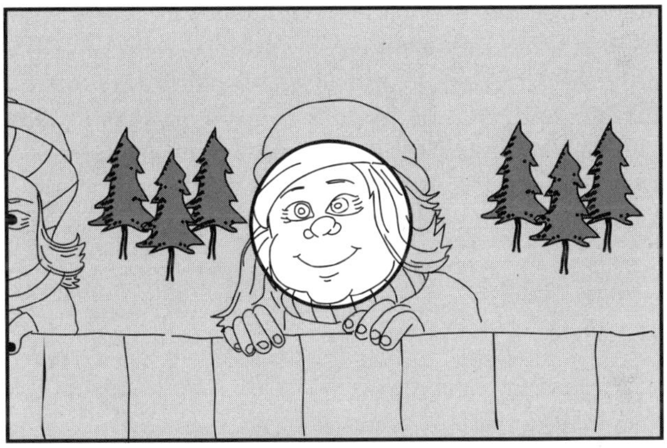

(2) To over-ride automatic features, aim the camera so that focus and exposure readings are made on the main subject, depress the shutter release button halfway or hold down exposure and focus lock buttons (see the owner's manual to find out exactly what to do on your camera) ...

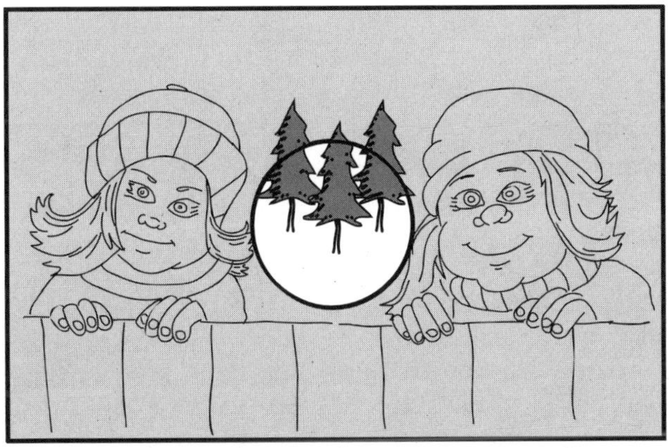

(3) ... then re-frame the image, holding down the exposure and focus lock buttons or keeping the shutter release partially depressed. Finally, depress the shutter release all the way to take the picture.

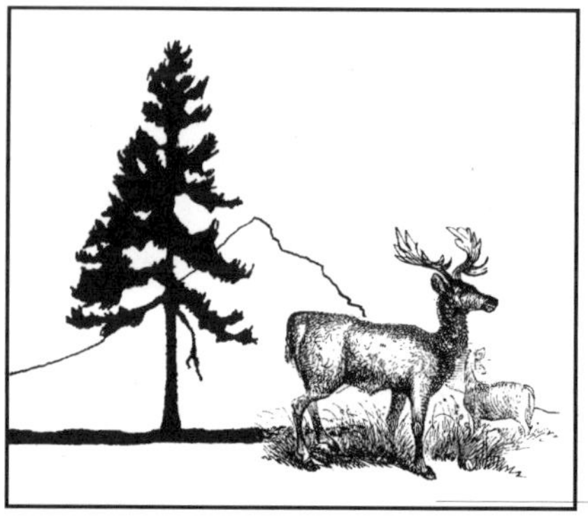
Wide-angle

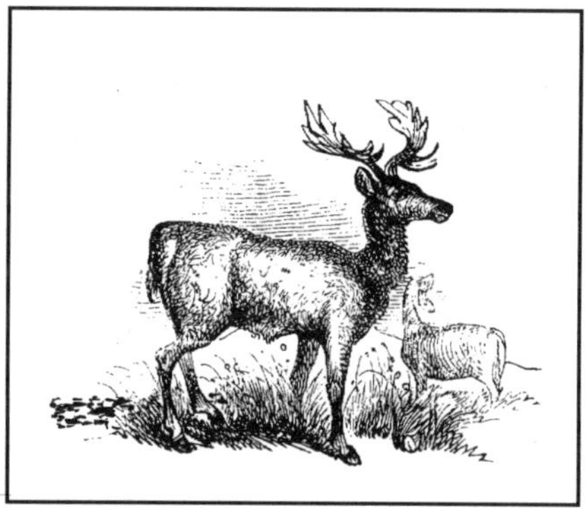
Normal

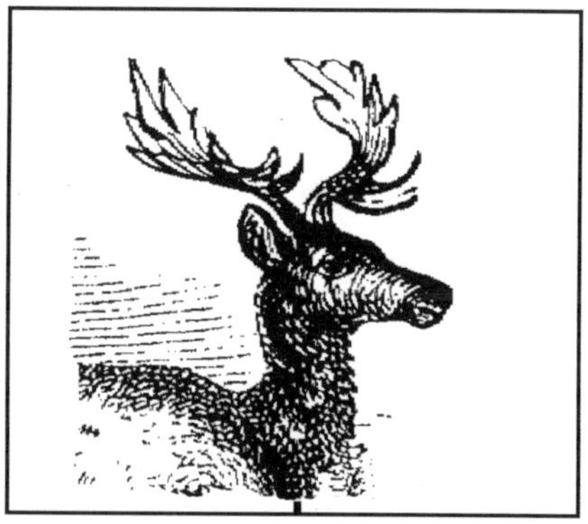
Telephoto

Focal length

The focal length of the lens affects how large the image will be on the film and how wide or narrow the angle of view. Because different cameras are designed to use different sizes of film, different lenses are needed. The size of the image projected onto the film by a lens and the distance the lens must be from the film to form a sharp image are directly related to its focal length. This number usually is engraved on the lens mount in millimeters, often preceded by f=, and is a measure of the distance between the optical center of the lens and the film when the lens is focused on a distant object (infinity). For example, f=55mm means 55mm focal length. Don't confuse f= with f/, which seldom appears on a lens. If you see 1: 2.8, the maximum aperture of that lens is f/2.8.

A so-called "normal" lens has a focal length about equal to, or slightly longer than, the diagonal of the image produced within that camera. For example, a square negative made on 120-size roll film measures about 80mm diagonally from corner to corner. Therefore, the normal lens for a 6x6cm reflex camera has a focal length of approximately 80mm. 35mm cameras normally are supplied with a lens of 50mm to 58mm focal length, slightly longer than the diagonal of the image. As you know 35mm refers to the *width of the film* in a 35mm camera. On a 35mm camera, a 35mm lens would be a moderate wide-angle (shorter than "normal" focal length).

An 80mm lens will always project the same sized image of a given object whether the lens is designed for use on a 35mm camera or on a 4x5. An 80mm lens will be a moderate *telephoto* if mounted on a 35mm camera, *normal* on a 6x6 camera, and *wide-angle* if its field of coverage is broad enough to cover 4x5.

When the focal length is much shorter than the film diagonal, the lens is said to be a *wide-angle,* projecting a smaller image of each object in its field but including a wider angle of view. When the focal length is longer than the image diagonal, the lens is said to be a long-focus or *telephoto* lens. It will form a larger image covering a narrower angle of view.

Image size is always directly proportional to focal length. That is, the image formed of a given object by a 200mm lens will be exactly twice as large as the image of the same object, at the same distance, formed by a 100mm lens, and four times the size of the image with a 50mm lens, regardless of the size and format of the film and camera. This rule applies also to variable focal-length zoom lenses.

Focusing

No lens is capable of recording all objects sharply at various distances within its view. Because of this, the lens must be adjusted (focused) within a certain range of distances so that all desired objects are sharp. Some adjustment of focus is possible on all but the simplest cameras. These are permanently focused at about 15 feet, which gives acceptable, although not sharp, focus on everything from about five or six feet from the camera out to infinity (as far as the eye can see).

Focusing is nothing more than moving the lens nearer or farther from the film plane with a threaded or geared mechanism. One of the latest trends in camera design is automatic focusing.

Autofocus lenses make it easy to "grab" unplanned shots but when the automatic feature is not needed, pros sometimes lock the focus on manual. Experienced photographers learn to prefocus according to estimated distances, and then to shoot when action is at its peak. Some autofocus lenses can be slow to react, and they will focus on the background or foreground unless the main subject is in the center of the frame. If your camera focuses automatically, you should study the owner's manual to find out how to "lock-in" the focus manually or turn off the autofocus feature.

"Photography ... is all about selection — of framing and focus ..."

— Phil Patton, writer

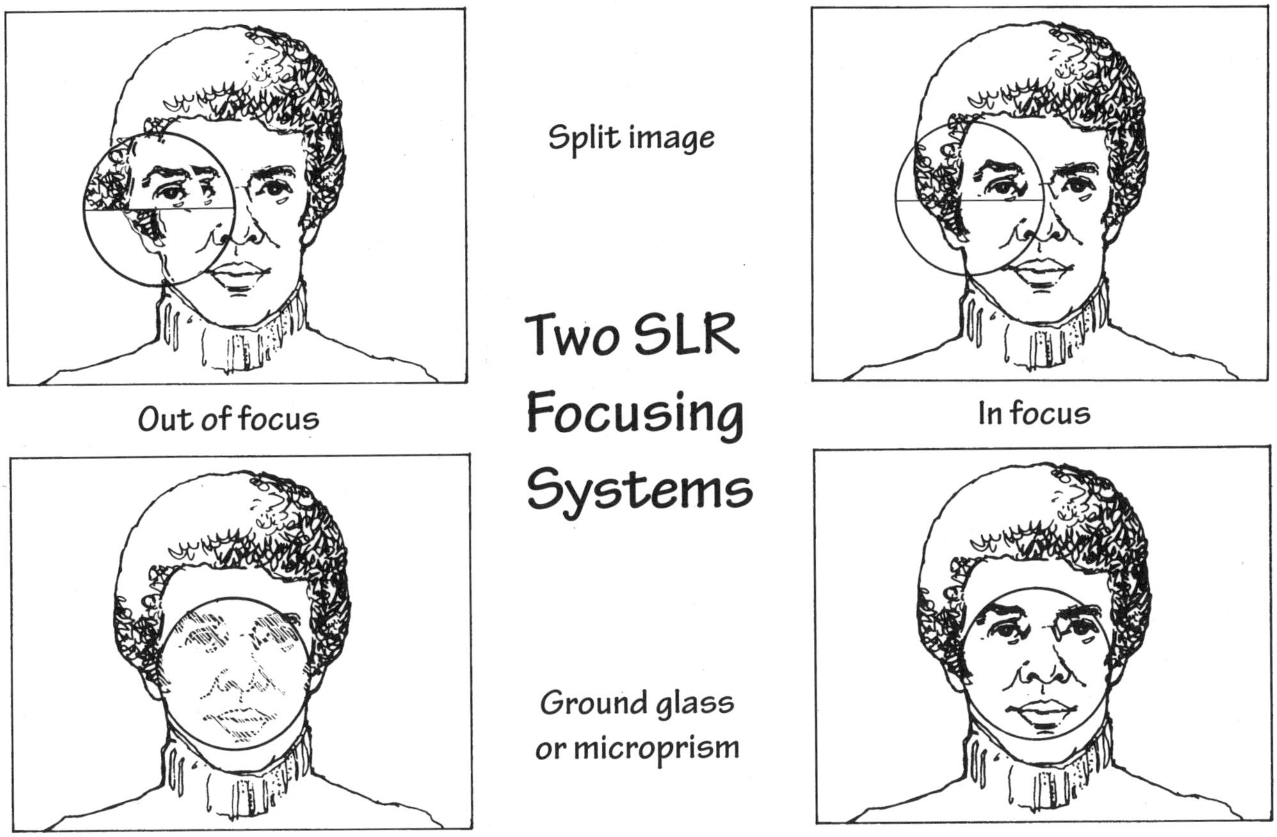

Close-Ups

"If your pictures aren't good enough, you aren't close enough."

— Robert Capa, photojournalist

Simple cameras do not permit the lens to be moved out far enough from the film plane to focus on close-ups. View cameras and some reflexes are provided with a flexible bellows, connecting the lens mount with the body of the camera, that can be extended for focusing on very near objects. Most 35mm SLRs focus as close as 1 1/2 to 3 feet, but they require extension tubes, a bellows attachment, or a supplementary close-up or macro lens to allow copy work and close-ups of nature and scientific subjects.

The viewfinder and parallax

With other than single-lens reflex and view cameras, the lens that actually takes the picture doesn't "see" exactly the same area that you see in the viewfinder.

This difference isn't noticeable on distant shots, but when focusing up close, this difference, called parallax, can result in the top of the picture being cut off or the framing being off-center.

With a single-lens reflex, parallax is not a problem, but precise framing sometimes is. Some tests on a copy stand (see pages 186-187) will show how much you may have to compensate. Usually the lens will include a little bit more than shown by the viewfinder.

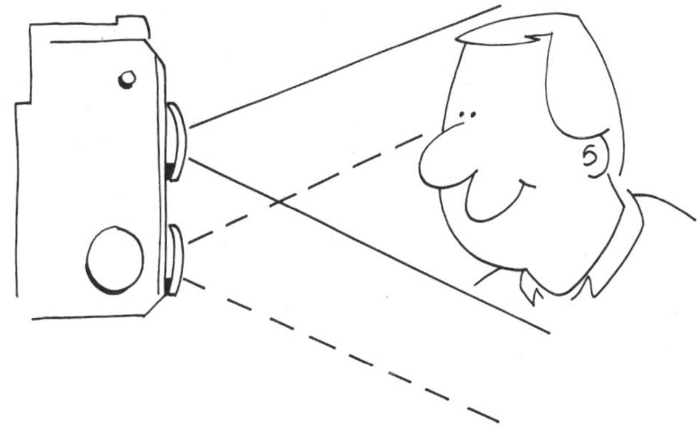

Abdel Alsoliman

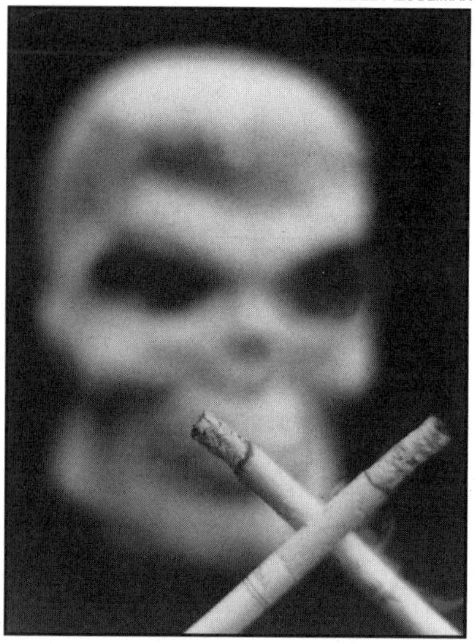

A large lens opening (f/2.8) and a close working distance resulted in a very shallow depth of field.

Nancy Miller

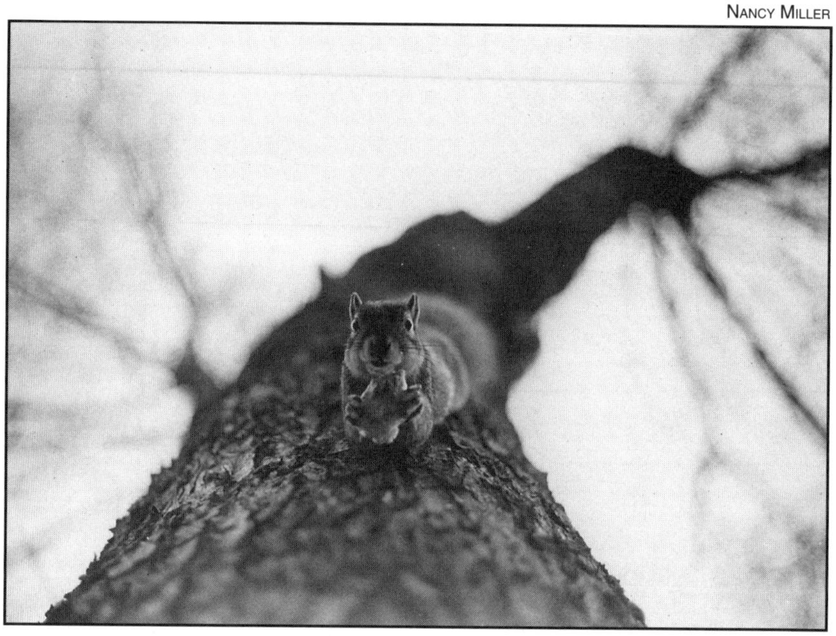

In the squirrel photo (upper right), not only has the photographer used selective focus to concentrate attention on her furry friend, instead of on what would have been a very "busy" and distracting background of branches and bark texture, but she has shown us the importance of looking elsewhere for pictures than straight ahead at eye level.

Erich Hammer

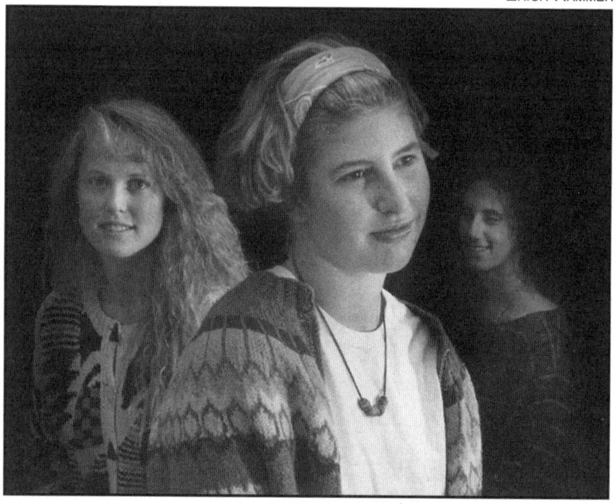

This studio photo illustrates depth of field. The camera was focused on the middle girl (on left in picture) and stopped down to f/16 to keep everyone in focus.

Jim Nixon

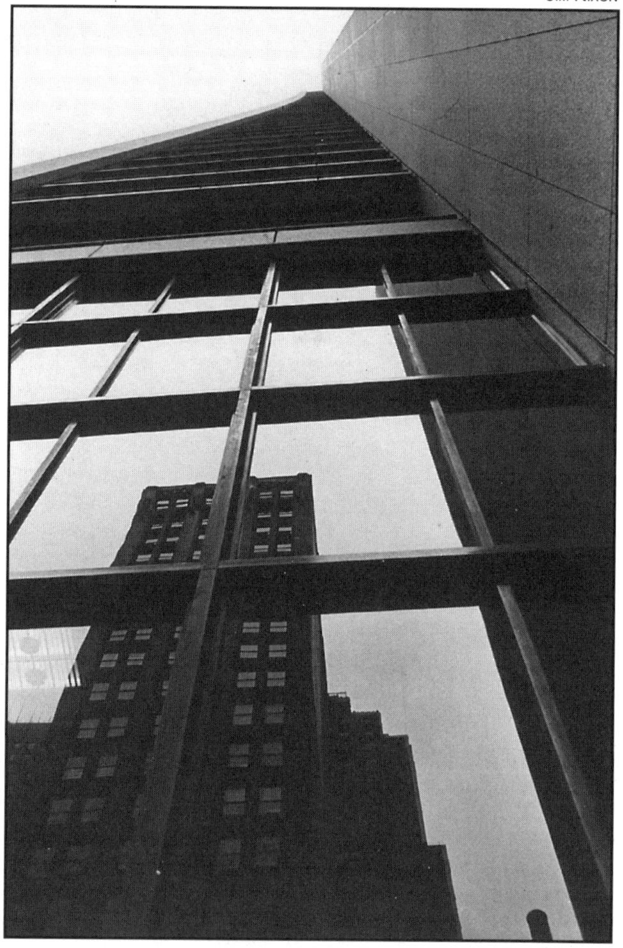

Here, the lens was stopped down to f/16 and focused between the plane of the windows and the reflection to keep all parts of the image in sharp focus.

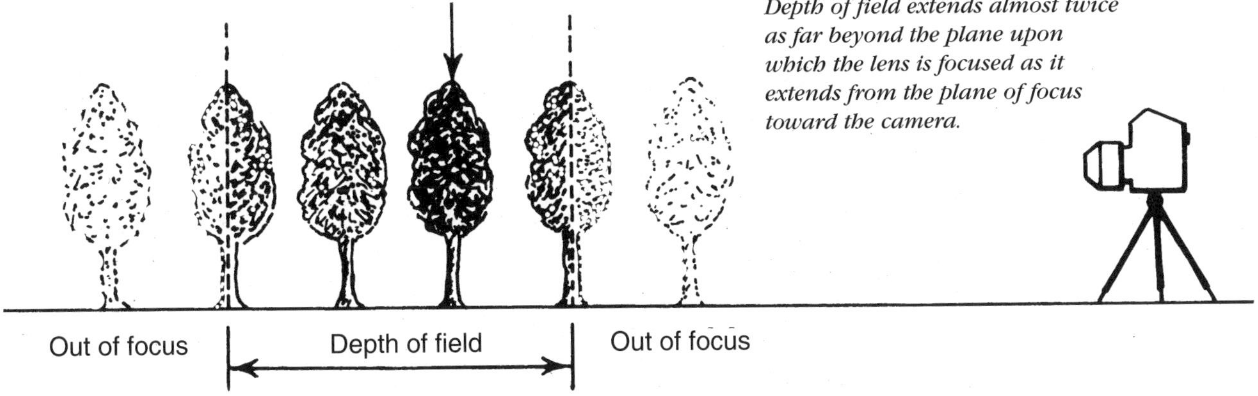

Depth of field extends almost twice as far beyond the plane upon which the lens is focused as it extends from the plane of focus toward the camera.

Depth of Field

Depth of field is the distance between subjects nearest and farthest from the camera that will be acceptably sharp in the finished image. Controlling sharpness is very important because most of the time you'll probably want the greatest depth of field possible. Except when the background would be distracting and should be kept deliberately out of focus, sharp detail in both foreground and background usually improves the picture. Depth of field increases when a smaller lens opening is used (f/16 instead of f/5.6) or when the camera is moved farther from the subject.

Lenses of short focal length give proportionately greater depth of field than longer lenses. View cameras, which employ long focal length lenses, can be adjusted to increase depth of field by bringing the lens mount or film plane of the camera more nearly parallel to the principal plane of the subject.

Many lenses on 35mm cameras have a depth of field scale engraved on the lens mount. With this scale you can predetermine whether certain subjects will be within the area of acceptable focus. Depth of field can be visually determined with a view camera or single-lens reflex by looking through the camera with the lens stopped down.

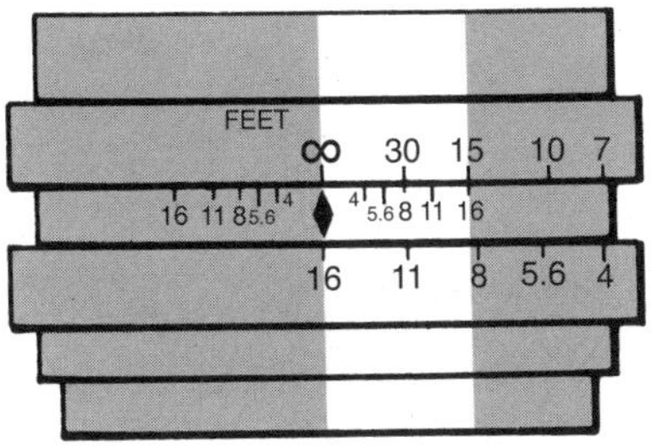

Focusing on infinity (∞) wastes depth of field. Note that the near limit is only 15 feet when the aperture is set at f/16.

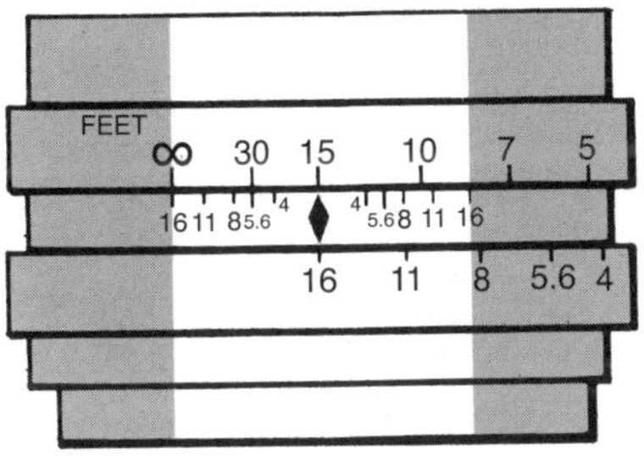

By focusing at the nearest limit of depth of field at infinity (hyperfocal distance) — in this example, 15 feet at f/16 — depth of field extends from 8 feet to infinity.

Hyperfocal focusing is a way to preset your camera for maximum depth of field, as for sports and travel photography

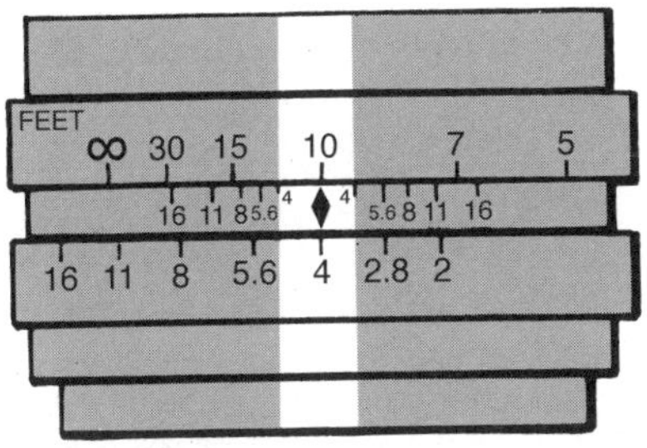

Lens focused at 10 feet. Depth of field from about 9-12 feet at f/4.

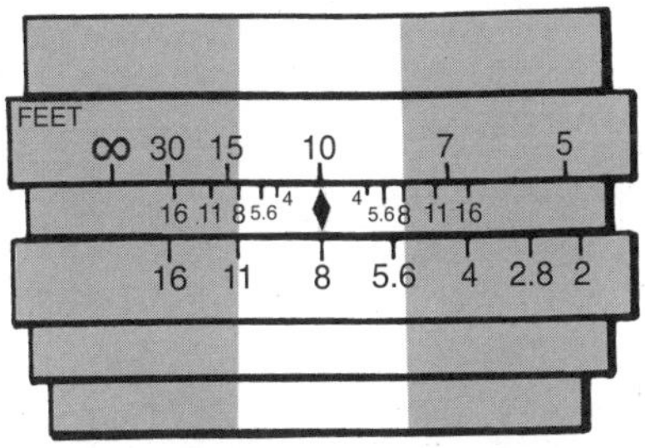

Stopping down to f/8 increases depth of field to about 8 to 14 feet.

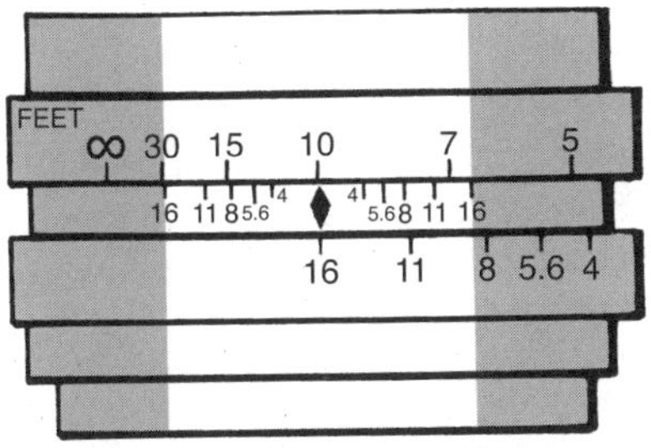

At f/16, depth of field ranges from closer than 7 feet to nearly 30 feet.

Depth of field depends upon both subject distance and lens opening. Some lenses have a "double f/stop" scale that indicates depth of field at any given setting (shown here within the white band).

Ardyce Czuchna-Curl

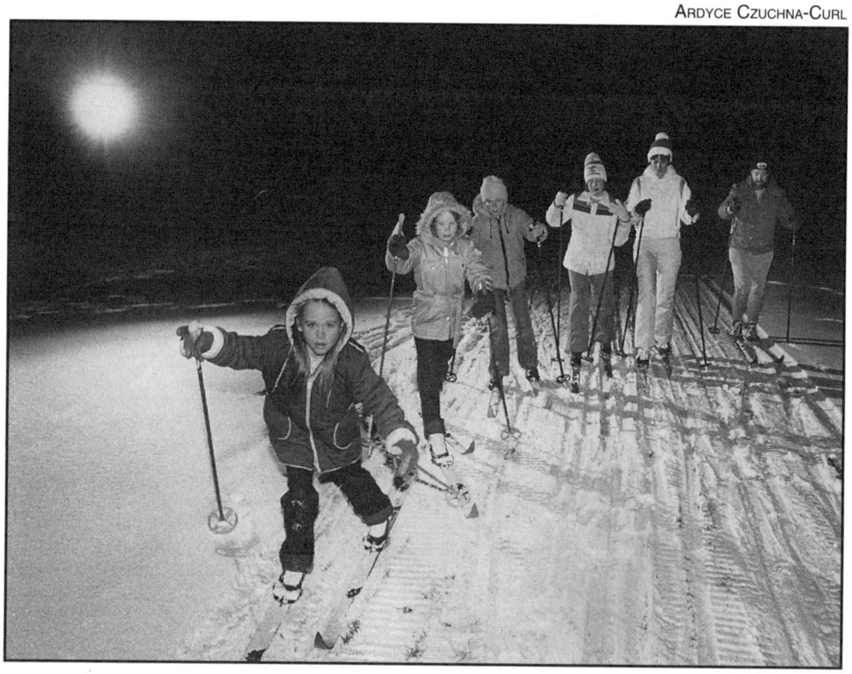

The flash determined motion-stopping in this photo. The shutter was set on the sync speed of 1/60, but the flash duration was more like 1/1,000 of a second. Two lights were used: A wireless slave flash unit (showing in the picture at upper left) simulated natural light, while a second flash on camera filled in foreground shadows.

Jeff Keyes

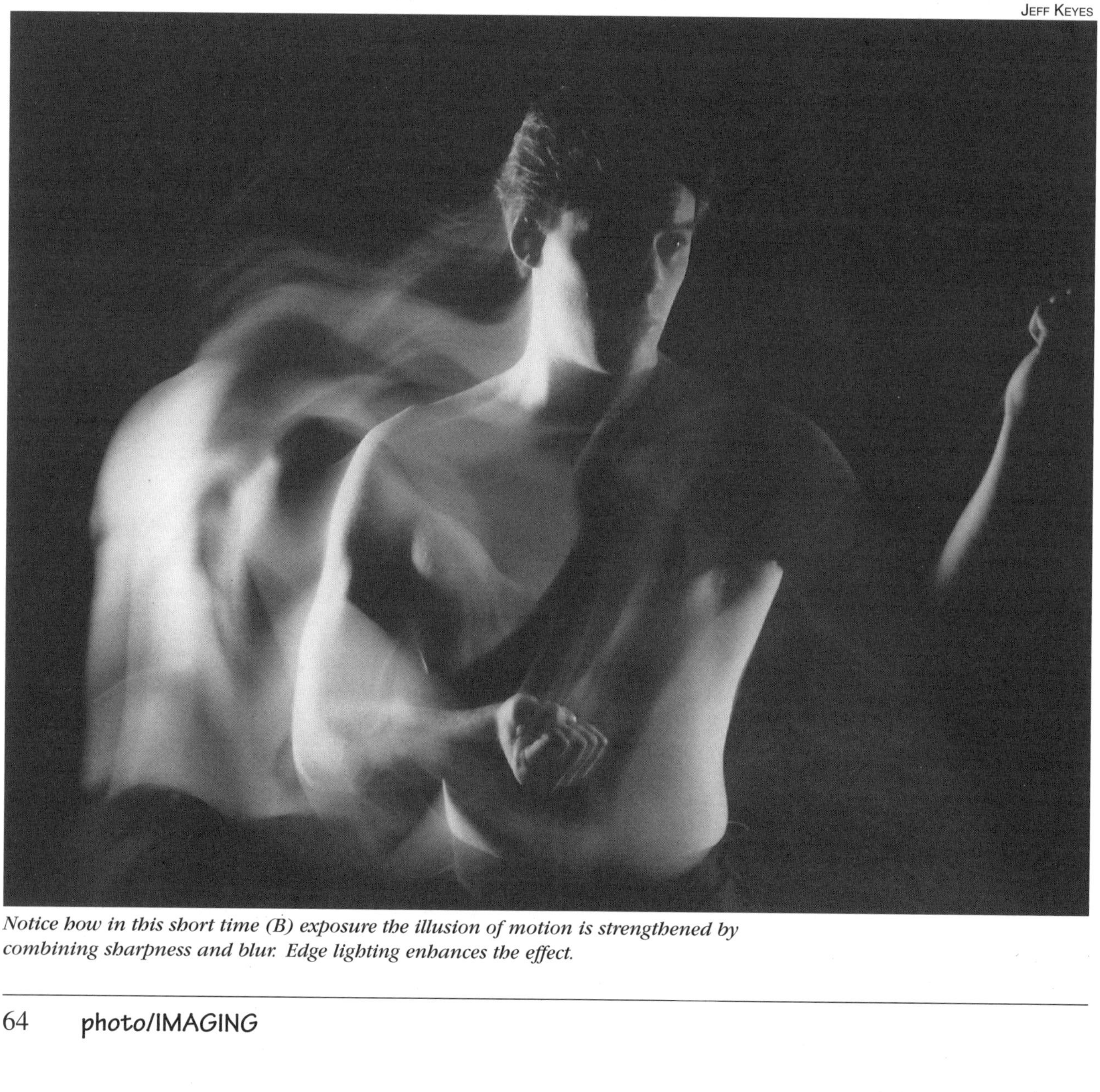

Notice how in this short time (B) exposure the illusion of motion is strengthened by combining sharpness and blur. Edge lighting enhances the effect.

The Shutter

Photography's most unique characteristic is the ability to preserve eternally a moment out of time. It is the camera shutter that makes this possible, together with sensitive film. We take these things for granted, but because of the limitations of their primitive equipment and materials, the first photographers were unable to record moving subjects. A portrait sitter had to hold unnaturally still or have his or her head clamped firmly to prevent movement during an exposure lasting anywhere from a few seconds to several agonizing minutes. Now you know why there are so few 19th century photographs of young children, animals, sporting events, or wartime combat.

Modern equipment and fast films let us choose whether to "freeze" the action for examination of minute detail, or to create an illusion of motion by deliberately allowing a moving subject to be blurred.

Stopping motion

The choice of shutter speed is yours (unless your camera is set on automatic). A speed of 1/60 of a second will "stop" a person walking toward you at some distance, but will take a higher speed, say 1/250, if the subject is closer to the camera or is walking directly past. Moving vehicles and fast-action sporting events usually call for 1/1,000 to freeze the action. If you're a nature photographer, you may find that the wind will move blossoms and leaves so much that you can't get a sharp image at less than 1/250 or 1/500.

Close-up photography often requires a very small lens opening to gain depth of field, but the resulting slow shutter speed can cause motion-stopping problems. This is when you need a tripod.

Camera movement can as serious as subject movement. Most people are unable to hand hold a camera steadily at shutter speeds slower than 1/60 of a second. The negative may look all right, but enlargement will show the telltale directional blur that proves the camera wasn't steady enough at the moment of exposure. Long focal-length lenses are especially hard to hold steady because they magnify movement by the same proportion that they magnify the size of the image.

"The goal of every artist is to stop movement, which is life ... and to maintain it fixed so that one hundred years later, when a stranger may gaze at it, it will once again move, because it is life."

— William Faulkner, author

SCOTT LAVACQUE

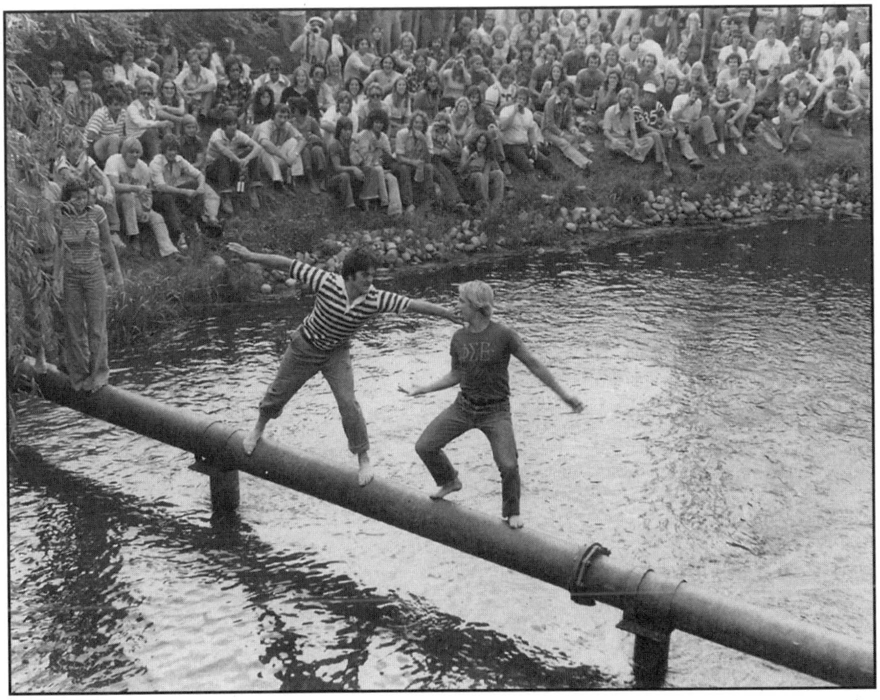

A shutter speed of 1/125 of a second was fast enough to "stop" the action because the photographer waited for a moment when the combatants' positions implied movement that was not actually happening (note the slight blur of the left hand of the man on your right).

Barbara Bergy

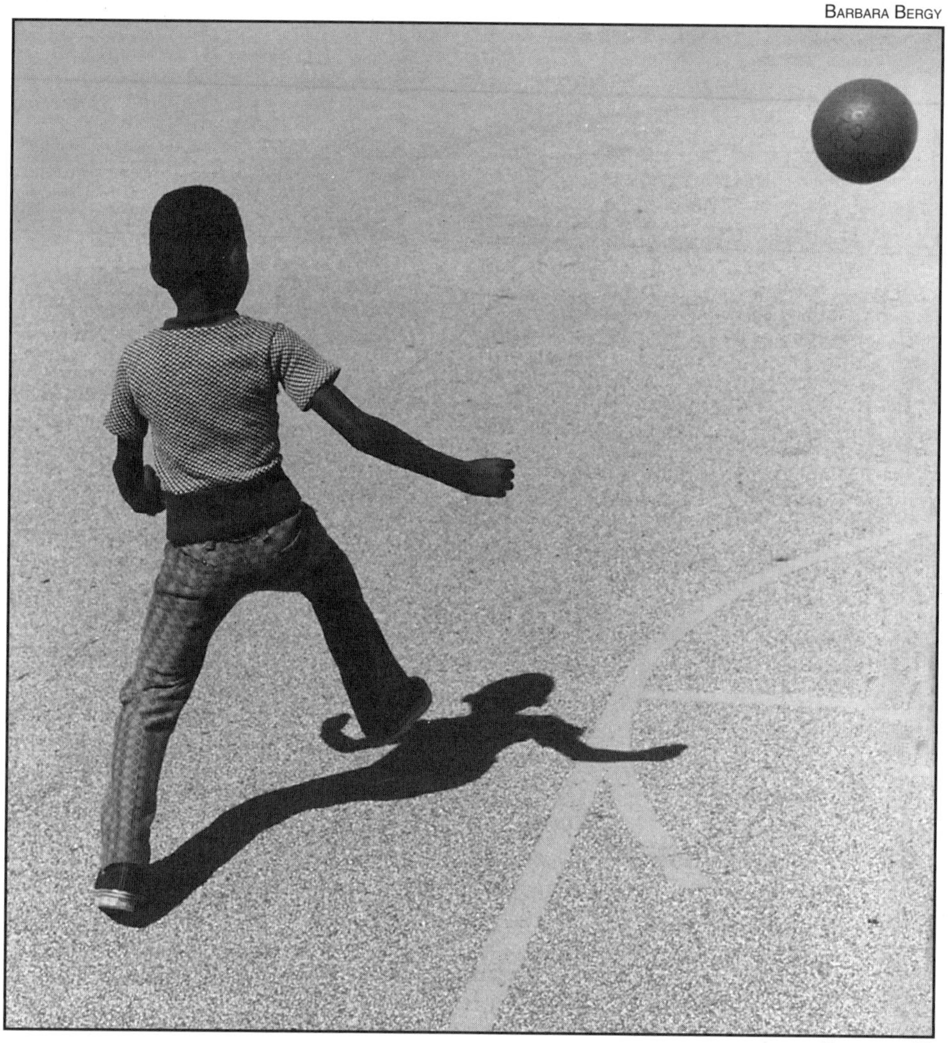

A shutter speed of 1/1,000 of a second froze the movement of this boy, his shadow, and the ball into a dynamic composition full of tension and graphic contrast.

Andrea Rubenstein (2)

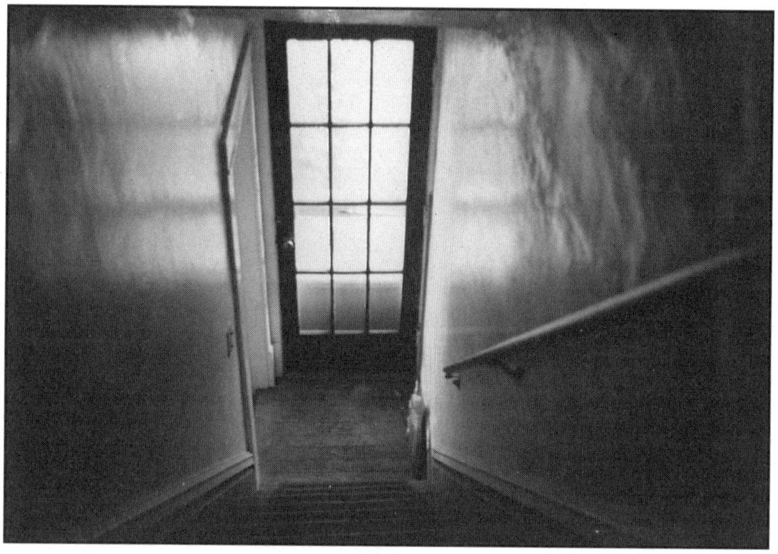

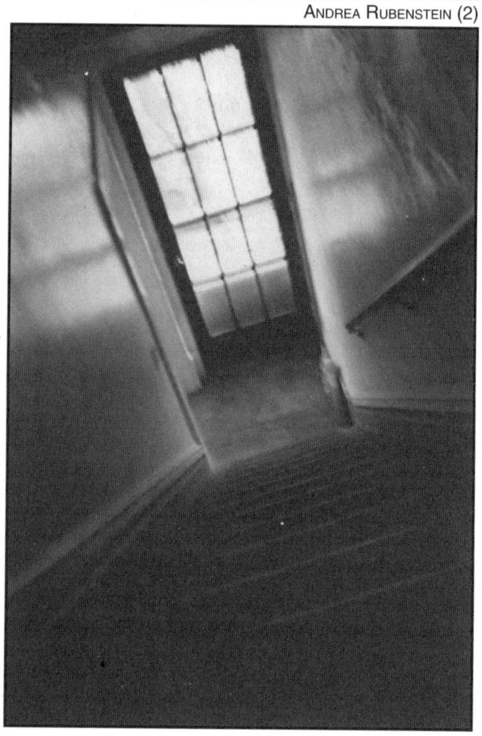

Do you react differently to these two images of the same stairway? In the picture on the right, do the vertical format, the tilted angle, and the blur from camera movement intensify the feeling — the fear — of falling?

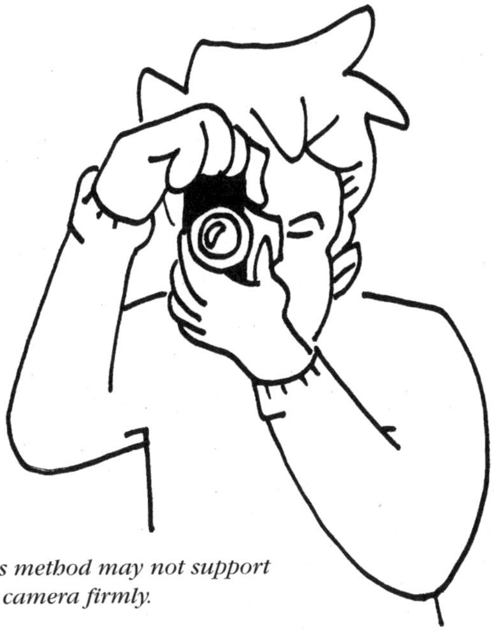

This method may not support the camera firmly.

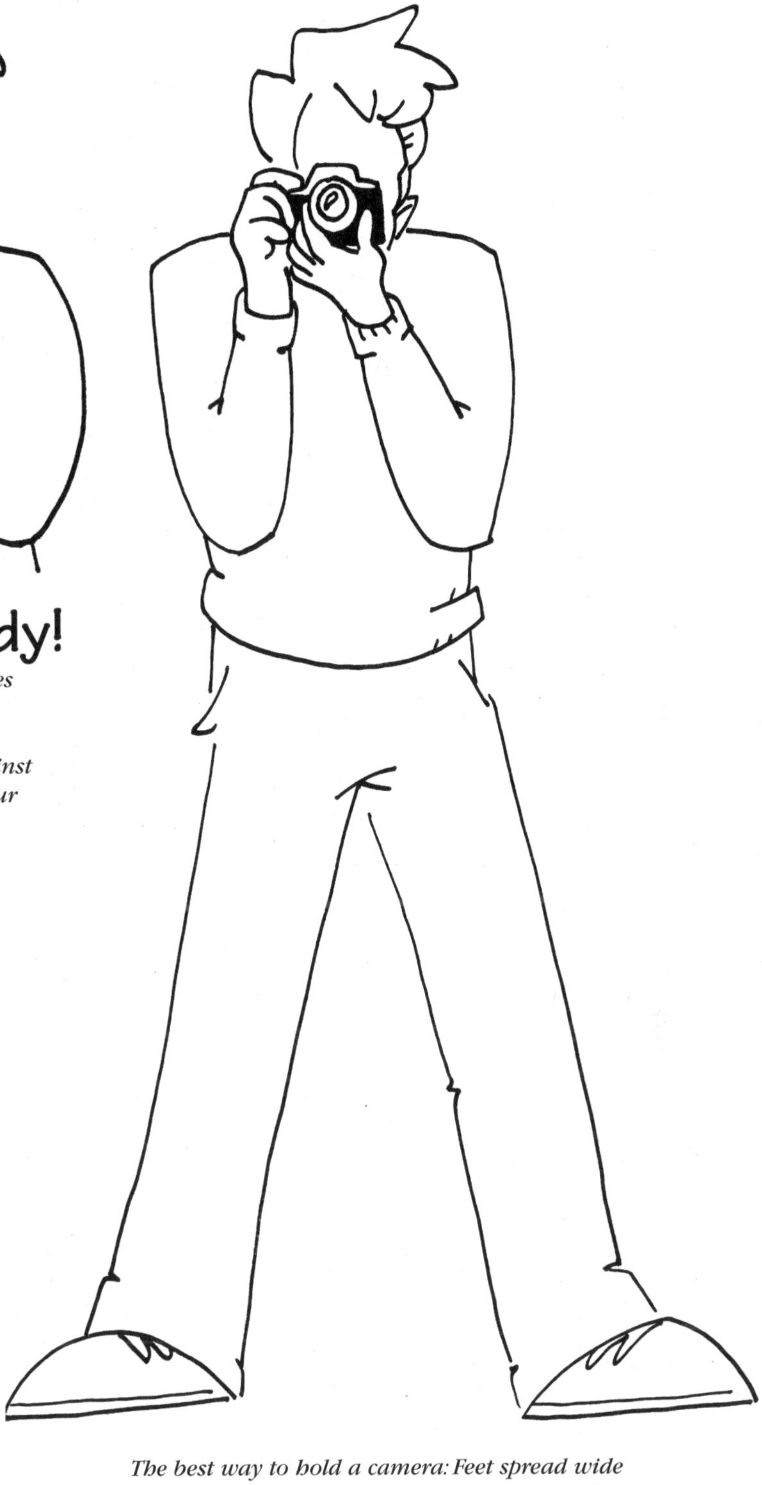

Hold the Camera Steady!

Hand-holding a camera requires the same steady nerves and concentration needed for accurate target shooting with a rifle. The camera strap can serve as a steadying sling if you stretch it tight. Hold the camera firmly against your face, even if you're wearing glasses, and brace your elbows firmly against your body. Squeeze the shutter release smoothly — don't punch or jab it! Whenever possible, use a tripod.

The best way to hold a camera: Feet spread wide apart, both elbows braced against your body. Left hand supports the lens and adjusts focus and zoom.

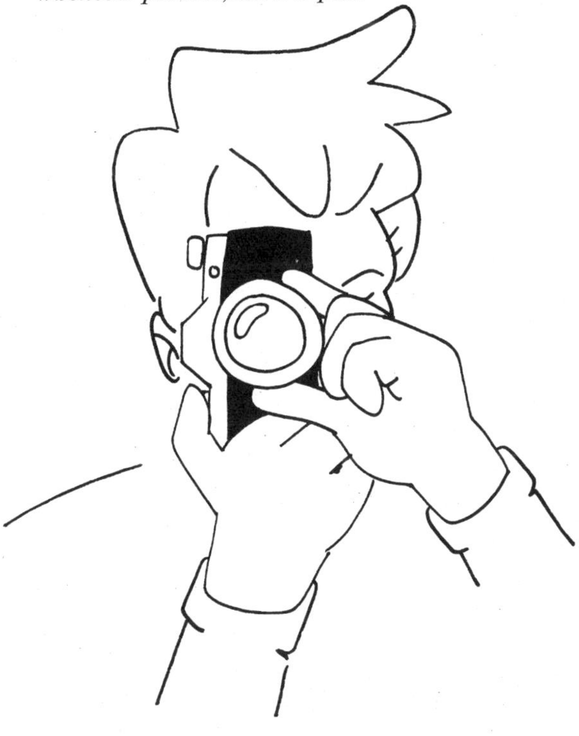

For vertical shots, the left hand supports the lens and adjusts focus and zoom. Elbows press against body. Right hand grips camera. Right thumb releases shutter.

Do you get the feeling of a surging crowd? The effect was obtained by hand-holding the camera at a shutter speed of one second, panning with the people as they burst through the turnstile at the opening of a carnival.

JIM NIXON

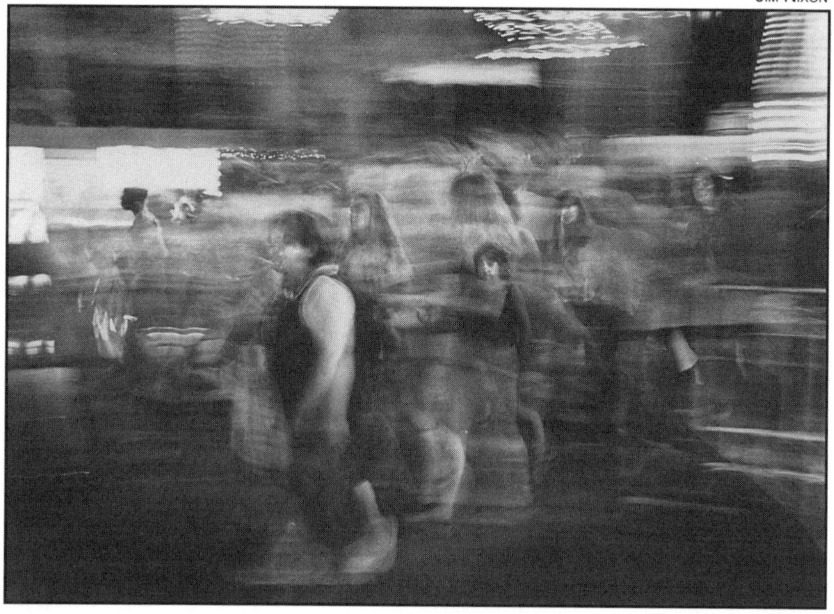

The unsteadiness of a hand-held one-second exposure adds interest to what otherwise would have been a routine burst of fireworks.

KAREN ERICKSON

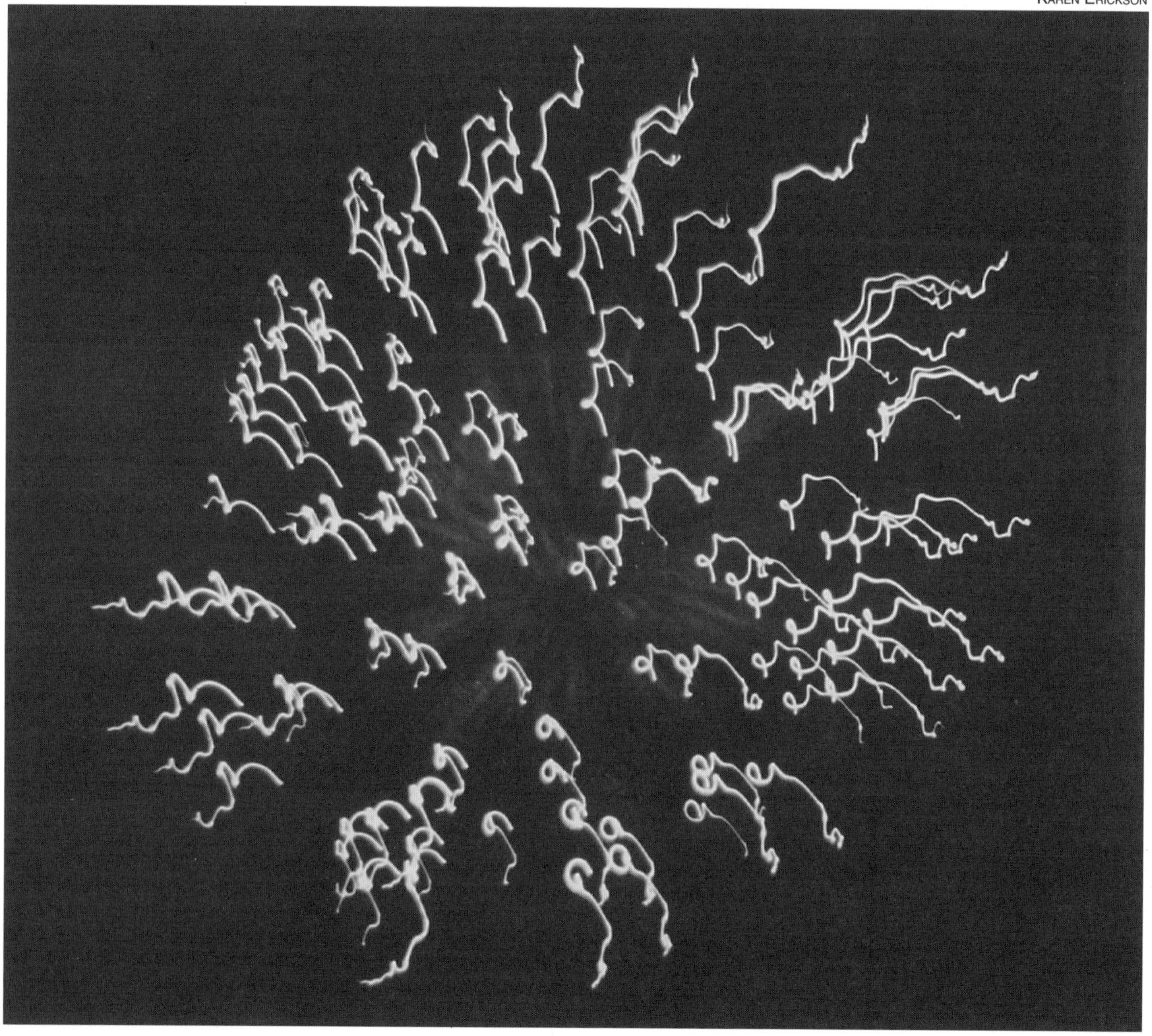

Creative Blurring

Usually we want to make *sharp* images, but can you imagine bad (blurred) pictures that are good? There are a couple of different ways to blur images creatively: (1) move the camera along with the subject (panning) and (2) hold the camera still while the subject moves past.

To pan, follow a rapidly moving subject through the viewfinder, using slow film (ISO 25-100) at a very slow shutter speed — perhaps 1/8 of a second. Continue moving the camera while you depress the shutter release. If your camera is an SLR the image will disappear while the shutter is open and the mirror is up, but you should follow-through with your body, trying to keep the camera lined up with the moving subject.

To show *subject* motion, mount your camera on a tripod and let the subject's movement trace a blur at various slow shutter speeds. You may be surprised at the interesting illusion of motion.

Nearly all modern 35mm SLRs use a focal-plane shutter — so called because the shutter curtain moves across the camera body, like a window shade, directly in front of the film. Lenses can be interchanged more conveniently and less expensively on a camera with a focal-plane shutter because each lens need not contain its own shutter. Most medium- and large-format cameras use between-the-lens shutters with maximum speeds of generally 1/500 of a second, allowing flash synchronization at all speeds. Unfortunately, the curtain of most focal-plane shutters is not fully open at speeds faster than 1/60. This is something to think about when buying a new camera. Certain 35mm SLRs will synchronize flash up to 1/250, or even faster, making it possible to use fill-in flash outdoors in sunlight, and to minimize "ghost" images when shooting with flash under bright ambient light such as at sporting events. Some cameras provide an option of "rear curtain sync," which allows the flash to be fired at the end of a long exposure so that a sharp image may be combined with a blurred one in a single exposure.

Ricky Don Meek

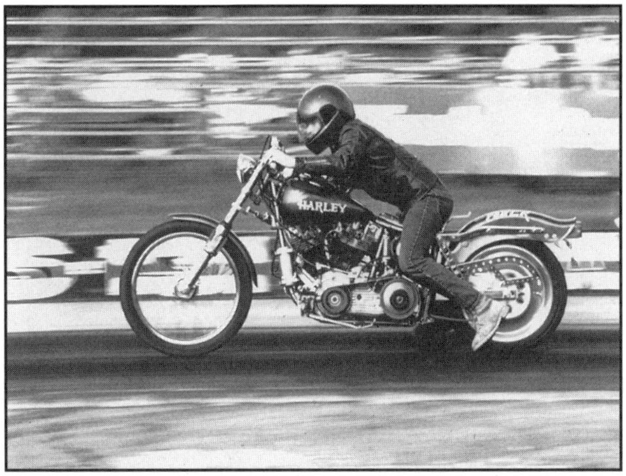

This motorcycle was moving so fast that panning at 1/60 of a second with a 200mm lens gave a strong illusion of motion.

The dancer moved in front of the camera, which was on a tripod, during a short time (B) exposure. Notice that her brief pauses left distinct images connected by flowing lines, suggesting the grace of the dance.

David Knight

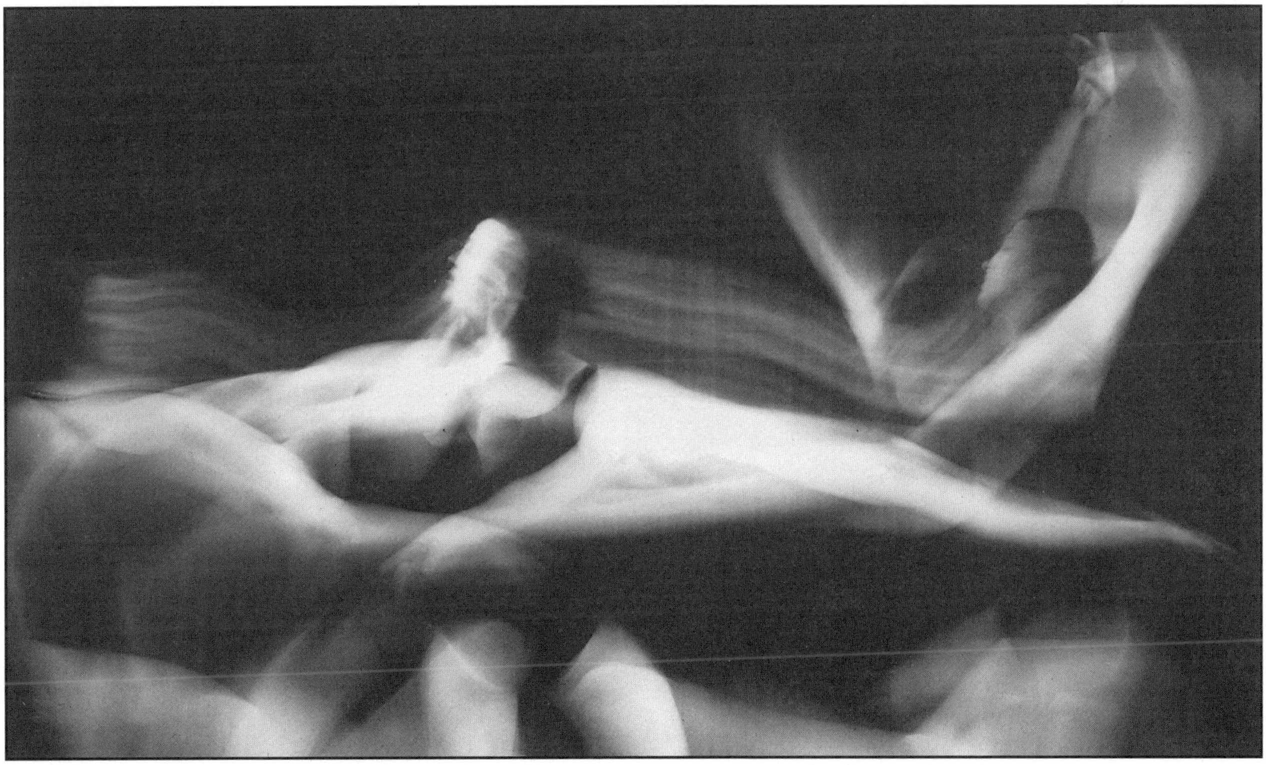

Erich Hammer (2)

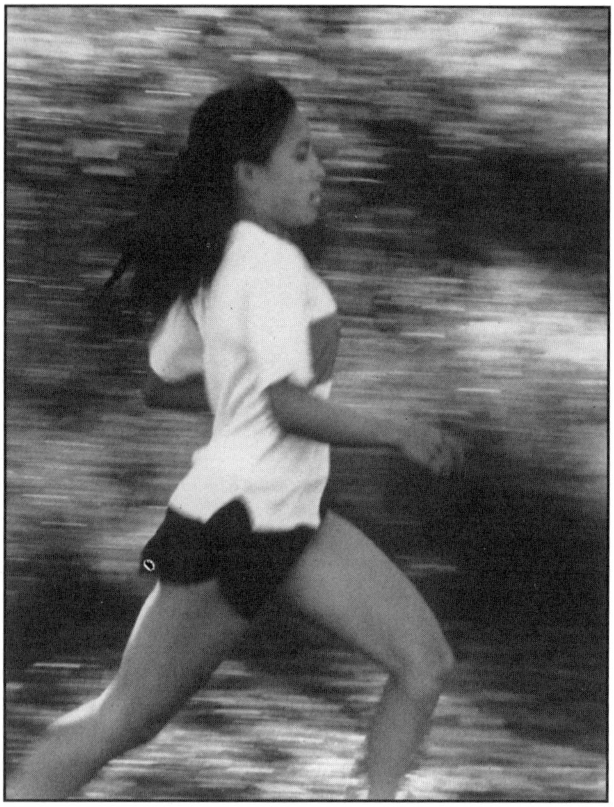

Panning the camera at 1/30 of a second as the subject ran past gave a feeling of breathless speed.

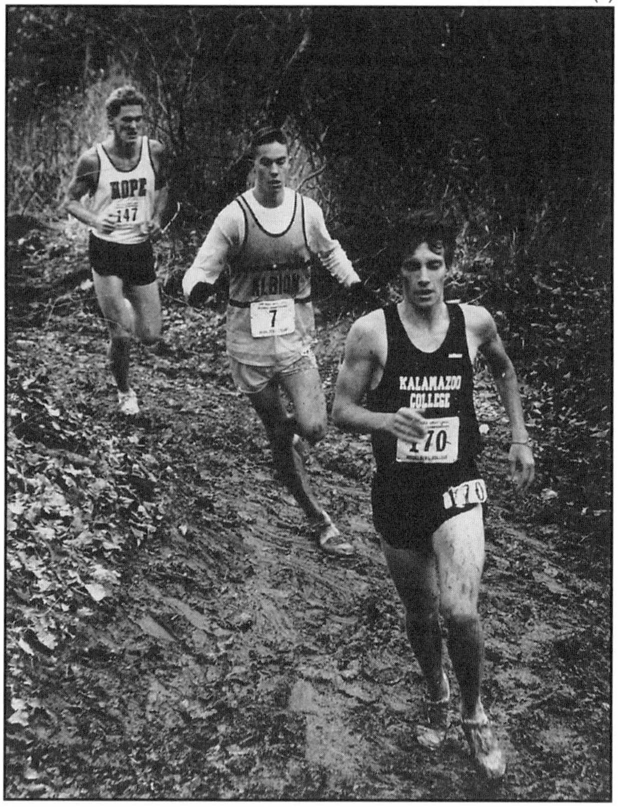

Because these runners were moving directly toward the camera, their motion was nearly frozen at 1/250 of a second.

David Knight

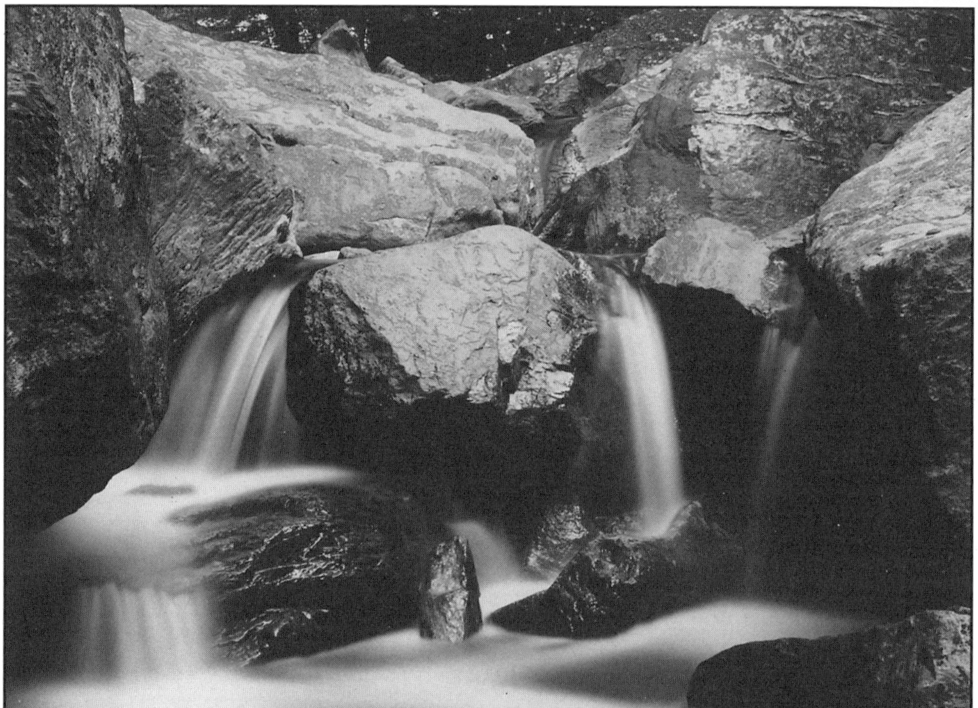

Obviously, rocks and camera remained motionless during this eight-second exposure, but the moving water has taken on a metallic, flowing quality.

Camera Care

Your camera is a precision instrument that deserves good care. It represents a sizable investment and it will give the best results when protected from dirt, moisture, and physical abuse.

Cleanliness is very important. A common misconception is that dust on the lens will cause spots on prints. This is not true — spots on images are the result of dust or lint on the film or in processing. A layer of dust on the camera or enlarger lens will at most reduce the contrast of the image, and it may degrade the sharpness. But dirt or sand on the lens may cause permanent scratches if you're careless about how you clean the glass surfaces.

The proper way to clean a lens is first to blow off surface dust with an air bulb, or gently wipe it away with a very soft brush. Sand or rough particles can make deep scratches if rubbed, so be especially careful. Here's how to remove fingerprints or water spots: wad a sheet of camera-lens tissue into a loose ball and moisten it with a few drops of lens-cleaning fluid, then wipe the lens surface gently in a circular motion. Don't pour the cleaning solution directly onto the lens because it can seep inside between the glass elements. Dry the lens with another loose wad of lens-cleaning tissue. Don't use cleaning products designed for eyeglasses or windows.

Although a little dust on the outer surfaces of the lens may not be very serious, dust, sand, and film fragments *inside* your camera may cause the mechanism to jam; or the tiny particles may leave images of themselves on your negatives. Blow out loose dirt with an air bulb, or wipe it out with a cotton swab or small brush; but be very careful not to touch the shutter curtain or the mirror. Never try to clean the mirror, other than by blowing off dust. The reflective surface is extremely delicate. Black spots that you see when looking through the viewfinder won't show on your pictures. The dirt probably is on the bottom of the prism where it should be removed only by a repair technician.

The best way to have a clean camera is to keep it from getting dirty. Invest in a durable, padded case for your equipment. Keep the protective caps on both ends of lenses when they're not in use. For the lens that stays on your camera most of the time, a UV, haze, or skylight filter (practically colorless) kept over the lens provides excellent protection against abrasion, dust, sand, and moisture. Opaque lens caps can be a nuisance, and it's a lot cheaper to replace a filter than to buy a new lens.

A few raindrops falling on your camera are not likely to cause permanent harm, although a good soaking probably will. Salt water is an especially voracious enemy of lens coatings and metallic finishes, so a filter over the lens and even a plastic bag over the camera will help protect it on a rafting or sailing trip. If your camera should ever become thoroughly immersed, especially in salt water, rinse it out immediately in a container of fresh water; then, if you can't get it to a repair shop right away while it's soaking, dry it out as rapidly as possible with warm air from a hair dryer. Operate the mechanism occasionally while it is drying to keep it freed up. Wet film can be saved if it is processed within a few hours. Seal the film in a jar of fresh water or a plastic bag until it can be processed.

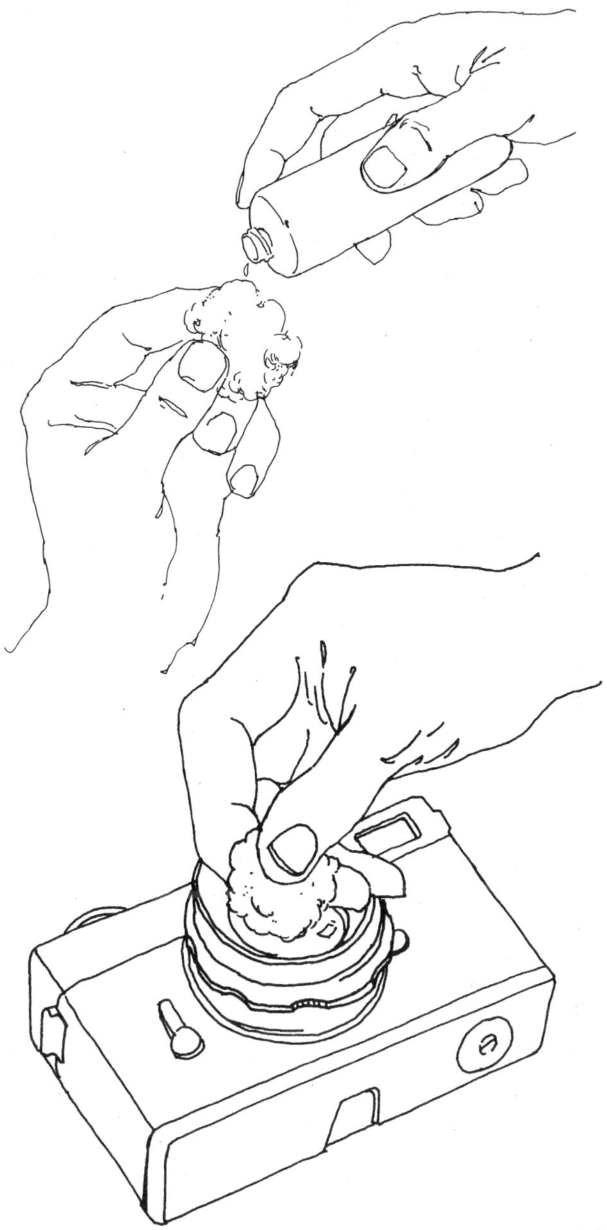

A clean lens is essential for clear pictures. Protect your lenses with lens caps or clear-glass filters, cleaning them only when necessary using the recommended procedure.

Travel tips

Photographers who travel, often encounter vibration problems. The vibration from a plane, train, motorcycle, or car eventually may shake loose some vital screws, so retighten the visible screws periodically with a jeweler's screwdriver. Plan to carry the camera around your neck or over your shoulder instead of having it travel in the baggage compartment.

Aside from customs difficulties and possible theft, another reason for carrying your camera is that you can request a visual security inspection at the airport instead of having your loaded camera pass through a potentially harmful X-ray machine. I have found that most airport-security personnel around the world usually will hand-inspect my camera and film when I smile and ask pleasantly. I remove film magazines from their opaque containers and place them in transparent, plastic storage bags so they can quickly be handed through security. An alternative is to purchase lead-foil containers from a camera store and leave the film in your luggage. One trip through most airport X-ray machines probably won't harm unprotected film slower than ISO 1,000, but the effect is cumulative.

Extreme heat and cold

The trunk or glove compartment and the ledge of the rear window of your car are among the poorest places to put a camera. Besides vibration, the intense heat within a close automobile in the sun not only can fog the film in the camera or cause color shifts, but it may actually cause lens elements to separate, lubricants to liquify, and batteries to deteriorate.

Tropical heat and humidity are especially troublesome, as fungus will grow rapidly on film and, if given enough time, may eat away some lens coatings and even etch itself into the glass.

Don't leave film in the camera any longer than necessary. If you're going to stay more than a few days in the tropics, store your camera in an air-conditiond room, a dehumidified closet, or in a sealed box containing a desiccant such as silica gel. An insulated picnic cooler will help protect your film and camera for a few hours.

Arctic conditions cause different problems. Although cold is less likely than heat to cause damage, low temperatures can weaken batteries and stiffen lubricants. Carry the camera under your coat between shots, and your body heat should keep it warm enough to keep working.

If your equipment has become thoroughly chilled, don't bring it into a warm room where moisture can condense on it (and inside). Let it warm up gradually, or seal the cold camera and lenses in plastic bags before bringing them indoors. Avoid putting equipment and film near heaters and radiators.

Another winter problem is static electricity, which can make lightening-like imprints on your negatives. Avoid generating static by manually advancing or rewinding film slowly.

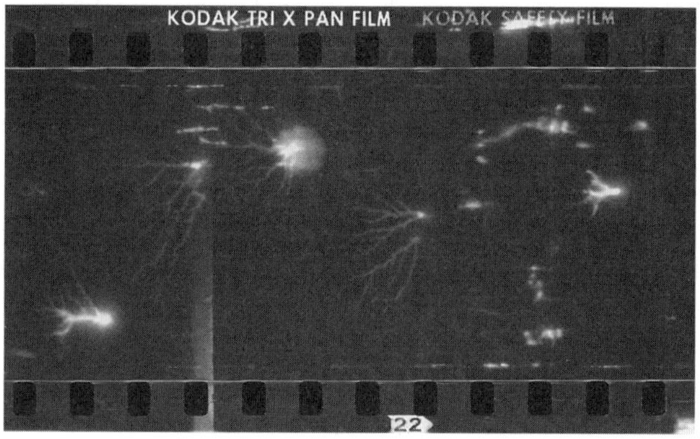

Static in action. This negative is an example of a very bad case of static electricity. Static discharge sometimes occurs at low temperatures and low humidity. It can be avoided in manually operated cameras by advancing and rewinding the film slowly.

Care of batteries

Batteries can fail without warning — working one day, dead the next. The tiny energy cells that power exposure meters and electronic features on most modern cameras should last a year or more. Put in fresh batteries before leaving on an extended trip, and carry spares.

Alkaline flash batteries require frequent inspection to remove the white powder that may collect on the terminals and cause flash failure. A rough cloth will clean the ends of batteries; a pencil eraser is a handy tool to reach down inside the battery compartment to clean the contact terminals there. Remove the batteries if your camera or flash isn't going to be used for several weeks; put them in a sealed plastic bag and store in the refrigerator. Freezing will prolong the life of film, but freezing is not good for batteries.

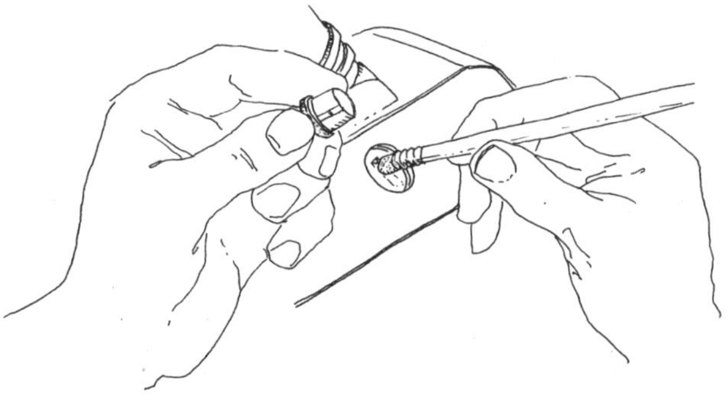

When batteries die, so may your camera. Sometimes operation can be restored by wiping the battery and internal camera contacts with a pencil eraser. But if batteries are more than a year old, assume their life is over.

Loading Film

Imagine shooting a roll of great pictures, then developing the film and finding it blank!

This happens, but it shouldn't happen to you. Dead batteries and careless film loading cause most of the problems people have when they begin using a camera. If the film isn't loaded correctly, most 35mm cameras will act as if everything is OK, and even the exposure counter will register.

Here's how to keep this disappointing experience from occuring: When you load your 35mm camera, be sure the film leader is firmly attached to the take-up spool or, if your camera is automatic-loading, it is pulled out to exactly the right length and laid against the indicator mark. Check to see that the film's sprocket holes are engaged with (or lying directly over) the sprocket teeth on both sides. Be sure the film is flat and lined up correctly before closing and latching the camera back.

If your camera has a motorized rewind and no hand-rewind crank, then you should consult the owner's manual to see whether there is a warning signal if something is wrong when you press the film advance to begin the roll.

Manually operated cameras are easy to check, because the rewind crank or knob will turn as the film advances. Here's how to take advantage of this feature:

After latching the camera back, press the film-advance lever until it stops. Then turn the rewind knob or crank in the direction of the arrow (clockwise, as if you were rewinding the film after exposure) until you feel slight tension. Stop. Release the shutter and advance the film two more frames, watching the rewind knob as you turn the advance lever. The rewind knob sould rotate counterclockwise, opposite to the arrow, showing that the film is moving. The film counter should now be on frame number 1. Check the rewind knob from time to time as you advance the film to avoid the embarrassment of shooting 36 exposures on the same frame!

Most 120-size roll-film cameras have an arrow inside the film magazine that must be lined up with an arrow printed near the beginning of the film-backing paper. Line up these arrows, then close and latch the cover to set the exposure counter. Stroke the advance lever or turn the knob until it stops on frame number 1.

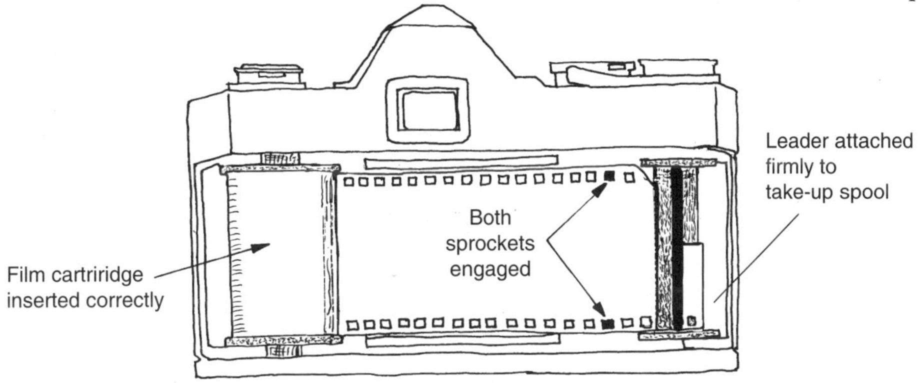

Most problems with film loading are caused by being in too much of a hurry. Take your time. Keep your fingers away from the shutter. Don't shortcut the procedure. Check every step.

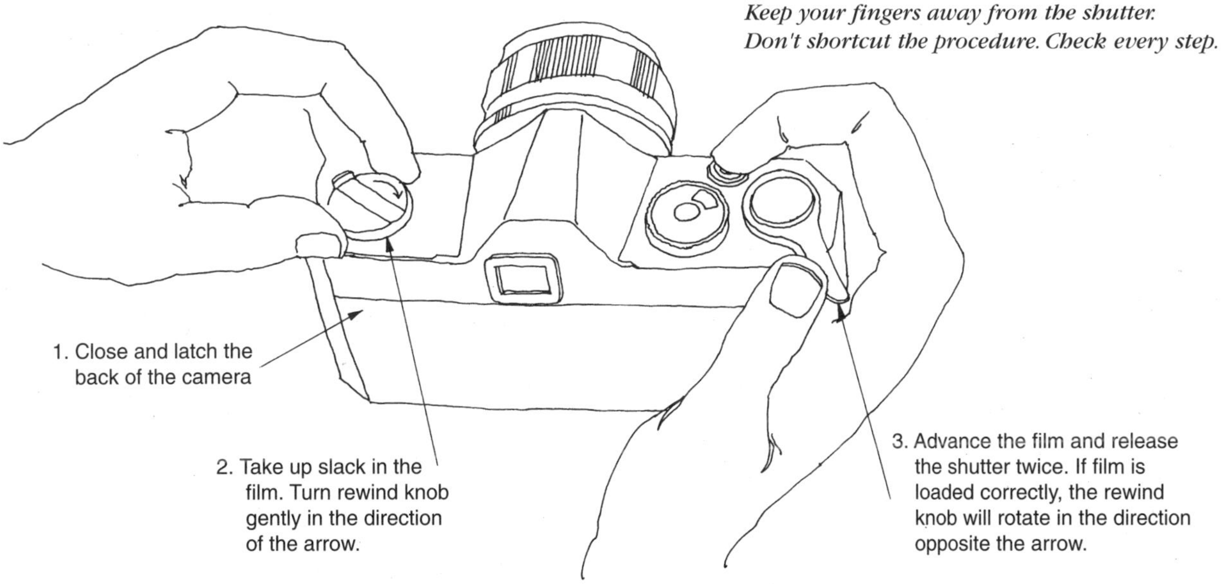

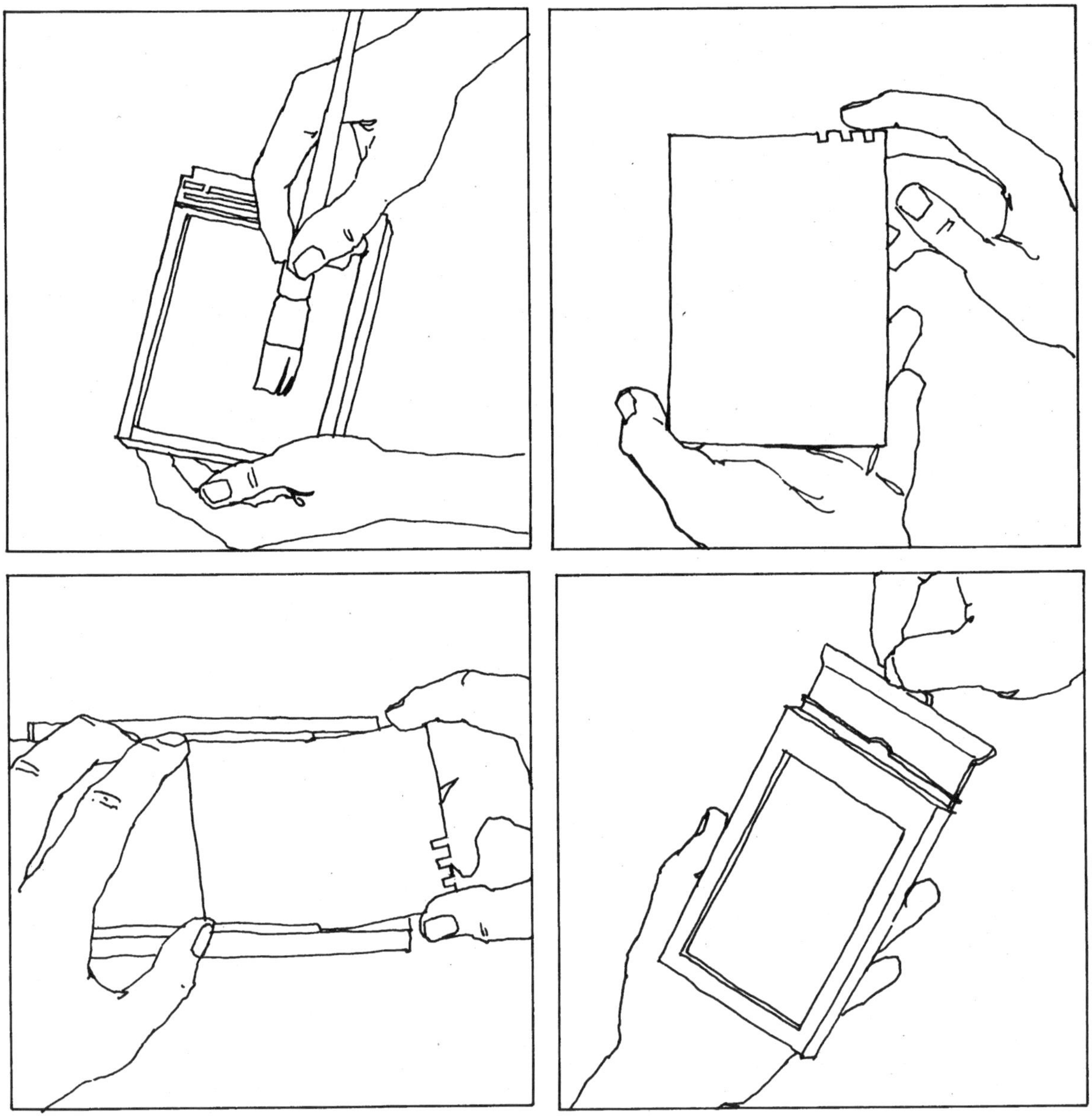

Sheet film holders must be kept free of dust. In the dark, each sheet of film is loaded separately beneath the retaining guides on one side of a holder. The dark slides should be inserted with the silver sides of the handles facing out to indicate unexposed film. After exposure, the slide should be reinserted with the black side of the handle facing out.

Sheet-film creates a set of different problems, because most films must be loaded in total darkness. Before turning out the lights, blow or brush the sheet-film holders free of dust before loading, and position the dark slides with the silver sides of the handles facing outward. Nearly all sheet films are notched so that in the dark, you can feel the notches with your right index finger if the film is held correctly for insertion into the holder. Guide the film into the retaining slots with your left hand, then fold over the hinged end flap and insert the dark slide all the way. Lock the latches. Don't forget to rewrap the leftover film and put it back into its light-tight box before turning on the lights!

All cameras should be loaded and unloaded in the shade or indoors — never in bright sunlight. Sheet-film holders tend to leak light if the dark slides are removed and inserted in direct sun; so shade the camera if possible when changing film. Never force any of the adjustments or controls on any camera. If the film should jam for any reason, unload the camera in a darkroom or inside a light-proof changing bag.

Although these tips and suggestions won't ensure that all of your photographs will be significant and visually exciting, avoiding the common mistakes mentioned above will help to increase the odds that your important images will not be lost forever because of malfunctioning equipment or a careless error.

Accessories 4

What Do You Really Need?

Buying a camera is only the beginning. There are many further ways to invest in photographic accessories and gadgets, and certainly even more to learn, once you begin the expansion from traditional photography into digital imaging.

A few accessories are essential. Some are useful for special purposes, while others merely are toys. This chapter will show you how to tell goodies from gadgets and help you get the most for your money.

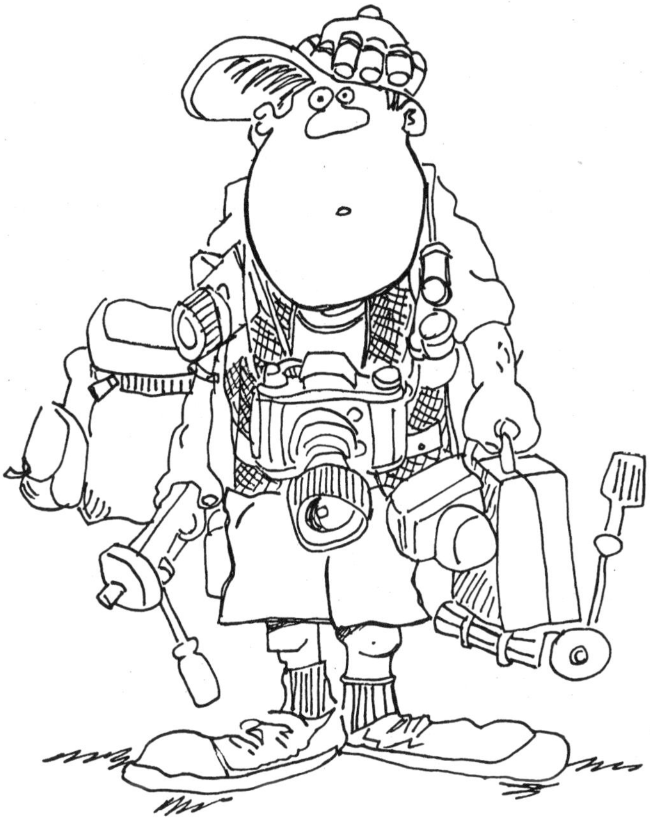

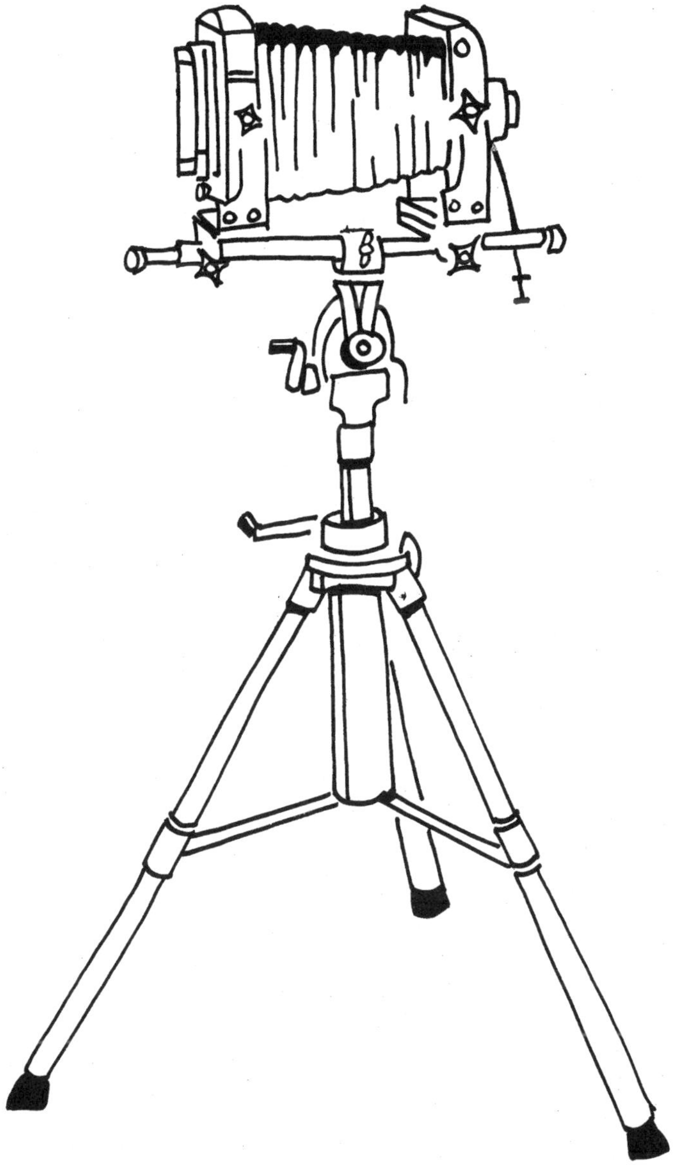

Tripod

First and foremost, you'll need a tripod. A sturdy tripod is essential for absolutely sharp pictures, although many beginning photographers don't believe they need one until they make their first big enlargements! Pick a tripod that won't wobble when you press down on the head with your hand and twist it. Also, get a bigger one than you think you need. Although you may curse the weight of a bulky camera support when you're backpacking or photographing in the field, you'll be glad when you finally compare your sharp negatives and prints with your former fuzzy ones.

Nature photographers often choose a tripod with legs that spread wide for low camera angles, while sports enthusiasts often are seen along the sidelines using a one-legged monopod. Check out different types of heads and camera-mounting devices. Some people enjoy the simplicity of a swiveling ball head and a quick-lock release plate. Others choose a pan head or the double-tilting kind. Many prefer flip-type leg locks to the kind that twist. Try before you buy!

Since you'll eventually need a tripod, find a sturdy one and make this important investment as soon as you can afford it.

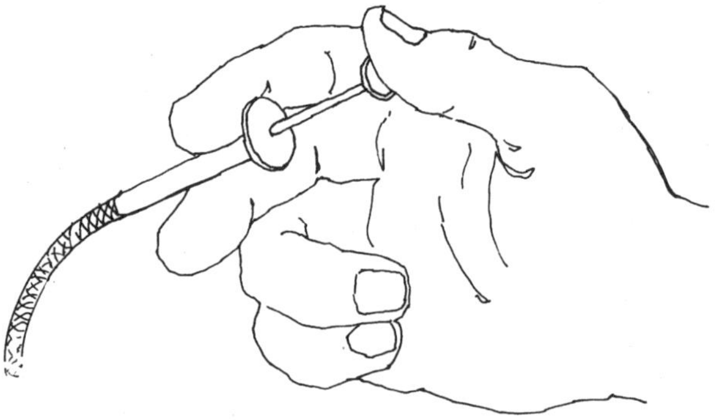

Cable release

When you're using a tripod, you'll need a cable release to trip the shutter without jarring the camera. A metal or cloth-covered cable release about 10 inches long will screw into a threaded socket in or near the shutter-release button of most cameras and permit you to squeeze the release much more gently than you can with your finger. Some newer electronic cameras don't have a cable-release socket. For these you may need a remote electronic release that plugs into the camera body.

Lens Shade

A lens shade, or lens hood, is another essential accessory. Screwing directly into the threaded outer rim of your lens, the shade will help prevent stray light from entering the lens from outside the field of view. This unwanted light can cause flare spots or streaks on the negative and may reduce the contrast of the image.

Either the rigid-metal or collapsing-rubber kind of shade is OK, but be certain that the threads are of exactly the right pitch and diameter to fit your lens (different lenses may require different shades). If you're not using a reflex camera, make certain that the shade doesn't obstruct the viewfinder or rangefinder window. You can't use a lens shade with some wide-angle lenses because it will cut off the corners of the image; so make sure the shade is the proper depth for each focal length.

Filters

Filters are useful for special effects, but you won't need nearly as many as you'll be tempted to buy. A UV, haze, or skylight filter will be a good investment as a permanent transparent lens cap. The filter will protect each expensive and delicate lens from moisture and abrasion, and minimize the number of times you'll have to clean the lens surface. Cleaning a filter is easier and much less risky than cleaning the lens. If the filter gets scratched, you can throw it away and buy another.

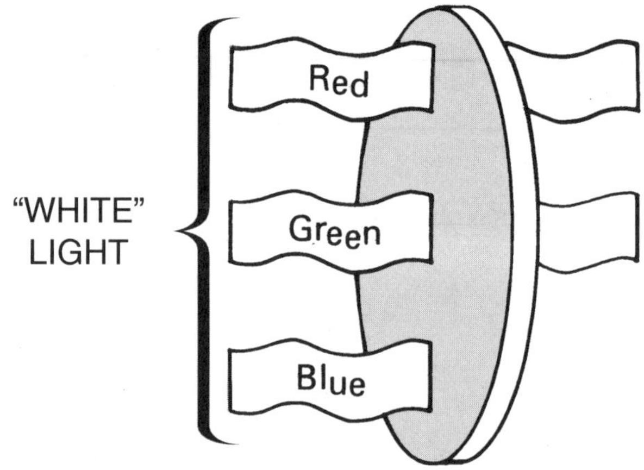

A YELLOW FILTER is commonly used to darken the sky in black-and-white photographs. It absorbs blue light and transmits other colors. Blue sky appears transparent in the negative, so the sky will print darker, and clouds will stand out in contrast to the sky.

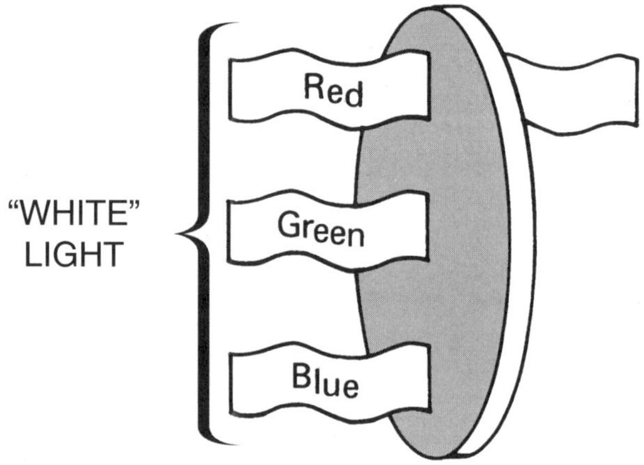

A RED FILTER transmits red light but does not pass other colors. Red objects will be rendered very light in a black-and-white print because these areas on the negative were darkened by red light. Objects that are green or blue will appear darker in the print and lighter in the negative, because light of those colors did not affect the film as much as the red.

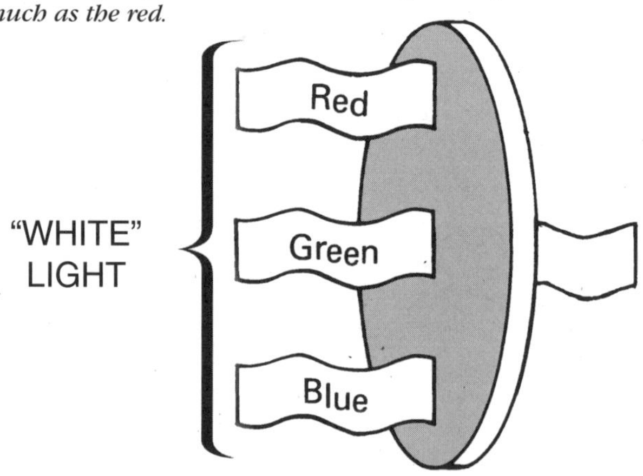

A GREEN FILTER transmits green light, absorbing red and blue. In black-and-white photography, what effect would a green filter have on the image of a red apple among green leaves?

Colored filters affect contrast

In color photography, filters are used mainly to modify color balance (see page 79). But with black-and-white films, colored filters are employed to darken or lighten a particular color as it will appear in the final print.

To understand how a filter works, you should know that visible "white" light consists of all the colors in the visible spectrum. The primary colors of visible light are red, green, and blue.

When you look at a red object, you are seeing reflected red light. The object has absorbed all the other colors, reflecting only red. If this red object is photographed through a red filter, red light is passed through to the film, but any green or blue light present is absorbed by the filter. Because the image is formed only by red light, the red object will appear dense on the negative and light on the print. Anything green or blue in the picture will not be recorded with much density on the film, so it will print very dark. Yellow light is a combination of red and green light. If you put a yellow filter in front of your lens, the filter will pass red and green light easily, but it will hold back the blue. The red and green light combine to form yellow, which records the image on the film. When a yellow, orange, or red filter is used with panchromatic black-and-white film, blue areas record as less dense on the negative, thus appearing darker in the final print. A common use for a yellow, orange, or red filter is to darken a blue sky, giving added contrast between sky and clouds or buildings. Here's a quiz question: Why won't a filter give this effect when the sky is overcast?

A green filter yields just the opposite result from a red filter, lightening greens and darkening reds and blues.

The effect of filters on black-and-white films is to lighten or darken colors. The rule to remember is: If you want to render a color *lighter* in the final print, select a filter the *same color* as the subject to be lightened or one that will transmit that color of light. If you want an object to appear *darker* in the print, use a filter that will block that color. A filter will darken objects that are its complementary or opposite color. For example, if you want to make a red object appear darker, use a blue or green filter. A red filter would make the red object photograph lighter than it actually appears; so would a yellow filter, although to a lesser degree.

Filters for copying

Other important uses of filters in black-and-white photography include the improvement of contrast between colored lettering or lines and the background on signs, posters, or architectural drawings. Blue printing on a white background, for instance, won't show as much contrast in a photograph as the original appears to the eye. Copying the document with a red filter will darken the blue considerably, increasing the contrast and readability of the reproduction.

Suppose that you want to copy a faded, yellowish-stained old document to make the writing (in black or blue ink) more legible. What filter would you use? A yellow or orange filter would record the yellow as white on the final print, increasing the contrast between the

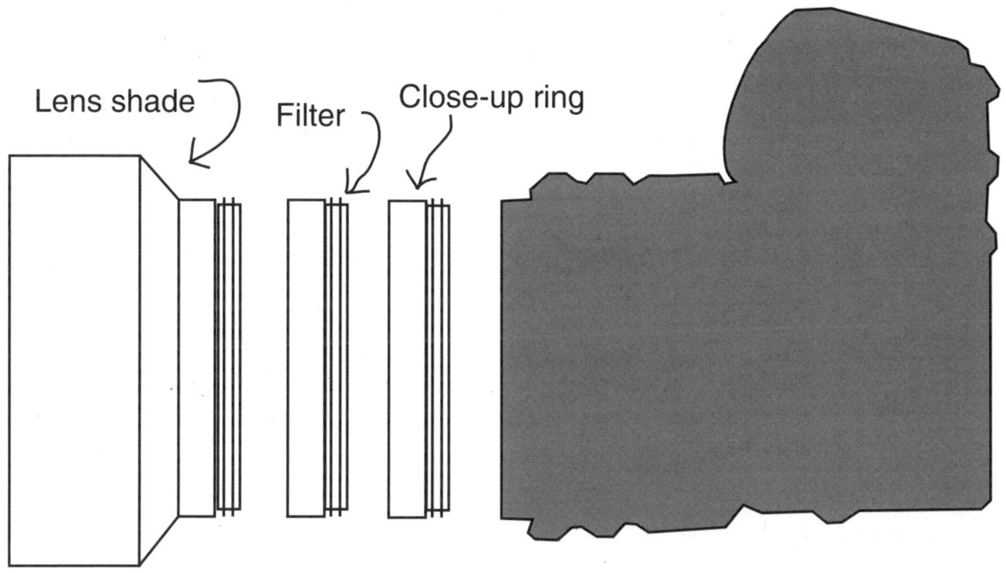

Filters, close-up lenses and lens shades can be purchased with screw threads to fit most lenses. Unthreaded gelatin and plastic filters can be attached with adapter rings and filter-frame holders. When many attachments are combined as in the illustration above, the corners of the image may be cut off (vignetted).

writing and the stained background. Here's another problem: What filter would you use to make a black-and-white copy of an old photograph stained yellow by age and improper storage? Right. Blue. The filter will render the faded, yellowish image darker and so it will be possible to restore much of the original contrast in a print made from the copy negative. Computer software makes it easier to enhance and restore many old images beautifully, but the best results sometimes come from scanning good photographic copies.

Remember the rule about filters transmitting their own and related colors and blocking opposite or complementary colors, and you'll be able to determine whether a filter will create the effect you want.

A polarizer reduces reflections

A filter useful with color films as well as black-and-white is a polarizer. For autofocus lenses and certain metering systems, you need a special type of circular polarizer. What this dark-gray-looking filter does is to remove many detail-obscuring reflections from non-metallic surfaces such as glass, water, and polished wood without affecting the relative intensities of colors. You mount the filter on the front of your lens and rotate it until you see the effect you want.

Because blue sky is polarized, the filter also will darken blue skies to some extent, depending on the angle between the sun and the lens. When shooting with color film, a polarizing filter will intensify the contrast between blue sky and clouds, snow, or autumn leaves about the same way as a yellow filter affects black-and-white. You'll get the most dramatic effects on a clear day, shooting upward at a right angle to the sun.

Polarizers can be placed over light sources as well as on the camera lens. When you do this you can completely eliminate surface reflections from printing inks and painted surfaces (see page 186). This technique is especially useful when making slides of original paintings and drawings and copying from books.

Filters require exposure changes

Although filters are very useful, there is also a drawback. Because all filters except the "transparent lens cap" variety absorb some of the light, you'll have to increase the exposure. Most cameras with through-the-lens exposure metering will compensate automatically for the density of the filter; however, for the most accuracy it's best to make the reading before putting the filter over the lens, then increase the exposure as shown in the

DAVID HARRISON (2)

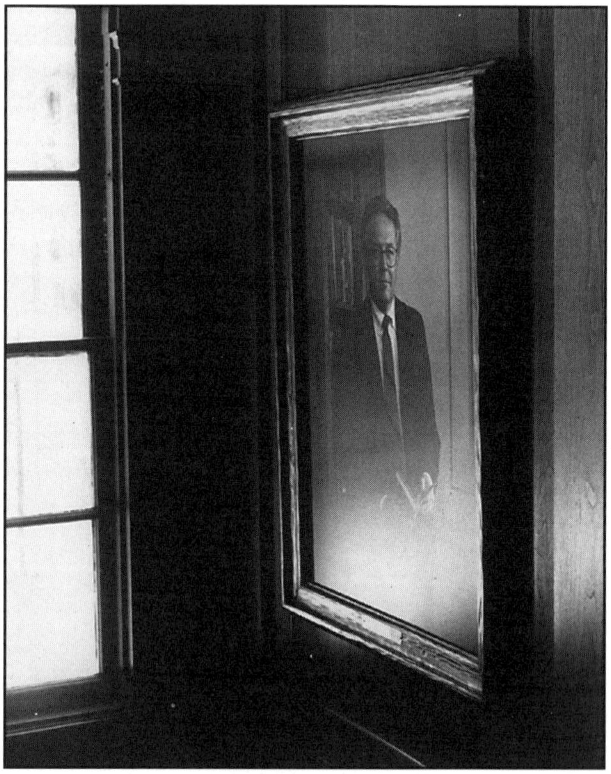

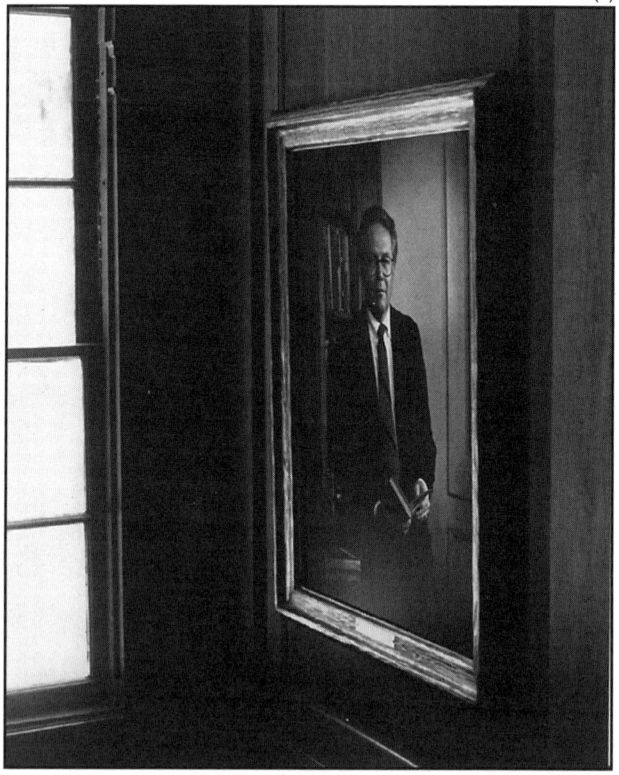

A polarizer can eliminate certain kinds of glare and reflections. In this detail from a building interior, notice the reflections on the surface of the portrait and the wall paneling in the photo on the left. On the right, a polarizer has made the reflections much less noticeable.

Filter Color and Type	Factor	Number of Stops Increase
Yellow (#8 or K2)	1.5x	two thirds of a stop
Orange (#15 or G)	2x	one stop
Green (#11 or X1	3x	1 and 1/2 stops
Red (#25 or A)	8x	three stops
Polarizing	3x	1 and 1/2 stops

table above. You can either open up the lens aperture or slow the shutter speed by the number of stops indicated. When using a hand-held exposure meter, you can divide the exposure index by the filter factor and set that lower ISO number into the meter. The daylight filter factors for the most commonly used filters used with most black-and-white films are shown in the table above. These factors should be verified against the film manufacturer's data sheets, especially when working with incandescent lights.

Neutral-density (ND) filters reduce exposure

Sometimes there's too much light, especially when working outdoors with fast film or in the studio with electronic flash. Neutral-density filters reduce the amount of light passing through the lens without affecting anything else. Use an ND filter when you need a slow shutter speed for panning or blurred-motion effects, or a wide lens opening for selective focus.

Neutral-density filters come in various densities and they can be stacked together. Most commonly used are ND .30 (1 stop), ND .60 (2 stops) and ND .90 (3 stops).

Filters can create special effects

Here's where it's easy to spend a bunch of money, buying an entire series of special-effects filters and the adapter kit to attach them to your lenses.

Several companies make filter sets, including close-up, diffusion, variable-density, fog, infrared, split-field, center-spot, cross-star, multi-image, multiple-exposure, and many more. Sales people will be happy to show these to you in a camera store.

Filters help control color

Previously, I have suggested using a UV or skylight filter as a lens cap. There are other good reasons. This filter also will absorb excess ultraviolet, improving color pictures taken in shade by reducing bluishness. With both color and black-and-white films, the UV or skylight filter also reduces the effect of haze in distant landscapes and aerial photos without requiring an increase in exposure.

Filters intended solely for color photography fall into three categories: *compensating, correction,* and *conversion.* Compensating filters (CC series) are for making minor changes in the color balance of light used to expose color films and printing papers. Correction filters — such as the FLD filter for daylight color film in fluorescent light, and the warming 81 series and cooling 82 series — are intended to improve the accurate reproduction of colors when the available light differs slightly from the color temperature for which the film was intended. Conversion filters — such as the blue 80 series and orange 85 series — enable the use of color film, balanced either for daylight or incandescent illumination, to be exposed with the other kind of light.

Filter factors for color-compensating, color-correction, and color-conversion filters are included in the film or filter manufacturer's exposure recommendations.

Filter formats

Although the most commonly used filters are available in either dyed or laminated glass for durability, each type is available also in less costly but more delicate gelatin or polyester sheets that are practical for studio use. All filters either screw directly into the front of the lens mount or they slip into an adapter ring or holder. Be certain to get the right diameter and thread size to fit your lens. If you own lenses with various front-thread sizes, you can buy filters to fit the largest lens and purchase step-down rings to adapt those filters to the smaller diameter lenses.

Exposure Meters

If your camera is equipped with a built-in, through-the-lens exposure meter, it isn't essential to acquire a separate meter. On the other hand, if you try to make very precise readings of small subject areas in order to place these areas in the proper exposure zones, you'll appreciate a precision, hand-held *spot* meter with a relatively narrow angle of view. Especially when photographing natural landscape and architectural subjects with larger formats, it's very convenient to be able to read the brightness of a small area from a distance. For studio and copy work with either incandescent lights or electronic flash, the appropriate type of *incident-light* meter is desirable because its spherical light-integrating cell gives precise "Zone V" readings regardless of back lighting or variations in background brightness (Chapter 5).

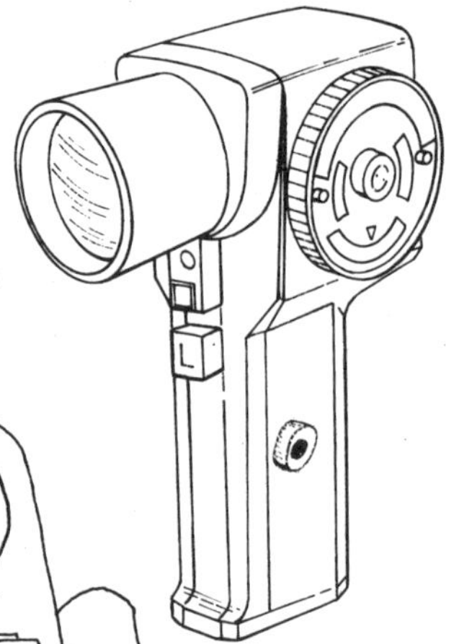

Spot-meters (right) are designed especially for making precise Zone-System readings (see Chapter 5).

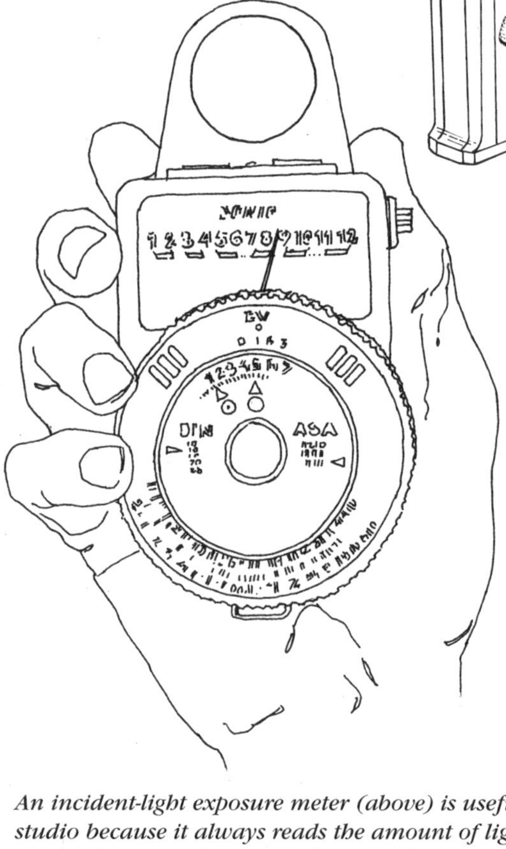

An incident-light exposure meter (above) is useful in the studio because it always reads the amount of light in a given place regardless of background brightness. Some incident-light meters will determine flash exposure.

Wide-Angle and Telephoto Lenses

Before buying expensive lenses, it's a good idea to wait until you discover your most comfortable shooting distance. For street photography with a 35mm camera, for example, many photographers prefer the wide-angle coverage and great depth of field of a 28mm focal-length lens because it allows them to work freely in the midst of a crowd without cutting off heads and feet. A wide-angle lens even allows shooting "from the hip" without putting the camera up to the eye. Other photographers prefer picking off their prey from a safe distance, hiding behind a 200mm or 300mm telephoto or a long zoom lens. Planned portraiture usually requires a moderate telephoto, so you're not literally in the subject's face.

JIM NIXON

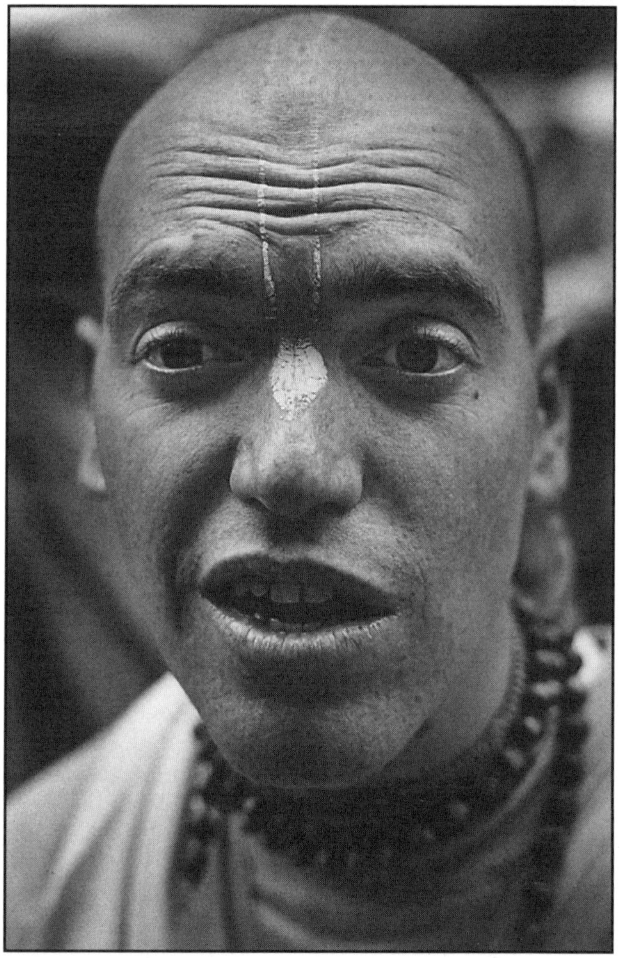

A pre-focused, wide-angle lens permitted this confrontational close-up. Would you feel more comfortable using a longer focal length?

Jim Nixon (2)

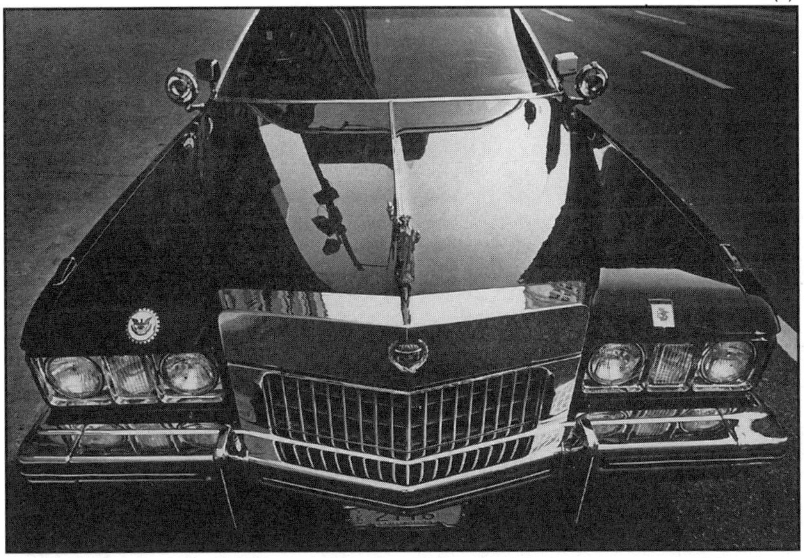

Wide-angle lenses tend to increase size differences between near and far objects, or between parts of the same object. In this photo, a 24mm lens made the presidential limousine appear even more massive and sculptural than it actually was.

(Below) a moderately wide-angle lens makes street photography more convenient in crowded places.

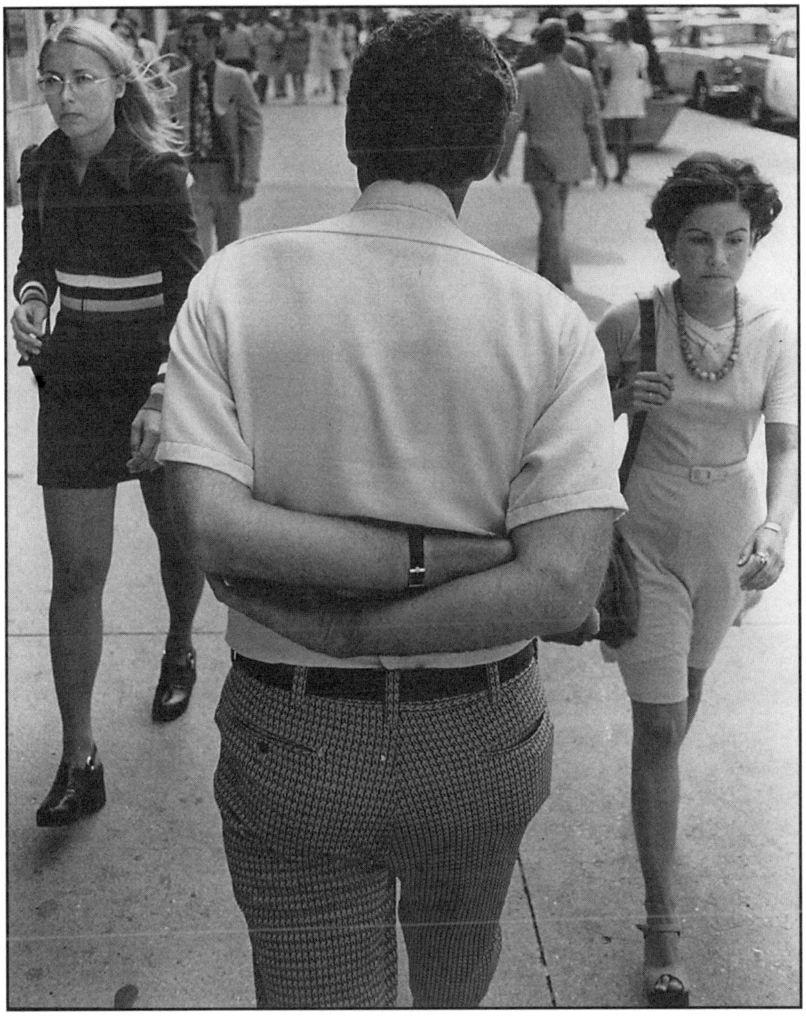

Raimonds Ziemelis

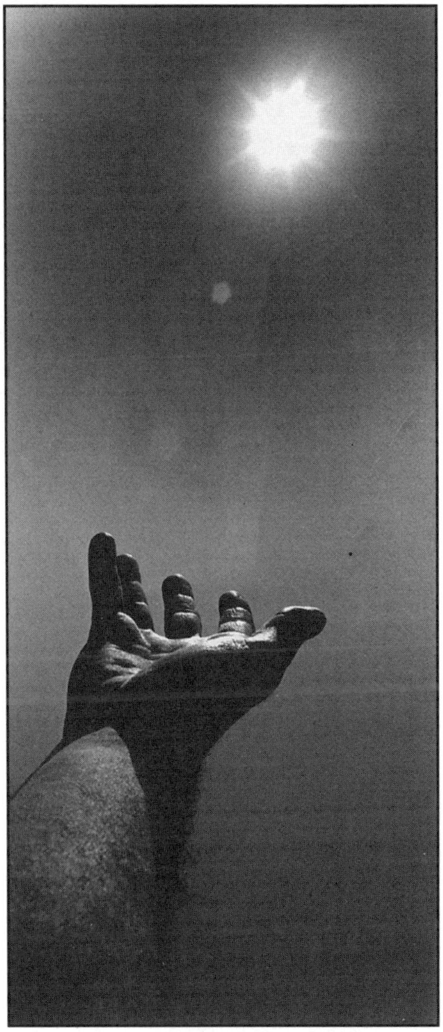

(Above) an extremely wide-angle lens (21mm) was necessary to allow the photographer to include his own right hand in the picture, while holding the 35mm camera in his left hand.

David H. Curl

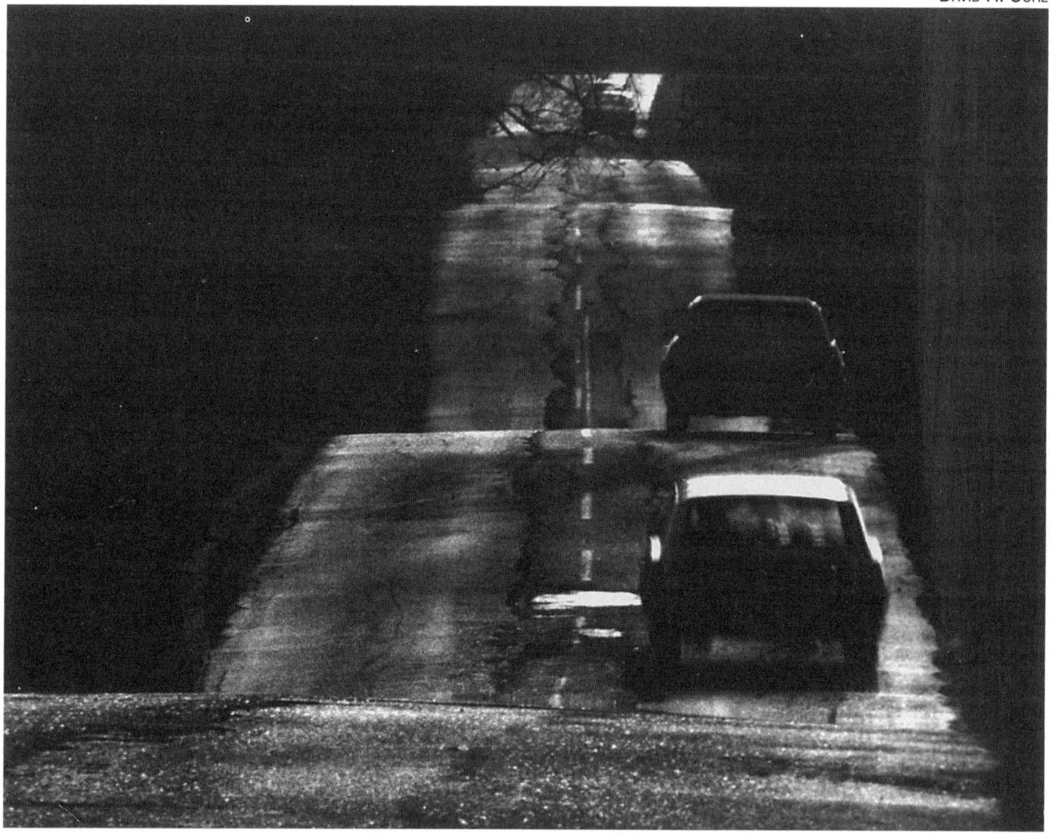

The cumulative compression of distance produced by telephoto lenses is especially apparent with long focal lengths. More than a quarter mile of roadway is visible in this photograph made with a 400mm lens on a 35mm camera.

Jim Nixon (2)

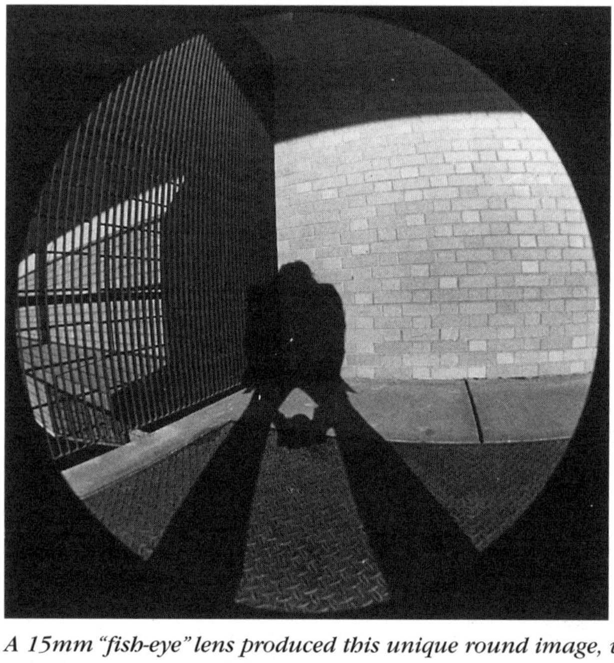

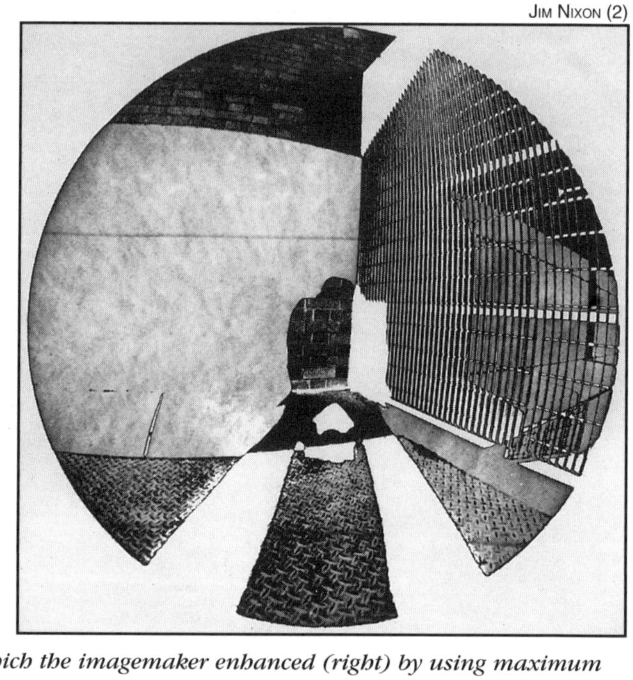

A 15mm "fish-eye" lens produced this unique round image, which the imagemaker enhanced (right) by using maximum printing contrast and the Sabattier effect. The image on the right is reversed because the final print was made by contact, using a "solarized" paper positive print as a negative (see Chapter 11).

"The lens reveals more than the eye sees."

— Edward Weston, photographer

Choose lenses you need

A focal length of about 105mm is very popular with portrait photographers who work with 35mm cameras because the 105mm lens gives a full head-and-shoulders image without the photographer having to be embarrassingly close to the subject. Wide-angle lenses tend to distort facial features on close-ups, whereas very long focal lengths flatten perspective and lose the feeling of roundness. Other than for specialized sports or nature photography, few people ever get their money's worth of use out of extreme telephotos (300mm and longer) or extreme wide-angles (less than 20mm).

Because variable-focal-length *zoom* lenses contain many elements, users generally sacrifice maximum aperture and some corner-to-corner sharpness in exchange for the convenience of carrying a single camera with only one lens. An alternative popular with professionals is to maintain separate camera bodies equipped with favorite focal-length lenses, switching rapidly between cameras rather than changing lenses or zooming. Beginners on a budget often start out with a mid-range zoom lens instead of the "normal" fixed-focal-length (for example: 28-85mm or 35-105mm).

Lens extenders

A lens extender is a cheap way to make a long telephoto out of a shorter focal-length lens. The trouble is that aberrations present in an inexpensive extender will bring down the image quality of a good lens to that of the extender. If you can afford it, usually it's a better investment to buy quality lenses of needed focal lengths (or a good zoom lens) then to try to stretch a normal lens into something that it isn't.

Close-focusing attachments

A macro (sometimes referred to as "micro") lens is the ideal close-up device for 35mm SLR cameras. Designed to give extremely sharp images at close distances, most macro lenses are designed to focus continuously from infinity to about 1:2 (half life size). Some zoom lenses have a macro range, focusing to about 1:4 (one - quarter life size).

The least expensive close-up attachments are diopter lenses that screw like filters into the front of a regular lens. Available in various strengths, these so-called "close-up lenses" each cost about the price of a filter and they fit easily into your camera bag.

Because the lens isn't physically moved out farther from the film, close-up lenses require no exposure correction. But they do tend to reduce the sharpness of the image, especially around the edges. Because of this problem, you should stop down the lens as far as possible, not only for sharpness, but because you'll need all the depth of field you can get when working that close to the subject.

Another way to focus a normal lens close to the subject is to attach extension tubes or a bellows attachment. These devices move the lens farther than usual from the film, so additional exposure will be required unless your meter reads through-the-lens and the coupling is retained between the lens and the camera body. If you need it, the table below will be a helpful guide.

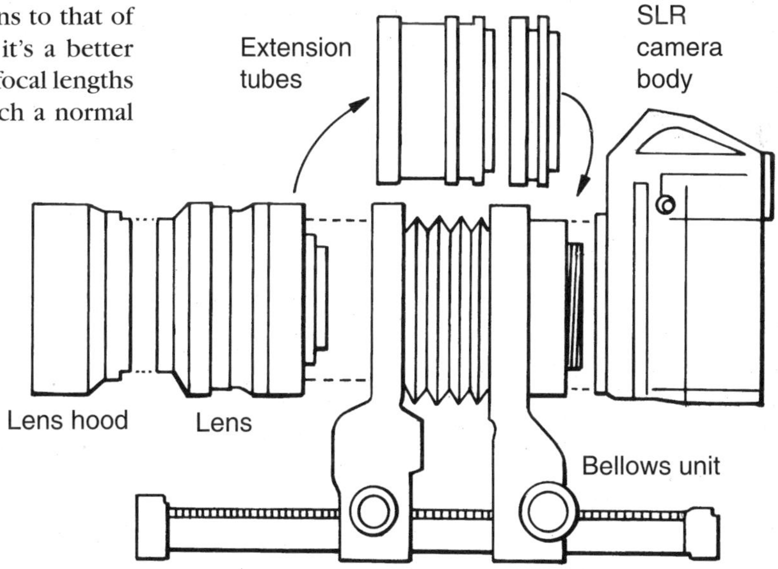

A macro lens is convenient for photographing objects down to about 1:2 (half the actual size). But extension tubes and bellows attachments permit getting even closer.

Exposure Correction with 35mm Cameras Using Extension Tubes or Bellows

Length of area Photographed (in.)	12	6	3	2.5	2	1.5	1	.5
Length of area photographed (cm)	30	15	7.6	6.5	5	3.8	2.5	1.2
Increase in exposure (f/stops)	$\frac{1}{3}$	$\frac{2}{3}$	1	$1\frac{1}{3}$	$1\frac{2}{3}$	2	$2\frac{2}{3}$	4

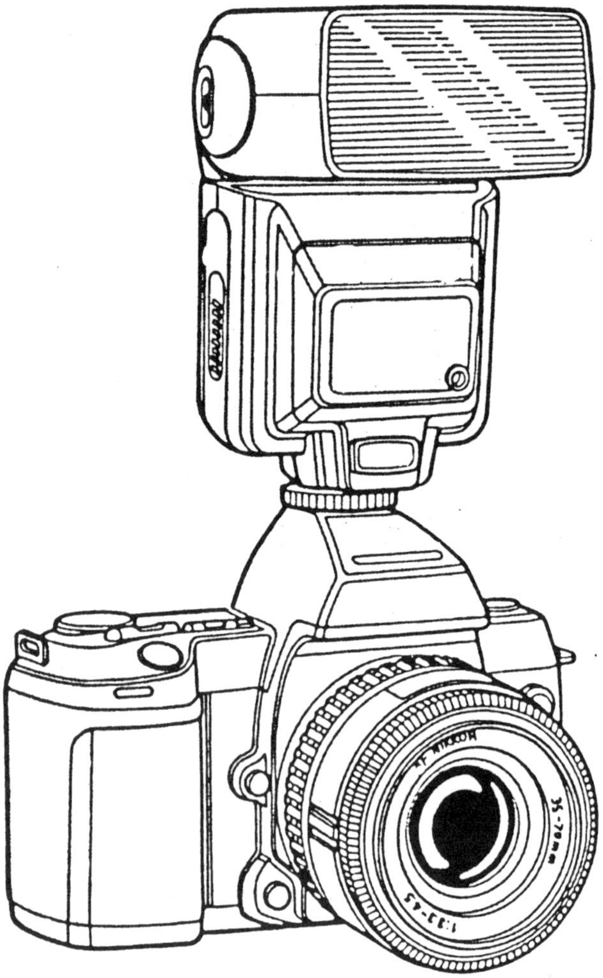

Flash

A flash unit mounted on the camera is hardly the ideal light source, as we'll discuss in Chapter 9, but it is a way of getting an image when there is not enough existing light.

The cost of an electronic flash unit varies with its light output and versatility. You will want automatic exposure sensing and the ability to swivel upward for "bounce" light. The best flash to buy will be a dedicated unit designed to take advantage of all the features of your specific camera.

If your flash is manually operated and lacks an exposure dial you can make the necessary calculations by using the following formula:

$$\frac{\text{Guide Number}}{\text{Flash-to-subject distance}} = \text{f/stop}$$

Guide number = 110
Distance = 10 feet

$$\frac{110}{10} = \text{f/11}$$

Flash exposure will be fairly even when everything in the picture is about the same distance from the camera. But when there is depth of field, near subjects may be overexposed while subjects farther away are underexposed. No one wants to print negatives like this. Automatic flash units don't solve this problem, because they expose for the nearest surface, whether or not that is what you want to emphasize. See Chapter 9 for the effect of removing the flash from the camera or "bouncing" the light. Bounce lighting may require about two stops extra exposure to compensate for the extra distance and for absorption of light by the ceiling or wall.

JIM NIXON

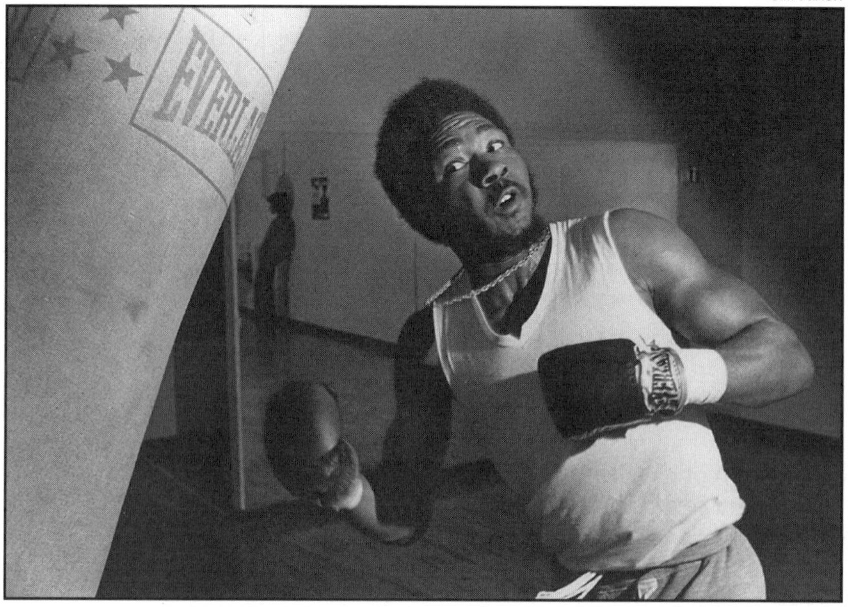

Electronic flash is the only practical way to stop very fast action when there isn't enough existing natural light. Although a slower shutter speed, such as 1/60 of second, may be required to synchronize the flash (notice in this picture that some background illumination has been picked up), the duration of the flash — usually 1/1,000 of a second or faster — determines the actual exposure time. Because the flash was held a few feet from the camera, a feeling of roundness was retained in the subject and the lighting appears to be from natural sources.

Buying Equipment

Your new camera or accessory is likely to serve you well if you buy it from a reputable dealer.The store probably will guarantee the equipment to your satisfaction, sometimes even extending the manufacturer's warranty. But if you're tempted to buy used equipment by mail or from an ad in the newspaper, you should know what to look for to avoid expensive repair bills.

Always be wary of equipment that looks badly beat up.That usually means the previous owner didn't take good care of it, and there could be serious internal problems. Manufacturers' service centers charge a minimum fee for handling a camera, whether the problem is simple or not. But you may be able to find a qualified local technician who will examine a prospective purchase or even make minor adjustments without charging for a complete overhaul. Major repairs could cost more than a used camera is worth, so a "bargain" may not be as good as it seems.

How to test a camera

Here are some things to look for if you're considering a used camera: Check the lens for scratches. Reject it if these are severe, especially if scratches or dust appear to be inside the lens — an indication that it has been disassembled. If the lens mount fits loosely or if the diaphragm setting ring or focusing ring turns hard, grabs, grinds, or turns too freely, suspect excessive wear or dirt in the mechanism.

Open the back of the camera and trip the shutter several times. Observe the diaphragm at several f/stop settings.The diaphragm should stop down quickly when the shutter-release button is pressed, and then open up again with no delay after each exposure.

Try each of the shutter speeds several times to see whether they are consistent and whether the settings seem to be proportional to the amount of time the shutter remains open. If in doubt about the shutter, have it checked by someone with an electronic tester. A shutter that sticks open at any of the speeds may need an expensive overhaul.

Check out the focusing system by focusing sharply through the camera eyepiece at objects at various distances; then compare readings on the lens distance scale with measured or estimated distances.

Test the exposure meter by reading light and dark subjects indoors and outdoors. Install fresh batteries, then compare the indicated camera settings either with another meter of known accuracy, or estimate with the "Sunny 16" rule (pp. 93) or with an exposure table. Be certain the meter needle doesn't stick or move erratically — a sign of needed repair. If the camera has either a liquid-crystal display or LED readout, the figures should be legible and should change appropriately as you measure areas of different brightness.

You can test the coverage and sharpness of a lens, as well as consistency of the shutter speeds, by photographing the classified ad pages of a newspaper. Mount the camera on a sturdy tripod, and tape the newspaper on a wall in strong, even light. Fill the entire viewfinder with the want-ads, focus very carefully, and then make an exposure at each f/stop on the lens.

You'll have to compensate by adjusting the shutter speed, of course, every time you change the aperture. Keep a written record so you can tell which negative was exposed at each f/stop; then when you study the negatives with a hand magnifier, you can tell easily whether you can read the printing out to the edges of each frame. You may find that your lens is like most, in that the edges of the negative tend to be somewhat less sharp than the center until you stop down to about f/4 or f/5.6, at which point the sharpness should become uniform.

Your strip of test negatives may reveal more than just the quality of the lens.The shutter speeds are OK if image density is consistent, but if any of the frames overlap or show uneven spaces between frames, the film-advance mechanism may require repair. If there are any light leaks inside the camera, you'll see dark streaks or spots. A scratch along the length of the film may indicate a rough spot, either on the camera-body aperture or on the film pressure plate.

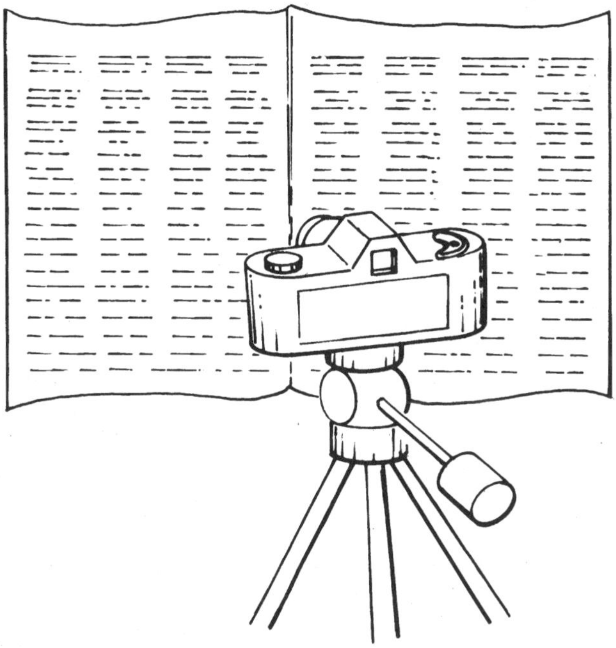

A practical way to test a lens, is to photograph a newspaper classified-ad page. Study the negatives with a magnifier loupe to check sharpness and covering power of the lens at different apertures.

Test flash synchronization

Mount the flash securely into its shoe, set the lens at its widest aperture and the shutter to the proper synch speed (usually 1/60 or 1/125). Turn on the flash unit and let it charge up (there usually is a "ready" light that comes on). Open the back of the camera (with no film in it, of course), aim the lens at a light-colored wall, look at the back of the lens and flash a "picture." You should see a brilliant flash through the lens at the exact instant that the shutter is open. If you see only a partial frame, either the wrong shutter speed has been selected or there is a real problem.

If there is any doubt about the condition of equipment you own or intend to buy, seek advice from a responsible dealer, a repair technician, your photo instructor, or an experienced photographer friend. If your equipment does need repair, take it to a reliable shop and ask for a written estimate of the cost and time required.

Modern cameras are marvelous precision instruments. Care for your camera respectfully and it will serve you well.

"I paint what cannot be photographed, that which comes from the imagination or from dreams ... I photograph the things ... which already have an existence."

— Man Ray, artist

Keith Alan Morris

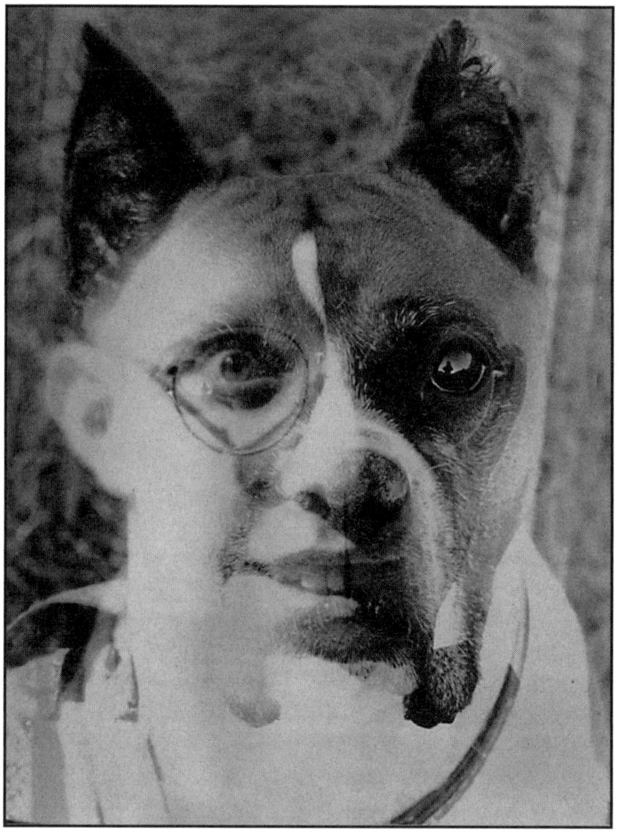

This image was created in the darkroom by double-exposing two negatives on the same sheet of paper. With computer software, a similar effect can be achieved more quickly and with infinitely greater control.

Sara Reschley

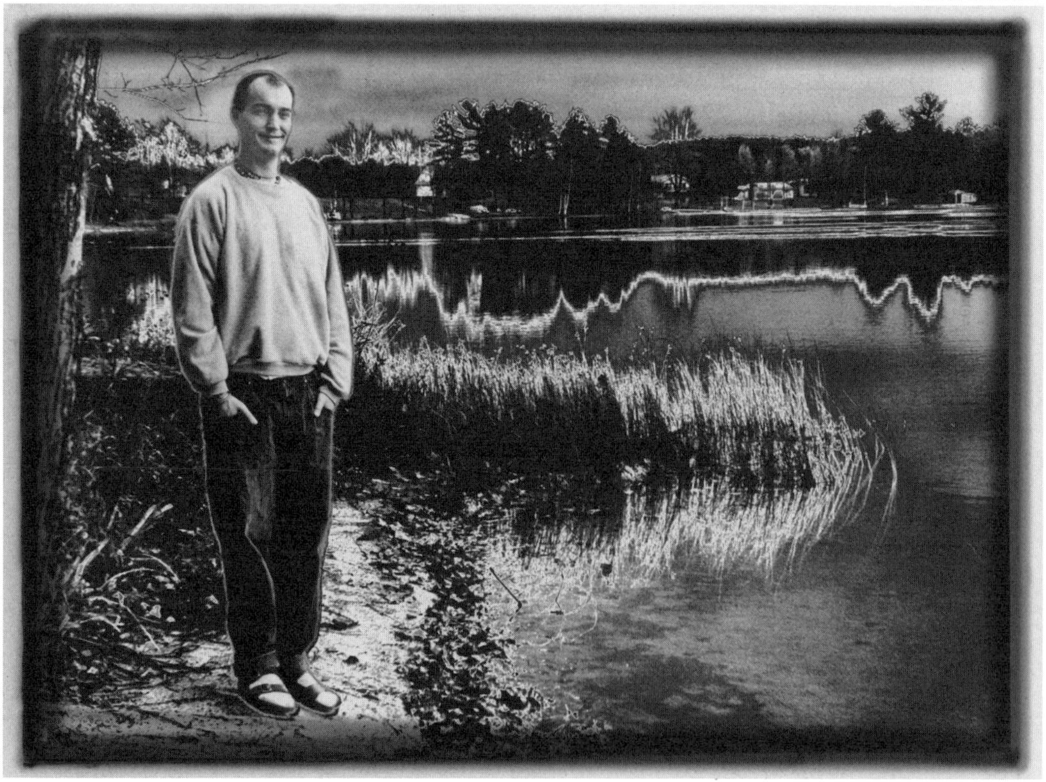

Ordinary pictures can be scanned into a computer, and quickly transformed into fantasy. The possibilities are limitless. Experimenting with the software is fun, because magical things happen. Incredible images can result when you previsualize an effect.

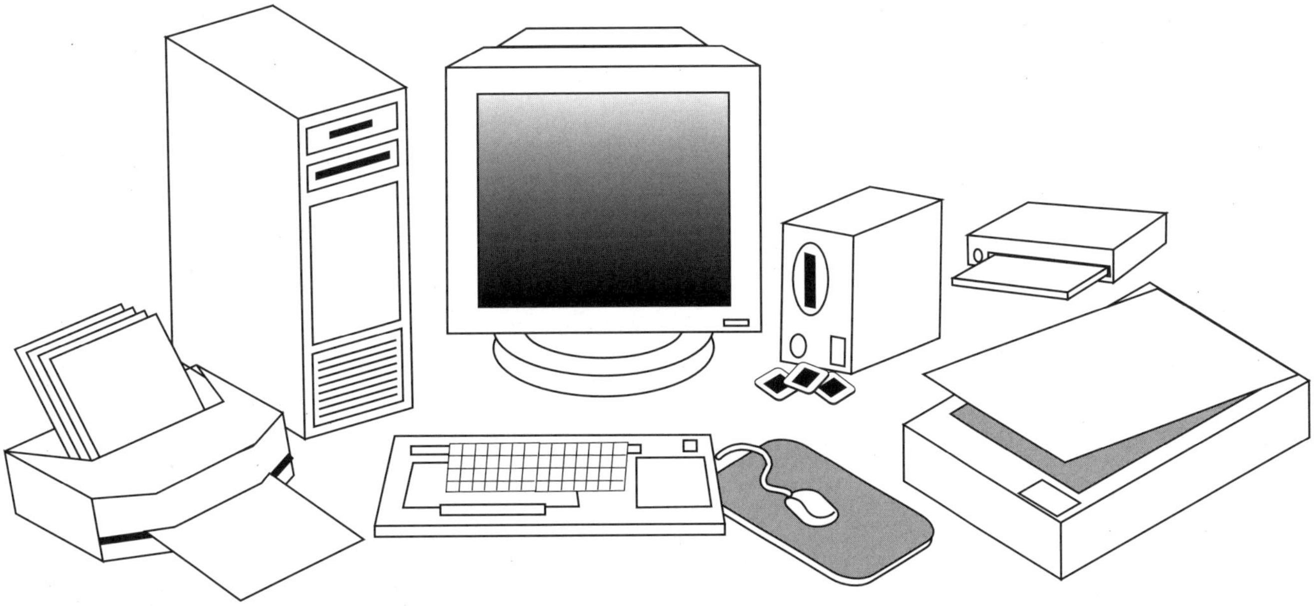

Going Digital

Most imagemakers who have been working digitally for a few years, have been using Macintosh systems. But the latest imaging software works similarly in Windows, so you can get good results with whichever platform is available. But not just any computer has enough power to make high-resolution (sharp, photographic quality) images.

> ***"You cannot say that a picture looks good or bad because a computer was used. ... it's just a different technique."***
>
> — Raymond Meier, imagemaker

Software and hardware

Adobe Photoshop is the most-used imaging software. You can master the tools and techniques of Photoshop and other image-editing programs with an ordinary computer if you keep your images small in size and maintain only screen resolution of 72 pixels per inch (ppi). But if you want to output large, color images that resemble photographs, you need some expensive equipment.

Photoshop requires at least four times the size of the file you are working with in order to process the image. This space should be a combination of random access memory (RAM) and virtual memory (free hard disk space). An 8x10-inch color photo at 300 ppi occupies almost 15 megabytes (MB). That means you'll need at least 60MB to process it. An 11x14-inch color image occupies about 43MB and requires nearly 180MB to work on. The rule is: the more RAM and the bigger and faster the internal hard drive, the better. Also you need a fast video card and a good monitor. As with purchasing a camera, there are advantages to buying computer equipment from a local source who will be there tomorrow to help you.

Input and output

You also need to get images into the computer and out. A digital camera is one way to input images. Another is a scanner.

Negatives and transparencies are digitized with a film scanner, and prints and flat objects with a flat-bed scanner similar to an office copy machine. In the printing industry, sophisticated drum-type scanners sometimes do both jobs. Digital cameras are common in commercial studios for product and catalog illustration and portraiture, and in sports and news photography when images need to be transmitted rapidly by telephone or satellite.

Output can be by desktop laser printer, high-resolution ink-jet or dye-sublimation printer, or by conversion back to a film negative or transparency from which photographic prints can be made. Removable magnetic and optical disk drives and CD-ROMs simplify transfer of digital images between computers and to imaging service bureaus.

On the horizon

Every year brings faster computers, easier interchange of files, greater storage capacity, improved cameras and printers, simplified, yet more versatile software, and lower prices. This is technological change unlike anything in the history of imaging. Climb onto the bandwagon as soon as you can, and learn the skills you need. Whatever computer you buy today, there will be a faster, cheaper one with more memory tomorrow, but it will work on the same principals you are learning now.

Jillian S. Sloan

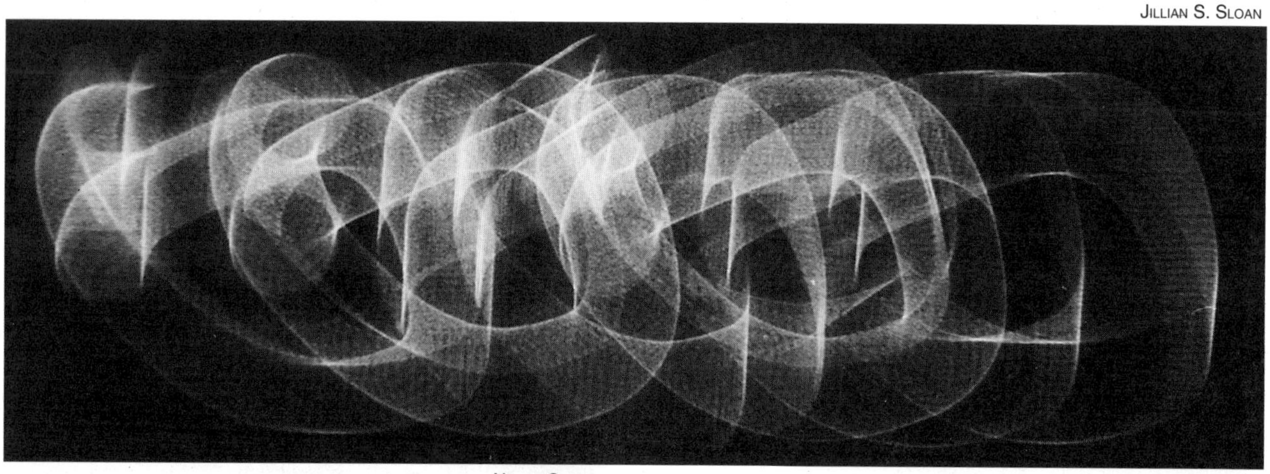

Nancy Snyder

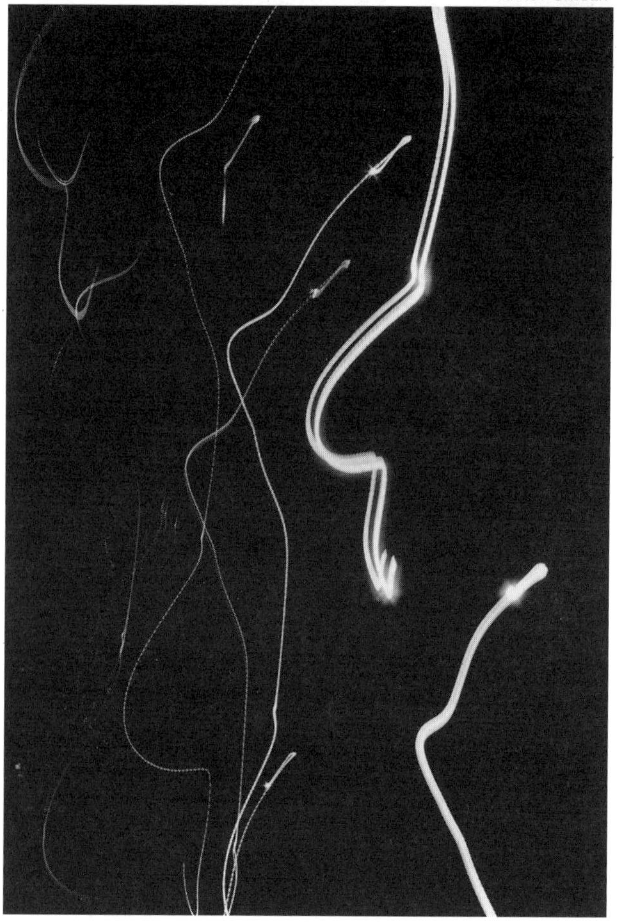

Michelle Campbell

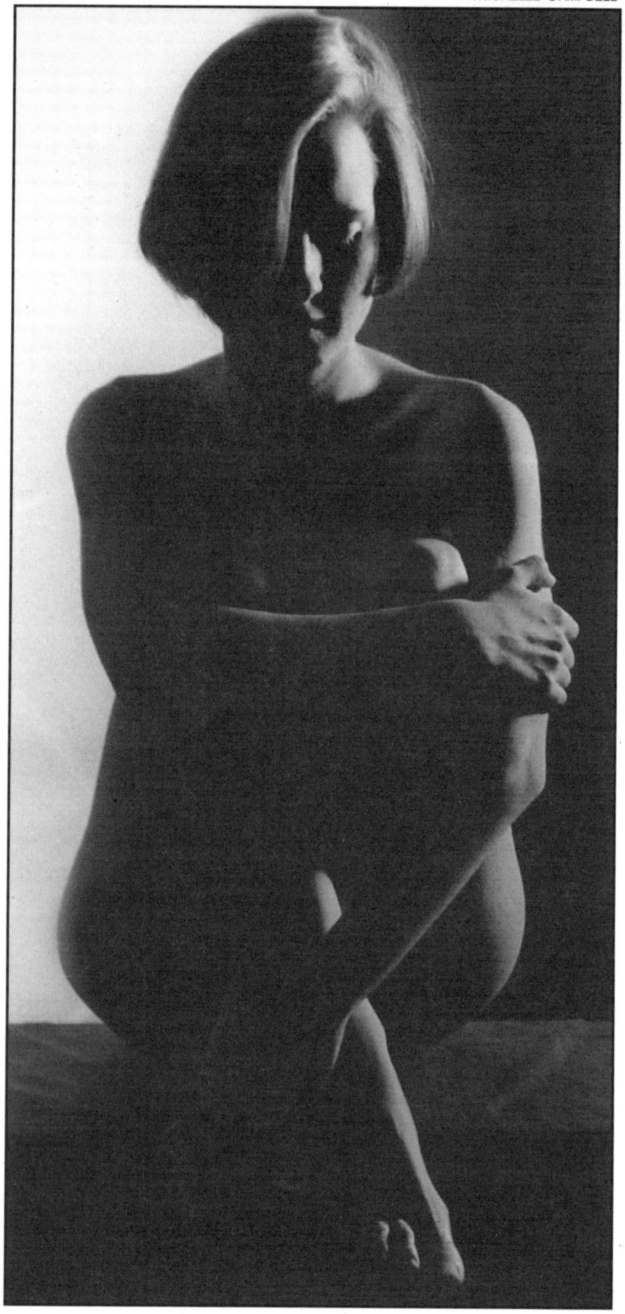

"The mastery of ... light is basic to the transformation of the ordinary into the special."

— Ken Marcus, photographer

Films and Exposure 5

Getting the Image

Although you'll discover soon how to work some "magic" in the darkroom and on the computer desktop, you must remember that if detail isn't present in the negative or in the scan, it won't be in the print. Films have certain inherent limitations that have to be learned about and accepted. In this chapter, you'll have a chance to find out how far you can err in exposure and development, and how you can compensate to make the best possible image.

Characteristics of Black-and-White Films

There are many types of film. Some, such as high-contrast copying and infrared, are intended for specialized use. But there is a wide variety of general-purpose emulsions. One type is chosen instead of another for one or more of the following reasons:

Speed

Exposure index (EI or ISO) is a measure of relative sensitivity to light. A film rated 400 by the manufacturer is assumed to be four times as sensitive as a film rated 100. The slower film (100), therefore, would require *four times* as much exposure (two stops more), than the faster film (400). Under certain conditions, experienced photographers sometimes rate film at a speed different from that recommended by the manufacturer.

Grain

Grain is the extent to which the tiny silver particles forming the image tend to clump together and form a mottled, or spotty effect. Generally, the faster the film (higher EI or ISO rating), the more tendency there is for grain to become visible upon enlargement of the negative. Color-transparency films are composed of dye images instead of silver grains, but high-speed color films also tend to show a grainy look when slides are projected or enlarged.

GRETCHEN POKORSKI

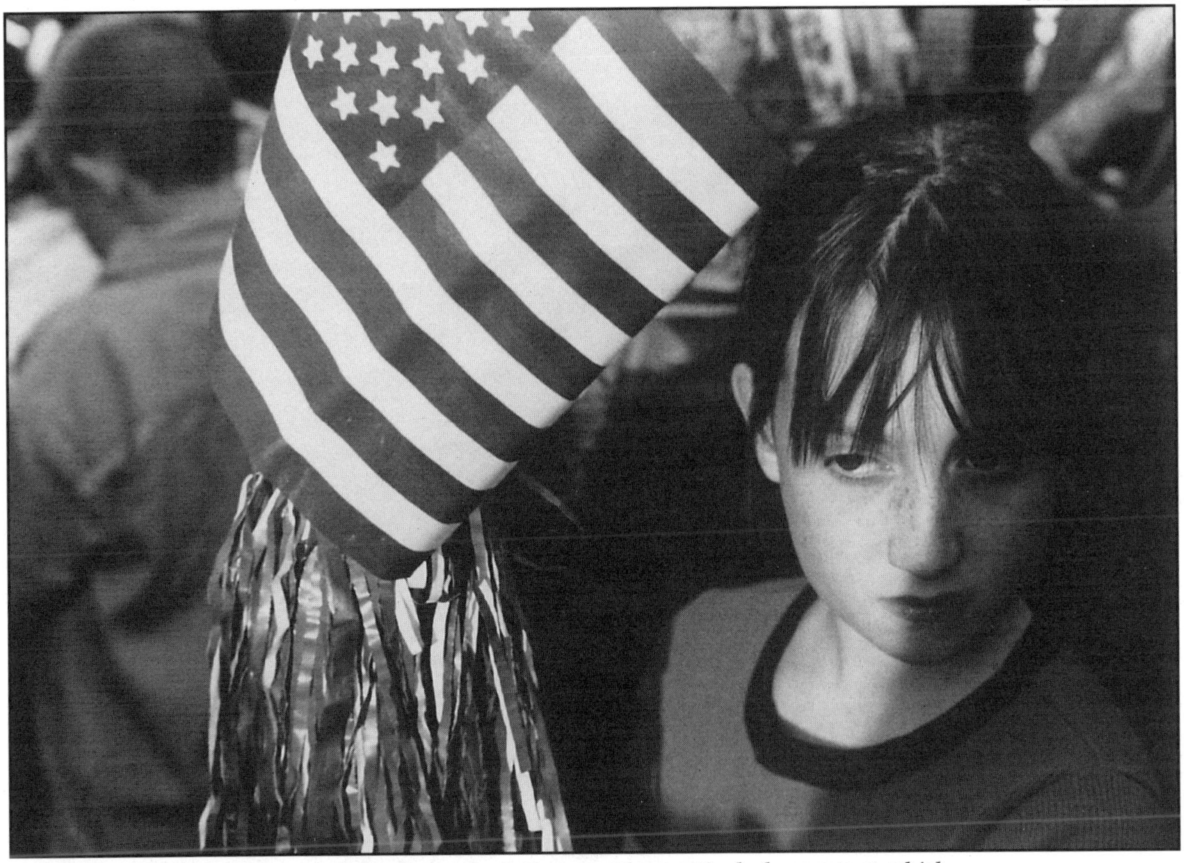

"Fast" film (ISO 400) is a good choice for general photography, particularly events at which you have to work quickly to preserve fleeting moments.

Robert Fleming

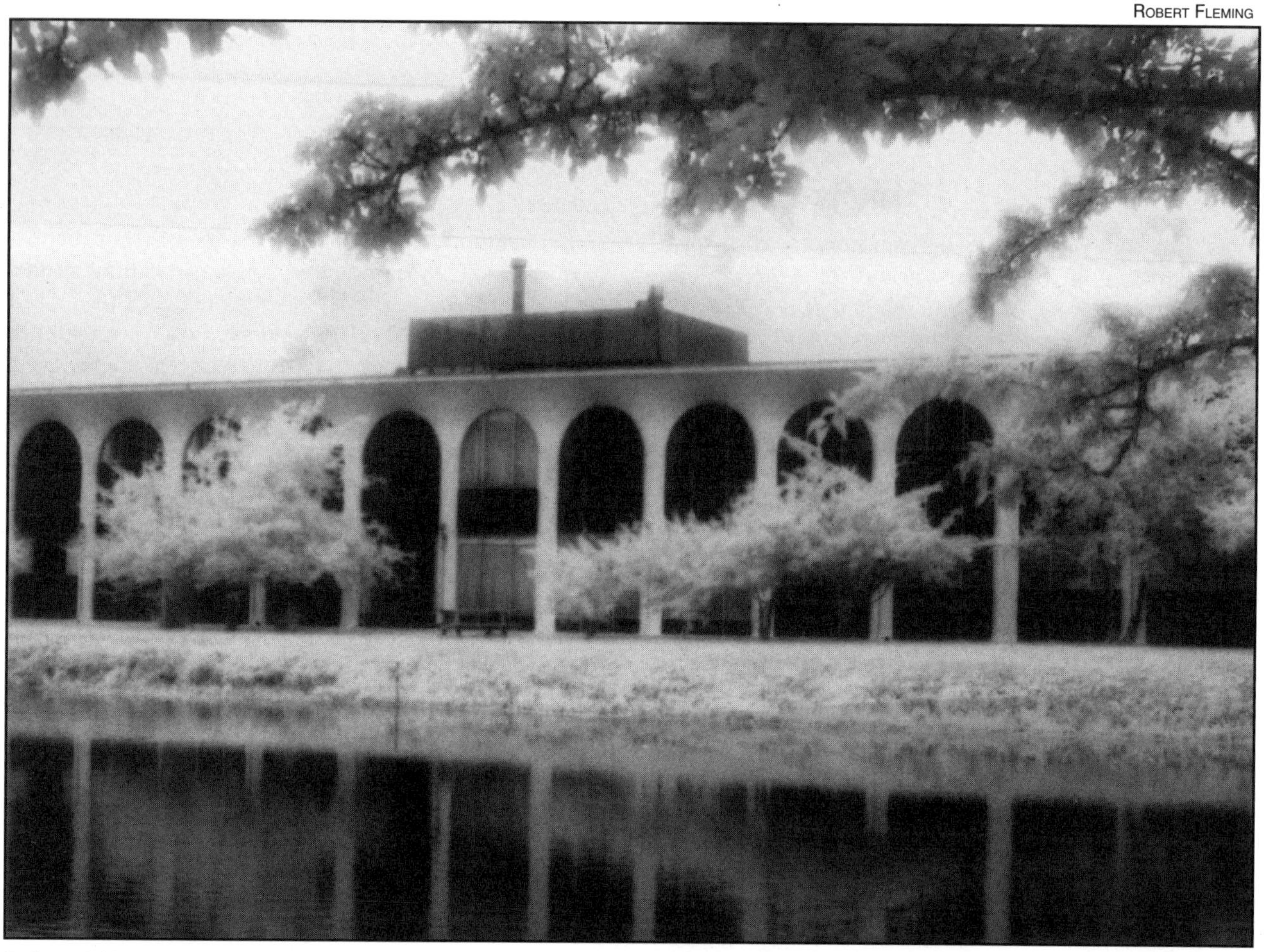

Infrared film records familiar things with an eerie difference. This specially sensitized film must be exposed throught a deep red filter to eliminate most visible light.

Todd Wickersham

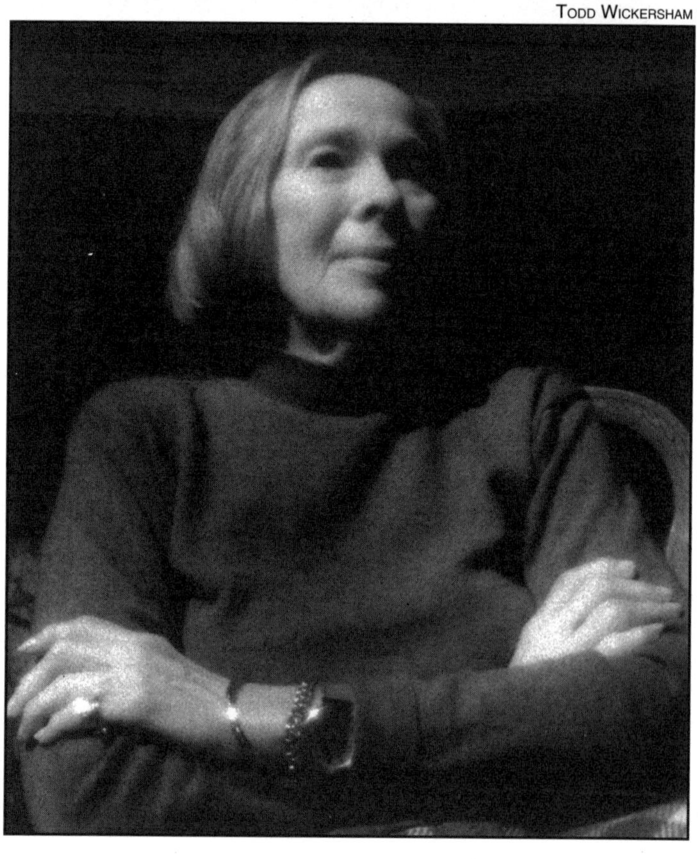

In another example of infrared, notice the unusual rendering of skin tones. Also characteristic of infrared film are accentuated grain and a soft, diffused image quality.

Color sensitivity

Black-and-white film is either *panchromatic* (sensitive to all colors of visible light) or limited in sensitivity to only part of the spectrum. Because nearly all films today are panchromatic, they must be kept in total darkness until processing is complete. A few special-purpose reproduction and copy films, however, may be handled and developed under a red or yellow safelight.

Contrast

Contrast refers to the relative differences in density between dark and light tones in the negative image. In both black-and-white and color, slower (lower EI or ISO) films tend to have more inherent contrast than faster films. Generally, low speed, finer grain and higher contrast tend to go together in some films, whereas high speed, more noticeable grain and lower contrast are common characteristics of others.

Latitude

Another important characteristic of film is *latitude* — the amount the film can be underexposed or overexposed without serious loss of image quality. Although color-transparency (slide) films are limited in latitude to within about one f/stop, modern black-and-white and color negative films can compensate for human or mechanical exposure error within as much as two or three f/stops and still produce printable negatives.

With negative films, it is better to err on the side of too much exposure rather than too little. If there is enough exposure to record density in the shadow areas of the negative, it can be printed; if there is not enough density, the missing shadow detail cannot be restored in printing. Greatly overexposed negatives produce grainy and unsharp prints with lost highlight detail. The rule is exactly opposite for reversal films such as color slides. Because of their limited latitude, color-transparency films usually should be exposed for the important high values, to prevent light skin tones, textured snow or sand, etc. from being too light and "washed out." Slides that are too dark are the result of underexposure.

Reciprocity

This will bother you when making lengthy time exposures. It also can be a problem with flash duration shorter than 1/1,000 of a second. Reciprocity is another word for the E = I x T rule that says lens-opening and shutter-speed relationships are linear. They are, except for very long and extremely short exposures. Reciprocity departure will affect exposures of one second or longer. For example, with Kodak T-Max 400 film and a metered exposure calling for one second, you should open the lens about 1/3 f/stop. Ten seconds should be increased to at least 15 seconds or open 1/2 stop. One hundred seconds should be 300 seconds, or open up one and one-half stops. For precise reciprocity corrections, refer to the film manufacturer's published data.

Choosing a Film

Because switching films can be confusing, my advice to beginners is to select one film and stick with it until another type is needed. Many people standardize on a 400-speed film because photos can be made in available light with a hand-held camera where a slower film would require a tripod. 35mm negatives from 400-speed film usually can be enlarged to 8"x10" before the grain becomes objectionable. Some photographers expose 400-speed film at a higher or lower exposure index. Described on page 120 is a method for determining an optimum "working" exposure index for your choice of film, exposed with your meter, in your camera, and developed following your own standardized procedure.

When fine print quality is more important than convenience or action-stopping, a slower film will be your choice. Except in extremely bright light, slow film will require a slow shutter speed, particularly when you stop the lens down to get depth of field. This will mean using a tripod.

Slow, fine-grained films are appropriate when enormous display enlargements are to be made, when increased contrast is desirable, as in copying documents, or when you want to reproduce extremely fine detail and texture in the subject.

Characteristics of Color Films

Speed, grain, contrast, latitude and reciprocity

These characteristics apply to color films as they do to black-and-white, but there are some differences.

Color films also are available in a wide range of speeds. As with black-and-white, grain is proportional to speed, so select fast film when you have to shoot hand-held under existing light. Use slow film when you can mount your camera on a tripod and stop down the lens, or when using bright studio lights or flash. Slower color films are the best choice when you want maximum contrast.

Color-negative films are almost as tolerant of over- and underexposure as black-and-white; but with color-transparency (slide) films, latitude is very limited. When in doubt, the rule with negative films is to give enough exposure to record detail in the shadow areas. Transpar-

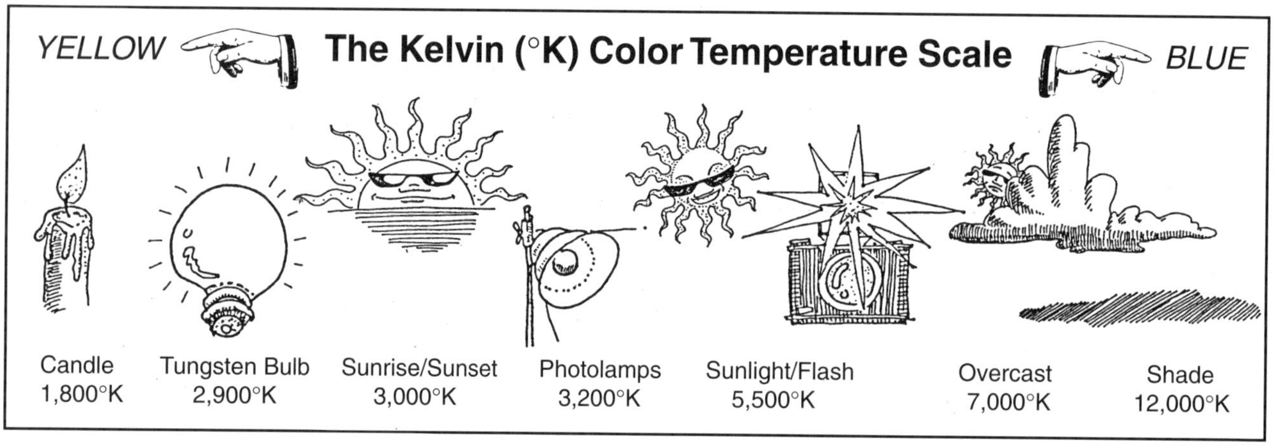

ency films require just the opposite: don't overexpose and "wash out" the important highlight values.

Reciprocity departure is even more critical with color not only because of the risk of underexposure, but because the color balance may shift in unwanted ways. Special color films intended for long or short exposures are available in medium- and large-format to aid the professional. Amazing improvements in color and density often can be made with digital software, but it is best to make the original film image as good as possible.

Color balance

Color-transparency (slide) films are manufactured specifically for exposure under predictable lighting conditions, either daylight or incandescent. Except for special effects, the colors of light should not be mixed. Fluorescent light is an example of misleading appearance and it doesn't even appear on the Kelvin scale (above). Because of their overall bluish appearance, fluorescent lights would seem to balance with daylight color film. But so-called "daylight" fluorescents usually are extremely weak in red. They give an unpleasant greenish color on film, unless compensated for with a magenta filter.

Electronic flash illumination is very close in color to the light for which "daylight" color films are balanced. Incandescent (tungsten bulb) lamps appear quite a bit warmer, more toward the lower end of the Kelvin color temperature scale. A picture will appear overall yellowish-orange if photographed under incandescent light on color film manufactured for daylight or electronic flash. Moonlight effects can be obtained by slightly underexposing tungsten-balanced color film in daylight, without the appropriate orange conversion filter.

Most color-negative films are balanced for daylight and flash. That's why photo finishers' prints from negatives exposed by incandescent light often look strangely orange. Automatic printers in labs are set for "normal" daylight/flash balance. Good custom prints can be made from these negatives, but the printing filtration must be adjusted. An alternative is to use a bluish filter over the camera lens when taking the pictures.

Although nearly any kind of color film can be filtered for acceptable color balance under standard kinds of illumination, it's best to use the right kind of film in the first place, making any minor adjustments in exposure or filtration according to the manufacturer's instructions. Starting with a better image will save you a lot of printing time, whether chemical or digital.

Storing Films

Whether black-and-white or color, you'll do best to buy fresh film and store it in a cool, dry place. Factory-sealed packages of film will keep well for two years or more in a refrigerator or freezer, even well past the expiration date printed on the box. But to prevent moisture condensation, try to wait 30 minutes for refrigerated film to reach room temperature before unsealing the package. Frozen film should thaw for at least an hour before the seal is broken. Film that has been stored in a hot, humid place may show gray or greenish overall fog or poor color quality. This is why outdated film may not be a bargain unless you can be certain that it has been refrigerated.

Loading Bulk Film

Should you buy bulk film? Some experts recommend it and others don't, although the economy of purchasing 35mm film in 100-foot rolls is very appealing. If you shoot enough pictures to use the nearly 700 exposures on a 100-foot roll before it goes out of date, the cost per shot with bulk film will be less than half what it would cost to buy factory-loaded film magazines. But on the other hand, you have to invest in a bulk-film loader and a supply of reloadable magazines. And bulk loading takes time and care.

The best reason for *not* using bulk film is the danger of scratches, fingerprints, or fog. With so-called daylight film loaders, the film may have to pass between felt light-trap pads four times instead of only twice with commercially loaded film. There may be more than twice the risk of an embedded speck of sand or grit gouging the entire length of a roll because the felt lips of the loader and the reused magazines are less likely to be clean.

Light fog will occur at both the head and tail ends of each roll (you have to be careful not to shoot right up to the very end — stop one or two exposures short), and there is always the possibility that someone might accidentally unscrew the lid of the loader and fog your entire bulk-film supply.

Some special films, however, are available only in long rolls. And it is convenient to be able to load short lengths of film for testing and for special processing. If you do load bulk film, be careful to handle the film only by the edges or by the very end; use strong enough tape (3/4-inch masking tape will do) so the film doesn't pull off the spool; inspect all felt light-trap lips for dirt; blow out dust from inside the magazines; and beware of light fog. Insert the spool in each magazine shell so that the long end of the spool will point toward the bottom of the camera when it is loaded. Most cameras will require that you trim the leader to fit the take-up spool.

Bulk loading, like everything else in photography, is subject to Murphy's Law.

> ***"Nothing is as easy as it looks.***
> ***It will take longer than you think.***
> ***If anything can go wrong, it will."***
>
> — Murphy's Law

Determining Exposure

A good exposure meter is a very valuable tool, but personal judgment is still important. If the meter in your camera is working correctly and you use it intelligently, you will make more printable negatives and projectable slides. Fine prints can best be made from properly exposed negatives. But since most exposure meters are programmed for "average" conditions, you will need to learn when to manually override the camera's settings.

Both your meter and your judgment will be needed when taking pictures in deep shade, indoors with available light, or whenever the subject is backlit or unusually light or dark. If in doubt, bracket — that is, expose at the setting you think is right; then, to make certain, shoot more frames at one-half or one stop more and less, depending on the subject. Even professionals do this. Many cameras have a "backlight" setting that gives one or two stops more exposure. Others provide plus or minus adjustments. Bracketing can be done by adjusting the shutter and aperture manually or by resetting the film speed. Read more about bracketing and exposure compensation in the Zone System section later in this chapter.

> ***"Good judgment comes from experience, and experience ... well, that comes from <u>bad</u> judgment."***
>
> — Anonymous

The "Sunny 16" rule

What can you do if your meter malfunctions or the battery dies? If you're working outdoors, there can be two solutions: First, refer to the film manufacturer's instructions printed on a data sheet or inside the box. The second alternative is to use the "Sunny 16" rule:

Exposure for an "average" subject, outdoors on a sunny day between about 10 a.m. and 4 p.m., equals the EI or ISO of the film as the shutter speed, at a lens opening of f/16. For example, with 400-speed film, the required settings under "Sunny 16" conditions would be 1/500 at f/16; 100-speed film would be 1/125 at f/16. (Your shutter probably isn't marked for 1/400 or 1/100, so use the closest setting).

But what if it's *not* a sunny day? Try this: under hazy sun, open up the lens to f/11. In light overcast, open up to f/8. If the sky is heavily overcast, or if your subject is in open shade on a sunny day, your basic settings for 100-speed film will be about 1/125 at f/5.6; 400-speed film will require 1/500 at the same f/stop range; 64-speed film would require 1/60, etc. Remember that this is the *basic* exposure. To increase depth of field, and for action photos, you can compensate between lens openings and shutter speeds all you want, as long as you maintain the basic relationship according to the speed of the film and the amount of light on the subject.

EASTMAN KODAK CO.

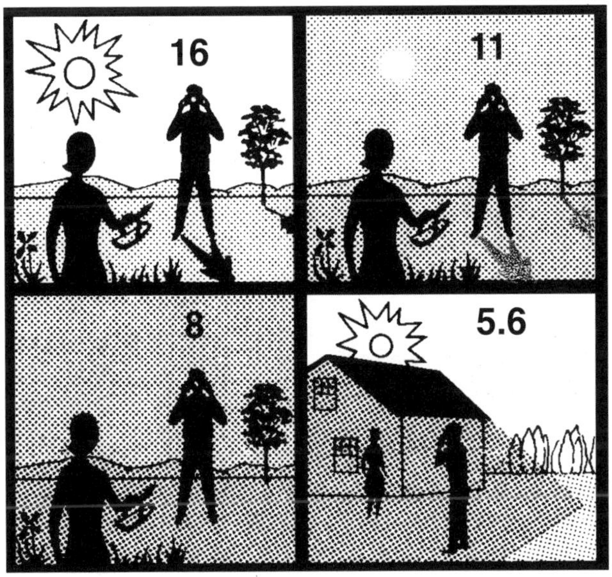

How meters work

Most built-in exposure meters average the brightness of the entire field of the lens by reading samples (see diagrams at right). Such meters are designed with the assumption that the average photographer will be shooting subjects of overall average brightness. So-called center-weighted meters assume that you're going to place the most important area of your subject in the center of the viewfinder and that you want that central portion reproduced as a middle gray. Spot meters scan an even smaller central area so you can move the camera around and compare the brightness of subject and background. Finally, matrix metering scans many areas of the camera's field of view, and feeds the readings to a microprocessor that attempts to figure out which is subject and which is background. The electronics integrates this data into a compensated exposure setting the way it would be calculated by an experienced photographer.

Exposure meters built into cameras are of the reflected light type, and they are all subject to the same limitation: they are designed to convert everything they read into an average middle gray. This averaging feature simplifies exposure determination, but it also can be seriously misleading if the subject is not of average brightness. With many types of subject matter, if you want to reproduce black and white with a full range of gray tones in between, you must learn to use a meter to help you previsualize what the final print should look like.

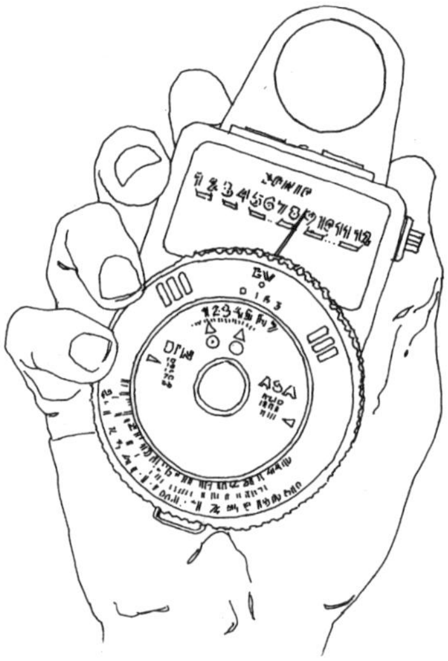

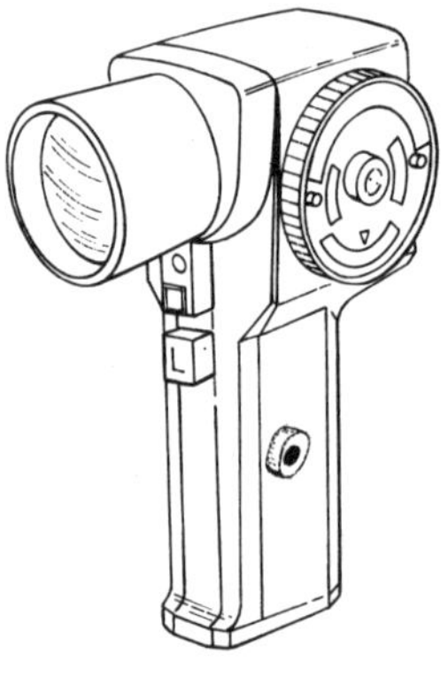

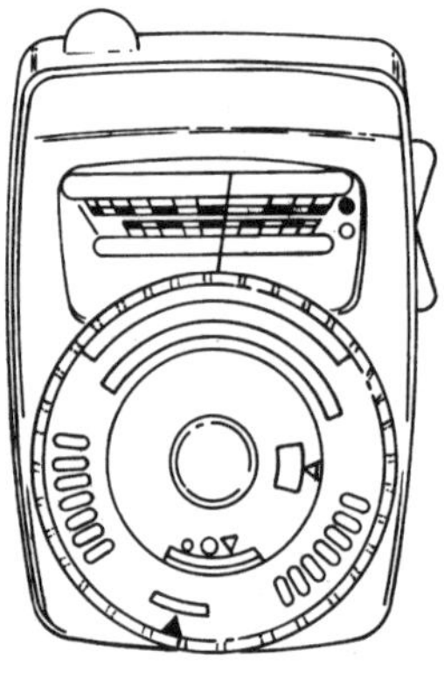

Basic types of hand-held exposure meters. (Above): Incident light. (Upper right): reflected-light spot meter. (Right): reflected-light meter with incident attachment.

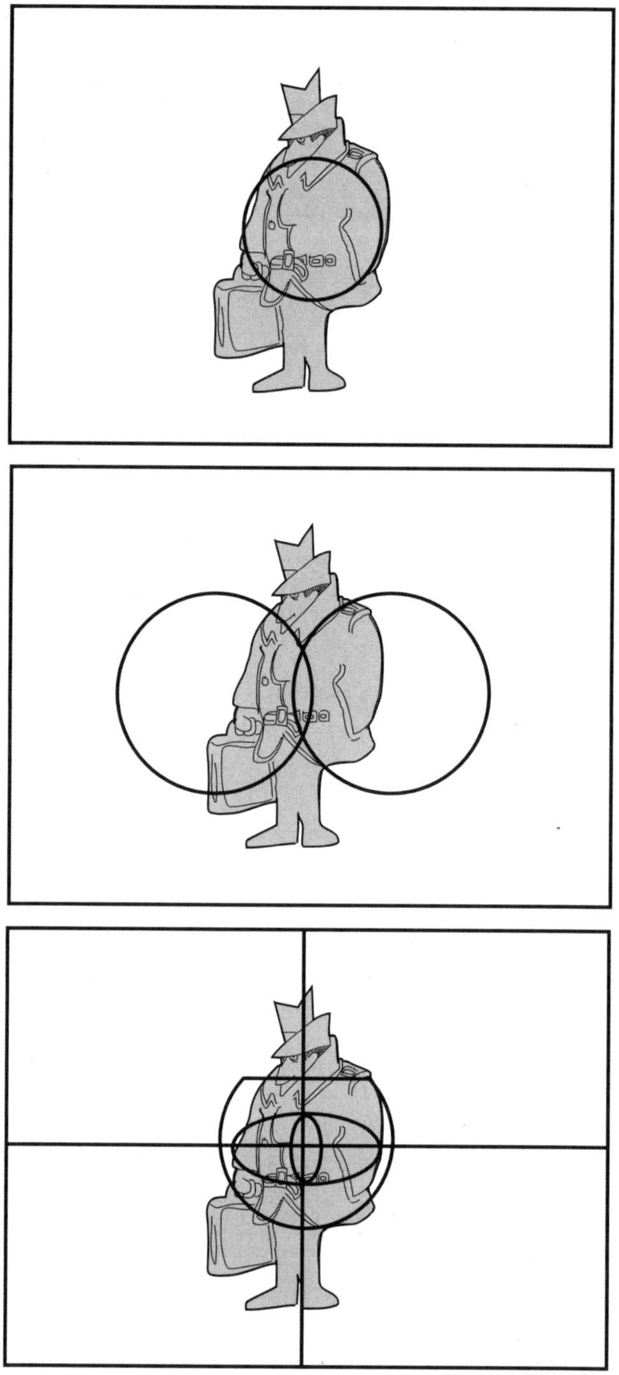

Cameras with built-in, through-the-lens exposure meters differ in the way they see the light. (TOP) A spot meter reads a narrow angle of view. (MIDDLE) A center-weighted system often has overlapping sensors that tend to pick up background brightness, unless you move in close to make the reading. (BOTTOM) Matrix metering integrates readings from several segmented sensors that cover the entire field of view. A computer chip attempts to separate subject from background. Matrix systems are surprisingly accurate and can be relied on when there is not enough time to make precise measurements.

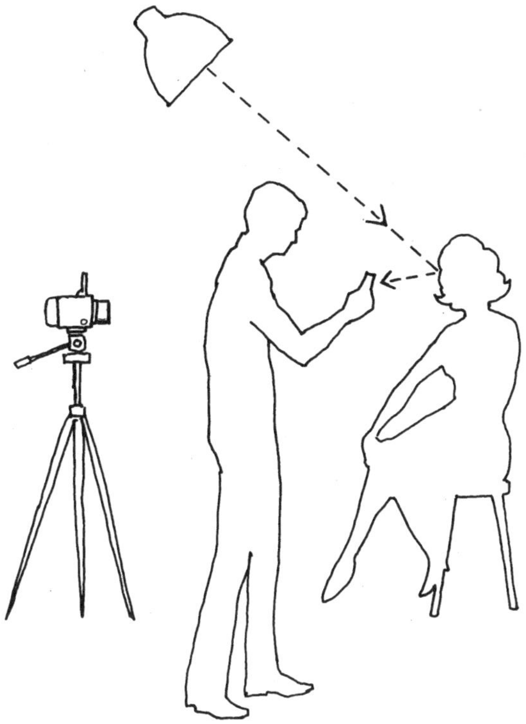

A reflected-light meter reads light reflected from the subject. The meter should be held so that it neither reads its own shadow nor is affected by background brightness

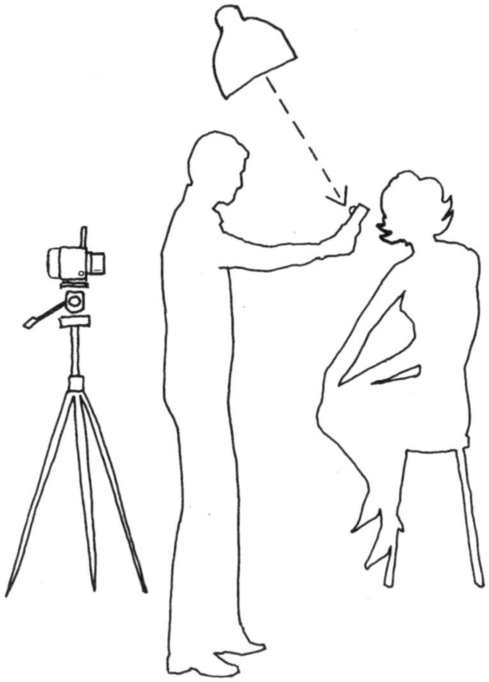

An incident-light meter reads light falling on the subject. It is not affected by variations in brightness of the subject or the background.

Reflected-light meters

A hand-held meter should be placed quite close to the part of the subject you're reading, but don't get so near that you read the shadow of the meter or your own shadow. Why get so close? Because if the background or adjacent areas are significantly brighter or darker than the area you want to expose for, the meter will include those areas and make the reading inaccurate. Spot meters, of course, are designed to read a very small area from farther away.

Cameras with built-in meters can be handled as if the entire camera were the meter: move in very close for the reading, note the settings called for, and then back off to shoot from the angle from which you made the reading. If the meter display changes, ignore it. Leave the camera set as indicated when you made the close-up reading. When in automatic mode, lock in the settings while making the reading, then back off to shoot.

> ***"The ability to anticipate ... the final print while viewing the subject makes it possible to apply the ... controls of the craft ... to achieve the desired result."***
>
> — Ansel Adams, photographer

Incident-light meters

Meters designed to read the light falling on the subject, rather than the light reflected from it, are called incident-light meters. Incident meters are especially convenient for studio use, and most flash meters are of this type. Incident readings should be made with the white light-gathering hemisphere of the meter pointing toward the camera from the subject's position (see diagram above). Extreme highlight and shadow values, stray light, and background brightness have little effect on an incident-light reading, so this technique is especially recommended for color photography, for copy work, and for situations in which the lighting is uneven or when small objects are being photographed against a contrasting background.

Because of their more limited exposure latitude, color-reversal films usually must be exposed close to the standard 18-percent middle gray to which meters are calibrated. Although the incident-light method will eliminate false readings from light sources and from the background, it does not distinguish between the important light and dark areas in the subject. These high and low values are very significant in black-and-white work because you can control the range of values in the brightness scale by manipulating exposure and development. The best way to get really superb black-and-white negatives is to use an accurate reflected-light meter, and follow a procedure known as the Zone System.

Nine Zones of Subject Brightness

Zone IX (N + 4 STOPS)	Glaring white surfaces. Snow in flat sunlight. White without texture. Light sources and reflections. (Maximum white of the printing paper).
Zone VIII (N + 3 STOPS)	White clothing with texture. Light-colored painted surfaces. Snow in shade. Highlights on Caucasian skin.
Zone VII (N + 2 STOPS)	Pale skin. Light-gray objects such as concrete walls and light-colored hair and fur. Snow or light sand with acute side lighting.
Zone VI (N + 1 STOP)	Average Caucasion skin value. Light stone. Average sand. Shadows on snow in sunlight.
Zone V (N)	Clear north sky. Dark skin in sunlight. Washed blue denim. Gray stone. Average weathered wood. (*Note: This is the 18-percent middle gray for which exposure meters are calibrated).*
Zone IV (N - 1 STOP)	Average dark foliage. Dark stone. Landscape shadows. Recommended shadow value for portraits in sunlight.
Zone III (N - 2 STOPS)	Dark, textured materials such as dark clothing, hair, and fur. Low values showing adequate texture in the print.
Zone II (N - 3 STOPS)	First suggestion of texture. Deep tonalities representing the darkest part of the image showing detail.
Zone I (N - 4 STOPS)	Slight tonality, but no texture. Unlighted interiors through open doorways. (Maximum black of the printing paper).

Adapted from Ansel Adams, *The Negative,* New York Graphic Society, 1981, p. 60
(Adams' original scale consisted of 11 zones).

"Most ... photographers ... forget that they are never photographing an object, but rather light itself. Where there is no light, they will have no picture; where there is remarkable light, they may have a remarkable picture."

— Galen Rowell, photographer

The Zone System

Developed by Ansel Adams for his own use and written about by Adams and many other photographers, the Zone System forces you to carefully previsualize your subject matter as you want it to appear in the final print. You must observe and compare the important tonal values in each scene, mentally placing each value at the desired place on a nine-step gray scale. Each step of the gray scale is one f/stop apart and is referred to as a zone (see table at left).

The Zone System is based on the ancient photographers' axiom: "Expose for the shadows and develop for the highlights." Photographers relied on this principle long before the invention of exposure meters and panchromatic films. The old-timers judged exposure by examining the brightness of the shadow areas of the image as they appeared on the ground glass back of the view camera, exposed according to experience, and then developed their slow glass plates or films by the light of a lantern or a dim red bulb until the highlights appeared to be of proper density.

The principle of the Zone System applies today with black-and-white films and can be very helpful in exposing color, although with color the development controls cannot be used.

This scene contains a full range of tonal values. So does the original photographic print. Although printing inks cannot show separation between the extreme values at both ends of the scale, zone numbers have been placed in the photograph to indicate approximately what the corresponding steps would be on the nine-step gray scale used in the Zone System. Each step, or zone, represents the equivalent of one f/stop difference in negative density.

RON NULL

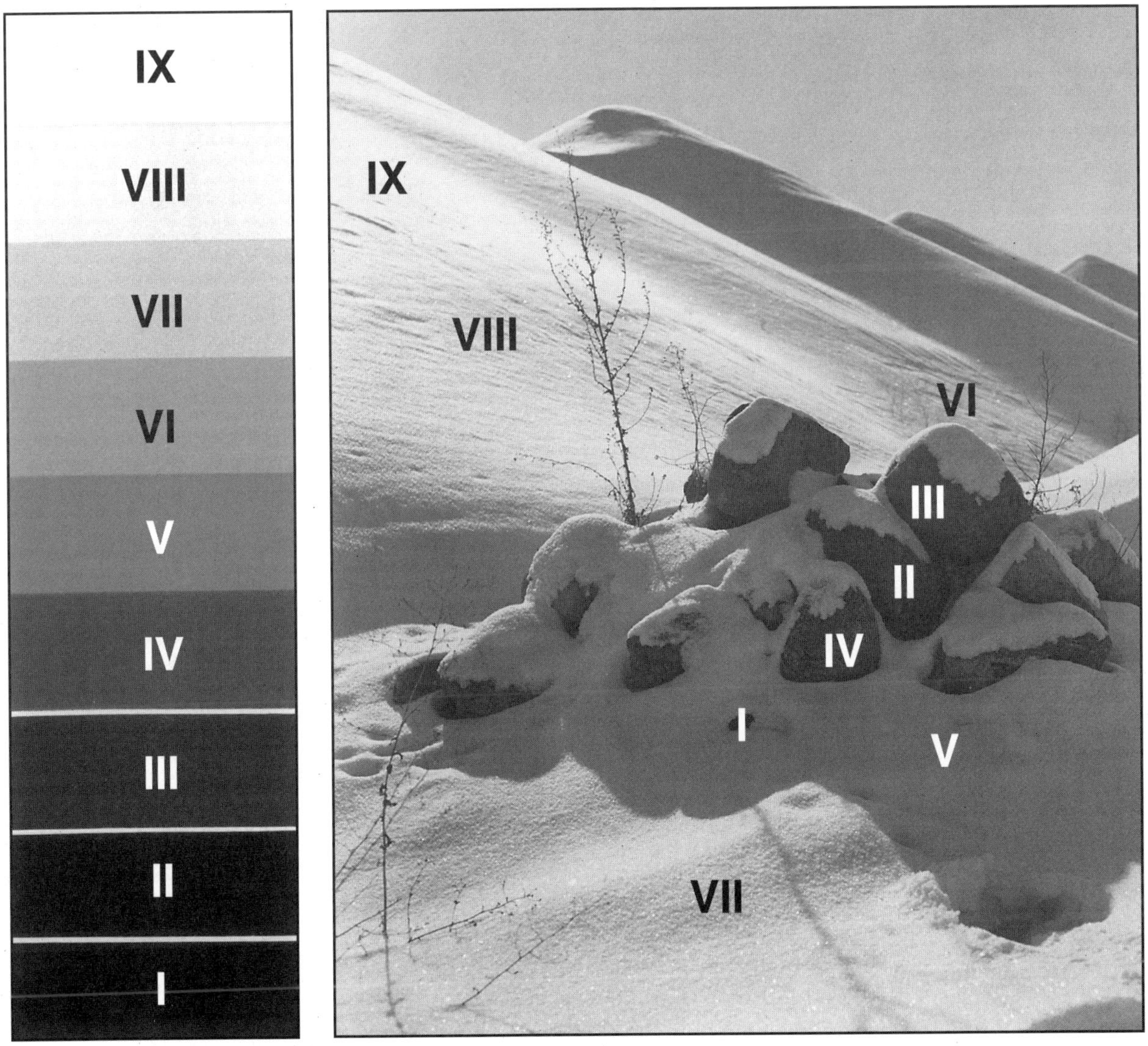

Shadow density in the negative is determined largely by exposure, more or less independent of development; whereas highlight density increases very rapidly in proportion to degree of development. If it weren't true that low and high negative densities respond differently to development, the zone system wouldn't work. Remember, the rule is to *expose for the shadows* (lower values — Zones I through IV) and *develop for the highlights* (higher values — Zones VI through IX). Ideally, you would read and place on the gray scale each important zone appearing in the subject. However, if you place even *one* zone correctly on the gray scale, all the other zones will fall into their relative places within the limits of the film used and the development given.

Placing Zone Values

There are five different ways of determining exposure with the Zone System, the first four of which are time-saving shortcuts: (1) the darkest important shadow method, (2) the most important highlight method, (3) the substitute reading method, (4) the standard reading method (recommended for color), and (5) the brightness range method, which gives you control over black-and-white negative contrast as well as density. When you understand the principle of the Zone System and are able to previsualize the zones into which significant subject brightnesses should fall, you'll be able to choose the best method for each situation.

1. Darkest important shadow

This method is simple, yet it keeps you from losing shadow detail in a subject such as a dark rock formation, dark animal, or a woodland scene with spotty areas of sunlight and shade. If you previsualize the zone into which the darkest important values should fall (usually Zone III) and expose so that zone is placed correctly on the gray scale, you'll record the textures in those dark areas. Other zones in the scene then will fall into place according to their relative brightness.

If the higher zones don't fit the gray scale, you can develop the film so they do. If the negative is properly exposed and developed, you should be able to tell the difference in the final print between areas that should appear as Zones VI, VII, VIII, and IX.

When you make a close-up reading of the darkest important shadow areas, the meter will give you a Zone V reading (middle gray). Unless you want those shadow areas to *be* Zone V, you'll have to convert the reading to the correct zone. The easiest way to do this is to count zones as you stop down the lens. If the chosen shadow area should be Zone III, simply read the meter to determine the f/stop for making that area Zone V; then count "Zone IV" as you close down one stop and "Zone III" as you close down another stop.

For example, a direct, reflected-light meter reading of a dark, textured area indicates an exposure of 1/30 at f/8. You know that this setting would be the correct exposure to render that area as Zone V, but you want it to reproduce as Zone III. So as you stop down from f/8 to f/11, you say to yourself, "Zone IV;" as you stop down one more stop to f/16, you say, "Zone III." Of course, you can leave the aperture alone and adjust the shutter speed instead. Suppose you choose f/16 because you want maximum depth of field. Your meter indicates 1/8 at f/16. How would you place Zone II? Increase the shutter speed two "stops" from 1/8 to 1/30.

The rule is to give *less* exposure than the meter says to place Zones I through IV. If you were basing exposure on higher values instead of lower values, you give *more* exposure than the meter indicates to place Zones VI through IX. No change is necessary to place Zone V, because the meter reads directly for Zone V. Count zones

Gary Cialdella

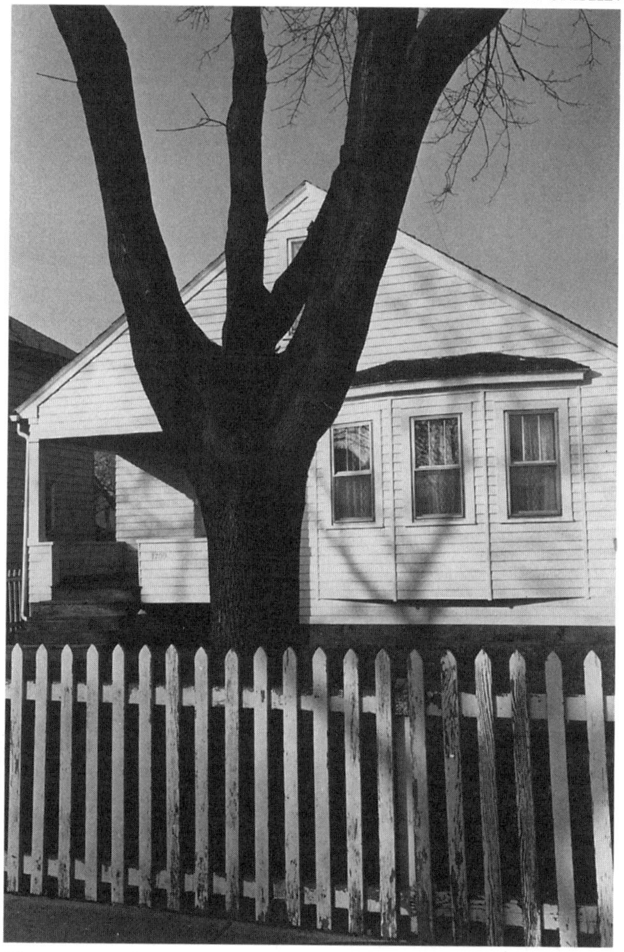

The extreme brightness range of this subject calls for N-(minus) development of the negative. Exposure should be based on Zone III to retain detail in the dark tree bark. The difference between reflected-light meter readings of the bark and the brightest portions of the white house indicated N-2 development to retain Zone VIII.

only on the marked shutter speeds or on the numbered f/stops of the regular scale (that is, f/5.6, f/8, f/ll, f/16, etc.).

Don't count the halfway click stops that may be on your lens. They are there simply to help you make slight adjustments in exposure.

2. Most important highlight

Choose this method when shadows are less important than light skin tones, snow texture, or other values above middle gray. This also is usually the most convenient metering method for color-reversal (slide) films.

Instead of reading the shadows, you read the skin tone or other light value directly with your meter and place that Zone reading on the chosen part of the gray scale. For example, in an outdoor portrait of a white person in full sunlight, the brightest side of the face reads 1/125 at f/16. You want the skin not to record as Zone V, but as Zone VI, so you open up the lens one stop from f/16 to f/11, saying to yourself, "Zone VI" as you set the aperture. If instead of a face, you've read side-lighted, textured snow or light sand, you would open up two stops from the Zone V reading to place the snow or sand on Zone VII. If you wanted to record flat-lighted snow or sand as Zone VIII, you would open up the lens three stops, from f/16 to f/5.6 or leave the aperture at f/16 and slow the shutter three "stops" from 1/125 to 1/15.

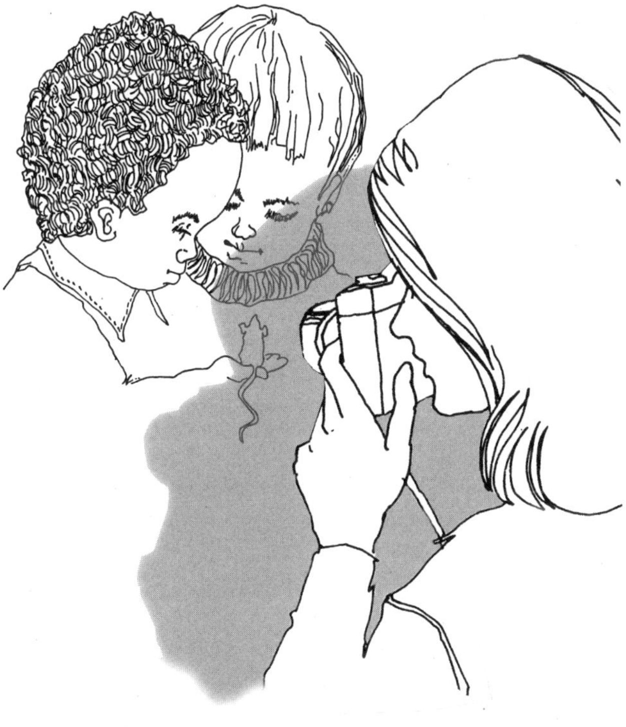

Read important light values up close. But when making a close-up reading, either with your entire camera or with a hand-held exposure meter, be careful not to include your own shadow!

In some cases, you may have to lose background detail in order to place the most important values in their proper zones. But be careful not to let your meter include those unwanted background areas in the reading. If you remember to read the *single most important value* (usually skin tones if people are in the picture) *and place that value in the desired zone*, you won't be misled by the background. Since your meter can't tell what the most vital part of the subject is, it will average everything you allow it to read into a Zone V middle gray.

3. Substitute reading

A variation of the most important shadow and highlight methods, a substitute reading is useful when it's impossible or inconvenient to approach the subject for a direct, close-up meter reading. You could read nearby snow to substitute for snow in similar light on a distant mountain peak. Or the trunk or foliage of a large nearby tree can substitute for trees on the other side of a river.

The important thing is to be certain the light conditions are the same, that you hold the meter (or entire camera) properly to avoid false readings from contrasting background values, and that you count out the zones correctly as you adjust lens or shutter settings from those indicated by the meter for Zone V.

> ***"Before [Ansel Adams], people thought mountains were made out of stone. He demonstrated they were made out of light and were never the same twice."***
>
> — John Szarkowski, museum curator

4. Standard reading

Appropriate for exposing color films of limited exposure latitude, the standard reading method is based on consistent Zone V readings from an 18-percent gray card or incident light meter or on reflected-light readings from some other standard value. Flash meters usually read incident light and are calibrated for Zone V. Other than a gray card, the most commonly used reflective value is the back (or palm) of the photographer's hand. Since light skin generally reflects at Zone VI in full light and dark skin at Zone V, this is a uniform standard that's always available.

Color films normally should be exposed for Zone V, allowing the higher and lower values to reproduce wherever they fall on either side of middle gray. Note that this is what you're doing when using the most important highlight method.

As with a black-and-white portrait, you would open up one stop in color if you've read Zone VI skin instead of a Zone V gray card. You would do this because the meter has read the skin tone not as Zone VI, but as Zone V middle gray. Color-reversal films ordinarily do not have enough exposure latitude to place zones more than about one stop away from the value read.

When your experience doesn't allow you to completely previsualize the result, bracketing is a good practice. Bracketing means making one exposure at exactly what your meter reading and calculations indicate, and then making another exposure at one-half stop, one stop, or more additional exposure and another at the same amount less exposure. When experience tells you that it's a waste of film to bracket both directions, such as long exposures when reciprocity is a problem, then simply extend bracketing as needed.

5. Brightness range

The brightness range method gives you greatest control over all the zones of subject brightness. At its most complex, this approach calls for reading each subject area separately with a spot meter, and plotting these readings on a gray scale so that the brightness of each part of the subject is matched to the optimum zone. If the subject's brightness range doesn't match the scale of zones, then plus or minus development of the film is indicated (only for black-and-white).

At its simplest, the brightness range method calls for reading only the lowest and highest significant values (frequently Zones III and VII) and averaging the two readings. You might choose, for example, to read both a Zone III tree trunk and Zone VII side-lighted snow. Reading from the tree trunk, the meter indicates 1/125 at f/5.6, while the snow indicates 1/125 at f/22. Remember that these exposures would render both the high and low values as Zone V middle gray. The difference between the readings is exactly four stops (four zones), which it should be, and an exposure of 1/125 at f/11, halfway between the extremes, would place both the tree trunk and the snow within the limits of the film, reproducing all values in between. This is exactly the same setting you would have obtained had you placed separately either Zone III or Zone VII or based the exposure on a Zone V gray-card reading.

Averaging the highest and lowest readings is a time-saving technique when both high and low values are the same number of zones above and below Zone V middle gray. But averaging doesn't work if all or most of the zones are skewed to either side of Zone V. In a very low-key subject, for example, the values may range from Zone II through Zone V, with nothing lighter than Zone V, except perhaps a tiny catchlight or reflection that isn't measured by the meter. In this case, the exposure should be based on the Zone V reading to place all of the low values properly. An average exposure would place the Zone V value between Zones III and IV, adding unnecessary density to the entire negative.

Similarly, a high-key subject with a tonal range extending from Zone VI through Zone IX may not contain any low values, or the low values may be so small as to be insignificant in determining exposure. An average setting halfway between Zones VI and IX would result in an undesirably thin negative, so the exposure should be anchored to Zone VI.

With many subjects, reading the highest and lowest important values and setting the exposure halfway between will result in a Zone V average, the same as a single overall reading of the entire subject or an incident-light reading. With other subjects, however, the averaging method may lead you astray either because the significant zones don't fall equally on both sides of Zone V or because the brightness range from highlight to shadow may be greater than the film can record. This may result in an unsatisfactory compromise of underexposure at the shadow end of the scale and overexposure of the high values. When this happens, the print will lack shadow detail and high values will be "washed out."

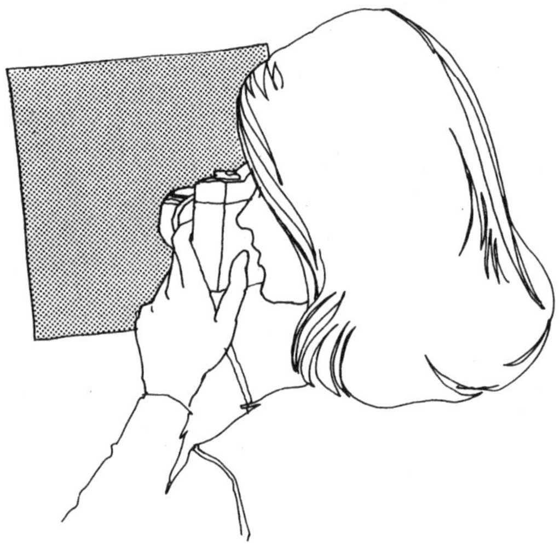

An 18-percent gray card (Zone V) is the standard to which exposure meters are calibrated. When you determine exposure by reading from a gray card, place the card so it receives exactly the same amount of light as the principal subject. Move in close (the card need not be in focus) but be careful not to read your shadow or the area beyond the card. Your hand, clothing, or some other surface can serve as a "gray card" if you place the reading on the appropriate zone.

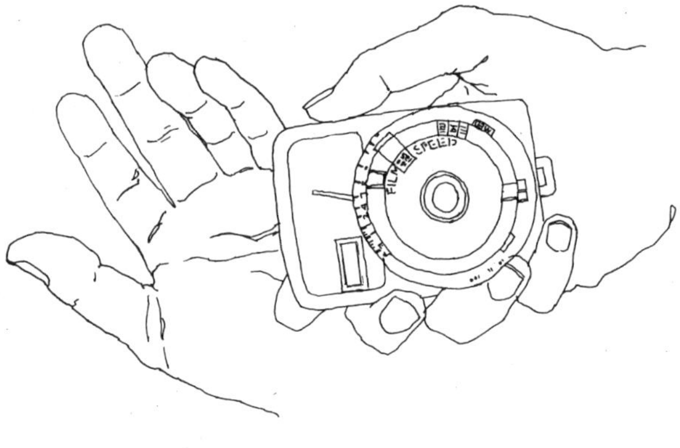

Adjusting Contrast by Development

Black-and-white film will reproduce at best a range of only nine zones. This means that Zone VIII can be no more than 128 times as bright as Zone I. If you detect a greater brightness range, you won't be able to record the entire gray scale properly unless you reduce the subject contrast. One way to do this (necessary for color) is to increase the amount of light in the shadows with flash or a reflector, or decrease the brightness of the highlights by shading them. With black-and-white you can reduce the contrast of the negative by developing it for less than the normal time.

JOHN GRIFFIOEN

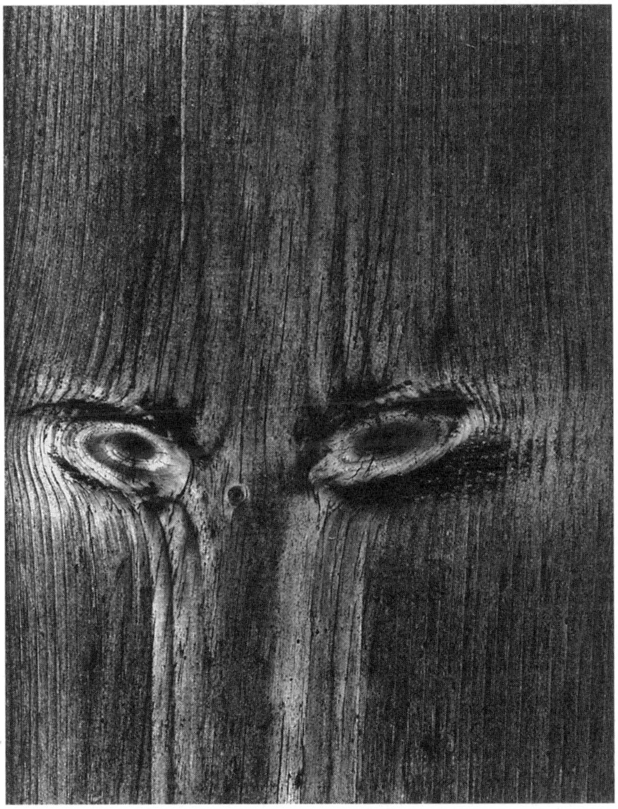

Do you see in this photograph a board or a baboon? Or is the image, for you, composed solely of textures and convoluted lines? With nearly all of the values darker than Zone V, this is an excellent example of the kind of low-key subject matter that requires normal plus (N+) development

"[Imagemaking is] like inventing a language at the same time I am using it."

— Jerry N. Uelsmann, imagemaker

Compression

Here's an example when development time should be reduced. Suppose a Zone III tree trunk reads 1/125 at f/5.6, while the Zone VII snow reads 1/125 at f/32. That's a *five-zone* difference instead of the desired four zones. In this case, normal *minus one zone* (N-1) development is indicated. If the tree trunk and the snow were *six zones* apart when the difference should be only four zones, correct development would call for normal *minus two zones* (N-2).

Expansion

Suppose you want to expand, instead of compress, the placement of the highest values. For example, you're shooting the scene just described, but on a very dull, overcast day. The Zone III tree trunk reads 1/30 at f/4, while the snow reads 1/30 at f/11. The difference between Zone III and Zone VII is only *three stops* instead of the desired four, so normal development *plus one zone* (N+1) would be indicated. If you wanted the snow to be rendered as Zone VIII, you'd want to extend development to normal *plus two zones* (N+2) to bring the high values up where they belong. Otherwise your print would seem gray and flat.

The brightness range method is very convenient for determining exposure if you're using sheet film and can develop single sheets according to whether you want to *expand* the brightness range (N+) or *compress* it (N-). Advanced photographers, who work with roll film and who can afford to own extra camera bodies or extra film backs, often load one camera or one back with film to be developed normally, reserving and marking another body or back for either minus or plus development. You'll learn much more about Zone-System development in Chapter 6.

Problems with Exposure

A sensitive and accurate exposure meter is indispensable for making fine quality photographs under varied lighting conditions. But the meter won't solve all of your problems. Your meter may not be entirely accurate; it may read consistently high or low. If the shutter speeds of your camera are slightly inaccurate in the same direction, you may find that the film speed for which you should set your camera will be different from the rating indicated by the film manufacturer. Slight differences in processing technique may also affect the way you rate the film. If you have doubts about the accuracy of your equipment or the quality of your results, ask your instructor or someone with a densitometer or an electronic shutter speed tester to examine your negatives and perhaps to test your camera.

Leslie Fitzpatrick

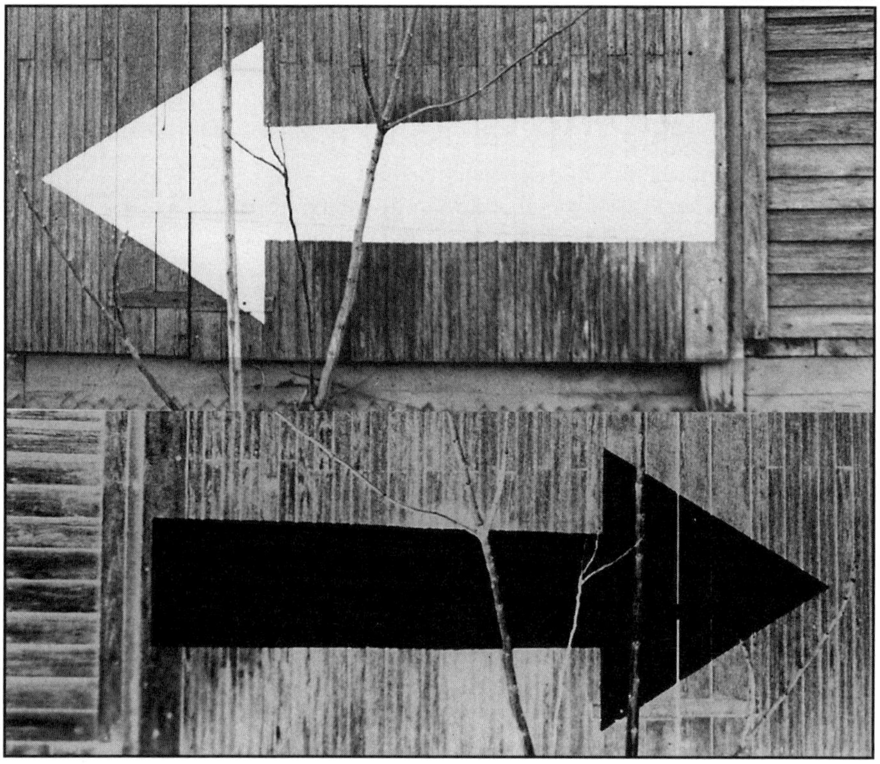

This positive/negative image (both halves were printed from the same negative) required contrast adjustment to match the middle gray values.

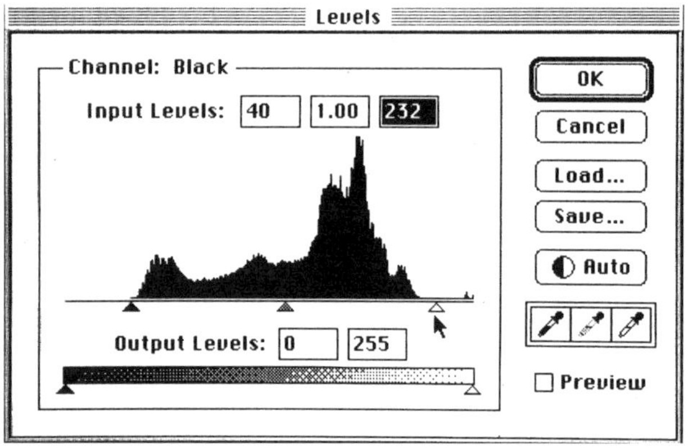

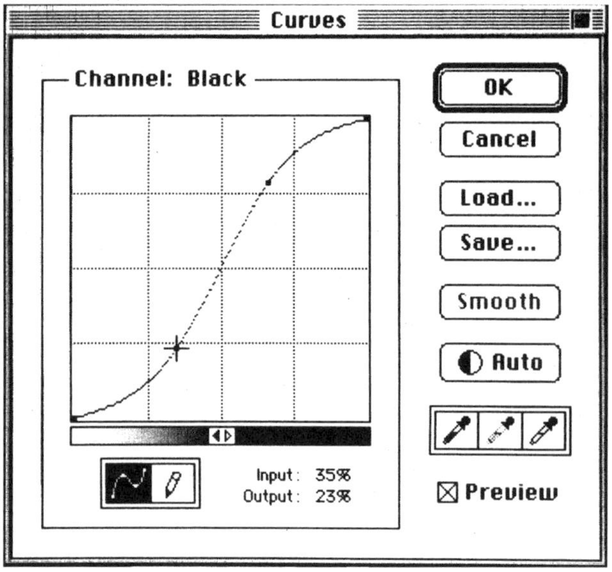

"Imagemaking is a little bit of science, a little bit of magic, and a whole lot of creativity."

— Anonymous

The Levels histogram (top left) shows the distribution of density values in the image. If there is much flat space at either end, moving the triangle sliders inward will place Zones I and IX where they belong. The Curves graph (bottom left) will initially be a straight line, but by selecting various values (Zones) you can place values on the gray scale where you want them. Often an ideal curve will take an "S" shape as shown here. Incredible image transformations can be done with the Curves palette (see page 211).

Adjusting Contrast with a Computer

The principle of the Zone System can be applied to digital images, with software features such as *Levels* and *Curves* in Adobe Photoshop. Instead of the nine separate light-value steps of the Zone System, *Levels* shows histograms, and *Curves* depicts a graph resembling the sensitometric curve applied in conventional photography (see examples at left).

Overall contrast of an image can be modified, or individual portions may be selected and adjusted. This process is easy to learn and is explained fully in the software documentation.

David H. Curl

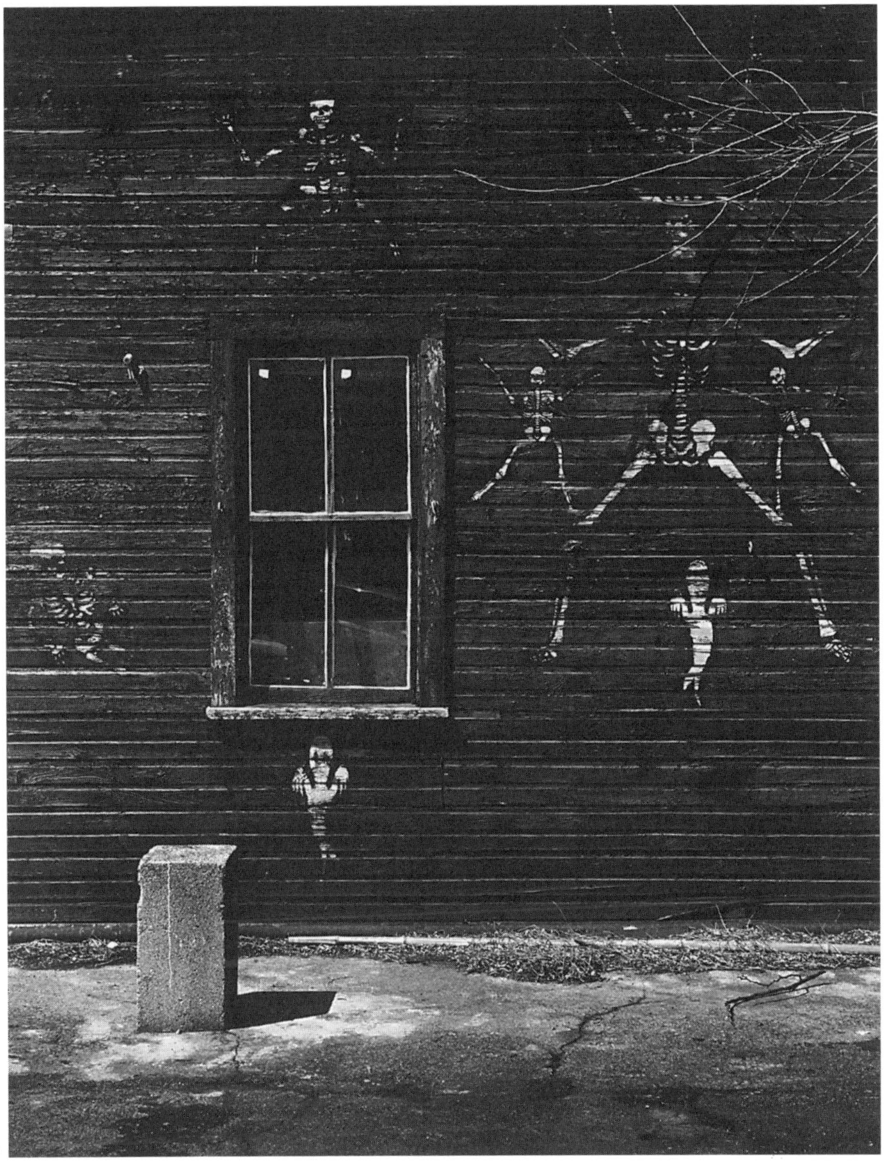

Nearly all the texture of this bizarre building was in its weather-beaten black paint. Careful placement of the wooden siding on Zone III was necessary to avoid underexposure. Extended development (N+2) increased the density of the painted, white figures, enabling them to print, with magenta added in the darkroom, as Zones VII and VIII, and the tiny white areas around the window panes as Zone IX.

> ***"A person who works with their hands is a laborer; a person who works with their hands and head is a crafter or artisan; and a person who works with their hands, head and heart is an artist."***
>
> — Anonymous

Take Notes

Don't be lazy about keeping records of your exposure settings, especially in unusual situations. There's nothing wrong with making a mistake the first time, but keeping careful records will save you the embarrassment, frustration and expense of repeating errors. You'll soon learn to estimate the proper exposure in many situations, verifying it with your meter. And you'll learn to compensate for unusual lighting conditions by varying exposure and development.

The only way to become a skilled photographer is to make lots of photographs. Be prepared to use plenty of film, but expose it systematically. Follow careful meter readings or printed exposure guides, but keep accurate records of every frame you expose. When the film is developed, compare your negatives with the exposure data. Then you won't repeat your mistakes.

You'll be wise to use a single kind of film most of the time and to standardize on processing. To learn the most about what your camera can do, don't limit your photographic activities to average scenes on sunny days. Look for chances to make pictures indoors, in bad weather, and under pressure. This additional experience will make you a much better photographer.

Kevin Miller

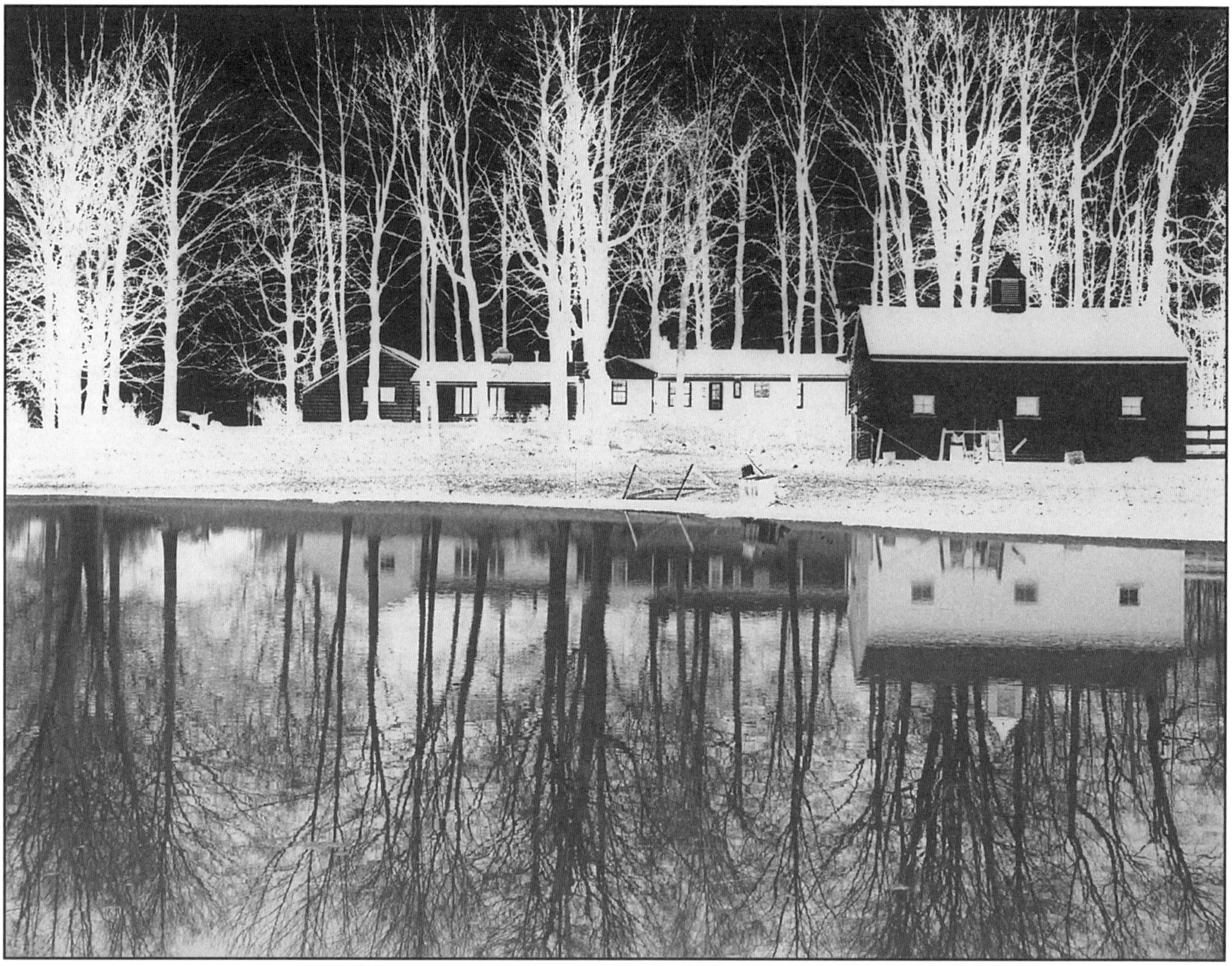

Both negative and positive images were cleverly juxtaposed in a single enlargement. The original negative was printed, and then a film positive was printed on the same sheet of paper. An opaque paper mask was cut carefully to parallel the shoreline. The same effect could have been achieved, but with less sharpness, by making a "paper negative" image from a positive paper print.

"Black-and-white photography has a potential for luminosity unequaled by any other medium. Its incomparable range allows me to contain both the material weight of reality and the ethereal weightlessness of light. I can create monochromatic images that appear to glow from within, radiating a strange and wonderful inner light."

— Sally Gall, imagemaker

Processing B&W Film 6

The Negative

Film exposed in a camera contains an invisible latent image made up of tiny silver particles that have been changed by light. These exposed silver particles suspended in the film's emulsion layer turn dark during development and form a visible negative image in which light and dark tones are opposite to what they were in the original scene.

Dark and light tones are reversed

Bright parts of the subject reflect more light onto the film, so those areas of the negative appear dark because they are filled with more opaque silver particles than the shadows. The darkest parts of the subject appear nearly transparent on the negative because very little silver has been deposited there.

Film is developed in an alkaline solution that chemically reduces the exposed light-sensitive halide salts to metallic silver, but the silver grains that were not used to form the negative image are still sensitive to light. An acid-hardening fixing bath dissolves the unexposed silver crystals, making the film safe to examine by ordinary light and more resistant to physical damage. After fixing, the amount of silver remaining in a given area of the negative determines its density or opacity.

Although not absolutely necessary, an acetic-acid stop bath or a water rinse often is used between developer and fixer to stop development quickly and evenly, and to make the fixer last longer.

Following the fixer, a bath in running water washes away chemicals remaining in the emulsion, so that the negatives do not become stained or faded.

Do it in the dark!

Most films must be handled in total darkness until after they have been through the developer and fixer. Processing may be carried out in ordinary room light if the film has first been loaded into a light-tight developing tank. The tank must be loaded in a completely dark room or changing bag.

Commercial labs process color film with automatic machinery, but you can develop color negatives and most slide films in exactly the same type of tank used for black-and-white. Different chemicals are required for color, and even more care must be taken with temperature, time and agitation.

Be careful; practice the process

Carelessness has no place in the darkroom. The only way to get consistently good negatives is to control accurately the temperature of the chemical solutions and the length of time the film is in each one. It's also very important to keep everything clean. Pictures can be ruined by chemical contamination or stains caused by hands and equipment that have not been washed and dried after being used.

Roll-film developing tanks are made from either stainless steel or plastic. The metal ones require more practice to learn to load, but they are more durable and require less chemicals per roll. Both types of tank are light-tight and have a hole in the cover through which solutions are poured in and out. Always follow the film manufacturer's instructions about development time and temperature unless you're quite sure of your reasons for doing otherwise.

"There is a painful lapse [of time] between the ... making of a photograph and looking at it. ... every photographer wants to rush right into the darkroom and see what he has done."

— Walker Evans, photographer

PREETI HANS

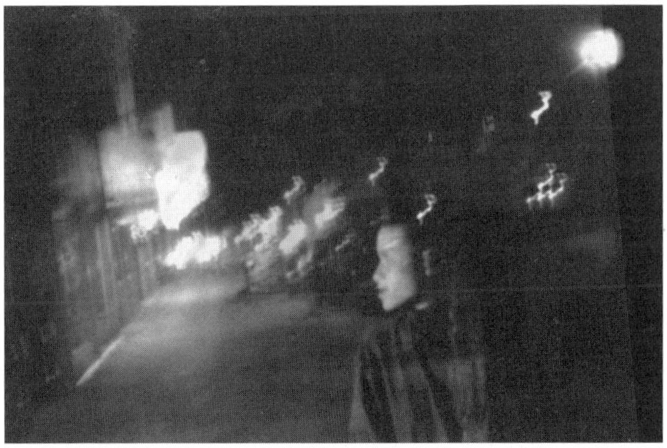

Can a tilted, unsharp image have more emotional impact than a sharp picture shot from a tripod? People often think the only way to shoot at night with a hand-held camera is to "push" the film to a higher exposure index. Pushing may not be necessary (see Chapter 9).

Ten Tips for Darkroom Safety

1. Be careful with chemicals!

Although few photographic chemicals are toxic in the concentrations generally used, the acetic acid in stop bath and fixer, and the bleach used in color processing could cause serious eye damage. Wear eye and hand protection when mixing solutions from powders and concentrates. Have copies of chemical safety data sheets available in case of emergency. If someone should drink photo chemicals, they should get medical help.

2. Never pour water into acid.

When preparing working solutions always start with water and add stock solution to make the amount needed. If any chemical gets splashed into your eye, flood the eye immediately with running water from a hose or eyewash, rinse it for several minutes, then go to a doctor.

3. Ventilate the darkroom.

Don't breathe chemical vapors in a closed room with inadequate air circulation.

4. Don't expose your skin unnecessarily to chemicals.

Learn to slide prints and sheet films into the tray without getting your fingers wet. Some people wear latex gloves or use print tongs to transfer prints and films between trays. Whenever your fingers touch chemicals, rinse in water and dry them immediately, especially if you're susceptible to skin allergies.

5. Keep your hands clean and dry.

Don't handle equipment or sensitized materials with wet or damp hands. To avoid constantly having to rinse and dry your hands while making prints, you may prefer to use print tongs or gloves. Some photographers like to keep one hand dry all the time for handling negatives, paper, and equipment, using the other hand for carrying prints through the solutions. Rinse your "wet" hand or tongs in water between processing steps.

6. Don't be sloppy.

Keep the dry side of the darkroom dry, and leave all chemicals on the wet side. Avoid dripping chemicals onto the darkroom floor or getting any chemicals on counter tops, squeegee boards, or equipment. If you do, your carelessness will become evident after the spilled solutions dry, leaving stains, corrosion, and airborne dust. If you want to take a print out of the fixer to inspect it, rinse the print in water and place it in an empty tray before carrying it around. Fixer is the greatest contaminator in photography. Always wash it off your hands before touching anything, even a towel. Don't let it splash around the darkroom.

7. Mop up spills.

Someone could be seriously injured from falling on a wet and slippery darkroom floor. So always clean up spills immediately, whether chemicals or merely water.

8. Dispose of chemicals properly.

Non-commercial amounts of photo chemicals do not pollute sewage disposal systems because the alkaline developer and acid stop bath and fixer tend to neutralize one another. But when you dump chemicals down the drain, rinse out the trays, tanks, and sink with plenty of running water. Not only does rinsing keep everything clean for the next user, but the water further dilutes discarded chemicals.

9. Beware of sharp instruments!

The safest kind of paper cutter for darkroom use is the rotary type with a covered blade. Never cut a wet print, because it may tear or jam the cutter. Be especially careful when using scissors in the dark.

10. Don't smoke.

You already know what this habit does to your own body and to the lungs of other people forced to breathe the same air. Darkrooms are very confined spaces, often without rapid ventilation. Ashes always make a mess, and an abandoned butt can burn down a building.

Safety is No Accident!

Getting Ready

It's easy to develop roll film, either black-and-white or color. The hardest part is getting the film loaded properly onto the metal or plastic reel that fits into the developing tank; but after a bit of practice, you'll feel confident of your skill. Try it several times with practice film. If you're using a stainless steel spiral reel, I recommend practicing at least100 times with your eyes closed! By then, your fingers will learn the touch they need to detect problems and you probably won't mess up your real film.

The following outline is presented to help guide you through the first few black-and-white rolls. Because each color process is somewhat different and the time and temperature requirements are more rigorous than black-and-white, it's important to follow the manufacturer's instructions exactly. You'll have few problems if you're careful and practice each step in the process several times until you feel fully acquainted with the procedure.

Have all chemicals and equipment ready

Items in **bold type** you'll need; others are optional:

- **Darkroom** with running water, or dark closet or changing bag and access to a sink
- **Developing tank with reel, cover and cap** (some tanks require a light-baffle tube)
- **Thermometer,** accurate photographic type
- **Timer**
- **Graduated beaker,** at least eight ounces (250 ml) for one 35mm roll in steel reel; 16 ounces (500 ml) for two
- (optional—recommended for color) Deep tray or dish pan for water bath, to keep solutions at the same temperature
- **Funnel**
- **Scissors**
- **Cassette opener** (for 35mm magazines)
- **Film clips** or spring-type clothes pins
- Drying cabinet or **clean place to hang film**
- **Towels,** clean and dry
- Lab apron (otherwise, wear old clothes)
- **Developer** stock solution
- (optional) stop-bath concentrate to conserve fixer
- **Fixer**
- (optional) washing agent to shorten washing time
- **Wetting-agent** concentrate
- (optional) sponge or squeegee (must be clean)
- **Filing/proofing pages** for negatives (transparent archival type)

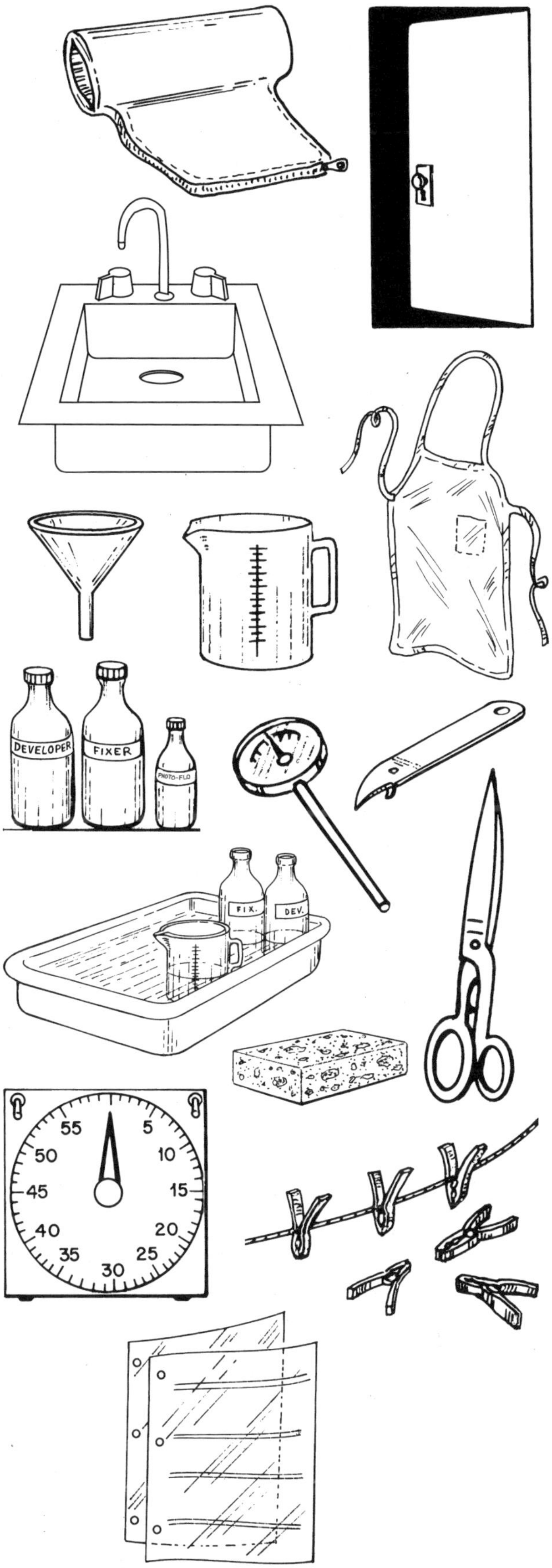

Now that everything is together, you're ready to start. Keep your wits about you, especially when working in the dark. That panicky feeling when you can't find the developing-tank cover in the dark is unlikely to occur if you practice ahead of time and lay everything out where you can find it by feel.

Control the water temperature

It is very important to maintain proper temperature. Turn on the tap water several minutes ahead of time and let it run into a beaker at a moderate rate until the temperature stabilizes. Adjust the hot and cold valves until the water is running at a steady 68°F (20°C). Keep the water running throughout the process if you can, but check it periodically because other demands on the water supply may cause the pressure and temperature to change. Use a thermometer that has been tested for accuracy; even one degree difference in the temperature of the developer can affect the quality of your negatives.

In hot weather, if your tap water won't cool to 68°F (20°C) you can work at up to 75°F (24°C) if you shorten the development time according to the film manufacturer's instructions (see table). Color reversal films may be processed at a much higher temperature, but all solutions should be kept within a degree or two of one another. The ideal temperature for developing most black-and-white film is 68°F (20°C) and even in hot weather you generally can maintain that temperature by circulating running water into a deep tray or plastic dish pan containing the tank and solution bottles. If your cold water isn't cold enough, you can immerse a plastic bag full of ice into the water as needed. But don't put ice directly into any of the solutions. If you can't keep solutions warm enough, try putting an electric immersion heater into the water that surrounds the chemical containers.

Preparing chemicals

For the same reason that you should stick with one type of film, I suggest that you start out with a standard developer and work with it unless you need to experiment with another formula. Although most developers are good for several rolls of film if used within a few weeks after mixing, and replenisher solutions are available to prolong their life, many photographers prefer to use fresh developer for each roll, discarding the solution after use. Developer will lose its strength if kept for more than a few months or if it is reused without adding replenisher.

For convenience and economy, and especially to reduce the possibility of contamination, I recommend that you try a basic "one-shot" developer, such as Kodak HC-110 or D-76, that you can afford to dilute for use and then throw away. For these developers, you mix a stock

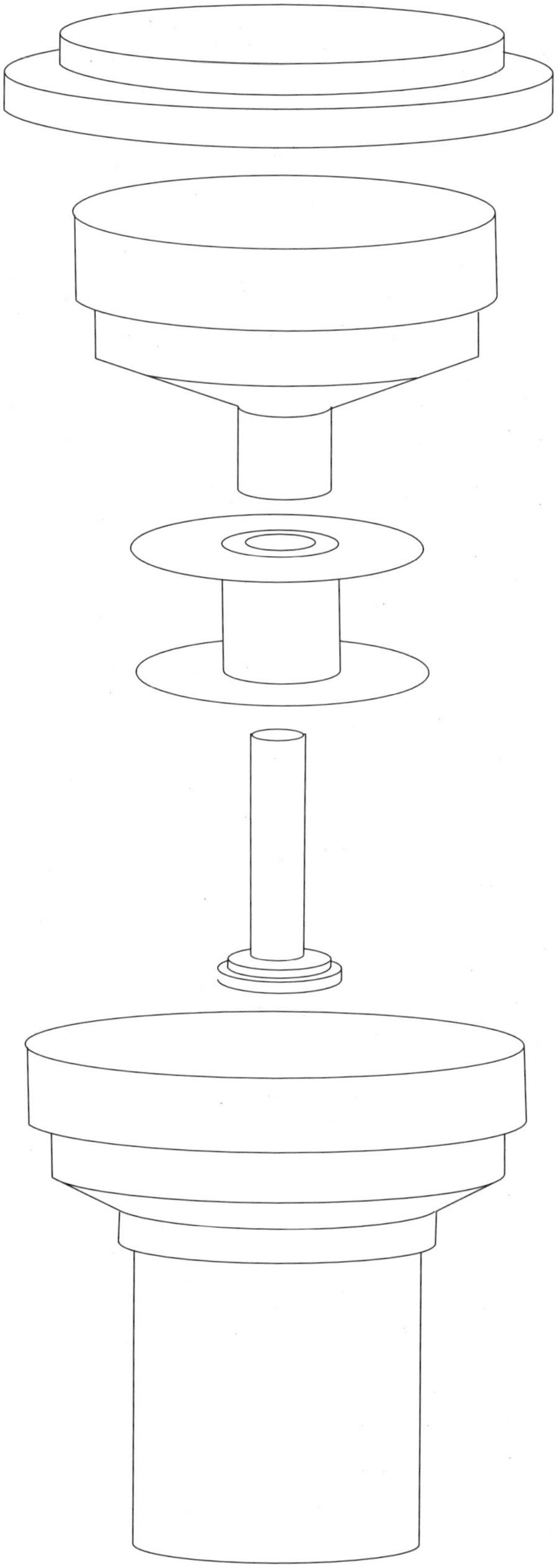

Plastic tanks and reels are popular with students because they don't require as much time and effort to learn to load. On the down side, they are breakable, usually require a light-baffle tube inside, and reels must be thoroughly dry before loading.

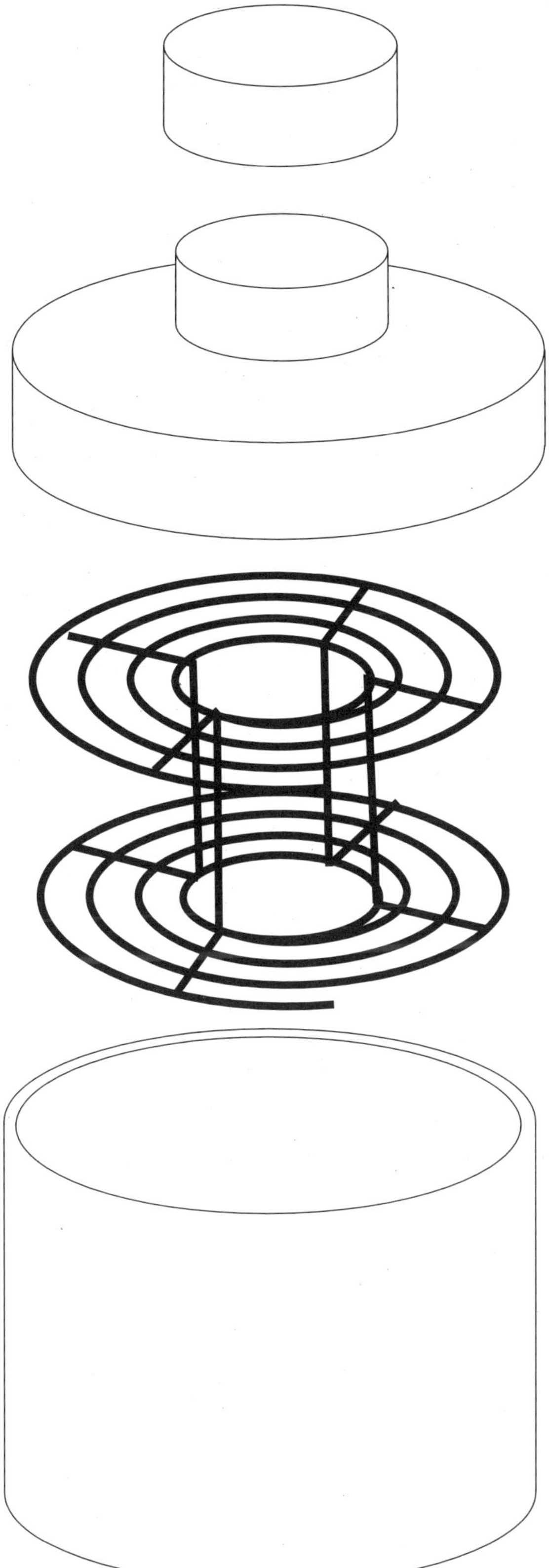

Most professionals and advanced amateurs use stainless-steel tanks with spiral wire reels. See the next page for how to load both steel and plastic reels. If you practice many times with either type before risking important film, soon your skill and confidence will rise

solution for storage from either concentrated liquid or powder. This stock solution usually is diluted still further with water immediately before use according to instructions on the film data sheet. For example, HC-110 stock solution usually is diluted 1:7 — that is, one ounce of stock solution is added to seven ounces of water to make eight ounces (250 ml) of working solution. Eight ounces is just enough to cover one 35mm reel in a stainless steel tank.Two rolls require 16 ounces (500 ml) etc. Plastic tanks may require 12 ounces (350 ml) per roll.A common dilution for D-76 is 1:1.

Mix the stock solution with 68°F 20°C) water and then put a thermometer into the beaker to verify the temperature.

Stop bath (if used) and fixer should be ready for use in beakers or bottles at about 68°F (20°C).

Typical Time-Temperature Development Chart

(Developing Time in Minutes)

Kodak T-Max 400 Film

Developer	65°F (18°C)	68°F (20°C)	70°F (21°C)	72°F (22°C)	75°F (24°C)
HC-110 (1:7)	6.5	**6**	5.5	5	4.5
D-76 (1:1)	14.5	**12.5**	11	10	9
D-76	9	**8**	7	6.5	5.5
T-MAX	NR	**7**	6.5	6.5	6

Kodak T-Max 100 Film

Developer	65°F (18°C)	68°F (20°C)	70°F (21°C)	72°F (22°C)	75°F (24°C)
HC-110 (1:7)	8	**7**	6.5	6	5
D-76 (1:1)	14.5	**12**	11	10	8.5
D-76	10.5	**9**	8	7	6
T-MAX	NR	**8**	7.5	7	6.5

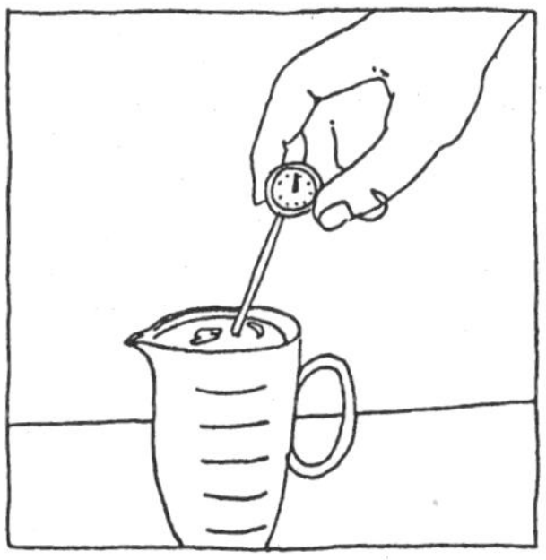

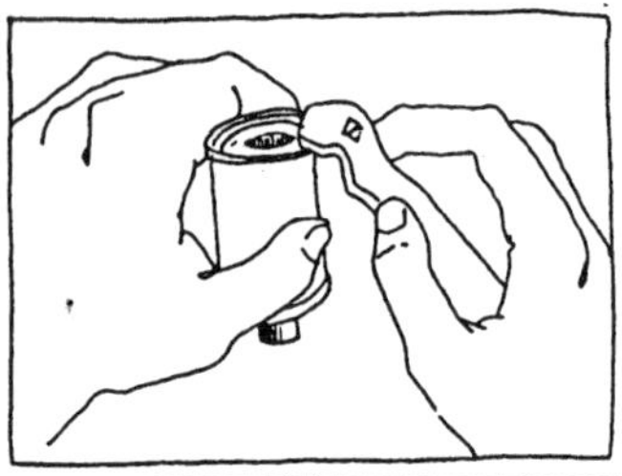

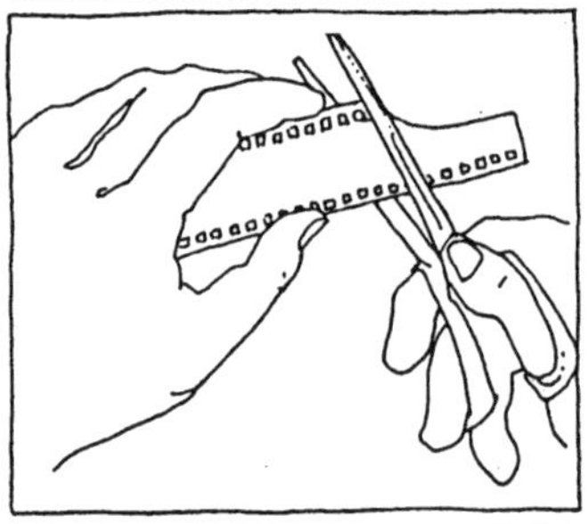

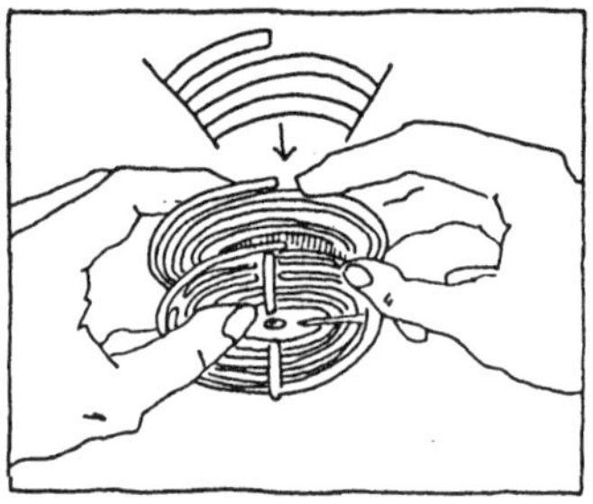

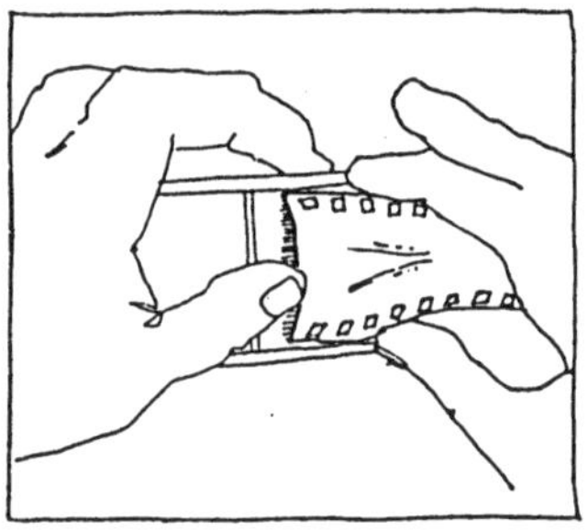

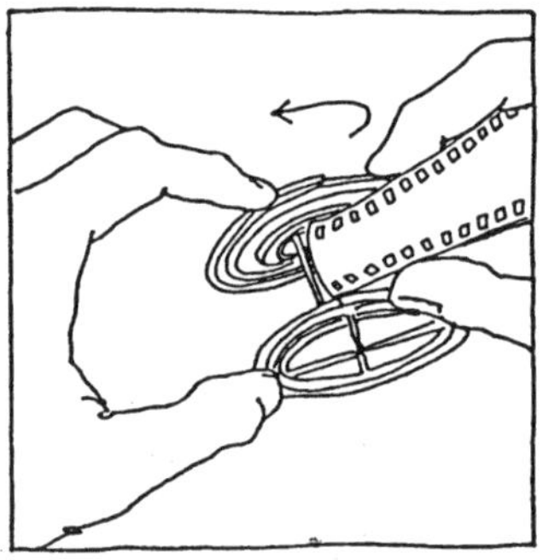

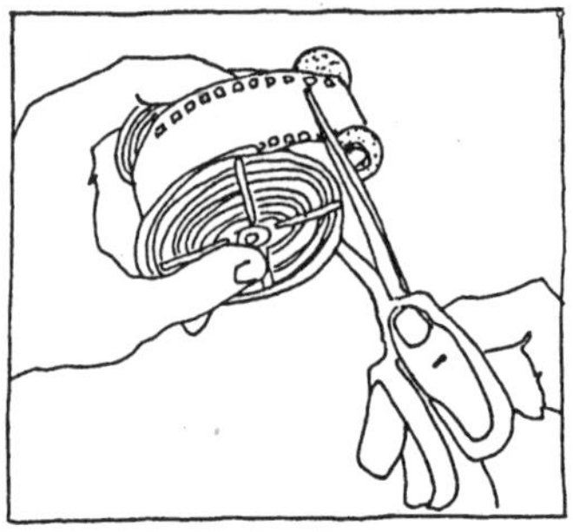

Developing 35mm Film Step-by-Step

1. (IN TOTAL DARKNESS)

Find the end of the spool that sticks out from the magazine and pry off the metal cap from the opposite end. Slide out the spool with the film wound around it. With scissors, carefully cut off the narrow part of the film leader. Try not to touch the flat surfaces of the film with your fingers.

2. (STILL IN TOTAL DARKNESS!)

Load the film onto the reel. Be sure the reel is completely dry and held correctly. The emulsion side (dullest appearing and lighter colored — although you won't be able to see this in the dark) should be facing the center of the reel. You can tell how it should go in the dark because roll film naturally curls toward the emulsion side. Feel for the open ends of the wires. The film must start from that side. Center the end of the film in the clip or slot at the hub of the reel; then rotate the reel, keeping the film curved slightly downward with your thumb and forefinger as it feeds onto the reel. You can feel it if the film buckles and misses a turn. When this happens, go back and rewind that section until it's going straight again. **The film must not touch itself anywhere, or undeveloped spots may result. Practice loading with a discarded film until you can do it smoothly 100 times in the dark.** If the film gets creased on the edges so it won't load, reverse it and start from the other end. Hold the film by the edges. Try not to touch the emulsion surface or scratch it with your fingernails.

Plastic reels are loaded from the *outside*, instead of from the hub. First, square off the end of the film with scissors between sprocket holes — it must be a smooth edge — then push the trimmed end under the outer flanges as far as it will go, then hold one half of the reel in each hand and rotate both sides back and forth until the film is drawn fully into the reel.

3. (STILL IN TOTAL DARKNESS!)

Put the loaded reel into the tank and put on the cover. Although the cover's cap can be removed to pour chemicals in and out, the main part of the cover must stay on until after fixing.

Alternative procedure: If your darkroom has running water, you can pour the developer into the tank first, then insert the loaded reel, put on the cover, and start the timer.

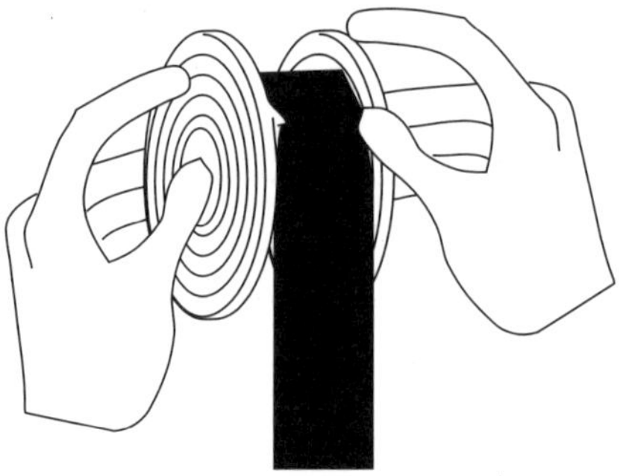

Plastic reels load from the outside, instead of from the center.

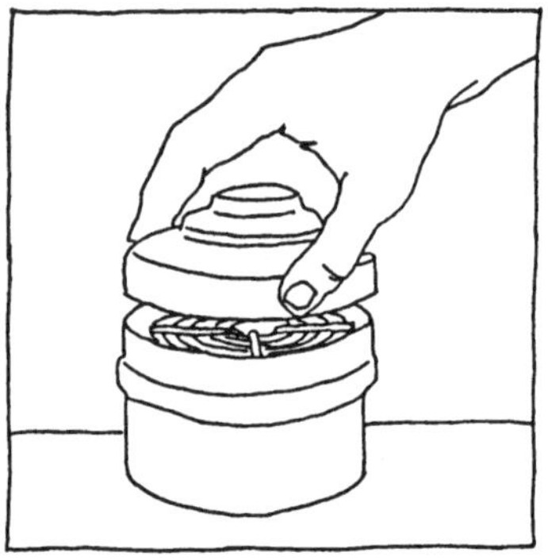

Now You Can Work in the Light!

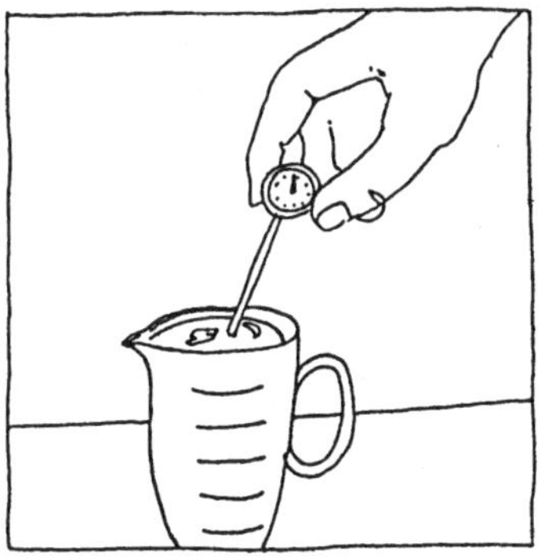

4. Recheck the developer temperature.

Set the timer according to the time-temperature chart.

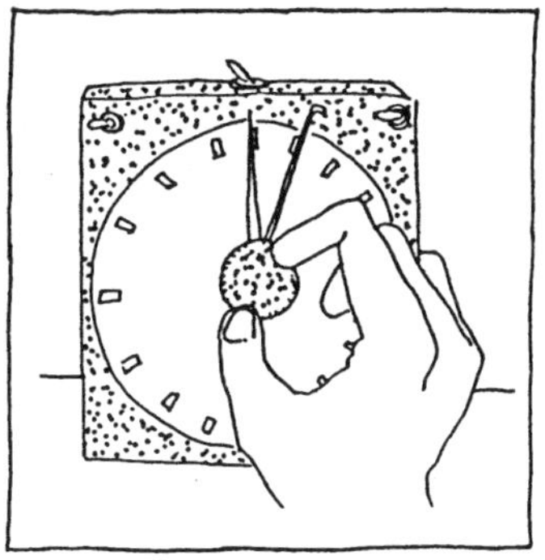

5. Start the timer.

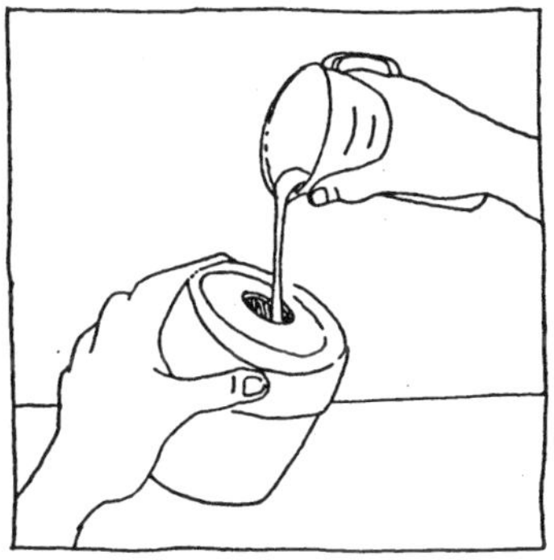

6. Pour in the developer.

Be sure there is enough developer to cover the reel(s). Hold the tank at an angle to let air escape, and fill it as quickly as you can.

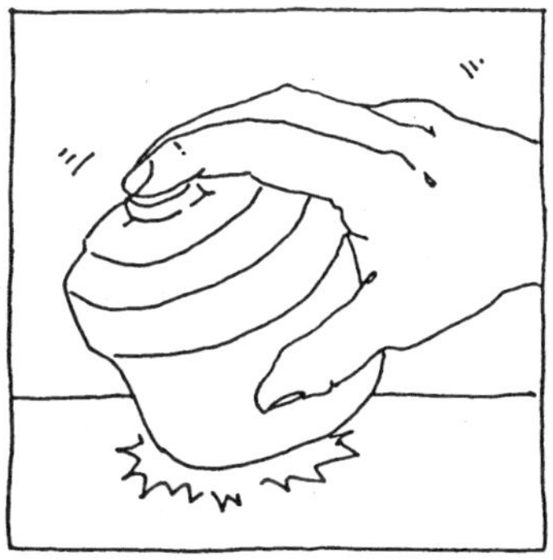

7. Put on the cap. Rap the tank.

Bang the tank three or four times on the bottom of the sink to dislodge any air bubbles, then immediately begin agitation.

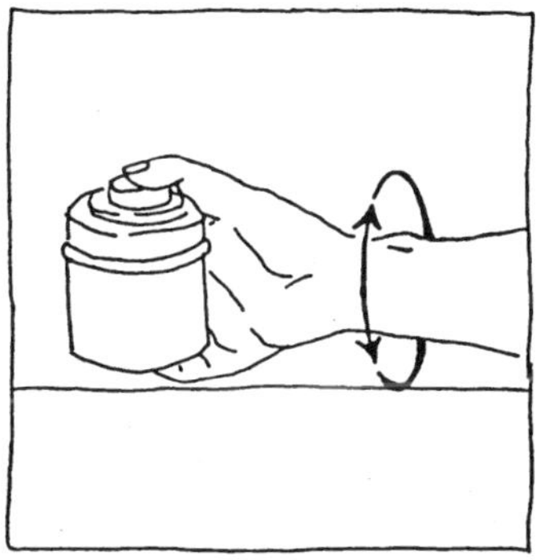

8. Agitate the tank.

Holding the cap on with your thumb or forefinger, turn the tank completely over with a gentle twisting motion five times in about five seconds. Be gentle — don't shake the tank. Repeat this five-second agitation procedure every 30 seconds. Rest the tank in the sink or in the water bath between agitation (if you hold it in your hand it will warm up). Some plastic tanks cannot be inverted, only rotated.

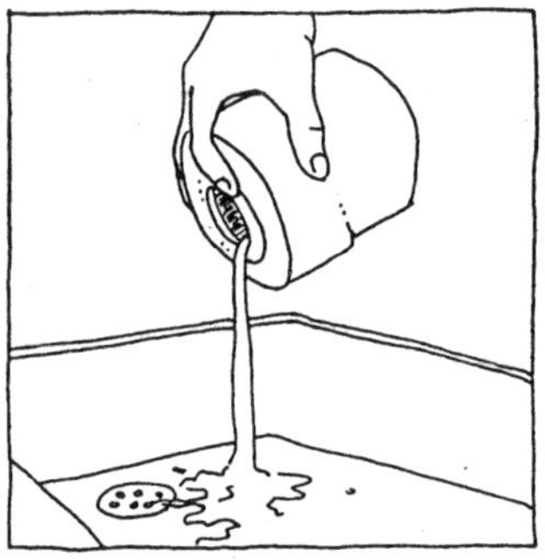

9. Remove the cap. Pour out the developer.

Take the cap off about 15 seconds before the developing time is completed. **DO NOT REMOVE THE WHOLE COVER!** Hold the tank so the cover can't come off, and quickly pour all the developer down the drain (unless your instructor tells you to save it).

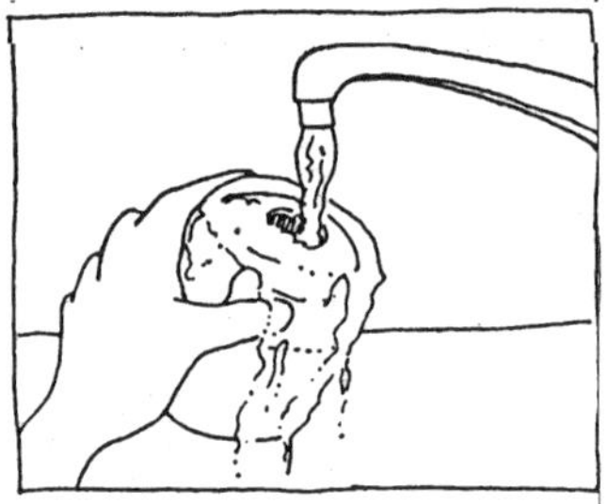

10. Fill the tank with running water.

The water should be the same temperature as the developer. (Option: use prepared stop bath). Put the cap back on and agitate the tank. If water is used, empty the tank and refill it again as quickly as you can.

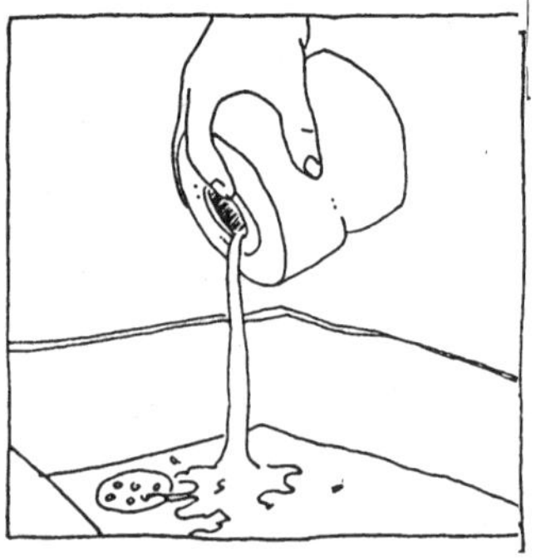

11. Empty the tank.

Drain it after about 30 seconds. **KEEP THE CAP OFF, BUT DO NOT REMOVE THE COVER.**

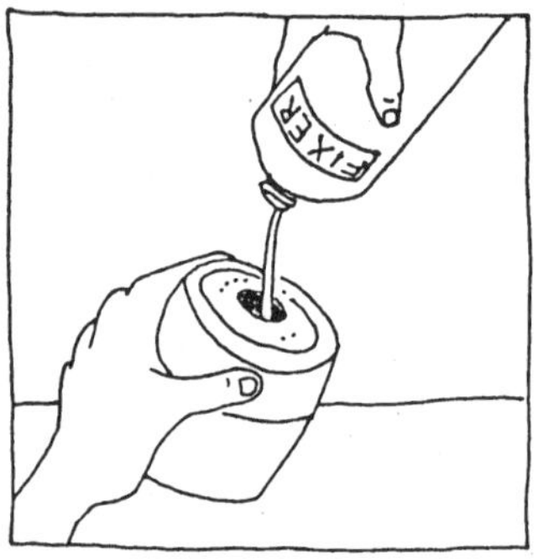

12. Pour in the fixer.

Be sure there is enough fixer to cover the reel(s). Set the timer for 10 minutes (or less if recommended).

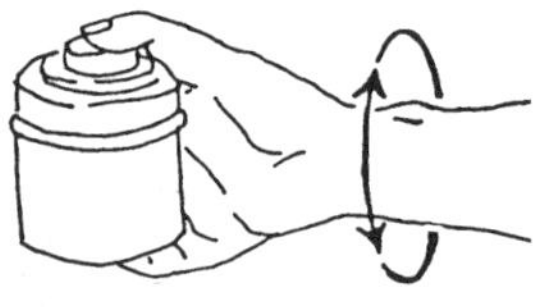

13. Replace the cap, and agitate the tank.

Use the same motion as during development. Exact timing intervals are not as important.

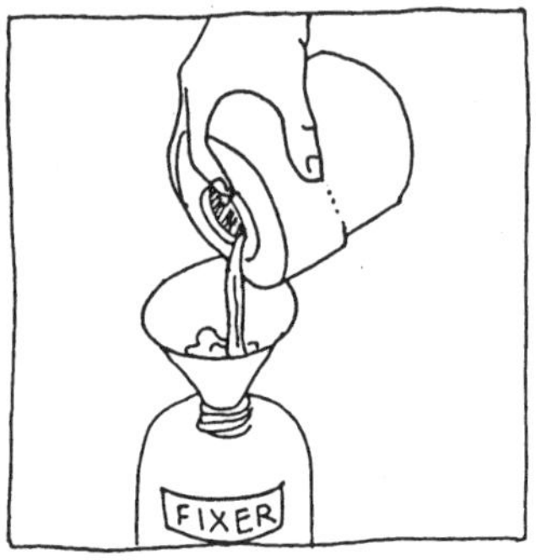

14. Pour the fixer back into its container.

BE SURE IT'S THE *RIGHT* CONTAINER! You can leave the tank cover off because the film is no longer sensitive to light. Fixer can be reused until it begins to take longer than five or six minutes for the milkiness to disappear, or more than 10 minutes for most of the magenta to leave T-Max film.

15. Inspect the film.

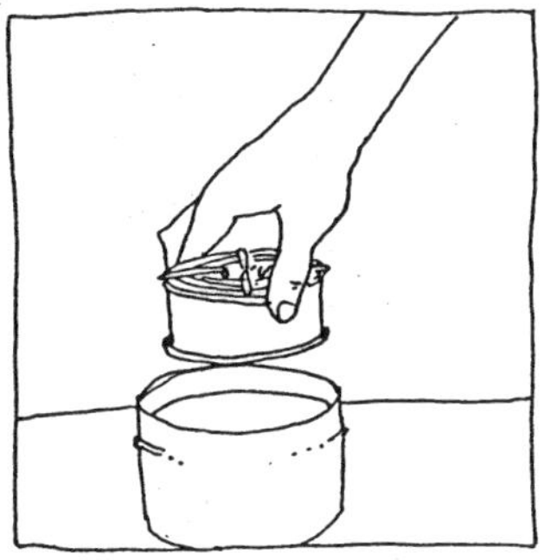

Remove the tank cover, rinse everything with water, then check the end of the film to see whether it is still cloudy-looking or magenta in color. If it is cloudy, or still strongly magenta after fixing time is up, put the film in fresh fixer until the color or cloudiness is gone or only a slight tint is left. Be careful not to drip or splash fixer around the darkroom — it dries to a messy white powder and contaminates everything. Rinse your hands and dry them before touching anything else.

16. Wash the film.

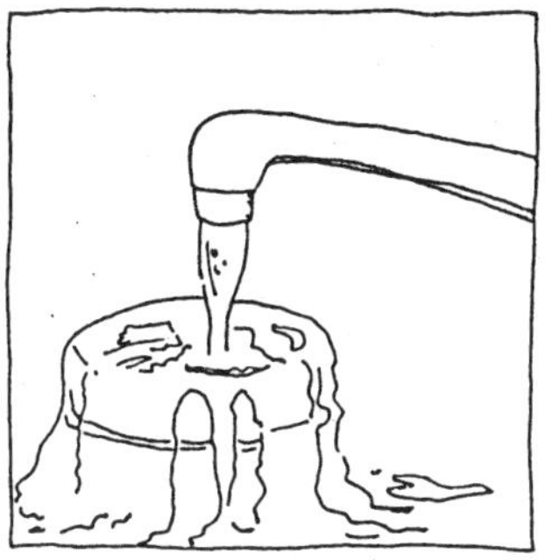

Leave the film on the reel and allow 68°F (20°C) water to run rapidly into the tank for 10 to 15 minutes. Empty the tank and refill it several times during washing. One or two minutes in an optional washing aid such as Kodak Hypo Clearing Agent or Orbit Bath can shorten washing time, save water, and ensure removal of all fixer (see manufacturer's instructions).

17. Add wetting agent.

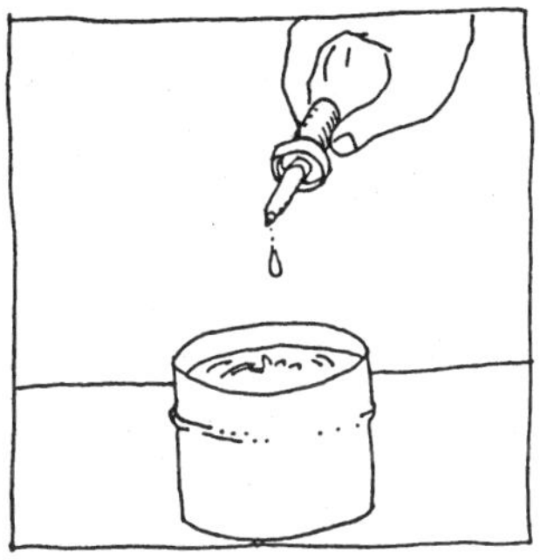

Turn off the water, leave the film in the tank, pour out water until the reel(s) are just covered, then add wetting agent such as Kodak Photo-Flo to the water. About one ml per roll will help prevent spots from forming on the film during drying, but too much wetting agent may cause oily streaks on the negatives. Agitate the reel gently, but don't make bubbles. Leave the film in the solution for about 30 seconds.

18. Hang the film to dry.

Attach a clip or clothespin to each end of the film and hang it in the most dust-free place available. Don't let anything touch the film while it is wet because it may get scratched, or pick up and hold dust and dirt.

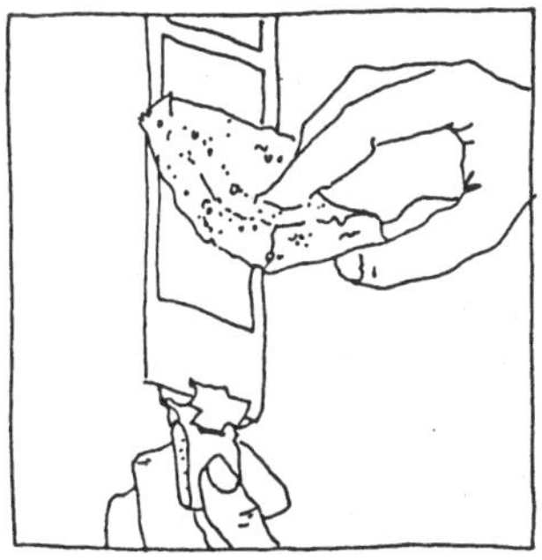

19. Wipe the film (optional).

Hard water or other contaminants may cause spots. These can be prevented by gently drawing a clean sponge (dampened with wetting agent, then squeezed almost dry) once down each side of the film. A clean squeegee may also be used.

20. Protect the negatives.

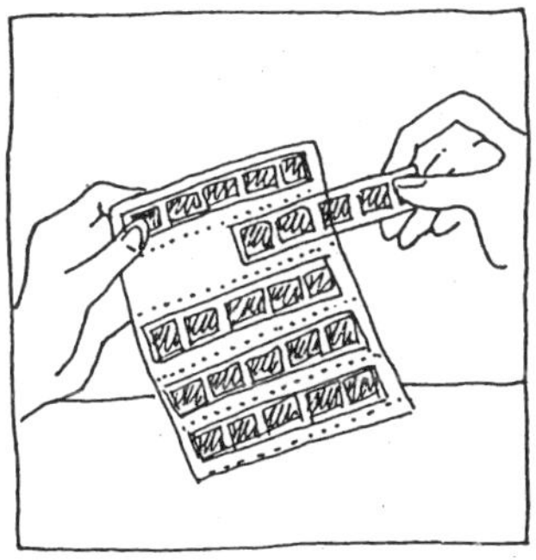

The film should be dry in one to two hours at average room temperature, or much sooner in a heated drying cabinet. As soon as the negatives are thoroughly dry, cut them into strips of five or six and slip them into archival transparent filing pages. Keep negatives in their pages to protect them from scratches, dust and fingerprints.

Processing Medium- and Large-Format Films

120 roll film is treated exactly like 35mm, except for opening the roll to load it onto the stainless-steel or plastic reel (see illustrations below). Sheet film follows the same processing steps, but it usually is handled in a very different way.

In the darkroom, sheet film must be loaded into special holders that take one sheet on each side. After exposure, each holder must be unloaded in the darkroom.

If a light-tight sheet-film tank is available, then the only difference will be in loading the tank and agitating it. When only a few sheets are to be processed, the tray method is convenient for controlling agitation and individualized development time. Some people are able to shuffle as many as a dozen sheets of film simultaneously in a tray — but the risk is great of scratching and gouging the soft emulsion of one sheet with a corner of another.

Stainless steel developing hangers in large tanks frequently are used by professional photographers, but with this method you have to agitate very gently by lifting the bunch of hangers and draining from alternate corners. Too vigorous agitation forces developer through the holes in the hangers, leaving streaks visible in the negatives and, subsequently, in the prints.

Sheet film (right) usually is processed either with hangers in open tanks, or in trays. Of course, with most films all steps through fixing must be carried out in total darkness, taking great care to avoid damaging the emulsion while it is wet and soft.

"Serious photography is always a craft and sometimes an art. ... I think ... using steel reels [is] one small measure by which professionals and serious amateurs are separated from ... hobbyists."

— Larry Thall, photographer and editor

To load 120 roll film, in the darkroom (below), break the paper seal with your thumbnail and separate the film from its backing paper. Let the paper hang down while the film rolls itself up in your hand. Handle the film by the edges only, except at the very end, when you have to tear off the tape. (If you tear the tape rapidly, you may see a flash of light — a harmless effect caused by static electricity). Loading the reels, either stainless steel or plastic, is similar to loading 35mm film.

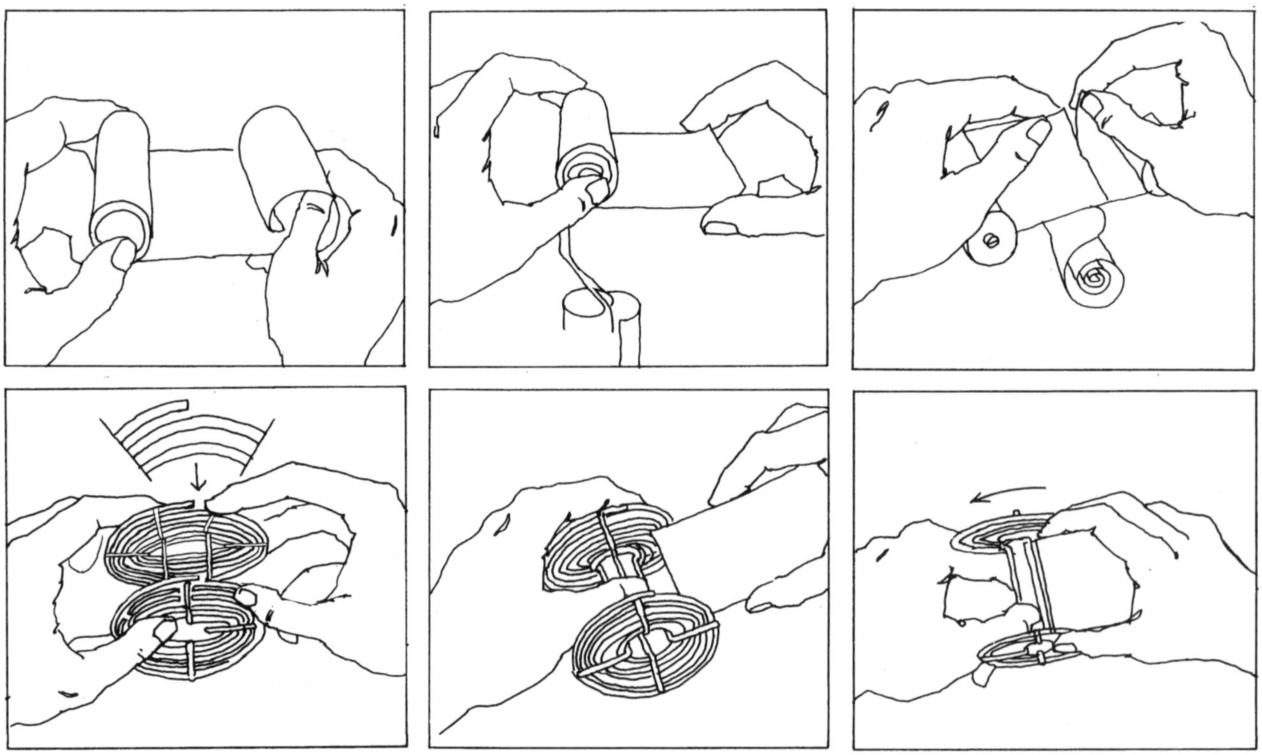

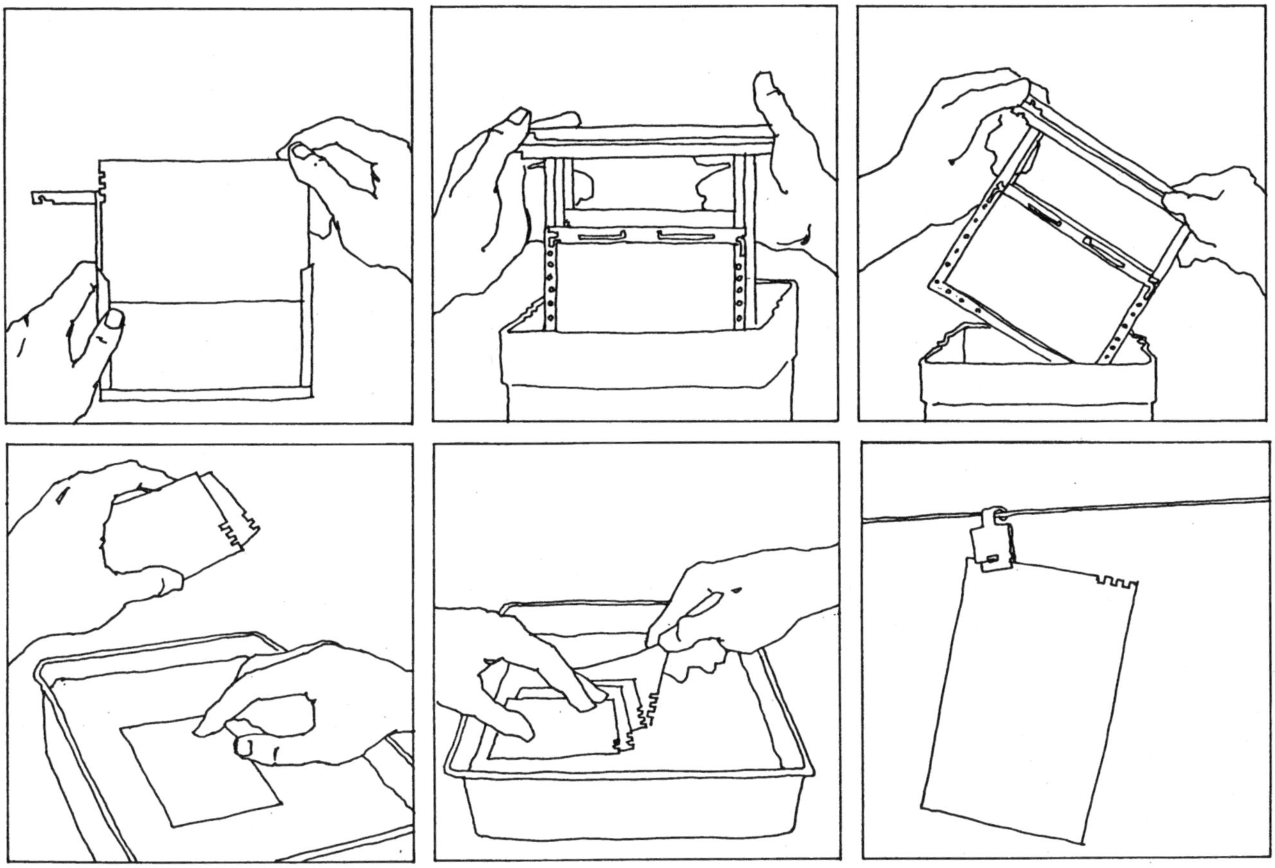

Some Hints for Better Film Processing

1. Use clean water for mixing chemicals.

City tap water usually is all right, but it should be filtered if it contains visible sediment. Well water often contains calcium, iron, and other impurities that can cause spots and streaks on negatives. Wiping the film when it's hung to dry will help eliminate these problems, as will mixing your final wetting-agent bath with distilled water. If water purity is a problem, you also might mix developer solutions with distilled water.

2. Mix developer gently.

Stir it according to directions and mix it at the proper temperature. Don't shake the bottle vigorously or stir the solution violently because oxygen in the air bubbles that are formed may partially reduce the strength of the solution.

3. Label all chemical containers clearly.

If you pour developer or fixer back into a storage bottle, be sure it's the right one. A solution should be thrown out if it becomes contaminated. Clean glass bottles and most plastic containers are safe for photographic solutions, but developer should be stored in a dark brown or opaque container to protect it from light. Never use a household bleach bottle for developer.

4. Don't touch the surface of the film.

Nor allow it to rub across a table top or along the bottom of a sink. The emulsion side is especially soft when wet, and it can easily be permanently scratched.

5. Wash everything every time, especially your hands.

Make a habit of rinsing utensils whenever they are emptied, and rinse your hands every time you get any kind of solution on them. If you always rinse your hands in water before touching the towel, the towel will stay clean and prevent contamination. Spilled chemicals may look like water when they're wet, but most of them leave a terrible mess when they dry. Sponge up any spills immediately, and rinse out and clean up everything when you're finished working. Avoid getting chemical stains on good clothing. But it you do get a stain, a product called *Stainout!* may make it less visible.

Controlling Contrast through Development

The old photographers' axiom that you should expose for the shadows and develop for the highlights was mentioned earlier. Half of the Zone System is based on placing readings of the lower values in the scene in the appropriate zones (I through IV) by adjusting exposure. Now, in developing the film, we have a chance to expand or compress placement of the higher values (Zones VI through IX) by increasing or decreasing the time of development. Obviously you can't vary the high-value density of each separate negative on a 35mm roll. The development control part of the Zone System is ideal for black-and-white sheet film, and for roll film when the entire roll has been exposed with special development in mind.

This process does not apply to color negatives or to color transparencies. Some speed "pushing" is possible with color films, but when you radically alter processing times you lose the ability to control color balance within normal tolerances. If you begin with an excellent color transparency or negative, you can achieve special color effects using computer software or duplicating techniques.

With black-and-white, as exposure is placed on the proper low zone by adjusting f/stops — one stop adjustment equals one zone — so development time can be adjusted by increments of one zone in the higher values. If "normal" development, as recommended by the film manufacturer and confirmed by your own tests, is represented by the letter N, then normal development plus one zone would be N+1; normal plus two zones would be N+2; normal minus one zone would be N-1, minus two zones would be N-2. Although further plus and minus extensions are possible with some films and with special developing techniques, two zones each way seems to be the practical limit for standard films and developers. The table below gives suggested development factors as a basis for trial. They represent a starting point for your own experiments with any combination of black-and-white film and developer.

Development Factors for Trial with Various Combinations of Films and Developers

	Multiply	Result
To *expand* gray scale (increase contrast)	N x 1.4 N x 1.8	N + 1 N + 2
To *compress* gray scale (decrease contrast)	N x 0.6 N x 0.4	N - 1 N - 2

"It's OK to experiment. Try anything you want. See what comes out!"

— David Posther, educator

Dennis Griffin

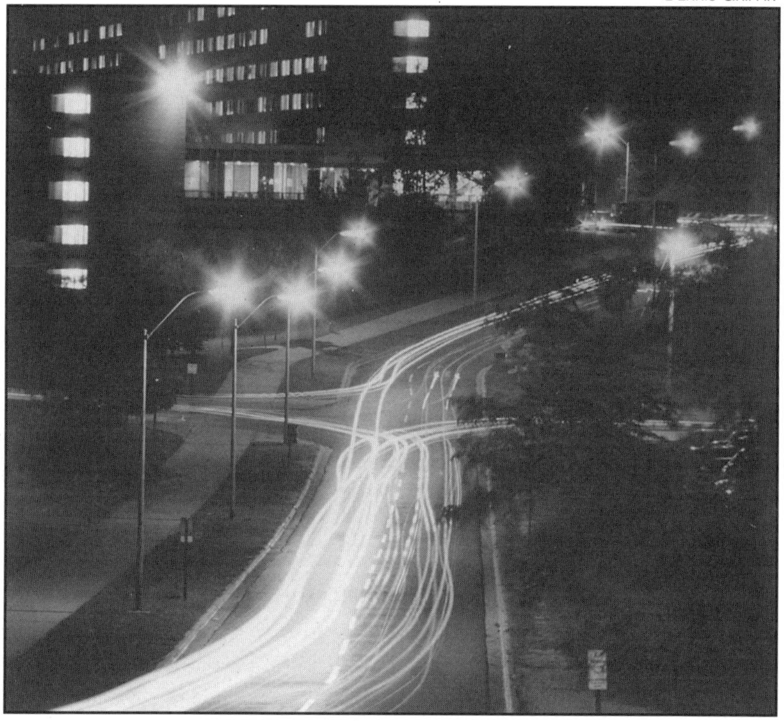

An exposure of five minutes at f/16 permitted the lights of moving cars to trace their patterns without being overexposed. Notice that the non-moving street lights have built up so much density on the negative that star patterns (halation) have been formed. N-2 development reduced the overall contrast.

Suggested Exposure Indexes (EI) and Developing Times for Kodak T-Max Roll Films in a Small Tank

Developer: HC-110 stock solution diluted 1:7 (Dilution "B") at 68°F (20°C).
Agitation five seconds every 30 seconds.

*If these short times produce uneven development, pre-soak the film in water at 68°F (20°C) for one minute before development.

	T-Max 100	EI	T-Max 400	EI
N + 2	13 min.	200	11 min.	800
N + 1	10 min.	125	8.5 min.	600
Normal (N)	**7 min.**	**100**	**6 min.**	**400**
N - 1	*4.2 min.	50	*3.6 min.	200
N - 2	*2.8 min.	25	*2.4 min.	100

BEATRICE RAY

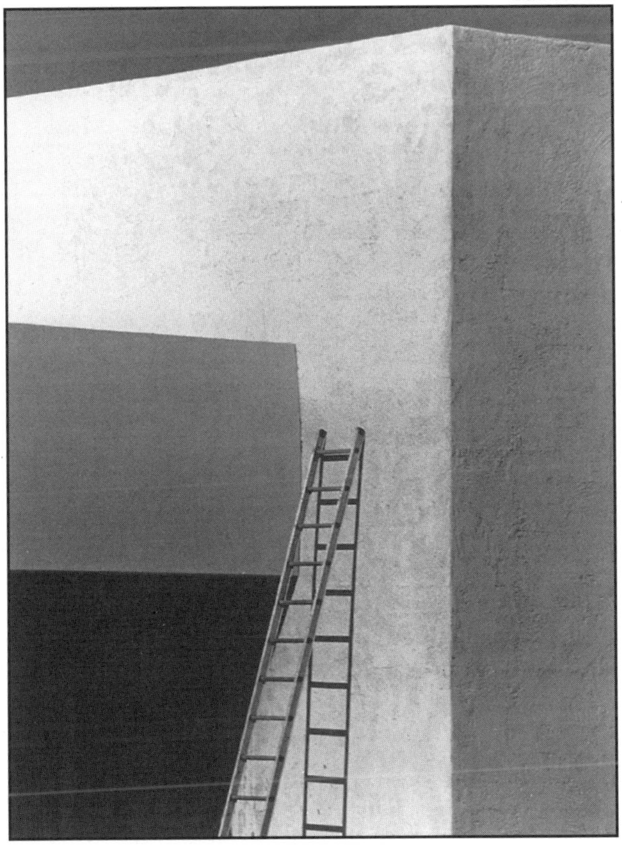

Applying the Zone System

One problem with the Zone System is that when you manipulate the developing time to expand or compress the contrast range of the negatives, you also change the effective speed of the film. If you don't compensate for this shift in speed when you intend to give N - (minus) development, your negatives may lack sufficient shadow density (you may not be able to separate Zones I, II, and III). On the other hand, giving N + (plus) development at the normal speed rating may result in unneeded density and excessive grain.

Exposing at a higher film speed and developing N + is not the same as "pushing" the film, which underexposes the shadows. See pages 166-167 for more about getting the maximum film speed possible under less-than-ideal lighting conditions.

The quality of your negatives can be affected by the accuracy of your camera shutter and exposure meter. If a densitometer is not available, you may not be able to make precise tests of effective film speed, but you can and should make practical tests.

To get started, you can use the effective film speeds and development times indicated in the table above. If you find that your experiments agree, fine! Otherwise, don't hesitate to work up your own table.

Evaluating Your Negatives

If you look at a group of negatives against the light, you'll probably notice that they differ in several ways. First, they will probably vary in overall density. Some may be nearly transparent all over because there was comparatively little silver deposited during exposure and development. Such a negative, low in density, transmitting a lot of light, is called a *thin* negative. Other negatives, appearing darker or denser because more silver was deposited, transmit less light and are called *dense.* A negative of very high density transmits very little light.

Besides differences in overall density, negatives vary in the relationship of dense and thin areas within each image. The brightest parts (high values) of each original scene appear most dense in the negative, and the shadows, or darkest areas (low values) of the subject appear thinner or more transparent.

The relative differences in density between the darkest and lightest important values within a single image is referred to as *contrast.* In a contrasty negative there is a great deal of difference in density between the high values (highlights) and the low values (shadows). In a flat negative, there may be very little density difference between high and low values. You must learn to judge the density and contrast of all kinds of negatives before you can expect to make good prints from them.

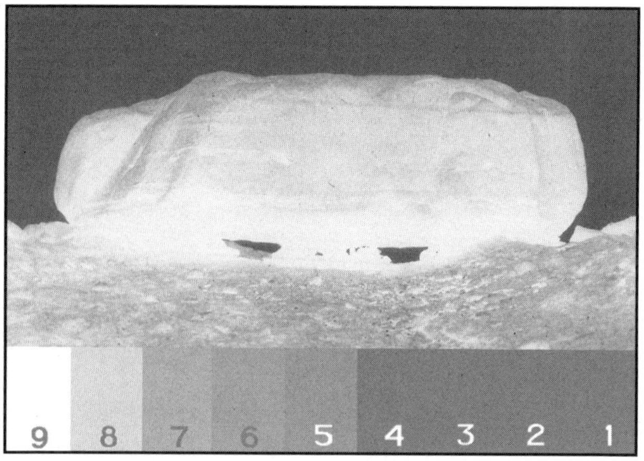

*A **thin** negative appears to be relatively transparent overall. Especially if the result of underexposure, the negative may not have enough density and detail in the shadow (clear) areas to properly separate the darker values in the print (Zones I through IV).*

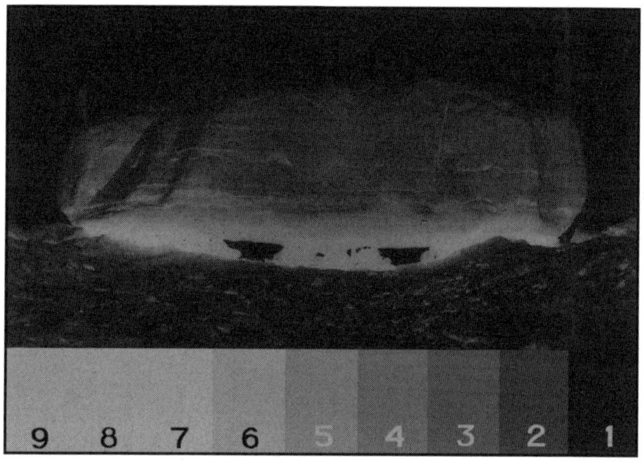

*A **dense** negative is relatively opaque. Although plenty of detail probably will be visible in the shadow areas, there may not be enough separation of bright areas to ensure visible differences between high values in the print (Zones VII through IX).*

The ideal negative

You can't make fine prints without properly exposed and developed negatives. A print can always be made again if it doesn't please you, but with negatives and color transparencies you have but a single chance. You have to do everything right the first time — or retake the photo.

Excellent prints will be made from negatives that are neither too thin nor too dense; neither too contrasty nor too flat; neither smudged, nor stained, nor scratched. Although you can burn and dodge and work minor miracles in the darkroom (see Chapter 7), the best prints will be made from "normal" negatives. You can be certain that most of your negatives will print well if you're always careful to set the camera for correct exposure, use fresh chemicals to process the film, and develop for the optimum time and at the proper temperature. Beginning with a good negative can save hours of darkroom effort.

Dense negatives usually are the result of overexposure. If an overexposed film is also overdeveloped — that is, developed too long or at too high a temperature or with too much agitation — the resulting negative may be so dense in the highlight areas that it cannot be printed. What happens is that Zones VII, VIII, and IX tend to merge, making it impossible to distinguish subtle differences between such high values as white clothing, pale flesh tones, and blonde hair. Such a negative is said to be *blocked up.*

There is a direct relationship between density and grain. Overexposure and overdevelopment combined can give skies and skin tones the texture of a concrete sidewalk. Unless you want this effect, don't let excessive grain occur as a result of negligence.

Thin, or extremely transparent, negatives may be caused by underexposure, underdevelopment, or both. Underdevelopment is the result of not leaving the film in the developer for long enough time, not agitating sufficiently, or using developer that is old and weak, contaminated with fixer or stop bath, or too cold. Thin negatives usually fail to record some of the lowest values

David Harrison (4)

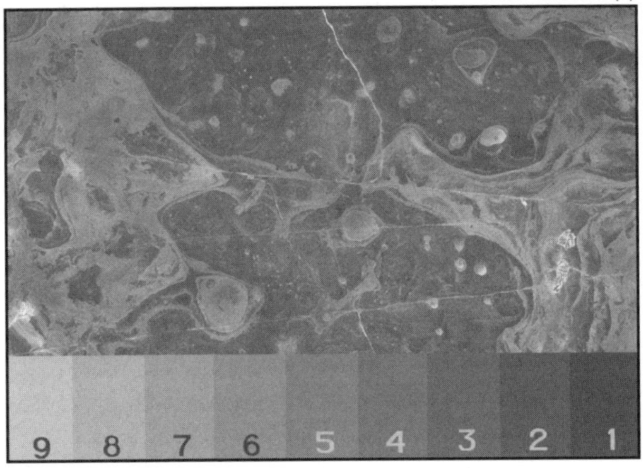

A ***flat*** *negative may not necessarily be thin, but it lacks contrast. The print will appear gray overall, and will require additional contrast to reproduce blacks and whites (see Chapter 7).*

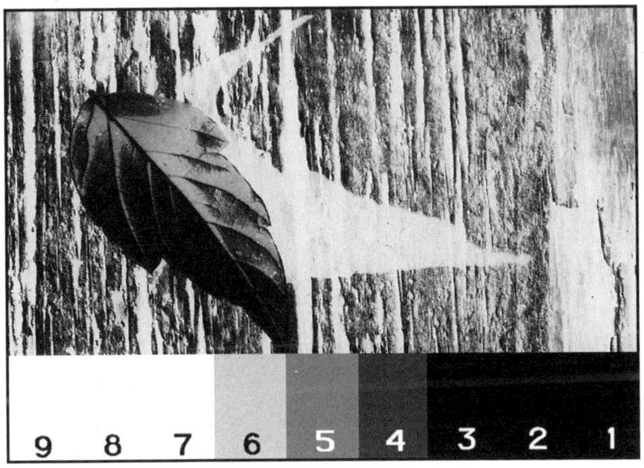

A ***contrasty*** *negative shows a wide range of densities. In the print, the shadows (Zones I through III) may merge together. The same problem may occur in the highlights (Zones VII through IX).*

(Zones I, II, and III), leaving clear film where there should have been shadow detail. These areas without density print either totally black or lifelessly gray. Very thin negatives also usually are flat or low in contrast.

Negative contrast depends mostly on the relative brightness values of important parts of the subject photographed. Contrast also is affected, and can be controlled to some degree, by development.

If your negatives always have too much contrast, you can shorten the normal developing time or try a different developer or dilution. Correctly exposed, but consistently flat negatives usually result from underdevelopment. Be sure that your agitation procedure is the same every time (over and back gently for five seconds every 30 seconds). Over-agitation increases contrast unevenly; under-agitation decreases contrast, leaving a mottled, uneven appearance.

Caitlin Lauchlin

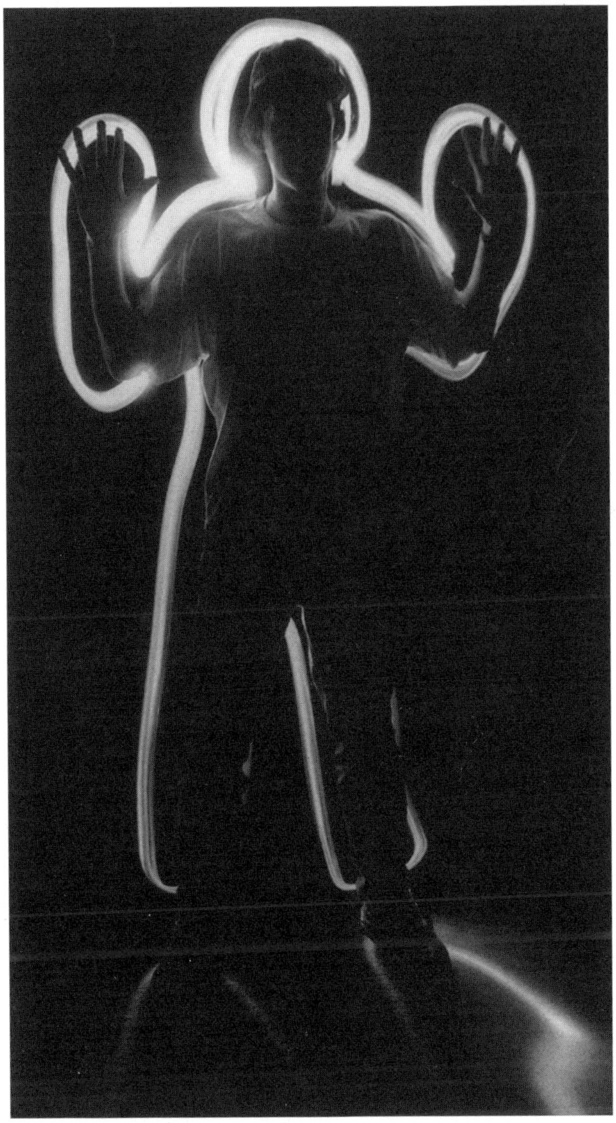

Print contrast is very important. Nearly every photograph looks best if there is a full range of tones (zones), even if some values are present only in small areas. In the original print of this low-key image, the whites are white and the blacks are black. With lower contrast it would have appeared flat and dull. To make this photo, Caitlin locked her camera's shutter open on "B", stood behind her friend and in a darkened room, "painted" her outline with a flashlight aimed toward the camera. She could have shown the model's face by firing a flash from the side or front during the exposure.

"How extraordinary the commonplace world can be."

— Robert Adams, photographer

Determining Exposure Index

Are your negatives consistently too thin or too dense? If you've been controlling everything — previsualizing zones, making accurate exposure meter readings, compensating the film speed for minus or plus development, developing in the proper solution at the recommended time, temperature and agitation — yet your negatives seem always to lack shadow detail (suggesting underexposure) or always are excessively dense (implying overexposure), you may need to determine your own "personal ISO" exposure index.

Although the manufacturer's ratings are scientifically determined and they usually are quite accurate, all kinds of problems may affect the way you should expose film in your camera. The shutter may be consistently fast or slow; the meter may read consistently high or low; or your film processing procedure may produce differences from the norm established in the film manufacturer's tests. Such errors occasionally fall in the same direction and the cumulative effect prevents optimum negative quality.

In black-and-white negatives, Zone I density should barely be distinguishable from the clear film (film-base density plus inherent fog) between frames and around the edges of the negative. By making the following test, you can determine which ISO meter setting yields the proper Zone I density. This will help you determine a modified exposure index for that particular film and processing combination that applies to your own equipment and method of working.

The film speed test involves photographing a standard 18-percent gray card at various exposures:

1. Place the gray card in even light.

The best site will be outdoors in deep shade or on an overcast day, otherwise the light will be too bright. Adjust the angle of the card so there is no glare.

2. Mount your camera on a tripod.

Focus the lens at infinity (you want the gray card to be out of focus — you're testing for negative density, not for detail). Move the camera close enough to fill the negative completely with the image of the gray card. Remember that your camera probably includes a little more than the viewfinder shows. Move in a little closer to allow for this. Be certain there are neither shadows nor glare on the gray card.

3. Read the gray card.

This reading will give you the exposure for Zone V. The camera (or hand-held reflected-light meter) must be close enough to the card so that you're not reading any background, but not so close that you read your own shadow.

4. Adjust the reading for Zone I.

Do this simply by stopping down (closing) the lens four f/stops. Count zones to yourself as you stop down. For example:

Meter reading (Zone V) 1/250 at f/4
Minus one stop (Zone IV) 1/250 at f/5.6
Minus two stops (Zone III) 1/250 at f/8
Minus three stops (Zone II) 1/250 at f/11
Minus four stops (Zone I) 1/250 at f/16

Of course, you can use any combination of shutter speed and lens opening that gives equivalent exposure, but avoid the fastest shutter settings (1/1,000 and 1/500) because they tend not to be as accurate as the other speeds. If you can't stop down far enough, place the gray card in a darker location and make a new Zone V reading.

5. Make a series of varied exposures.

The first exposure should be at the manufacturer's film-speed rating for Zone I placement (1/250 at f/16 in the preceding example); then repeat the test at 25 percent, 50 percent, 75 percent, 100 percent (a duplicate of your first exposure), 150 percent, and finally 200 percent of the film manufacturer's exposure index. For example, in testing a film rated ISO 400, you would set your exposure meter at ISO100, 200, 300, 400, 600 and 800. A test of ISO 100 film would include meter settings of ISO 25, 50, 80 100, 160 and 200. For each different ISO setting, calculate the exposure for Zone I and keep very careful records of the sequence of exposures. If you have some frames left over on the roll after finishing your tests, either repeat the tests or make pictures to finish up the roll. This is so the developer will have a normal amount of silver to work on and not skew the results of your tests.

6. Compare the negative densities.

After normal processing, read each of the test negatives with a densitometer. In most cases, the Zone I negative closest to a densitometer reading of 0.10 above film-base density will have been exposed at the correct exposure index for that type of film and your particular combination of camera, exposure meter, and processing procedure. For this test to have any meaning, however, you must keep very careful records. You also have to standardize your developing procedure.

A practical test

If a densitometer isn't available, you can make a simpler, practical test that will indicate your working exposure index. Photograph a subject containing a large, very dark area with detail that would fall into Zone II. Dark, textured tree bark would be a good subject, or rough black soil or stone. Shoot at the various ISO settings suggested for the densitometer test, deliberately placing the dark, textured surface on Zone II (three stops less than the Zone V meter reading). Again, keep very careful records. After the negatives are processed, examine them through a magnifier, selecting the least-dense negative that seems to contain printable detail in the Zone II area. The ISO setting used to expose that frame is your working exposure index for that film.

> ***"Do not be afraid of the practical and mundane aspects of the medium; they will strengthen your technique and discipline and give you a broader perspective of the world we live in."***
>
> — Ansel Adams, photographer

Negative Faults

If you see negatives that have noticeable overall-gray "fog" density extending beyond the picture area into the margins of the film, you can suspect that the film was unintentionally exposed to some light before or after exposure or during processing. Or it could have been outdated film, or film that has been x-rayed or stored at high temperature. Dark streaks on negatives mean that some light probably got to the film either when it was in the camera — opening up the camera back, or a light leak — or while the film was being loaded or unloaded in bright light. Color-transparency films, of course, show fog and light leaks not as gray or black but as white or yellow.

Don't be alarmed if you notice a slight bluish or purplish cast to your negatives. This is the effect of antihalation dyes and is normal on many kinds of film. A slight overall magenta tint is typical of Kodak T-Max films, but if the color is intense or uneven, the film should be refixed in fresh fixer and rewashed. An orange or brownish appearance is to be expected of color negatives, the coloration being caused by a contrast-masking layer built into the film during manufacture.

Mysterious blotches or "fireworks" effects on negatives may be the static-electricity fog that occurs in cold weather and low humidity when roll film is advanced or rewound too rapidly or the dark slide of a sheet-film holder is withdrawn or inserted too quickly.

Sometimes finger marks and scratches from careless handling of undeveloped film will show up as dark spots or lines on the finished negatives. Dark crescent-shaped marks result from pinching the film too tightly while loading the developing reel.

Processing problems like these usually are caused by carelessness. Most of the common negative problems that you are likely to encounter are described on pages 122-125. With care, most of them can be avoided.

> ***"The camera should be used for recording of life, for rendering the very substance and quintessence of the thing itself, whether it be polished steel or palpitating flesh."***
>
> — Edward Weston, photographer

David Harrison

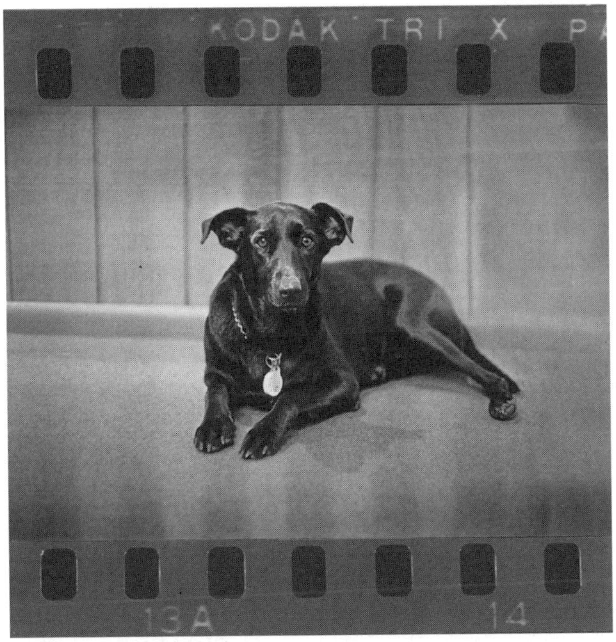

Careful and consistent agitation is very important. If agitation during film development is too vigorous or too frequent the negatives may be too contrasty and may show streaks like these. Insufficient agitation can result in flat negatives that are mottled and uneven in density. Agitation problems will show up especially in smooth middle tone areas such as skin tones and sky.

What's Wrong with My Negatives?

Images pale and light (negatives very thin and transparent), but frame numbers dark and legible. Shadow areas lack detail. (Color slides too dark.)

Cause: Underexposure.
Prevention or Correction: Print with magenta filtration. Reshoot if possible.

Images and frame numbers thin and weak.

Cause: Underdevelopment.
Prevention or Correction: Print with magenta filtration. Reshoot if possible. Mix fresh developer. Verify dilution, time, temperature and agitation. Chemically intensify negatives, or scan and improve in computer.

Images very dark, dense and grainy, but frame numbers appear normal. (Color slides too light and "washed out".)

Cause: Overexposure.
Prevention or Correction: Increase print exposure time, using filters if needed. Reshoot if possible.

Images very dense and contrasty, highlight areas opaque. Frame numbers extremely dense and fuzzy.

Cause: Overdevelopment
Prevention or Correction: Increase print exposure time, using yellow filtration. Reshoot if possible. Verify developer dilution, time, temperature and agitation. Chemically reduce negatives.

Negatives evenly gray (fogged) all over, including area between frames and around sprocket holes. (Color slide film may appear yellowish or greenish overall, even outside the image area.)

Cause: Film exposed to light, extreme heat, or radiation.
Prevention or Correction: Check darkroom and bulk film loader for light leaks. Be sure not to remove tank cover during development. Store film away from heat. Protect from x-rays.

Image area gray-fogged, but area outside and between frames is clear. (Color slides may appear washed out or yellowish, while area outside image is opaque.)

Cause: Light leak in camera — probably shutter, lens mount, or bellows.
Prevention or Correction: Refer to camera-repair technician.

Film fogged with dark streaks or blotches. (On color slide film, the streaks are clear or yellow.)

Cause: Light leak
Prevention: Load camera in shade. Keep film holders, magazines and rolls from bright light. Check reusable magazines and film holders for light leaks. If same fog pattern appears on more than one roll, consult a camera-repair technician.

Film overall fogged very densely over a few frames; rest of roll normal.

Cause: Camera back opened before rewinding film.
Prevention: THINK!

Strong overall magenta cast to entire roll or sheet of T-Max film.

Cause: Insufficient fixing.
Prevention or Correction: Return to fresh fixer until color clears. Rewash.

Milky translucency to all or portions of film.

Cause: Insufficient fixing.
Prevention or correction: Return to fresh fixer until milkiness clears, plus a few minutes more. Rewash.

Purplish-gray, opaque areas within image area of otherwise normal roll. (Or odd-shaped clear areas if film was taken off the reel before fixing.)

Cause: Film stuck together during processing.
Prevention or Correction: Next time load reel more carefully.

Purplish-gray, opaque areas along edges of film, but outside image area.

Cause: Film stuck to flanges of reel during processing.
Prevention or Correction: This is normal. Ignore it.

Clear, or less dense, round spots; may have dark edges.

Cause: Air bubbles clinging to emulsion during development.
Prevention or Correction: Pour developer quickly into tank. Immediately rap tank three or four times. When putting reels or hangers into filled tank, rap reels or hangers against the tank.

Tiny clear pinhole or irregular spots.

Cause: Dust, lint, or film fragments on emulsion during exposure, or too-strong an acid stop bath.
Prevention or Correction: Blow and brush inside camera and film holders before loading. Dilute stop bath or use water rinse.

Dense streaks in even areas of image such as skies, especially near sprocket holes in 35mm film.

Cause: Excessive or too-vigorous agitation.
Prevention or Correction: Agitate gently and consistently.

Mottled or uneven density or streaking from densest areas.

Cause: Insufficient agitation.
Prevention or Correction: Agitate gently and consistently.

Light (underdeveloped) stripe across the length of all negatives on the roll.

Cause: Not enough developer in the tank.
Prevention or Correction: Measure carefully the amount of developer needed for each roll.

Slimy or crystalline scum on negatives.

Cause: Insufficient washing.
Prevention or Correction: Use washing agent; rewash; use fresh wetting agent.

Rounded spots or streaks dried on surface of film (usually on base side).

Cause: Deposits left by impurities in wash water or wetting agent.
Prevention or Correction: Remove spots gently with cotton swab moistened with photographic film cleaner or lens cleaner. Mix wetting agent with distilled water. Wipe wet film with clean sponge or squeegee before drying.

"Dirt" particles embedded in emulsion.

Cause: Impurities in wash water or wetting agent. Wet film has touched a dirty surface.
Prevention or Correction: Soak film in washing agent and rewash. Bathe film in distilled water/wetting agent solution. Wipe film gently with clean, moist sponge or squeegee. Filter water supply if problem persists. **NEVER LET ANYTHING TOUCH WET FILM!**

Emulsion blistered, frilled, or reticulated.

Cause: Extreme changes in temperature during processing.
Prevention: Monitor temperature, especially during rinse or wash to avoid surges of hot water.

Dark, crescent-shaped marks.

Cause: Film bent or crimped during loading of reel.
Prevention: Handle film carefully.

Lightning-like lines or blotches.

Cause: Static electricity
Prevention: In the camera, when the weather is very cold and dry, avoid very rapid film advancing and rewinding. In the darkroom, separate roll film slowly from its backing paper; unload sheet-film holders slowly. Avoid static.

Corners of image less dense than center (or corners rounded off).

Cause: Lens not covering film size; lens shade or filter cutting into field of view (especially with a wide-angle lens). This problem is referred to as vignetting.
Prevention: Use proper lens and attachments.

Thin, dark lines parallel with edges of film. May start and stop or may go entire length of roll.

Cause: Scratching before development.
Prevention: Check camera back, film magazines, and bulk loader for burrs or embedded particles of sand or grit. Never cinch film (pull it tightly into a roll).

Light scratch lines.

Cause: Cinching roll, rubbing strips of negatives together, or other rough handling after processing.
Prevention: Cut roll-film negatives into short strips. File all negatives in individual archival sleeves or pages. Keep them there.

Excessive curling or brittleness.

Cause: Too-rapid drying.
Prevention: Rewash and redry. Air dry with minimum heat.

Hazy, diffused, indistinct images.

Cause: Lens or filter may be severely smudged or very dirty.
Prevention: Inspect and clean with lens-cleaning fluid and lens tissue.

Entire image blurred equally.

Cause: Camera movement during exposure.
Prevention: Hold camera steadier. Use tripod whenever possible.

Moving subject blurred (when you don't want it that way).

Cause: Shutter speed too slow
Prevention: Use faster shutter speed; pan camera to follow subject movement.

One plane of subject in sharp focus, remainder out of focus.

Cause: Too-large lens opening or lens focused incorrectly.
Prevention: Focus on principal plane of subject. Stop down lens for desired depth of field.

Corners of image unsharp, especially at wide apertures.

Cause: Poor-quality camera lens; or supplementary close-up lens or extender used at too-wide aperture.
Prevention: Use smallest lens opening possible (e.g., f/16 or f/22).

One side of image or irregular area consistently unsharp.

Cause: Lens or film pressure plate out of alignment.
Prevention: Refer to camera-repair technician.

Multiple or overlapped images.

Cause: Accidental double-exposure; camera loaded incorrectly, or film transport malfunction.
Prevention: Check shooting and loading procedure. If problem persists, refer to camera-repair technician.

Space varies between frames.

Cause: Film transport malfunction.
Prevention: Either live with it, or replace camera or have it repaired.

Part of image normal; part totally unexposed or underexposed.

Cause: With flash: improper synchronization — shutter probably set at too high a speed (the edge between light and dark will be sharp and straight). Without flash: Something in front of lens, such as camera case or strap, coat collar, part of hand, etc. in front of lens.
Prevention: Most 35mm cameras synchronize flash at 1/60 or 1/125 second — see owner's manual. Be careful how you hold the camera.

Film completely blank (clear) except for frame numbers and edge printing. (Color slide film opaque with legible frame numbers.)

Cause: Film not exposed. Camera probably not loaded correctly or dark slide not withdrawn from film holder.
Prevention: Load film carefully. Be sure sprocket holes are engaged in 35mm camera. Don't forget dark slide when using sheet film.

Film completely blank (clear) with no frame numbers or edge printing visible.

Cause: Film probably "developed" accidentally in water or fixer.
Prevention: Check procedures. Label all solution containers.

Film completely opaque with no evidence of image. (Color slide film transparent.)

Cause: Film totally exposed to light or strong radiation before development.
Prevention: Be careful!

Film heavily fogged, but with traces of image. (Color slide film may appear yellowish or greenish.)

Cause: Film exposed to light or radiation before or during development.
Prevention: Be careful!

An evocative image such as this requires a full range of tones to reproduce subtle form and texture. Everything must be correct: lighting, exposure, film processing, and printing.

JEN MROZOWSKI

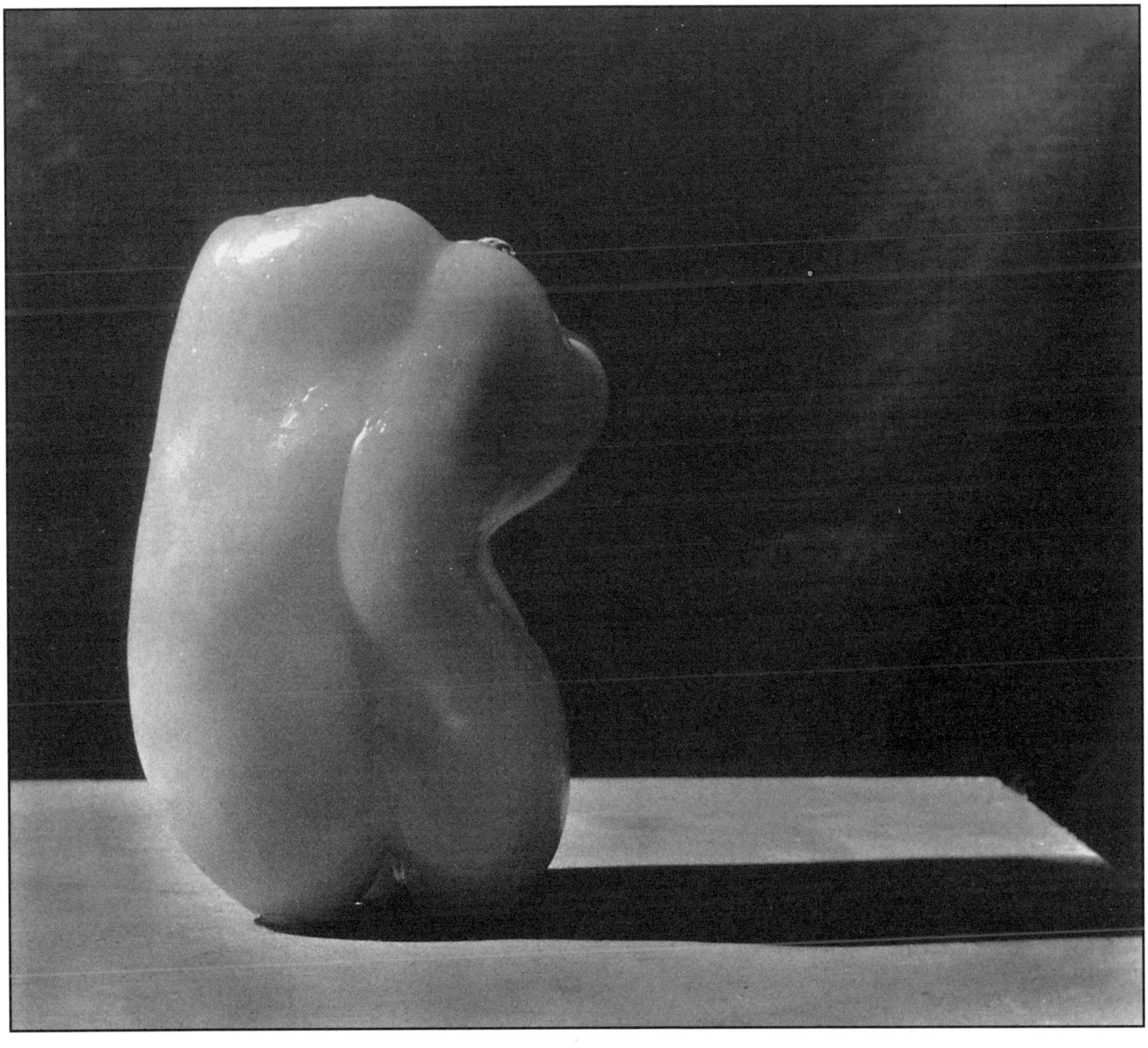

"What motivates me to take pictures? ... It's my chance to seize the moment and create something that is just as revealing, and insightful as anyone else could or would produce. I'm not saying that I can do it better. I'm just saying that I believe I can do it and create images that are mine."

— David Gremp, imagemaker

CAITLIN LAUCHLIN

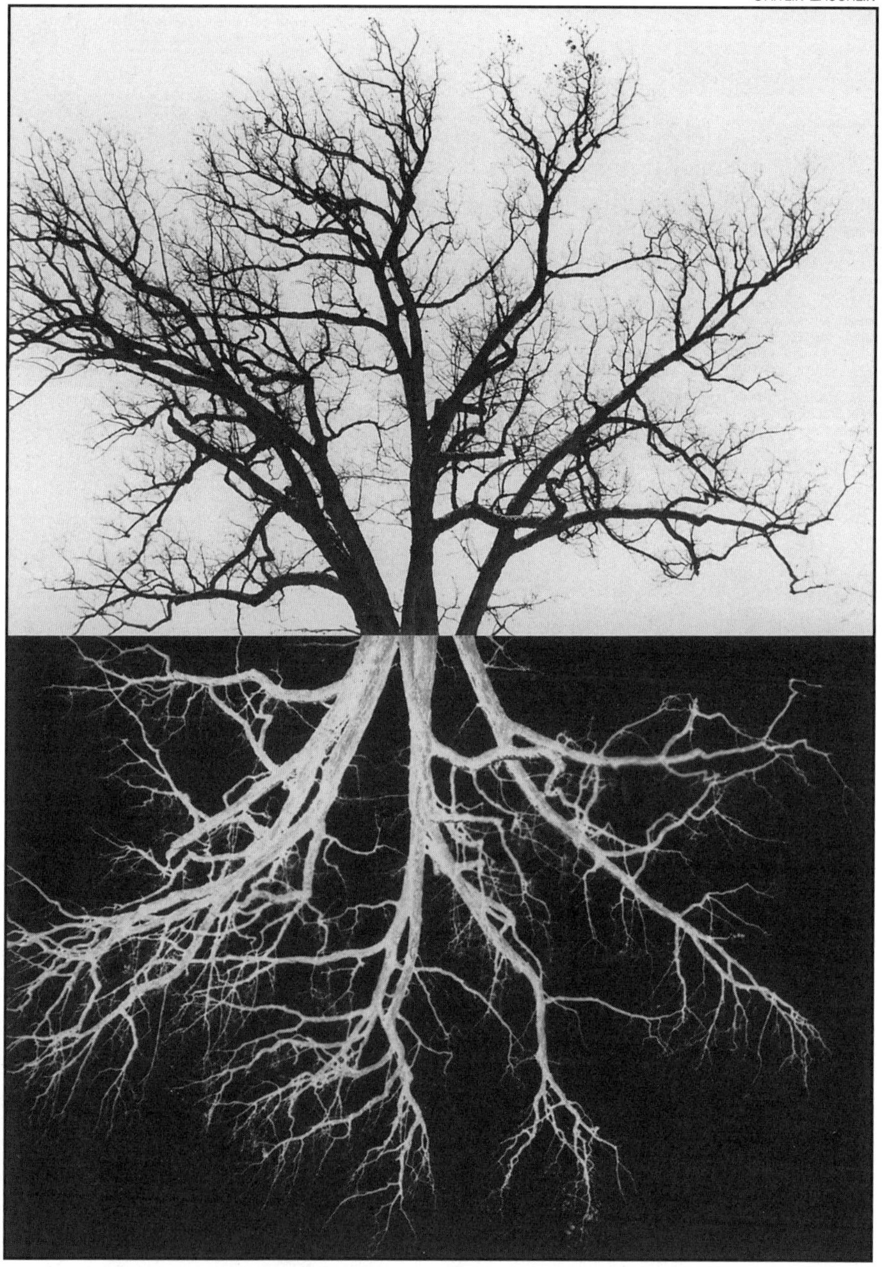

A positive print and a negative print were trimmed and mounted together to create this expression of line, texture and contrast. In this image, what is the importance of negative space?

Making Quality B&W Prints 7

"The negative is comparable to the composer's score: the print to its performance."

— Ansel Adams, photographer

"Combine the optimum moment with the ambiance of a fine print, and perhaps a successful photograph is achieved."

— Ansel Adams, photographer

The Print as a Performance

The print you make is the final revelation of what you saw, thought and felt when you were in the presence of the subject matter. Ansel Adams was a talented musician, and a photographer whose awe-inspiring landscape prints are among the finest ever made. Adams' musical training influenced his photographic work and his performance analogy (above) tells us that, in the darkroom, creative interpretation can improve your message.

It's at this final stage that you bring to bear everything you know about communication and about technique to make the print speak for you as eloquently as possible.

Aesthetically, printing is alchemy: chemicals are converted magically into images. Technically, however, a print is made by exposing light-sensitive paper to light passing through a negative. A corresponding positive image is formed on the paper, the image appearing upon development. To make the image permanent, the print must then be fixed, washed and dried.

"I have been asked many times, "What is a great photograph?" I can answer best by showing a great photograph, not by talking or writing about one."

— Ansel Adams, photographer

Photographers who work with view cameras, as Ansel Adams frequently did, produce very large negatives that can be printed by contact. A contact print is the same size as the negative and is made by sandwiching the negative between a sheet of photographic paper and a sheet of glass. The great photographic artist Edward Weston worked in this way, most of his work being contact printed from 8 x 10-inch negatives. The contact-printing technique is very convenient for proofing roll-film negatives, but smaller format negatives usually must be enlarged for final viewing or reproduction.

When is bigger, better?

Besides the spectacular effect of making big pictures from little negatives, the enlarging process allows many controls with which you can improve on a somewhat less-than-perfect negative. With these controls you can lighten or darken areas, alter the scale of values, modify perspective, soften or strengthen lines, combine images, or print only a selected portion of a single image.

Although color printing from both color negatives and transparencies is becoming much simpler and less costly — hence much more popular — the process of producing fine black-and-white prints for exhibition and reproduction will be emphasized here. If you master the equipment and controls required to make quality black-and-white prints, you certainly will be able to follow the manufacturer's instructions for whatever color printing process you may choose later to attempt.

Grow into digital

Digital imaging is the newest option. Shown in Chapter 11 are several examples of conventional darkroom techniques and how similar effects can be achieved with a computer and digital printer. But learn the printing procedures in this chapter first. Traditional optical/chemical processes will still be around for a long time, because they provide the foundation for the art and science of imaging. Learn to make excellent conventional prints and your digital images not only will be better, but much easier to make because you will have learned to use the tools around which the software has been designed.

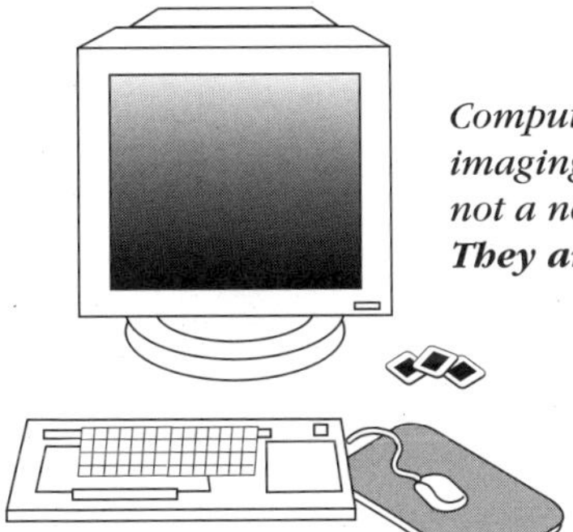

Computers and digital imaging software are not a new medium. ***They are new tools.***

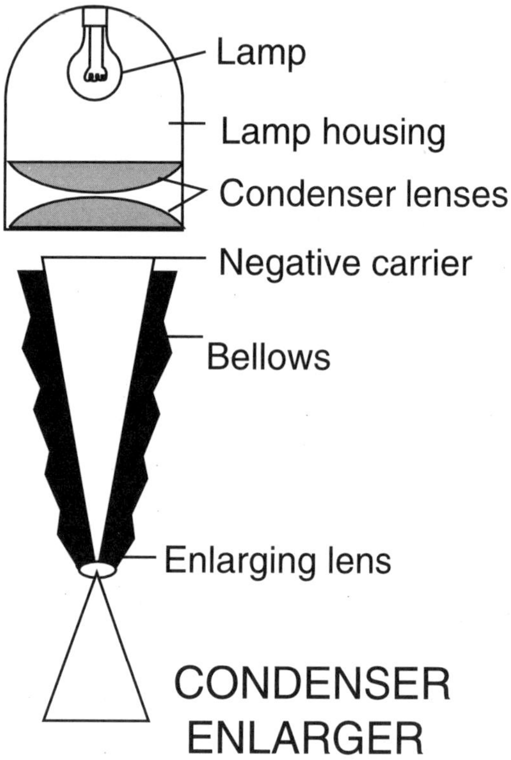

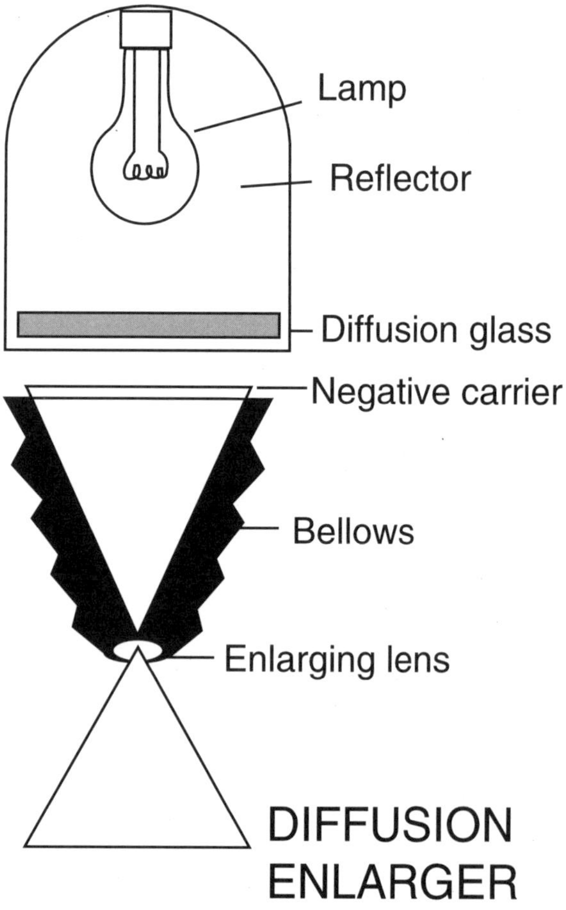

The Enlarger

The two most common types of enlargers are referred to either as *condenser* or *diffusion,* depending on how the light is passed through the negative. Some enlargers combine both types of illumination, having a relatively large, diffused light source plus one or two condensing lenses above the negative to concentrate the light. A "cold light" fluorescent head is a diffusion source.

In comparing enlargers, we find that the condenser enlarger will yield prints of comparatively higher contrast than those made with a diffusion enlarger; but the condensing lenses have an unfortunate tendency to emphasize all the defects in the negative, such as grain, scratches, and dust. Some people claim that condenser enlargers yield sharper images, but the appearance of sharpness is only the effect of higher relative contrast. Assuming a sharp negative, the actual sharpness of the print depends on the quality of the enlarging lens, how flat the negative is held in the carrier, and how accurately it is focused. Sharpness has little to do with the type of illumination.

Filters control contrast

Variable contrast or color printing filters are placed either in a holder beneath the lens or in a slot above the negative.

Separate filters aren't necessary with enlargers that have built-in dichroic filters. These enlargers generally are of the diffusion type and are very convenient to use because you can dial in the exact amount of magenta or yellow filtration needed to print on variable-contrast black-and-white papers as well as color materials.

Match lens to negative size

Most enlargers are designed to accept more than one negative size. You must use a negative carrier (film holder) of the right size, a lens of the appropriate focal length, and you may need to change either the condenser lenses or their position to match the negative size to be printed.

If either condensers or the enlarging lens fail to "cover" the negative, the edges of the enlargement will receive less exposure than the center. The result can be light corners and a "hot spot" in the middle. The normal focal length for 35mm negatives is 50mm; for 6 x 6cm, 75 to 80mm; and for 4 x 5-inch negatives it should be at least 135mm.

The Darkroom

On the dry side, you'll need:

- Enlarger
- Set of filters, and holder if required
- Electronic timer
- Adjustable easel
- Contact-proofing easel
- Focusing magnifier
- Anti-static brush
- (optional) Canned compressed air (environmentally safe type only!)
- Dodging and burning tools
- Negatives in file pages
- Enlarging paper (8 x 10 variable-contrast RC recommended)
- Paper trimmer (rotary blade for safety)

On the wet side:

- Four 8 x 10 trays (one may be larger, for washing)
- Safelight(s) (Type OC yellowish orange or sodium vapor)
- Timer or clock with sweep second hand
- Graduated container (one quart or liter)
- Thermometer (dial-type preferred)
- (optional) Print tongs or latex gloves
- Towels
- (optional) Lab apron — or wear old clothes
- Print-developer stock solution
- Stop-bath concentrate
- Fixer concentrate
- (optional) Washing-agent concentrate (needed only for fiber-base paper)
- (optional) Print washer or tray siphon (needed for fiber-base paper)
- Squeegee board and squeegee
- (optional) Print dryer or screen frames

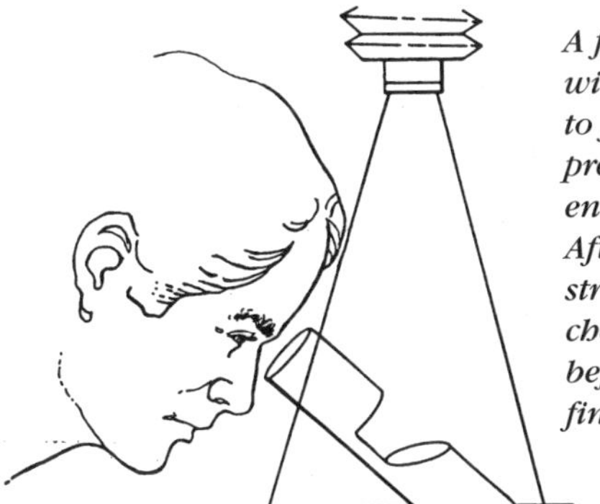

A focusing magnifier will make it easier to focus the image precisely on the enlarging easel. After making test strips, always re-check the focus before making the final print.

Choosing paper

Because there are so many brands, types, and surfaces, your choice of enlarging paper will be influenced by availability and personal preference. A good beginning choice is 8 x 10 variable-contrast RC (resin coated) paper.

RC papers are available either with a smooth glossy surface or with a smooth or lightly textured matte (dull) or semi-matte finish. Examine the package carefully or ask advice before buying, because the coding can be confusing. For example, Kodak labels their Polycontrast RC glossy paper "F," their smooth matte "N," and a lightly textured semi-matte surface "E." Ilford Multigrade RC papers come either in *"Deluxe"* for tray processing or *"Rapid"* for processing either in trays or in a roller-transport machine. Ilford surfaces include *glossy,* similar to Kodak's "F," *matte,* and *pearl,* which is a unique, lustrous semi-matte.

Another reason to read the label carefully is that Polycontrast and Multigrade papers are available with fiber base as well as resin-coated. Both RC and fiber papers also are available from several manufacturers with many names, contrast grades, weights and surfaces. Papers labeled with contrast grades one through five cannot be used with variable-contrast filters. The paper in a given package will yield prints only of that contrast level.

Although many fine art photographers prefer graded, premium fiber-base paper for museum quality exhibition prints, RC paper has many advantages for everyday work.

Using RC paper

Prints made on RC paper require much shorter washing and drying time. They usually dry with a smooth finish and lie perfectly flat for filing and mounting. The biggest disadvantage of RC paper is that if it is allowed to soak too long, water or chemicals may creep into the paper that is sealed between plastic layers, separating the edges and possibly affecting the permanence of the print. The most practical procedure is to batch-process your prints. Fixing requires less than one minute. Shuffle the prints to keep them from sticking together. Prints can accumulate for a few minutes in a fresh-water holding tray. Each batch then should be washed for two to three minutes, either in a rapid-flow archival washer or in a tray that is filled with running water from a hose and dumped and refilled frequently. If you are using the tray method, shuffle the stack of prints a few times to keep them from sticking together. These prints should be placed immediately into a hot-air dryer, or squeegeed and laid out on screen frames. Then you can return to the darkroom to expose and process the next batch.

Defeating dust

In the printing darkroom, dust is the biggest enemy. If your darkroom is air-conditioned or ventilated so that filtered, temperature- and humidity-controlled air is blown into the room at slightly higher pressure than outside, you'll have much less trouble with dust. In any event, good housekeeping is an absolute must. Vacuum away the dust regularly, but do this *after* a printing session rather than immediately before. This gives the dust a chance to settle elsewhere than on your negatives. You'll probably notice the worst dust problems during dry weather when the air is heated and the humidity is low. Dried chemicals produce dust, so don't splash chemicals around. Mop up any spills immediately, because chemical dust can leave horrible spots on sensitized materials. For this reason, it's best either to purchase concentrated liquid chemicals or to mix solutions from powders *outside* the darkroom.

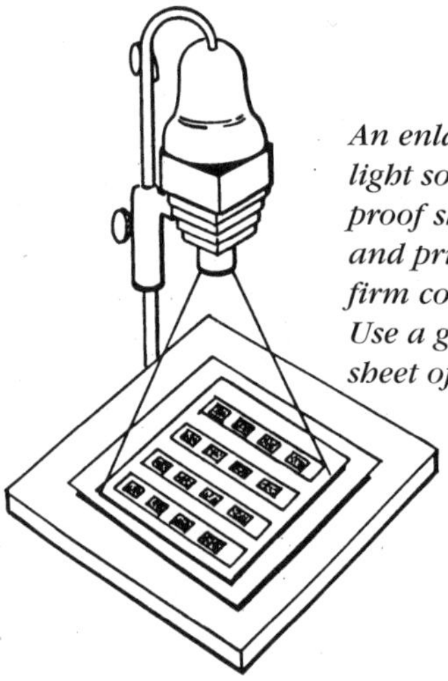

An enlarger makes a convenient light source for exposing a contact proof sheet. Be sure that negatives and printing paper are held in firm contact emulsion-to-emulsion. Use a glass proofing easel or a sheet of heavy plate glass.

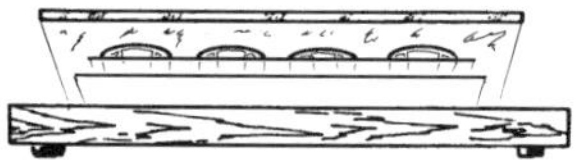

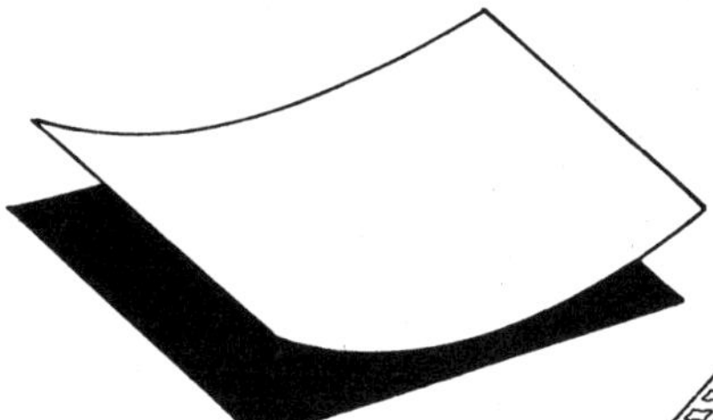

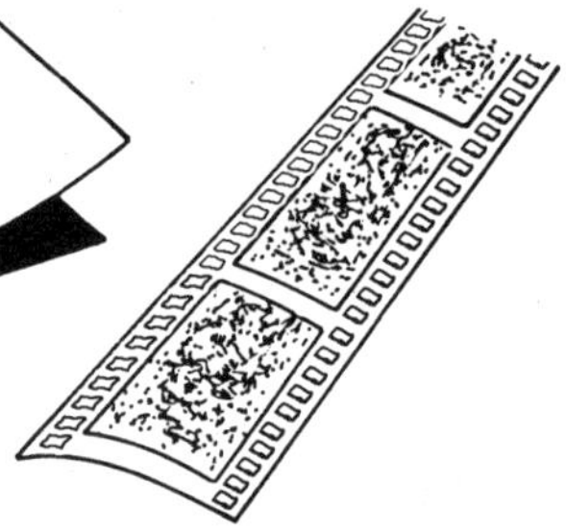

Negatives and fiber-based papers normally tend to curl toward the emulsion side. Learn to tell the emulsion side of the brand of RC paper you use either by the gloss of the surface or by the printing on the back.

Making a Contact Proof Sheet

Contact proofs simplify filing and will make it easier to choose the best negatives from a series. You can make a contact sheet very easily using your enlarger as a light source. Besides printing facilities, you will need either a glass-topped proofing easel or a sheet of plate glass about 10 x 12 inches. Here's how:

1. Set up chemicals.

These will be the same as for enlarging (see page 132).

2. Place the easel on the baseboard.

It should be directly below the lens. Put an empty negative carrier in the enlarger.

3. Set the enlarger timer.

For the first test, try 5 seconds.

4. Turn on the enlarger light.

(Switch the timer to FOCUS).

5. Open the lens to its widest f/stop.

6. Raise the enlarger head.

Adjust the height until the light beam covers the entire proofer, and an inch or two around the edges.

7. Turn off the enlarger light.

(Switch the timer to TIME).

8. Place the paper.

Under safelight, lay a sheet of 8 x 10 paper face up on the bottom of the proofing easel. (Fiber-base paper usually curves toward the emulsion; RC paper lies flat. You can tell the emulsion side because usually it is shinier than the base. Sometimes the back has printing on it. If you can't tell the difference by looking, moisten a corner of the paper between your lips. (The slightly sticky side is the emulsion). Place your transparent file page full of negatives emulsion side down over the paper. Lower the glass and hold it down firmly.

9. Make the exposure.

Holding down the glass, press the timer button and wait until the light goes out. Remove the paper, but leave the negatives in the easel in case you have to make another exposure. Process the contact sheet according to the procedure on pages 132-138.

10. Evaluate the print.

If the entire sheet is too light, add a few seconds exposure time; if too dark, give less time or close the lens opening one stop (one click). When you get a good contact sheet, write down the time, the lens opening, and the height of the enlarger so you can repeat what you did. If your negatives are consistently exposed and developed, the settings for future contact sheets will remain about the same.

Unless all your negatives are perfectly exposed, some of the images on the contact sheet will be lighter, some darker. But you'll find that the proof sheet is very helpful in deciding which negatives to print. Examine each frame with a magnifying glass to check sharpness, facial expression, etc., and mark cropping directly onto the proof sheet with a marker or wax pencil.

"I have never lost that initial thrill of watching an image surface in the developer."

— Jerry N. Uelsmann, imagemaker

Enlarging: How-To-Do-It

Follow the procedure shown on pages 132-138 to make enlargements of some of your favorite negatives. Your enlarger, timer and darkroom setup may differ slightly from the illustrations, but this is how it's done.

A contact sheet is a handy way to evaluate your negatives, and to make choices for enlargement. If your negatives are of consistent density, and the exposure is correct for the contact sheet, none of the negatives will appear excessively light or dark on the contact sheet. In the example (below) the light frames are ***over****exposed negatives and the dark frames are* ***under****exposed. A wax pencil has been used to indicate cropping of frames chosen to be enlarged.*

ARDYCE CZUCHNA-CURL

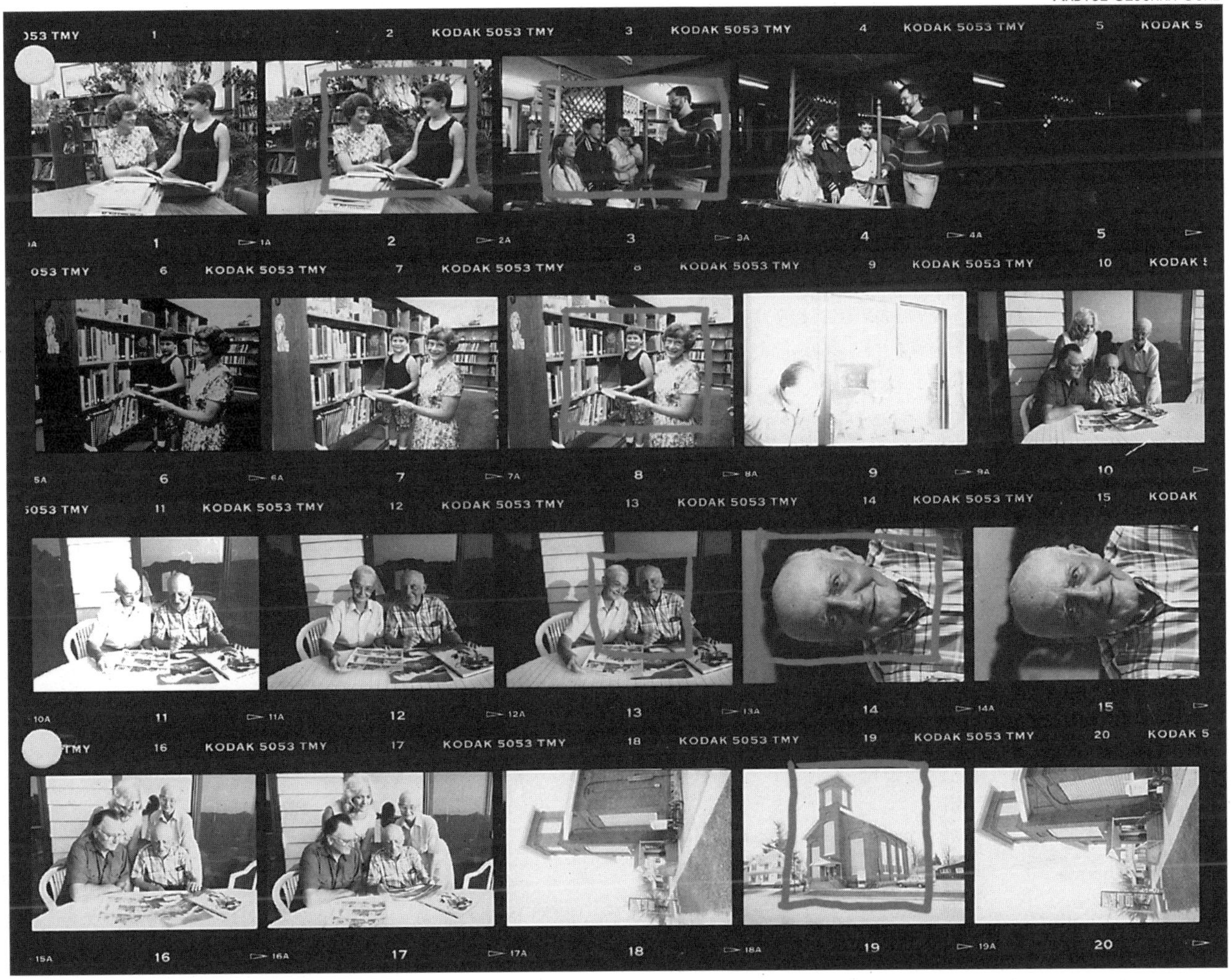

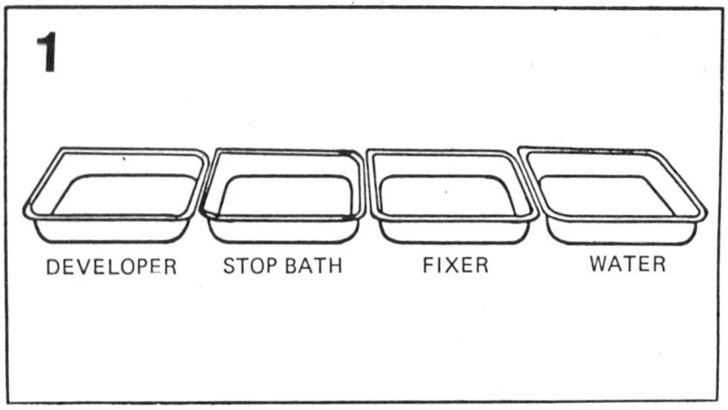

Arrange four clean trays in a row. Use trays that are slightly larger than the biggest print you plan to make.

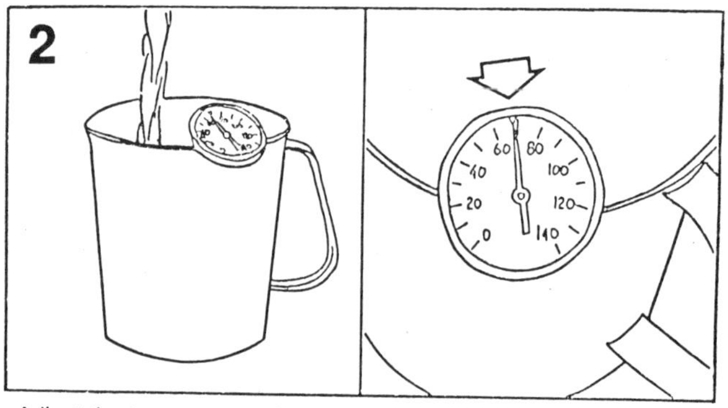

Adjust the tap water to about 68°F (20°C). In hot weather, if you cannot maintain 75°F (24°C) or below, you can use a plastic bag full of ice cubes to keep down the temperature of the developer.

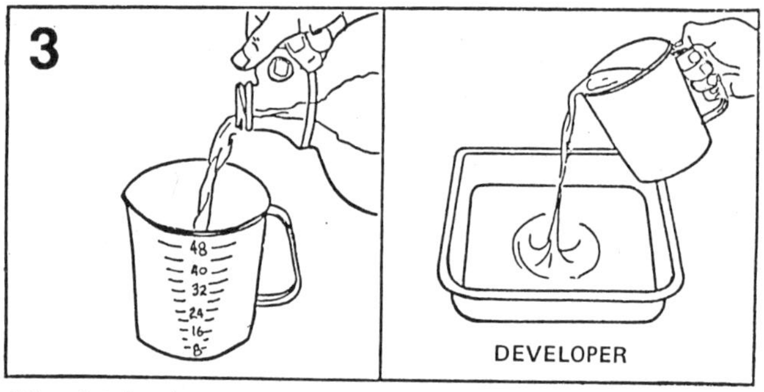

Mix print developer stock solution with approximately 68°F (20°) water according to the manufacturer's instructions to make 1 quart (1.1 litre). Pour developer into the FIRST tray. Rinse the beaker with water.

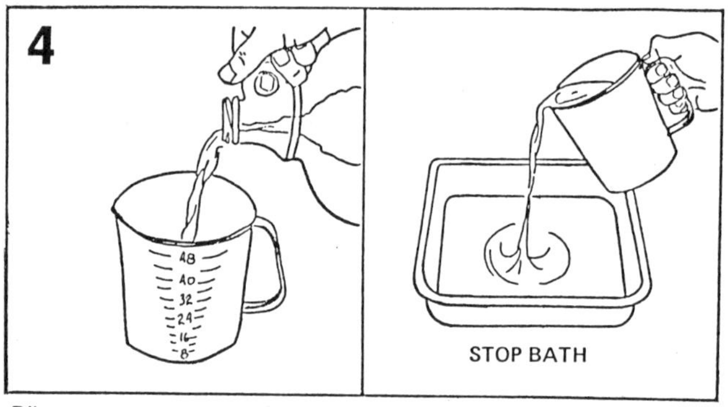

Dilute stop bath stock solution with water. The usual dilution is one ounce (30 mL) to make one quart (1.1 litre). Pour stop bath into the SECOND tray. Rinse the beaker.

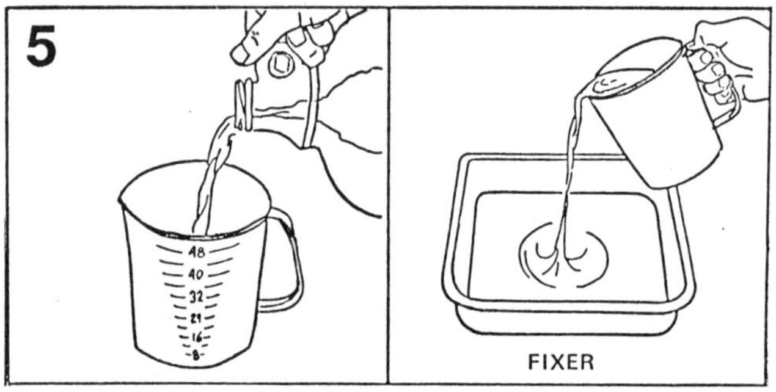

Dilute fixer stock solution according to manufacturer's instructions to make 1 quart (1.1 litre). Pour fixer into the THIRD tray. Rinse the beaker.

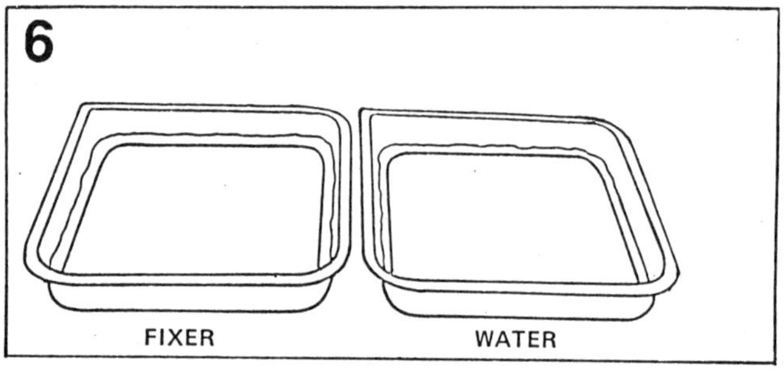

Fill the FOURTH tray with water as a holding bath.

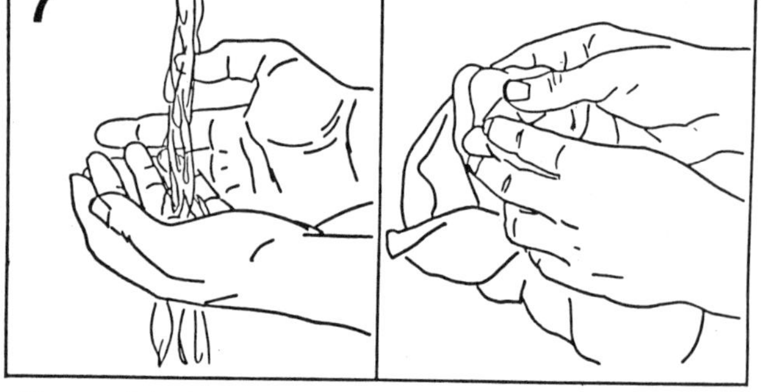

Rinse and dry your hands thoroughly before touching negatives, paper, or equipment.

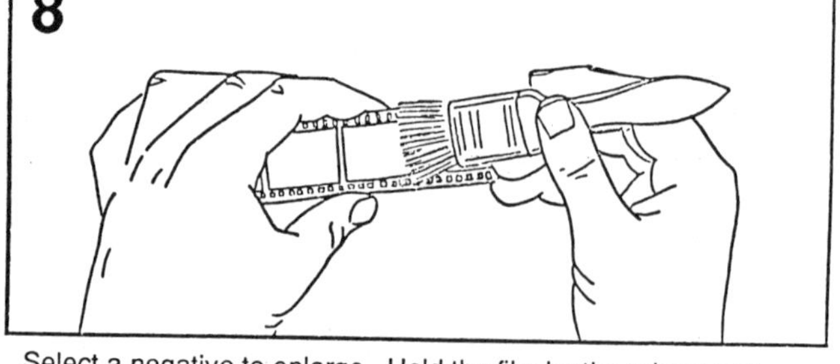

Select a negative to enlarge. Hold the film by the edges and gently remove dust from both sides of that frame with a soft brush.

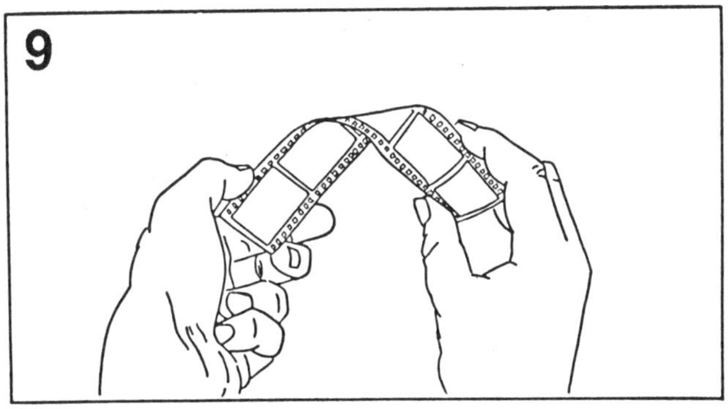

The emulsion side of the film is the *dull* side.

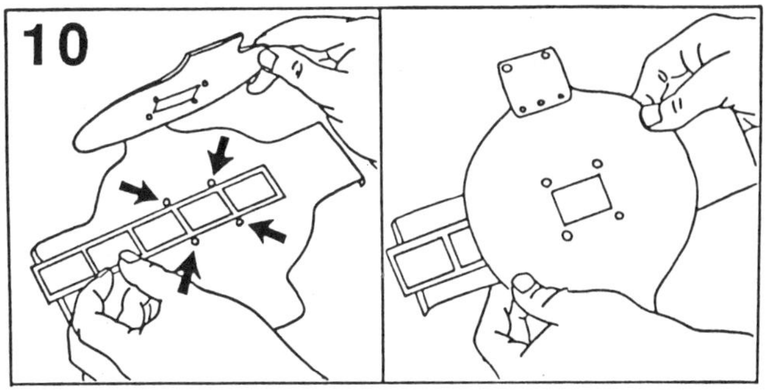

Place the film in the negative carrier with the emulsion (dull) side *down*. Center the negative between the pins. Close the carrier.

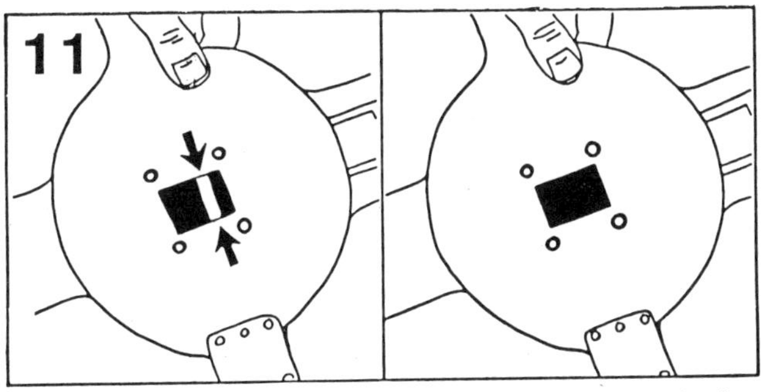

Hold the negative carrier toward the light to see if the negative is centered. Look for dust. Don't move the film without opening the carrier.

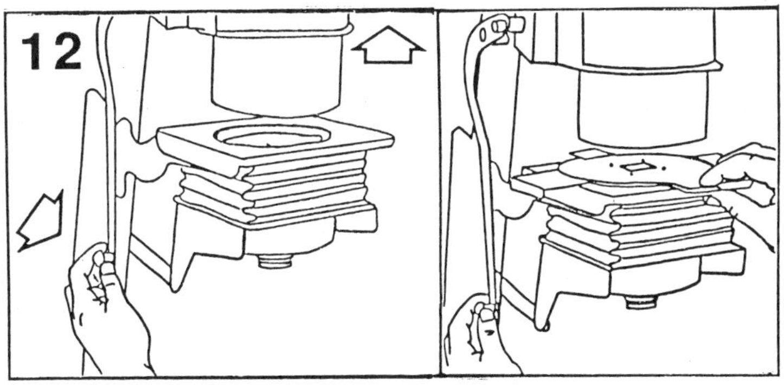

Raise the enlarger lamp housing and insert the negative carrier so the emulsion side of the film faces *down* toward the baseboard.

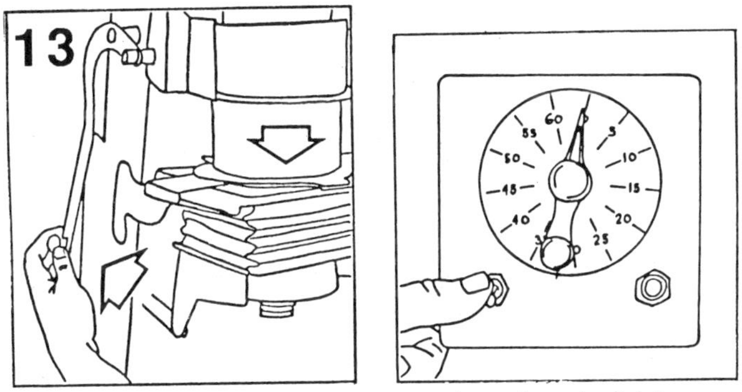

Lower the lamp housing. Turn on the enlarger lamp (switch to FOCUS on most timers).

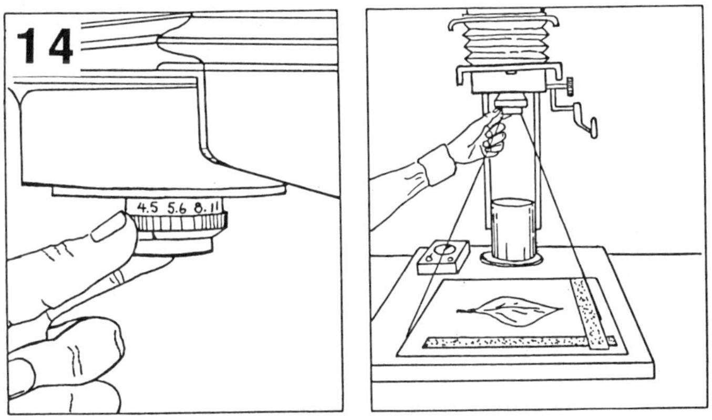

Rotate the aperture ring on the enlarger lens so the brightest image is projected onto the easel.

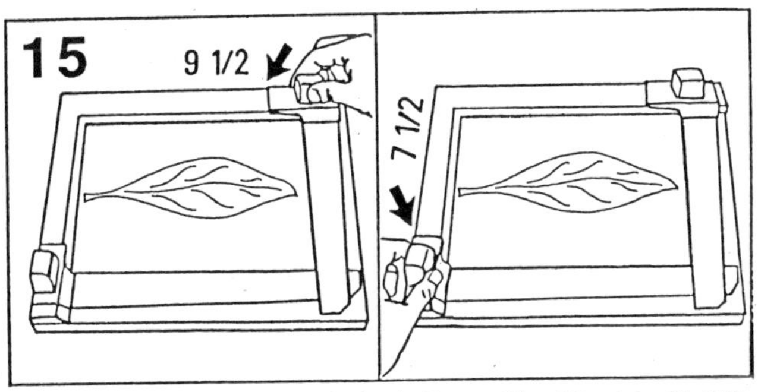

Adjust the easel to the size desired. For an 8" x 10" print with 1/4" borders, slide the side adjustment to 9 1/2" and the bottom adjustment to 7 1/2".

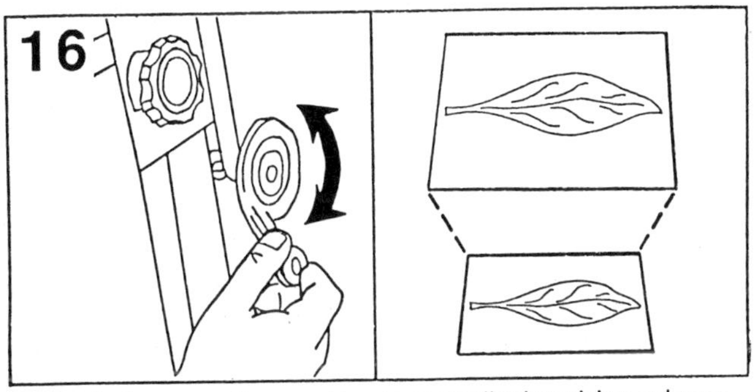

Make the image on the easel larger or smaller by raising or lowering the enlarger head.

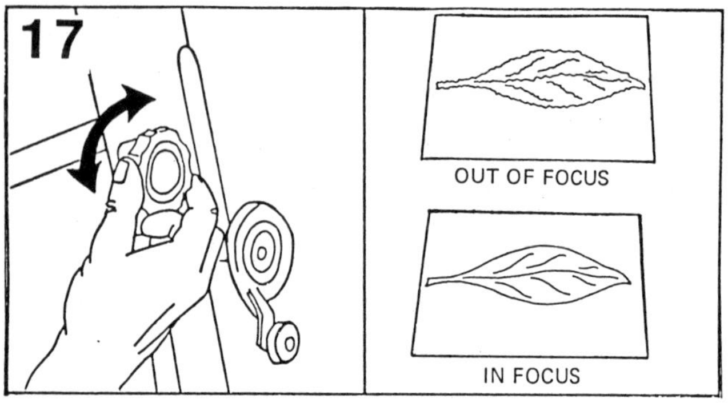

Focus the image on the easel by turning the focusing knob. Use a focusing magnifier if one is available.

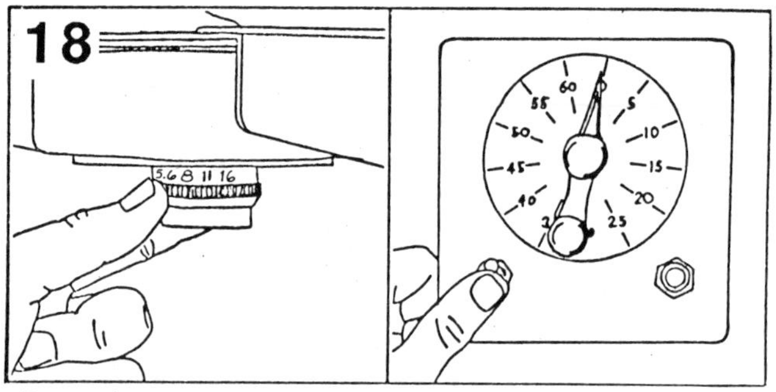

Rotate the aperture ring on the enlarger lens to decrease the brightness of the projected image by two click stops (f/8 or f/11). Turn off the enlarger lamp.

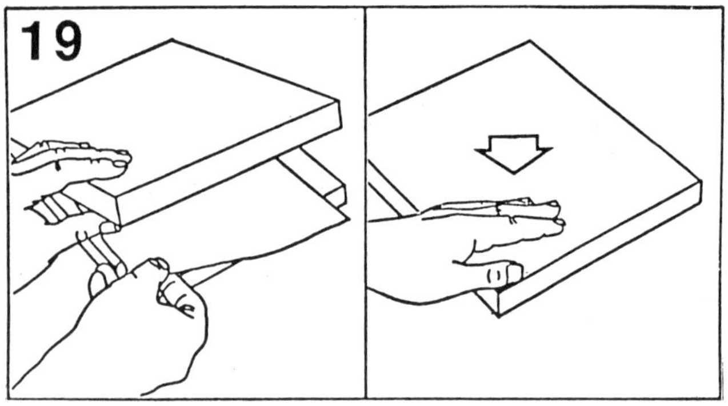

Remove a sheet of photographic paper from the box or envelope. Handle the paper only by the edges. REPLACE BOX COVER or CLOSE ENVELOPE!

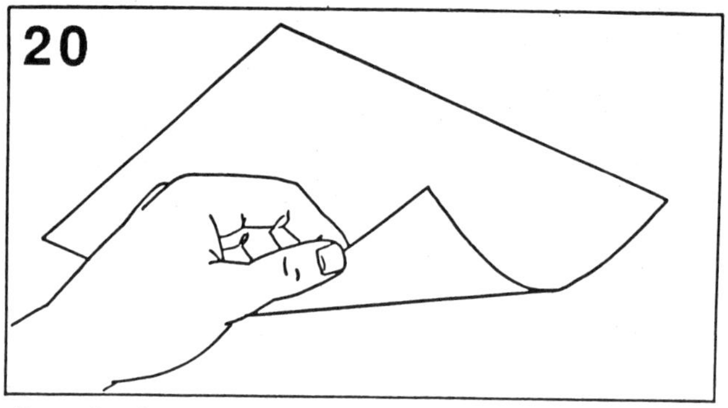

Determine the emulsion side of the paper. Usually it is the *shiny* side (the opposite of film). Handle the paper by the edges.

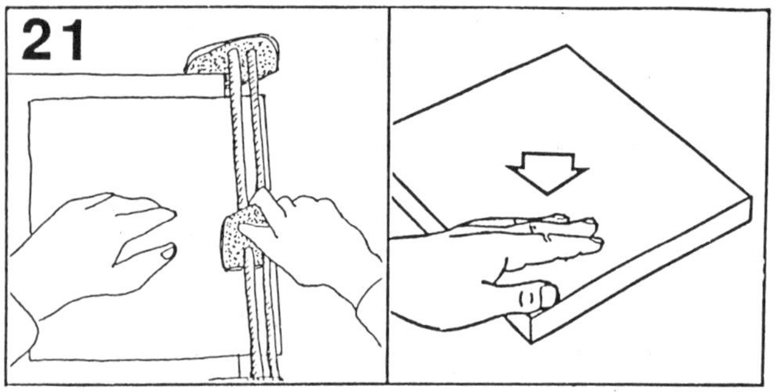

Cut the sheet of paper into test strips about one inch wide. Return the strips to the box or envelope and reclose it.

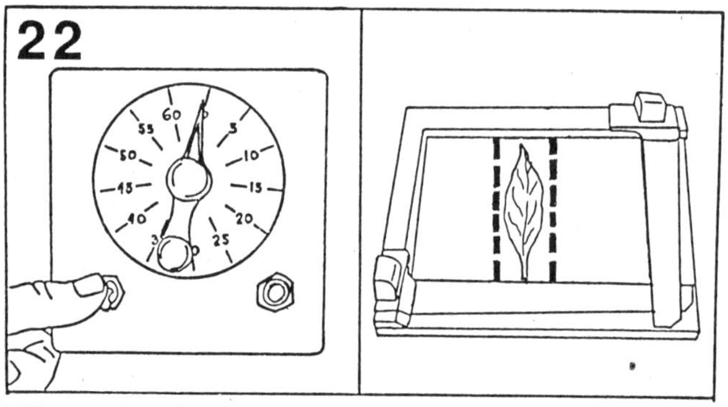

Turn on the enlarger lamp. Find an area of important detail with high values, such as skin tones or highlights in the image.

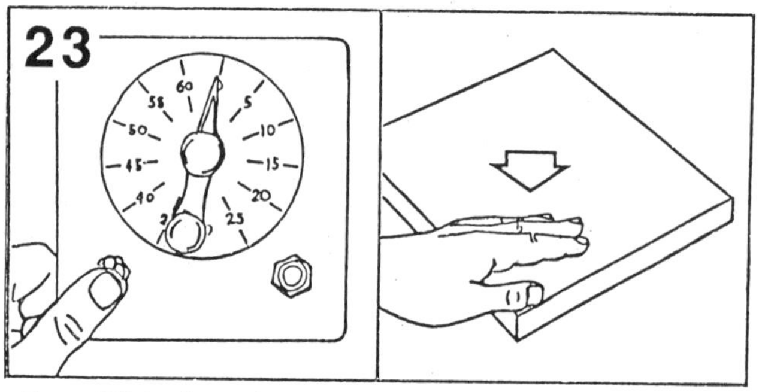

Turn off the enlarger lamp. Remove one of the strips of paper from the box or envelope and reclose it.

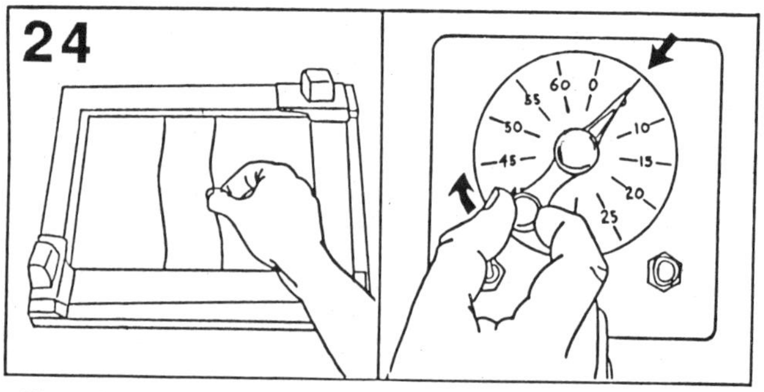

Place the strip of paper with the emulsion side (shiny side) up on the easel where the important detail will be projected. Set the timer for 2 seconds.

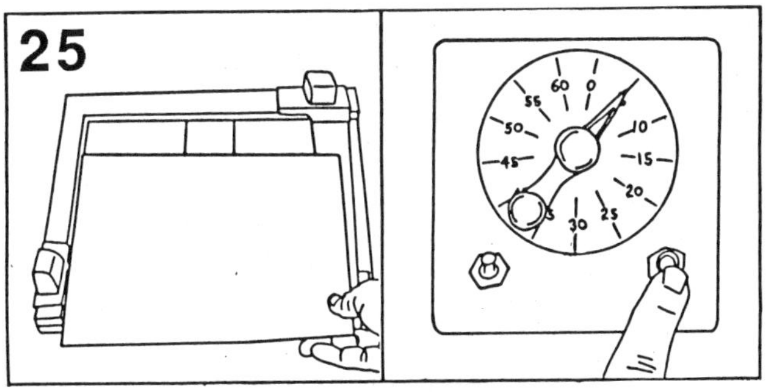

Cover 3/4 of the test strip by holding a piece of cardboard slightly above the easel but not touching the paper. Press the timer button to make a 2-second exposure.

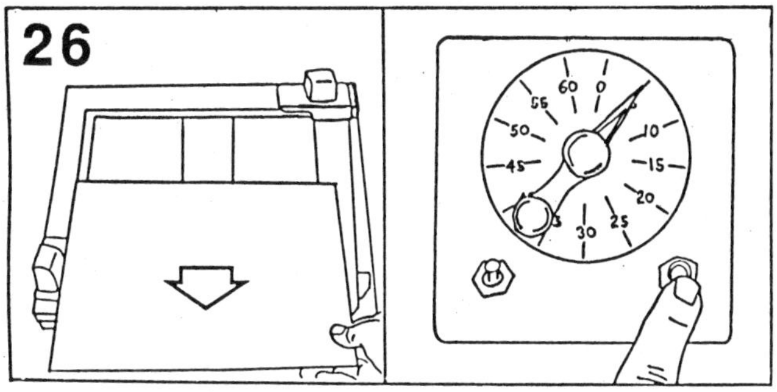

Move the cardboard to uncover another 1/4 of the test strip, but don't touch the paper and make it move. Press the timer button to make another 2-second exposure.

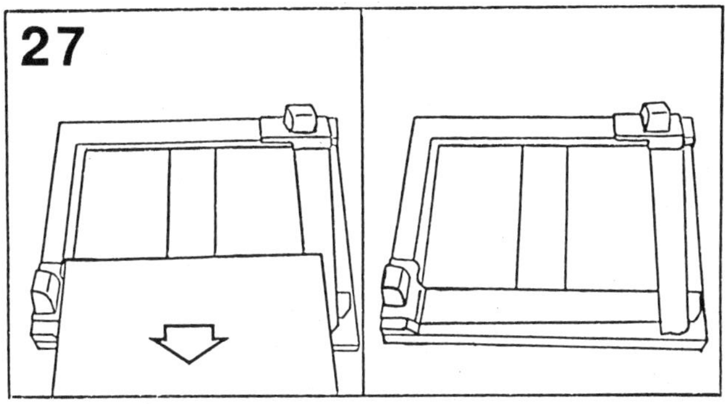

Continue until you have made four exposures of 2 seconds each. After developing, you will have a test strip with four exposures: 8, 6, 4, and 2 seconds.

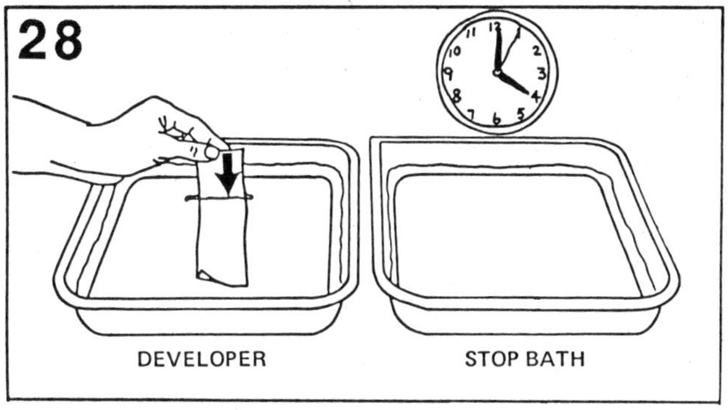

Without getting your hand wet, slide the test strip into the DEVELOPER so that the solution covers the entire strip. Note the time.

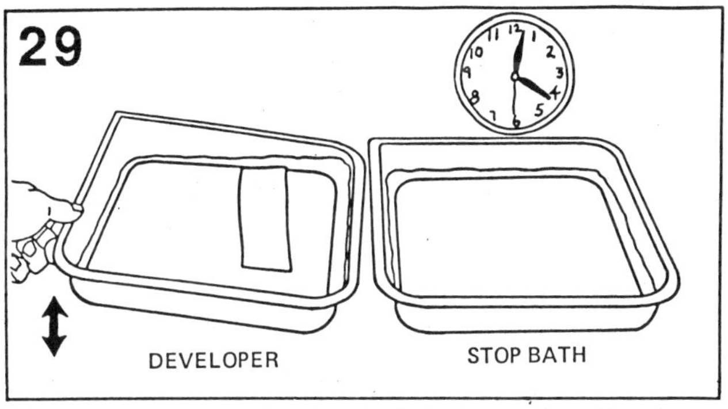

Constantly agitate the developer solution by gently rocking the tray. After 1 minute...

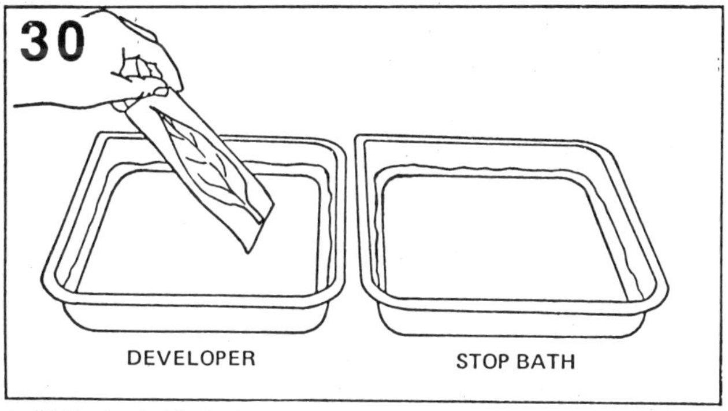

...lift the test strip by one corner and drain into the DEVELOPER tray for a few seconds...

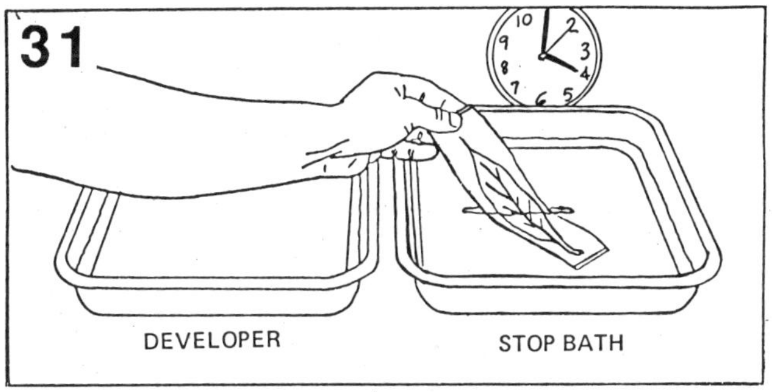

...then slide the test strip into the STOP BATH so that the solution covers the entire strip. Agitate. After about 10 seconds...

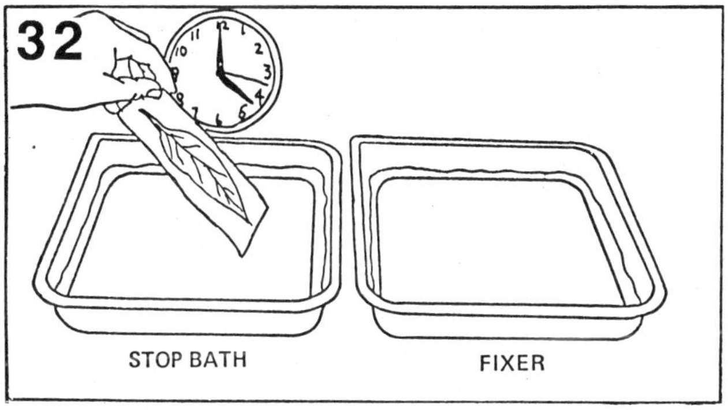

...lift the test strip by one corner and drain into the STOP BATH tray for a few seconds...

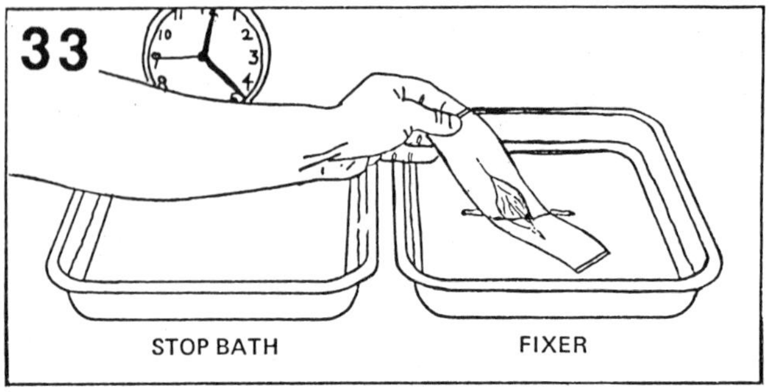

...then slide the test strip into the FIXER so that the solution covers the entire strip. Agitate. After about 30 seconds...

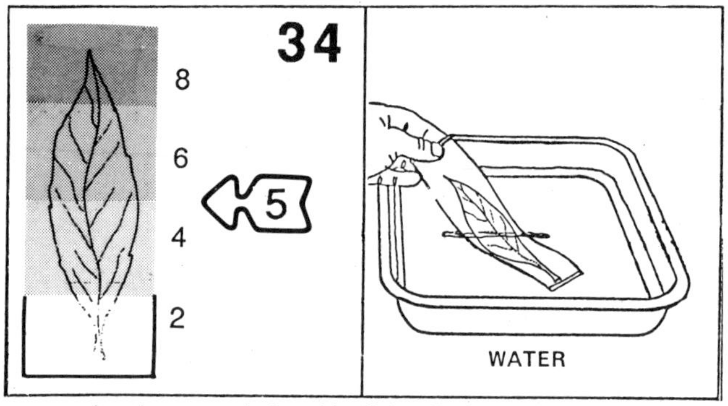

...examine the test strip by white light. If others are working in the darkroom, rinse the test strip in water, place it in a clean tray, and carry it outside the darkroom.

Determine the best exposure from the test strip and note the time. If the best time appears to be between two of the test sections, use an intermediate time.

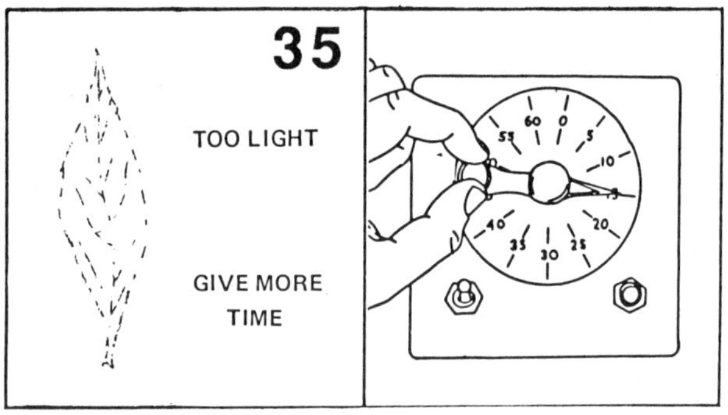

If the entire test strip is too *light,* make another test giving twice the time for each step.

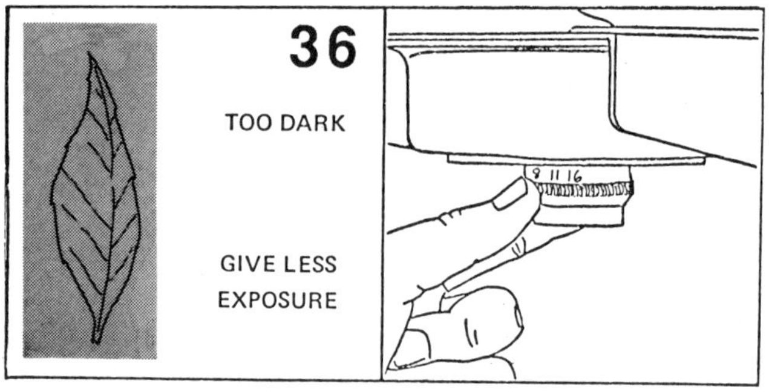

If the entire test strip is too *dark,* make another test at the same times as before, but *decrease* the brightness of the image by one more click stop on the lens (e.g. f/11 instead of f/8).

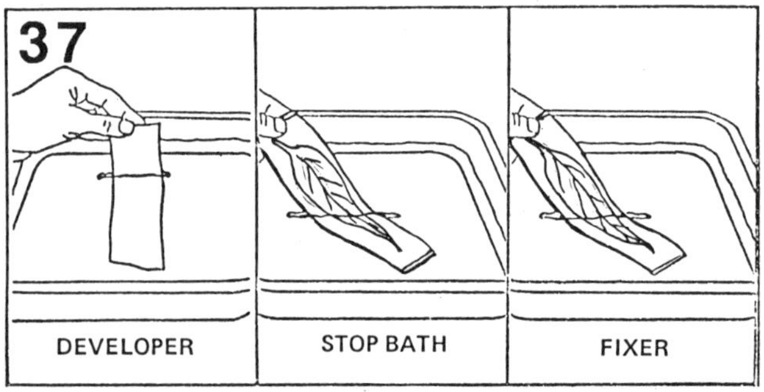

Process the test strip as before. Rinse it in water and examine it in white light. Afterward, rinse and dry your hands thoroughly.

When the test strip looks right, you're ready to make a full-sized print. Turn on the enlarger lamp.

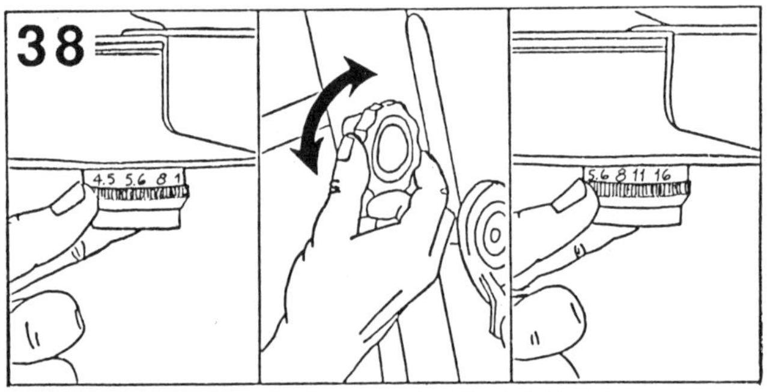

Rotate the lens aperture ring to project the brightest image. REFOCUS. Decrease the brightness of the image by stopping down the number of click stops determined by the test strips.

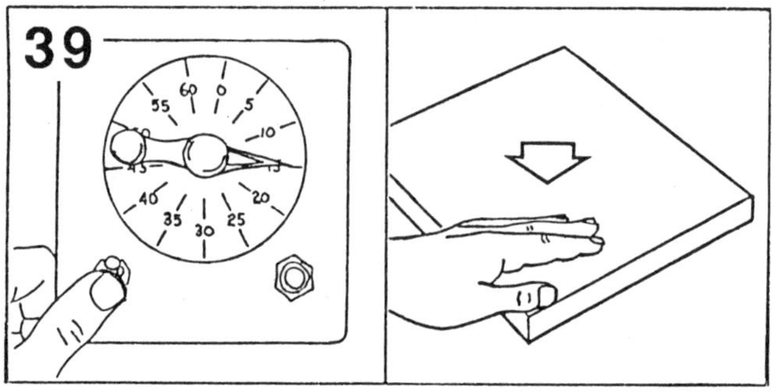

Turn off the enlarger lamp. Take a full sheet of paper from the box or envelope and reclose the package. Handle the paper only by the edges.

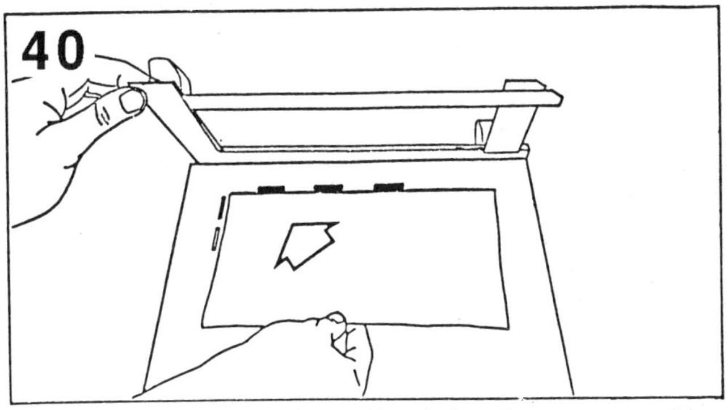

Raise the metal frame of the easel and place the paper—emulsion side up—against the corner guides. Lower the frame.

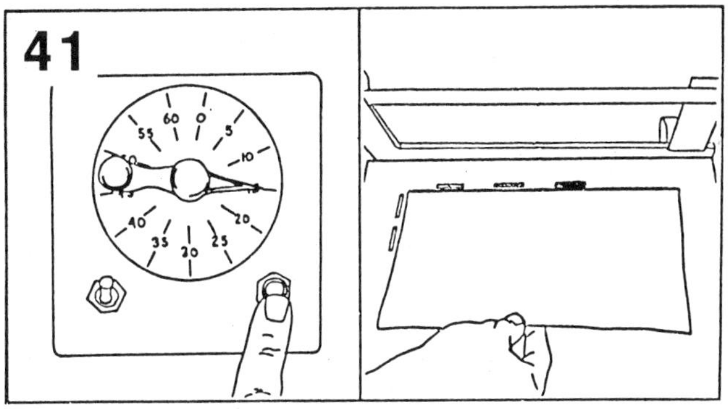

Expose the paper for the time determined by the test strip.

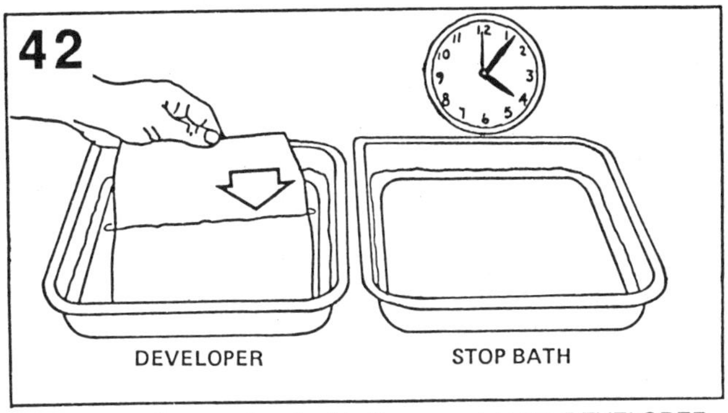

Without wetting your hand, slide the paper into the DEVELOPER so that the solution covers the entire sheet. Note the time.

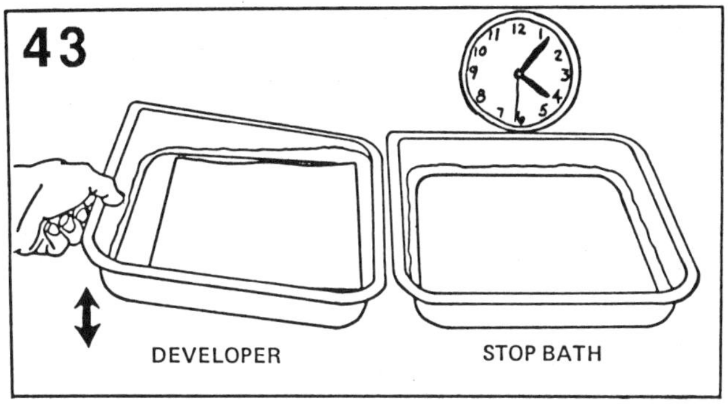

Constantly agitate the developer solution by gently rocking the tray. After 1 minute...

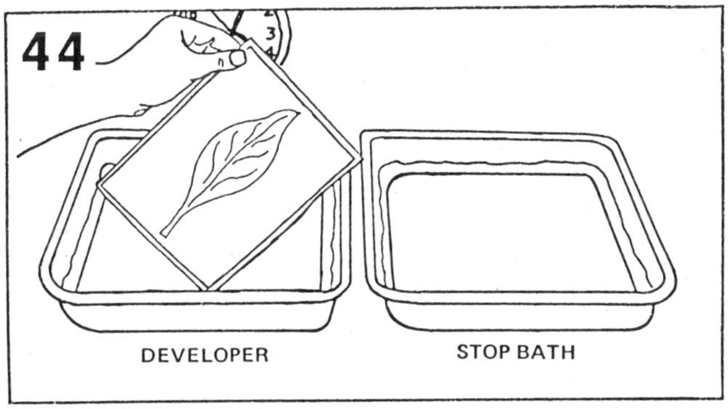

...lift the print by one corner and drain into the DEVELOPER tray for a few seconds...

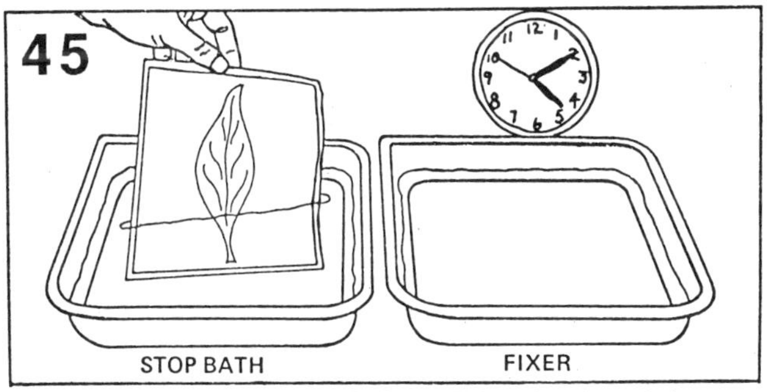

...then slide the print into the STOP BATH so that the solution covers the entire print. Agitate the tray. After about 10 seconds...

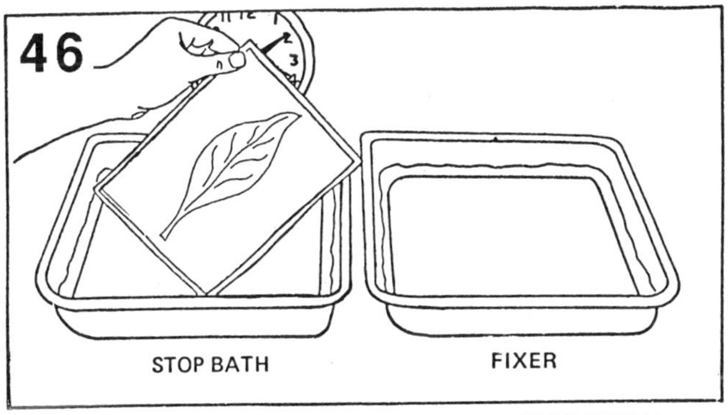

...lift the print by one corner and drain into the STOP BATH tray for a few seconds...

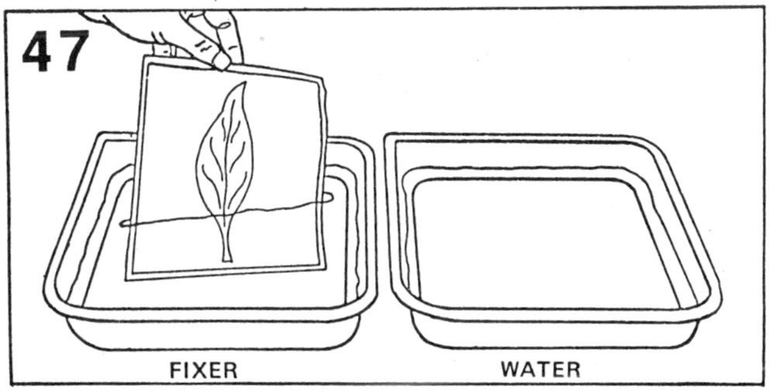

...then slide the print into the FIXER so that the solution covers the entire print. Agitate the tray. After about one minute you can rinse the print in water and inspect it in white light.

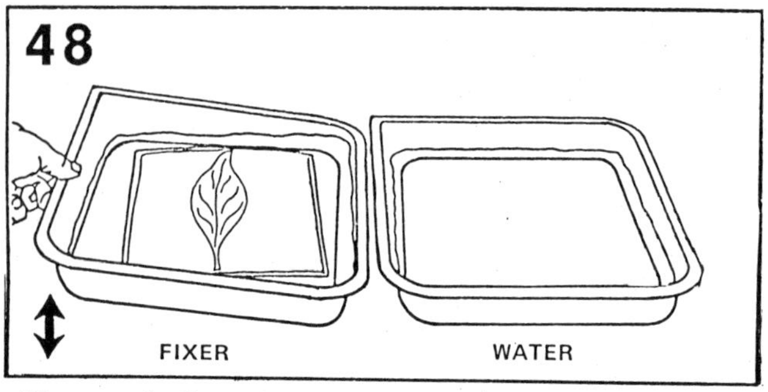

When you finally are satisfied with your print, let it remain in the FIXER for about 2 minutes. Agitate the print every half minute or so by rocking the tray so the print always is covered by the solution. If several prints are in the tray, shuffle them so they don't stick together.

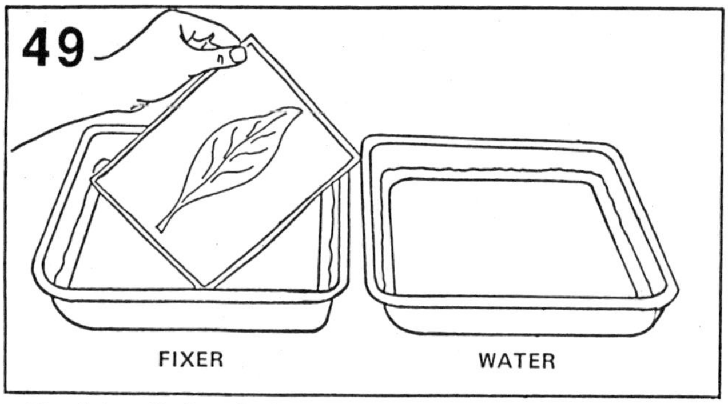

After fixing, lift the print by one corner and drain into the FIXER tray for a few seconds...

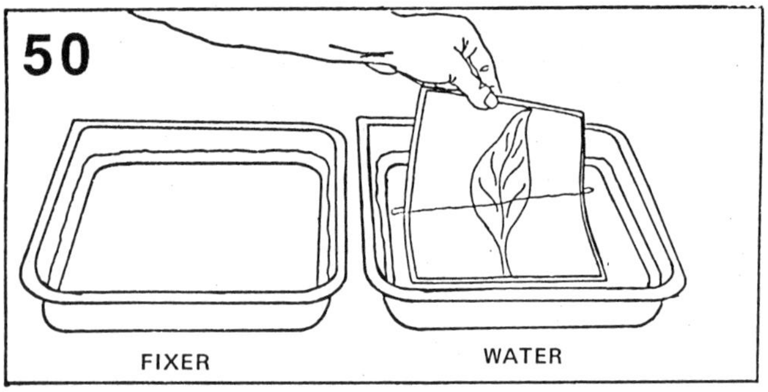

...then transfer the print into the water holding bath. If you're making several prints, they can accumulate in the water tray for as long as half an hour. Dump the tray occasionally and refill it with fresh water. Keep the prints separated so they don't stick together.

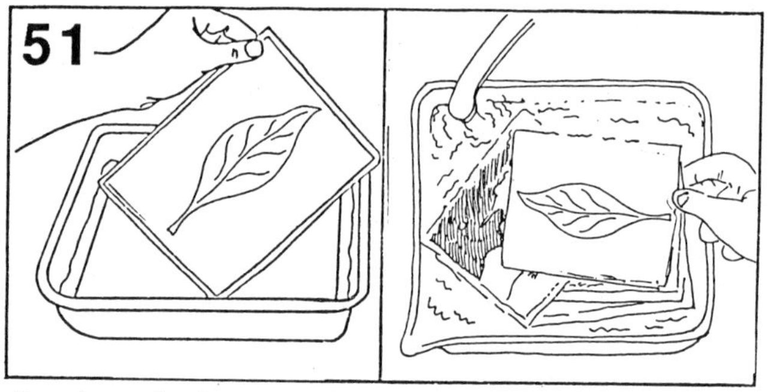

Transfer each print separately to the washing tray. Water should be flowing at about 68°F (20°C) if possible. Shuffle the prints gently to keep them separated. Dump and refill the tray a couple of times to accelerate washing.

While prints are washing, discard all solutions and rinse and drain all trays and accessories.

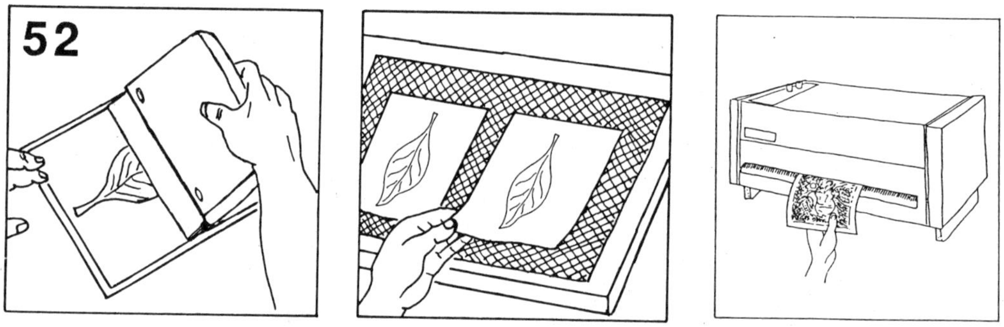

Transfer washed prints into a clean tray. Squeegee the face of each print and place it *face up* to dry on a screen frame or feed it into a hot-air dryer. (Fiber-base prints should be placed *face down* on a screen frame or dried in a blotter roll or canvas belt dryer.)

David H. Curl (7)

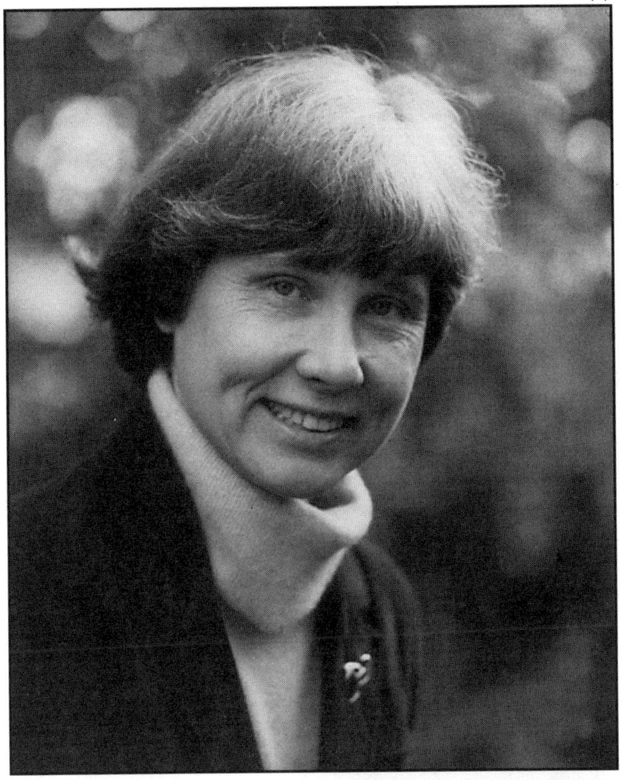

Evaluate the Quality of Each Print

If the print is too light, give the next one longer exposure time or open the enlarger lens. If it is too dark, give less time or stop down the lens.

If the print is dull-looking and the deepest shadows are gray instead of black, make another print using a higher-numbered filter or add more magenta.

If the print shows chalky highlights and black shadows without detail, make another print using a lower-numbered filter or less magenta. If it is extremely contrasty, take out all magenta filtration and add yellow.

Determine exposure and contrast changes by making new test strips as necessary. Place the test strips so they include important tonal values.

Check for white spots on the print. If you see any, look for dust or lint on the negative and brush it off.

Before making the next print, make certain the negative has not shifted out of focus.

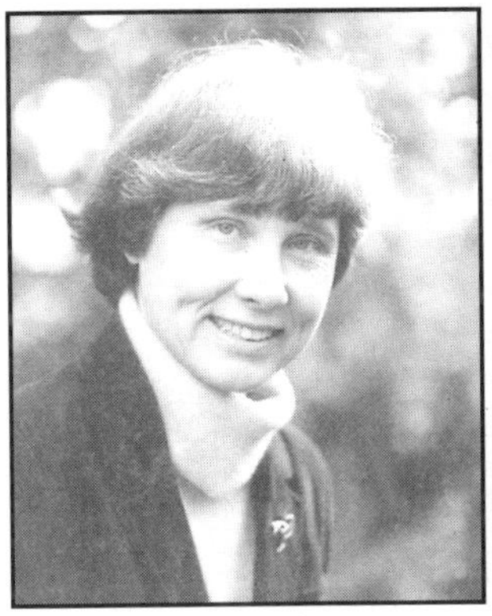

Too light? ***More time.***

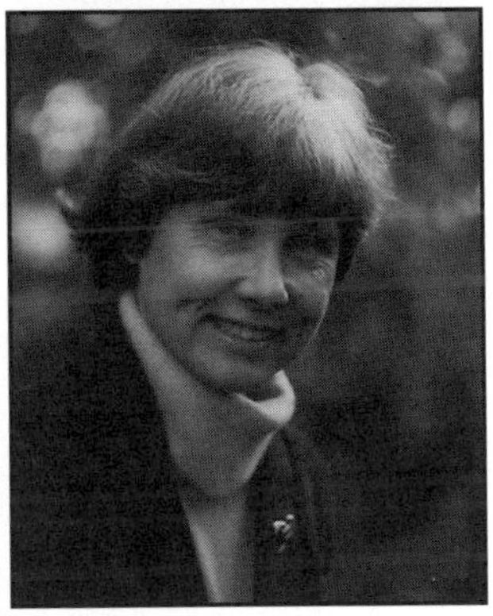

Too dark? ***Less time.***

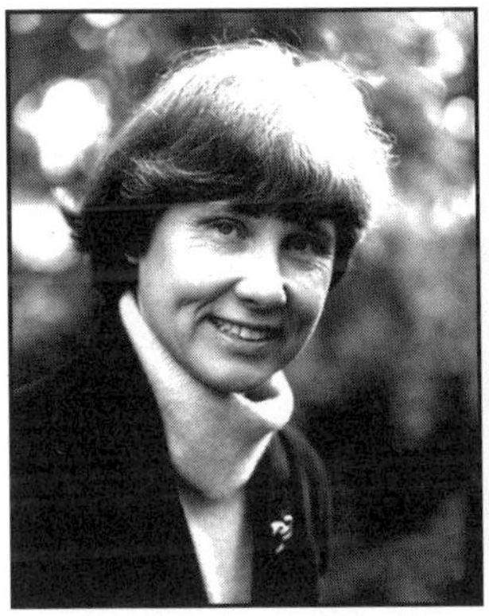

Contrasty? ***Less magenta.***

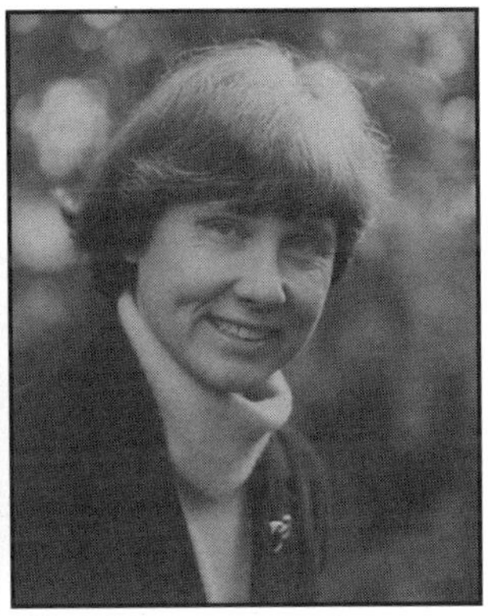

Flat? ***More magenta.***

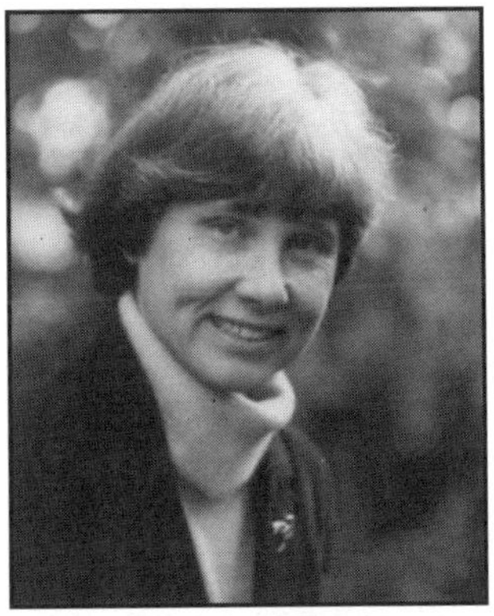

Fuzzy? ***Check focus.***

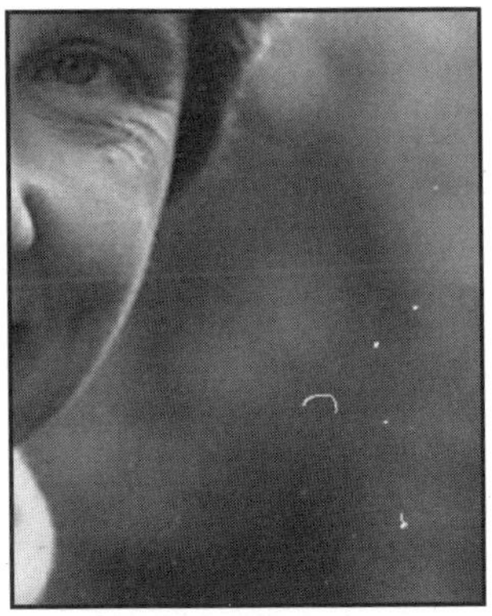

Spots? ***Brush the negative.***

"... a fancy thing done badly is not craftsmanship at all, yet a simple thing done well is the essence of such work."

— Llewellyn Seibold, architect

Printing Controls

Exposure

After you've made a good print from one negative, try working with other negatives of different density and contrast. While a normal negative may print well at 10 seconds, a very *dense* negative may require as much exposure as 30 or 40 seconds. On the other hand, a *thin* negative may need only one or two seconds to avoid coming up too dark in the developer.

Around 10 seconds is a practical exposure time — not too long to be boring, nor too short to preclude control. You may find that if you set your enlarger lens to about f/8 or f/11, the time may be about right. Otherwise, keep adjusting exposure time and lens opening as necessary. Make test strips. The rule about time vs. aperture is the same as adjusting a camera lens and shutter.

A group of so-called "normal" negatives all will print at about the same time. That's one of the advantages of using the Zone System: your negatives will be much easier to print because they'll be more uniform in overall density and contrast.

Expose for light areas

Although "expose for the shadows" is the rule for negatives, you'll discover that exposing a print for the *high* values will give you better control. Once your tests show satisfactory tone and detail in the lightest important areas of the print (skin tones, snow, etc.), you can adjust relative values of the darker areas by filtration or choice of paper grade. By dodging (holding back some of the light), you can lighten shadow areas that print too dark. Incidentally, you'll have to increase the exposure if you raise the enlarger head to make a larger print, or if you change filtration or use a different grade or type of paper. Each time you change something, make a new test strip.

Standardize development

Development time, with most papers, is not a control. A print developed for the recommended time (usually one to 1 1/2 minutes) will have the best quality. If the print comes up too dark in the tray in less than a minute, it's because it was overexposed. Leaving a light print longer than a couple of minutes in the developer won't help much, and the print may become fogged or stained. In either case, go back and make another test.

> ***"I hear and I forget. I see and I remember. I do and I understand."***
>
> — Chinese proverb

DAVID H. CURL

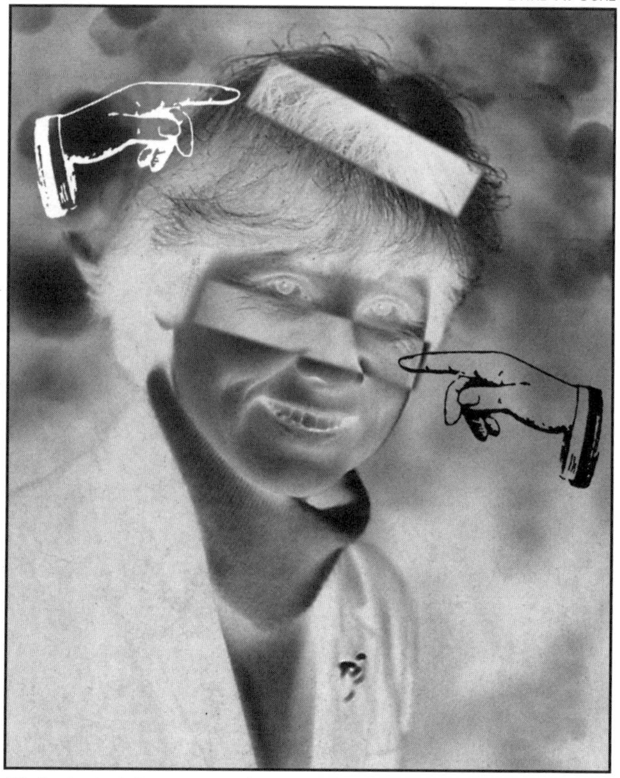

Make test strips across the most important values in the image. These will be skin tones if people are in the picture. If burning and dodging are required, place a test-strip in each significant area (the hair needs "burning-in" in this portrait — see page 144).

Allow for "dry down"

You'll soon discover that prints always look slightly darker under the safelight than they do when viewed under white light. So remember this when evaluating your prints. Let each print develop out for the full recommended time, then examine it under white light. If you're working in the darkroom with other people, I suggest that after fixing your print, you rinse it in water, then place it in a clean tray and take it outside the darkroom where you can evaluate it properly.

But this isn't the end of the story. Your print will "dry down" somewhat darker and flatter than it looks while wet. Some very particular photographers actually sponge or blot off surface water from a print to get a preview of what it will look like when it's dry. RC paper requires such a short wash that you can go ahead and dry the print. Another alternative is to re-wet an extra print that has dried to your satisfaction, and keep it in a tray of water as a sample to match similar values in the prints you're going to make later.

If you take a print out of the fixer to be viewed, rinse it off in water first to keep from contaminating the work area. If you're going to keep that print, don't forget to put it back into the fixer for one to two minutes for RC papers or 10 minutes for fiber-base.

DAVID HARRISON (3)

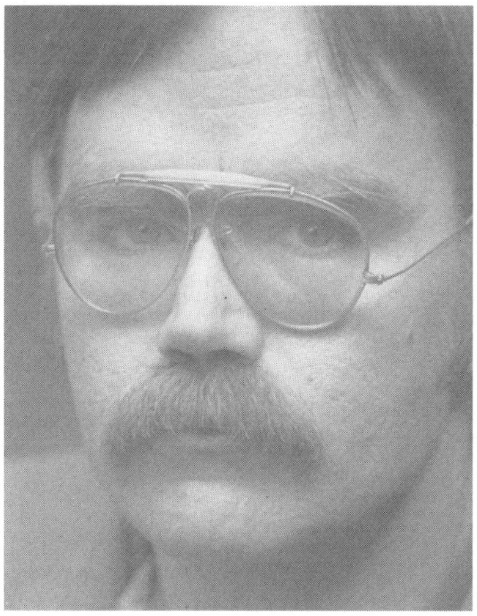

100 Yellow

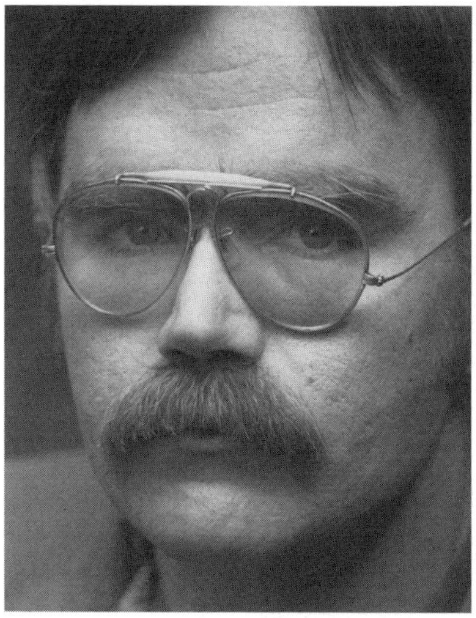

No Filtration (white light)

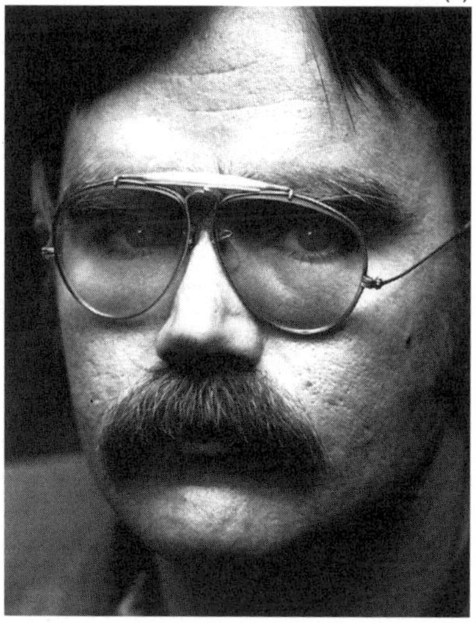

200 Magenta

Control the contrast

Each print, with few exceptions, should have within it some tones of pure white and strong black. Sometimes these black and white areas will be very small, but usually they should be there. Also, with most subject matter there should be a full range of gray values in between the white and the black.

If you could use the Zone System on every picture, controlling the entire process exactly, you could print every negative at a standard exposure setting and without adjusting the contrast. In reality, each of us produces our share of negatives that aren't quite perfect, and it's helpful to be able to do some compensating in the darkroom.

A flat, low-contrast negative may print very well when you add quite a lot of contrast, while a reduction in contrast may be needed for a negative that includes a range of brightness too great to record on the paper without help. Excellent prints never can be made from very thin negatives in which shadow detail has been lost because of underexposure. The same is true of extremely dense negatives with opaque "blocked-up" highlights.

If you make your test strips on skin tones or other important values above zone V, and base your print exposure on those tests, then the dark values will indicate the contrast control you need.

When the areas that should be black in the print come out merely gray, then higher contrast is called for. To increase contrast with variable-contrast paper, use magenta filtration. If the shadows are so dark that important detail is lost and high values also lack texture, then you may want to reduce contrast by using either less magenta or yellow alone. Contrast grades 1.5, 1, and 0 give progressively less contrast than "normal," while grades 2.5, 3, 3.5, 4, 4.5 and 5 give increasingly more.

Color enlargers allow you to dial in magenta, yellow and cyan filtration. Only one color is used at a time because they will cancel each other out. Cyan is not used for printing black-and-white.

White light (no filtration) is considered "normal" contrast, the same as grade 2 paper or Polycontrast or Multigrade filter number 2.

Filters may change exposure

Make a new test strip whenever you change contrast. Exposure will be consistent between steps with some filter sets except for 4, 4.5 and 5. Others may vary over the entire range. Color enlargers require adjustment in time with every change of filtration (see table below). As magenta or yellow filtration is increased, less light is transmitted through the negative to the paper. Each time you change filtration or paper grade, there will be a change in exposure; so make a new test strip across the same high value as before. The greater the density of filtration, the more exposure increase will be required, but the increase will not always be predictable. Some electronic enlarging systems can meter for these changes, but most of us will have to use test strips.

Magenta	Seconds
0	5
20	6
40	7
60	8
80	9
100	10
120	11
140	12
160	13
180	14
200	15

Beth Sturgis (2)

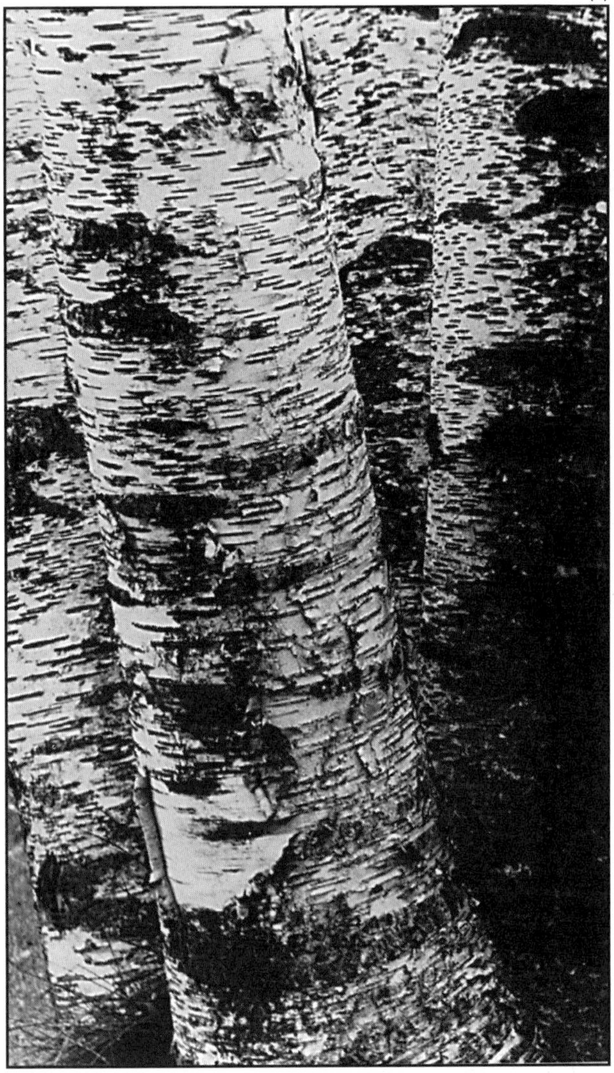

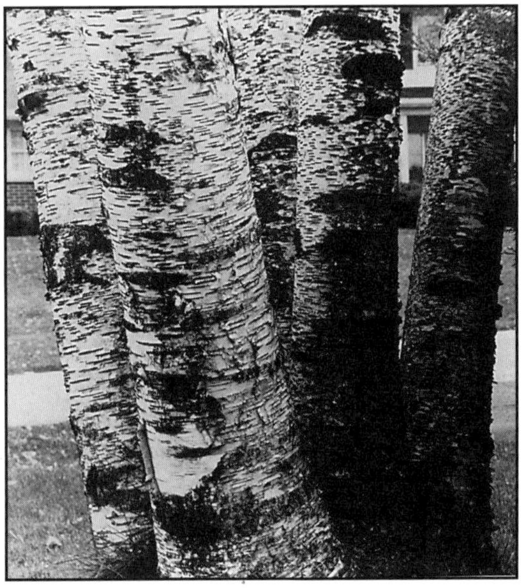

Usually it's not necessary to keep the shape of the image to the exact format of the paper. A little bit of cropping sometimes makes a lot of difference. Simplify ... simplify ... simplify!

Approximate Contrast Filter Equivalents

Paper Grade or Filter Number	Color Enlarger Filtration
0	80 Yellow
1/2	55 Y
1	30 Y
1 1/2	15 Y
2	0
2 1/2	25 Magenta
3	40 M
3 1/2	65 M
4	100 M
4 1/2	150 M
5	200 M

"Extraneous things get into photographs that you really have to weed out."

— Brian Lanker, photojournalist

[Amateur photographers are] "... not aware of edges — the casual snapper just points the camera at something without noticing the composition."

— David Hockney, artist

Cropping removes distractions

Cropping is the most basic control in projection printing. Although some of the most highly respected photographers — including Edward Weston and Henri Cartier-Bresson — apparently never trimmed any of their pictures, cropping is a way that we who do not yet see as clearly can have a second chance to recompose our images. Don't be afraid to crop; hindsight is a lot better than lack of sight. We learn by making mistakes, recognizing them, and correcting them. Just don't blow up a tiny portion of a 35mm negative and expect it to equal the quality you would have achieved had you been able to enlarge the entire image.

As sometimes we second-guess on composition, we also can have a second chance to improve on lighting. The technique is called *burning* and *dodging*.

Combining contrasts

Sometimes an image, where part of the subject was in sunlight and part in the shade, needs increased contrast in the shadows and decreased contrast in the highlights. This kind of control is possible with variable-contrast paper: the shadow areas are exposed with magenta filtration while the rest of the print is covered with opaque paper or cardboard. Then the shadow areas are covered while the high values are exposed with yellow light (usually a much longer exposure). Making a separate test strip for each area will help you to determine the different exposure times.

With Adobe Photoshop software in a computer, select the different areas and adjust the contrast of each in Image>Adjust>Curves.

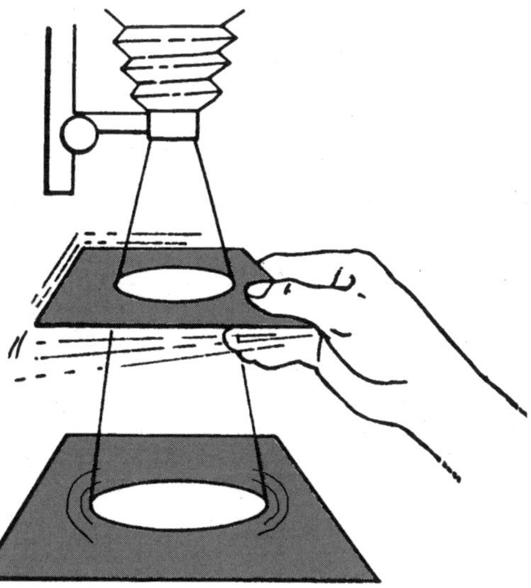

***Vignetting** means "burning-in" the selected subject, while "dodging" the rest of the image during the entire exposure.*

Vignetting isolates a subject

Vignetting (pronounced vin-yet-ting) means burning-in the portion of the image that you want, while totally dodging out the rest (for example, taking one person's head out of a group picture). A commercially made adjustable plastic vignetter can be purchased, or you can make your own by tearing out an oval opening or whatever shape you want from a piece of black construction paper. Make the edges of the opening sawtoothed or tear them raggedly. To avoid leaving a distinct edge, hold the vignetter well above the enlarging paper and keep it moving.

A computer will permit you to invert the selection, feather it, and then fill the background with white or any value or color you choose.

Tilting easel cures convergence

The most common example of convergence distortion occurs when the camera has been tilted upward to photograph a tall building, causing the sides of the building to come together toward the top. A lot of convergence can be dramatic, but a little bit can be annoying when you're trying to keep the edges of a rectangular subject parallel with the margins of the print. You can correct this by tilting the easel, propping it up with a book or other support until the image looks right. You should focus about one-third of the distance down from the highest point of the image and then stop down the lens far enough to bring the entire negative into sharp focus on the easel. If you can't get the image sharp enough by stopping down the lens, try tilting the negative carrier opposite the tilt of the easel by blocking it with a couple of pencils or strips or cardboard. Refocus carefully if you do this, and wrap a dark cloth around the negative carrier to block stray light from fogging your paper (or someone else's if others are in the darkroom).

In Adobe Photoshop, use Image >Effects>Perspective.

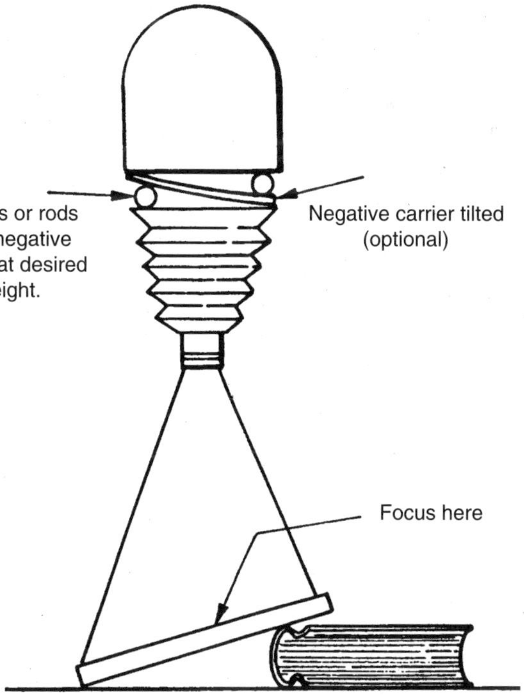

***Correcting perspective distortion:** Focus carefully. Stop down the lens to achieve depth of field. If you tilt the negative, wrap opaque cloth arund the bottom of the enlarger lamphouse to block stray light.*

Ardyce Czuchna-Curl (4)

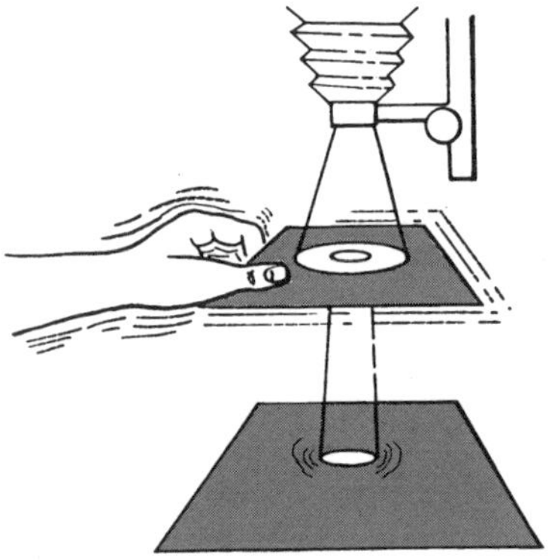

Darkening the corners improves many pictures, especially portraits. Notice that burning-in the edges (dodging the center) concentrates attention on the subject's face.

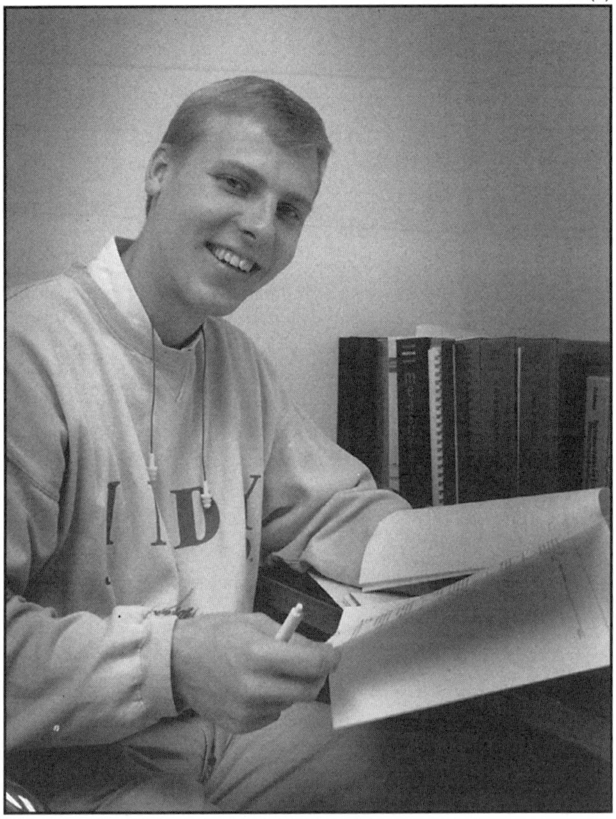

Burning-in. *After the overall exposure, more time is given selectively to darken parts of the image.*

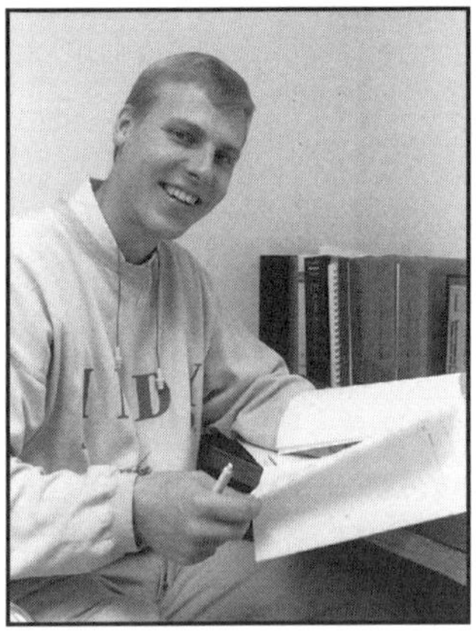

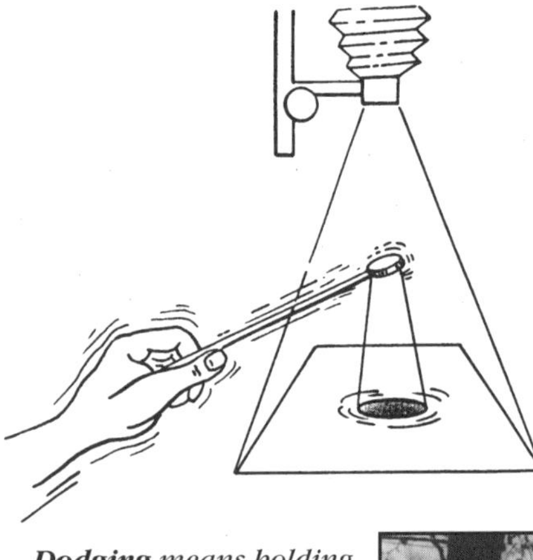

Without dodging, the man in the cab printed much too dark. The same result could have been achieved by exposing for his face, and burning-in everything else.

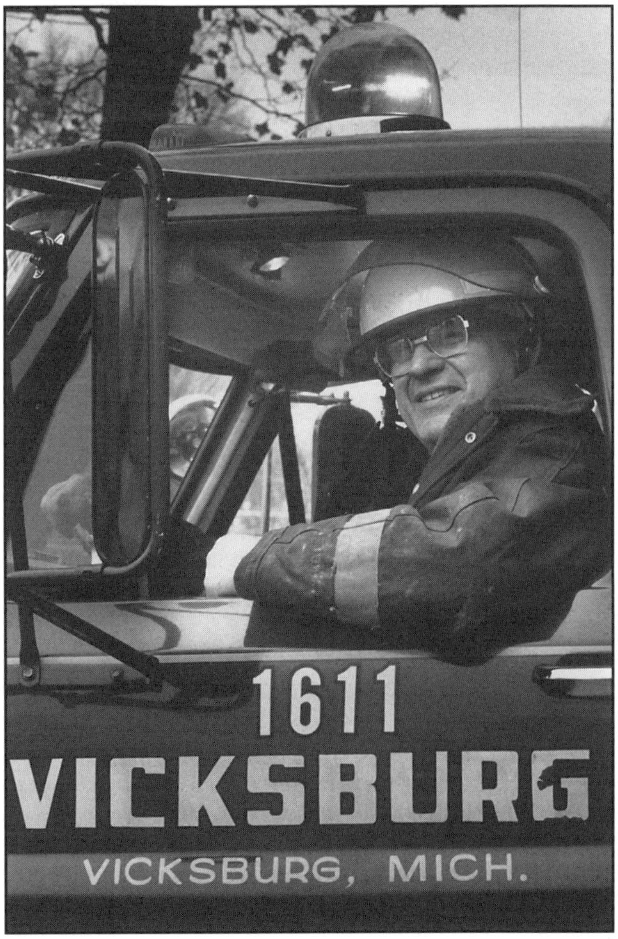

Dodging *means holding back light from part of the image during the exposure. Keep the tool moving so it won't leave a shadow noticeable in the final print.*

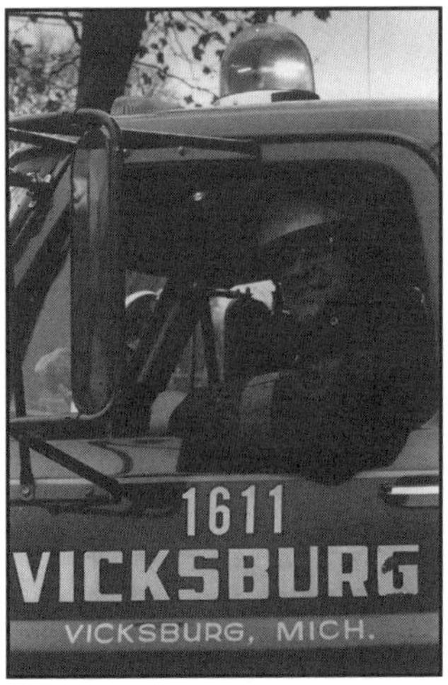

DAVID H. CURL (2)

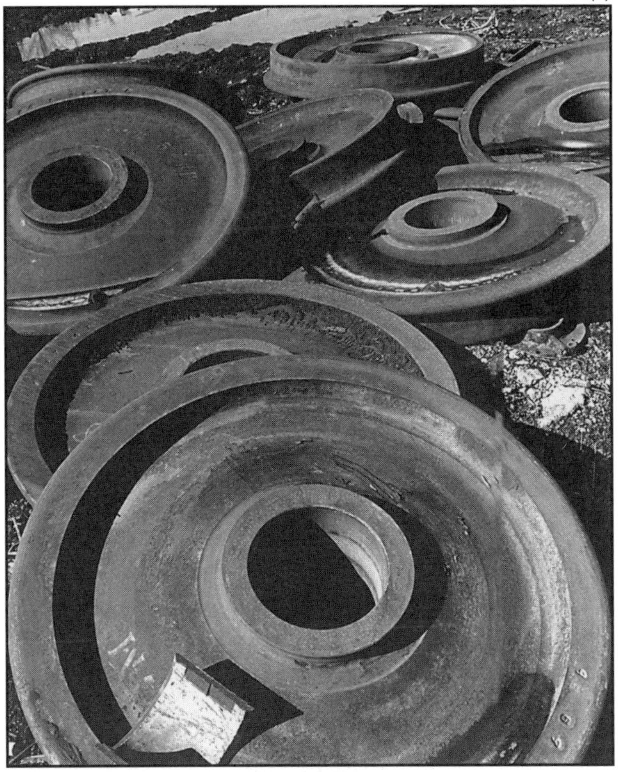

Straight print without flashing. Light areas of contrasting shape and texture tend to compete for attention with the repeated oval forms of the wheels. Burning-in these areas would darken, but not eliminate them.

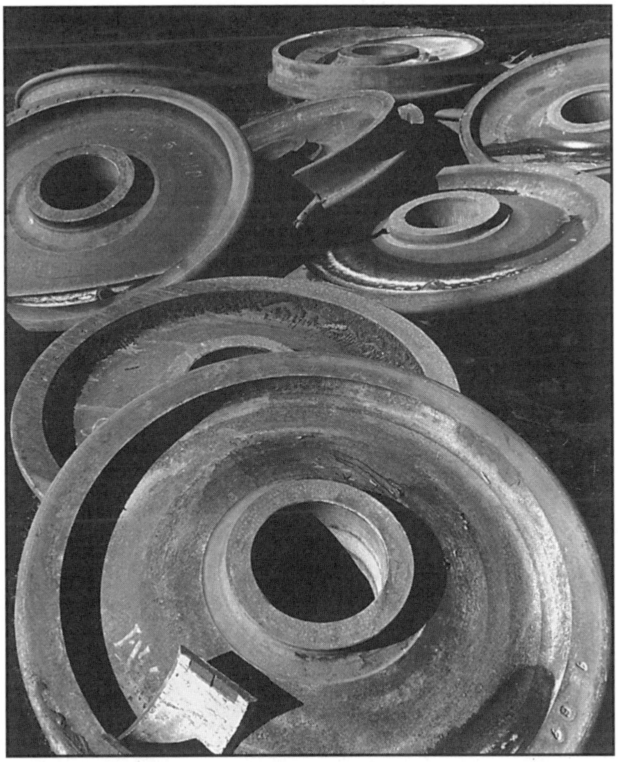

A small flashlight masked with black tape was used to darken light areas around the edges of this print. A red filter under the enlarging lens allowed the image to be visible so that the places needing flashing could be seen.

Dodging lightens areas

When part of the image prints darker than you want, you can shade that area during part of the exposure time. This process, called dodging, can be done with your hands or with a piece of opaque paper attached to the end of a length of thin, stiff wire. The dodging device must be held well above the printing paper and kept moving to avoid a noticeable line between dodged and undodged areas. To find out how much dodging is needed, make a separate test strip of that area.

Burning-in darkens areas

The opposite of dodging — burning-in — gives more exposure to selected parts of the print. This can be done by shaping your hands to cover all of the picture except the part to be darkened. But you probably can get better control by giving the extra exposure through a hole cut into a sheet of opaque paper or thin cardboard large enough to cover the entire print. Keep the paper with the hole in it well above the print and keep it moving so the effect isn't made noticeable by a sharp edge or a dark spot. Pictures with light sky or a bright background often are improved by darkening the corners or edges by burning-in with a sheet of opaque paper or cardboard shaped to fit.

Flashing eliminates light areas

Flashing is burning-in with raw, white (or filtered) light to darken distracting highlights in a print. Either remove the negative and use the enlarger as a light source, or use a small flashlight with a paper or foil cone attached to selectively darken small, light areas. Like dodging and burning-in, the flashed area must be blended smoothly into the rest of the image to avoid an artificial appearance.

***Dodging, burning-in** and **flashing** all can be done best in Photoshop by selecting areas and changing them in the **Image > Adjust** menu. **Curves** gives the most control. The dodge and burn tools work more like an airbrush.*

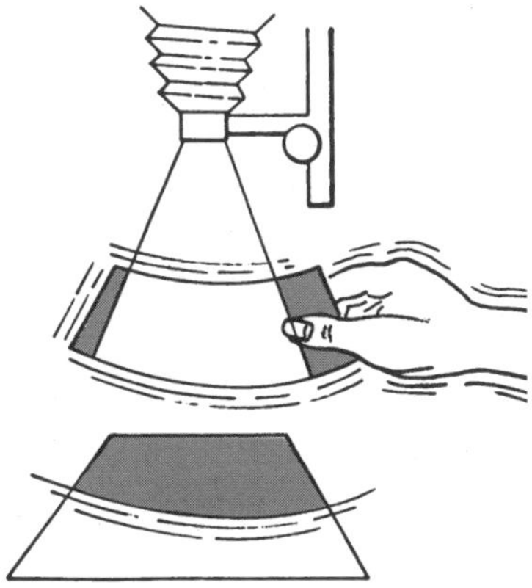

***Flashing** edges of a print, such as darkening the sky, can be done with an opaque card. Keep the card moving to avoid a noticeable shadow line on the final print.*

Diffusion softens the image

Diffusion is the deliberate softening of an image. It is not the same as having the image out of focus. Diffusion makes dust, scratches, blemishes, retouching, and grain much less noticeable. And because it also tends to hide skin wrinkles, diffusion is a favorite trick used by some portrait photographers to make aging subjects appear more youthful and glamorous. The process works best when a diffusion filter is attached to the camera lens, but it also can be done in the darkroom. You can make your own diffuser by holding beneath the enlarger lens a stretched out piece of panty hose, fine-metal window screening (black is best), or cellophane (crumpled, then smoothed out). The diffuser should be kept moving slightly during the print exposure, and you should make a new test strip because the exposure probably will be longer than without diffusion. More contrast may be needed, also. You can vary the effect by holding the diffuser under the lens for only part of the exposure time.

In Adobe Photoshop, the diffusion effects are found under Filter > Blur. Try various levels of Gaussian blur.

Giant prints and posters

Most enlargers can be pivoted either at the base or at the head to enable a negative to be focused on the floor or on a wall. You may need to do this if you want to make a print 16x20 or larger. Stack heavy weight on the baseboard so the enlarger doesn't fall over. If your easel isn't large enough, simply attach the corners of the paper to a flat support with loops of tape. Focus carefully!

Giant digital prints can be made by transfering your image files on a removable disk to a service bureau equipped with an ink-jet or electrostatic roll printer. Another option is to have your digital files converted to film by a lab with a film recorder, then make, or have made for you, enlarged silver or chromogenic prints.

Black-and-white prints from color negatives

Kodak makes a special panchromatic paper called Panalure that makes excellent black-and-white prints from color negatives. The trouble is, it has to be handled in the dark, like color paper. You can make pretty good prints, however, on regular paper if you dial in plenty of magenta filtration (equivalent to grade 3 1/2 or 4). Black-and-white negative prints can be made directly from color slides (page 203), but normal-looking prints require that an internegative be made on film. This can be done most easily with a slide duplicator.

In *Photoshop*, switching between color and grayscale is done under Mode.

Washing and drying prints

As you saw in the step-by-step instructions, prints on RC paper can be processed very quickly. Fiber-base papers, however, should be washed in a rapid flow of water for at least one hour, or about 20 minutes if a washing agent is used to remove fixer and silver salts from the paper. In either case, prints should be agitated frequently and kept separated while washing.

Where water is scarce, an alternative method is to use a washing agent, and then soak the prints for a minute or two in each of six or more changes of water. Agitate the prints often and drain them well at each change.

Stains and fading are the results either of improper fixing or of not washing prints long enough. This effect may not be noticeable until several months, or even years, later. When permanence of the print is not very important, thorough washing is not necessary from the standpoint of the print itself. A serious side effect of insufficient washing though is contamination of blotters, drying racks, or the canvas belt of a print dryer. Fixer left in prints by incomplete washing is transferred to other surfaces, and soon even properly washed prints become contaminated by the drying equipment. Don't let this happen!

RC prints and matte prints on fiber-base paper may be dried in a number of ways. When a lot of prints need to be finished in a hurry, an electrically heated dryer can be very helpful. Special beltless dryers are available that quickly remove the moisture from RC prints with a breeze of heated air. Some people use a roll or stack of lint-free blotting paper, but the most popular drying technique for both RC and fiber-base prints is to squeegee the surface gently and spread the prints (RC prints face up, fiber usually face down) on fiberglass screening stretched over wooden or aluminum frames.

For that emergency rush job, an electric hair dryer will dry an RC print in a hurry!

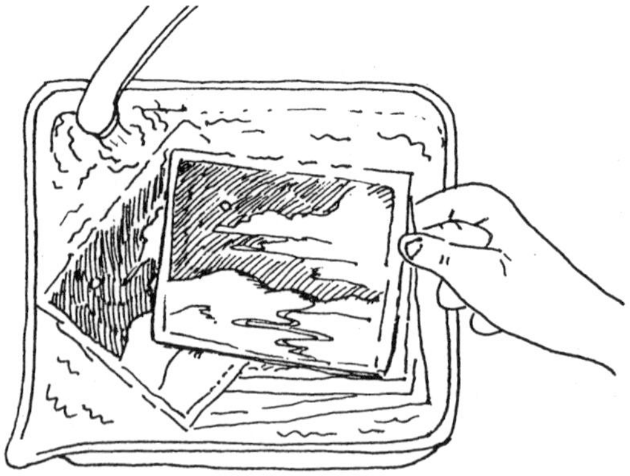

Batch-process RC prints. Don't let them accumulate in the water. Shuffle the prints frequently in the washing tray so they don't stick together during a two- to three-minute wash. Drain or squeegee them, then dry either face up on screen frames or in a hot-air dryer.

A Dozen Paragraphs of Darkroom Advice

1. Operate equipment gently.

Learn where the adjusting and locking knobs are on the enlarger and please don't use brute force on them. Timer levers and switches will last years longer if operated with care.

2. Keep reference information.

Read the printed data sheets that come with films, papers, and developers. File a copy of each for future reference or tape them to your darkroom wall.

3. Touch only the edges.

Fingerprints can be forever, and they are almost certain to occur if you handle film or paper with damp or chemical-contaminated hands.

4. Wear an apron or old clothes.

Developer leaves a brown stain that's very hard to remove from clothing. According to Murphy's Law, the spots will occur on the front of your best white blouse or shirt!

5. Open paper carefully.

Open each new package of photographic paper so that it can be resealed. Cut off a few strips of paper from one sheet for test exposures; then put the strips in the top of the package where they'll be handy when you need them.

6. Don't leave paper sitting out.

Remove only one sheet of sensitized paper from the package at a time and then close the package. Even under safelights, photographic paper will fog if left out too long or kept too close to the light. Lifting the head of your enlarger with the lamp on to insert a negative or to check for dust will fog any paper that's on the counter top or in the developer tray. Accidentally turning on the room lights while the lid is off a full box of paper will be a memorable and expensive experience!

7. Never reverse processing steps.

If you return a print or film to the developer after it has been in stop bath or fixer it will contaminate the developer. Always rinse your fingers or tongs before putting them back into the developer. Some photographers who use tongs reserve one pair for the developer and others for the stop bath and fixer.

8. Ask before switching on lights.

Don't turn on the white lights unless you check first to be sure that other people's paper is covered, as well as your own. Ask permission of anyone else working in the darkroom before turning on the lights or raising an enlarger lamphouse with the light on.

9. Refocus before reprinting.

During the interval between the test strip and the final print, heat from the enlarger lamp may cause the negative to buckle or sag enough to throw your print out of focus. Try using a focusing magnifier — this device makes it easier to focus sharply on the grain or fine detail of the negative. Don't forget to stop down the lens again after focusing!

10. Reshoot poor negatives.

Don't waste time trying to salvage a technically bad negative through the use of extreme paper-contrast grades, chemical reducers or intensifiers, and so on. If possible, correct your error by making another negative.

11. Wash prints in batches.

Washing time begins when the last print is put from the fixer or washing agent into the wash water. Another print will contaminate the batch if added to others already washing.

12. If in doubt, throw it out!

Beware of chemical solutions in unmarked containers. The best practice is to not use any solution if its identity or age is in doubt. Developer and stop bath should be dumped after every printing session, even though only a few prints were made. Penny-pinchers may want to reuse fixer and washing agent, although none of the four solutions should be used for processing more than about 25 8x10 prints or the equivalent per quart (liter) of working solution. Developer turns brown with extreme exhaustion; some types of stop bath become purple. Worn-out fixer may appear frothy, but by then it's too late. Keep track of the number of prints processed and make up fresh working solutions whenever they are needed.

What's Wrong with My Prints?

Image already too dark before one minute in the developer.

Cause: Overexposure.
Prevention or correction: Expose another print either for less time or at a smaller aperture. Make a test strip before exposing a large sheet of expensive paper.

Image still faint after 1 1/2 minutes in the developer.

Cause: Underexposure.
Prevention or correction: Expose another print either for more time or at a larger aperture. Make a test strip first.

Print exposed and developed properly, but the image looks gray and dull.

Cause: Not enough contrast.
Prevention or correction: Make another print using magenta filtration or grade 3 or 4 paper. First, make test strips to determine exposure and contrast.

Print dark enough overall, but lacks detail in high values.

Cause: Too much contrast.
Prevention or correction: Make another print using less magenta or all-yellow filtration, or grade 1 paper. First, make test strips to determine exposure and contrast.

Corners of print very light; center appears normal.

Cause: Vignetting.
Prevention or correction: Use 50mm enlarger lens or longer for 35mm negatives, 80mm or longer or 6x6cm, or at least 135mm for 4x5. If there are condenser lenses, be sure they are the right size and spaced correctly. See if the filter holder is cutting off part of the light.

One side of print very light, rest of print normal.

Cause: Partial vignetting.
Prevention of correction: Straighten negative carrier; insert it all the way. Check alignment of enlarger and filter holder.

Highlights of print gray, but margins pure white.

Cause: Light fog.
Prevention: Check for light leak in enlarger: around negative carrier, filter holder, or lens mount.

Print overall gray, including margins.

Cause: Light or chemical fog.
Prevention: Be sure paper is fresh and has been stored at cool or moderate temperature. Inspect darkroom for light leaks. Check safelights for proper filter and brightness. Be sure developer is fresh, diluted properly, and not too warm.

Black streaks on edges or corners of prints.

Cause: Paper partially exposed to light.
Prevention: Be sure lid is on paper box or inner envelope is folded over before turning on white light.

Thin white line in same place on all prints from same negative.

Cause: Small scratch on negative.
Prevention or correction: Handle negatives carefully. Print with diffusion-type enlarger to hide the scratch.

Thin black line in same place on all prints from same negative.

Cause: Deep scratch on negative.
Prevention: Handle negatives carefully.

Blurred double-image effect.

Cause: Vibration.
Prevention: Don't bump the enlarger during exposure.

Small white spots and "snakes" in sharp focus.

Cause: Dust and lint on negative.
Prevention: Blow and/or brush off dust before exposing print.

Fuzzy, unsharp light patches on print.

Cause: Dirt on enlarger lens, filter, or condensers, or obstruction in lamphouse.
Prevention: Clean lens and filters; inspect inside of lamphouse.

Print fuzzy and diffused overall, but in focus.

Cause: Very dirty enlarger lens or filter. Poor quality lens or lens taken apart.
Prevention: Clean lens and filters. Check lens. Don't unscrew anything!

Print partly out of focus.

Cause: Negative buckled, not held flat in carrier, or enlarger misaligned.
Prevention: Reinsert negative. Check alignment. Refocus.

Short, dark random lines on faces of prints.

Cause: Abrasion.
Prevention: Handle prints gently in developer.

Dark oval or teardrop-shaped stain in corner or along one edge of print.

Cause: Holding onto the print with thumb and forefinger while it is in the developer tray or draining.
Prevention: Don't hold print more than a few seconds with your fingers. Use tongs.

Muddy-looking, mottled print.

Cause: Uneven development or underdevelopment.
Prevention: Slide print under developer solution quickly and completely. Develop for full time, agitating tray constantly.

Irregular dark stains on face of print.

Cause: Excessive handling in the developer.
Prevention: Keep your hands off the print while it's developing. Lift with tongs. Agitate by rocking the tray.

Brown or yellow stains on back of dried print.

Cause: Chemical contamination.
Prevention: Wash prints fully. Clean squeegee board and clean or replace print-drying surfaces.

Overall yellow or purplish stain.

Cause: Insufficient fixing (overall yellow stain on RC prints may be from insufficient washing).
Prevention: Fix and wash for proper time. Don't let prints stick together or float on the surface. If you inspect a print from the fixer tray, be sure to return it for complete fixing. Shuffle the prints gently two or three times in fixer and wash.

Cracks in emulsion.

Cause: Wrinkling or folding.
Prevention: Handle prints gently — don't let them get bent sharply or tumbled roughly in washing. Hold prints straight as they go into the dryer.

Scratches or gouges on face of print.

Cause: Abrasion.
Prevention: Be careful with tongs. Trim long fingernails. Don't let sharp corners of one RC print scrape the surface of another.

Emulsion frilled or separated on corners or edges of print.

Cause: Wash water too warm, or print soaked too long in water or washing agent.
Prevention: Keep temperatures below 75°F (24°C). RC paper shouldn't stay wet more than about 15 minutes; fiber-base papers no more than a couple of hours.

Fiber-base prints curl excessively.

Cause: Prints dried too fast or humidity too low.
Prevention or correction: Flatten in a mounting press or under weight. If necessary, moisten backs of prints and re-dry in a blotter roll.

Prints stuck together.

Cause: Prints not completely dry when stacked.
Prevention or correction: Soaking stuck fiber-base prints in water may permit them to be gently peeled apart without damage. RC prints probably cannot be separated without tearing off the emulsion.

David H. Curl

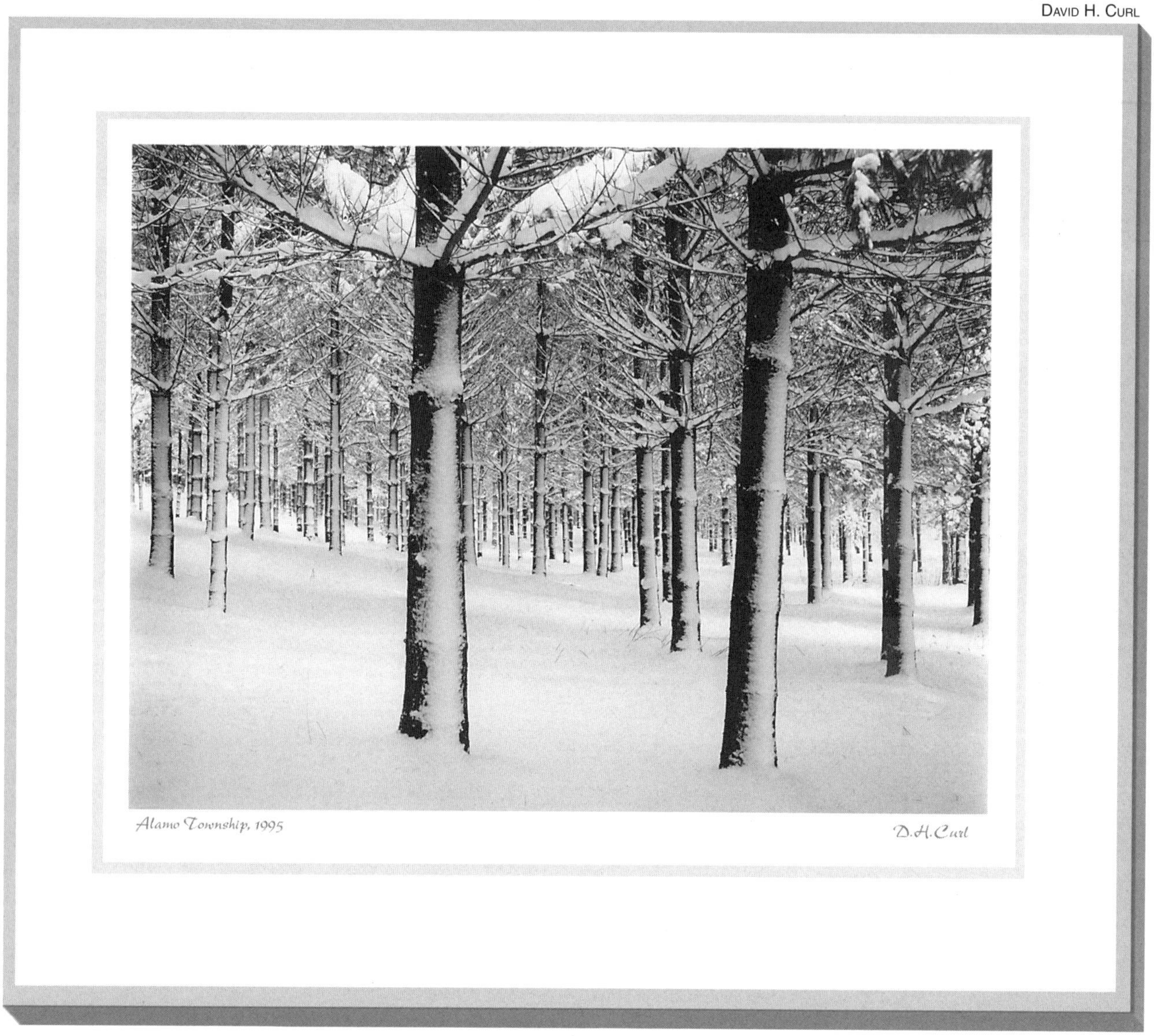

A print, finished, mounted, matted and framed. Photographs, whether black-and-white or color, traditionally are mounted on white, or off-white archival rag board. If an overmat is used, it should be cut from the same board used for mounting. Occasionally black or gray mounts and mats are used, but only if white doesn't work. Colored mounts and mats may be appropriate to blend with a home decorating scheme, but seldom for gallery exhibition. Notice that equal space has been allowed at the top and sides of the print, and slightly more below. If a title is penciled in, it normally is placed at the lower left, and the artist's signature at lower right.

> ***"Photography is observation. It's studying how people move; how light plays on surfaces; how time of day affects color. It's noticing what goes on around us and recognizing that yes, here is an observation worth recording, a moment worth saving."***
>
> — Barry Tanenbaum, editor

Print Finishing and Display 8

"The name of the game is to get your work seen."

— Ed Paschke, artist

Neatness and permanence

Making a quality print is only part of the process. You probably want to show your prints to people and you want your work to look its best — permanently. That means mounting, and/or matting and framing, and effective display. It may mean toning. And you may be concerned with archival processing so that your photographs can be enjoyed by future generations.

Archival Processing

Most photographic materials, including prints on RC papers, will last for many years without apparent deterioration if they are processed carefully in fresh solutions, according to manufacturer's instructions, and stored with reasonable care. So unless you're producing prints for a museum collection, you might not have to worry about archival processing. If you are concerned, here are some major points to consider:

1. Don't overfix RC prints.

If RC prints remain too long in the fixer, chemicals can creep into the paper base that is sandwiched between plastic layers. Fix RC papers as briefly as 30 seconds in fresh fixer; wash immediately for two minutes in rapidly changing water (don't let the prints stick together), and dry immediately.

2. Fiber-base paper is different.

Fiber-base prints should be treated four to five minutes (with agitation and separation) in each of two successive baths of fresh fixer. Use a water holding bath — don't allow prints to accumulate in the fixer. Change the water in the holding bath every few minutes and wash batches of prints frequently.

3. Protective toning.

The life of fiber-base prints can be extended by toning in gold-protective or selenium toner according to the manufacturer's instructions. An economical and satisfactory short-cut procedure is to transfer prints directly from the final fixing bath into a solution of selenium toner and washing agent:

Kodak Hypo Clearing Agent working solution 1 gallon (4 liters)

Kodak Rapid Selenium Toner concentrate 3.5 ounces (100 ml)

Kodalk Balanced Alkali 2.5 ounces (75 grams)

Agitate prints constantly while they are in the toner solution, watching for any noticeable shift in image tone. Three minutes is enough time for protective toning. With some papers, a longer time in the toner solution will pleasantly intensify the blacks and may give a warm effect to the image. Discard the solution after about ten 8x10 prints, or the equivalent, have been treated per liter.

4. Wash prints thoroughly.

Wash treated fiber prints in an archival washer that completely separates the prints, or dump the wash water every five minutes and manually separate the prints, placing a different one on top each time. A total washing time of 30 minutes at 68-75°F (20 -24°C) is probably adequate, although maximum permanence is attained by using a bath of Hypo Eliminator (Kodak HE-1 formula), followed by an additional 20-minute wash.

5. Remove surface moisture.

Squeegee or sponge both the front and back of each print. Use only a clean squeegee or sponge for this purpose, and lay the print on a smooth, nonabsorbent surface such as a stainless-steel plate or sheet of plexiglass. The bottom of a plastic photo tray should not be used, as it may harbor chemical residue.

6. Air dry the prints.

Place them face down on thoroughly clean fiberglass screening stretched onto frames.

7. Prepare for display.

Attach prints to 100-percent rag or other sulfite-free board with dry-mounting tissue or archival corners, or acid-free tape. Nonbuffered board should be used for dye-sublimation, ink-jet, and chromogenic prints. If an overmat is to be used, it should be cut from the same board. Some kinds of cold-adhesive sheets are archival, but never use household tape, spray-adhesive, glue, or rubber cement.

Betsy Hornbeck

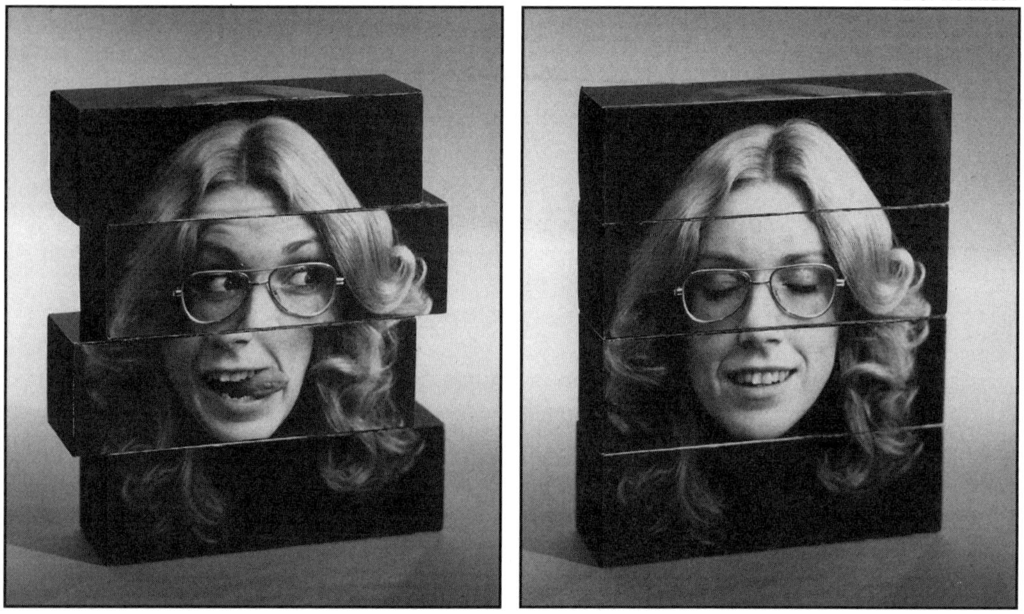

Only two of the many combinations of this entertaining, three-dimensional self-portrait are shown here. The photographer cut enlargements of four different poses into four equal-sized strips, mounting each strip on one side of a wooden block.

Selecting the size

Your portfolio will look more professional if the prints are uniform in format. 8x10 prints usually look best on mounts cut to 11x14, 12x15, or 13x16. 11x14 prints often are exhibited on 16x20. You probably will want to use 4-ply board, which is about 1/16" (1.5mm) thick. The size can depend on whether you buy ready-cut board or cut it down yourself from large sheets that come in various sizes: (A 22x28 sheet cuts perfectly into four 11x14s, 30x40 cuts into six 12x15s, and 32x40 makes six pieces 13x16 with very little waste). Keep the dimensions to even inches because sectional frames come that way.

What kind of mounting board?

White, or off-white, acid-free "museum" board is ideal, but expensive. Good quality illustration board usually costs less and may be satisfactory for class projects. It pays to shop around because the college bookstore or a local art-supply store may offer bargains in "slightly shop-worn" smooth-surfaced illustration board that can be cut down perfectly for mounting photographs.

How to cut it

The kind of heavy-duty guillotine trimmer found in print shops is ideal for cutting mounting board, although you can do very well in your own studio with a razor-sharp, stout-bladed utility knife and a metal carpenter's square. When cutting with a knife and square, cover the work surface with a piece of scrap cardboard or building board and make several straight, decisive cuts until the knife penetrates clear through. A few circular swipes on a pocket carborundum hone will keep your knife blade sharp and lessen the chance of leaving ragged edges. Cut away from the "good" part of the mounting board so you won't damage that part if the knife slips. The same cutting technique applies to foam core, which is a convenient backing material if you frame your prints. Be careful with the knife!

Separating tonal values

When light image tones tend to merge with the mounting board, you could consider adding a thin black line around the photograph. Some photographers print all their negatives full-frame, using an oversize negative carrier that automatically leaves a slightly irregular black border around each image. A more flexible approach that permits cropping is to add a black border by flashing the edges when the print is made (see photo below), or create an appropriate frame with software tools. Other alternatives include offset mounting using two contrasting boards, or careful ruling with a technical pen after the print has been mounted.

Brian Kuehn

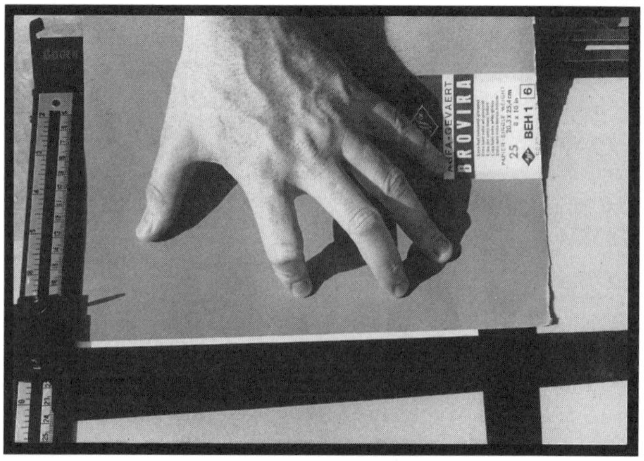

Permanent Mounting

Archivists insist that valuable museum prints be displayed only with reversible methods such as archival mounting corners or acid-free tape. But for their own portfolios, many imagemakers prefer dry mounting for convenience, and because carefully dry-mounted prints are neat, flat, and relatively permanent. Several types of adhesives are available including some "cold" processes using an adhesive with peel-off backing, but hot mounting with a press usually is preferred. The following procedure is for mounting RC prints using Seal ColorMount tissue. This same material can be used to mount fiber-base papers and the process is very similar. Other adhesives are available, some of which are intended for use at different temperatures. For best results, read the manufacturer's instructions.

Dry Mounting with a Press

1. Turn on the press.

For RC and dye prints, adjust the temperature control to 175°F (79°C). Fiber-base prints require 200°F (93°C). Allow half an hour for the press to warm up.

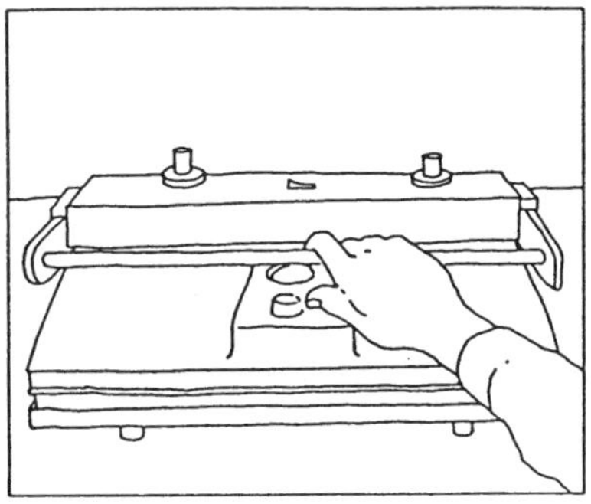

2. Plug in a tacking iron.

Set it for medium temperature. Allow it to warm up.

3. Pre-dry the mounting board (optional).

Place a sheet of mounting board between clean paper. Close the press, but don't lock it. Open the press to allow moisture to escape, then repeat the process, leaving each sheet in the press for 30 to 60 seconds. Fiber-base prints should also be pre-dried in the same way. It is not necessary to pre-dry RC prints. No pre-drying should be required when the humidity is low and all materials are thoroughly dry.

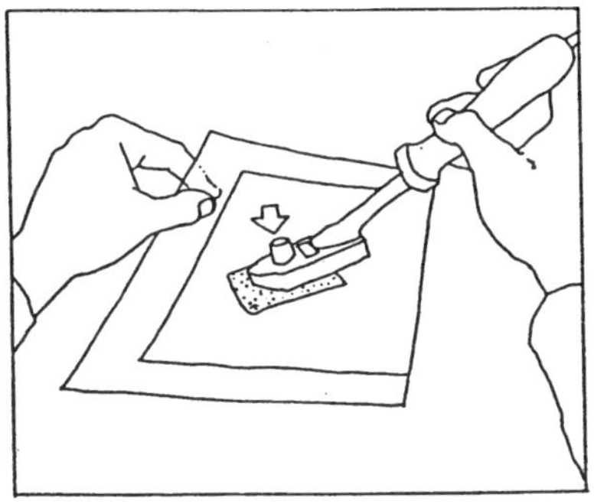

4. Attach tissue to the back of the print.

Lay a sheet of mounting board or clean paper on the table top to protect the face of the print. Be sure there are no particles of dust or grit between the print and the tissue. Bond a sheet of ColorMount tissue to the center of the back of the print by holding the flat tip of the tacking iron against a small piece of teflon release paper for about five seconds. A shiny patch on the print is the result of pressing too hard.

5. Trim the edges.

Cut both print and tissue at the same time. Now you can make last-minute cropping decisions. Cutting is easiest and most precise with a rotary trimmer. With a guillotine paper cutter you may have to hold the materials firmly to keep them from slipping and cutting crooked.

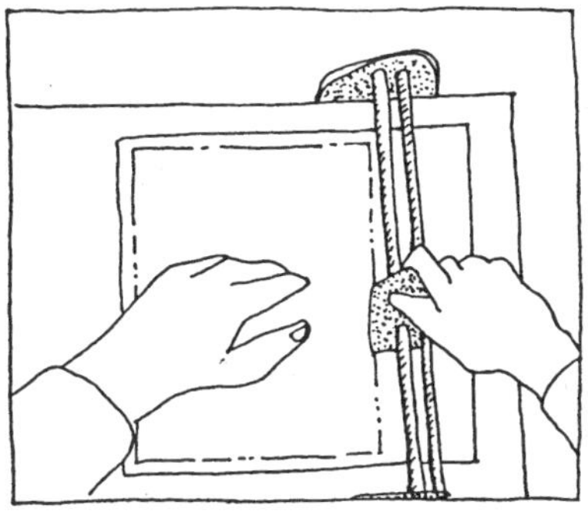

6. Center the print on the mounting board.

Measure carefully and mark the corners with a pencil. If you're going to use an overmat, it's easier to cut the mat first and use the mat as a guide for locating the prints.

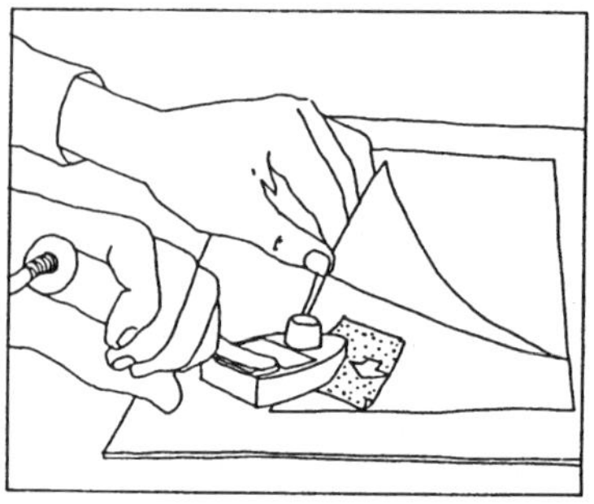

7. Attach two corners.

Be sure there aren't any particles of dirt or grit between the tissue and the print and the mounting board. Fasten two diagonally opposite corners of the tissue to the mounting board. Hold the flat tip of the tacking iron against a small piece of teflon release paper for about five seconds. Press outward slightly with the tacking iron toward each corner so you don't gather a fold of tissue back under the print.

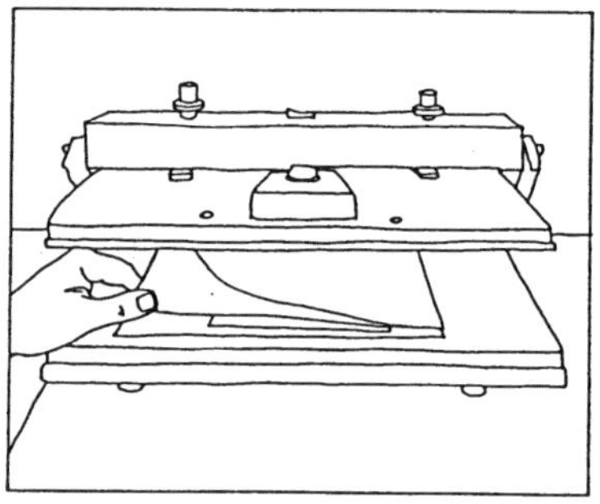

8. Place materials in the press.

Place the print, with two corners attached to the mounting board, face up inside a folder made from teflon release paper. Lay this folder in the press on top of the foam-rubber pad. (For color prints, lay a ColorMount cover sheet over the top). Be sure no particles of dirt or grit are present.

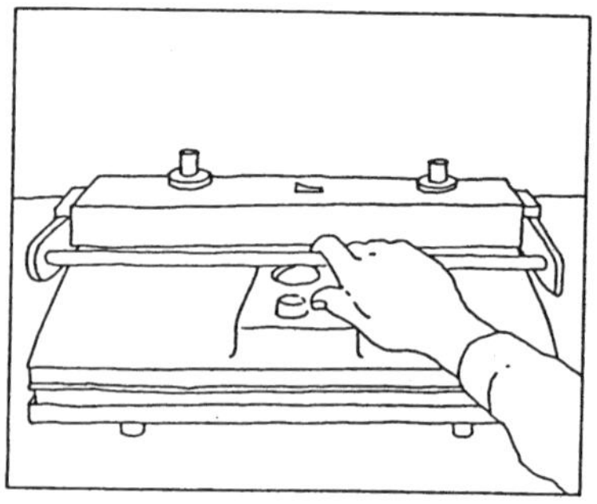

9. Lock press closed for about 30 seconds.

10. Open the press.

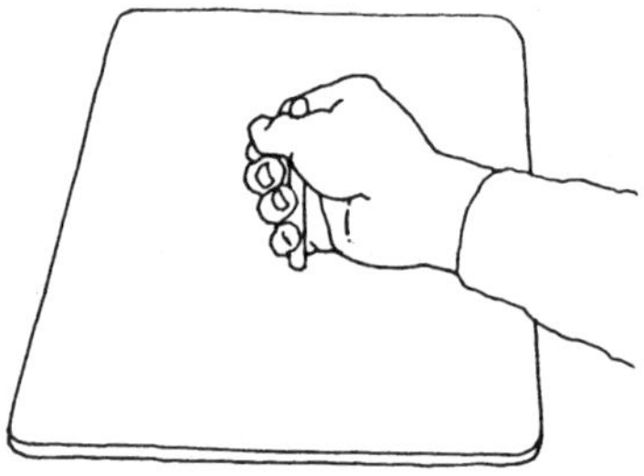

11. Cool under weight.

Quickly transfer the print in its release-paper jacket to a clean, flat surface. Cover immediately with a heavy metal plate (bonding occurs during cooling). After allowing a minute or so for cooling, inspect the bond. If the print has not adhered completely, return it to the press for a longer time and/or increase the heat slightly. If blisters or dull spots show on the surface of an RC print, the press temperature is too high. Remember Murphy? He always advises: "Never mount your best print first!"

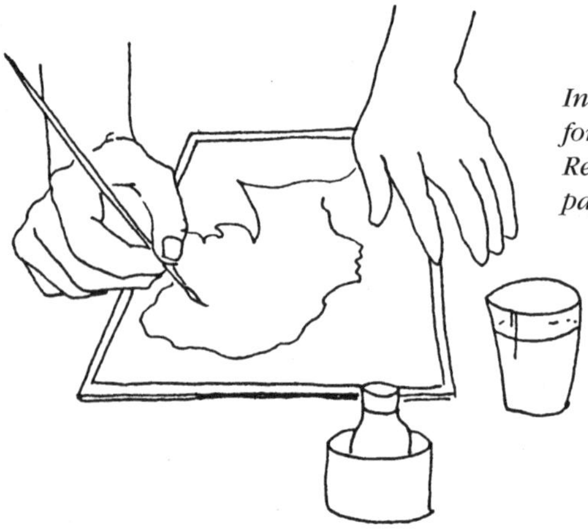

Inspect your mounted print for dust and lint spots. Remove them as shown on page 155.

Camouflaging White Spots

Retouching digital images is so easy and perfect that one dreads going back to hand-work. But when you're working with conventional materials, you'll always need to make a few minor corrections.

Along with dry mounting, spotting is another factor that sets apart professional-quality prints. No matter how carefully you brush and blow before enlarging, a few specks of dust will cling to the negative. To conceal those remaining dust spots, you'll need a very fine (00), high-quality red-sable watercolor brush and SpoTone dye, number 3.

Some people like to prepare a palette of various SpoTone dilutions, but you may find it easier to work directly from the bottle cap following this procedure:

1. Prepare the dye.

Be sure the cap is on tight. Invert the bottle and then right it again. Unscrew the cap and leave it on the worktable. Put the uncapped bottle someplace where it won't get knocked over (make a tip-proof bottle holder from the plastic cover of an aerosol spray can). Allow the dye in the bottle cap to dry for a few minutes.

2. Prepare the brush.

Moisten your brush enough to point it, then draw the tip over the dried dye in the bottle cap. Although it might not seem genteel, the tip of your finger moistened with saliva makes an excellent palette for moistening and pointing the brush. Or you can use a little water in a shot glass or small beaker, and a paper towel or tissue for wiping the brush. Rest your hand on a piece of paper to avoid marking the face of the print.

3. Apply the dye.

If you're spotting within a dark area, apply the dye full-strength directly to the spot with the very tip of the brush. Don't try to paint on the dye, but stipple with several tiny touches of the brush tip, working from the center of the white spot outward to blend the edges with the background.

4. Dilute the dye.

When the background of the spot is lighter, you'll have to dilute the dye. Use more water or saliva on the brush when you pick up the dye. Then draw the tip of the brush across the end of your finger or a paper towel to get a lighter color and a drier brush before touching the brush tip to the print.

Keep the brush almost dry, and always dilute the dye more than you think necessary; then go back and add more. If you put on too much dye, it's permanent — you make another print! Scratches and hair lines can be hidden with spotting dye, too. You do lines by drawing the tip of the brush very slowly and very lightly along the length of the white line, going back several times to make the blend undetectable. Badly damaged images can more easily be scanned, then restored using the cloning tool in Adobe Photoshop.

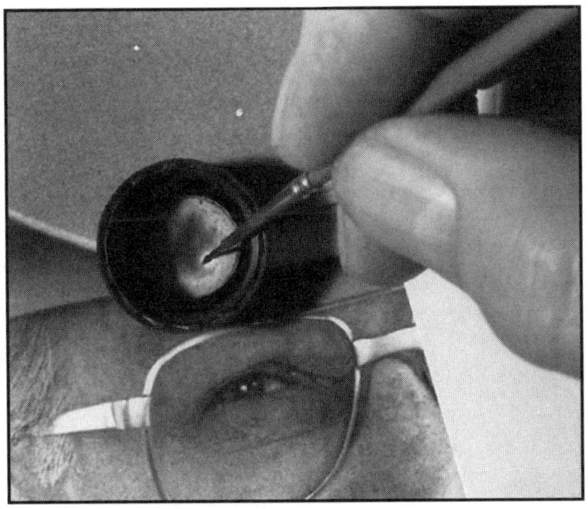

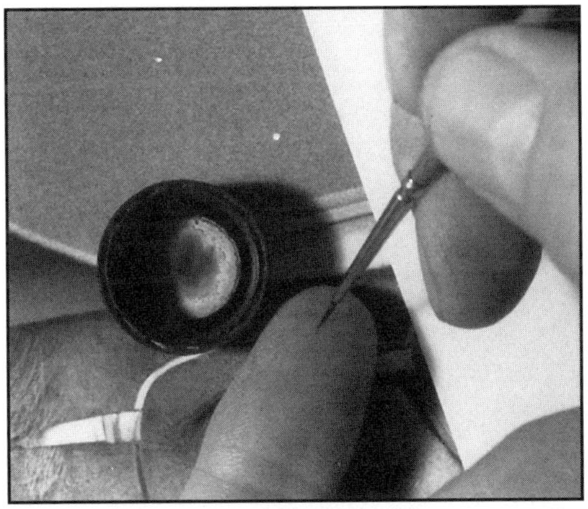

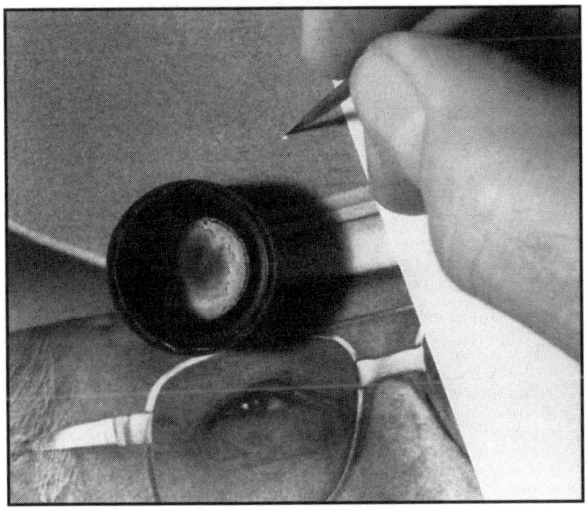

Cutting an Overmat

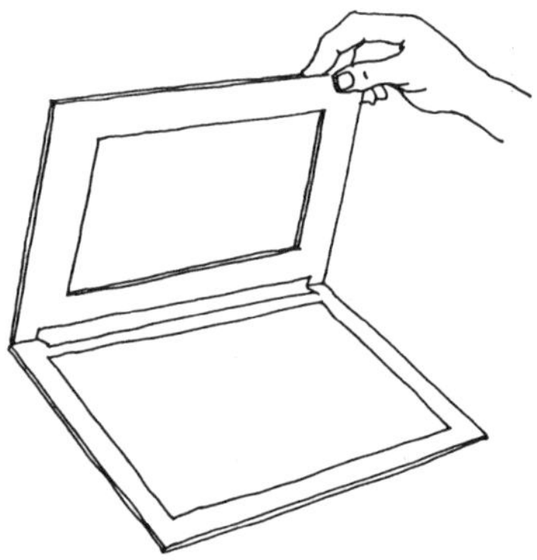

An overmat is a sign of professionalism that adds elegance to a print, especially if it is to be framed. The mat separates the print emulsion from the glazing, lessening the possibility of moisture condensation and fungus growth inside.

Mats are easy to make if you have access to a mat-cutting machine or jig. They also can be cut by hand with a beveled knife holder and a metal square. The blade should be very sharp, so be careful with the knife! Practice first with scrap board. Be sure to cut against a smooth and expendable surface such as a discarded sheet of illustration board.

A mat may be cut from the same board used for mounting, unless the color of the inside laminations is unsuitable.

Here's how to cut a mat for an 8x10 print mounted on 11x14 board:

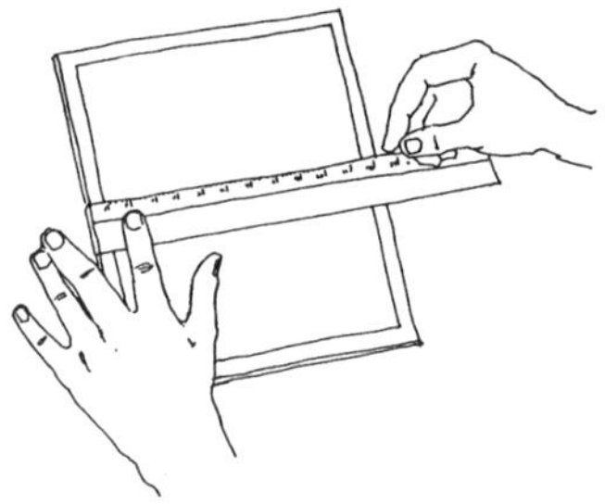

1. Measure the width.

Decide how wide you want the mat opening (7").

2. Calculate the side margins.

Subtract the width of the opening from the width of the board (11 - 7 = 4), then divide by two to figure how wide the side margins should be (2").

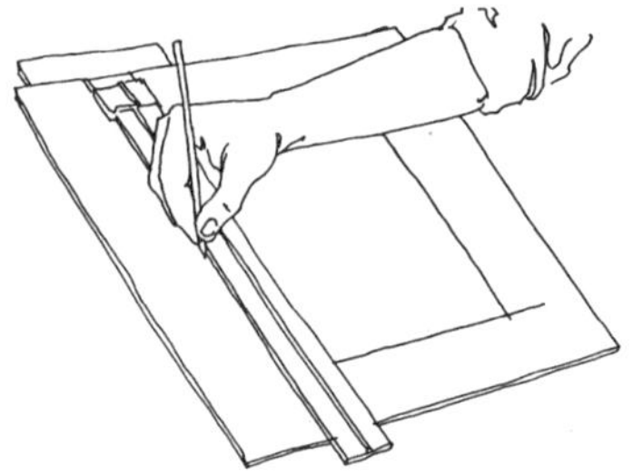

3. Measure the height.

Decide the height of the mat opening (9").

4. Calculate top and bottom margins.

Subtract the height of the opening from the length of the board (14 - 9 = 5), then divide by two if you want equal spacing top and bottom. Often, artists leave slightly more space below the print and make the top margin the same as the sides. If we do that, the top margin will be 2" and the bottom 3".

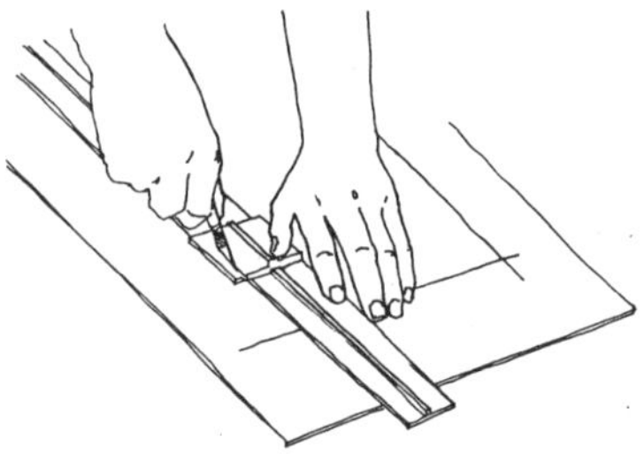

5. Mark the margins.

On the back of the mat board, pencil mark the margin widths for the top and sides of the opening. Use either a carpenter's scribe or a T-square.

6. Prepare the knife.

Insert a new or sharpened blade. Place the knife into the slot for either a straight or beveled cut (X-Acto knife holder is shown. There are many types).

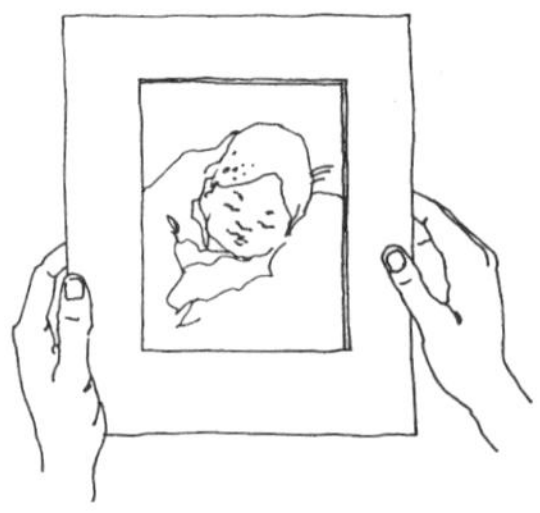

7. Cut carefully.

Hold your body against the base of the T-square and press down firmly on the end of it with one hand so it doesn't slip. Carefully cut each of the marked lines in turn, from the back of the board, cutting barely into each of the corners but not beyond them.

8. Finish the corners.

If the corners don't fall right out, finish each cut with a new single-edge razor blade. Be careful to maintain the angle of the cut, and don't cut too far.

9. Place the print.

Line up the finished mat with the mounting board and insert the print so it is centered the way you want it within the opening in the mat. Lift the mat and mark the corners where the print should be mounted.

10. Dry mount the print.

Trim and mount as described on pages 153-154. If the mat opening is smaller than the photo, the edges won't show, so you won't have to be as careful about trimming them. Photographers who prefer full-frame images often cut the mat opening oversize and align the print within, leaving a wider space at the bottom for a signature. Oversize mats also have the advantage of interchangeability. Assembling exhibits is much easier if all mats are cut to a standard size.

11. Hinge the mat.

Attach it to the backing board with a non-bleeding, non-drying tape made for library or office use. (Hinges aren't needed if the print is to be framed).

To mat or not to mat ...

A window mat can be cut from almost any kind of board, but it usually looks better if all layers of the mat board are of the same color and texture, especially if the edges of the mat opening are to be beveled. Of course, sulfite-free board should be used for both mat and backing if archival permanence is important.

What about colored mats and mounts? In photography, the general rule is to use white unless there is a very strong reason not to. Some prints do look better with a gray or buff mat, and a few prints — very few — require black. Sometimes color prints can be matted effectively with a harmonizing color, but this is a matter of taste, and colored mats seldom are seen on gallery walls.

Generally speaking, a photograph should be complete within its own borders and not need the mat to complete the graphic balance or to enhance the tonal range of the print. A colored or textured mat seems more often to compete with, rather than to complement, most photographs. The support should be just that — a background to support the image; a mat is a window through which the image is viewed. Neither should distract or call attention away from the photograph.

Etching Black Spots

SpoTone will take care of white spots on a print, but it won't do anything about black spots. Black spots can be removed by etching or bleaching, but the cure may be worse than the problem. Etching nearly always mars the surface, although tiny spots on matte paper can be worked down with the tip of a very sharp razor knife. The idea is to shave away the emulsion a layer at a time, stopping before you remove everything down to the white paper base.

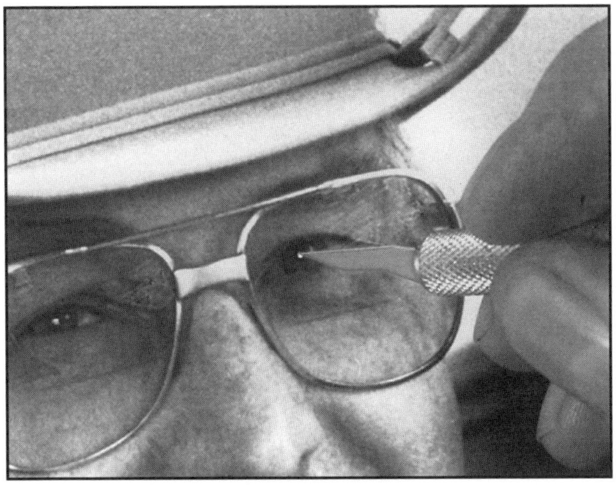

Creating catchlights. *With a sharp blade and a steady hand, you can etch reflections into eyes that otherwise would be dark and lifeless. In Photoshop, you paint them in with a small white brush.*

Bleaching

Another way to get rid of a dark spot is to bleach it with potassium ferricyanide bleach (Farmer's reducer) or with 2-percent Tincture of Iodine. The same technique can be used to "dodge" very dark shadow areas or bleach out backgrounds. Here's what you do:

Lay the damp print over the back of a tray. Apply small amounts of the bleach solution with a brush or cotton swab, blotting away any excess bleach with a sponge or paper towel before it spreads. Bleach and blot several times until you get the desired result, then refix and wash the print. Fixer accelerates ferricyanide bleaching, so for major lightening of tone you can alternate between applications of bleach and fixer. The process may leave a yellowish stain that usually goes away when the print is refixed and rewashed.

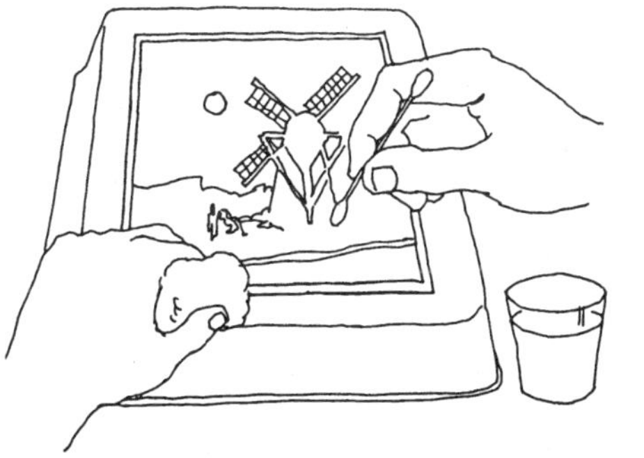

Framing and Glazing

Framing adds a final touch of elegance to your work for public exhibition or permanent display. (How can it be art without a frame?) Ornate frames usually are inappropriate for photographs, but a tasteful silver or black narrow-edged frame can add a lot to the appeal of a print, as well as keep it flat and protected.

Ordinary single-strength window glass is commonly used in frames, however acrylic sheet is popular because it is light, unbreakable (although it will scratch easily), and may help to protect the print from harmful ultraviolet radiation. You can buy either glass or acrylic and have it cut to size at a full-service hardware store. So-called non-glare glass is seldom used to frame photographs because its semi-matte surface tends to gray out the blacks in the print. Reflections are annoying. Avoid them by hanging framed prints on walls that don't face windows, lights or other light-colored walls.

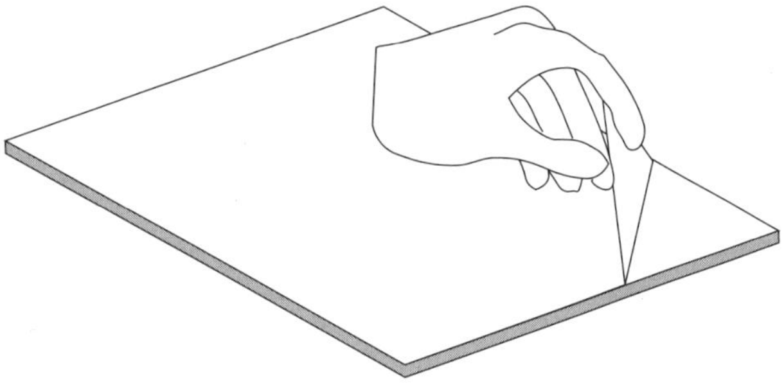

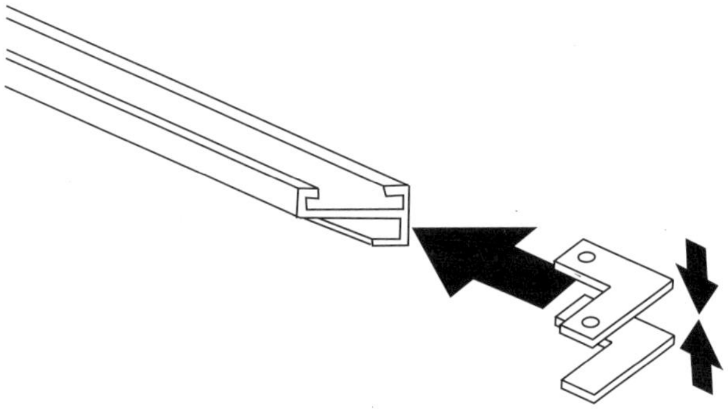

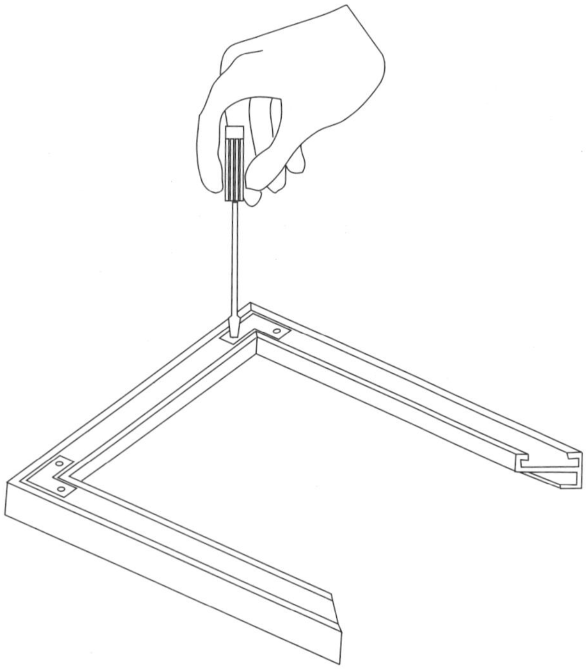

Assembling a Sectional Aluminum Frame

Neilson sectional frames are simple and practical, relatively inexpensive, and available at art-supply and photo stores and mail-order distributors. They are quick and easy to assemble. Here's how:

1. Lay out all the frame pieces.

Open the bag of hardware and be sure you have four pairs of corner angles with screws, two hangers and two bumper pads. Also there probably will be several flat metal springs. Lay out the parts on your work table.

2. Prepare the glazing.

Clean the glass, or slowly strip the covering from the acrylic sheet. Gently brush off dust. If static electricity attracts dust to the plastic glazing, try grounding the sheet against a water pipe for for a few minutes or simply let it stand until the charge goes away.

3. Assemble the "package."

Stack the glazing, mat, mounted print, and backing. Foam core makes a convenient backing. Because of the thickness of foam core, you probably won't need to use the metal springs to hold the materials package in the frame. Be sure that no dust, lint or hair is trapped where it can be seen under the glazing.

4. Put together one side.

Insert one pair of corner angles (with the name facing up on both pieces) into the track at each end of one short section of the frame. The thin angle goes inside and the thick one with the screws outside. Don't tighten the screws yet.

5. Assemble three sides.

Slide the two long frame sections over the angles, making a "U". Holding the corners tightly together, tighten all four screws.

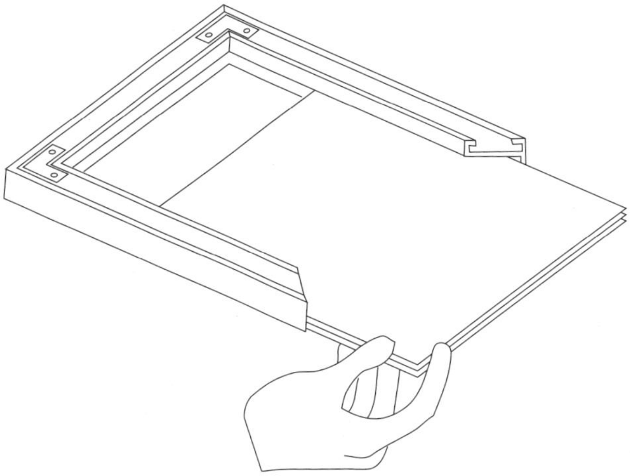

6. Insert the "package."

Slide the assembled glazing, mat, mounted print and backing into the channel in the frame.

7. Attach the final side.

Insert the remaining pairs of corner angles into each end of the final frame section. Slide the exposed ends of the angles into the side pieces of the frame, draw the corners together, and tighten all four screws.

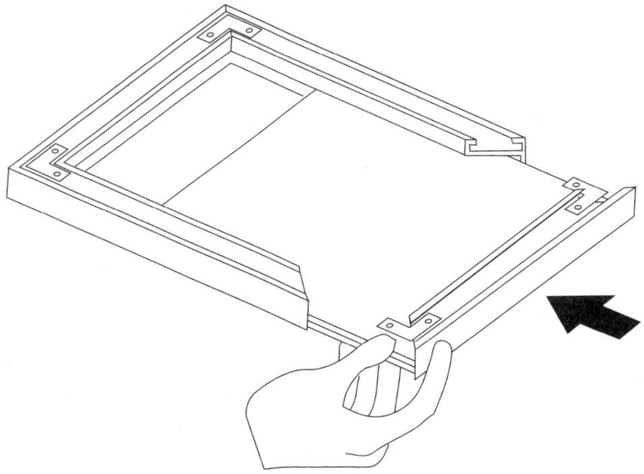

8. Inspect the front of the frame.

Be certain the corners are correctly aligned and that no dirt is trapped inside. Then check the tightness of all the screws.

9. Slip-in the springs if needed.

If the backing isn't thick enough to fill the channel, space the flat springs around the inside of the frame and slide them into place. If you do use the springs and you want to take the frame apart, be sure to remove them before unscrewing the corner angles.

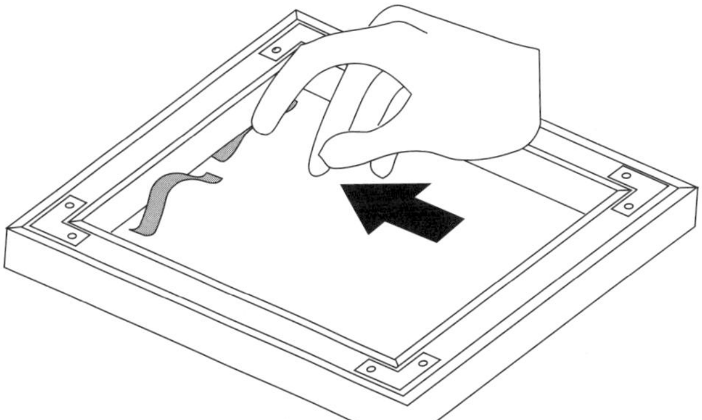

10. Attach two hangers.

Snap one hanger into each side of the back of the frame, just below the top corner angles. (There also are other types of hangers. See instructions). Picture wire may be strung between the hangers, but the best method is to suspend the frame by its top edge over two nails. If the nails have been leveled on the wall, the picture will never hang crooked!

11. Attach two wall bumpers.

Peel off the backing and attach one bumper to each bottom corner of the frame.

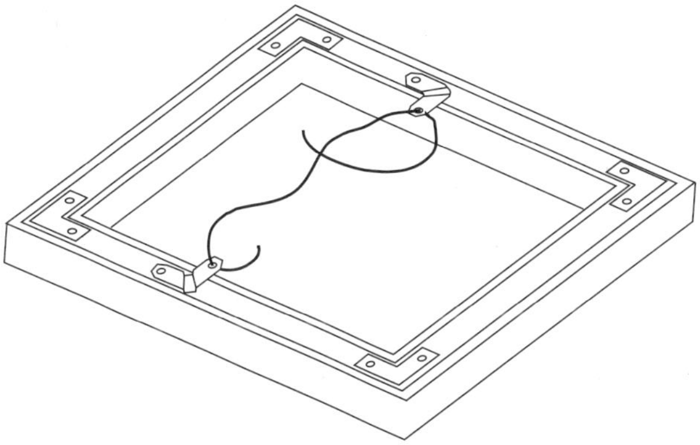

> ***"A ... photograph need not be explained, nor can it be contained in words. My photographs are presented as ends in themselves, images of the endless moments of the world."***
>
> — Ansel Adams, photographer

Bebe Lloyd

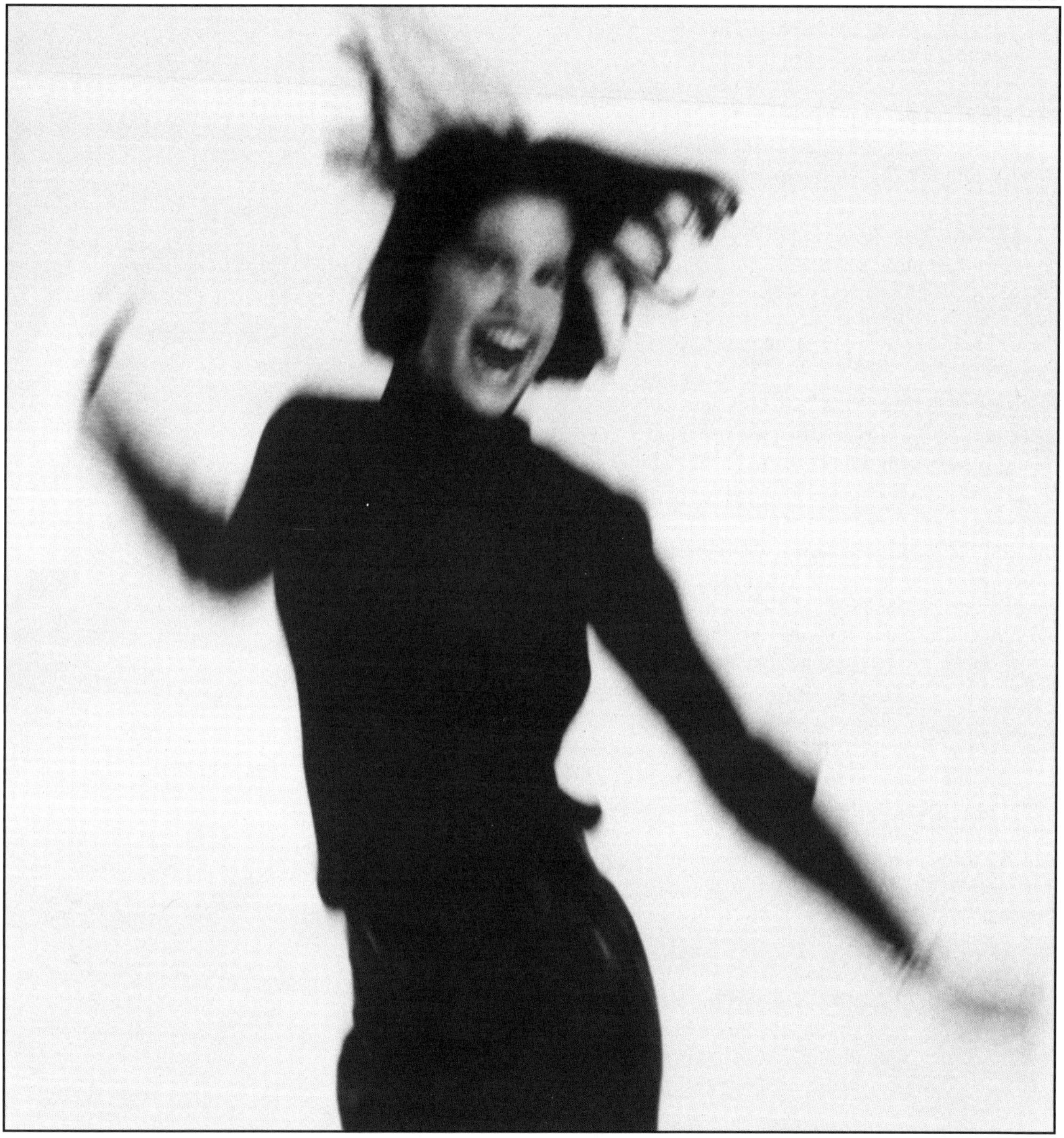

Is this a "portrait"? Does every picture have to be sharp? The shutter speed was one-half second. Only two lights were used: one 45° key light on the girl, and one aimed to separate her from the background. (See Chapter 9)

"Nothing great was ever achieved without enthusiasm!"

— Ralph Waldo Emerson, essayist and poet

Photographing People & Things 9

> ***"Camera lens, film, developer and printing paper have but one purpose: to capture and present light ... light is too often unknown, unstudied, and abused by photographers."***
>
> — Edward Weston, photographer

In photography, light is everything! Light is the force that illuminates subjects so we can photograph them. Light reveals form and texture. If you're going to make successful photographs of people and objects, first you must learn to observe light as it falls naturally on shapes and surfaces; then you must control the quality, direction, and intensity of light so that your subjects are most significantly revealed.

Notice the Light

Wherever you are, observe the effect of light on human faces. Notice how light can envelop a subject softly and gently, or harshly highlight irregularities. The way we see texture depends on whether light floods the surface with general illumination or skims the surface. Light coming from an angle creates shadows that emphasize and strengthen the natural feeling of roundness or roughness.

> ***"Become aware of distance, become aware of direction, become aware of bounce, become aware of the absence of light, become aware of reflectiveness ... "***
>
> — W. Eugene Smith, photojournalist

There are certain clichés about light. Light that is bright and all-encompassing can imply a feeling of airy openness, space, and happiness. Lightness also may be associated with innocence or femininity. Absence of light creates mysterious shadows that may appear ominous and threatening — or deep tones that may suggest drama, dignity, or strength.

Whether you're picturing people, pets or products; boats, buildings or boxes; rivers or rocks; snow or sand, the same general lighting principles apply. When planning a picture, determine first the quality, direction and intensity of the main or key source of light. Study the desirable, or possibly unsatisfactory effects of the light as it falls on the subject. Note how the light will affect the exposure and development required to reproduce the subject naturally. Then decide how you will change the light or its effects to get the result you want. You may decide to return to the scene when the light is different.

> ***"Light is never stable and never the same a second time ... Light makes each succeeding minute of every environment a new experience, and gives each situation the potential for aesthetic discovery."***
>
> —Charles Swedlund, educator

Because we're accustomed to seeing the world bathed in various degrees of sunlight, "natural" photography of most subjects usually means reproducing the general feeling of sunlight — or room light — coming from above. Any other illumination may seem contrived. Except when experimenting for unusual effects, the aim usually is not to call attention to the lighting, but to reproduce things the way they would naturally appear.

The "natural look" calls normally for a single *main* or *key* light source that appears to come from somewhere above and to one side, casting shadows that emphasize the form and texture of the subject. If additional lights produce more than one set of shadows, the picture may look weird, and facial features may seem distorted.

> ***"Every time you change position — every time there's a change in the light — there's a new world to see."***
>
> — Frank Gohlke, photographer

Look at pictures, observe people

You can learn a lot about lighting by studying other people's pictures. Most of the examples in this book were produced by students, and these pictures will be a good place to start, but get into the habit of analyzing the lighting and composition of every photo and painting you see. Also watch people as they sit in class, in the office or plant, at home, or outdoors, and notice the way their faces and bodies are illuminated.

Steve Gusfa

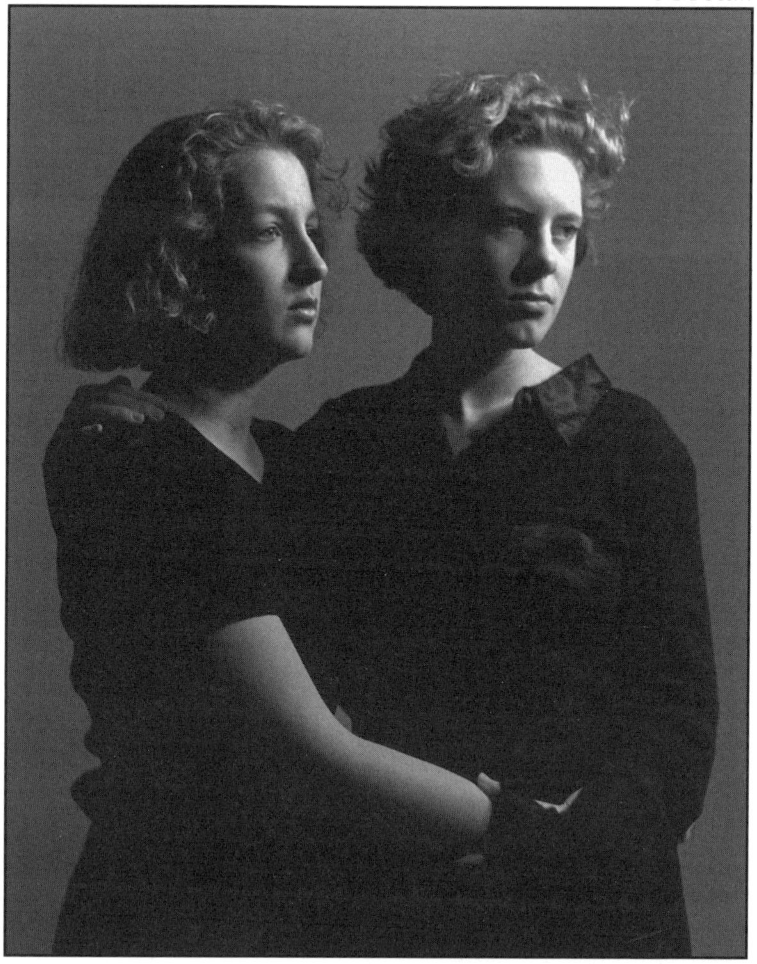

(Above) A single 45° light created a low-key mood, illuminated both faces, and spilled enough light on the gray background to prevent tone mergers.

(Below) Large classroom windows provided soft, directional light; a chalkboard was a convenient background. Notice the vitality obtained by having the subject turn her head at an angle to her shoulders.

William Beverly

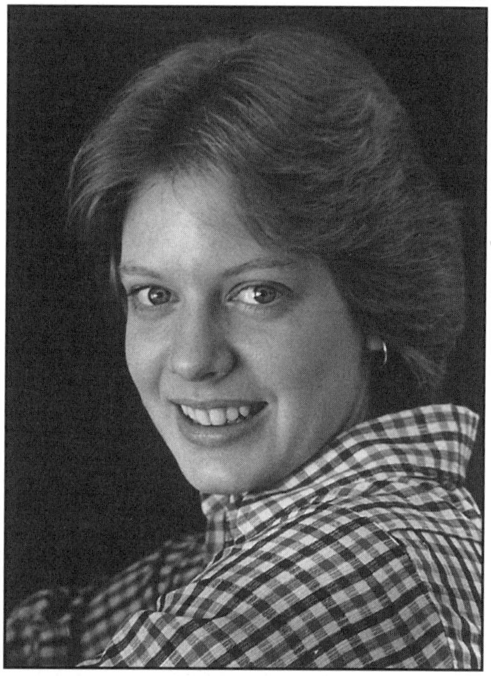

Larry Allen

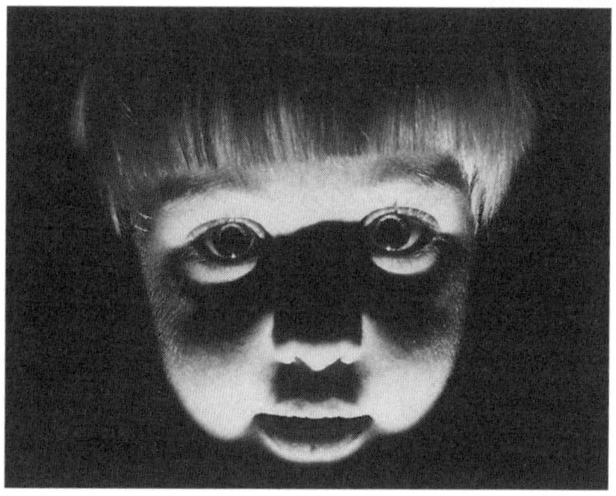

(Above) Lighting from underneath seems mysterious, even sinister, as the head appears to be floating in space.

Robert Fleming

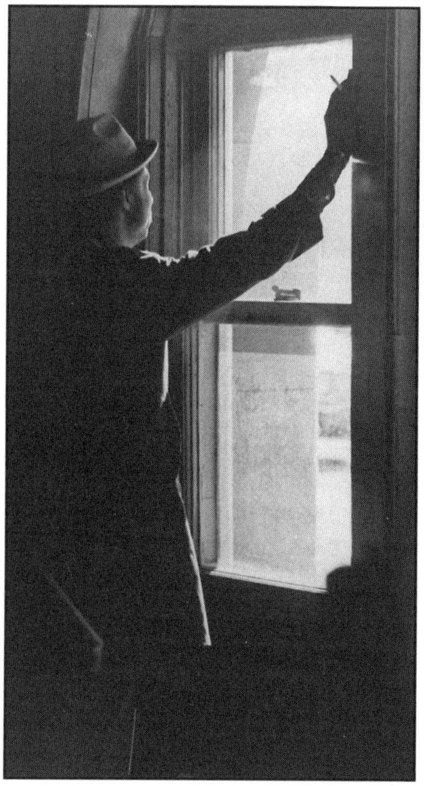

(Right) Natural window light is everywhere. It can be excellent for photos, especially when the subject faces toward the light. Here, the mood suggested that no fill light or reflector be used. What exposure problems needed to be solved?

MARY CAIN

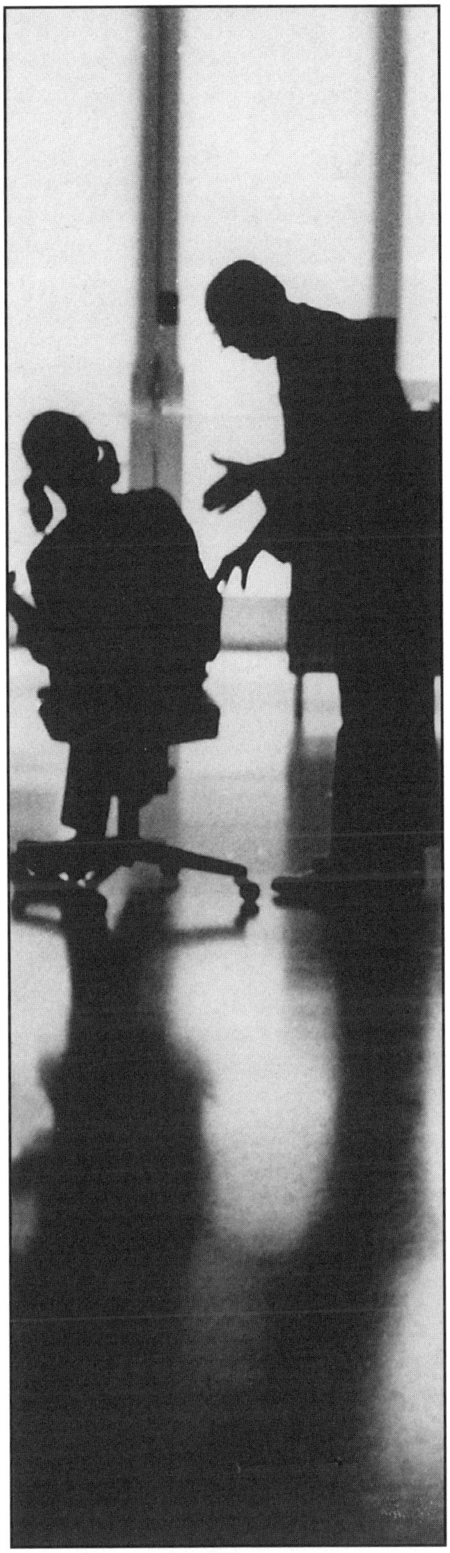

(Above) Could this silhouette be more provocative than if the image portrayed a full tonal range?

WILLIAM T. O'BRIEN

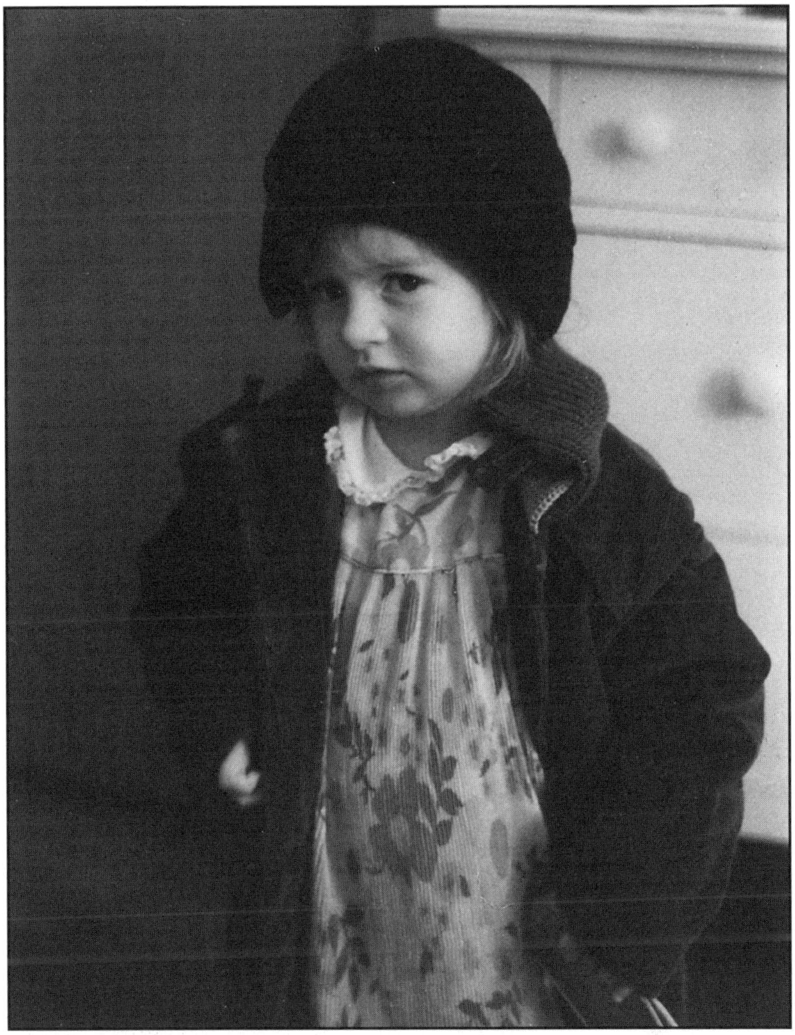

(Above) Soft, existing room light was sufficient for this appealing portrait

R. VANDER ZWART

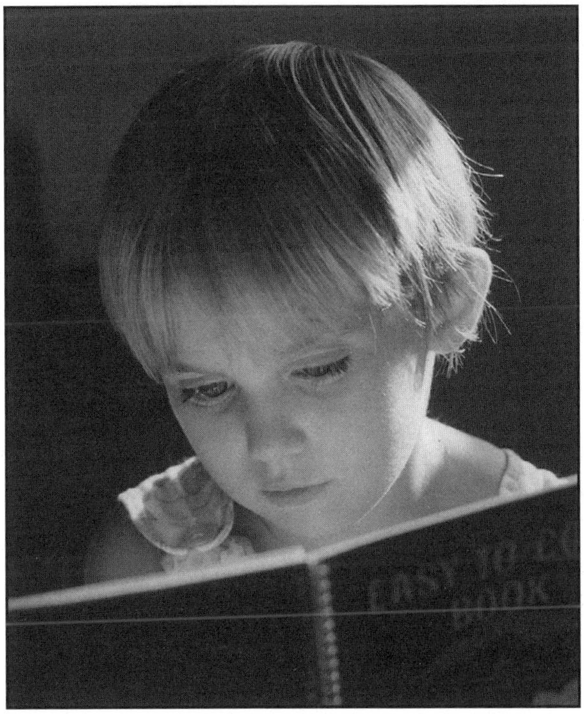

(Left) An open book makes an excellent reflector to balance the extreme contrast caused by backlighting in direct sunlight.

Ardyce Czuchna-Curl (2)

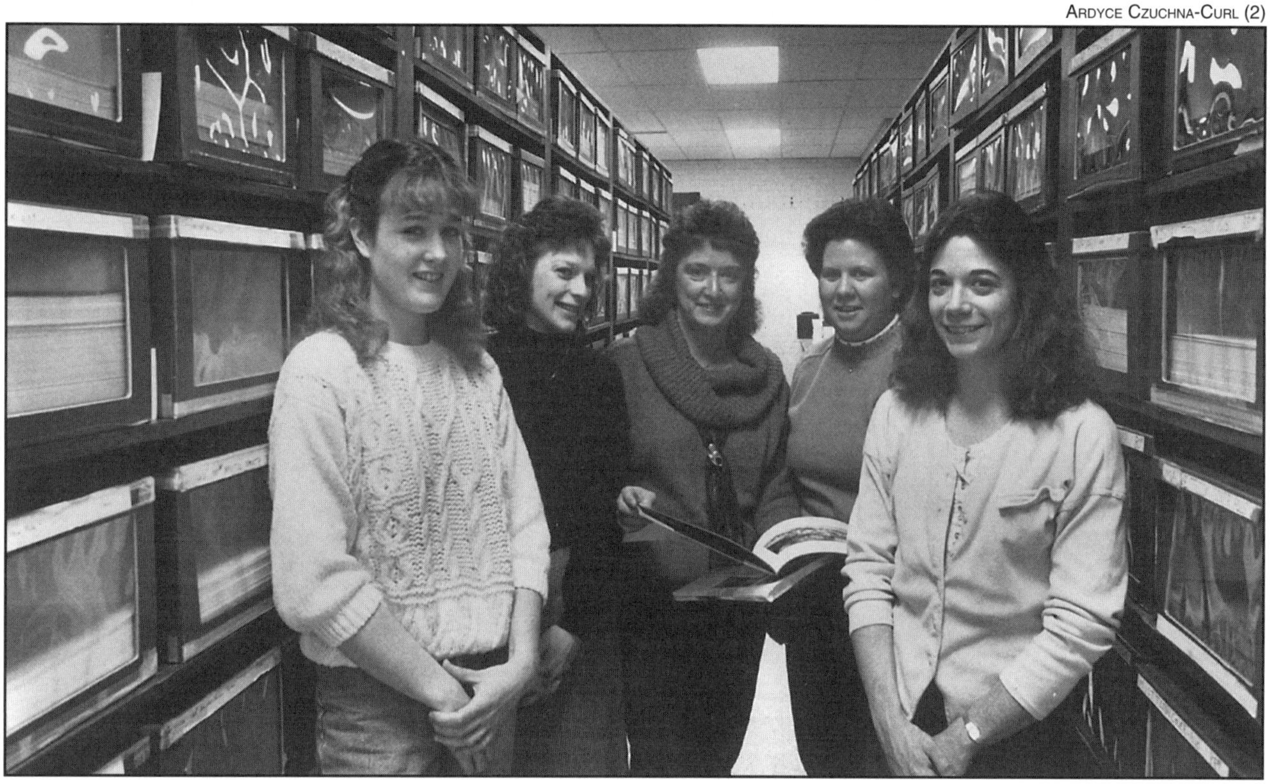

Available light from fluorescents in the ceiling gave a natural look to this obviously posed, but believable group portrait for the company newsletter. 400-speed film was used. Exposure, with the camera on a tripod, was 1/8 second at f/11.

David H. Curl

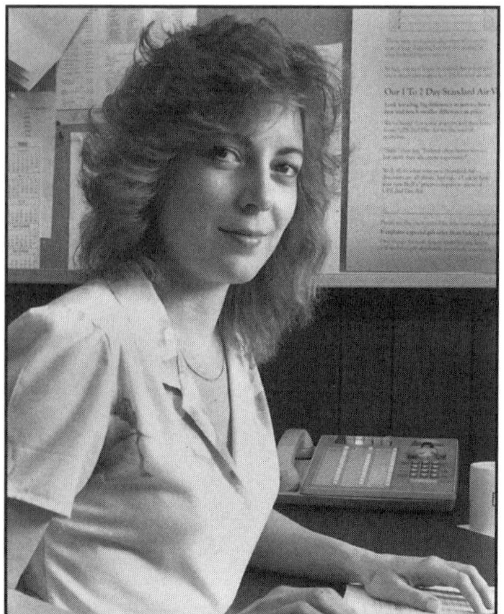

Existing light in the office was appropriate for this employee portrait. Notice that perfect 45° "short" lighting was achieved by asking the subject to turn her head until the existing light created the desired effect. Shot on a tripod with 400-speed film at 1/8 second.

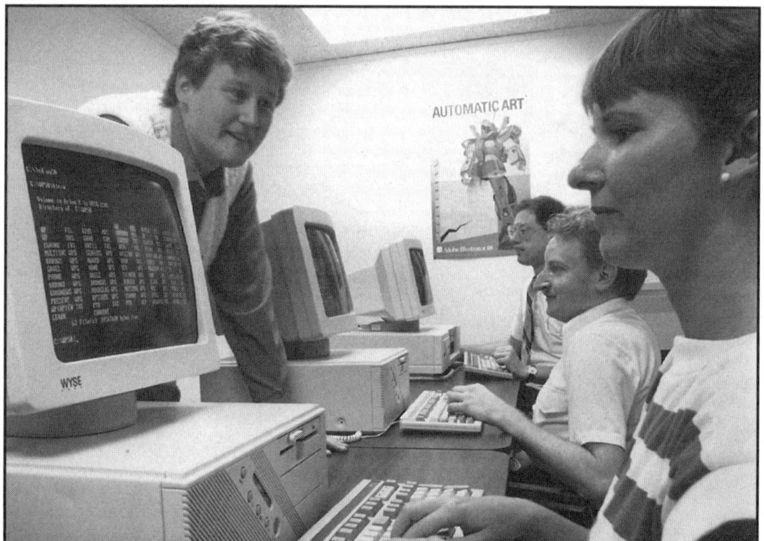

*Overhead fluorescent lights were adequate for a "posed-unposed" exposure of 1/4 second at f/22 on 400-speed film. Visualize this same picture taken with direct flash on camera or with bounce flash. When would you **not** choose the tripod and existing light?*

Make the Most of Existing Light

Excellent pictures can be taken by existing light, without using flash or heavy studio lights. Existing room light, together with "fast" films, can create realistic photographs. Instead of moving the light to the subject, as in a portrait studio, the secret of success is in moving your subjects in relation to the light. If you're shooting a group activity, for example, arrange everyone so that each person faces a light source, whether that source is a window, a lamp, or a fireplace fire.

Try the "posed-unposed" technique

Arranging people doesn't necessarily mean posing them stiffly. You can group people informally and direct them to go ahead with some natural activity such as talking, working, playing a game, or examining an object. When you're ready to shoot, ask the people you're photographing to "hold it just like that" for an instant if your shutter speed is slow. Make several exposures, and pretty soon your subjects will lose their self-consciousness. Before the people are in place, if possible, use your exposure meter to determine a basic overall exposure setting, but be extra careful not to let the meter pick up any stray light that might affect the reading. Move some people closer to the light source, if necessary, so that all important parts of the picture are receiving about the same amount of light.

Evenly lighted rooms present few problems for existing-light photography, except perhaps that the light may be perfect for uniform exposure, yet uninteresting. If the light is strong and bright from windows along one wall and two or three stops darker on the other side of the room, you have two basic choices. First is to face the subjects toward the windows as a key light and allow the background to remain dark. The second approach would be to work for a dramatic effect by backlighting the subjects. With backlighting there is a risk of underexposing shadow detail, so either make incident-light readings or meter the shadow areas. As in other situations of extreme subject brightness range, the lowest important values should be placed in the proper zones. Another solution is to reduce the range of brightness.

Fill in the shadows

When the main subject is backlighted, a reflector may introduce enough light to supplement the shadows, or you can try bouncing light from the ceiling or walls. The bounce technique works well with either flash or flood, yet allows you to preserve the believable effect of natural illumination.

Don't forget to carry a tripod with you for shooting interiors. The extra trouble will pay off when you need more depth of field and you're forced to shoot at a slow shutter speed, such as 1/2 second. Some interiors are just too dark to permit using a hand-held camera.

Some typical existing-light exposures (400-speed film)

Classrooms, offices	1/60 @ f/4
Home interiors	1/30 @ f/2
Auditorium stage	1/30 @ f/2
Bright stage show, concert	1/125 @ f/4
Night football, baseball, races	1/125 @ f/2.8
Indoor sports	1/125 @ f/2.8
Neon signs	1/125 @ f/4
Night street scenes, carnivals	1/30 @ f/2.8
Candlelit close-ups	1/2 @ f/5.6
Floodlighted buildings	1/2 @ f/5.6
Traffic, carnival ride patterns	B @ f/16
Fireworks	B @ f/16
Lightning	B @ f/11

David Harrison (2)

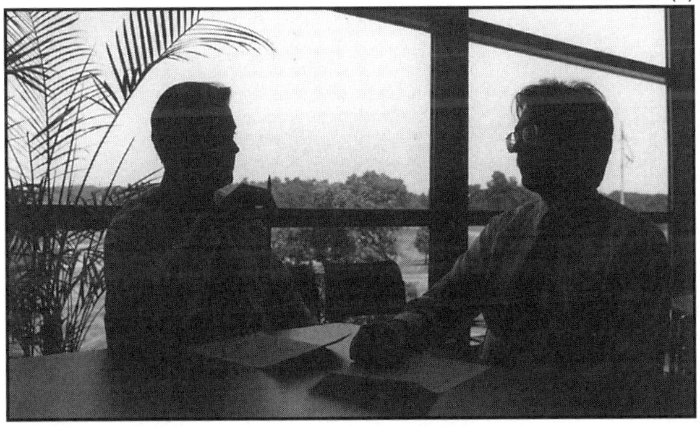

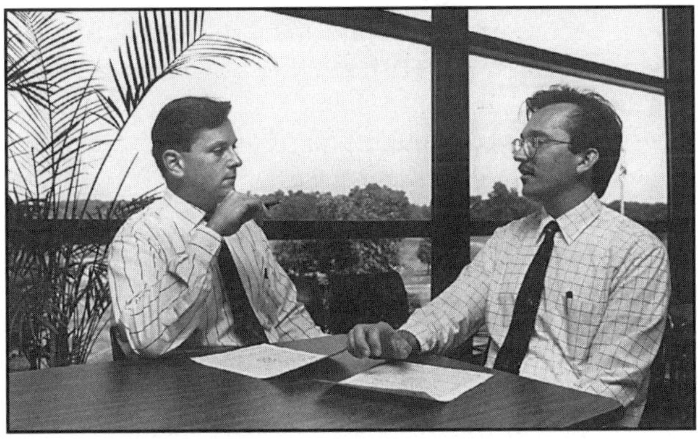

Bounce flash can fill in the shadows when subjects are facing away from existing light. When the subject is stationary and the camera is on a tripod, a reflector may be the best choice because you can see its effect.

PAM VOGEL

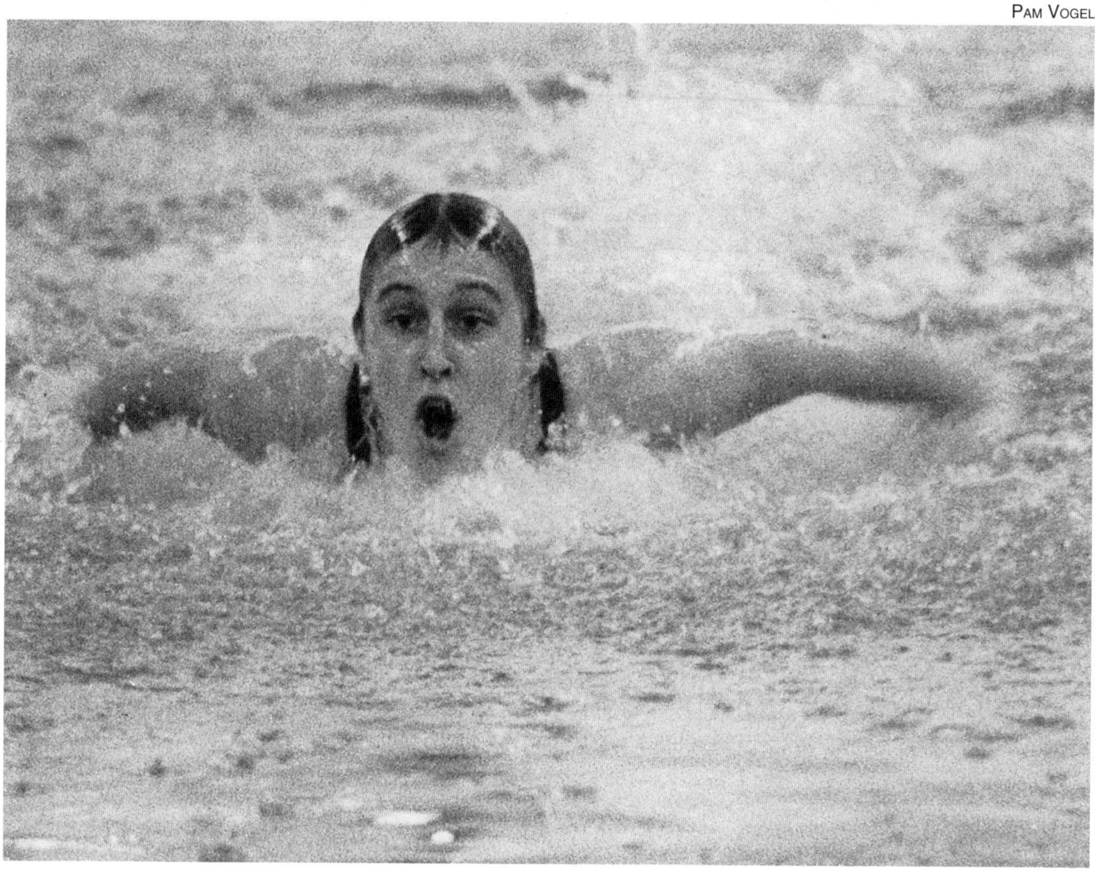

In low-contrast lighting, underexposing 400-speed film at EI 1600 and push-processing with N + 2 development results in a negative that appears about as grainy as ISO 3200 film also shot at EI 1600.

Push-Processing

If you want to take pictures of moving subjects in relatively dim light, such as stage action, indoor or night sporting events, or industrial machinery in action, something has to be sacrificed to be able to use a fast shutter speed. What you give up is fine grain and shadow detail. The super-crisp, color action shots of basketball or hockey that you see in sports magazines may have required setting up around the arena thousands of watt-seconds of electronic flash so exposures could be made on films rated EI 100 to 400. But for reproduction in newspapers, good-enough photos are made every day using faster film under existing light.

Films such as Kodak T-Max P3200, Ektachrome P800/1600 and Ektapress 1600 all are intended to be exposed at EI 800 or higher, depending on processing. The instructions packed with these films give guidelines. Manufacturer's instructions for commonly used EI 400 films such as Kodak T-Max 400 and Ilford HP5 Plus also indicate processing for EI 800, 1600, or higher.

Film manufacturers build into their products a safety margin of about one stop, which means that if your equipment is correctly calibrated, you can expose most films at double their normal speed and still get an "acceptable" rendering of average subject matter. The penalty you pay for minimizing exposure is the risk of loss of shadow detail. By doubling the speed from 400 to 800, you're underexposing by one stop; in Zone System terms, you're lowering the low values in the subject brightness range one full zone. For example, a dark, textured Zone III area photographed on T-Max 400 film would be rendered at EI 800 as Zone II. Doubling the speed again to EI 1600 will place that Zone III area in totally textureless Zone I, losing all shadow detail below Zone IV and resulting in an extremely thin negative.

The price of pushing

"Pushing" means underexposing the film and overdeveloping it — sometimes in concentrated or high-energy developer. Developing underexposed negatives for extended time or in strong developer increases the density of the higher values (Zones VI through IX) without doing much for the shadows. This increase in highlight density makes the negative more contrasty, but it is also very likely to "block up" the high values so that the lighter zones cannot be separated in the print. High-energy developers often build up a false shadow density through overall fog and increase the tendency for grain to clump together and become visible.

BLAIR BEITNER

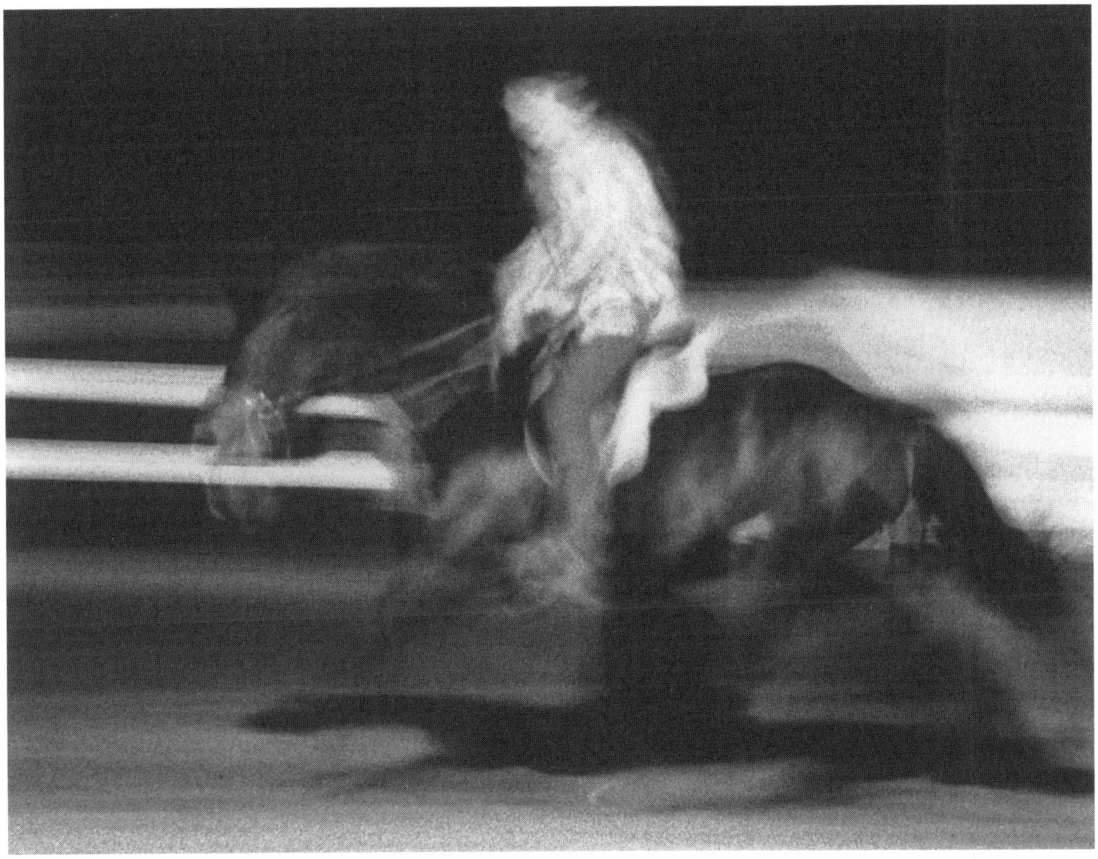

Kodak T-Max P3200 film was exposed at EI 3200 outdoors at night. At f/2, a one-second shutter speed gave the negative printable density and the picture an exciting illusion of movement.

Because of the loss of shadow detail, pushing is poor practice when the subject has a wide brightness range, such as people doing things in an unevenly lighted room. Sometimes, as with night football, pushing is the only way to get pictures. But be ready for problems printing underexposed negatives, especially if there are dark-skinned players wearing dark-colored uniforms.

Pushing is useful, however, when you need to stop fast action in limited light and when the brightness range is so narrow that you would want to give N + (plus) development anyway. Some examples could include football or soccer on an overcast day, or a swimming meet or ice hockey in an evenly lighted arena. Under such conditions, there are few significant low values to lose; hence, an underexposure of one or two stops (rating 400-speed film at 800 or 1600) and N + 1 or N + 2 development would be appropriate. Perhaps a better approach than push-processing would be to try a very fast film such as T-Max P3200. The negatives may be thin and somewhat grainy, but they should have a satisfactory tonal range and adequate contrast for printing and reproduction. If light is adequate, exposing P3200 at EI 1600 will give a one-stop margin that will improve shadow detail.

Pushing color films

The higher the exposure index, the greater the grain; and "push" processing increases contrast. These rules apply to color films as well as to black-and-white. But you have to decide whether a sacrifice of shadow detail and a gain in contrast are acceptable prices to pay for results. Aerial photography is one field in which it is routine to push color film. An extra stop or two of speed is desirable, and the extra contrast from push-processing helps reduce the effects of haze in the air.

Since magazines and newspapers are printing many more color photos, staff photographers and correspondents have to come back with color negatives or transparencies that will stand reproduction. Fortunately, grain doesn't show as much in the halftone reproduction on a printed page, so many photojournalists routinely shoot 400- or 1600-speed color-negative film on daily assignments.

This is the most important rule to remember about pushing: Do it when you have to, but don't expect the same quality as when you give correct (Zone System) exposure and processing.

JOHN WILLERTON (2)

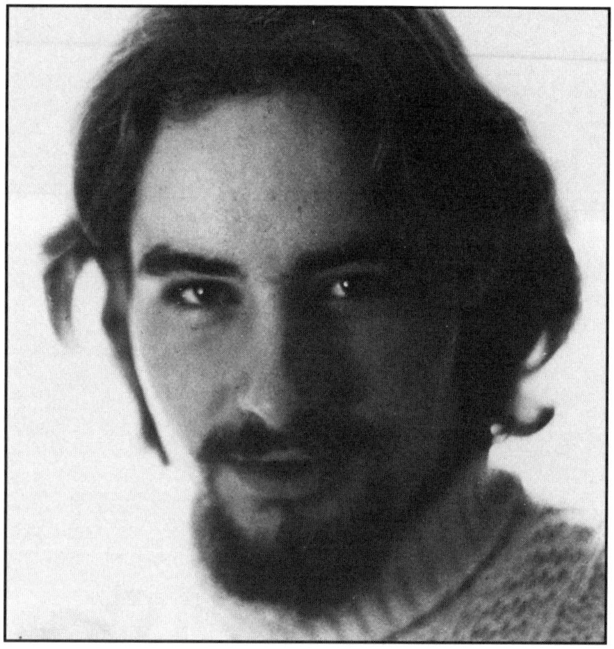

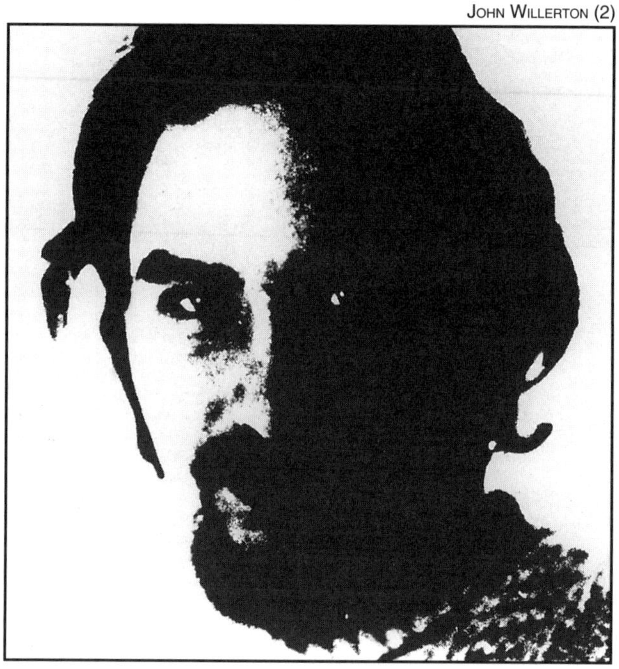

Does the difference in contrast affect your reaction to the person in the portrait — as you imagine him?

Portraiture

"If you wait long enough and someone is looking at you — sooner or later you will see their soul, providing you don't talk too much."

— Bruce Davidson, photographer

A portrait should emphasize the subject as a person. A good environmental portrait can reveal much more about the subject than merely what he or she looks like. Surroundings or background may contribute by indicating something about the person's home life, work, or interests. A fleeting expression on the subject's face may reveal deep truth.

"A portrait ... if it's handled right ... is the closest thing to climbing inside somebody's mind and experiencing what they are about."

— Brian Lanker, photojournalist

Careful selection of pose and lighting by the photographer can bring out grace, poise, dignity, and character, as well as emphasize or de-emphasize certain features. The subject's eyes, facial expression and body language often will reveal a great deal about your own relationship with the individual you are photographing — tense and formal, casual and relaxed, amiable and intimate. You might be surprised to realize that your instinctive choice of camera angle, subject distance, and lighting will reveal something of your attitude toward the person.

"The good photographic portrait is a collaboration, a transaction between photographer and sitter. It reveals the personalities of both. ... Photographer and ... subject are connected by a thread that is delicate and tenuous. If the two establish rapport, the photograph will be a success. The subject will feel that the photographer has had the insight to see his best qualities, and the photographer will feel that he has perceived the essential human being. Thus, it is the photographer's responsibility to choose the particular fraction of a second by which the person would wish to be remembered."

— Margery Mann, photographer

"The attitudes of people are so different in front of a camera. Some are embarrassed. Some are ashamed. Some hate to be photographed and others are showing off. You feel people very quickly. You see people naked through the viewfinder ... and it's sometimes very embarrassing."

— Henri Cartier-Bresson, photojournalist

At one time, a 4x5-inch or even larger negative was thought to be necessary, for portraits always were believed to require retouching. But many excellent portraits now are being made with 35mm and 120-size roll film cameras. Small negatives are difficult or impossible to retouch with pencil and an etching knife, but much of the demand for retouching has disappeared. Many portraits are made for publication, and reproduction processes suppress enough detail to effectively diminish many facial faults. When it's important to satisfy the subject, soft lighting and simple diffusion techniques either at the camera or in the darkroom can soften the appearance of wrinkles and blemishes. Digital photography simplifies retouching and makes possible immediate selection of images from a shooting session.

"The difference between a portrait and a snapshot is that the portrait is [made when] the person agreed to be photographed. It's not at all like somebody you see and catch on the street."

— Henri Cartier-Bresson, photojournalist

Although excellent informal portraits can be made in existing light with a small hand-held camera, a tripod and controlled, artificial lighting are still important equipment for making "formal" portraits. You also will need a plain, neutral background.

It's hard to converse with your subject and observe spontaneous expressions while looking through a viewfinder (it makes your subject uneasy). However, with a tripod and a cable release, you can concentrate on the subject and forget about the camera, except to trip the shutter. If you have a choice of lenses, a lens about twice the normal focal length is ideal for portraiture.

LIN CHILDS

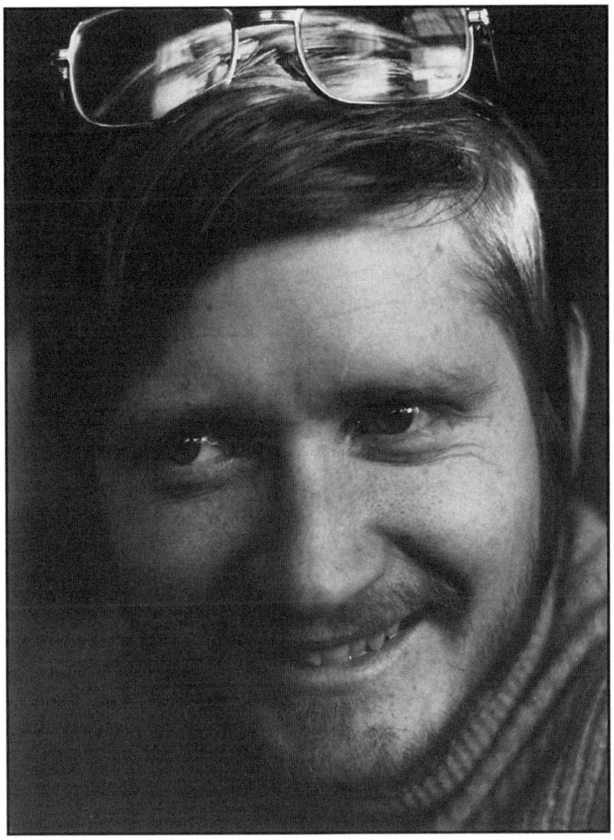

Awareness, spontaneity, intimacy — all elements of an effective portrait. Does this one suggest something about the relationship of subject and photographer?

A shorter focal-length lens at close range tends to make the subject uncomfortable and to distort facial features, making whatever part of the anatomy is closest to the camera appear abnormally large.

"One reason photographs don't look natural is that photographers always tell their subjects to look pleasant."

— Author unknown

Professional Studio Lighting

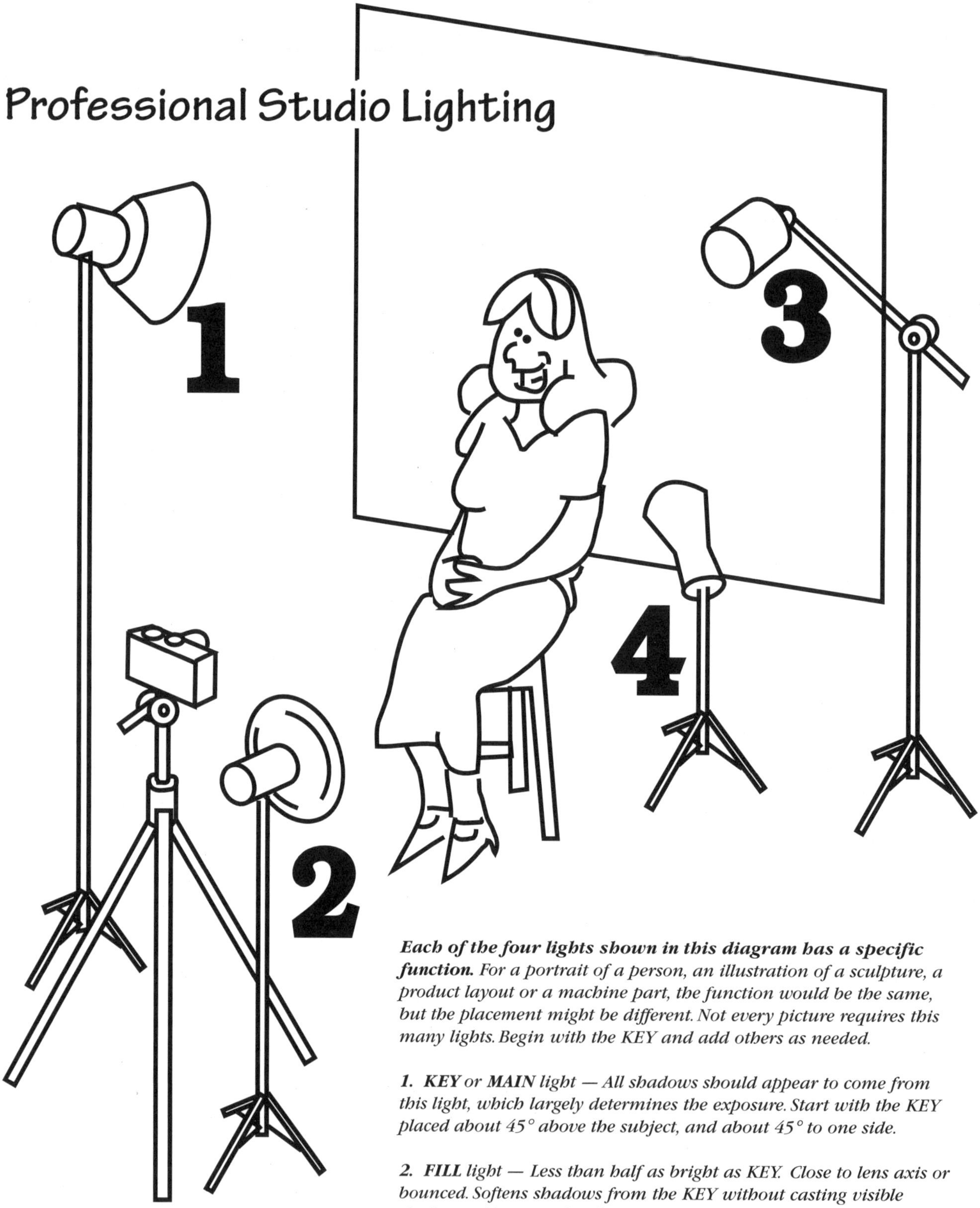

Each of the four lights shown in this diagram has a specific function. *For a portrait of a person, an illustration of a sculpture, a product layout or a machine part, the function would be the same, but the placement might be different. Not every picture requires this many lights. Begin with the KEY and add others as needed.*

1. ***KEY*** *or* ***MAIN*** *light — All shadows should appear to come from this light, which largely determines the exposure. Start with the KEY placed about 45° above the subject, and about 45° to one side.*

2. ***FILL*** *light — Less than half as bright as KEY. Close to lens axis or bounced. Softens shadows from the KEY without casting visible shadows of its own. A reflector sometimes is used instead of a lamp.*

3. ***ACCENT*** *or* ***BACKLIGHT*** *— Adds highlights on hair and shoulders. Should not shine into camera lens or on subject's face.*

4. ***BACKGROUND*** *light — Separates the subject from the background. Eliminates any shadows cast on background by FILL.*

Placing the key light

"Studio" portraits usually require a minimum of two lights: the main or key light and a fill-in light, or one light source plus a reflector for fill. Most professional studio portraiture and illustration is done with electronic flash systems with built-in "modeling" lights to aid positioning. Maximum control is possible with flash (sometimes referred to as strobe) lighting. Large tent-like softboxes, reflectors, grid and focusing spot attachments all make it easier to get exactly the quality, intensity and direction of light desired. The very quick, bright flash eliminates the problem of motion, and its brightness permits great depth of field.

Incandescent "hot" lights will do almost as well. They're just not as convenient for the photographer nor as comfortable for the sitter.

Whatever the light source, the key or main light should be the brightest and it should cast the only noticeable set of shadows, comparable to the sun's light outdoors.

The 45° formula

Usually the best place for the key light is high enough so that the light falls on the subject's face from about 45° above eye level, and 45° from the subject's face on the side away from the camera. In other words: 45° high and 45° from the far side. And place the camera on the dark side of the face. This 45° formula produces a result that, among pros, is referred to as "short" lighting because, assuming the subject isn't facing squarely toward the camera, it illuminates the short (narrow) side of the face. Short lighting is appropriate for most faces. Notice the examples in this chapter and look for other examples of short key-light placement everywhere: still photos, movies, television, and on the stage.

An alternative 45° key-light placement is broad lighting; so-called because the camera is looking at the lighted (broad) side of the face instead of the shadow side. Butterfly lighting places the key light 45° high, directly above the subject's face, producing a "butterfly" shadow directly below the nose (see illustrations on page 172).

Light the eyes

If your subject has deep-set eyes, or is wearing a hat that shades the eyes, either tilt back the hat or lower the key light until the eyes no longer are in shadow. Try to get a "catchlight" in each eye from the key light. These tiny bright sparkles add life to the portrait.

Susan Thole

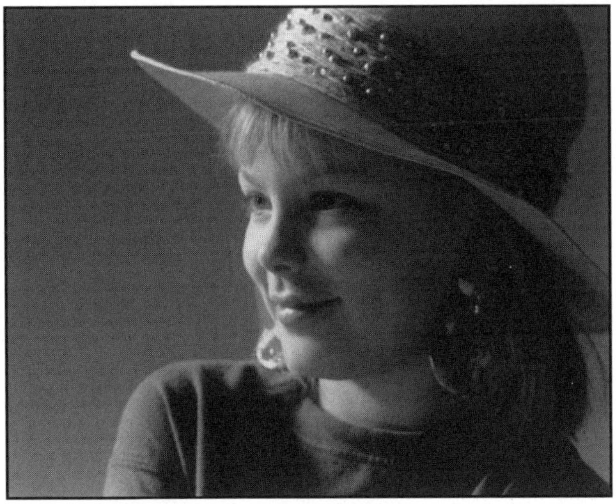

This is a good example of 45° key light placement. Notice that the highlights are on the far side of the face, forming a triangle of light on the cheek nearest the camera. The shadows are on the camera side of the face, and have been made transparent by a weaker fill light near the camera. The catchlights in the eyes were created by the key light.

"I like to try to feel what the artist felt [at the moment of creating the work]. That's how you know what art is."

— Alice Walker, poet and novelist

David Harrison

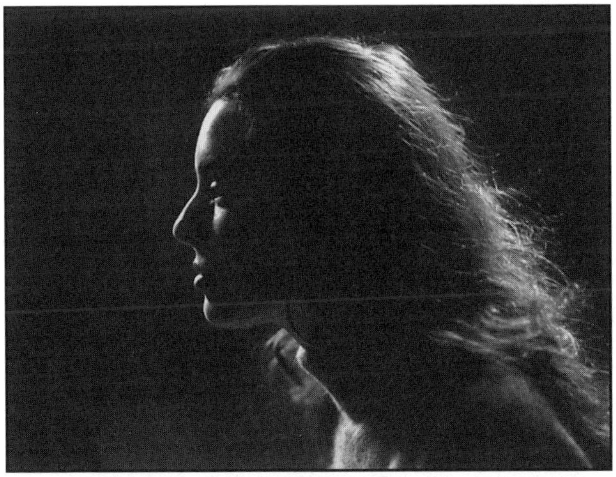

Do you like this low-key profile portrait? Only two lights were used: The key was 45° behind the model's face, to the left. The accent was 45° behind her, to the right. The two lights were set at 90° to each other. This effect, a variation of the basic 45° short light, is called "rim" lighting.

W. A. Moss

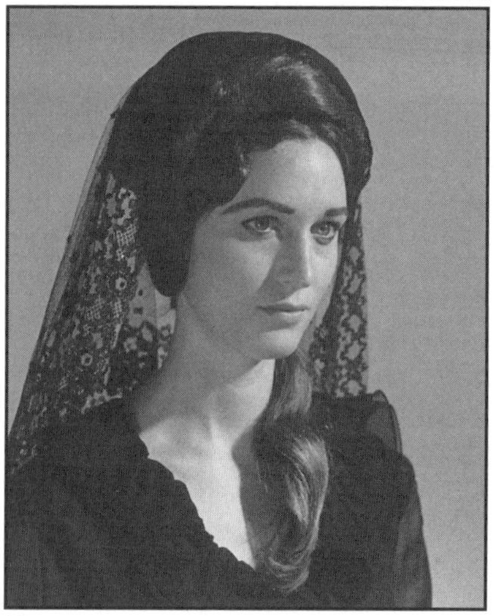

The portrait above illustrates placement of the 45° key light and diffused fill. Notice how the key light forms a triangle of light on the model's right cheek. This is what is referred to as short lighting, because the key is placed to illuminate the short, or far side of the subject's face. Notice that the camera is on the shadow side.

Ashaki Smith

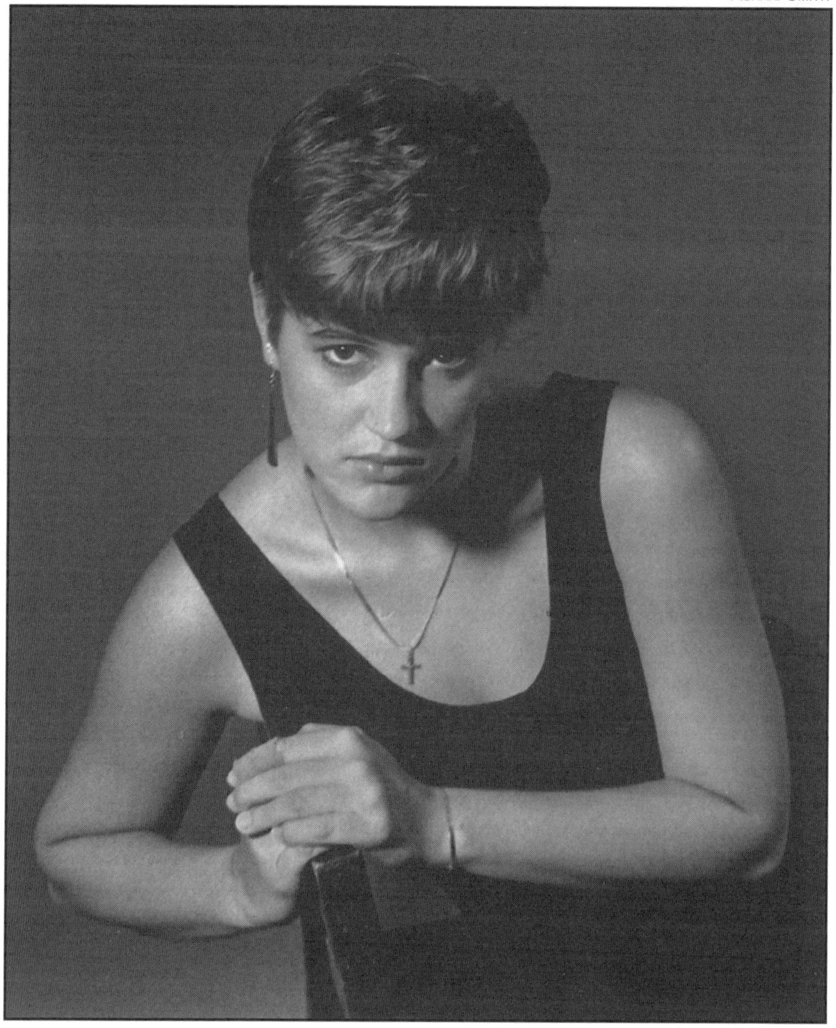

A sophisticated theatrical appearance has been achieved with broad lighting, no fill, and a subtle accent light behind the subject's left shoulder. Notice how her hands and arms are carefully posed to unify the composition.

David H. Curl (3)

Short light

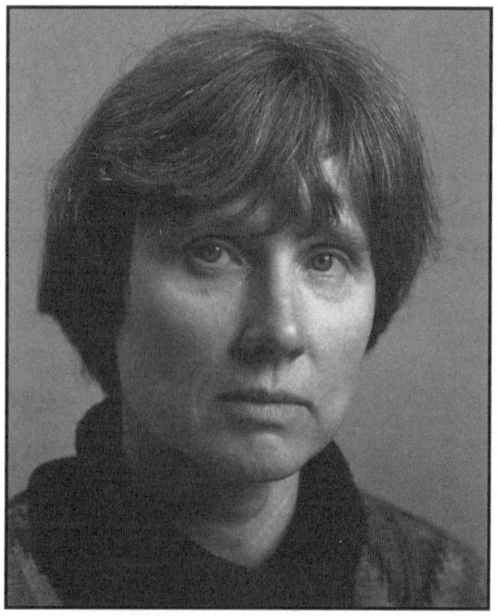

Broad light

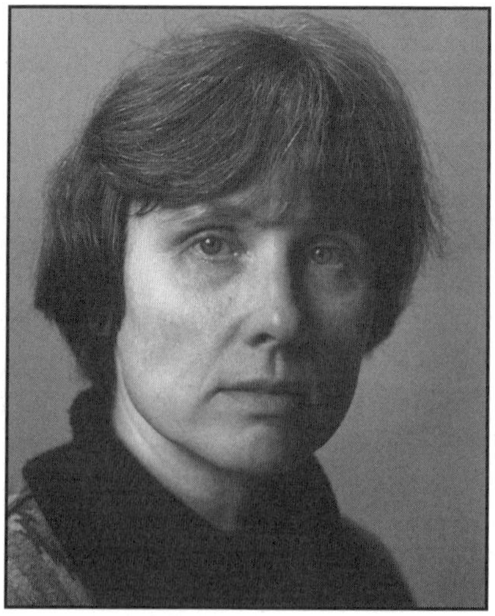

Butterfly light

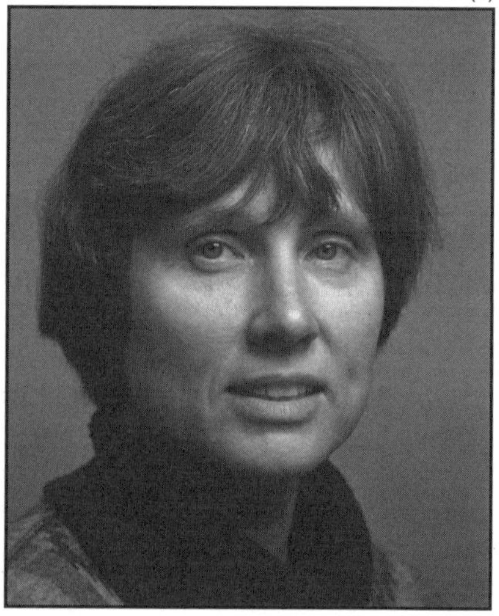

Placement of the key light emphasizes facial form. Compare short lighting (left), broad lighting (center) and butterfly lighting (right). In each example, the key was the same — a single quartz lamp bounced off a silvered umbrella. The only change was moving the key light. No other lights were used.

Fill in the shadows

Because the shadows cast by the key light alone usually will be too dark for anything but a dramatic theatrical effect, you probably will want to add a fill light or use a reflector to reduce the subject contrast. Using too much fill is a common mistake. If the fill is too bright it will wash out the effect of the key light and cast shadows of its own. The fill light should be only one-half to one-fourth as bright as the key, and it should be placed as near as possible to the camera (or bounced) to prevent secondary shadows.

Experiment with the lighting ratio, remembering that for a one-zone difference in brightness the fill should be half as bright as the key. If the fill is one-fourth as bright, the difference will be two zones.

Caucasian skin in full light should ordinarily be Zone VI and the shadow side of the face no darker than Zone IV. Dark faces often reproduce well at Zones V and III. You can control the relative brightness of the fill by moving it toward or away from the subject, or by "feathering" the light by turning it toward one side to control its intensity. Other good techniques are to attach a translucent diffuser over the fill light, or to "bounce" the light from a convenient white wall or reflecting surface. Remember that a two-zone difference in brightness represents a lighting ratio of 4:1 between key and fill. You can verify the ratio with your exposure meter, reading first the highlight side of the face and then the shadow side.

Separate the subject from the background

When dark-haired people are being photographed with only one or two lights, their hair sometimes lacks detail and sparkle, and it blends into the background. Dark hair can be brought up to Zone III, improving its texture and adding some sparkling highlights, by using a third light, called an accent light, high above and behind or to one side of the subject. Carefully aim the accent light at the area you want to brighten, being careful not to let any of the light spill over onto the subject's face or into the camera lens. When you add an accent light, it's generally a good idea to put a lens shade on your camera and use "barn doors" or a "snoot" on the accent light to keep glare out of the lens. The accent light won't affect an incident meter, but don't forget to switch it off before making a reflected-light reading of the face.

If the background seems too dark, a fourth light can be placed behind the subject and directed onto the background. Move the subject farther from the background if an objectionable shadow of the subject falls on the background from the key or fill. If the shadow is weak, the background light can eliminate it; if not, move the subject still farther from the background. A painted wall or plain drapes can serve as a portrait background if you don't have a roll of seamless paper or a painted canvas flat. A makeshift background rigged from a blanket or sheet usually shows wrinkles and looks fake. For environmental portraits, a natural background is best of all. Try to avoid strong patterns and lines unless you can include them as part of the composition. Bold background elements often distract by competing with the subject for the viewer's attention.

Camera angle

Most portraits of a seated subject look best if the camera height is near to the subject's eye level. Looking down on a person can make them appear submissive (children often are photographed from an adult's eye-view). Looking up at a person either adds stature or a feeling of aloofness. If your camera is on a tripod, as it should be, direct the subject's eyes to the lens or to wherever you want them to look. Otherwise, in trying to get an animated expression, the subject's eyes might follow you — if you're not standing directly behind the camera, you might get a lot of "white of the eye," which looks unnatural.

Often, a head-on front view of a person (passport style) is unflattering and gives an unpleasant feeling of confrontation. For most subjects, a three-quarter view is better, showing only one ear. Turning the head in relation to the body gives a feeling of poised action. You'll learn a lot by trying to emulate portraits that you like. Invite your favorite model to help you experiment with variations in posing and lighting.

MIKE DEINES

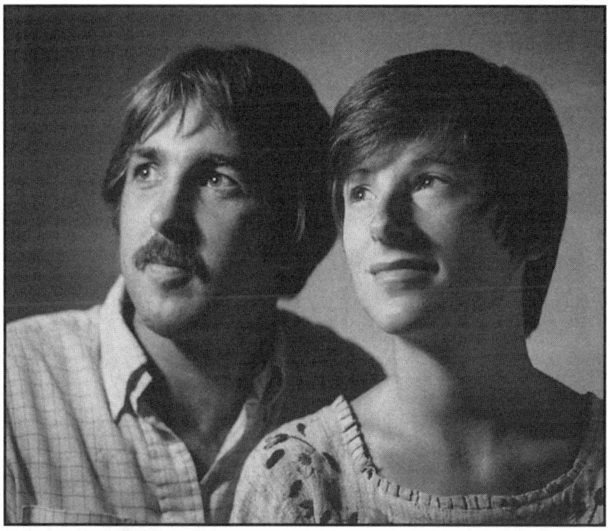

This informal portrait illustrates the use of a single key light on two people. A window can give this effect, or any kind of direct light source. Enough light was scattered around the room from light-colored walls to fill the shadows with some reflected light.

Jorg Jasper (3)

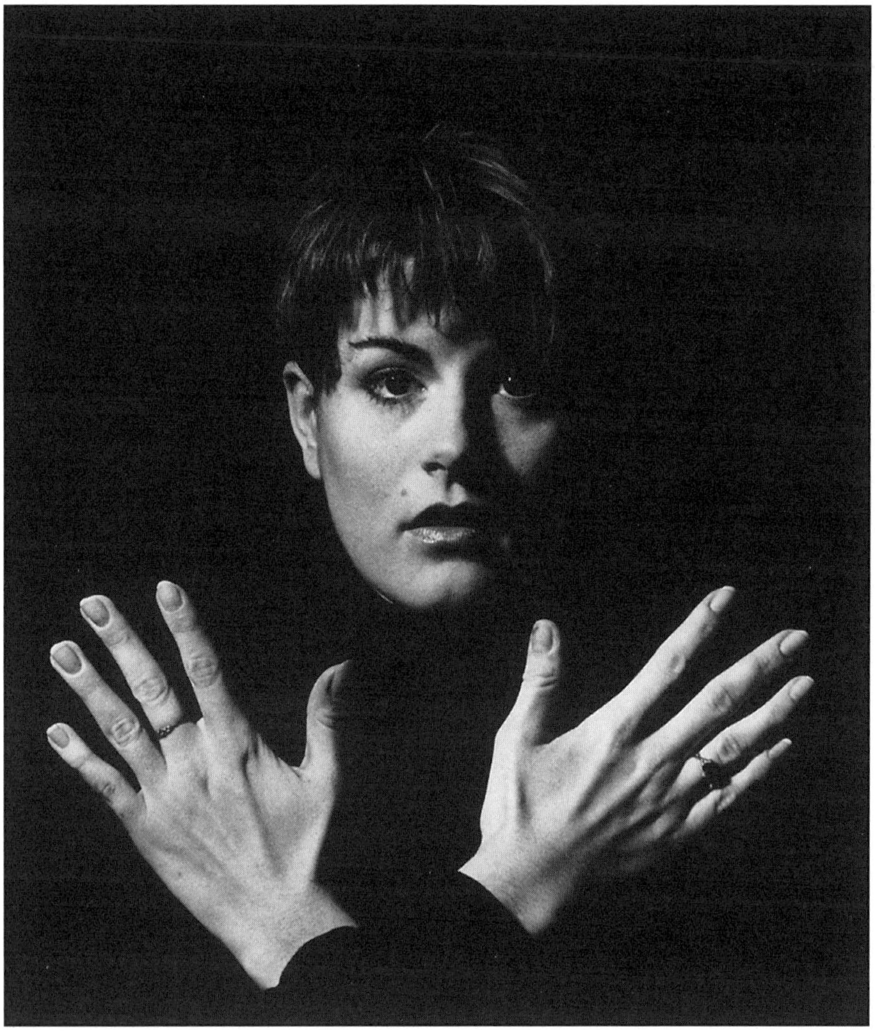

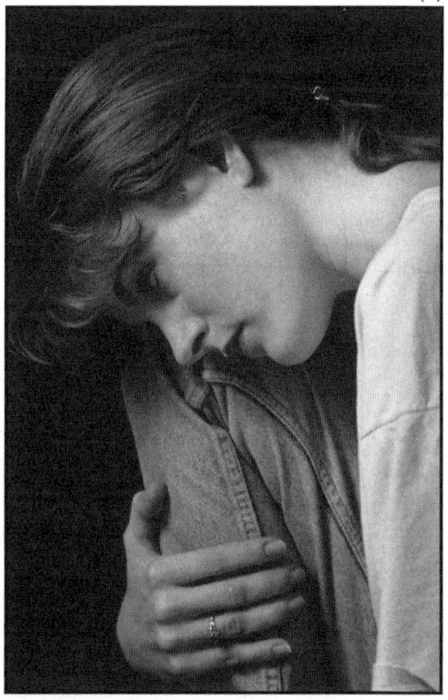

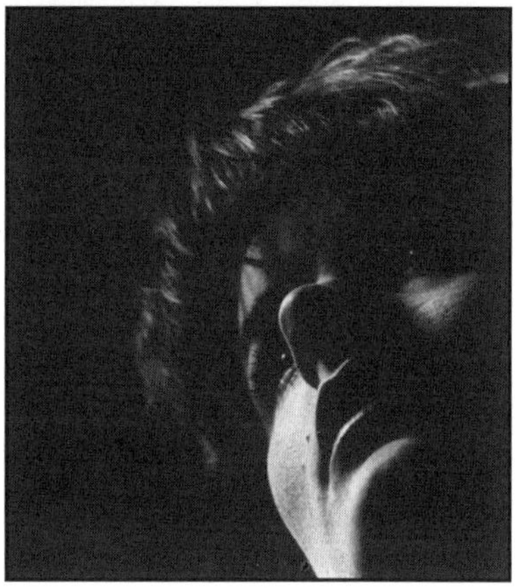

Did you recognize that the same person is the model in all three portraits above? How is your impression of the personality of the subject affected by variations in pose, lighting, camera viewpoint and image contrast? How far can (or should) photographers go toward creating a persona for a subject in front of the camera?

Darren Hathaway

Notice the perfect 45° short lighting in this available-light portrait. Because of the wide lens opening, the depth of field is very shallow.

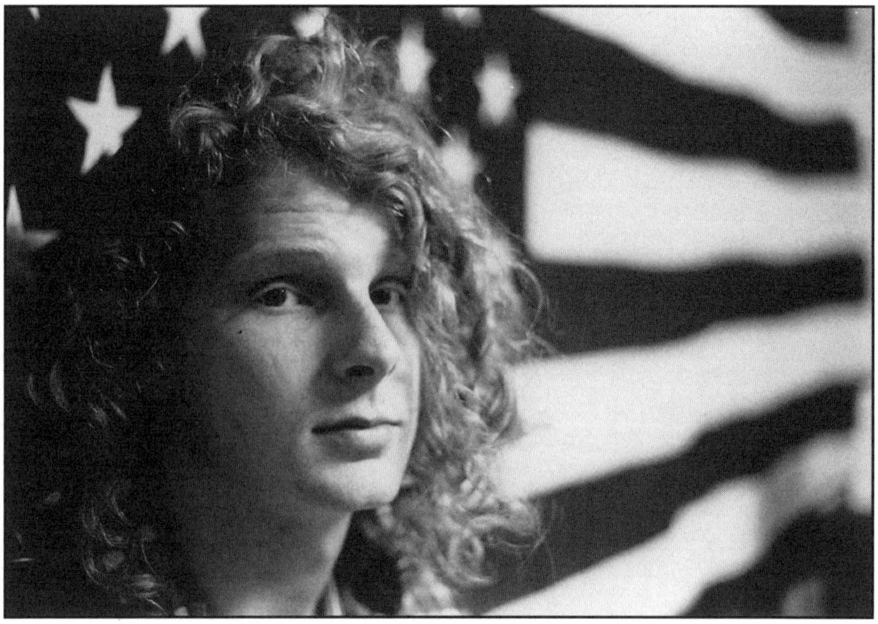

WALLACE KIRK

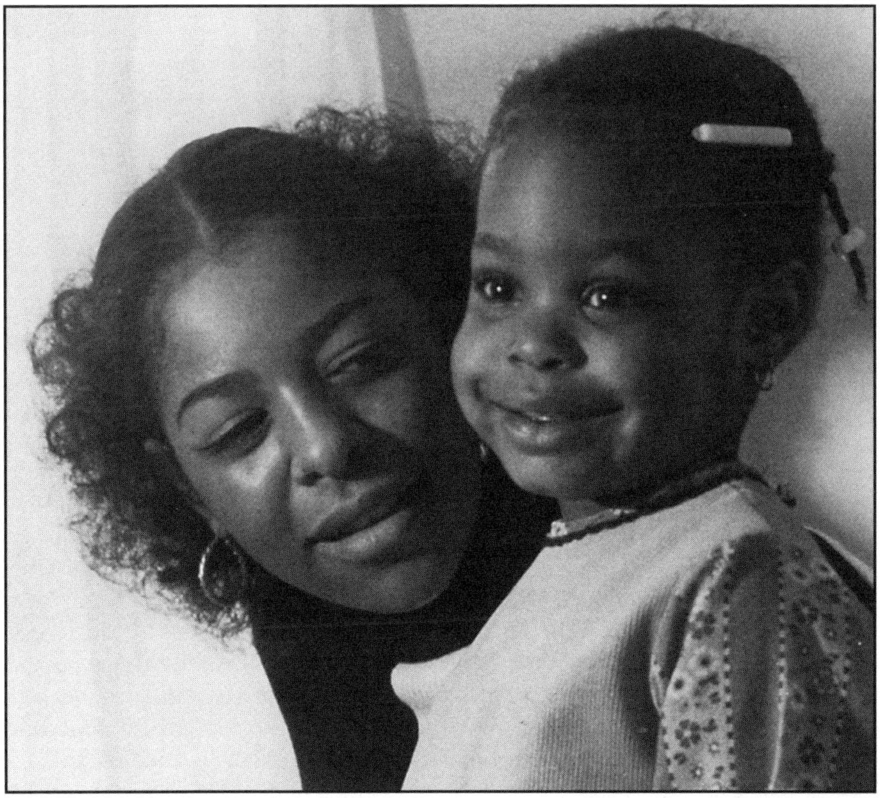

A single key light plus fill provided sparkling short light to both faces in this informal home portrait. Notice that the fill is just bright enough to show detail in the shadows without eliminating them.

ARDYCE CZUCHNA-CURL

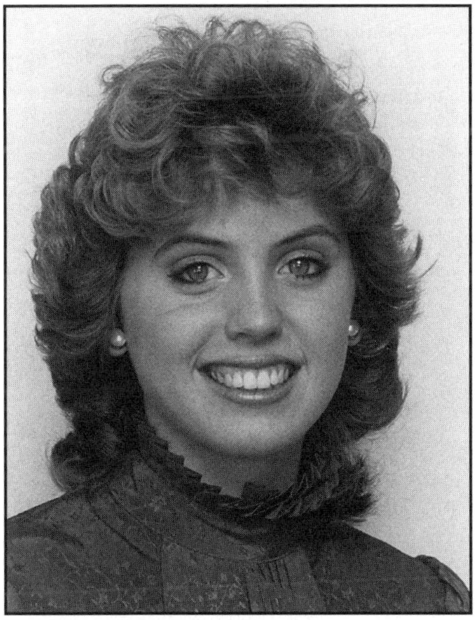

Bounce lighting gives a very soft, nearly shadowless effect without casting an annoying shadow on the nearby background. The bounce technique can be used with any kind of light source, anywhere there is a low, white ceiling or other reflective surface.

JOHNNY YEE

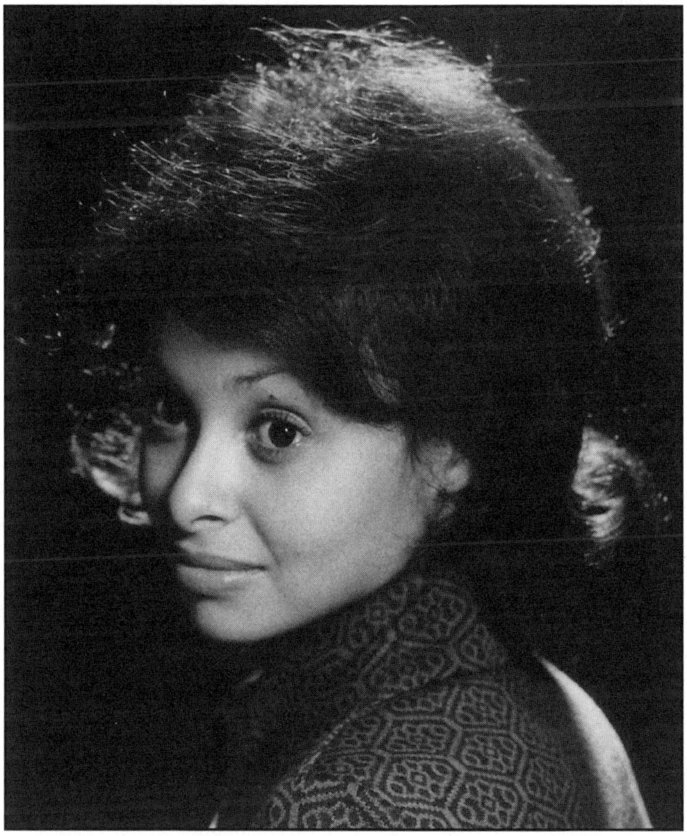

Here is another example of broad lighting, in which the key light illuminates the broad, or near, side of the face. No fill has been used, but a strong accent light adds sparkle to the hair and separates the model's shoulders from the background.

Solving Portrait Problems

"So many people dislike themselves so thoroughly that they never see any reproduction of themselves that suits. None of us is born with the right face. It's a tough job being a portrait photographer."

— Imogen Cunningham, photographer

Professional portrait photographers have to lie a little — and sometimes a lot — to make a living. Very few people really are willing to be photographed the way they actually look, especially when they're paying for the pictures!

But you can be a portrait photographer and not resort to photographic sorcery or hand or computer retouching to make your subject appear at his or her best. If you study your subject carefully, you'll see that camera angle, lighting, and choice of lens all can affect a person's appearance for good or ill. Let's look at some examples of how to solve the most commonly encountered portrait problems:

"After a certain age you've got the face you deserve, I think."

— Henri Cartier-Bresson, photojournalist

"As people grow older, there is written on their faces not only what life has brought to them but what they have brought to life."

— John Mason Brown, essayist

Texture

Wrinkles, crow's feet, and laugh lines are signs of life, and everyone past the age of 20 has a few. A middle-aged or older person pictured without wrinkles would seem ridiculous (look at a portrait-studio window display). Nevertheless, when you photograph your mother, maiden aunt, or a favorite friend, the facial lines may seem a bit severe. But take heart; soft lighting will soften the lines. Diffusion can do the rest. Try using a filter made for the purpose, or produce your own diffuser from a snippet of mesh window screen, a piece of pantyhose, or a sheet of cellophane that has been wrinkled up and then flattened again. Either put the diffuser over the camera lens, or diffuse during enlargement. While enlarging, you can control the effect by holding the diffuser under the enlarging lens for only part of the exposure time. Keep it moving. Avoid retouching altogether with careful lighting. You can hide wrinkles on a person's neck or conceal a double chin by "short" lighting the face and throwing the neck into shadow.

105mm lens

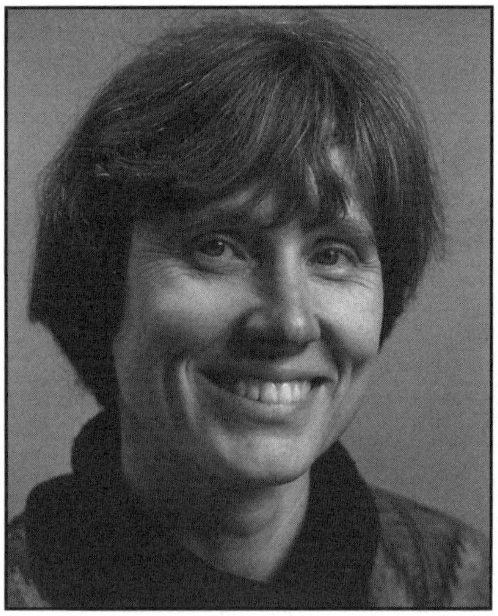

55mm lens

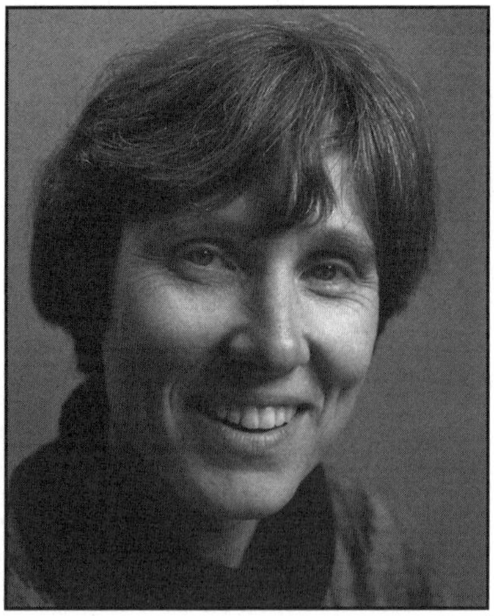

35mm lens

David H. Curl (3)

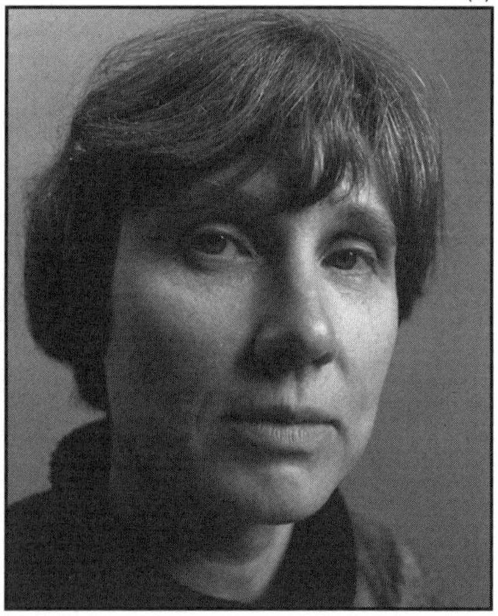

The lens makes a difference. Compare the rendition of facial features, especially the nose and chin, in the photograph on the left that was made with the equivalent of a 105mm lens on a 35mm camera, with the version in the center made with the equivalent of a 55mm lens, and the result on the right equivalent to a 35mm wide-angle lens on a 35mm camera. (The camera was moved for each exposure to keep the same image size).

Distorted facial features:

On close-ups of people, a normal focal-length or wide-angle lens tends to enlarge the nose or chin or whatever part of the anatomy is closest to the camera (see examples on page 176). A long telephoto lens tends to flatten out the features, giving a paper-doll effect. The favorite focal length of most portrait photographers is about twice "normal," that is, about 105mm for 35mm cameras, 150-180mm for 6cm cameras, and 300-360mm on 4x5.

But suppose you have a subject for whom you want deliberately to emphasize or suppress a facial feature — a weak chin, for example. Choosing a relatively short focal length and a low camera angle will strengthen the chin in proportion to the rest of the face. Shooting slightly down on a person with a large forehead will emphasize the brainy or "egghead" feeling. A long nose can be shortened by approaching the subject from a slightly low camera angle, and a crooked nose sometimes looks better from the side toward which it bends. When eyes aren't at the same height, shoot from the side where the eye is lower and the face may appear normal.

A burly person tends to look even heavier when photographed full-face. Heavy-set people appear slimmer with a three-quarter pose and short lighting. Or you can add a few pounds to a thin-faced subject by use of broad or butterfly lighting.

Deep-set eyes:

The problem is to get enough light into the eye sockets. Either place the key light lower than usual, or lower the lighting ratio by moving the fill closer or using a reflector to bounce light into the eyes.

Glasses:

A person who wears glasses only occasionally can be shown holding them in the hands, perched on top of the head, tucked into the shirt collar or pocket, or hung by a chain around the neck. But if the person wears glasses all the time, he or she often looks and feels strange without them.

Leave the glasses on, but be extra careful about shadows and reflections, adjusting the lights or positioning the subject's face so that shadows from the frames don't cut across the eyes. Tilting the face slightly downward usually will get rid of reflections from the key and fill lights. With existing lamp or window light, the key often is reflected in the glasses; in the studio, reflections usually are caused by the fill. Raising the bows (ear pieces) of the glasses or tipping the face down slightly will usually get rid of the most severe reflections. If reflections remain, try bouncing the fill from a surface above the camera. In digital images, remaining reflections can be toned down or eliminated by using Adobe Photoshop's cloning (rubber stamp) tool.

Heavy eyeglass frames require careful placement of the key light to avoid shadows across the eyes. Watch out for secondary shadows from frames if the fill light is too bright or too far from the camera position. When very thick lenses are worn, sometimes the only way to eliminate reflections in the glass and distortion of the face through the lenses is to ask the sitter to borrow a pair of empty frames from an optician.

DAVID H. CURL (2)

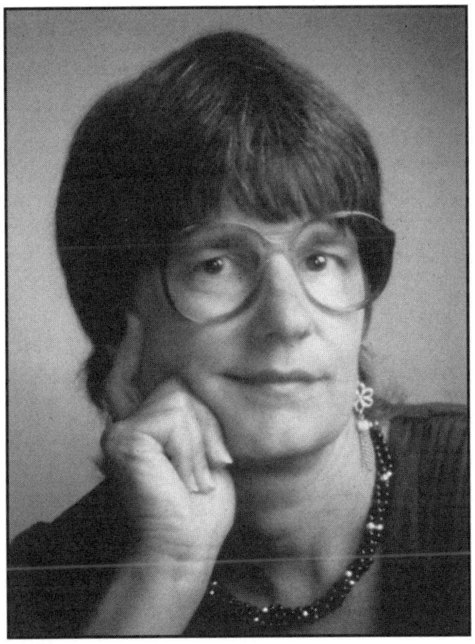

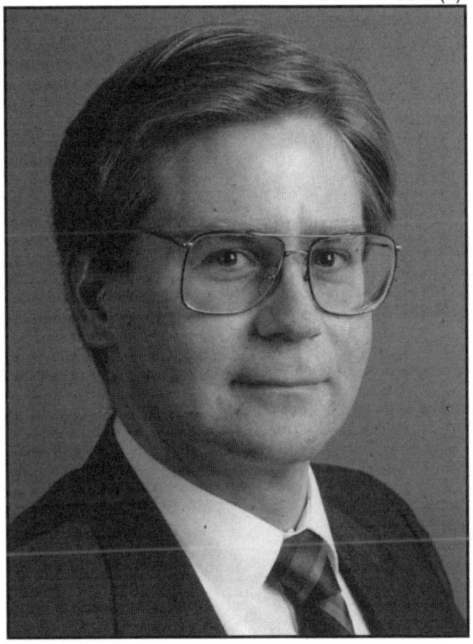

Notice that short lighting was used on both of these portraits. The lighting ratio was about 3:1 (key light three times as bright as the fill). No reflections are visible in the glasses because the key light was high enough and the fill carefully adjusted. Also the bows (ear pieces) of the glasses were raised slightly to direct reflections downward. Shadows from the key light would conceal texture and any blemishes on the near cheek and neck. The portrait on the left was softened by placing a diffusion filter over the camera lens.

Facial Blemishes:

Look carefully at your subject to see whether you can conceal acne scars and other marks by choosing your subject's "best" side; then use short lighting to throw the offending areas into shadow. In severe cases, makeup may be needed, but diffused short lighting usually will do the trick.

Prominent Nose:

A good look at your subject will tell you whether the nose requires special attention. Tilting the chin up will minimize a long nose, while carefully controlled short lighting will straighten a crooked or an arched nose. A person whose nose points to one side should be photographed from that side.

Baldness:

The rule here is simply to keep the light away from the top of a man's head and not to emphasize his baldness with a high camera angle. To save burning-in time in the darkroom, pre-dodge a bald head by using barn doors on the lights or block some of the light with a head screen made from a piece of cardboard clamped or taped to a light stand. The same trick can be used to keep an ear or shoulder from being too light and distracting attention from the face.

Clothing:

Plain dark clothes usually are best, because the face, being lighter, tends to stand out. Loud designs and bright, complex patterns draw attention to themselves. Unless the lighting is carefully balanced, bare arms and shoulders may compete for attention with the face and require burning-in in the darkroom. So, unless it's a glamour session, it's best for the model to cover up.

NANCY BLY

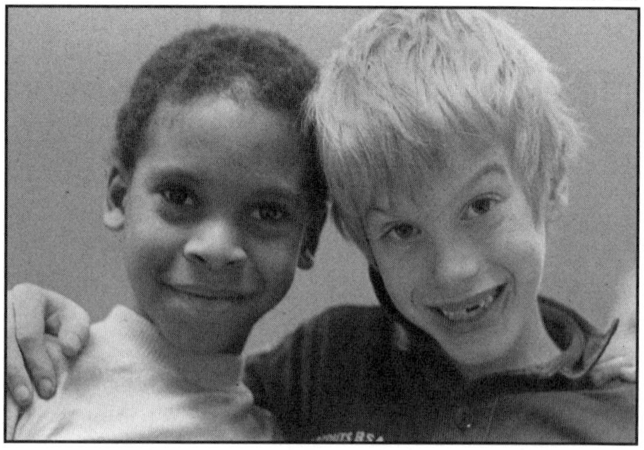

Children often "mug" for the camera. But soon, unlike adults, they will resume their activities and forget that a photographer is present.

Get to Know your Subject

Take the time to talk with people you're photographing. They'll feel less uncomfortable in front of the camera. You don't have to entertain your subject. It's usually better not to try to dominate the conversation, but to ask sincere questions to assure them that you are really interested in them as a person.

If you study each person intelligently and perceptively, you can capture his or her likeness, as well as some of the person's essence and spirit. Fortunately the heavily retouched ("mortician's ideal") portraits of the past are no longer very popular. Good posing, lighting and camera techniques will keep you from having to resort to much retouching. Perhaps you will become one of those happy photographers who genuinely enjoys working with people. If so, you may be able to make a career of portraiture or photojournalism, because the public is beginning to appreciate informal and more natural-looking pictures of themselves, their families and associates.

FUMIKO YARITA

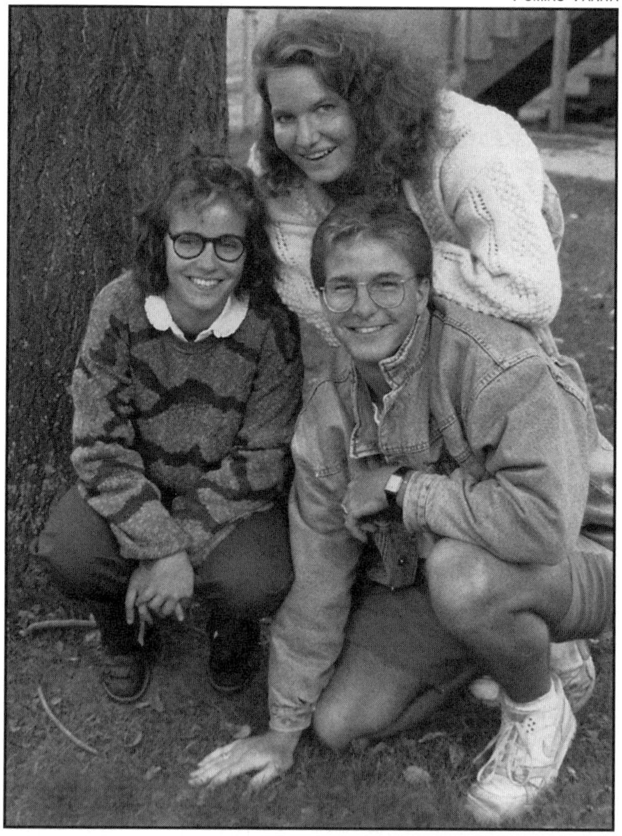

Instead of allowing them to stand stiffly in a row, the photographer directed her friends into an informal triangular pose that appears spontaneous and natural.

Full-Length and Group Portraiture

A good group portrait consists of several individual portraits taken at the same time. Each face and figure should be properly lighted to bring out the form and best features of each person. But in group photography, the whole actually is greater than the sum of its parts because the total effect must be compositionally interesting, as well as technically well-lighted and photographed.

Play the role of "Director"

Avoid deadly, static, row-on-row groupings. Use enough imagination to arrange everyone in a unified and varied way. When people agree to be photographed, they look to you, the photographer, for guidance and direction. Tell them what to do, whether you merely want them to look toward the camera and "Smile, please," or pretend to be doing something.

This is your Big Chance to act like a Hollywood director. And the most successful method of preparing your "actors" will often be the posed-unposed technique. First decide how to arrange people, props, and background the way you want them in relation to the lighting, and then determine exposure and focus. After all the technical problems are solved, direct the people either to continue what they would normally be doing (working on machines, examining an object, or talking informally with one another), or give directions: "Joe, please hold up the trophy like this, with both hands and be telling about how you won it; Mary and Jim, you'll be looking right at Joe." Or, "Pick up the phone, Sally, and pretend that you're having a pleasant conversation with your boyfriend." Or, "Be adjusting the horse's bridle with both hands, Jennifer, then turn and look directly at me ... now smile!"

Ardyce Czuchna-Curl

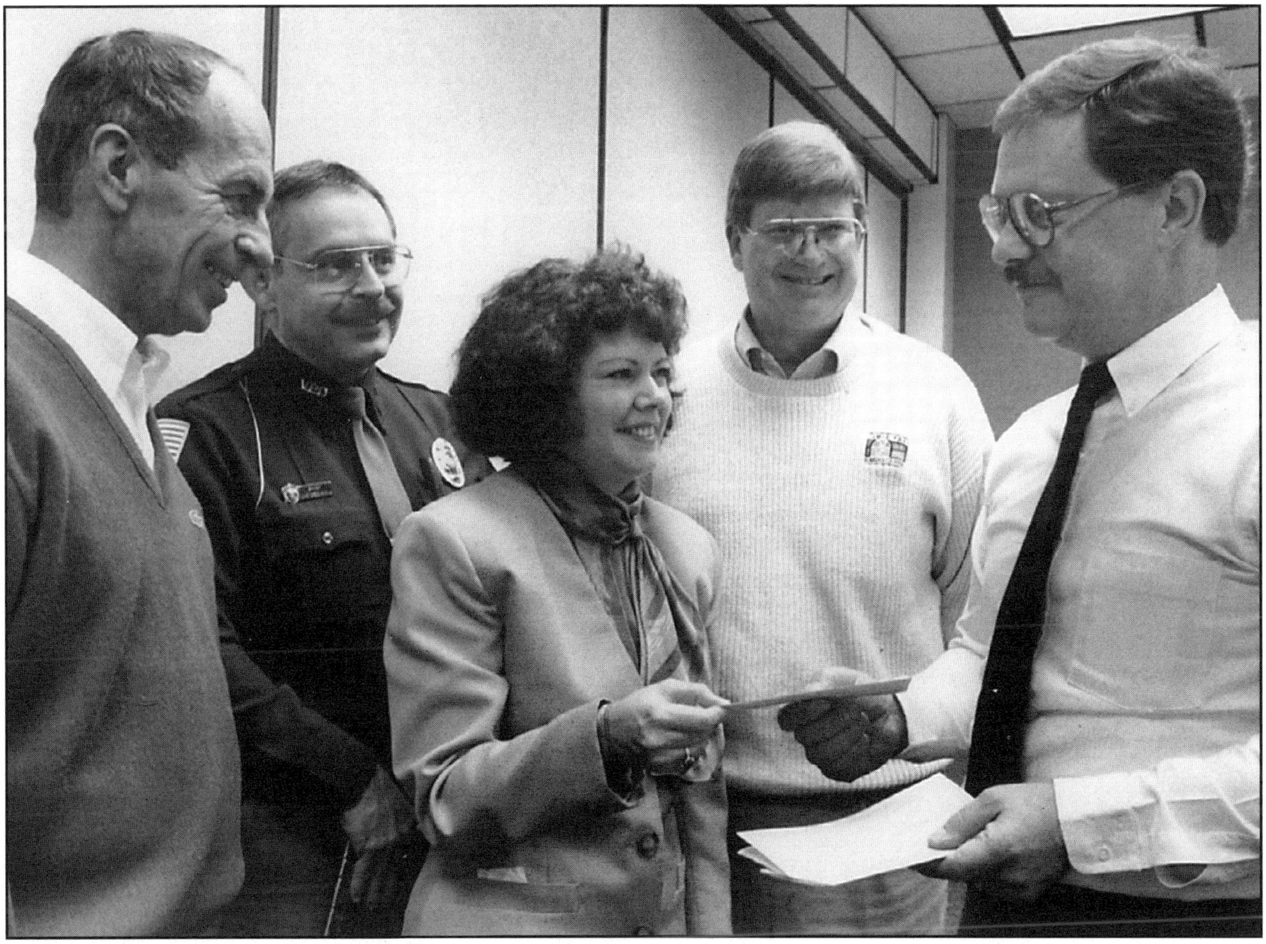

Every photojournalist has to do the "people with a piece of paper" shot. Unless directed by the photographer, people will simply stand in a row with their arms hanging down at their sides. Notice here that the three key people (on the right) are arranged in an informal triangle and they have been given something to do with their hands.

Posing the whole person

Full-length portraits require much greater attention to background detail and to the pose, especially outdoors. Obvious things to be on the lookout for include avoiding wires, poles and branches growing out of people's heads, eliminating excessively bright or "busy" areas, especially in corners or along edges, that might distract from the main subject(s), and not allowing awkward placement or amputation of arms, hands, legs, and feet.

Hands should be holding something, tucked into belt or pockets, or posed together in a natural way. Arms should not be just hanging down. Legs and feet ought to be placed naturally and comfortably, but usually not "at attention." Fashion models learn to place most of their weight gracefully on one foot, with the other foot slightly forward and at an angle. A seated figure looks more active if the weight is shifted slightly to one side instead of distributed equally onto both buttocks.

Body grace is especially important in fashion and figure photography because an awkward pose and crude lighting can make even a beautiful person appear grotesque. For a full-length figure, the camera angle generally should be lower. Eye level usually is right for a head-and-shoulders portrait, but a chest- or even a waist-high camera position often lends grace and dignity to a standing figure.

"Beauty is its own excuse."

— Ralph Waldo Emerson, essayist and poet

Nudes

The human figure is the most challenging of all to photograph. Because art is never absolute, but relies on the sensibilities of the beholder, a clear distinction has not always been drawn between conscientious representation and crass pornography. A beautiful photograph of a nude body should not be thought of as a portrait of a specific person unclothed, but should be viewed as an impression of an aesthetically satisfying natural form. Perhaps, in such a fine photograph, some will discover metaphoric meaning.

"To make a photograph of the human body express something more than mere physical nakedness or suggestive sex, one has to look for qualities that make the human body a ... beautiful part of nature. The nakedness of a body is as natural as the nakedness of a tree."

— Wynn Bullock, photographer

"When the subject is in any way uneasy, the personality goes away where the camera can't reach it."

— Henri Cartier-Bresson, photojournalist

Jim Nixon

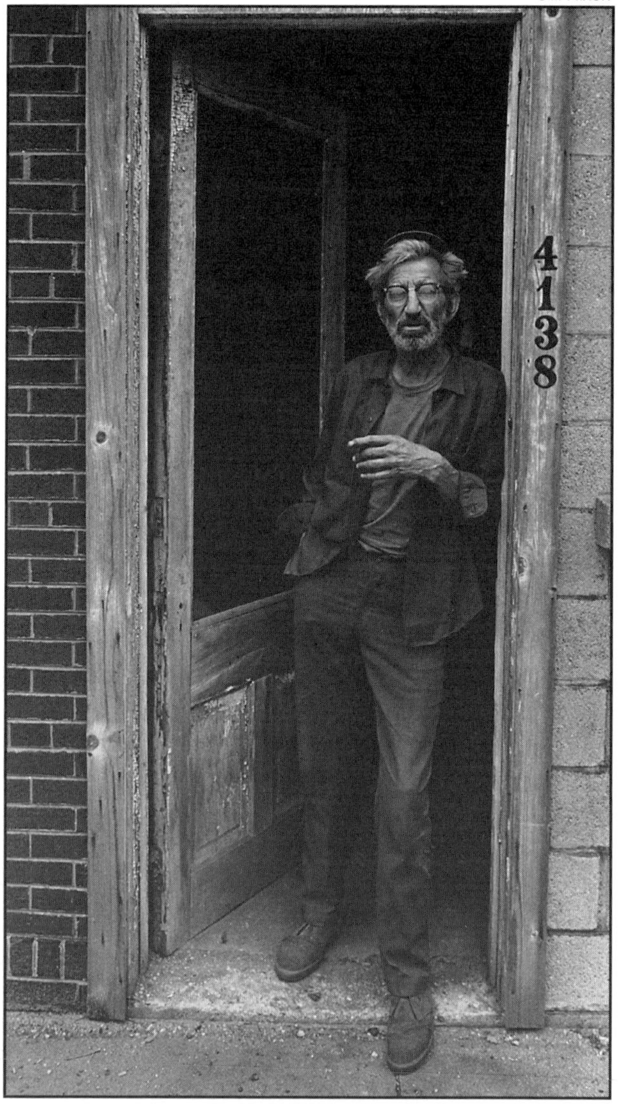

A full-length portrait — straightforward and eye to eye. Notice the relaxed, natural positions of hands and feet.

Self-Portraiture

"Promote visual health ...
photograph a friend."

— Walt Burton, photographer

Making a revealing photo of one's self can be fun and challenging. Knowing how it feels to be in front of the camera helps us to empathize with people who pose for us. The biggest difficulty is judging light, focus, depth of field, etc. from the other side of the lens.

Of course, the simplest solution is to have a stand-in pose for you until everything is ready, then you take his or her place as model, letting the stand-in release the shutter. Another way is to work with a large mirror placed near the camera. Or you could use a video camera and monitor, although seeing exactly how one looks before the exposure tends to take away some of the spontaneity and surprise. If you're working alone, the shutter can be released with the camera's delayed-action self-timer, with a long cable release, or with a remote-control electrical release.

Do we reveal our real self, try to create an image of our ideal self, or attempt to realize a fantasy? Think of self-portraiture as a way to release inhibitions and develop empathy for those we photograph. Posing for pictures, one learns quickly the awkwardness and discomfort felt in front of a camera by most inexperienced models.

KOLEN MACKEY

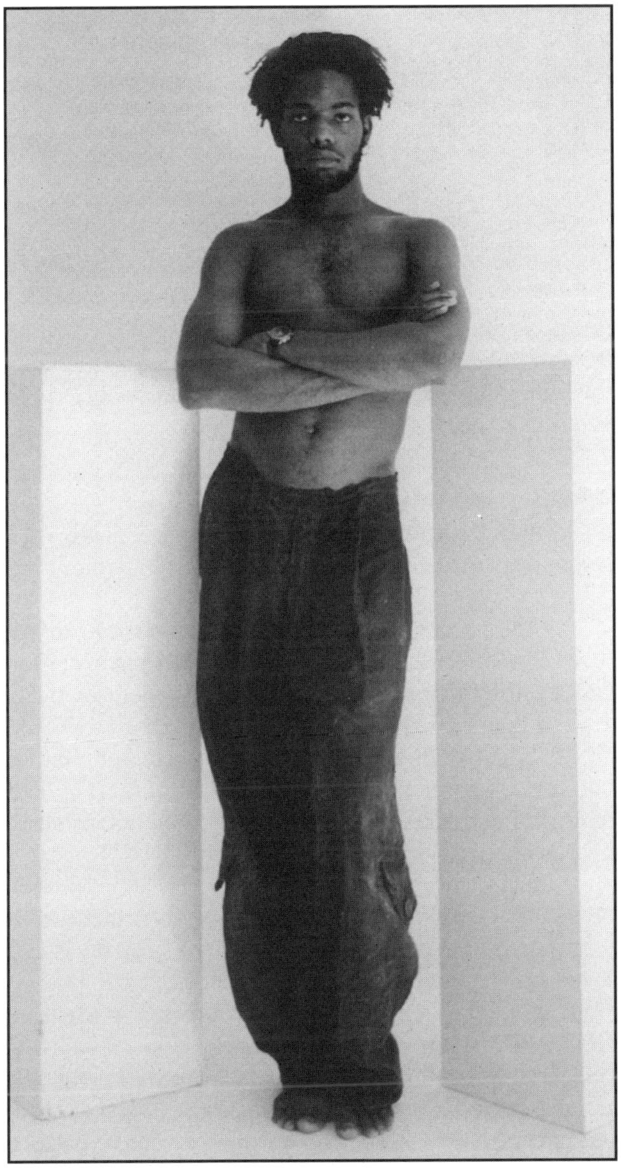

MARION GRZANOWSKI

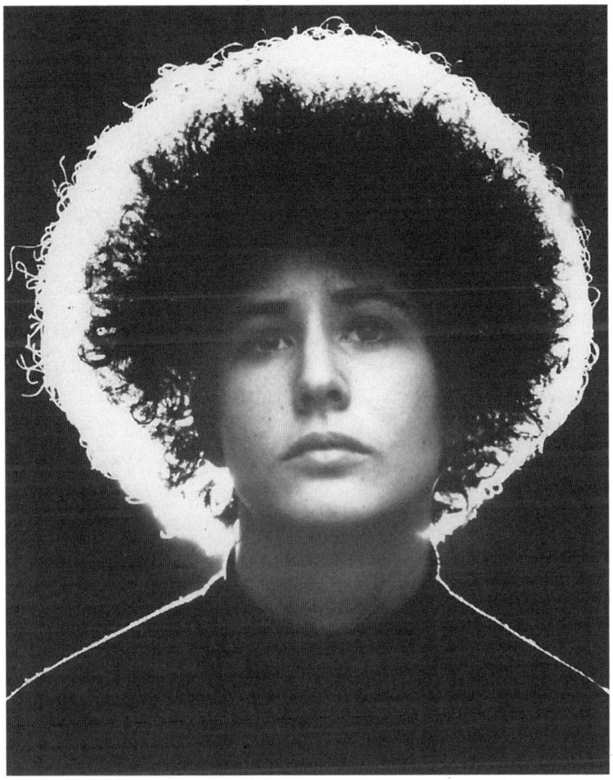

Extremely strong backlighting provided the halo effect, balanced by diffused butterfly lighting on the face.

Richard Strader

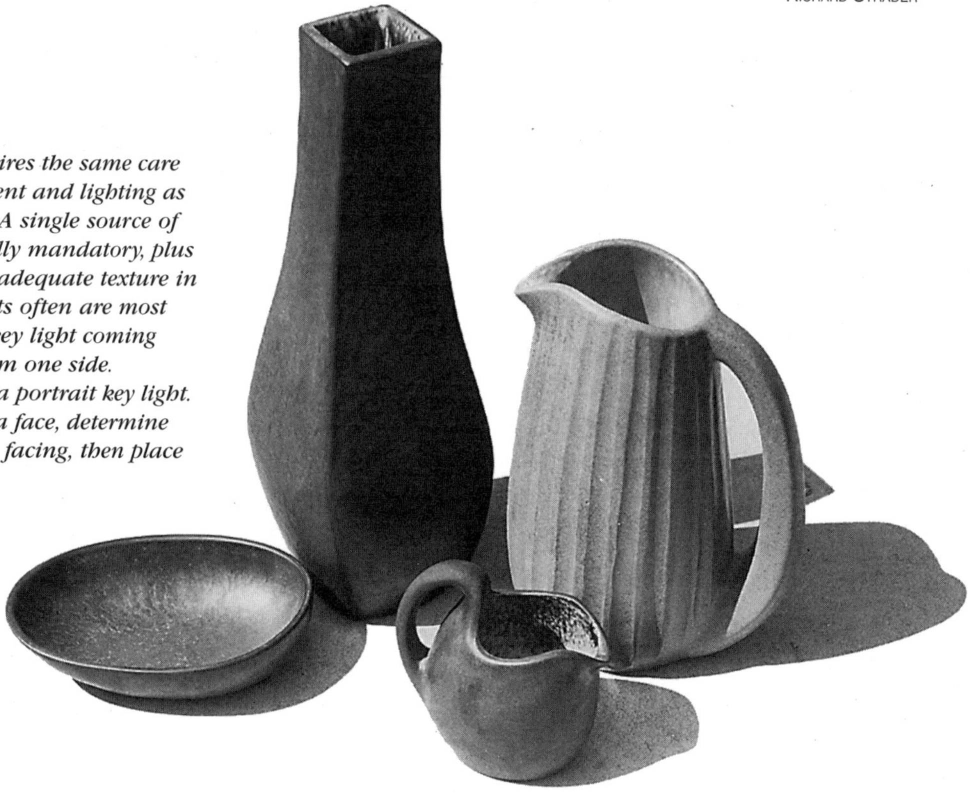

Photographing objects requires the same care and attention to arrangement and lighting as making portraits of people. A single source of shadows (key light) is usually mandatory, plus sufficient fill light to retain adequate texture in the shadows. Still-life subjects often are most effectively lighted with the key light coming from behind or strongly from one side. Remember the 45° rule for a portrait key light. Imagine that the subject is a face, determine which direction the "face" is facing, then place the key light accordingly.

Product Illustration

Most of the principles that apply to creating portraits of people apply also to photographing a structure, a sculpture, or a cereal box. The lighting principles are similar (key, fill, accent, background), and so are the elements of perspective and composition. Always think first in terms of reproducing the shape or form and texture of any subject. Then you'll be able to work out the details of lighting, lens choice, camera position, and so on — one problem at a time.

Find the "face"

As each person has a face, so does each building. Because of this, the most successful architectural photographs will be made at a time of day and season when light creates the strongest feeling of form and texture. It is the same with large outdoor sculptures, fountains, storage tanks and silos, and certainly with natural forms such as mountains, rocks, and trees.

Photographing small objects in the studio offers a great opportunity to find the "faces" of products and to study the effects of light placement. Working with a miniature model, you can simulate the sun with a lamp. As you shift lights about in the studio, you should notice the way shadows fall and the way in which lighting angle can reveal and emphasize texture. Strong shadows may add to the effectiveness of studio illustrations, even to the point where the shadow may be more interesting than the object itself. Dramatic lighting can produce a three-dimensional effect, the highlights tending to come forward while the shadow areas recede.

Start with the simplest lighting

So that you can see what you're doing, it's always a good idea to begin with only one light, but there are two basic approaches:

(1) Start out with a key light, as in portraiture, to reveal basic shape and texture through shadows; then add a fill light or reflector, and finally accent or background lights if required.

(2) Begin with a broad, diffused "base" light, either bounced or from a large translucent softbox. Then add direct key and accent lights to create highlights and shadows as needed within the composition.

Instead of using many lights, commercial photographers often employ large and small reflectors made from cardboard, foam core, or foil to brighten small areas and to bring substance to reflective surfaces.

Your choice of background will depend on the tone and texture of the subject. If the background is white or very light in color you can vary the contrast between it and the subject simply by directing more or less light on the background. Unless background texture or pattern

Doug Hauk

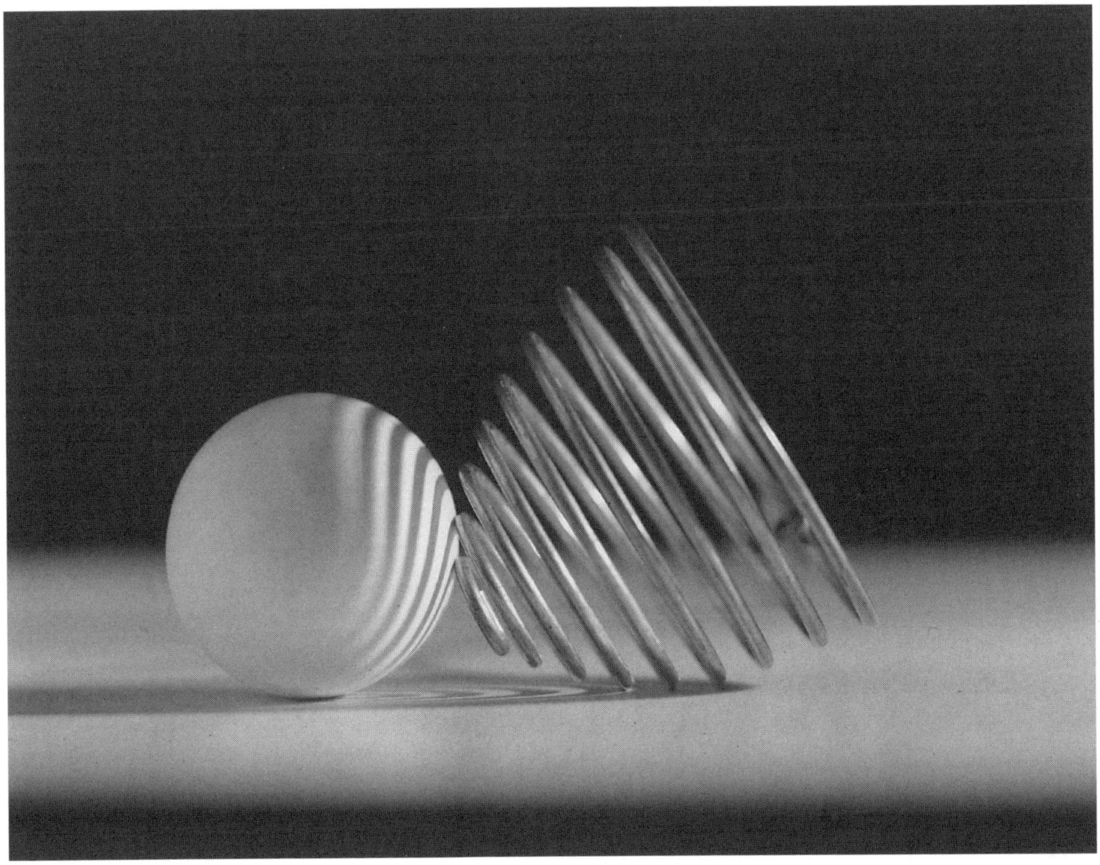

In this commercial subject, imaginative use of lighting has emphasized and repeated the basic pattern of lines and forms.

contributes to the picture, as it does frequently when illustrating food, the background should be unbroken by seams, edges, or wrinkles.

Some small objects can best be photographed on a pedestal several feet from the background. For others, a miniature stage can be improvised by curving and taping a large sheet of lightweight poster board or seamless paper along the top of a small table and part way up a wall. If the background is large enough to allow the subject to be placed well forward, the table can be pulled away from the wall far enough to allow lights to be placed behind it (see illustrations on page 184).

Instead of a plain paper background, you might choose a material that can give added information about the subject, if you're careful not to introduce too much additional texture or pattern. Native backgrounds such as stone, sand, cloth, woven matting, or tree bark can establish location and add character and realism to certain illustrations.

"I respond initially to the texture, form and the effect of light on my subject."

—Susan Carr, photographer

David H. Curl

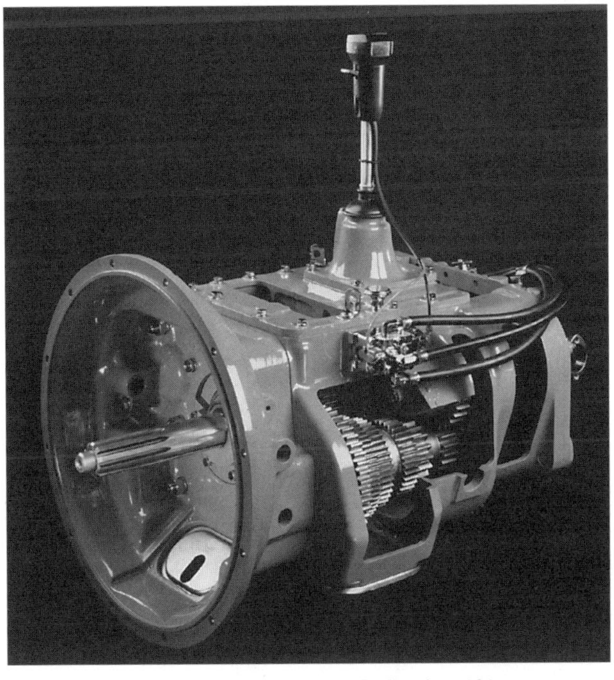

This large truck transmission was lighted as if it were a sculptural form. The general shape was noted, then five lights and three reflectors were placed to emphasize form and surface, and to separate light and dark values.

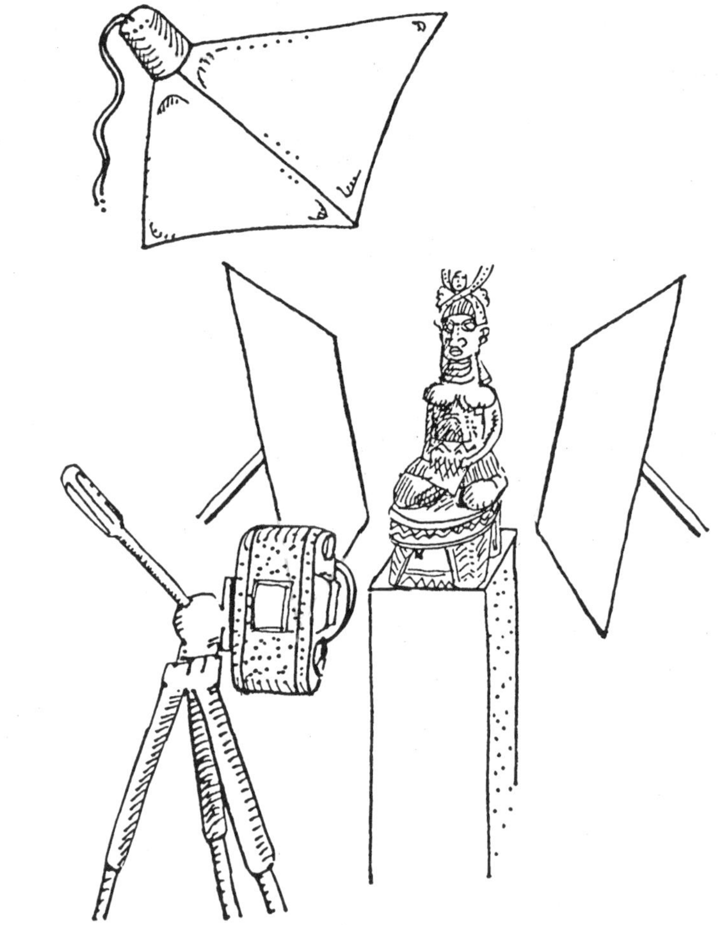

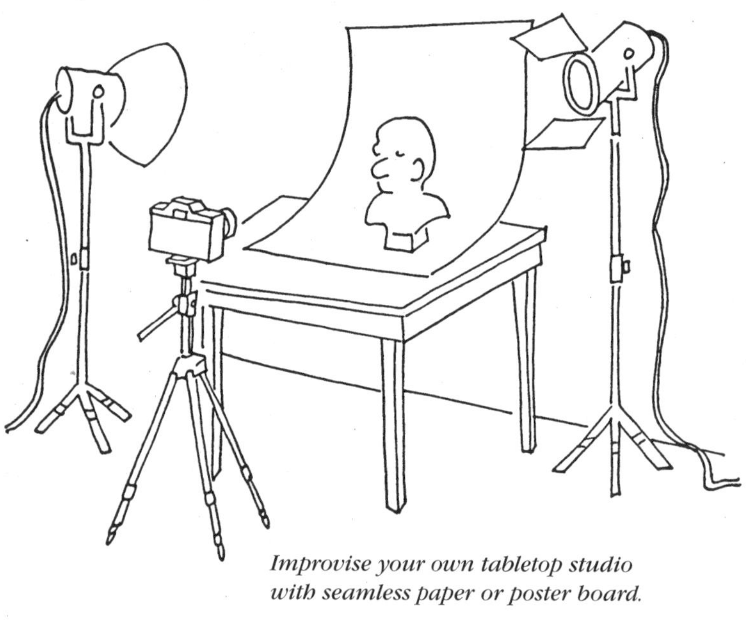

Improvise your own tabletop studio with seamless paper or poster board.

David H. Curl

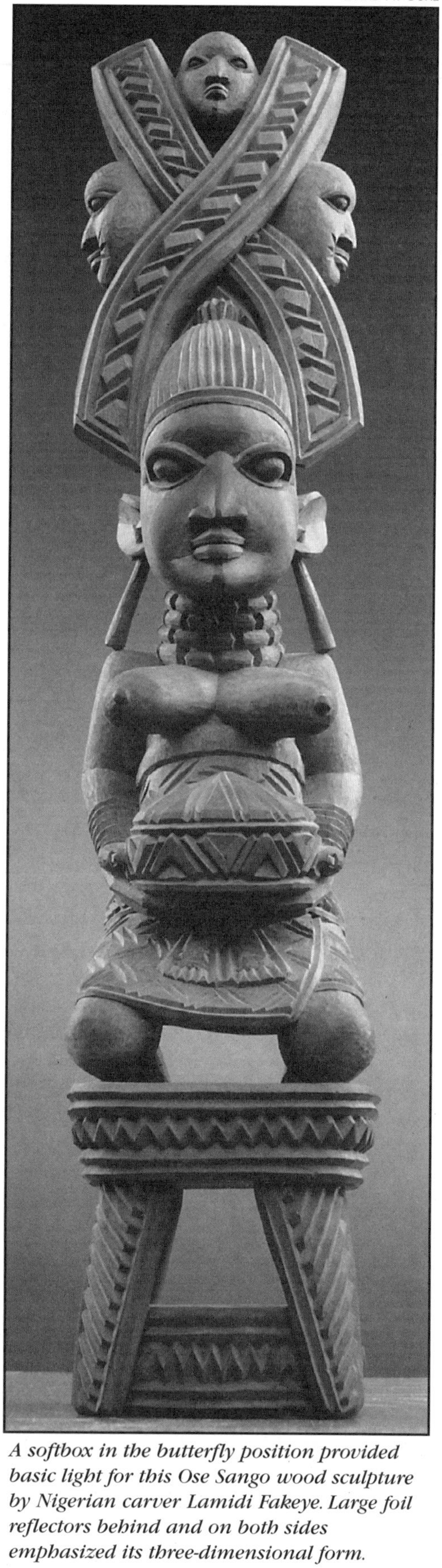

A softbox in the butterfly position provided basic light for this Ose Sango wood sculpture by Nigerian carver Lamidi Fakeye. Large foil reflectors behind and on both sides emphasized its three-dimensional form.

DAVID HARRISON (3)

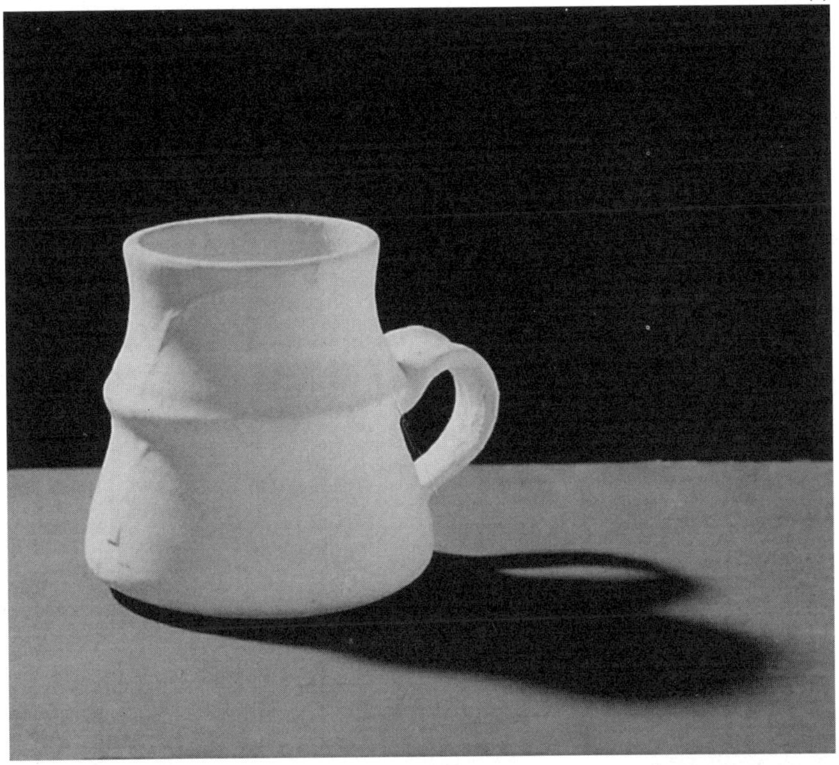

This cup was photographed with a single light to the left (notice the shadow). A reflector card was placed directly below the camera lens to retain detail in the near side. Compare this placement to 45° short portrait lighting.

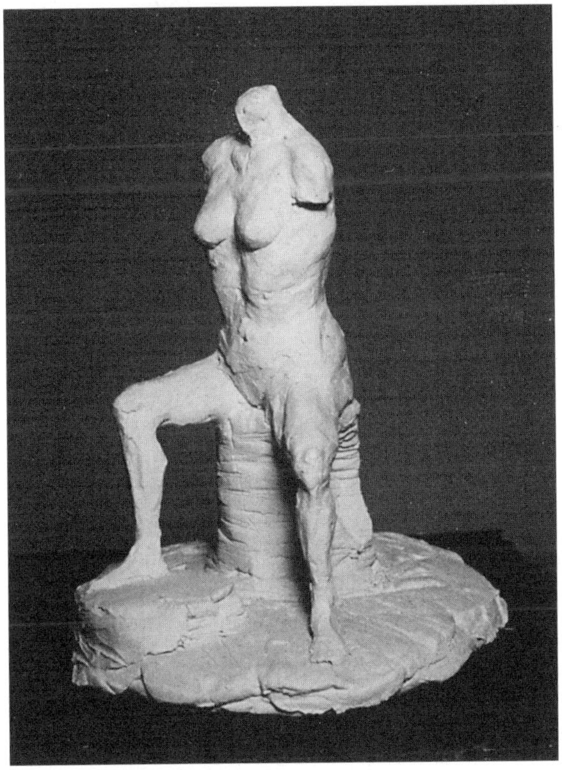

This one-foot-high sculpture was photographed with a single light. Notice the dramatic difference between the flat effect (above) when the light is near the camera, and the roundness and texture (right) when it is moved to the side and behind the figure.

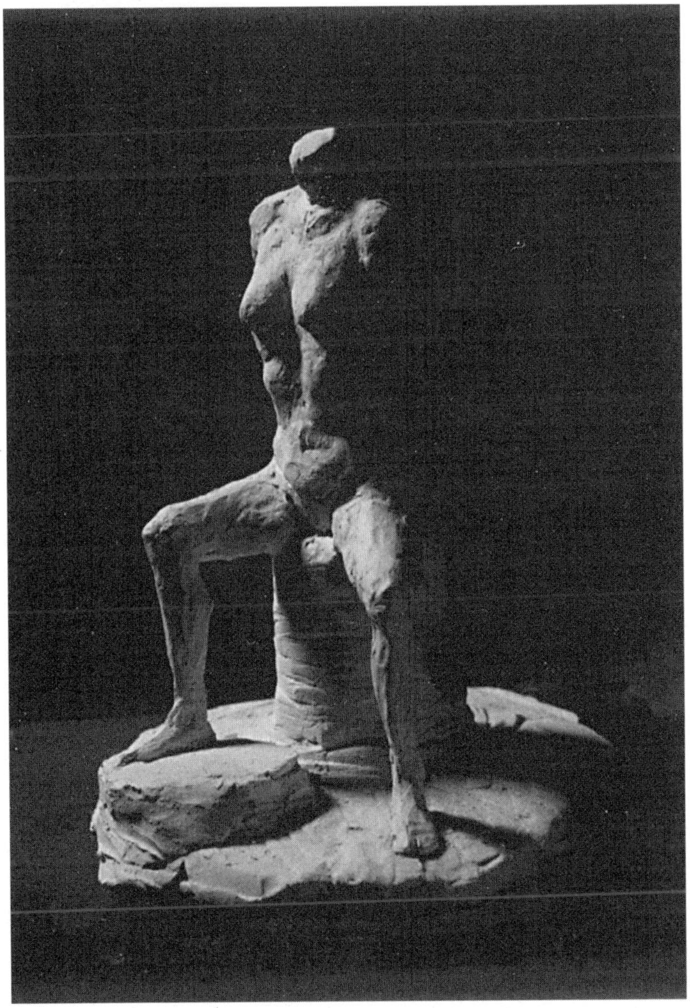

Copying and Close-Ups

The photographic reproduction of flat objects is known as copying, whether you're making a new negative from an old photographic print, or reproducing a map, an illustration from a publication, or a painting or drawing.

Line copy is just black and white

Black-and-white material to be copied usually is divided into two categories: *line* and *continuous tone*. Line copy materials consist only of black-and-white without gray tones. Examples of line copy are the kinds of things we would first think to reproduce on an office copy machine: a printed or typewritten page, an ink drawing, or a screened halftone reproduction (the image being broken up into a pattern of black-and-white dots). Such materials are best photographed on special film such as Kodalith Ortho or High Contrast Copy film. If high contrast film is not available, you can use ordinary film, but you should reduce the Zone V exposure by one or two stops and give N + 2 development to increase the contrast. (NOTE: get a Zone V exposure either by using an incident meter or by reading a standard 18-percent gray card).

Continuous-tone includes grays

Continuous-tone originals contain many shades of gray between the lightest and darkest tones. A good photographic print fits into this category, as does a painting or drawing containing various shades of tone or different values and intensities of color. Slow, fine-grained films are suitable for most continuous-tone copying. The highlights may tend to print with a grayish cast, however, so special copying films are available in sheet film sizes that are designed to make reproductions that more exactly match the tonal values of the original.

Special techniques for color

Copying in color requires a film balanced for the light source. While natural light can be used, the most consistent results will come from using a sturdy copy stand with two studio lights to ensure even illumination. Either quartz lamps or 3,200°K incandescent bulbs are commonly used because they match tungsten-balanced color films such as Ektachrome 50 and 160. An 80A blue filter will balance tungsten light with daylight color films, or you can use blue filter gels over the lights or blue-tinted bulbs. Color negative films can be corrected in printing. The color of the light isn't important with black-and-white.

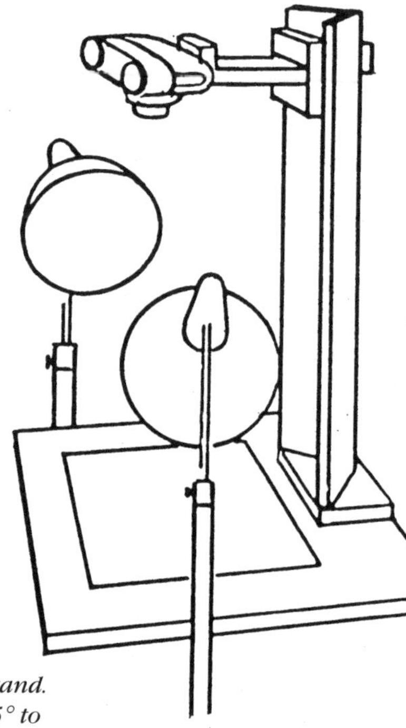

A typical copy stand. (Lights are at 45° to copy board).

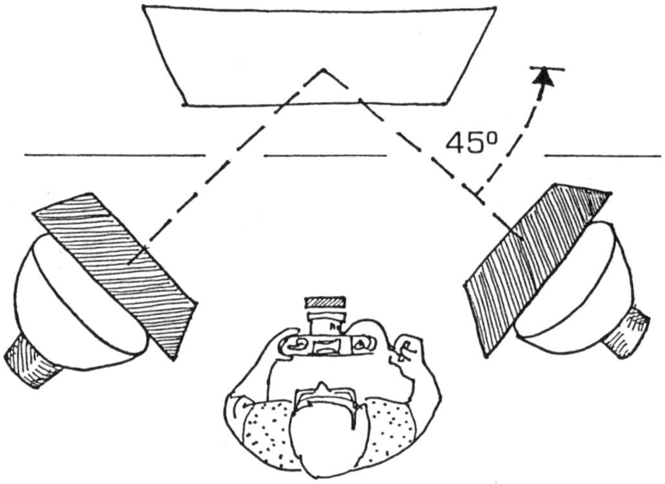

Color saturation in copies of paintings and other artwork can be improved by placing a polarizing filter over the camera lens (rotate it to see the effect), and large polarizers over both lights.

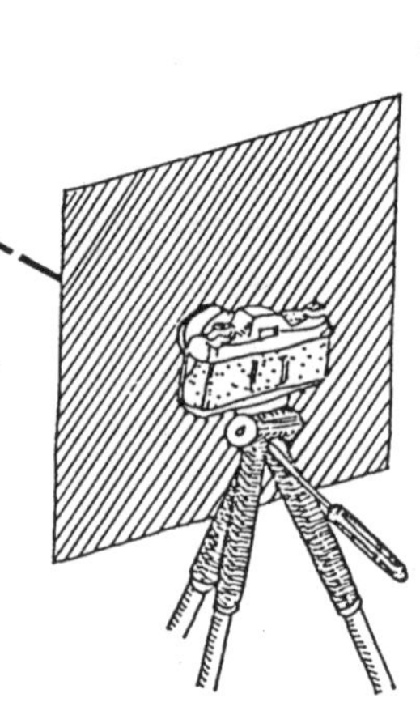

Reflections of the camera in the glazing of a picture frame or display case can be minimized by shooting through a hole cut in a black card or cloth. Polarizers also should be used.

Place lights at 45°

The lights should be placed at equal distances from the material to be copied, set at an angle of 45°, and aimed so they slightly overlap the center of the copy. Check the evenness of the light with a hand-held, incident exposure meter, if possible, and readjust the lights as necessary. Determine exposure with the incident meter or, if you must use the meter in the camera, read from a standard 18-percent gray card held directly in front of the material to be copied.

Polarizing filters properly placed over each light and on the camera lens will eliminate nearly all traces of surface reflections from glossy inks or paints and improve the color saturation of the copy. The axis of the polarizer on the camera must be set 90° from the axes of the lamp polarizers. This combination usually will require about 1 1/2 stops more exposure (a factor of three).

Increase exposure up close

Additional exposure will be needed when photographing things that are very small. This is in addition to any increase required at one second or longer because of reciprocity. A general rule is to give four times normal exposure (two stops) if the subject is about the same size as the negative — for example, a postage stamp or an insect photographed life-size on 35mm film. If the subject is reproduced approximately half natural size, such as copying a small snapshot photo with a 35mm camera, the exposure should be increased by one stop or double the exposure time (see table on page 83). Always base the exposure for close-up and copy work on a Zone V reading from a gray card or an incident meter. If you don't have an incident meter or a gray card, read a non-glossy white card and divide the ISO setting on the camera by five. This will give you Zone V because a white card reflects about 80 percent of the light, five times as much as an 18-percent gray card.

Sharpness

While copying flat material doesn't require much depth of field, small three-dimensional objects usually need all the depth of field possible — usually f/16 or the smallest opening on your lens. With flat materials, many lenses are sharpest overall around f/5.6 or f/8. Some zoom lenses and very fast lenses, however, are not very sharp in the corners except when fully stopped down. Test your lenses to find out how good they are (see page 85). Always use a sturdy copy stand or tripod, and increase the exposure time as necessary to account for both reciprocity and close-up factors.

Restoring old photos

CORAL GIBBS COLLECTION (2)

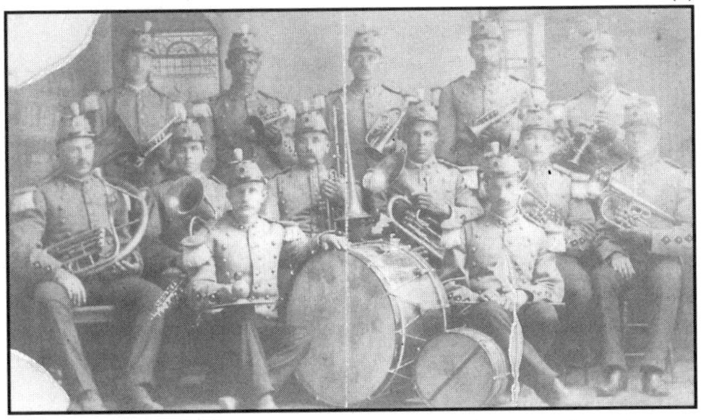

Historical photos that are faded, stained, creased and torn can be improved dramatically by using special copy films, filters, and processing. Computer software makes restoration much faster by eliminating the need for hand-retouching and re-copying. This photo had been faded to a faint yellow and physically damaged.

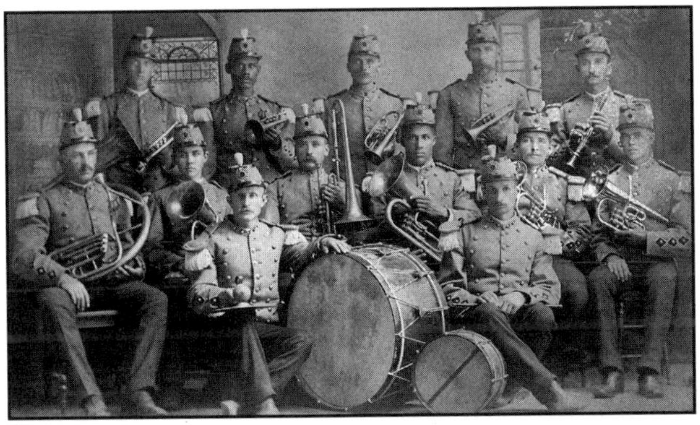

Here is the result of restoration of the scanned image in Adobe Photoshop. First, the curve was adjusted as shown below, to increase the contrast. Then the damage was repaired with the cloning tool. This photo was kept in grayscale mode. Sometimes a better image can be created by scanning the monochrome original in RGB color, then selecting and improving the best of the color channels.

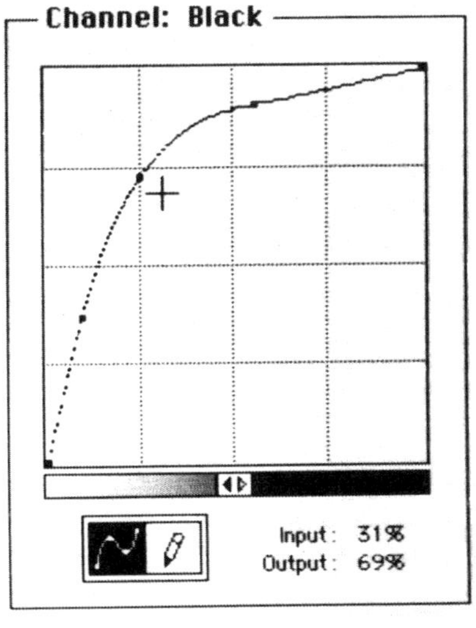

ARDYCE CZUCHNA-CURL

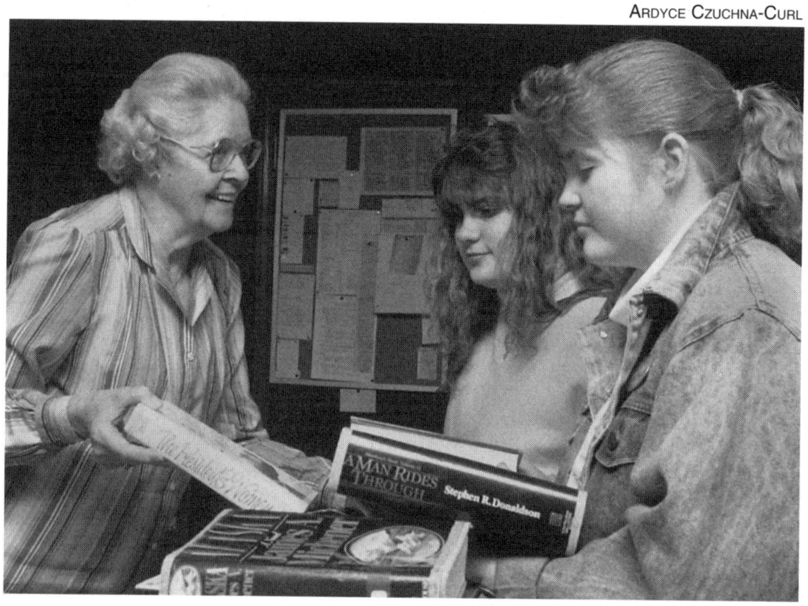

Bounce flash has given the effect of natural overhead light, but the picture was made with the camera hand-held instead of on a tripod. Although the room was large, the ceiling was white and low enough for adequate exposure. The sensors on camera-dedicated flash units will compensate exposure automatically.

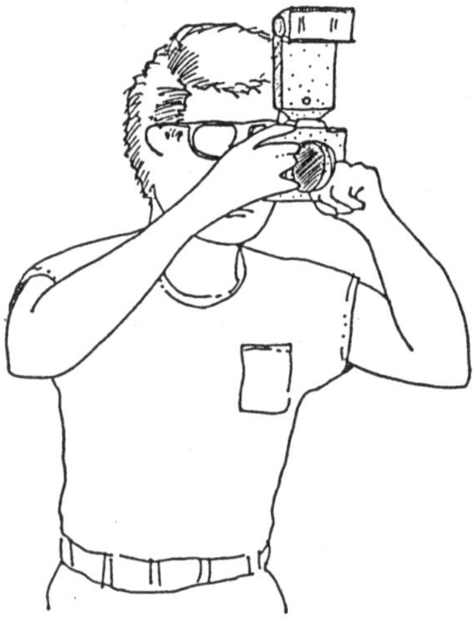

Direct-on-camera

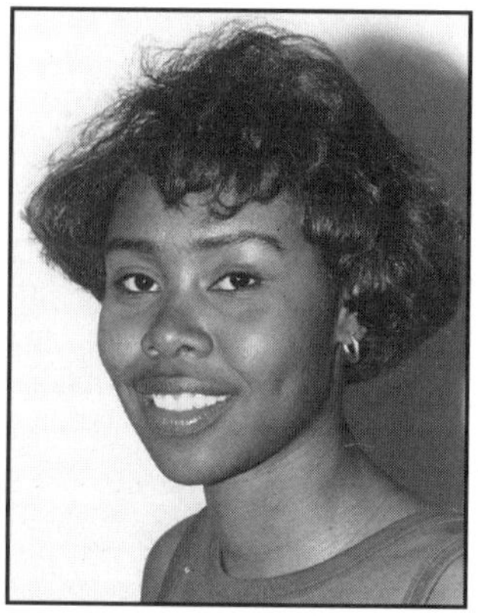

Direct-flash-on-camera. *This is the "point and shoot" method — convenient and quick, but the lighting is so flat it gives a "paper-doll" effect with little form and texture. Notice the typical dark shadow on the background. Flash-on-camera often results in the dreaded red-eye.*

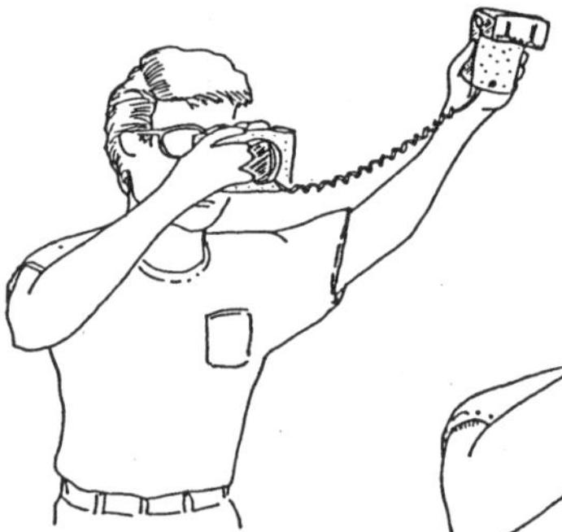

Direct-off-camera

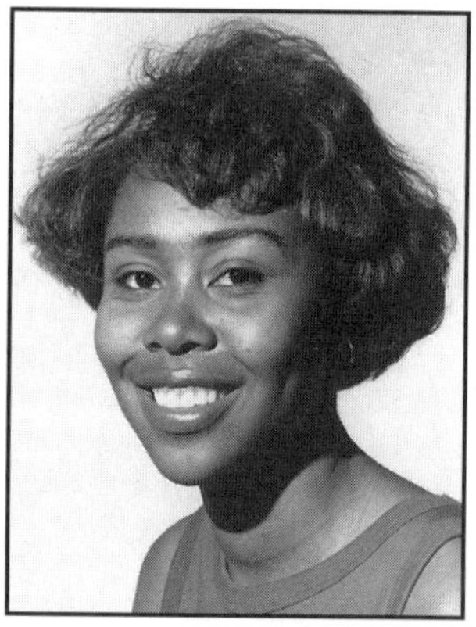

Direct-flash-off-camera. *Hurried photojournalists use this technique to get some feeling of roundness when there isn't time to set up lights or to use a tripod. Aim the flash carefully, because lighting can be uneven. The shadow on the background is hidden behind the subject.*

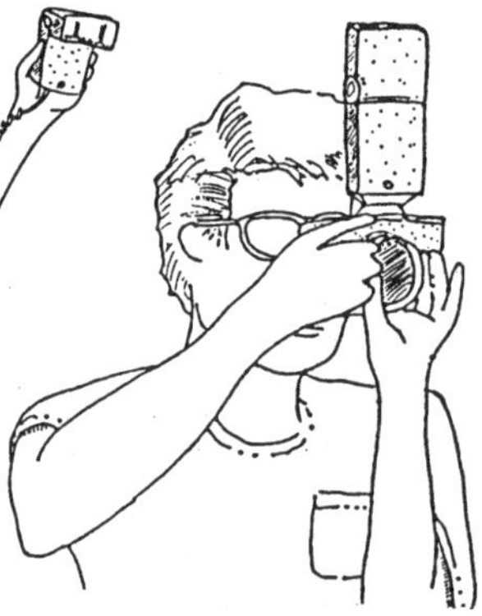

Bounce from ceiling

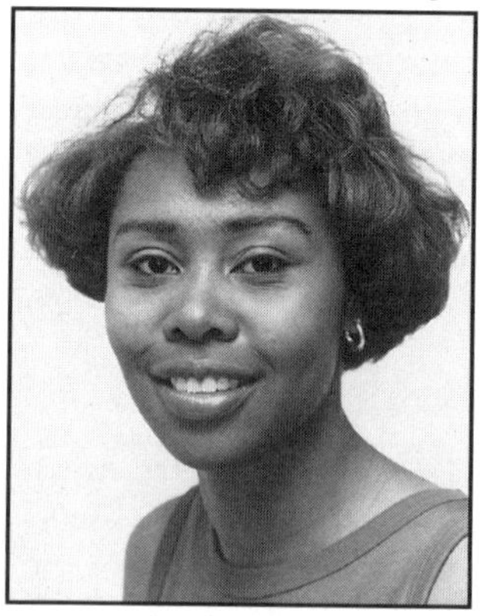

Bounce-flash-on-camera. *This soft lighting is convenient, flattering to most subjects, and works well in smaller rooms with white ceilings and light-colored walls. In this example, the flash was aimed straight up at the ceiling.*

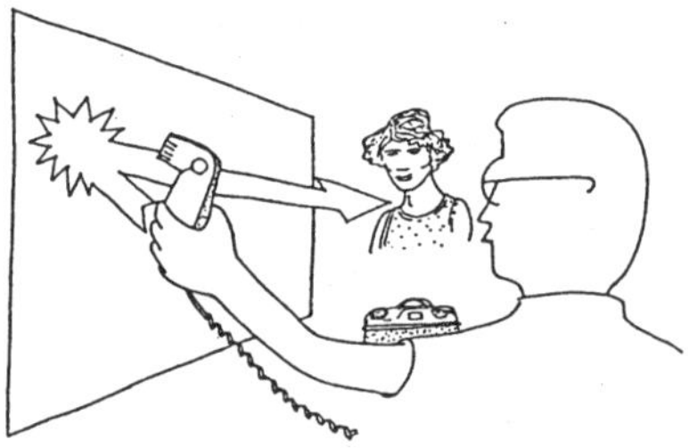

Bounce from wall

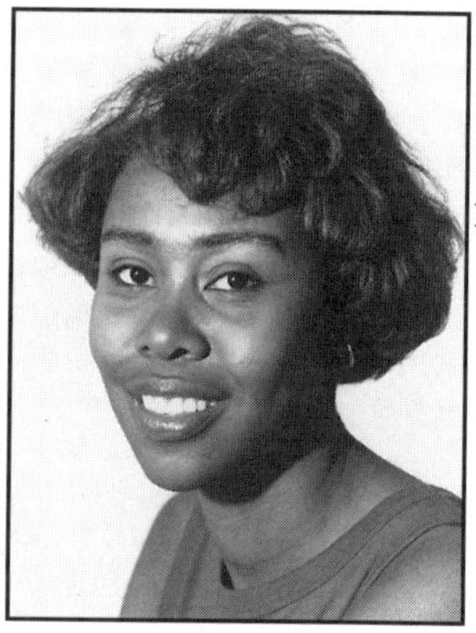

DAVID H. CURL (4)

Bounce-flash from a white surface. *Softer than direct-flash-off-camera, but shadows are more distinct than flash bounced from the ceiling, because the reflecting surface was closer. A reflective umbrella is often used, or a nearby wall.*

Using Flash

Flash is a handy way to get a picture when there isn't enough existing light. Most professional portrait and commercial studio photographers use flash almost exclusively for their work because of its uniform quality, consistent high intensity, incredible motion-stopping ability, and lack of uncomfortable heat and glare — whether the subject is a person, an animal, or an ice cream sundae. But these professionals seldom shoot anything with only a small flash unit on the camera. They work with expensive, heavy-duty multiple-lighting units.

Effective lighting with flash, like good lighting with any other source, is the result of previsualizing the effect you want to achieve. Do you want shadows to be harsh, soft, or nonexistent? Do you want to emphasize texture, or accent a certain part of the subject? Do you want to use light to separate the subject from the background? All of these questions should be answered before photographing any subject with flash, or with any kind of light.

On-camera

The common method of using flash — with the flash unit clipped into a metal shoe mounted on top of the camera or held by a bracket at one side of the camera and aimed directly at the subject — violates all of the principles of good lighting. Use direct-flash-on-camera only as a fill-in to illuminate harsh shadows cast by the sun, for personal "snapshooting," and as the sole light source only when there's no other way to get the picture.

ARDYCE CZUCHNA-CURL

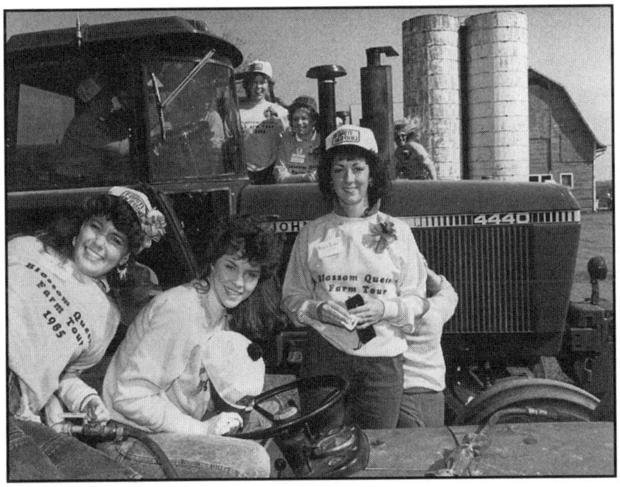

Fill-in-flash on the camera erased dark shadows on the womens' faces. Use this technique outdoors when you can't control the light in other ways. Set the maximum synchronized shutter speed on your camera. Determine the sunlight exposure first, then adjust the flash or camera distance for the lens opening required.

Red-eye

A flash on the camera aimed directly at the subject gives flat, uninteresting lighting. It may cause an ugly black shadow on the background, overexpose foreground objects, and underexpose subjects farther away. Another problem with flash-on-camera is red-eye, which is caused by people's eyes reflecting the flash the way the eyes of animals on the road reflect car headlights. The solution to this problem is to move the light source away from the camera.

Off-camera

By placing the flash unit to the side or above the camera, shadows are cast on the subject more from the ideal 45° key-light position, giving a feeling of form, texture, and depth. Red-eye is eliminated. Off-camera flash requires a cord sufficiently long to hold the flash at arms' length, or farther if you want to mount the flash on a stand. Carefully aim the flash so that the light goes where you want it. It's easy to tilt the flash unknowingly up or sideways. This can cause uneven lighting.

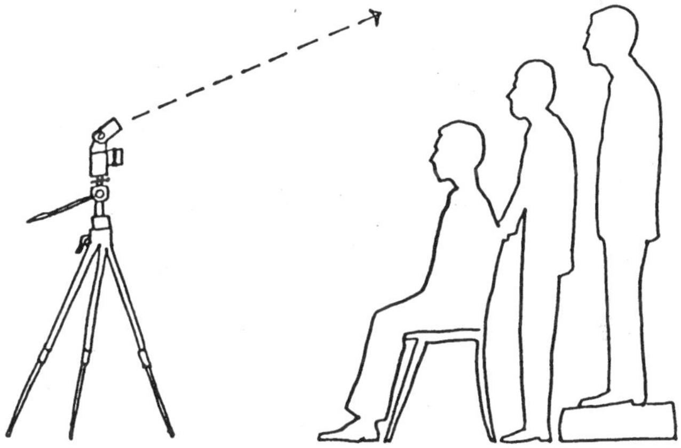

Have you wondered why your flash swivels to various angles? For most pictures, it should be aimed straight up at the ceiling to avoid uneven light coverage.
But when you have to photograph people at various distances from the camera, aiming the flash at or slightly beyond the farthest subject will reduce the tendency for the nearest subjects to be overexposed. Use this technique outdoors or in a large gym or banquet hall when bounce lighting is impractical.

Bounce

The simplest way to get decent lighting with a flash mounted on the camera is to tilt the flash straight up at the ceiling or sideways to a nearby wall. Called "bounce" flash because the light is bounced off a reflective surface and back down to your subject, the bounce technique gives soft, low-contrast lighting that looks very natural. But bounce flash works only in relatively small rooms with white ceilings or light-colored walls. It won't be effective outdoors, of course, or in a gymnasium or auditorium. With color film, unless the bounce surface is white, the picture will take on the color of the ceiling or wall.

Aim the flash straight up at the ceiling or directly at a reflecting surface. A flash that is partially tilted may cause the picture to be too light at the top and too dark at the bottom.

Flash exposure

Most small flash units automatically give the right amount of light if their controls are set to the proper f/stop and distance range. Exceptions may be with bounce and when shooting direct flash outdoors at night or in a very large room. Since some light is lost under these conditions you may need to open the lens one or two stops more than indicated. Be sure to run tests with new equipment, and attach a label to your flash so you won't forget the settings.

"Dedicated" flash units that read light through the lens usually will compensate for these conditions. They also make it easier to fill in shadows outdoors on a sunny day.

If your equipment doesn't have automatic fill flash, begin your tests by setting the maximum shutter speed that your camera will synchronize (see owner's manual or set at 1/60 if the shutter-speed dial is not clearly marked). Then, either by meter or "Sunny 16" rule, set the lens opening. For example: 100-speed film on a sunny day should be 1/60 at f/22. Check the charts on your flash to find out the distance range within which you can work at f/22. If your tests show that the flash is too intense, either use the next lower brightness setting or tape translucent diffusion material over the flash.

Simple 45° lighting emphasizes the repetition of forms and textures.

JORG JASPER

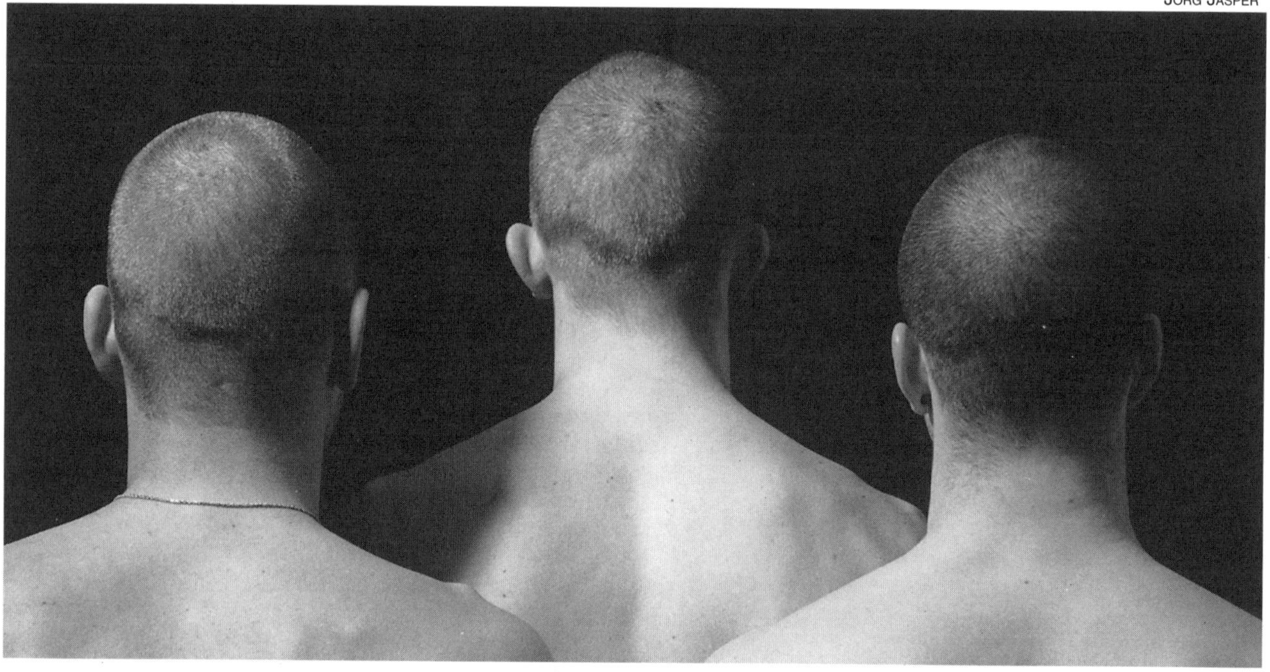

Special Imaging Techniques 10

"Events that never happened—photographs of strange things and strange visions in strange places."

— Peter Gold, photographer

Seeing the Unexpected

People believe in photographs. Because most of us subconsciously accept the old adage that "the camera never lies," photographs can shock us by twisting what we have quietly expected to be a faithful reproduction of reality into an unexpected experience.

"Show me something I haven't seen before, don't tell me what I already know. ... Disturb my assumptions about reality, don't reinforce them."

— Duane Michals, imagemaker

Computers add another dimension to photographic reality. Now any careful craftsperson can create images that look like photographs, but that cannot be. Digital imaging makes much simpler and more perfect the tricks that we already know how to do with a camera and in a darkroom, and makes possible countless new ones.

"The universe is full of magical things patiently waiting for our wits to grow sharper."

— E. Phillpots, philosopher

Frequently, there is conflict between interesting subject matter and interesting photographs. Great photographs exist that are superb renditions of compelling subject matter, yet in other great photographs the subject matter is scarcely recognizable. Artists use the term *surrealism* to describe work that transcends reality. But unique to photography is the ability to produce an image that exists in a world of its own, halfway between the real and the imaginary.

"Surrealism is freedom. It is the power of imagination. What you dream. ... What comes out of you when you don't know it."

— Henri Cartier-Bresson, photojournalist

Sometimes, because of subtly revealed textures and forms or bizarre juxtaposition of subject matter, a "straight" photograph may offer us a surrealistic surprise. But more often, such interesting images are the result of inspired manipulation.

"I frequently attempt to show in my work ... the unreality of the "real" and the reality of the "unreal." This may result, at times, in some disturbing effects. But art should be disturbing; it should make us both think and feel; it should infect the subconscious as well as the conscious mind."

— Clarence John Laughlin, photographer

DIANE OSBORNE

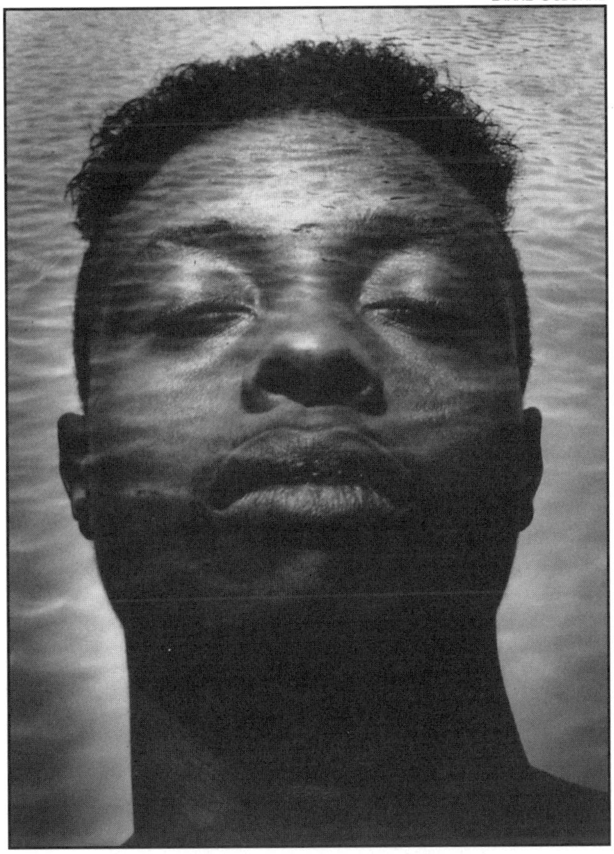

Two negatives were sandwiched in the enlarger to create this provocative image that served as the lead picture in an exhibition. It could have been an in-camera double-exposure, or a computer composite. Regardless of the production technique, what matters is the result..

When examining the work of certain contemporary imagemakers, sometimes it's hard to tell for certain where photography has ended and handwork or optical/electronic manipulation begun. Widespread overlapping of technologies is creating an ethical dilemma, as well as an artistic "gray area" within which it is sometimes difficult to distinguish concept from craft, and message from technique.

Some photographic special effects are good, clean fun. Some of the more obvious "tricks" that can make a strong artistic statement, produce a visual joke, or sometimes sell a product include special films, lighting illusions, multiple exposures, optical effects with lenses and filters, and digital enhancement and manipulation.

Darkroom and computer effects range from the obvious to the amazing, with many steps in between. Photographic effects are created in one of three ways: by accident, by trial and error, or by deliberate design. In this chapter, we will describe several special effects that you can achieve.

"Great photographs exist ... in the electric tension between real and unreal."

— Charles Harbutt, photographer

Reflections

"The mark of an educated person is to see something in a mud puddle besides the mud."

— Anonymous

One rainy day as I was stepping off the curb to cross a street, a little girl splashing around nearby shouted, "Mommy, Mommy, look at the pretty rainbow in the gutter!"

"Silly girl," replied Mom. "Can't you see that's just dirty oil floating on the water. Don't get it on your boots!"

So much for imagination. When that little girl goes to school, will her teacher show her how to draw a Thanksgiving turkey by tracing around her hand? Will she be told that the country landscape she has crayoned isn't right because the sky is not blue and the grass is not green?

"It's OK to trust your instincts."

— Ed Paschke, painter

DAVID HARRISON

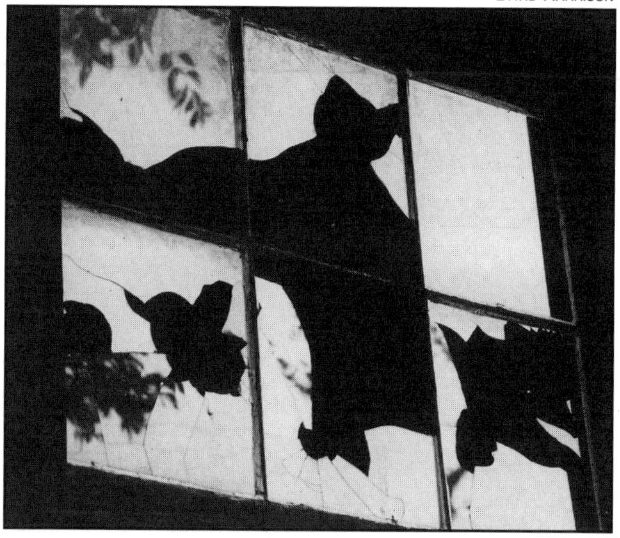

Which form is surface, which form is behind the glass, and which is the reflection? Reflective surfaces can yield endless relationships between positive and negative space.

I hope you will learn to see puddles, polished metal and stone surfaces, windows and glass doors as mirrors, too. Notice what you see in reflective surfaces, what's on the surface, and what may be revealed beyond.

Special Filters

Special filters can create stunning effects. Camera filters differ from enlarger filters. Most different of all are computer filters, hundreds of which are available to literally transform images to which they are applied.

Placed in front of the camera lens, any colored filter will create an overall tint of that color on color film, and sometimes that's what you want. One interesting technique is to make a triple exposure (on a tripod) through each of three colored filters (#25 red, #61 green, and #38A blue). Ignore the filter factors, exposing each time for the basic exposure without a filter. Bracket, of course. The effect is most dramatic when part of the subject remains stationary during all three exposures, while other parts such as flowing water, blowing leaves, or other moving objects appear in the scene. For this project your camera must permit multiple exposures without moving the film.

On a camera or enlarger lens, a diffusion filter gives a soft-focus "romantic" effect to landscapes and, when used on portraits, tend to obscure wrinkles and facial blemishes. Experiment, because the strength of the effect often depends upon the lens opening (larger openings show more diffusion).

A piece of black metal screening or nylon mesh will diffuse the image, but glass filters seem to give more sparkle to the highlights.

Some filters are available with a clear center and a diffusing effect around the edges, or with color surrounding the center. You can make your own diffusion filter by smearing a circle of petroleum jelly around the outer portion of a clear UV filter (don't do this on the lens!)

Computer software diffuses the image with various "blur" commands. The best diffuser for photographic effects in Photoshop is Filter > Blur > Gaussian Blur.

Some split-field filters increase apparent depth of field by giving near and far sharpness. Others are half-clear and half-graded neutral density (useful for darkening a light sky or the top of a snow-capped mountain); others consist of bands of color. Split-field effects are achieved in a computer by pasting separate images together.

A star filter can add a dramatic cross-line flare effect to light sources and slightly diffuse the image. A piece of silver aluminum screening over the lens also will give this effect. Other filters use a diffraction pattern to create various starburst and rainbow illusions. All are most effective with backlighted subjects including light sources or bright highlights. Software star filters permit variations of number of points, length and breadth, brightness and color.

Multi-image filters repeat the image of a person or object three or more times. Some designs give an illusion of linear motion. All perform best when a distinct subject is separated from a relatively dark, plain background. The multiple images appear closer together with a wide angle lens and farther apart with longer focal lengths.

D. Morenz

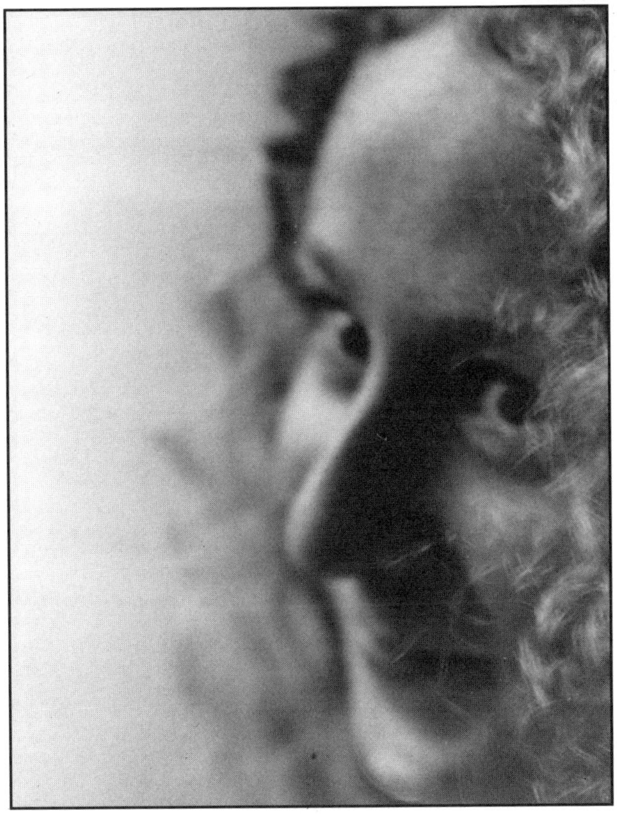

Diffusion is not often used in this era of super-sharp images, except by some portrait photographers. In the intimate photo above, does unsharpness detract, or does it contribute to a feeling of motion and fun?

David Harrison

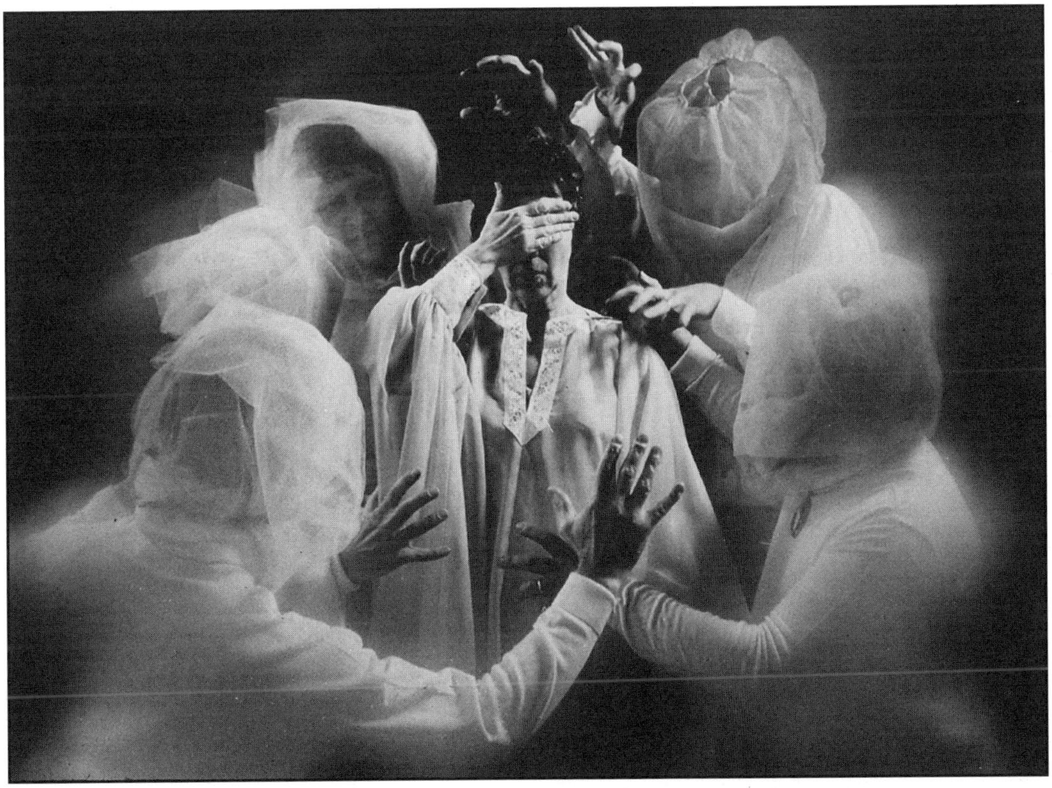

The desired dreamlike quality of this fantasy image resulted from smearing a ring of petroleum jelly around the outside surface of a UV filter, leaving only the center clear. A center-sharp filter could have achieved a similar effect. In Adobe Photoshop, the center of the image could have been selected, broadly feathered, inverted, and the Gaussian blur filter applied to the outer areas.

MICKEY HOWELL

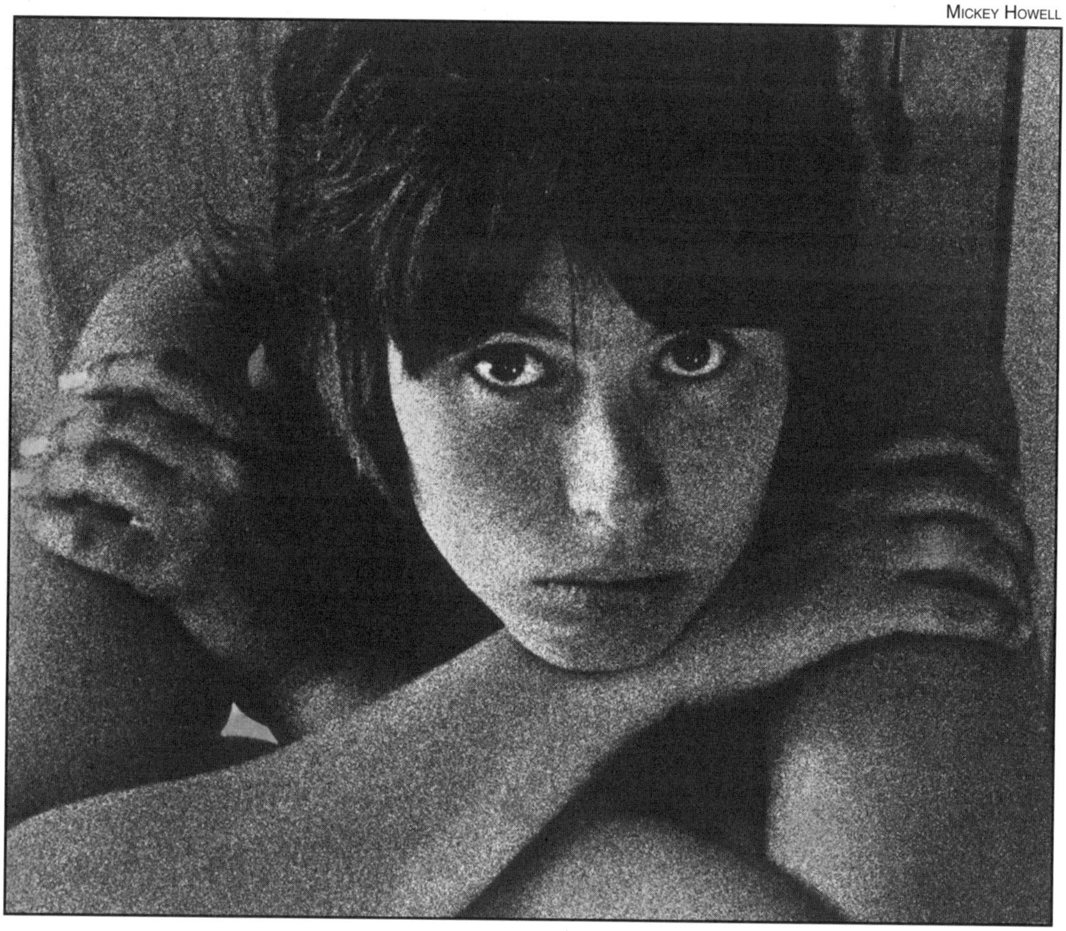

Although grain usually is something most photographers try to minimize, course grain texture sometimes can strengthen the statement. The portrait at right was enlarged from a samll portion of a 35mm negative made on very high-speed film that had been push-processed. In imaging software, film grain effect can be achieved by applying a "noise" filter.

Special Films

For special effects, sometimes the "wrong" film can be right! For example, if you want grainy texture in a portrait, instead of ISO 100 film, choose a very fast emulsion such as Kodak T-Max P3200, then push-process the film, and make a big, high-contrast enlargement from the negative. You'll be sure to get grain!

Extreme contrast effects such as silhouettes and outlines are easier to achieve when special film is used for the original camera negative. Kodalith Ortho film, when processed in Kodalith developer, yields black-and-white negatives with no grays. Ektagraphic HC Slide Film can be processed either for ultra-high contrast or moderately high contrast such as when copying faded old photos or low-contrast drawings. Kodak Technical Pan film also depends upon processing to determine its contrast. This slow, ultra-fine-grain film is intended for scientific photography, but has many other uses.

Infrared film is another scientific tool that has been adopted by experimenters for bizarre pictorial effects. Unusual because its speed varies widely according to subject and lighting conditions, infrared must be exposed through a dark red (#25) or visually opaque (#87) filter. It also requires extra care in focusing.

Color "Temperature"

"Color should be convincing, appealing and enjoyable; but not necessarily accurate."

— Eliot Porter, photographer

Accurate color sometimes is very important, as in commercial work. But at other times the impression of color may enhance a picture's mood and meaning. Once you know how to get correct color, you can use this knowledge to create variations and fantasy effects.

Each type of color film is designed to be exposed by light within a particular part of the energy spectrum, which is known as the Kelvin temperature scale (see diagram on page 92). To put it very simply, candlelight and firelight are on the very "warm" or reddish end of the Kelvin scale; tungsten lights such as household bulbs and studio "hot" lights are still on the warm side (most studio tungsten and quartz lights are 3,200°K). Electronic flash is on the bluer side, similar to mid-day sunlight (5,500°K), while the extreme blue end of the spectrum consists of light reflected from the blue sky, which can measure 12,000°K or more.

Because the color of light varies so much, color films have to be selected and/or filtered to match the light when accurate color values are wanted. But what about dramatic effects? Well, one common Hollywood technique is to shoot "day for night." Scenes that appear to take place under the blueness of moonlight really have been shot in sunny daylight, but on film balanced for tungsten — and underexposed to drop out shadow detail. You can do the opposite to enhance the colors of neon signs, fireworks, etc., or if you're using gelled (filtered) lights in the studio. Daylight-balanced film may cause the colors to appear more intensely saturated.

Unintentional use of the wrong color film for the light is a common beginners mistake. So when the skin tones come out orange, what happened? That's right. You probably exposed daylight film under tungsten light. What about when an outdoor color picture is very blue? Well, if it's in sunlight, it probably was shot on tungsten film. But if the picture was taken in heavy shade, it may simply have required a warming filter. With color slides these mismatches can be catastrophic, but color-negative film usually can be corrected when it is printed. Computer software gives you a wide spectrum to correct or distort hue, saturation and brightness.

David Harrison

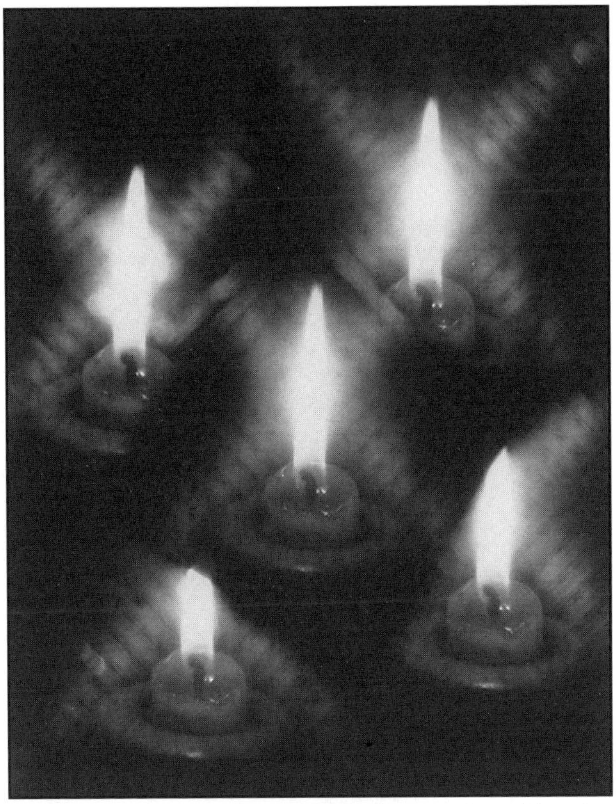

Novel and sometimes spectacular effects can be achieved with special filters. Here, multi-image and star filters were combined to glorify a single candle flame.

Debi Reda

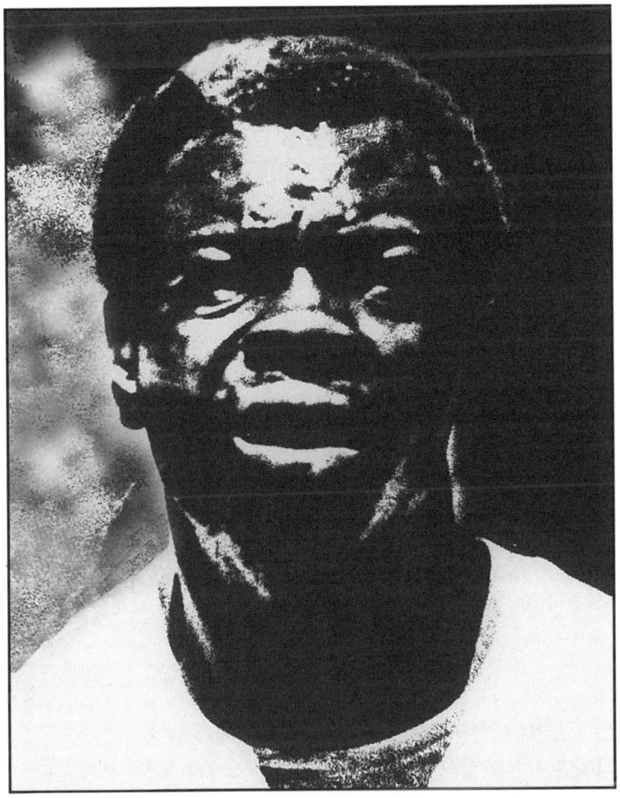

High-contrast film transformed an ordinary continuous-tone image into a dramatic abstraction

"I found that I could say things with color and shapes that I couldn't say in any other way — things that I had no words for."

— Georgia O'Keeffe, painter

"Perhaps the biggest surprises will be found not in the far reaches of outer space, but rather in the near reaches of inner space — that special space where wonders are wondered, new worlds are imagined, and happenings are understood."

— Bill Stonebarger, educator

Fumiko Yarita

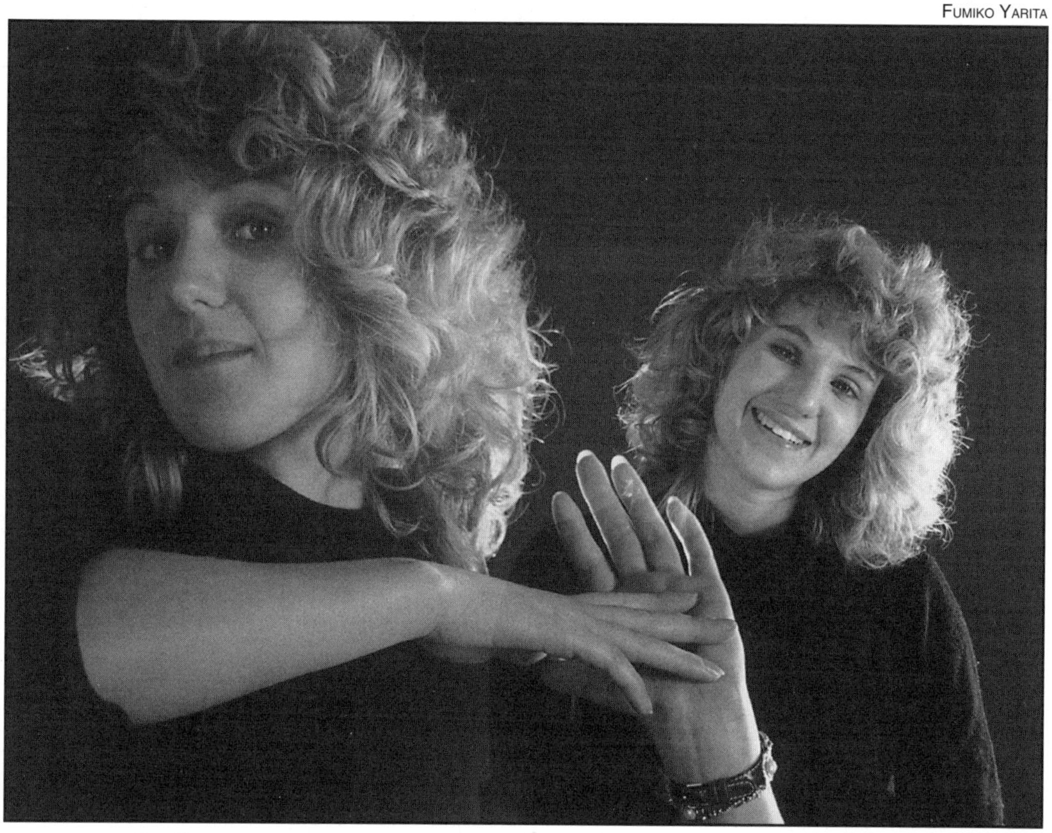

The black background of this double-exposure kept "ghosting" to a minimum. (Note the slight overlap that shows only in the center). Because each exposure was at a different distance, the camera had to be refocused.

Rene Poch

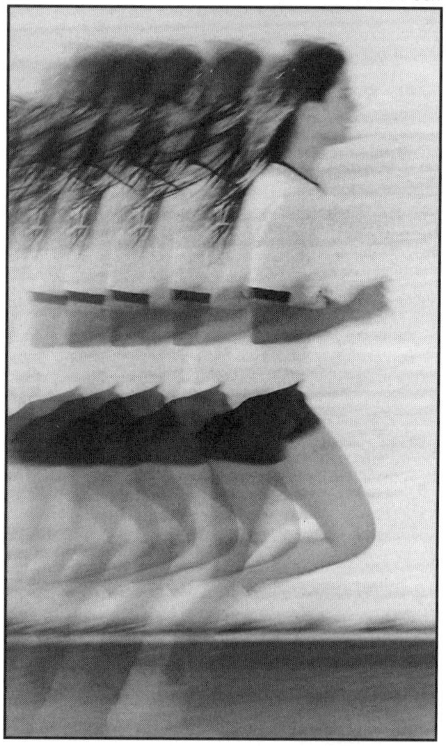

This illusion of motion was achieved by making five separate exposures on the same sheet of enlarging paper, moving the easel one inch each time. The white background enabled the runner's face and form to stand out because the paper remained unexposed in those areas.

Steve McNut (2)

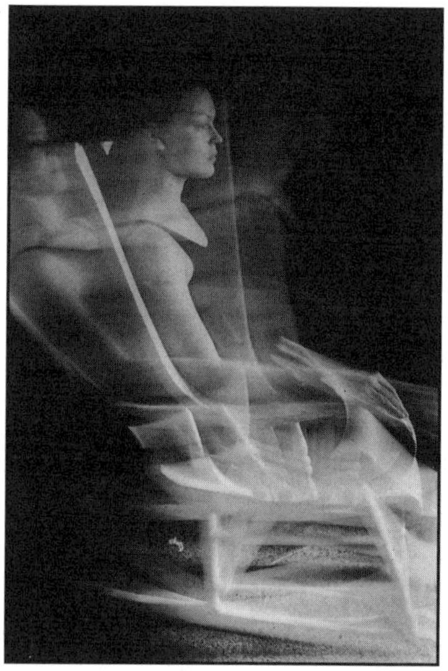

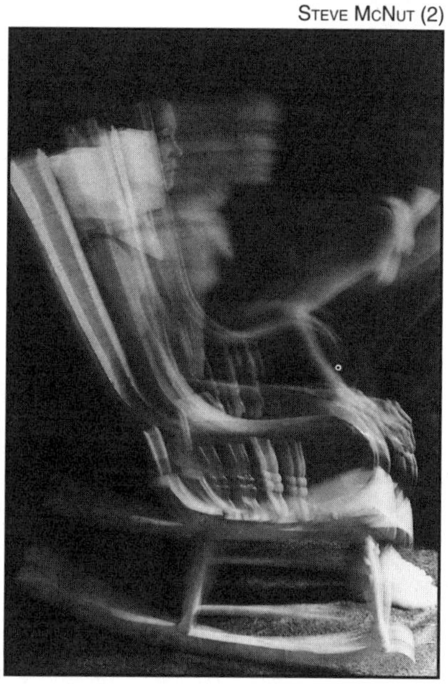

Sharp images were recorded as the model paused briefly, blurred images as she moved during the brief time exposure (shutter set on B, cable release depressed for about five seconds).

"It is the relationships between things that gives meaning to them."

— Hans Hofmann, philosopher

Multiple Exposures

Repeated images of an animated subject can be done with a multi-image filter, but more control is possible with an in-camera multiple exposure or with flash fired in sequence during a time exposure.

Multiple exposures are easy if your camera provides a means for cocking the shutter without moving the film. Many 35mm cameras do, but not all. Check the owner's manual to see whether yours has this feature. If not, you could consider acquiring an inexpensive older camera that does, such as a venerable Argus C-3.

When using a dark background for a multiple exposure, normal exposure should give good results. But if the background is light or if the subject overlaps much of itself, you may need to divide the total exposure by the number of images (for two exposures, stop down one stop; for four exposures, two stops). Experiment!

With the camera on a tripod and the shutter locked open at "B" setting, a flash can be fired repeatedly as the subject slowly moves across the picture area. Combining sharp with blurred motion images is another interesting technique. If you're using only hot lights, direct the subject to move, then hold; move, then hold; leaving sharp images connected by blurs to give the appearance of motion. A variation is to direct your subject, side-lighted with tungsten lights, to move slowly and then end the blurred sequence with a single pop of the flash. Of course, all of this must take place either in a darkened room or outdoors at night; otherwise light reflecting from the background will build up too much density and obscure the subject.

A final variation, useful to photograph a large unlighted interior or an outdoor space at night, is "walk-around" flash. You lock open the shutter and walk around within the picture area firing the flash. Be sure to direct the light away from the camera, hiding yourself if possible behind pillars, doorways, furniture, etc. The lens opening will depend on the power of the flash unit at the chosen flash-to-subject distance.

Time Exposures

Night can be an exciting time to photograph city skylines, buildings, fountains, etc. A tripod is necessary, and so is exposure bracketing. You can start with an exposure table such as the one on page 165, but since every subject is so different you'll still want to bracket to be sure (don't forget that reciprocity departure may require increasing exposure). Motion effects such as panning and zooming can be done at shutter speeds from about 1/30 down to 1 second. But holding the camera shutter open (set on "B" and operated with a locking cable release) for several seconds or even several minutes can give a dramatic illusion of time and motion as lights from moving objects trace themselves onto the film (turn back to the example on page 116). A small lens opening usually works best to keep lighted objects from losing shape and color from overexposure. Also you may need to use a slow film.

TODD WICKERSHAM

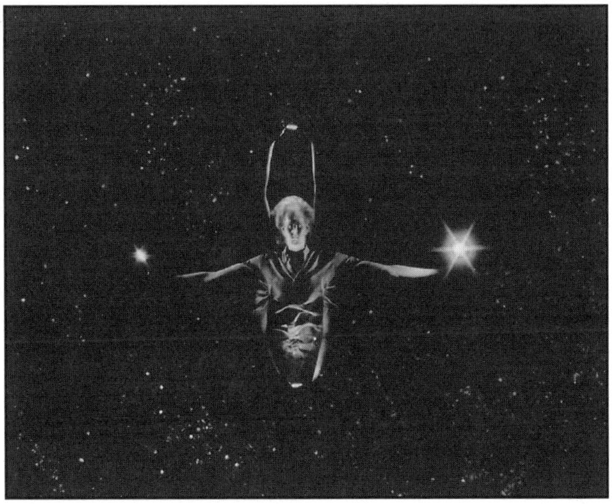

In this unusual self-portrait, a flash unit was held and fired manually at each of four positions while the camera shutter was held open on B setting with a locking cable release. The lens was set at f/16. The star-field background was created by sprinkling baby powder on the enlarging paper before exposure, then blowing it off before putting the print into the developer.

DAVID HARRISON

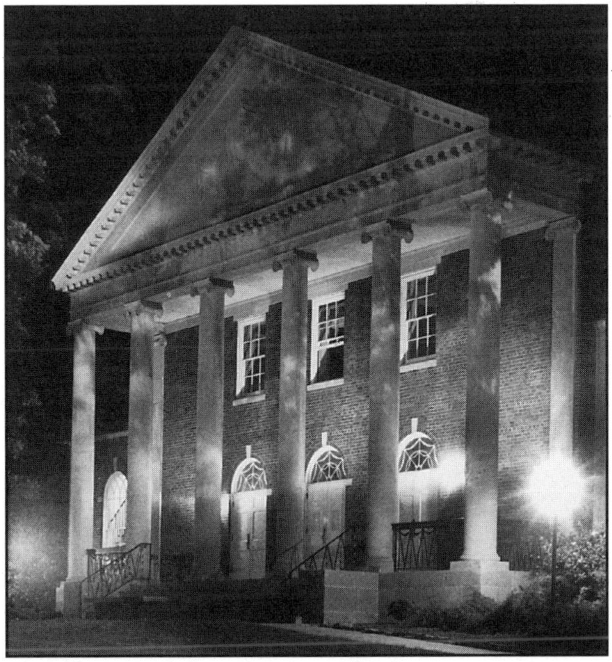

This night-time image was created by firing a hand-held flash unit 15 times as the photographer walked around the building and hid behind columns.

Darren Hathaway (2)

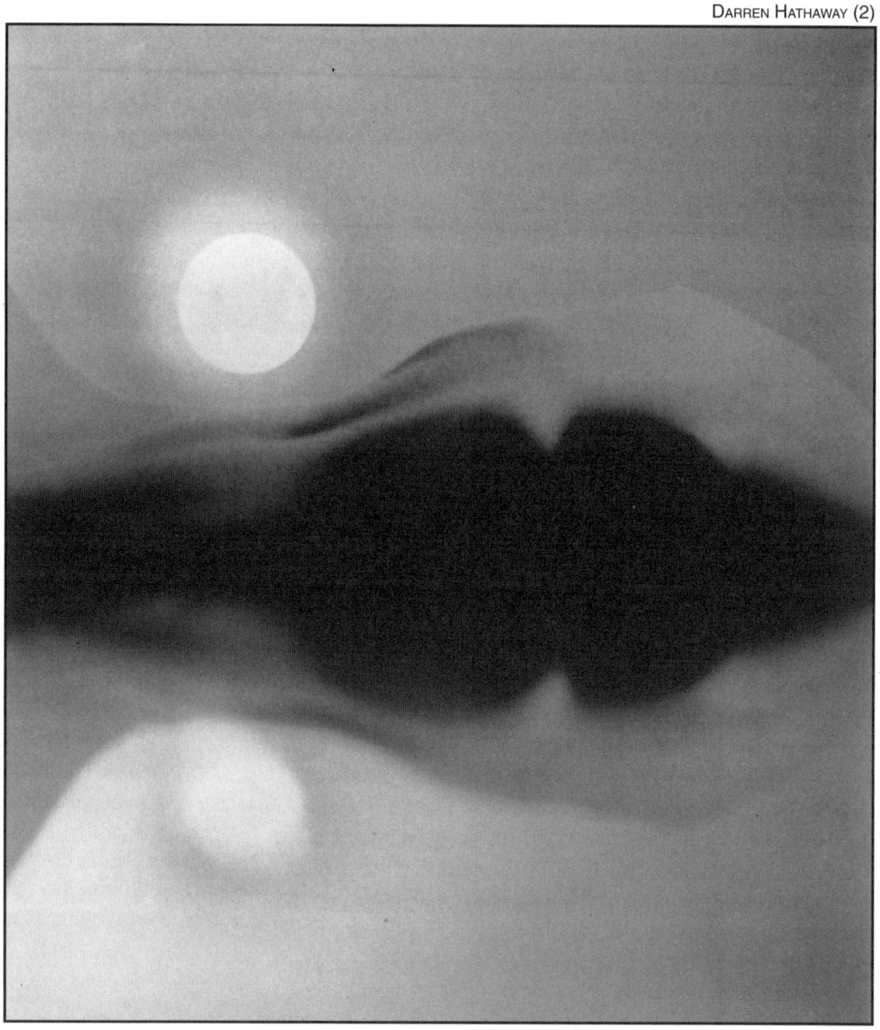

Carefully masked images from four slide projectors were superimposed to blend the "landscape," the moon, and both reflections. Re-photographed off the screen with 35mm color-negative film, the final result was a spectacular 16x20 color print. With a computer, the four slides would be scanned in, pasted to separate layers, then assembled into the final photomontage.

"Art is the only way to run away from home without leaving home."

— Twyla Tharp, choreographer

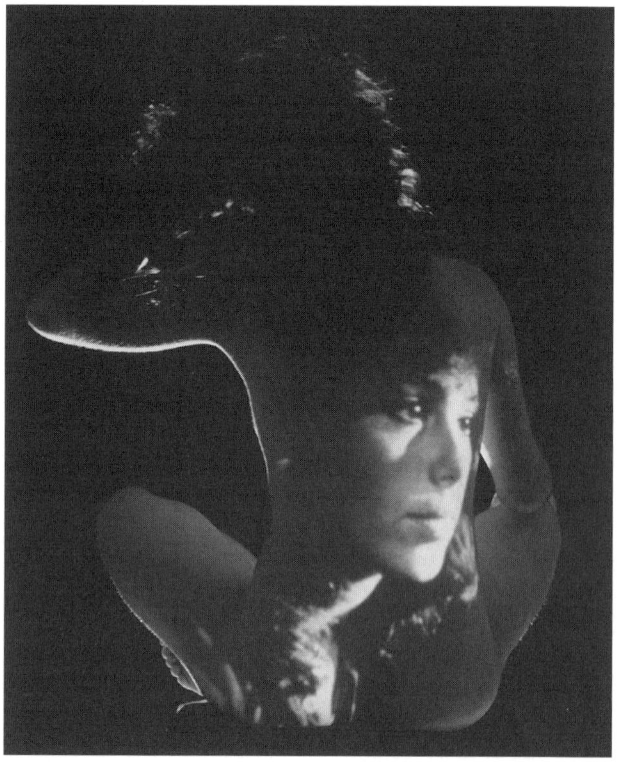

A color slide was projected onto the model's back in a darkened room, and then re-photographed. Notice how backlighting prevents the outline of the model's body from blending into the background. Whether superimpositions are done in the camera, in the darkroom, or in a computer, each part of the image must be lighted and scaled to fit with the others.

Projected Images

If you're working with color slides, ingenious combinations are possible. Slides with objects against light backgrounds can be removed from their mounts, sandwiched together, and remounted for projection or printing. If two, three, or more projectors are available, try projecting together slides of subjects against dark backgrounds. The pictures can be overlapped and blended by moving the projectors around. Brightness can be adjusted simply by stretching strips of black masking tape across the front edges of projector lenses (don't stick the tape to the glass). Projected images can be overlapped and blended together seamlessly by using soft-edge slide masks available from audiovisual suppliers.

When you get an arrangement on the screen that you want to keep, take a picture of it directly off the screen surface with your 35mm camera. Distortion can be minimized by setting up the camera on a tripod slightly above and behind the projectors, framing the projected image tightly with a zoom or telephoto lens. The closer the projectors are to the screen, the brighter the projected image will be.

Either tungsten-balanced slide film or color negative film can be used. With 100-speed film, you may have to expose for several seconds with the shutter on "B." Make tests based on meter readings made from the screen (avoid reading your own shadow). Bracket toward longer times, because reciprocity will lengthen the exposure needed.

Photomontage

A few artists, especially Jerry N. Uelsmann, have mastered negative sandwich and multiple-exposure printing techniques to create collages — or more precisely, montages — that extend our perceptions of reality. But it is easier, now, to superimpose images with software. Selecting, copying, and pasting layered images in Adobe Photoshop is fun, challenging, faster at the keyboard than in the darkroom, and environmentally friendlier. In Photoshop, the layers palette is the key, because image components saved there can be infinitely modified, transparentized, and recombined.

"The problem with fantasy is that it's not real. And the problem with reality is that it is!"

— Marilyn Rowens, photographer

Leonardo Brito

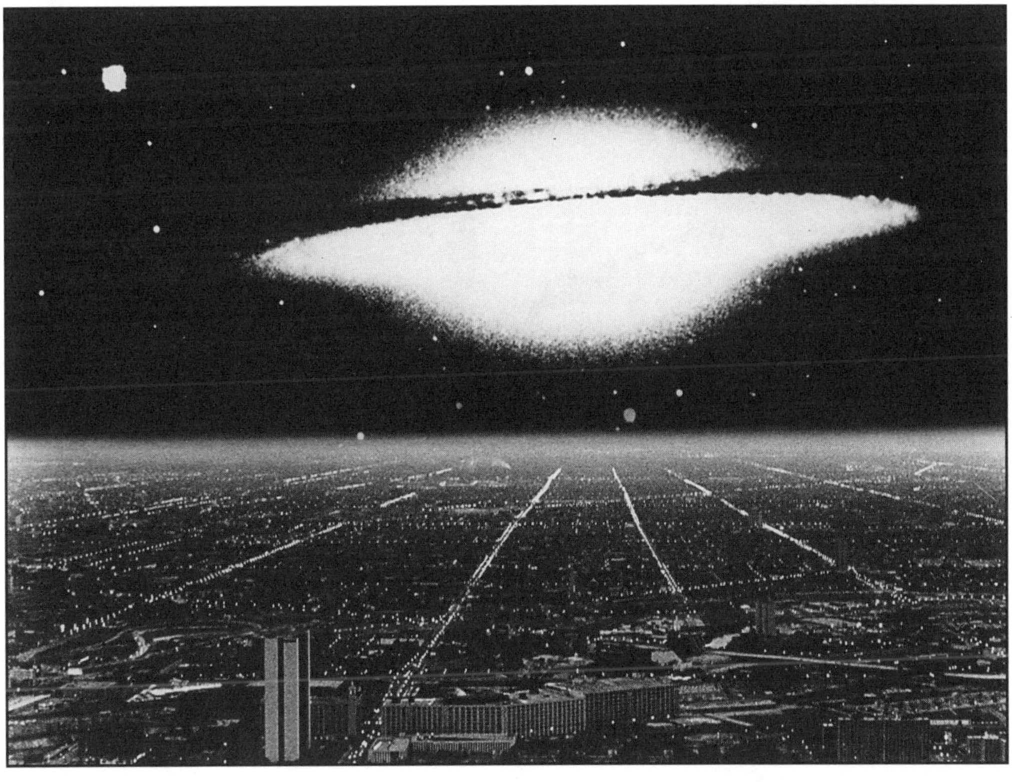

In the darkroom, a level horizon line simplifies blending two images. Complex images are much less tedious to mask with the selection tools in computer software.

DAVID HARRISON (2)

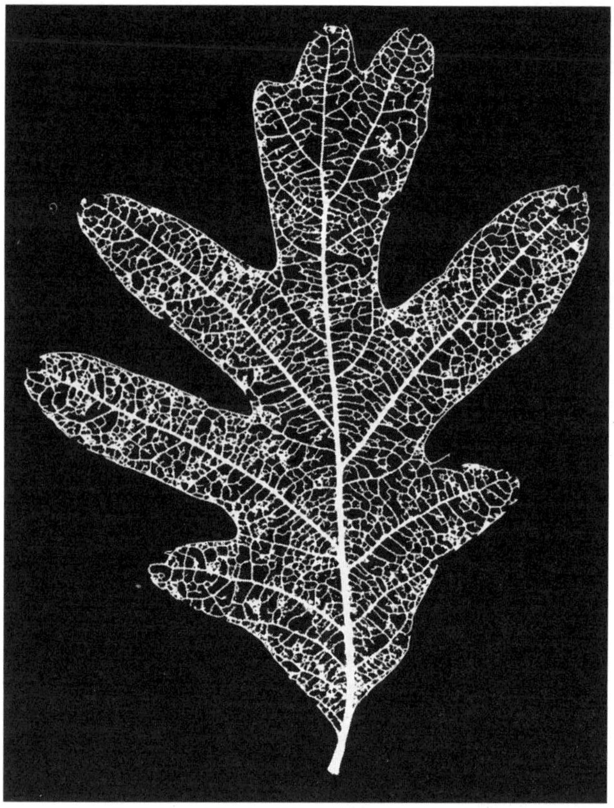

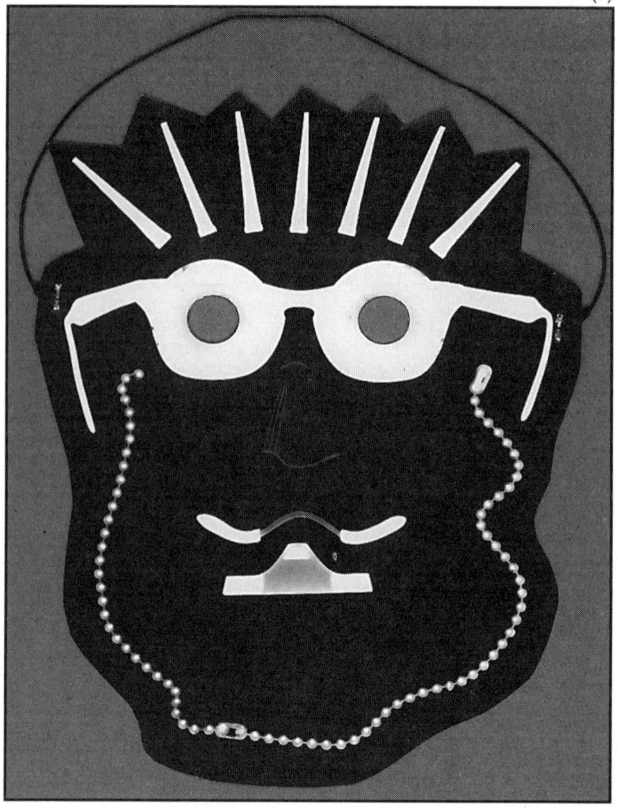

(Above) A leaf skeleton found on the ground was placed between glass in a 4x5 enlarger and projected with maximum contrast.

LOIS HENRY

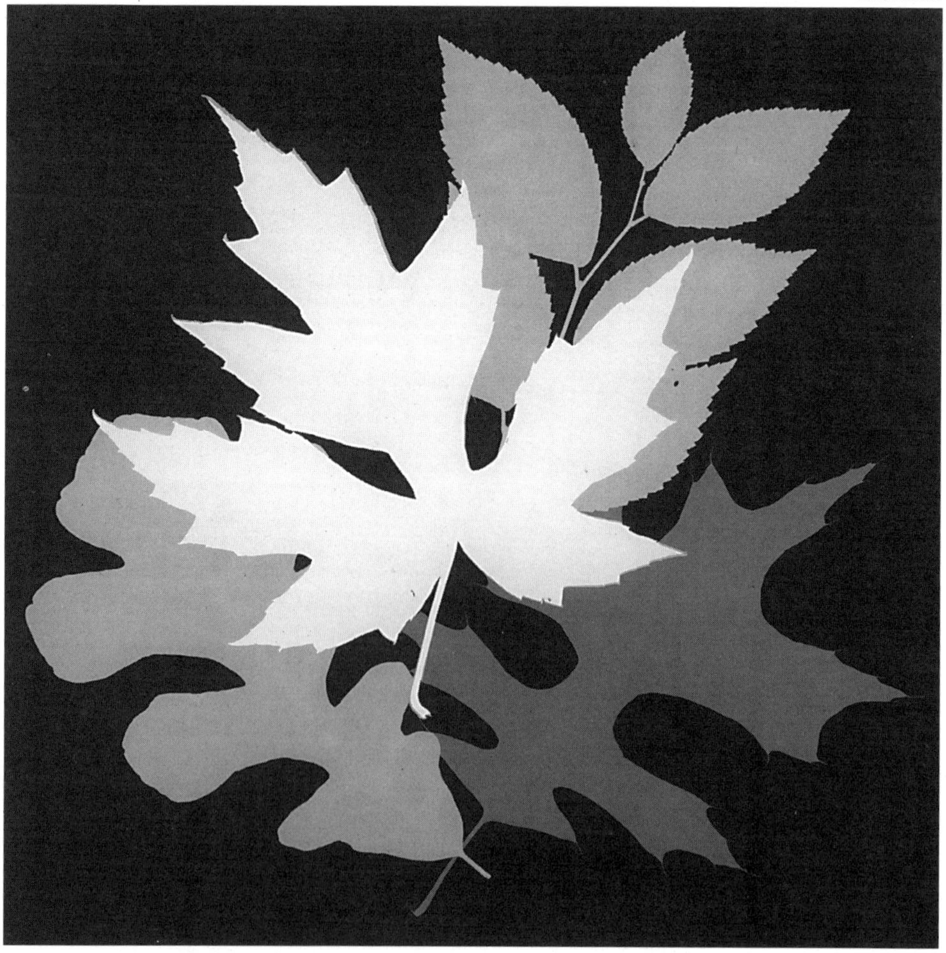

(Right) The various tones of gray in this photogram were achieved by giving a series of short exposures, removing one leaf each time until only the part of the paper beneath the maple leaf in the center received no light and remained white.

Photograms and Scannergrams

A cameraless, shadow picture is the first assignment given by many teachers of photography. Because a photogram project requires no negative, it can be done on the first day of class. The experience with chemicals and an enlarger or other light source provides an excellent initiation for beginners into the mysterious rites of the darkroom. But making photograms can be more than an exercise. Exploring this simple process may challenge your imagination to find forms that will reproduce themselves in varied tones, and to place them in graphically interesting patterns.

Any photographic paper will do for photograms — in fact, this is a good way to use up surplus paper of any size, surface, weight, or contrast grade. Simply make a trial exposure to determine the deepest black you can get without producing flare around the images of the objects you've placed on the paper.

Also, instead of placing objects on the paper, thin, flat cutouts and patterns that will fit into a glass negative carrier can be inserted into an enlarger and projected as large as the paper available.

A scannergram is created by arranging objects on the glass of a flat-bed scanner. In addition to the shadow outlines, surface texture is revealed, and sometimes with three-dimensional objects, amazing color fringes and rainbow effects can occur.

James Alvaro

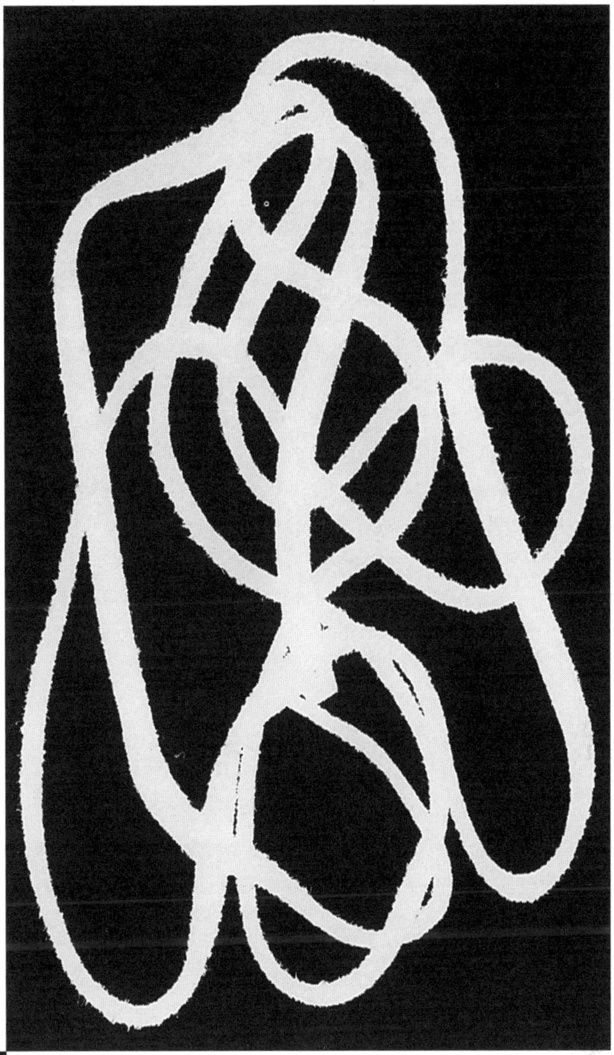

Aurelia Spengler

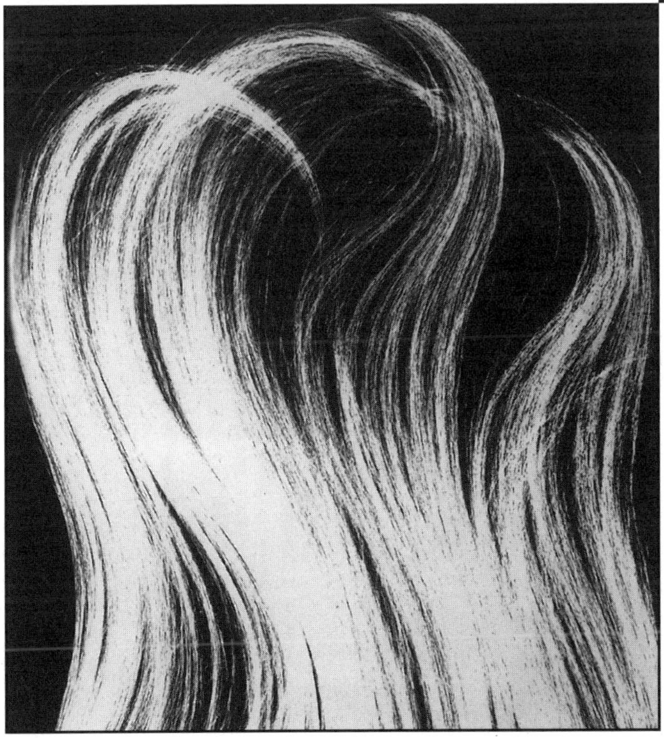

"The darkroom is capable of being ... a visual research lab; a place for discovery, observation, and meditation. ... Let us not be afraid to allow for "postvisualization"... willingness ... to revisualize the final image at any point in the entire photographic process."

— Jerry N. Uelsmann, imagemaker

JORG JASPER (2)

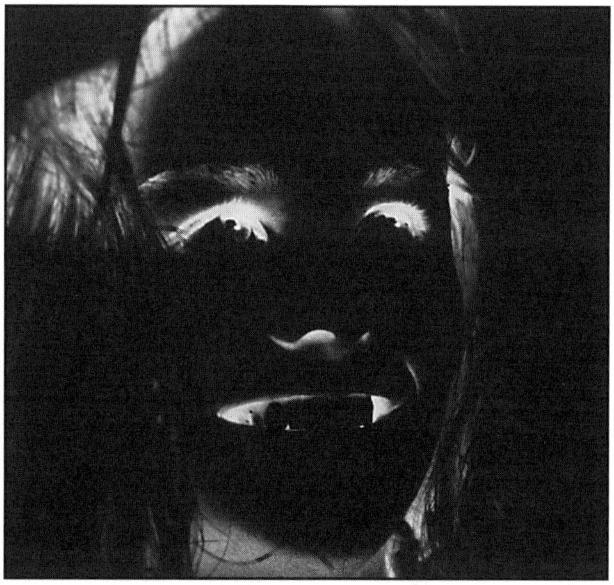

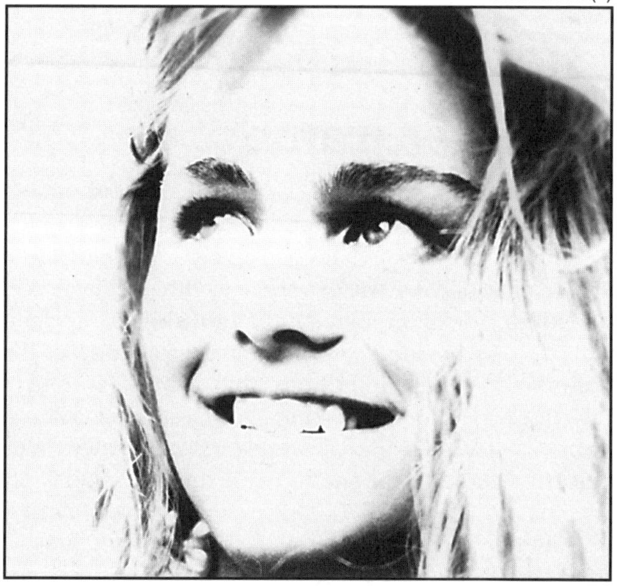

The negative print (left) was made directly from a color slide. The high-key positive print (right) is a contact print from the negative print. Expect increased contrast.

LINDA CHICK

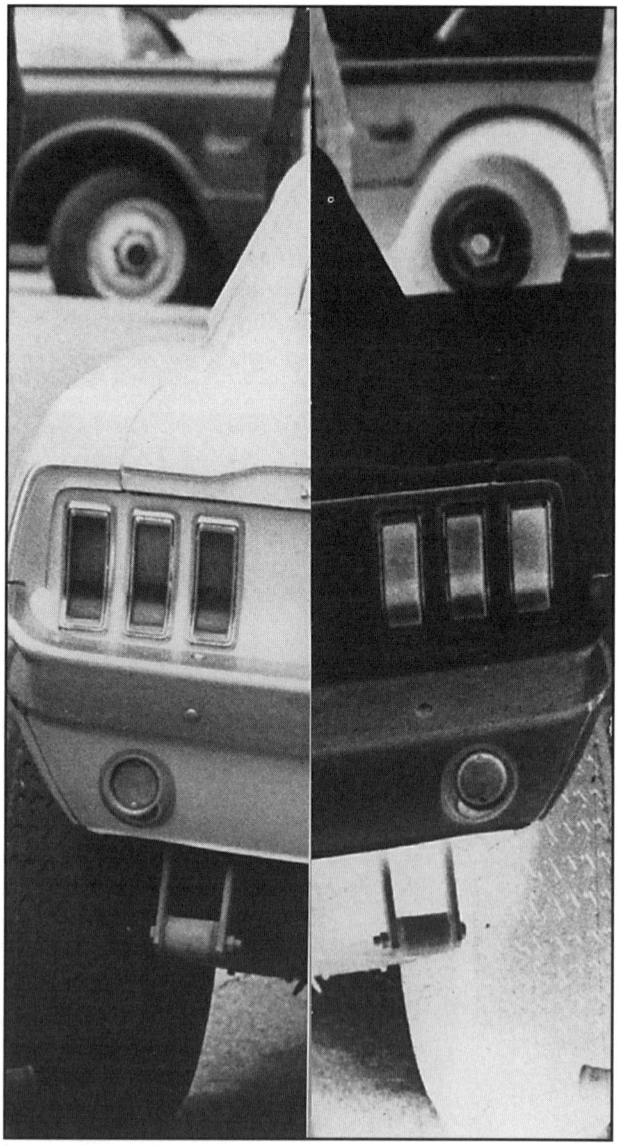

Negative Prints

A negative print? Why not! If you put a positive image such as a color slide into the negative carrier of an enlarger and make an enlargement, the result is a print that is reversed in tonal values and, usually, increased in contrast.

Starting with an ordinary negative, you make first a normal print, then produce the negative print by contact — paper to paper. For maximum sharpness, contact imaging of dry prints should be done emulsion-to-emulsion, either in a vacuum frame or a spring-backed, glass printing frame. Lacking either, you can use a contact-proofing easel if you firmly hold down the glass. If the positive print has just been processed and is still wet, try soaking the unexposed paper in a tray of water and laminating it against the paper positive, emulsion-to-emulsion, with a print roller or squeegee. After exposure, peel apart the two sheets and develop the final print normally. During exposure you can make parts of the image lighter or darker by dodging and burning, as with a conventional print.

In Adobe Photoshop, Image > Adjust > Curves will bring you to the Curves graph. Reversing the high and low ends will convert the image to a negative.

> ***"Constant creativity and innovation are essential to combat visual mediocrity."***
>
> — Jerry N. Uelsmann, imagemaker

Steven Hunt

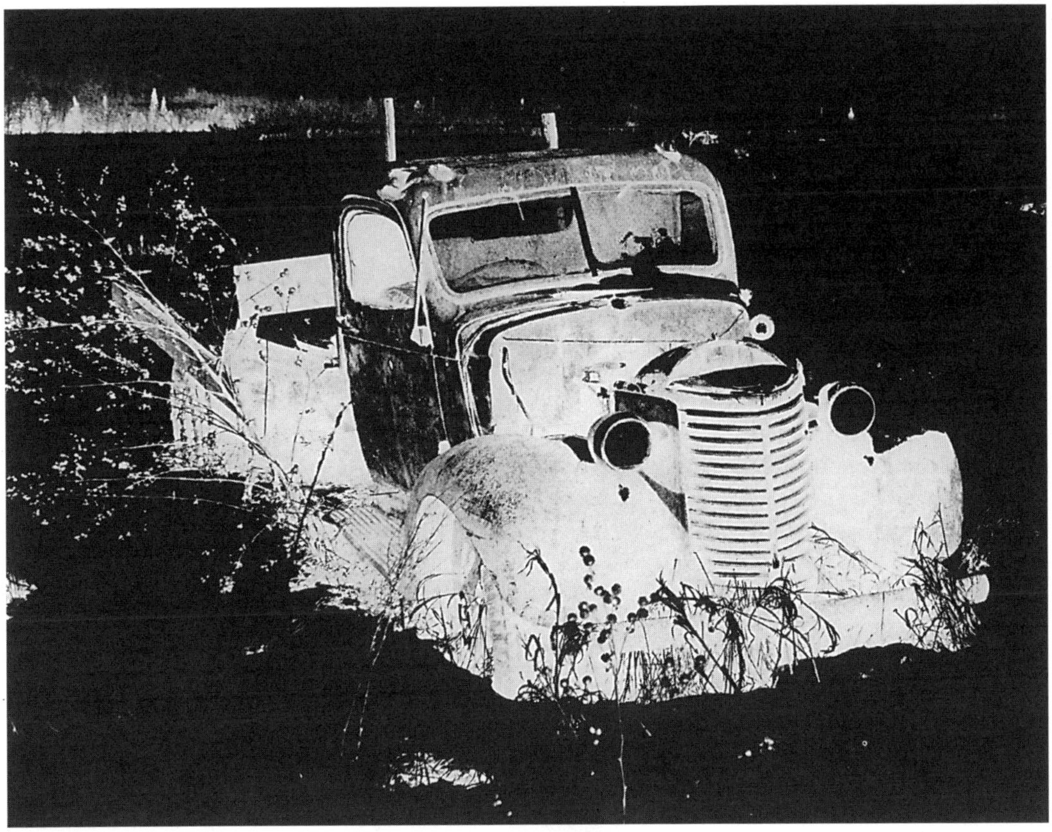

An image like this can be enlarged directly from a color slide or made by contact from a positive print. In the computer, reverse the value scale (see page 211).

Jim Scherrer

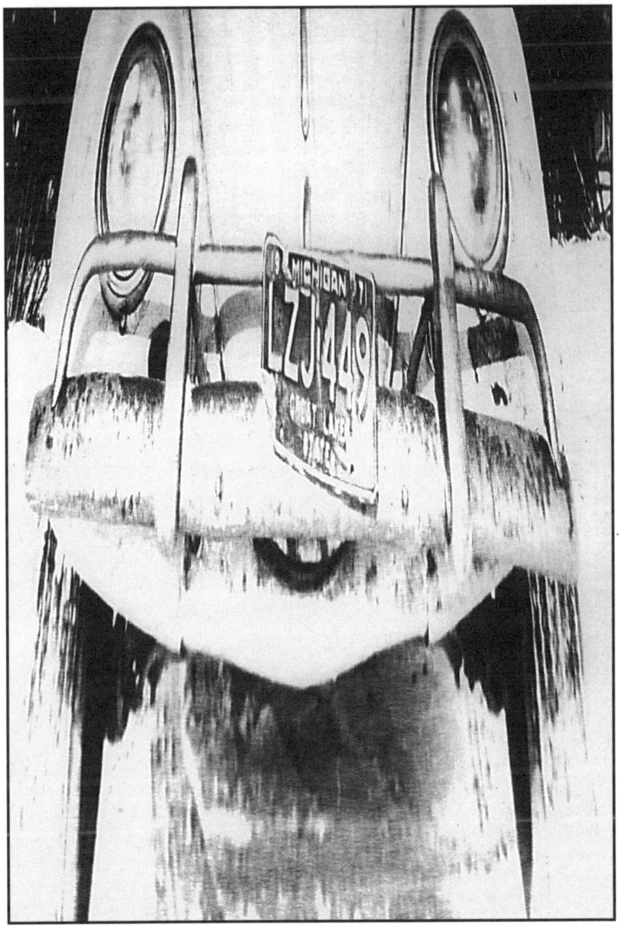

Image Distortion

The same technique that corrects for converging verticals and similar errors in perspective can be reversed to produce distortion in a normal image. Try going even further than tilting the easel. Curving the paper, for example, can make a "stopper" from an ordinary photograph. Another idea you might want to try is to aim your camera into a highly polished, distorted surface and then add to the effect by holding the paper out-of-square when printing. Further distortion can be achieved by copying (re-photographing) the distorted print. This is one way graphic artists make lettering appear to conform to an angled or irregular surface.

In different upgrades of Adobe Photoshop, either Image > Effects > Perspective, > Skew, > Distort, or Layer > Transform will permit variations either subtle or extreme. With 3D software you can stretch a photograph or pattern to cover the surface of an object.

Combination Printing

Sometimes it's effective, and often amusing, to print from more than one negative onto the same sheet of enlarging paper. There are several ways of doing this so that the images combine to form one. The choice of method depends on the relationships of the images, the size of the negatives, and whether their backgrounds are black (transparent on the negative) or light (dense on the negative). If you have a pair of negatives with transparent backgrounds, and if the subjects are in scale with each other, a simple negative sandwich in the enlarger will work. To judge whether two negatives will sandwich effectively, simply hold them up to the light together and move them around to see whether they will register satisfactorily. Beware of dust on the negatives and dust trapped between them, or you may have a lot of spotting to do.

Negatives with dense backgrounds must be printed separately. The background of the second negative, if it is dense enough, will mask out all but the image you want to print, so as not to affect the image from the first negative already printed. Careful dodging or vignetting will be necessary if the backgrounds of the negatives are not dense enough. A carefully cut mask can be useful when you want to print in a background, such as sky, around a clearly defined object.

Most difficult of all is the blending of portions of two or more separate negatives to create what appears to be a single, unmanipulated image. It is easier to do this when each negative is in a separate enlarger and focused, masked, and with exposure determined in advance and timer set. Then you can produce several prints nearly alike, and perfect the process with a minimum of mistakes. Although a great deal of setup time and testing is required to make a blend line that doesn't show, the results can be strikingly surreal.

"The true magician can explain his trick, but the magic is still there."

— Jerry N. Uelsmann, imagemaker

David H. Curl

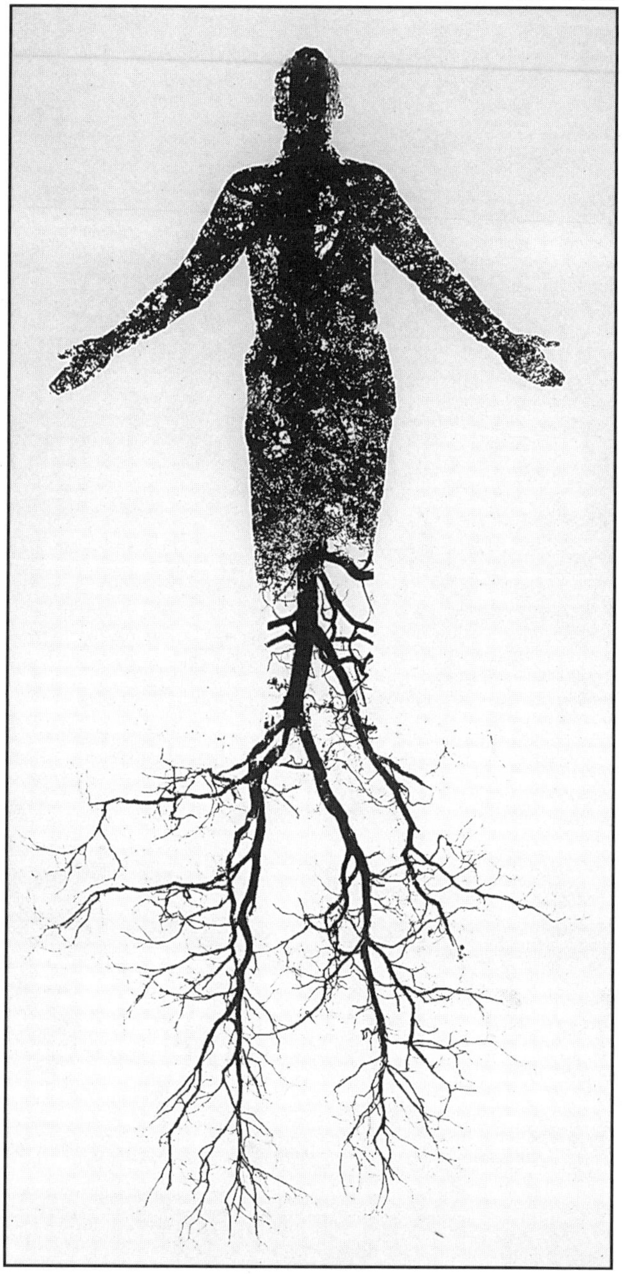

Dan Fetters

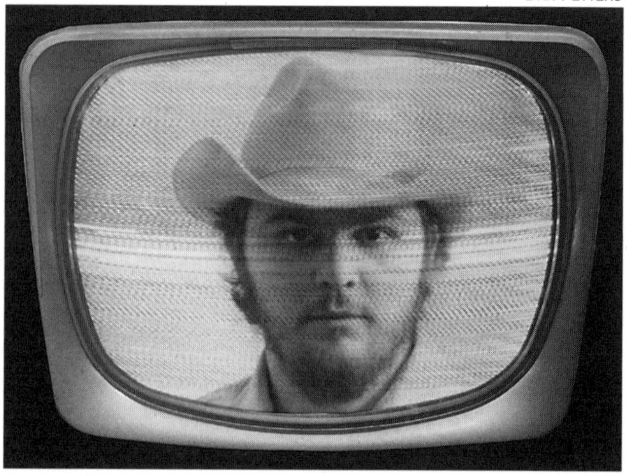

(Above) Two negatives were sandwiched, one of them upside down, to produce a "roots" effect from bare branches. The background remains white because the backgrounds of both the tree and the silhouette-figure negatives were very dense and overlapped when the two negatives were sandwiched for printing.

(Right) This man put himself on TV by exposing the same sheet of enlarging paper separately to two negatives, using two pre-set enlargers. A mask was cut from black paper. With a computer, the portrait would simply be selected, copied, and pasted into the screen.

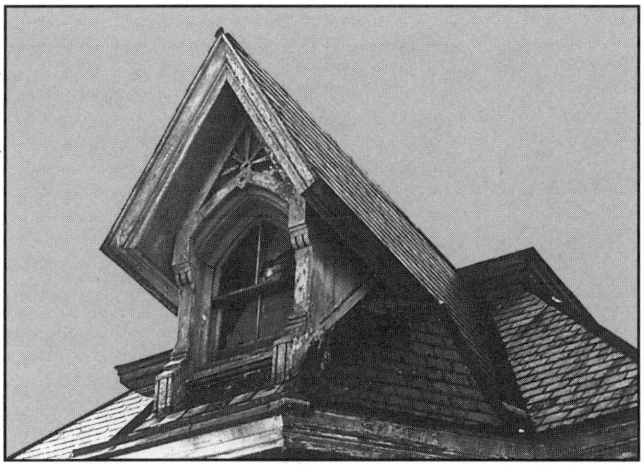

***(1)** This old house gable is interesting because of its form and texture, but the dull gray sky is not very exciting. Dramatic clouds are needed to increase the illusion of depth and heighten the mystery.*

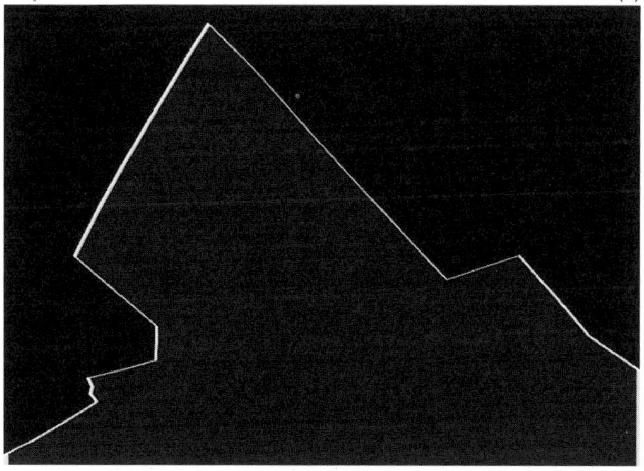

***(2)** Under an enlarger, the projected image is traced with a pencil onto black construction paper, and a two-part mask is cut out carefully with scissors. The gable negative remains in the enlarger, with exposure time, lens opening and contrast filter unchanged.*

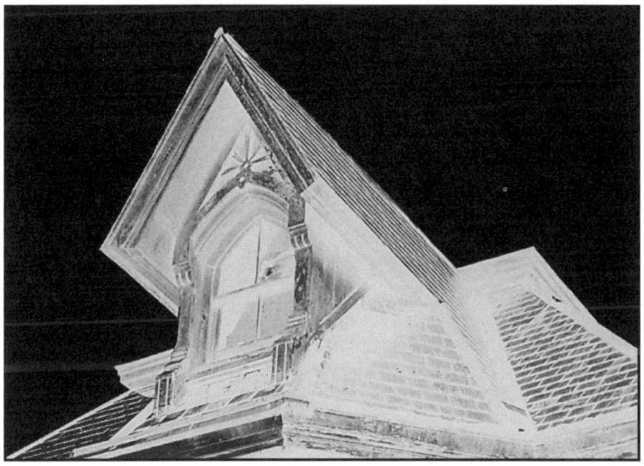

***(3)** The sky mask is taped to the easel around the projected image of the gable.*

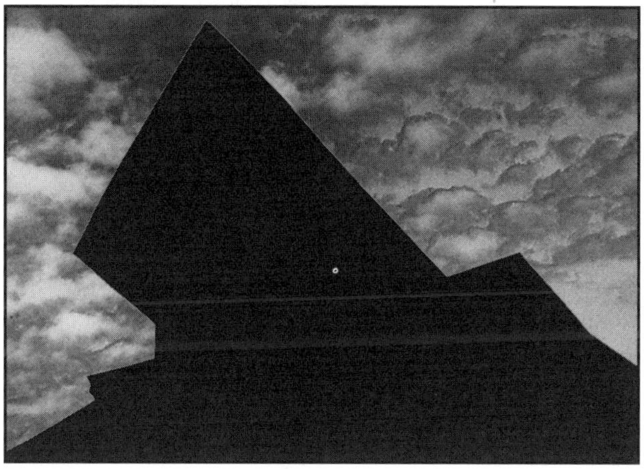

***(4)** The gable mask is taped to another easel and positioned under another enlarger. The sky negative is framed and focused. Exposure and contrast for the sky are determined by test strips.*

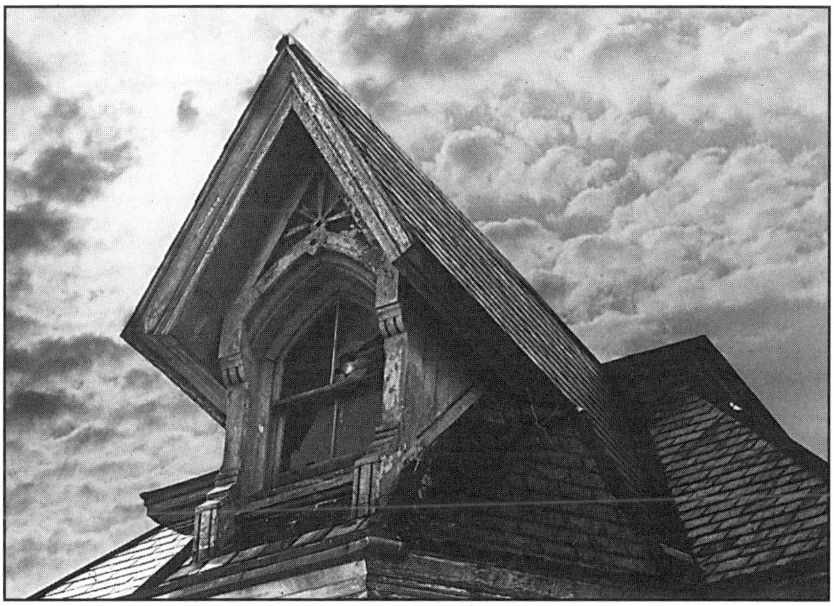

***(5)** A sheet of enlarging paper is first exposed to the gable negative, then the paper is moved to the other easel and exposed for the sky. This picture was easy to blend because there was a distinct separation line between images. When the blend line must be soft, a thin sheet of transparent plastic clamped under the enlarger lens can serve as a shelf to place a mask. Experiment with the height of the mask and with the lens opening (re-adjust the time) until the blend is smooth. In the computer, the process would be: select, feather, copy, and paste.*

Jeff Keyes

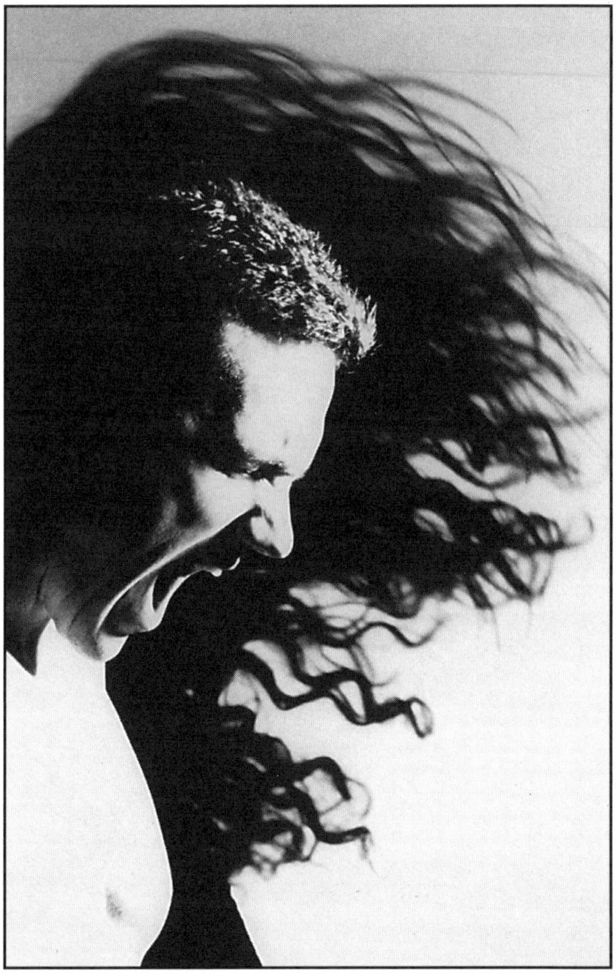

(Right) To produce this negative sandwich, the man was photographed against a black background so that his head would fit inside the silhouette of the larger head.

Brien Kuehn

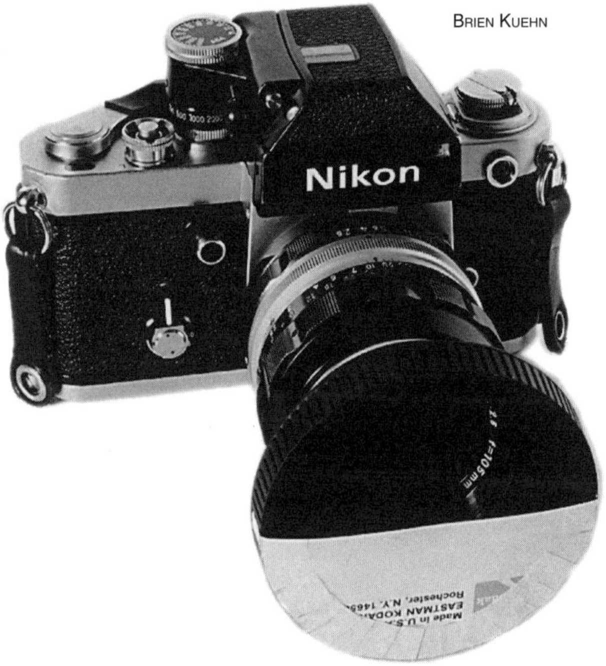

Lowell McCoy

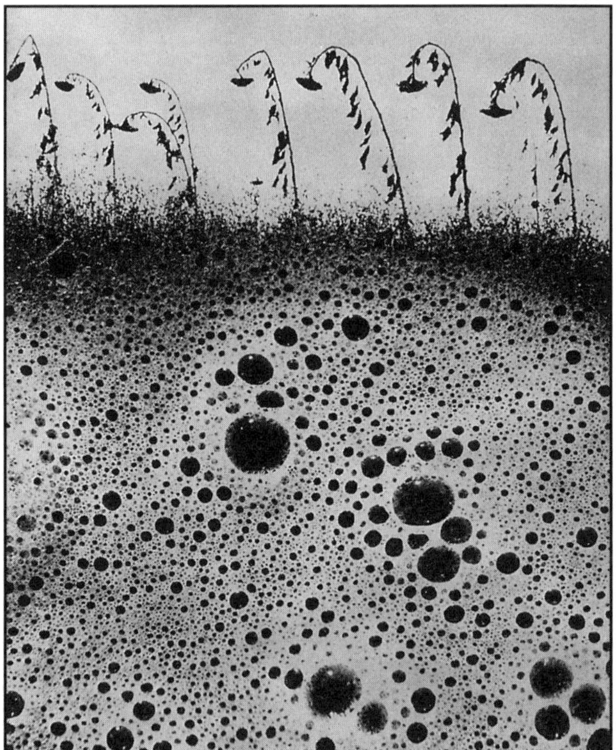

(Right) A soft blend like this can be achieved by shooting two negatives with a graduated filter, or by masking the lens. A piece of opaque paper taped to the lens shade (above) can leave half the negative as clear film that blends smoothly into the image. Rotate the filter or mask 180° when the other half of the image is exposed, and you may have two negatives that will sandwich or blend perfectly. The lens opening will affect the sharpness of the blending edge, so experiment with different f/stops. A perfectly symmetrical image can be created by exposing two identical negatives with the soft-edged mask, flipping one, and blending the images together.

Mike Bombich

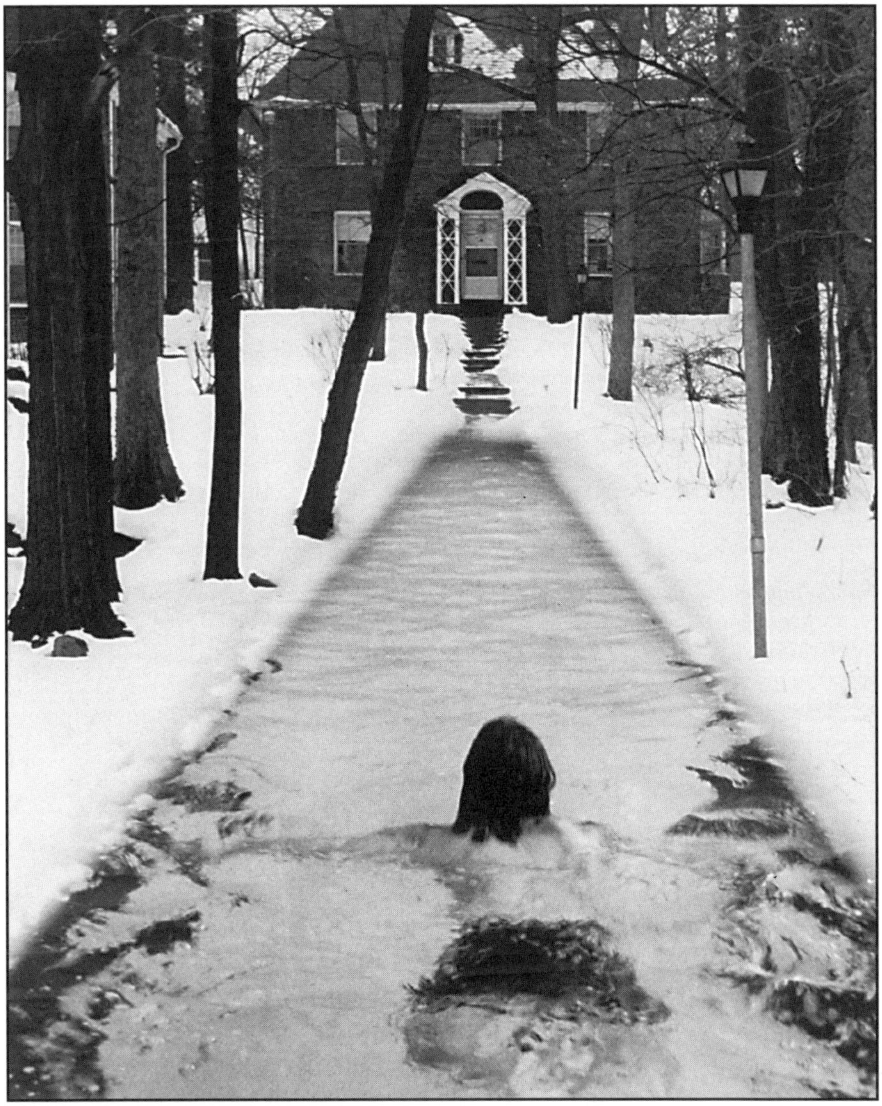

This surreal campus scene was double-printed with paper masks and two enlargers as shown on page 205. The soft blend required that the masks be held far enough above the paper to prevent a sharp line. When you learn the software tools, a computer can save time and make it easier to create images even more complicated than this.

(Below) This negative sandwich was preplanned. The face and sculpture were photographed at the same size against a black background so the negatives would superimpose easily without needing to be masked.

Darren Hathaway (3)

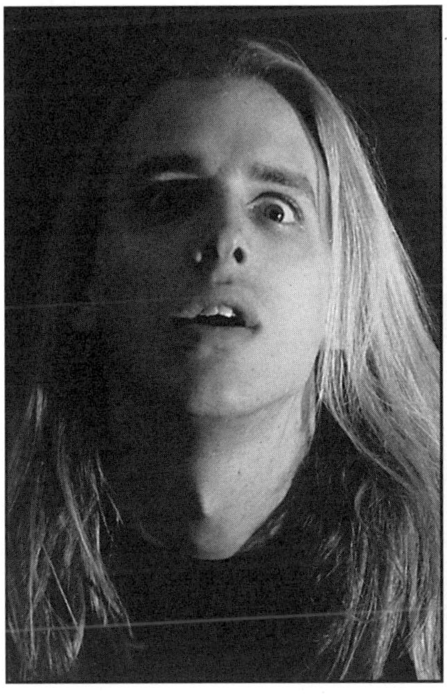

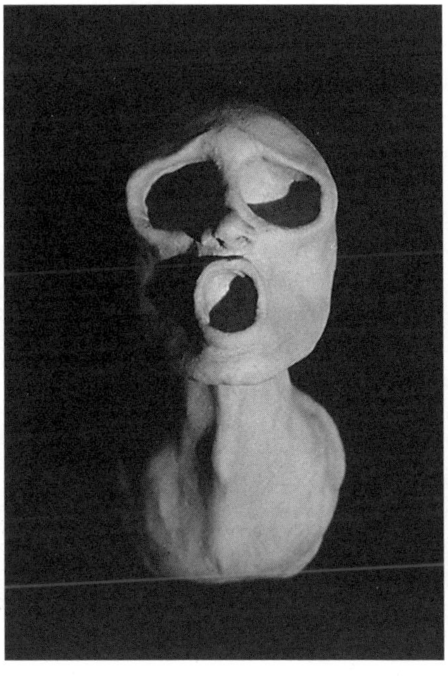

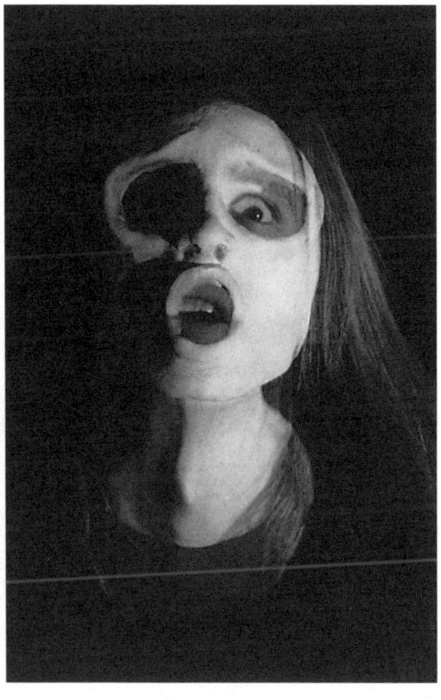

David Harrison (2)

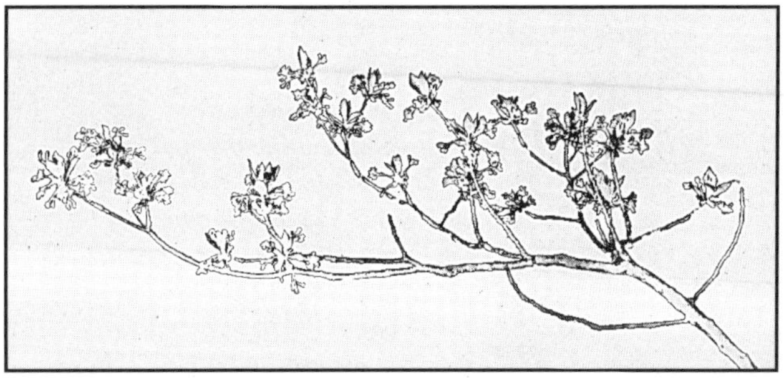

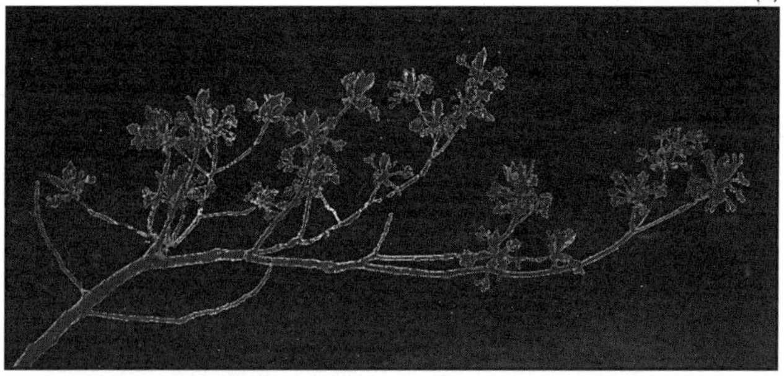

This sassafras branch illustrates an alternative to the solarization process described on page 209. The very dark image on the right was exposed from the original negative with 200 Magenta (#5 filter). After one minute of development, a 100-watt bulb in the darkroom ceiling was turned on and then immediately turned off. The print was allowed to develop, without agitation, for 30 additional seconds before being stopped, fixed and rinsed in water. This dark print then was squeegeed face-to-face with an unexposed sheet of wet enlarging paper, and the sandwich exposed to 200 Magenta (#5 filter) enlarger light, through the back of the paper "negative" for about 10 seconds. The two sheets of paper were then peeled apart and the second sheet was processed normally, resulting in the print on the left.

Lowell McCoy

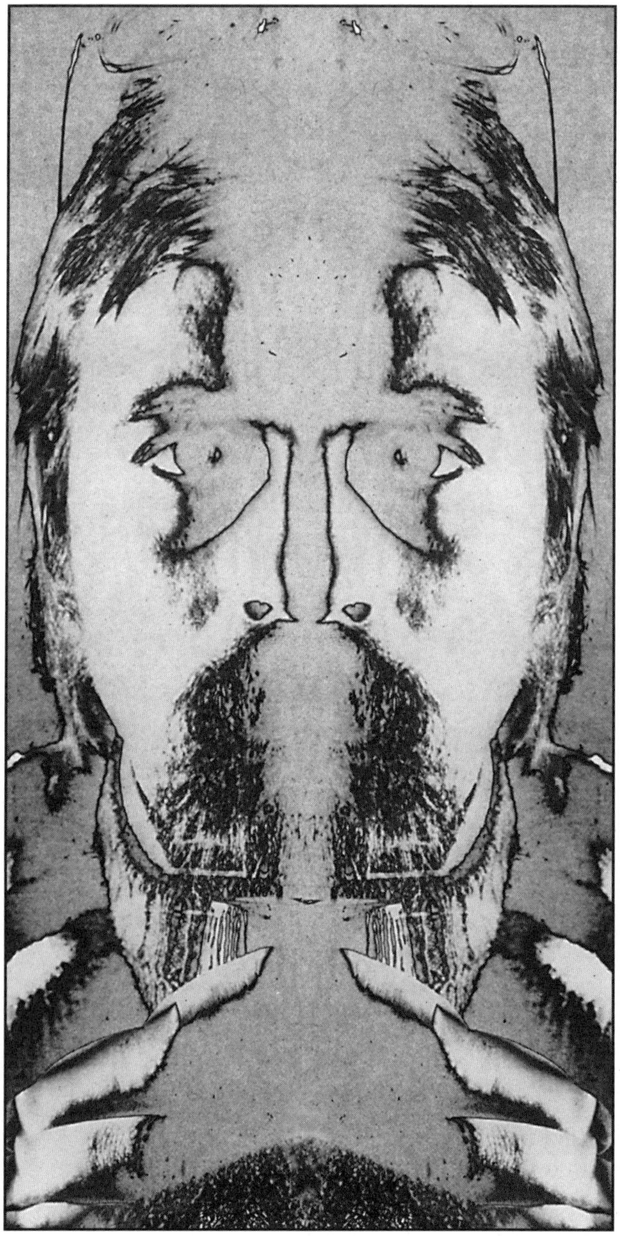

(Right) Double-exposure, paper-negative, and solarization techniques were combined to create this unusual image.

Solarization (The Sabattier Effect)

Intriguing, partly negative-partly-positive images can result from exposing either film or paper to white light after development has been partially completed. The part of the image already developed acts as a mask, while the previously unexposed emulsion is being exposed to light. If the image has strong contrasts between light and dark areas, delicate white or black outlines, called Mackie lines, may be formed.

Don't give up in despair if the first results aren't what you expected. Part of the fun of the Sabattier effect is its unpredictability. You'll find that you can vary the effect if you experiment with the duration of the white-light "flash" exposure and also if the exposure occurs when the print or negative is only partially or almost fully developed. When you try the Sabattier effect on film, of course, you have only one chance — if the effect isn't right, you have to make another negative. For this reason, I suggest you expose several duplicate negatives on sheet film, or space your frames on roll film so you can cut the roll into perhaps three sections for separate development and solarization. Kodalith Ortho film is recommended when you want to make duplicate sheet-film positives or negatives for solarization. These films give the added contrast usually needed, and can be developed by inspection under a safelight either in Kodalith developer or in print developer if you don't need maximum contrast.

Rebecca Allen (6)

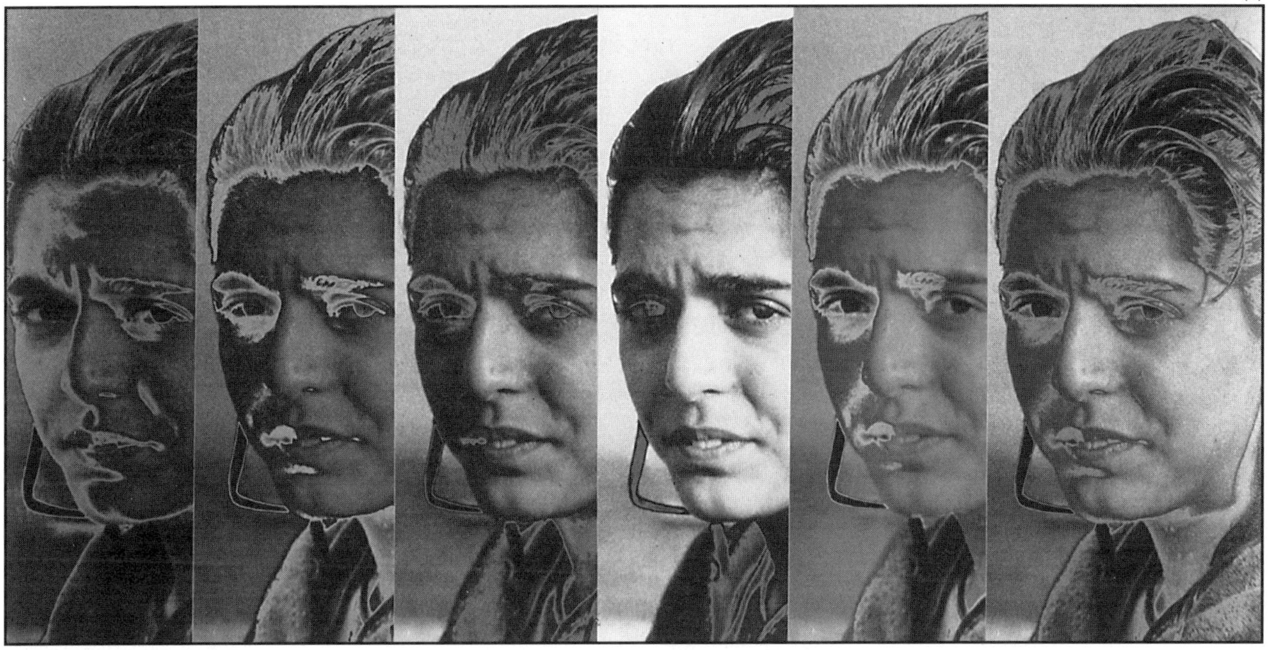

Each of the six prints above was produced on variable-contrast paper using maximum magenta filtration (200M). The process used was the double-exposure method described below. Differences were created by varying the first and second exposure times, but the 1:3 ratio between the exposures remained the same. Dull-looking prints usually result from using paper or filtration that is less than maximum contrast, or from trying to work with a negative that lacks tone separation.

How to "solarize" an 8x10 print by the double-exposure method

1. On the enlarger baseboard, lay a piece of glass or Plexiglass at least a couple of inches larger all around than the size of the paper. Focus a negative with good separation between black and white onto a sheet of plain white paper the same size as your printing paper that is laid on top of the glass.

2. Mark with tape on the baseboard where the corners of the image will be.

3. Set the enlarger lens at f/5.6 and the timer at four seconds for your first trial.

4. If you are using variable-contrast paper, set the enlarger's color head for maximum magenta, or insert a #5 filter. Graded paper should be #5.

5. Soak a sheet of enlarging paper in fresh print developer at normal dilution for about one minute.

6. Remove the focusing paper and move the glass to the sink. Lay the wet photo paper, emulsion side up, on the glass and gently remove all of the developer from the surface. The best method is to make one continuous sweep across the paper with a rubber squeegee blade. You can create a textured background by wiping several times or blotting the surface with a paper towel.

7. Without dripping developer, move the glass back to the enlarging easel and position the glass so that the paper is where you want it.

8. Make the first exposure. Try four seconds at f/5.6 for your first test. After making the exposure, don't move the glass or the paper!

9. Without moving the glass, watch the print develop under the enlarger for about 30 seconds. The image should appear rather light and very contrasty.

10. Make a second exposure three times the length of the first exposure (12 seconds for your first test).

11. Peel the print off the glass and slide it back into the developer tray for at least 30 seconds to deepen the blacks.

12. Stop, fix, wash and dry the print as usual.

13. If the print seems too light and the Mackie lines are not well shown or values not sufficiently reversed, try another print, exposing for five and 15 seconds, or six and 18, and so on.

14. When finished, clean up everything especially well. Be sure to wash the glass!

If you don't like your first "solarized" print, try varying the exposure times, but keep the 1:3 ratio. Dull looking prints usually result from using paper or filtration that is not maximum contrast, or from attempting to work with a negative that lacks adequate separation of light and dark tones.

"One must learn by doing the thing; for though you think you know it, you have no certainty until you try."

— Sophocles, philosopher

Therese Douville

Dropping out the mid-tones can eliminate extraneous detail, focusing attention on the underlying graphic design. Notice in this example the strong interplay between positive and negative space (foreground and background).

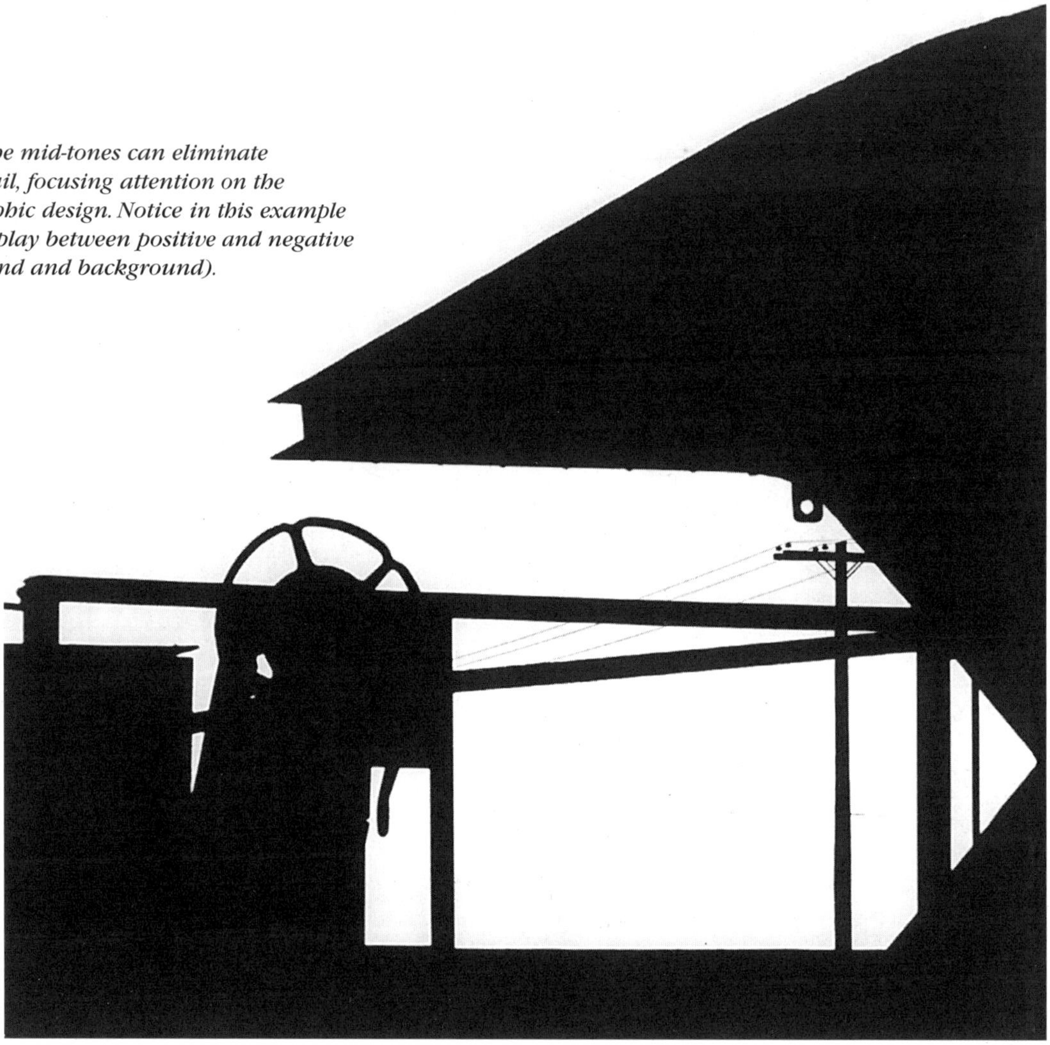

The high-contrast derivations below are typical of effects possible in the darkroom by printing superimposed Kodalith positives and negatives. In the computer, a continuous-tone image can be traced with pen tools or manipulated with Filter > Stylize > Trace Contour or > Find Edges. Further adjustments can be made in Image > Adjust > Curves.

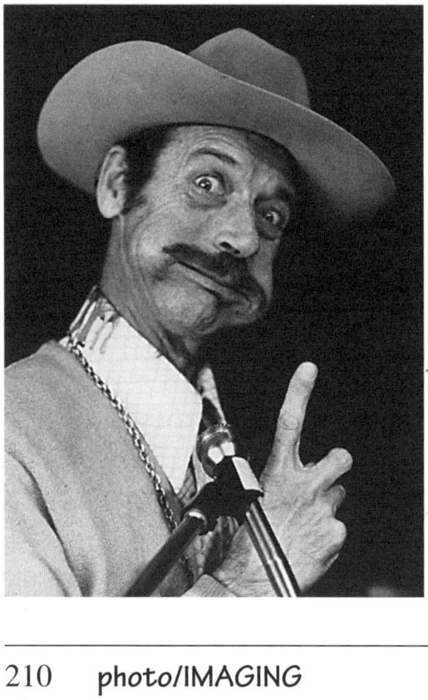

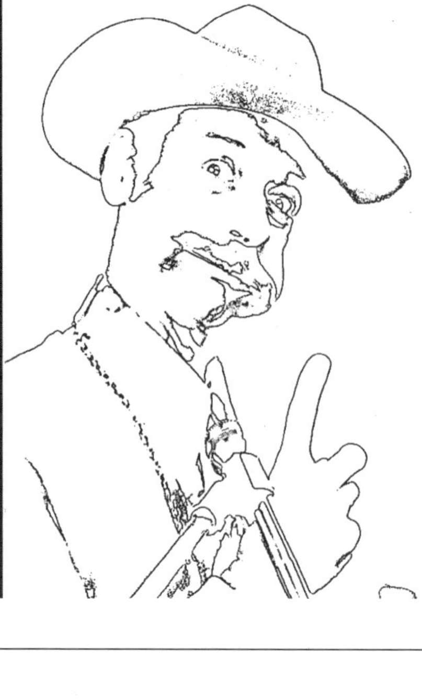

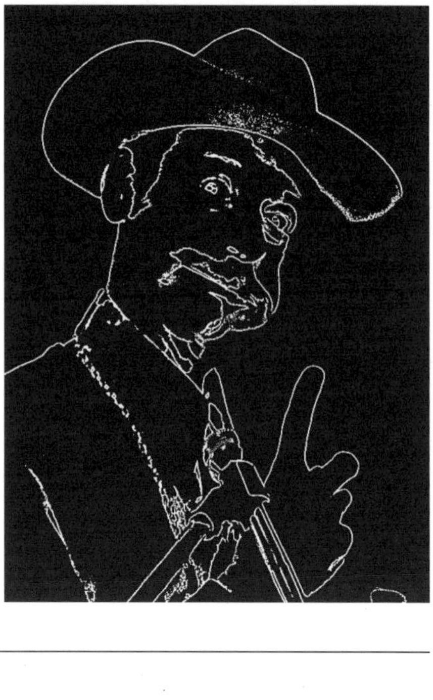

John Stites (3)

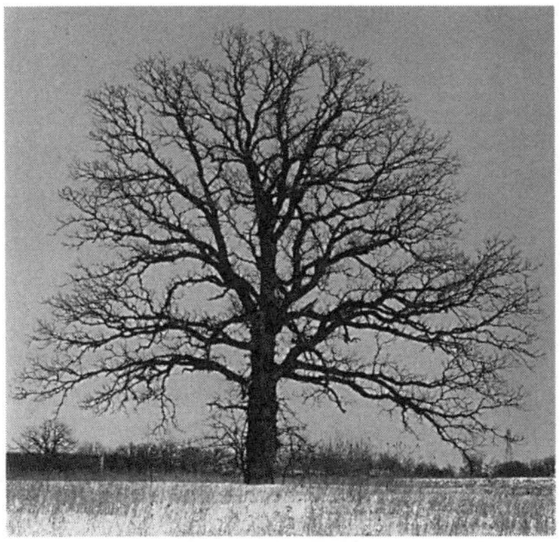

Continuous-tone image

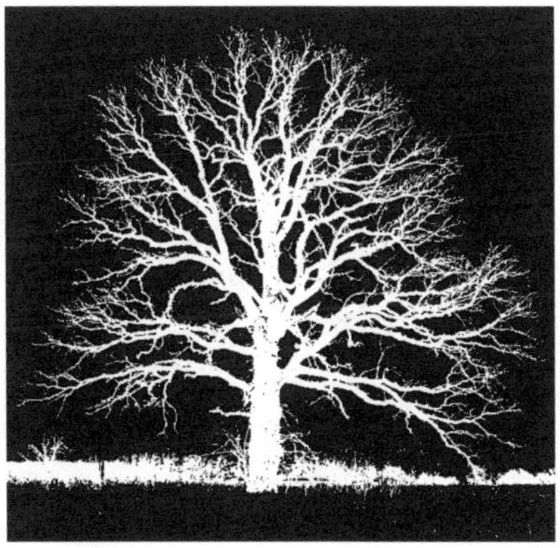

Kodalith negative

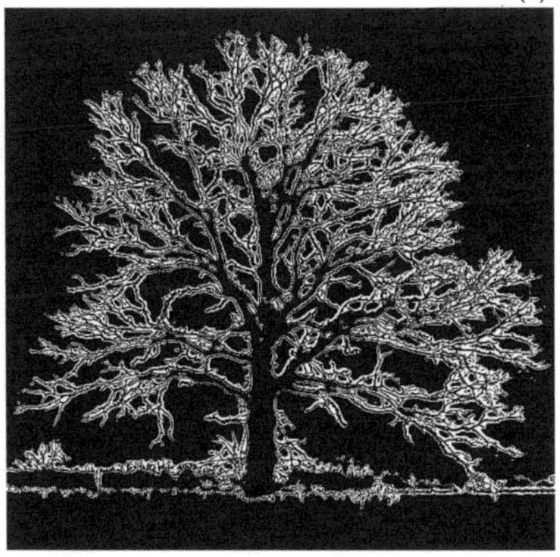

Solarized Kodalith negative

High-Contrast Dropout

Some photographs have more impact if the middle tones are "dropped out"— that is, if the image is reduced from a full scale of tones to pure black and white. Maximum magenta filtration (contrast grade 5) often will yield a satisfactory high-contrast print from a negative that already is a near-silhouette, or that includes prominent light and dark elements. Additional tones can be dropped out by making an intermediate positive or negative by projection on Kodalith Ortho film.

Kodalith is a graphic-arts film that is intended to yield completely clear lines against an opaque black background if exposed properly (ISO 3-6) and developed in Kodalith developer. Kodalith solarizes beautifully, and it can be developed to lower contrast in ordinary print developer. A red (1A) safelight lets you develop by inspection until you see the result you want. Although Kodalith can be exposed in-camera, the exposure is extremely critical, however, and it's much easier to control the results when you convert a normal negative or color slide to high contrast in the darkroom.

A continuous-tone image that has been converted to high-contrast sometimes is referred to as a tone-line or line-conversion. In Adobe Photoshop, the conversion is accomplished in the Image > Adjust > Curves dialog box. Another method is Image > Map > Threshold.

Dropping out only the background requires careful masking and, usually, airbrushing. But in Photoshop all you need to do is select the background with either the lasso or the magic wand tool, then fill it with white, or with whatever value, color or texture you want.

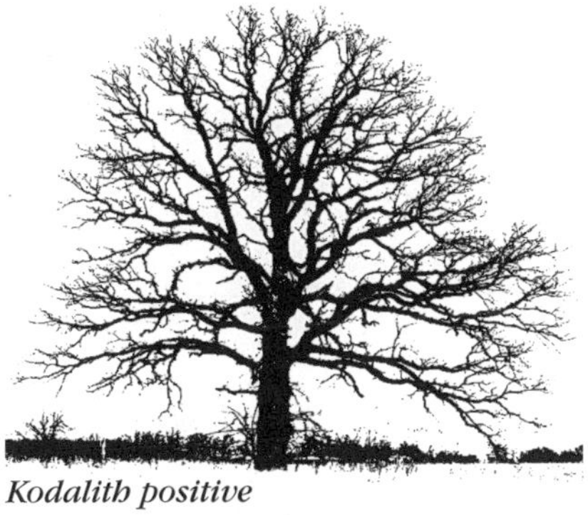

Kodalith positive

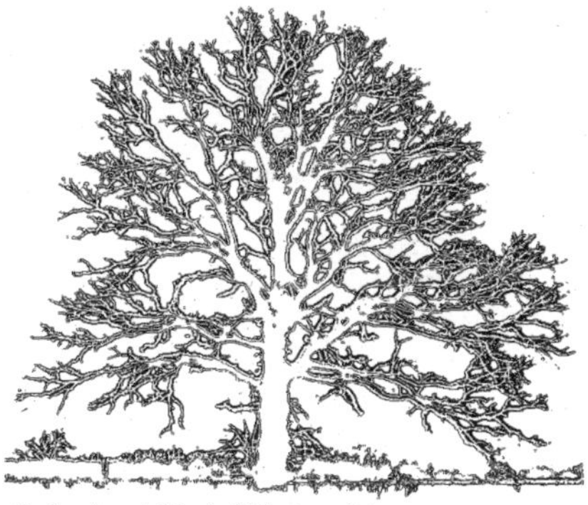

Solarized Kodalith positive

These oak-tree images all were created from Kodalith negatives and positives made from the negative of the image at upper left. The double lines resulted from solarization. Exposure was one second, to the light of a 25-watt bulb four feet above the developing tray.

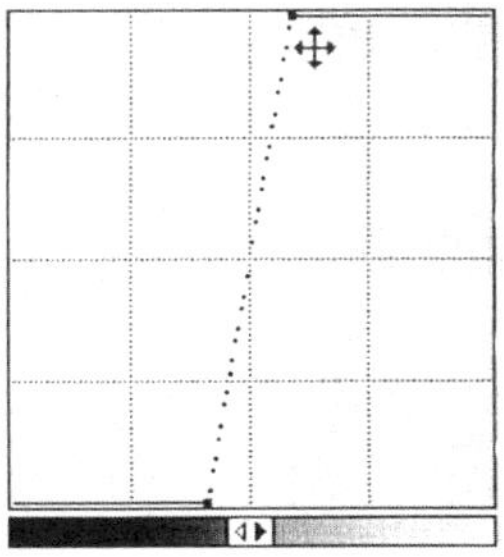

In Adobe Photoshop, Image > Adjust > Curves lets you drop out gray tones by steepening the slope of the line.

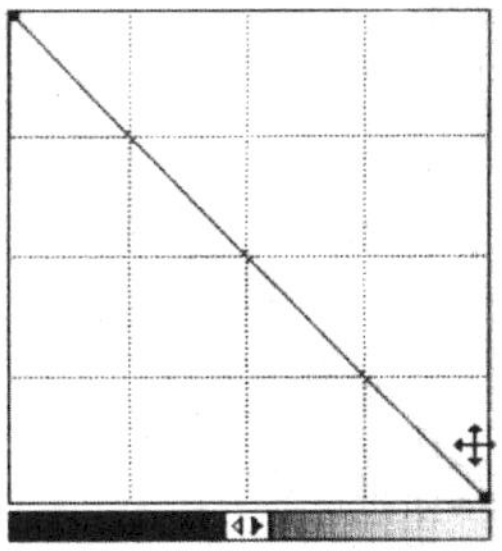

Reversing the high and low points converts the image between positive and negative.

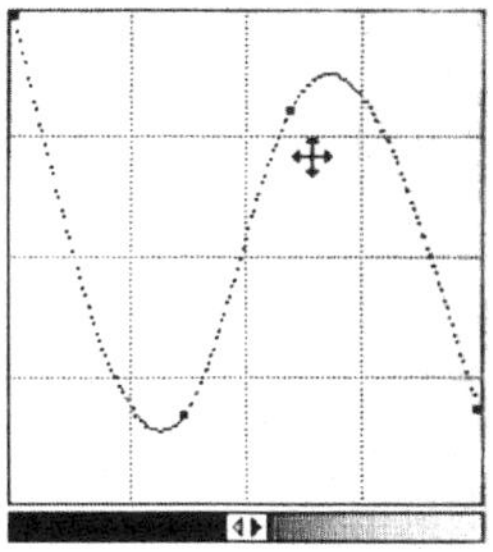

Shaping a sine curve "solarizes" the image.

JOHN STITES (5)

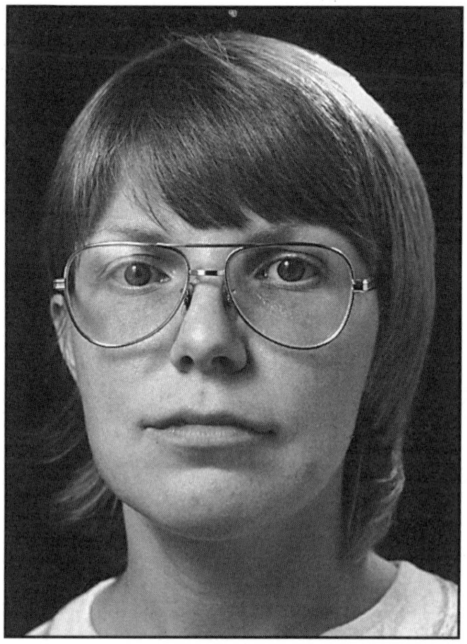

Straight print from original negative (above) and final result of posterization process (right).

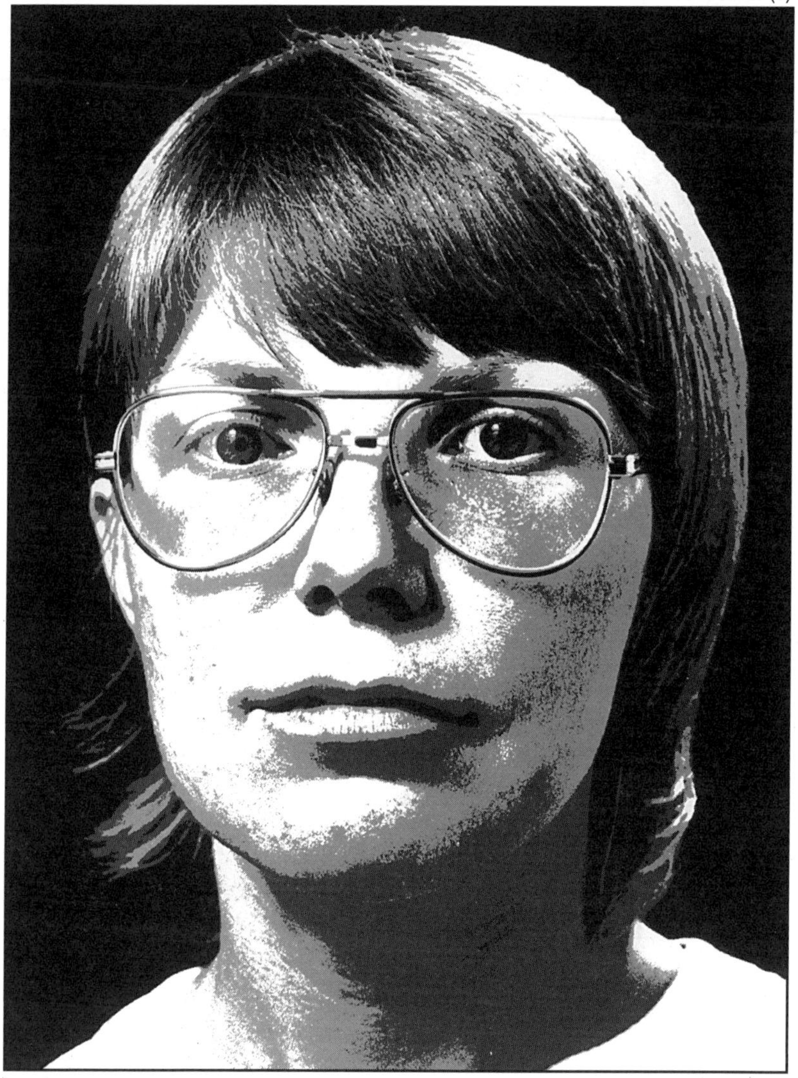

Posterization converts a conventional photograph into something resembling a screen print. Instead of a full range of gray tones, the scale is limited to three or four values. It is easier to keep the Kodaliths in register while printing if separate enlargers can be set up. The sheet of paper is transfered from easel to easel. Determine exposures by test strips.

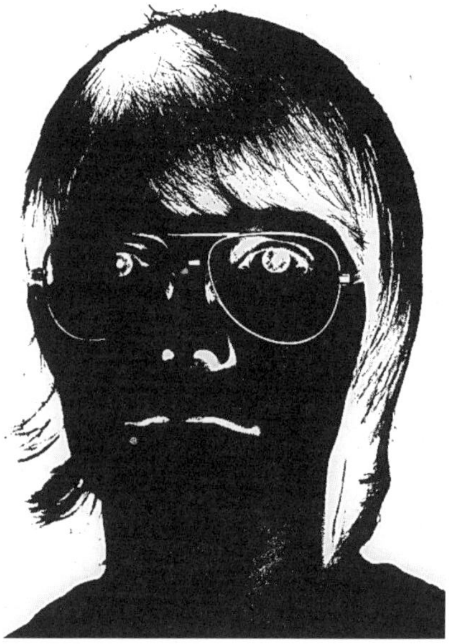

Shadow negative ***35 sec.***

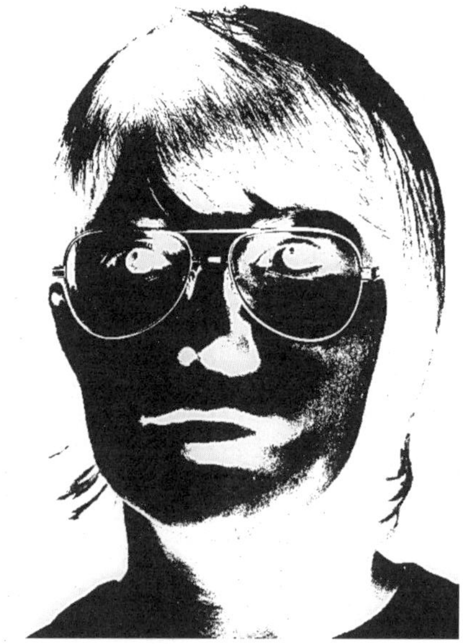

Mid-range negative ***7 sec.***

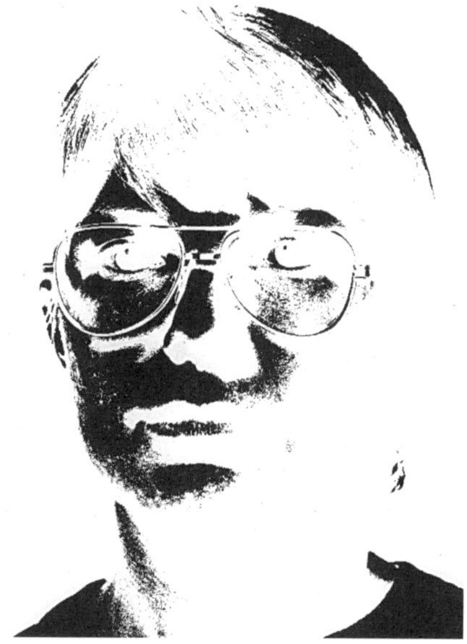

Highlight negative ***4 sec.***

These three Kodalith negatives were made from Kodalith positives made from the original continuous-tone negative at exposures of 10, 5, and 2 1/2 seconds. Each negative was printed separately, in register, on the same sheet of paper, at the times shown above (final result is at top right).

Tone Separation (Posterization)

Another way to produce a strong graphic image from an "ordinary" photograph is to make a posterized print from three or four high-contrast separation negatives on Kodalith film. Start with a fairly contrasty film positive and expose the duplicate negatives either by contact or by projection. You should deliberately underexpose one negative so that only the highlight areas are recorded. The intermediate negative(s) should receive somewhat more exposure, therefore the opaque areas will be larger. Finally, the negative receiving the most exposure will record the largest area of density and cover the deepest shadows that you'll be able to reproduce. The separation negatives must be printed in sequence of the most dense through the least dense, and they must be registered exactly with one another, similar to the way in which screen-process stencils are registered when printing with inks. In Photoshop, the sequence is Image > Map > Posterize. Then vary the number of levels until you are satisfied with the result!

Reticulation

One of my students "discovered" reticulation quite by accident. She came to me in tears, having "ruined" an entire roll of negatives. Luckily, however, the subject matter had been enhanced by the neat pattern embossed onto the film by her "mistake." Deliberate reticulation can yield extremely interesting texture effects, but I suggest that you try the process on a roll of film that contains copy negatives made from prints of simple subjects with large areas of even tone. Here's how to do it:

Immediately after normal development (before fixing), place the film in a rinse of hot stop bath at least 140°F (60°C). Leave the film in the hot stop bath for one minute, and then plunge it immediately into a bath of ice water for another minute before fixing and washing. Dry the film quickly with hot air. Any of several computer software filters can be applied to obtain reticulated texture or mosaic effects.

"A painting can be abstract from the beginning; a photograph, to be nonobjective, must either be selected with infinite care from a corner of nature or tortured out of all recognition in processing."

— Thomas W. Leavitt, photographer

Mary Kay Payne

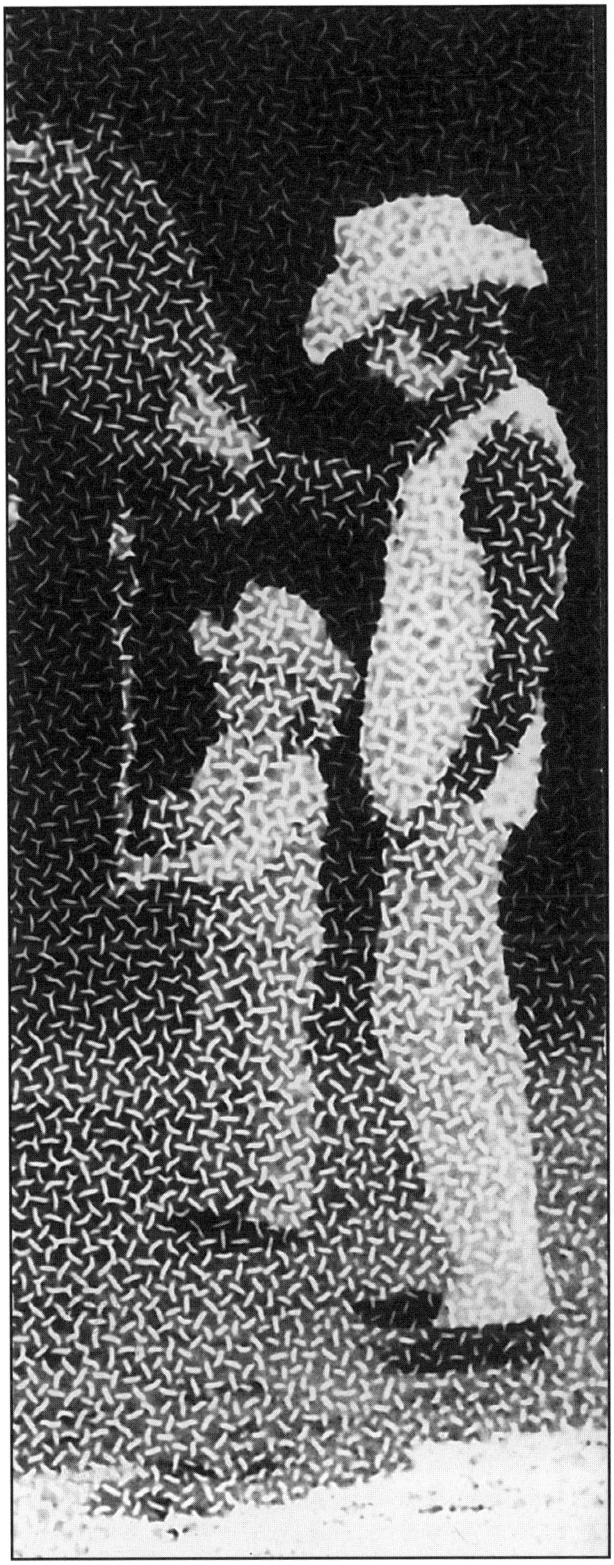

This image was reticulated during processing. The abstracted shapes of positive and negative space have been reinforced by replacing eliminated detail with superimposed texture. The Filters menu of your imaging software offers several exciting possibilities.

Texture Screens

Besides grain or reticulation in the negative, another way to superimpose an overall pattern onto a photograph is to print through a transparent material with the desired design. Texture screens can be purchased, or you can make your own by photographing a textured surface on high-contrast film. Graphic-arts textures and patterns can be reproduced with Kodalith film, and some materials such as lace, netting, or rice paper can be used directly as texture screens. The screen either can be sandwiched with the negative or placed over the enlarging paper when the print is made. Ordinarily, you should use a sheet of glass or a negative proofer to hold the texture screen and the paper in firm contact. A glass negative carrier may be needed in the enlarger, too, but usually stopping down the lens will keep both negative and screen in good focus.

Halftones are texture screens

Continuous-tone photographs must be printed through a kind of texture screen called a halftone screen, if they're to be reproduced in ink on a printed page, such as in a book or magazine. The special screens used for this purpose break up the image into a regular pattern of black dots of various sizes that, if the screen pattern is small enough, give the illusion of various tones of gray. You can get a sort of "pop-art" effect by superimposing a photolithographer's halftone screen on your negative and then enlarging it until the dot pattern becomes visible. A transparent contact screen can be placed tightly against the enlarging paper in a proofer, or sandwiched with the negative and then enlarged, or a duplicate negative can be made on Kodalith Autoscreen Ortho film. Autoscreen film has a built-in 133 lines-per-inch dot pattern that can be enlarged to the degree desired. Such a screened negative can be used to produce a screened positive on regular Kodalith, the first step in making photographic screen process prints.

Computer software includes built-in screen patterns for reproducing continuous-tone images on laser-printers, and with imagesetters that prepare high-contrast film negatives to make offset-printing plates. Digital images consist of pixels that, when enlarged enough become visible as a checkerboard pattern on the monitor. Many effects available in the Filters menu of your software also can superimpose an interesting and functional pattern or texture.

DAN KLAASEN (TOP), BOB LANE (BOTTOM)

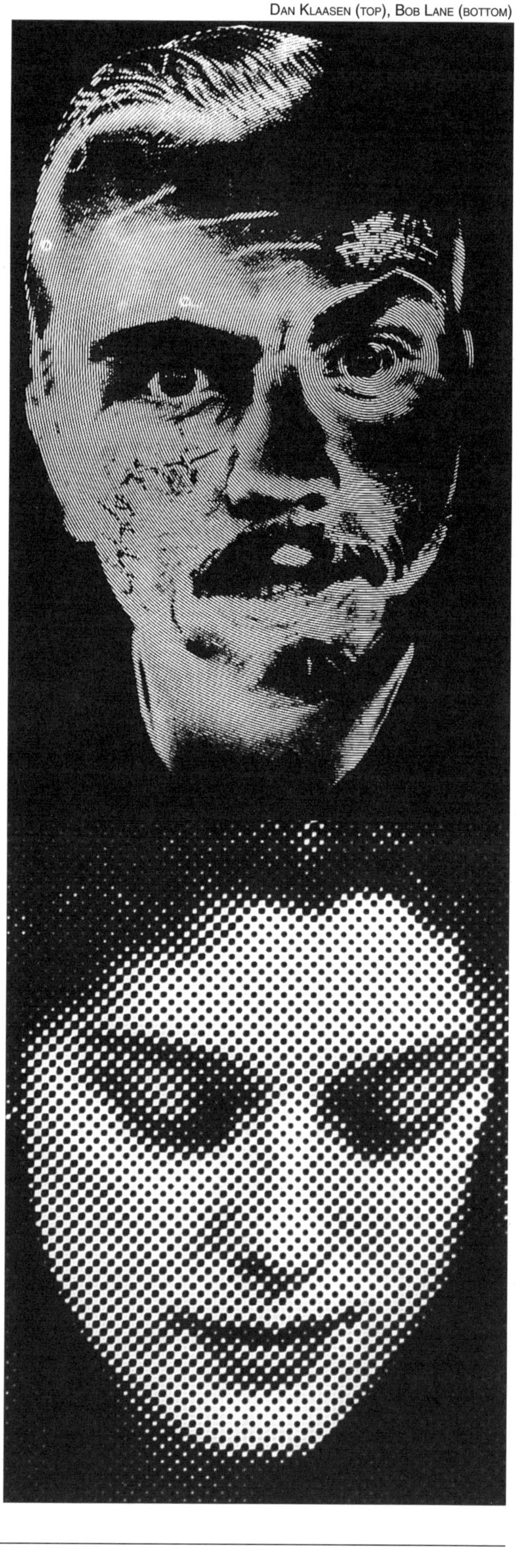

(Right) The concentric-circle pattern at top is from a commercial texture screen placed over the negative. The "Pop Art" effect at bottom is a 133-line printers' halftone screen (enlarged).

DAVID HARRISON (2)

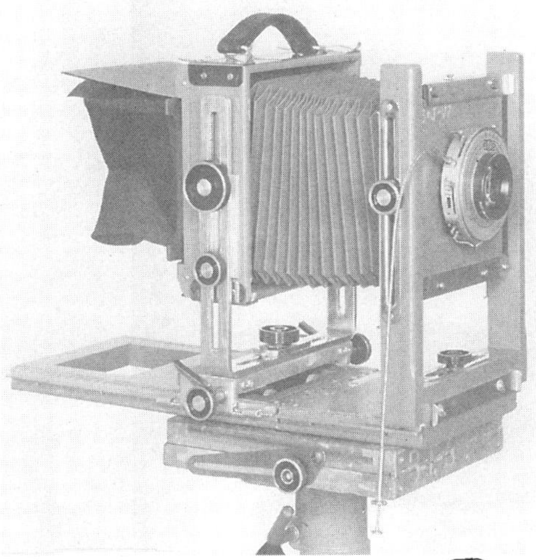

Original print

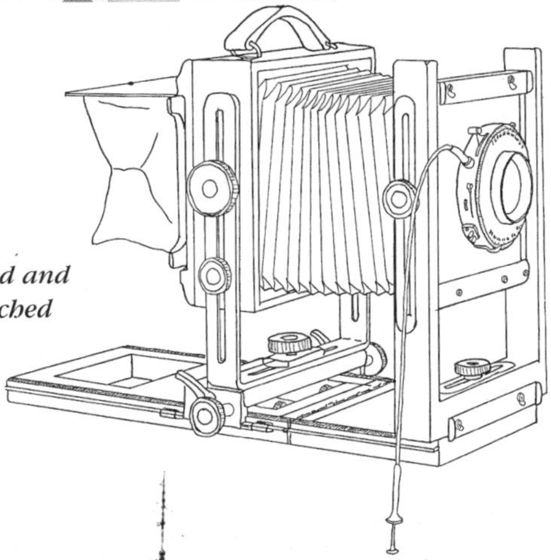

Inked and bleached

Photo-Sketching

Another way to produce a tone-line conversion requires some hand-drawing, and eliminates the photographic image altogether. Many technical illustrators and commercial artists use similar methods regularly, only instead of ink, they will trace selected parts of the image with a graphics stylus using software such as Adobe Illustrator or Macromedia FreeHand. Another manual method simply is to place a negative or a slide into the enlarger and trace the outline of the projected image with pencil or marker the size you want it onto paper on the baseboard. Shading effects and other details can be added later.

The photo-sketching process involves making an enlargement and bleaching away the photographic image after tracing over it. Here's how it's done:

1. Make an enlargement of the desired size. This print should be light and flat — just dark enough to see the wanted detail (low contrast, underexposure, and underdevelopment will produce this kind of print).

2. Process and air dry the print. A long wash is not required.

3. Ink-in the detail you want, using a draftsman's technical pen and waterproof black India ink. (If the print is made on matte surfaced paper, the drawing can be done with a pencil). Detail you don't want should not be traced. Shading can be done by stippling. Allow the ink to dry thoroughly.

4. Bleach away the silver image in a solution of Farmer's Reducer. You can buy packets of prepared powder or mix up a longer lasting two-solution bleach consisting of 25 grams potassium ferricyanide crystals dissolved in 1 liter of water in the first tray and regular fixer in the second. Alternate the print between the two trays until the bleaching is complete.

5. Agitate the print in ordinary fixer until the yellowish stain is gone. Wash, then air dry.

J. SAVAGE

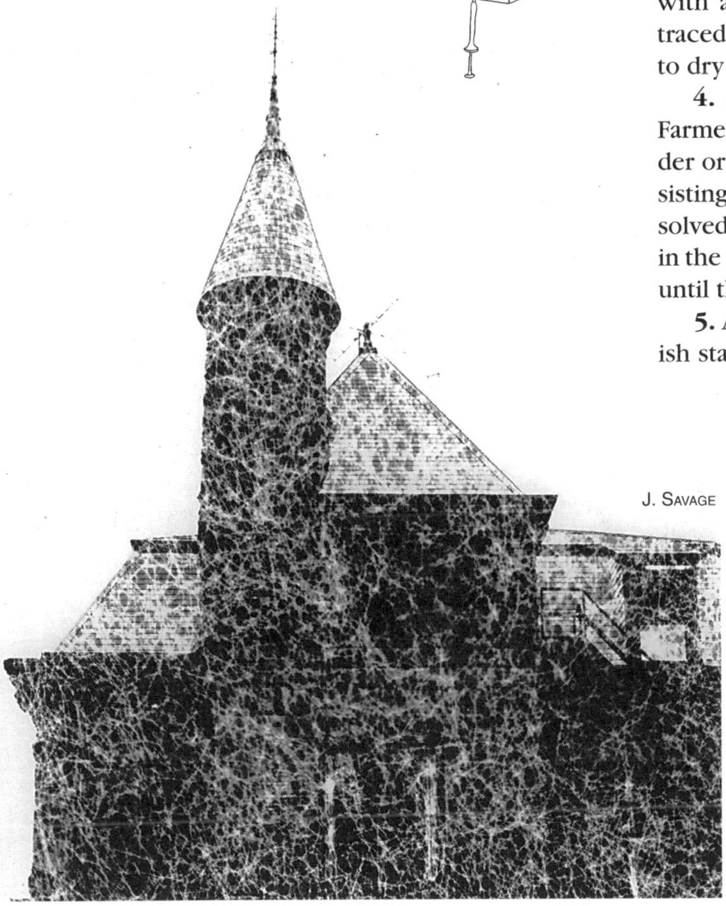

(Left) Texture effects can be simulated by placing a transparent pattern in contact with either the negative or the paper, and printing through the combination. This cobweb effect was obtained by sandwiching a sheet of lens-cleaning tissue with the negative.

Keith Alan Morris

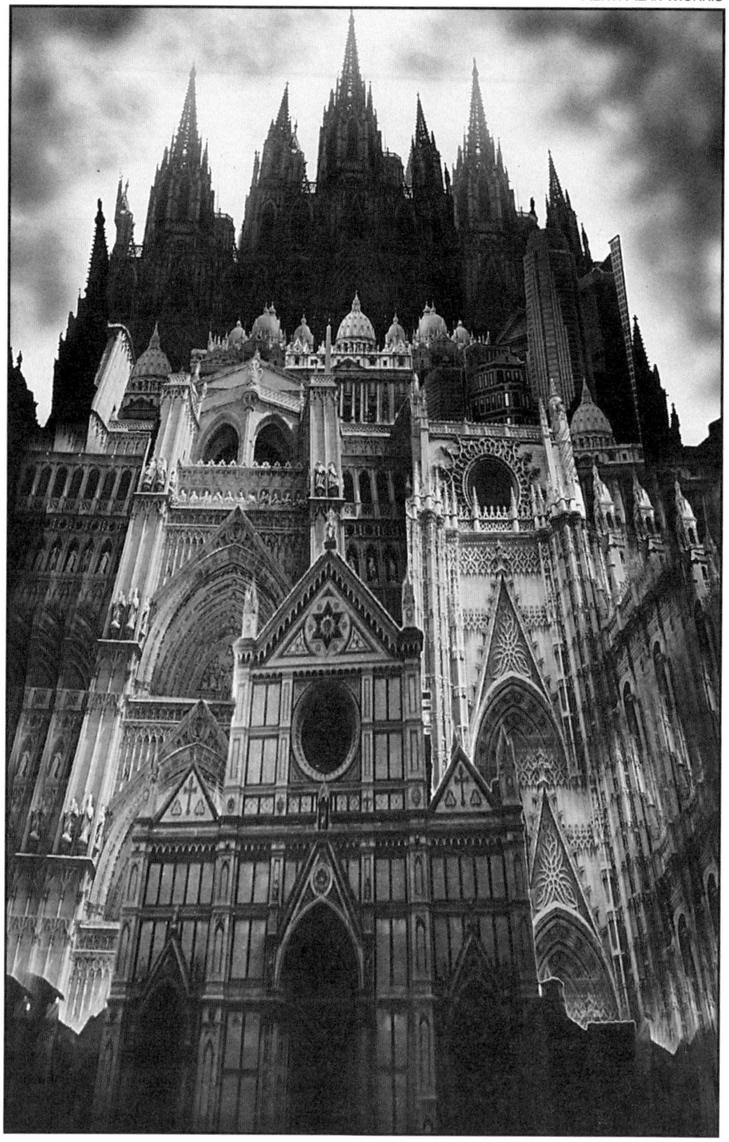

"Any technology sufficiently advanced, is indistinguishable from magic."

— Arthur C. Clarke, author

Digital Imaging

Craftsmanship never goes out of style. There is a certain dignity and satisfaction from doing something well with one's own hands that is never enjoyed by masters of machines. There will always be painters using brushes, furniture makers working with hand tools, and imagemakers processing fine prints. But the faster tools will not go away — digital cameras and printers, computer graphics software — these are the imaging tools of the 21st century. Optical/chemical photography is not dead, but it has already been replaced in the graphic arts by electronic publishing. As old concepts expand to include technologies undreamed of only a few years ago, there is reason to preserve the past even as we embrace the new.

Everything described in this book can be done digitally. But every image has to be *created* before it can be modified.

Processes such as tone- and line-separations and posterization can be done electronically: First you scan a conventional image; then with digital "darkroom" software in a personal computer, you crop, eliminate, combine, retouch, modify, distort, reverse, adjust contrast, insert text, add color, change color — anything imaginable. You see what you're doing on a video monitor, and experiment until you get just the effect you want. Then print it out with a couple of keystrokes or transfer it directly into a page-layout program.

There is good reason to study traditional techniques, because they are the basis of modern methods. So what should each of us be doing about digital technology? Learning it. Don't be left behind!

"If you want to go somewhere, you gotta get on the bus."

— Tom Bodett, author

Imaging as a Profession 11

Q. "As an ethical professional, I'm compopelled to do things as well as I know how, but I'm frustrated by the corporate liaison who insists that I do everything her way. I have a difficult choice to make. Do I compromise my artistic judgment to please her, or do I stand firm and risk offending her? So far I haven't made a decision and I'm a nervous wreck."

— N.H., Los Angeles, CA

A. "We all must choose, but we cannot choose not to choose. Fortunately for you and your client, the choice is very simple. You were hired to produce exactly what the client wants and it must be done exactly as the client, through its corporate liaison, wants it done. That nonsense about artistic integrity must come to a screeching halt. Use your ability to produce great work to your client's specifications, not to second-guess the world."

— Adapted from a column by Leo Lukowsky, *Industrial Photography* magazine's Answer Man

Creativity vs. Craft

If you truly love photography, there is a down side to turning pro. On the other hand, the idea of being paid to do that which you most enjoy is enormously appealing. In spite of having squarely faced this dilemma throughout more than forty years of earning a living from imagemaking, I haven't fully resolved the conflict between creative freedom and financial security. But then few photographers have resolved it, and in other media even fewer artists have. Nevertheless, students constantly are asking for advice on how to make a living by making pictures.

"It's not easy being in love with photography and trying to make a living from it."

— Ralph Gibson, imagemaker

The source of the dilemma remains the ancient paradox of creativity vs. craft. Craft sells regularly and predictably; creativity sells sporadically. The best compromise is to approach your craft creatively (but not too creatively, because in the changing marketplace the value of "art" lies less with the artist than with the beholder).

"Whoever pays the piper calls the tune" is not just a folk saying. It is equally true that whoever pays the photographer sets the rules for the assignment. If eventually you become one of the celebrities in our industry, some clients may give you blanket assignments and be delighted with whatever images result. You then will be able to measure your success by the size of your bank balance. To reach this exalted status, however, requires much more than mere talent. It requires an extraordinary knack for both salesmanship and showmanship.

Another paradox is of more recent vintage — the incredibly rapid advances in technology from the traditional optical/chemical to the electronic. Foreward-looking visual communicators today refer to their field as "imaging." Think of that when you're deciding whether to sign up for video and computer courses. Remember it when writing your resume.

"Work consists of the things you have to do that you dislike doing — everything else is either play or a labor of love."

— Roger E. Greeley, humanitarian

To earn a living as a professional imagemaker, I see three choices: (1) seek a salaried staff position, (2) be a self-employed free-lancer, or (3) set yourself up in business as an entrepreneur. A fourth option may lie on the periphery of the profession — in one of the allied fields related to imaging or in a profession or trade that makes use either of photographs themselves or visual communications technology. Obviously, the prerequisites for success vary greatly, depending on which road you decide to take.

The Corporate Imaging Technician

Industrial firms, government agencies, publishers and large imaging studios need to hire competent technicians. These big organizations already know the kinds of work they want done, and they will buy the services of skilled craftspeople who will come to work in the morning, do the assigned job promptly and acceptably, and then go home in the evening (although overtime is all too frequent in our industry).

What about creativity? Yes, definitely — and you might eventually get praises — and raises — if you can make images of an automobile, a milling machine, a stylish dress, a bottle of beer, or a group of people so that the composition is subtly balanced and the lighting adds sparkle to the subject. But too often the corporate imagemaker is expected only to carry out the ideas of the "Creative People" in the advertising or public-relations department. I remember how disillusioned I felt when I realized that the benevolent Fortune 500 corporation I was working for in the midwest actually sent out to a New York advertising agency all the jobs that called for imagination and originality. The agency then farmed out the work to a commercial studio and added the agency's sizable commission to the cost. It doesn't often occur to an executive that creative visual work of all kinds could be produced by people within the organization.

Working for someone else

Perhaps the greatest challenge facing you as an employee will not be how to solve technical and creative problems, but how to sell yourself, to raise your own stature — subtly — in the eyes of your employers. Being active in professional organizations will provide some opportunities for recognition through seminars, awards, publications, and continuing education

Corporate imaging offers important trade-offs that help to compensate for the frustrations. When you sell your services to a large employer, you do so in exchange for relief from such problems as hustling to find clients, filling out endless small-business paperwork, and considering anxiety-provoking issues like hospitalization and disability insurance for yourself and for your dependents. Most big corporations also will relieve you from part of the responsibility of putting aside money for your eventual retirement. That biweekly paycheck and employee-benefit-package can look pretty good when you consider the alternatives.

"Luck is when preparation meets opportunity."

— Harvey Frye, educator

How to get and hold a job

Landing a staff job doesn't always require a college degree, but getting — and holding — a job with advancement potential does demand mastery of the fundamental skills of imaging, video/electronics, and computer graphics. Graduates of recognized technical schools, colleges and universities with highly regarded degree programs generally have an advantage not only because of the degree, but because they can show a portfolio of good work. The most successful job seekers will have mastered certain prerequisites such as how to write up an application and resume. Some employers are wary, however, of hiring advanced-degree holders to fill technical positions. A master's degree could even be a handicap. Employers often are unwilling to pay the higher

David H. Curl (2)

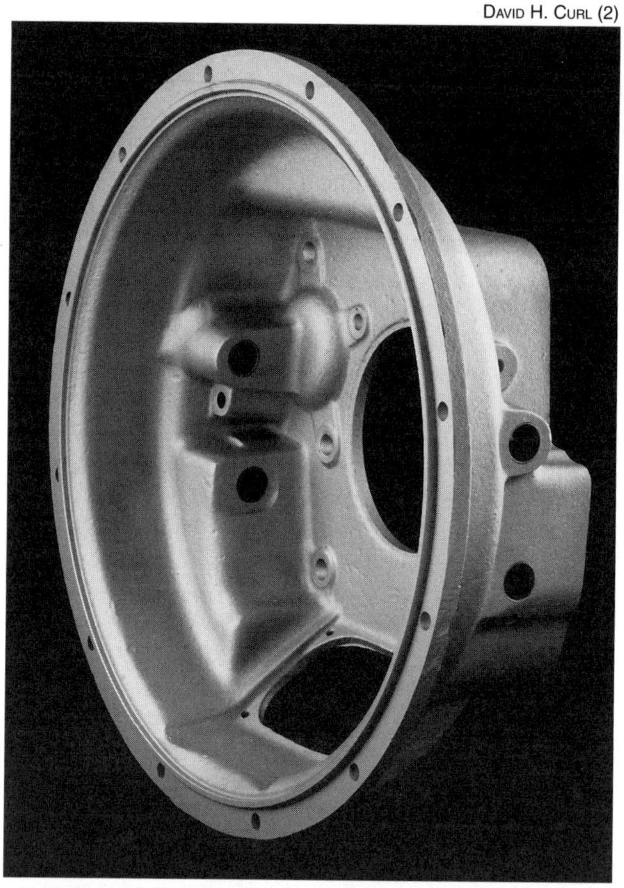

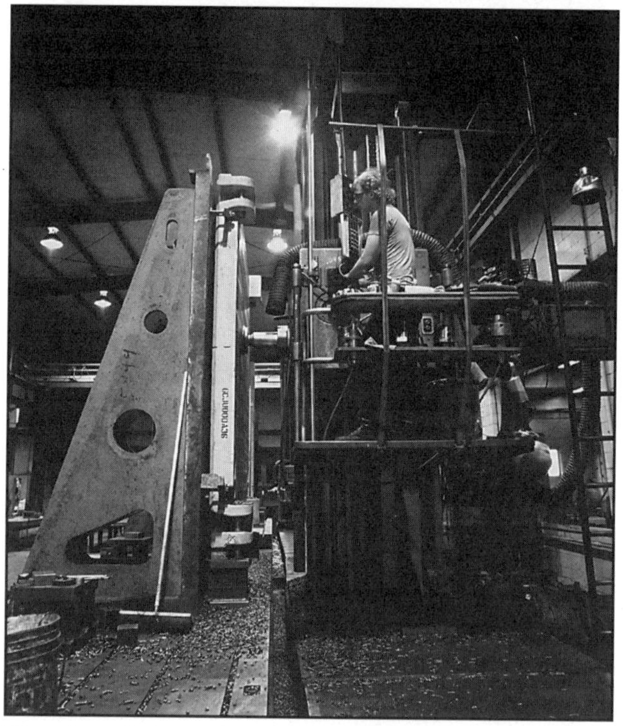

These two photographs are typical of daily assignments facing an industrial photographer. The challenge is to record all the detail wanted by the client, but produce images that are both excellent and interesting. The more you know about the plant and products, the better you will be able to anticipate the client's requirements..

PREETI HANS

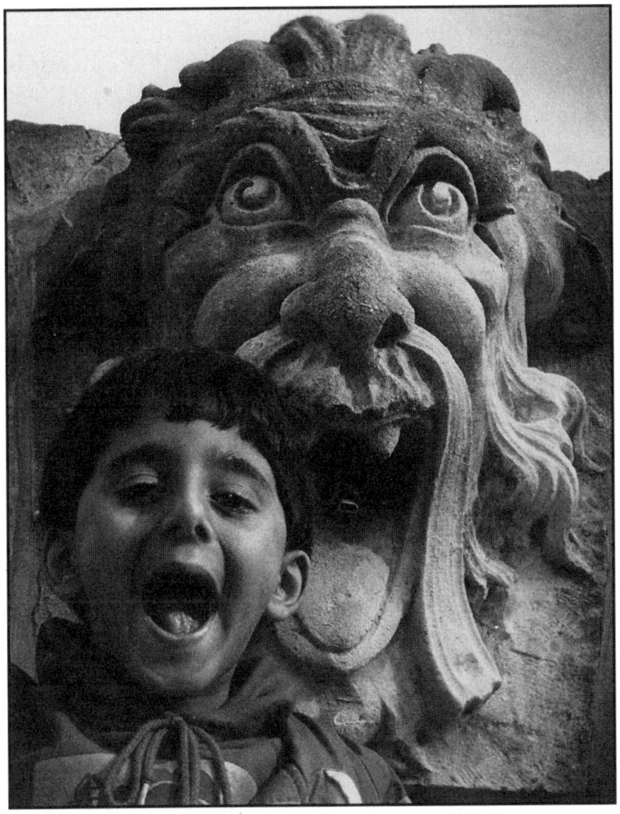

Publications buy pictures that catch the reader's eye. When you travel, always look for fresh picture ideas.

salary that an MFA (Master of Fine Arts) would seem to demand, and a few "School of Hard Knocks" managers have been known to feel intimidated by an applicant's degree. But such academic jealousy seems to be largely a problem of the past. In many industries and organizations today, the winning combination would seem to include photo, video, graphic arts and computer experience plus a bachelor's degree in business administration or communication. "Here's a young person," goes the logic, "who can do a good technical job for us now, yet who may be potential management material."

Corporate imaging can be a very interesting way to make a living. Skilled visual communicators contribute significantly to the productivity of the organizations that employ them, but few of my colleagues who are "staff" photographers take pictures for a hobby. Most of them prefer to play golf or go sailing.

"When [things] go on in my town, I've got to photograph them. There aren't any big events here. The rest of the world really doesn't care ... But they're very important ... to everybody who lives here."

— Brian Lanker, photojournalist

Consider the Media

Daily and weekly newspapers occasionally hire an ambitious young photographer, but usually the jobs go to the best graduates of journalism schools, and the openings are not created by expansion, but by retirement. Often, staff positions are filled by interns learning the business before moving on. Many newspaper photographers at first find their jobs fulfilling because they feel involved in community happenings. But it soon becomes quite a challenge to keep coming up with fresh, new ways of handling routine assignments and still meet daily deadlines.

Most magazines that once retained large staffs of adventuresome and imaginative photojournalists now either are defunct, or they buy much of their photography from free-lancers who work independently through stock-photo agencies or cooperatives, or on contract to the publisher.

"Photo departments ... need photographers who think. Don't just be a shooter. Anticipate the editor's needs and become part of the team."

— Scott McKiernan, photojournalist

Television has changed forever the public's media habits. The evening news and various talk shows and specials have replaced, for most people, the daily newspaper and weekly magazines as major sources of current information and entertainment. As advertisers have shifted much of their marketing budgets from print to television, so also have changed the opportunities for photojournalists.

The demise and reformatting of many magazines, however has created a larger demand for specialized publications, on-line services, and multimedia. There seems to be at least one magazine or newsletter for every hobby, interest, and profession in the world, and most of them use photographs!

Production of documentaries and news for television is almost a totally different field from still photography. Although the "good eye" and human sensitivity of the photojournalist are needed by the filmmaker/videographer, the still photographer making the switch to professional motion pictures or video finds it very difficult to finance and complete a production independently. Because of the enormous costs involved and the tremendous amount of work, producers nearly always need to draw a salary or to have a commercial sponsor. One person rarely completes a production alone. A crew consisting of director, camera operator, and sound, lighting, and editing technicians usually is required. Videography and special-effects production certainly is where much of the action is, but to get to the top one needs specialized training, intensive experience, and often labor-union affiliation.

"Talent doesn't come in a box. It comes from within us. It can't be bought, but it can be rented."

— Joe Farace, imagemaker

Sell Yourself Enthusiastically!

There's psychology in applying for a job in imaging, as in any career field. First you have to do a good job of building yourself up in writing. Your resume, or vita, must provide prospective employers with the basic facts about your personal status and educational background, plus a chronological listing of your previous work experience. Make this section of your vita brief, but emphasize those aspects of previous jobs and internships that relate to the position you seek.

For example, if you're applying for work as an imaging technician with an aerospace firm, and you shot video and stills of aircraft activities and tests while you were a photographer in the Navy, say so. Remember that your resume represents you to someone you haven't met. Try to impress the human-resources office with your effectiveness and your neatness, if not with the depth of your experience.

Don't send your resume and portfolio off unannounced. Make a phone call. Find out who does the interviewing and reviewing, and how to spell and pronounce their name. Make an appointment and be there early.

Show only your best work

If you're not sure what you do best, take stock of your abilities. Spread out your work and look at it as if you were hiring yourself. What would stand out? What might someone else think of you from looking quickly at your images?

Your portfolio shows what you have actually accomplished, and suggests the kind of work you can be expected to do without additional training. Your pictures and sample videos or CD-ROMs should look good and so should you. Just as you wouldn't show up for an employment interview wearing tattered jeans and unkempt hair, you shouldn't expect an employer to be impressed by dog-eared, unmounted, unspotted prints or sloppily-edited video clips, no matter how good the content and technique. Don't try to show more than 20 to 30 prints unless you're asked for more, and select examples that show you have an idea of the kind of work the company does.

You wouldn't include abstractions, nudes, or fashion illustrations in a portfolio intended to show how well you might handle a nuts-and-bolts industrial job. Your prospective employer will probably be looking for well-corrected view camera illustrations, competently lighted product photos, and perhaps an example of your best "company magazine" style picture-story feature. A prospective employer wants to hire someone who can produce the kinds of images he or she expects.

"If I can see the world through my employer's eyes, then I can sell my employer what my employer buys!"

— Ed Forman, motivator

What employers look for

The expectations of advertising and publishing executives can be a bit different. An art director or picture editor will want to see your most imaginative work to determine whether to take the risk of offering you a challenging assignment. The editor or art director sees competent professional work every day. What he or she probably is looking for is not only someone who can cover routine assignments in an unusual way, but someone who can be counted on to deliver promptly and according to client specifications. Competition is so keen that ad executives seldom are willing to take a chance that might cost them a client. Editors have pages to fill and deadlines to meet. Your portfolio and your personality have to inspire confidence that you can do what you say.

"Say what you mean. Mean what you say. Do what you say you're going to do."

—Morris Massey, author and motivator

The pictures in your portfolio should show exactly what you can do. Begin with several attention-getting images, include a sequence showing your skill and versatility in the prospective employer's field of interest, then close with a few more blockbusters. And don't talk too much. Let the pictures speak for themselves. A good mount size is 16x20; 11x14 is adequate and more portable, but the mounts should all be the same size. Put your prints in a neat nylon or vinyl case, and you will have an attractive presentation that will help you to sell yourself.

The Free-Lance Business

If you begin to feel restless in the security of corporate employment, you may soon begin to look longingly at the glamorous life of the free-lancer who, it would seem, flits care-free from client to client like a butterfly, sampling the nectar from only the choicest opportunities. Don't you believe it! Free-lancing can be a killing grind. It is a fierce competition in which only the very fittest survive.

Nevertheless, the flame of free-lancing attracts, like moths, thousands of aspiring young imagemakers every year. As a successful independent entrepreneur, you can be an artist, but you also have to be a canny businessperson. Many among the self-employed choose to work through a "rep" (agent), who can relieve them from making sales calls and free them from some routine business matters in exchange for a percentage of each assignment contract.

> ***"The phone does not always ring. Sometimes you have to pick it up and dial."***
>
> — Scott McKiernan, photojournalist

Free-lancing, demanding and uncertain, is, nevertheless, a good way to make some pocket money, especially if you're good at a specialty and if you research your specialized market carefully. Nearly every young professional starts out by free-lancing or moonlighting (moonlighting is part-time free-lancing). There will be more on how to break into the business a little later on in this chapter. Meanwhile, let's look at some other career possibilities.

DAVID HARRISON

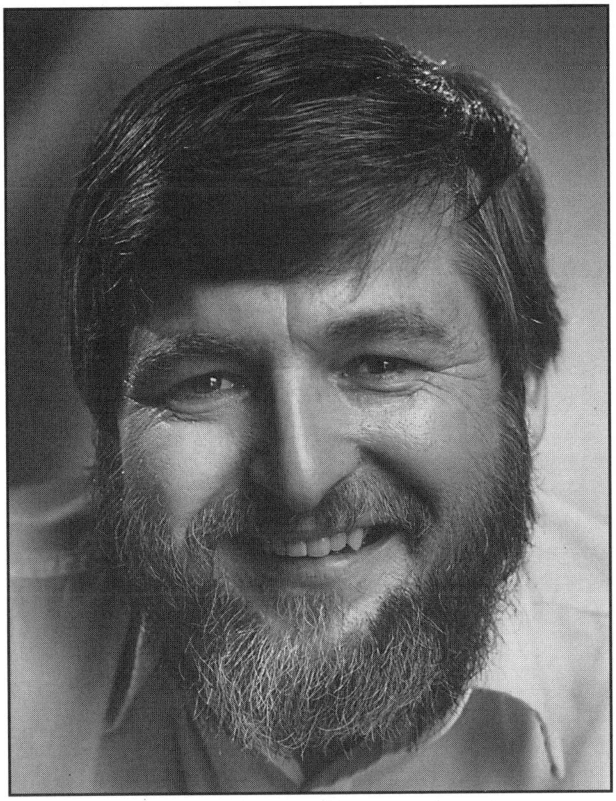

Portraiture is perennially profitable. Many free-lancers and owners of small studios have begun their business by doing model and performer portfolios for friends and acquaintances, then for others as the word spreads.

Opening Your Own Studio

There's always money to be made from portrait, wedding, and general commercial photography. Although the field is somewhat crowded, there seems to be room in almost every community for a quality studio. Usually there is an untapped market for photographic sales that cries for an enterprising person to develop the market through advertising and through offering excellent service at a fair price.

But to be successful at establishing and operating a studio, you must have an insatiable drive for achievement. You and your spouse or partner should expect to work 16-hour days routinely, at least for the first few years, to earn a modest financial return. You have to enjoy running the business fully as much as you enjoy photography, perhaps more. And because human contact is such an important aspect of operating a studio, it's essential to develop a friendly, open, somewhat-extroverted personality. Contacts made through service clubs and community activities will pay off for you at the cash register just as they do for other business people. Like the florist, the real-estate broker and the neighborhood merchant, the successful photo-studio owner becomes an integral part of the community as he or she goes about earning a living.

> ***"One of the best things about being on my own is that when a client calls, I know that they're calling for ME. I try to treat each client like they're the only one I have. The bottom line is ... if they're happy, they'll come back."***
>
> — Bill First, imagemaker

Brian Kuehn

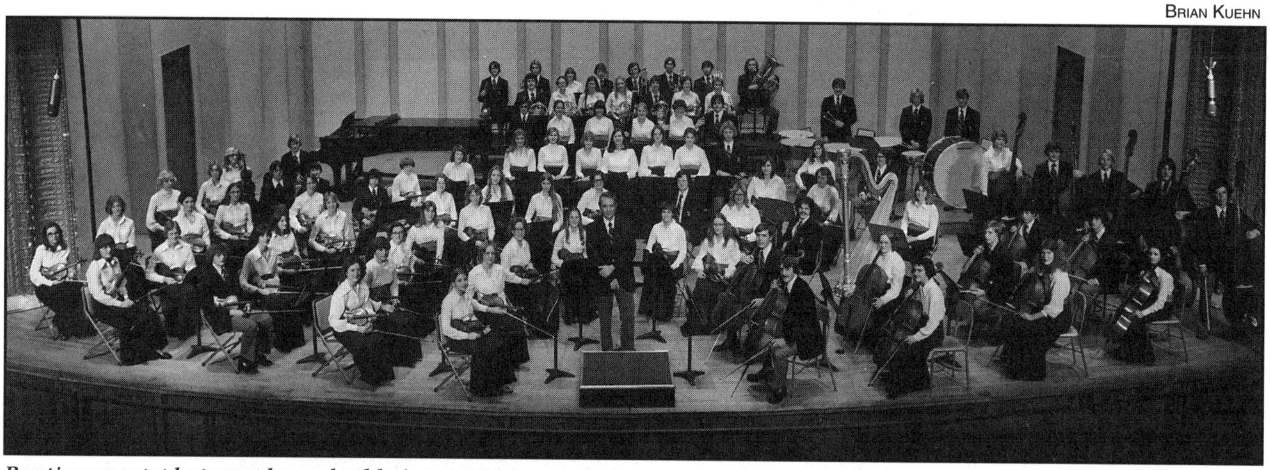

Routine group photographs and athletic team pictures can be a recurring source of income for anyone with a medium- or large-format camera, some patience, and lots of hustle. Every face must be recognizable so everyone (or their parents) will want to buy a print. A wide-angle lens will be very useful, along with one or two large flash units with umbrellas or softboxes to supplement uneven existing light. Most group pictures are shot in color, so look for a professional lab that offers wholesale prices on quantity "packages" that may include folders and captions as well as processing and printing.

Other Career Opportunities

Many careers related to photography are open to men and women who are interested in the field in some capacity other than as a practicing photographer. Video is an attractive field of its own, and the graphic arts encompass the wide world of printing, color separation, and computer imaging. Scientific and biomedical imaging include photomicrography, photogrammetry, spectroscopy, metallography, ballistics, and many other finely differentiated specialties in industry, medicine, and law enforcement.

Photographic and electronic manufacturing and retailing is a multibillion-dollar industry in itself, employing scientists, engineers, managers, technicians, and salespeople, most of whom require considerable knowledge of at least certain aspects of photography. Although much of the imaging equipment sold in the United States and Canada is imported, the distributors of equipment and manufacturers and distributors of materials and supplies employ experienced imaging professionals as trainers, technical representatives and salespeople.

Photofinishing, film and video postproduction, and computer imaging provide further career options for those who have technical skills and management ability. Custom laboratories and service bureaus provide high-quality processing, printing, film transfers, editing, duplicating and digital output services for professionals, while huge automated finishing plants and shopping-mall mini-labs process and print the billions of images exposed each year by weekend snapshooters.

"Photography is a magic thing. Nothing will ever be as much fun!"

— Jacques Henri Lartigue, photographer

How important is a degree?

A two-year degree from a community college or technical institute often is the entry-level qualification for many jobs in the career fields mentioned here, a position as a corporate imagemaker or assistant, or a studio intern/assistant. A bachelor's degree is required by some employers, and is often a prerequisite for advancement to a management role or, if photography is combined with science or engineering, to a specialized technical or supervisory position.

"After graduating from college, I got my education from two years working in a studio."

— David Kamm, imagemaker

The MFA (Master of Fine Arts) is considered by most colleges and universities as a terminal degree for the individual who will teach in a department of art, with the Ph.D. being a credential for the academic administrator, researcher, or art historian. Teachers in secondary and elementary schools require a bachelor's degree plus a teaching certificate. For permanent certification, most states require teachers to obtain further credits in education, leading eventually to a master's degree.

Full-time jobs teaching photography are rare, there being many more aspiring teachers than vacant positions. Part-time teaching, however, is pleasant and relaxing for some working imagemakers. More of these opportunities are becoming available as public interest increases in photography, video and computers as leisure-time activities. For teaching evening or weekend courses, community colleges, art centers, and adult-education programs often employ experienced professionals who have demonstrated a talent for teaching.

How to be Successful

Back, as promised, to free-lancing. Many successful professionals started out this way, often gaining experience and making pocket-money-plus while in high school or college. Here's advice on how to begin:

1. Specialize!

Become especially skillful at photographing certain types of subject matter that you particularly enjoy and know something about. One of my former students is a model-airplane buff. He submits regular how-to-do-it, illustrated articles to the model-building magazines. He has become so well known in this field that editors send him assignments and he has sold a number of color covers. What is your hobby: horses, dogs or cats, wildlife, hunting and fishing, gardening, weaving, woodworking, custom cars, antique aircraft, spelunking, stamp collecting? You name it and there are special-interest publications, organizations, and individuals who will buy photographs. One student was taking pictures of some of the animals she admired at a pet show. Some of the animals' owners asked her for prints, and now she has become official photographer for all of the cat and dog shows in her corner of the state — and she has all the reprint business she can handle. Another former student follows his passion to all of the regional motor speedways and auto shows. He makes good money every summer and sells stock photos during the off-season. But the work wouldn't continue coming along if these individuals weren't interested enough to keep going after it. That brings us to point No. 2:

2. Hustle!

Another student enjoys architectural photography. While still in high school, he made a series of construction-progress pictures of a public building being erected in his home town. Putting 8x10s of those photos neatly into a ring binder, this enterprising young photographer went to see the contractor on the job. The contractor, very impressed, bought the book on the spot and commissioned the young man to shoot aerial and ground progress pictures at regular intervals of every subsequent project that his firm did in the area. Out of this contact grew sales to subcontractors, architects, and eventually to occupants of the buildings. But the photographer had to go around and see these people. They would never have come to him.

If you study collections of photographs made in the 1880s and 1890s, you notice that itinerant photographers traveled about photographing families posing out in front of their houses or farm buildings. Many of these century-old photos not only are historically valuable, they are technically excellent — sharply focused, well-exposed, and obviously made with a properly adjusted view camera. But George Eastman's snapshot Kodak killed much of this business, convincing most people that they could take their own snapshots of their homes and families. Today, people still will buy photographs of themselves and their property, but not many will call up a photographer and order the work done. Maybe you don't feel comfortable doing door-to-door sales, but one neighbor does tell another, and if you can wangle a few jobs — even for free or for barter — other people will want photographs made if you're on the scene at the right time.

"Kidnapping" is another way to collect some cash (this term means *photographing* children, of course, not abducting them). In formal child and baby photography, you're competing with the established studios as well as with cut-rate operators in shopping malls. It doesn't occur to many parents, however, to have their kids photographed around the home, or in a park, in natural childhood settings and typical activities. Even if the parents own an expensive camera, chances are their snapshots of the kids are stilted, too far away, and poorly exposed.

Another of my former students, who now makes his living as an elementary school teacher, started out making informal portraits of children in his classes. When parents saw the photos, they loved them. Parents told other parents. Now this teacher enjoys a lucrative home-portrait business that keeps him busy every summer and on weekends, and adds a nice supplement to his salary.

Other photo and video opportunities in every community include kids' athletic teams, adult sports leagues and Corporate Olympics groups, scouts, 4-H, and local pageants and festivals of all kinds.

The quality free-lancer cuts into the established professional's business less than you might think. The smart free-lancer will use imagination and hustle to profit from a largely untapped segment of the community's portrait and commercial photo market. Most studio operators depend on the formal and conventional walk-in and telephone trade, so they often make little effort to go out to the public. The part of the potential market that the pros overlook is your fair share! Then, after you gain enough experience, you, too, can become part of the established profession — if you choose.

3. Be professional!

You become a professional as soon as you begin earning a substantial amount of your income from photography. If you're operating as a professional, the public will expect you to be dependable, to produce quality work, and to price your work fairly but competitively. If photography is a moonlighting business for you, don't try to take work away from established studios, but try to mine the gold that they may be overlooking. Above all, don't compete unfairly on price. If your work is as good as the studio operator's, your price should be competitive.

The established pro has overhead expenses that you don't have, so you can charge less — right? Wrong! People often tend to value services according to what they have to pay. Not only does a competitive price make your work appear to be of higher quality, but if your costs actually are less than the studio's, you can pocket the profit without feeling that you're taking away someone else's livelihood by undercutting prices.

Weddings are a case in point. With so many automated color processing and printing laboratories providing a complete wedding package at a very low price, the wedding photographer can spend all of his or her time shooting and selling, and no time at all in the darkroom. If you're a moonlighter and you like to shoot weddings, leave the upscale formal bridal portraits to those who do the job best, and concentrate on providing a uniquely personal type of candid wedding coverage tailored to the desires (and the financial resources) of the bride and groom and their parents. Through friends and satisfied customers, you could create a demand for quality custom wedding coverage, including video, that might actually increase business for some of the better studios, as well as give you a comfortable extra income.

Since weddings are such important occasions, you must deliver like a professional or your budding business will evaporate overnight! Plan ahead with the bridal couple, be punctual and polite, be neat and courteous, yet boldly competent. And whatever happens, don't goof up technically. These rules apply not only to weddings, but to any assignment. The professional is competent and confident, dresses like a business person, and behaves maturely.

4. Keep trying!

If you're determined to make money at photography, you've got to keep at it until you develop a reputation for quality and dependability. It may take a while before the work begins to come to you, instead of having to go out after it all the time. This is especially true of sales to publications, as all free-lance writers know. In publications work, you'll be dealing with many of the same markets as writers, and you can expect to collect rejection slips and polite letters at about the same rate. There are excellent references available at your public or college library that can give you up-to-date information about publishers and agencies, and how they should be approached.

If you sell directly to publications or to commercial and advertising markets, it's very important to price your work fairly and competitively because you're competing directly against full-time professionals. Find out what the going rates are. Many publications specify the rates they will pay. This and other valuable information can be found in some of the guides, such as *Writer's Market* and *Photographer's Market*. The price for assignment work should be negotiated based upon the intended use of the image(s), the client's budget, and your costs of doing business. Pricing guidelines and marketing ideas will be available from colleagues you meet through organizations such as the Professional Photographers of America (PP of A), the National Press Photographers Association (NPPA), the American Society of Media Photographers (ASMP), and state and local imaging groups. The membership benefits usually far outweigh the cost, so you should consider joining one or more of these organizations. One of the major benefits is continuing education.

5. Keep learning!

Most of the best professional imagemakers are happy to share their secrets with young people entering the field, because they have not forgotten that they learned much of what they know from others. Every year there are hundreds of workshops in all aspects of professional imaging and fine-art photography that are attended by working pros from all specialties. Many of these programs occur in pleasant resort areas so participants can simultaneously relax and recharge. Professional organizations, manufacturers, and vendors often sponsor clinics and short courses in hotels and on college campuses. The industry's most comprehensive schedule of intensive, hands-on courses is offered year-round in Atlanta, Georgia by the Winona School of Professional Photography. (For a Winona catalog, call 1-800-742-7468). A list of other organizations offering workshops is on page 258.

"All things come to one who waits — if you work while you wait!"

— Anonymous

RAIMONDS ZIEMELIS

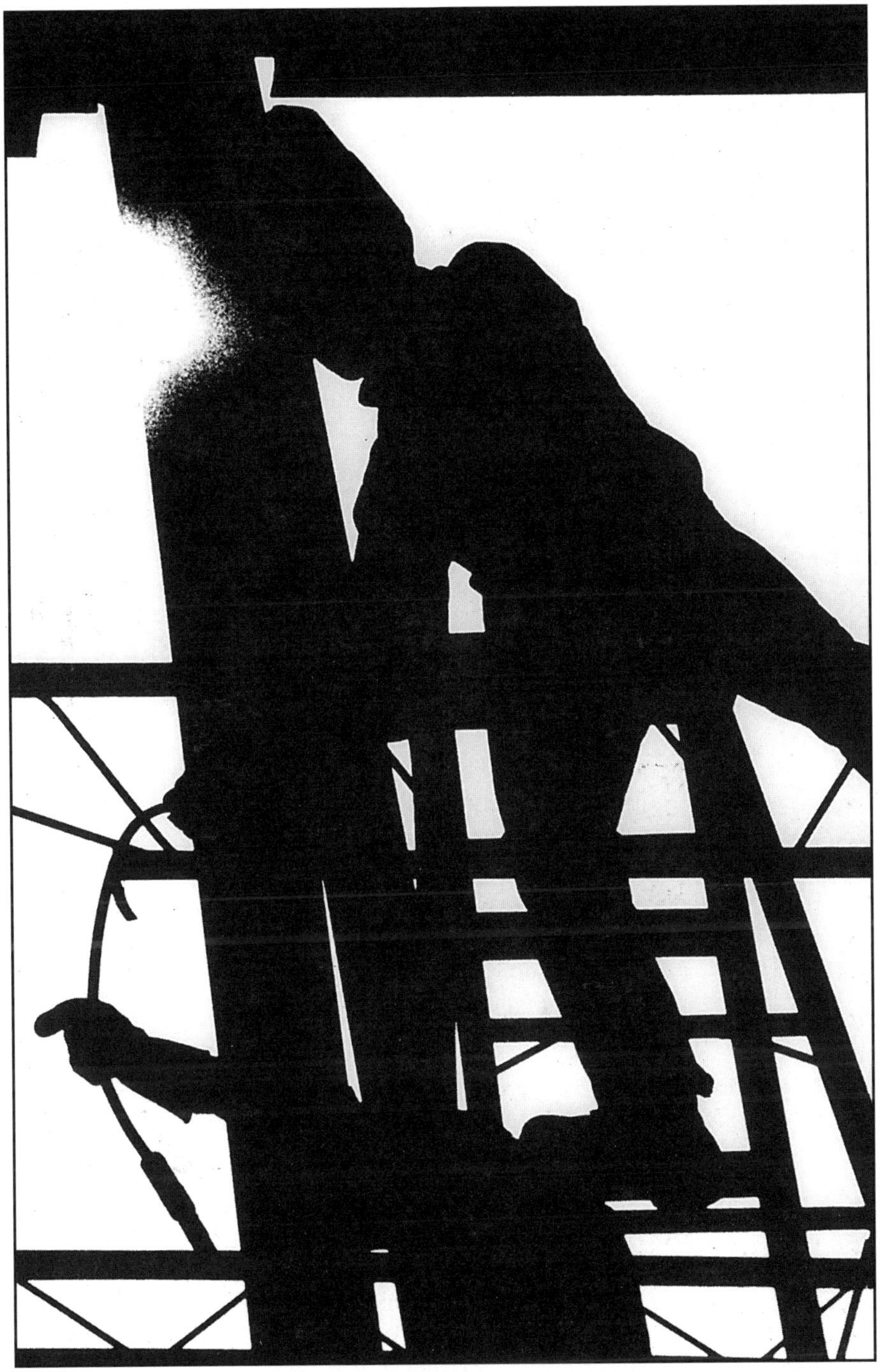

Stock photos should be eye-catching and dramatic. Try to visualize subject matter in its most abstract or graphic form, even when working on a routine assignment. The high-contrast dropout technique simplified this construction photograph to forms in positive and negative space. If you can consistently produce images with impact, they can produce extra income for you as stock photos placed with an agency.

Selling Stock Photos through an Agent

Editors looking for specific kinds of pictures, usually make their first call to an image library. These research and sales agencies are referred to in the trade as stock houses. When you first start out as a free-lancer, you should try to sell some pictures directly to publishers, especially if you have a strong specialty. You might be lucky with sales, and if you can establish a name for yourself, your chances of having work accepted by a stock house are greater than if you've never had anything published. Agencies work on a 40-to-50 percent commission, but an active agent will show your pictures to markets that you might never have imagined, nor had the time to send work to. Barbara Van Cleve, formerly an agent specializing in travel and textbook markets, offered my students some pretty sound advice:

"Young photographers," she said, "usually have an inflated sense of their ability and a naive knowledge of the market, which makes them very impatient should sales not be forthcoming immediately. They need to know that their work is competing with the work of famous professionals who market on their own to all kinds of clients, with whom we also deal. Further, to be really involved in this business they ought to be sending us at least 50 new slides per month, until they build up a file of around 1,000 shots with us. These should cover a wide range of subjects in order to be most saleable."

The advice offered by Van Cleve to aspiring young photographers is to "look at a lot of pictures as they appear in ads, textbooks, and magazines, make assignments to themselves to shoot these assignments, do a lot of highly selective shooting, edit their work carefully, send it to us ... and be patient." Furthermore, she added, "All sales through an agent should be considered 'gravy' or 'icing on the cake.' No one can live on stock sales alone, and no professional does. Some work from very good photographers will sit in our files for a year before we can market it, because textbook publishers follow cycles in their revisions."

"If young photographers want to bypass a service such as ours," suggests Van Cleve, "they can use the *Writer's Market* [or *Photographer's Market*] as a guide ... and send out letters of inquiry accompanied by some sort of inexpensively printed brochure as a sample of their work. When a buyer contacts them, they can send out their slides for review and take their chances. But they will soon learn the economics of postage!" When you send out work to a publication, you're trying to get the attention of an appropriate editor.

Dealing with Editors

Every day major publications receive so many unsolicited manuscripts, photos and story ideas that sometimes the best they can do is to return them unopened. Editors like to receive material they can use, but they don't have time to handle photos and articles that are wildly inappropriate or of unsatisfactory quality. If you want to hit a particular market, first study recent issues of the publication you are aiming for, then query the editor briefly by letter, enclosing a few representative samples of your work. Always enclose a self-addressed, stamped envelope (SASE) with enough postage for the return of anything you want to get back. Editors expect a SASE and most won't return your material unless you enclose one.

Publications pay for accepted work either upon receipt (desirable but uncommon) or upon publication. When you do sell photographs or an article, be certain there's written agreement on whether the editor is buying full, exclusive rights to your material, or only reproduction rights for one-time publication. Naturally, you're entitled to much more money when exclusive rights are involved. Rates vary widely for single photographs, from a pitiful low of only a few dollars for a single black-and-white print, $100 to $250 or more for color, up to more than $2,000 for an illustrated article purchased by a major magazine.

Some editors, if they like an article idea that you've queried them about, will give you some suggestions for making it more saleable and then "assign" you to do the story. Unless you're a well-known pro, however, this kind of assignment is still on speculation — the editor is not obligated to publish your material nor to pay you for it if the results don't measure up to expectations. But on the other hand, the editor is ethically bound not to "steal" your idea and assign it to another photographer or writer until you've had a good crack at it. You're bound ethically, too, not to submit the same story or photographs to competing publications at the same time. You could, for instance, submit similar fishing photos to an outdoor magazine and to a calendar publisher, but not to another hunting-and-fishing magazine until your material has been rejected by the editor of the first magazine. Simultaneous submission of queries is OK, though, because it often takes so long to receive replies.

Contract for your services

Some picture editors, especially those who publish magazines and annual reports for industrial stockholders and employees, may prefer to contract for your services by the day, rather than by the picture or by the story. Day rates are individually negotiable, of course and should be based on your costs, but remain close to what others are charging for similar work. The photographer usually retains the negatives, transparencies and digital files, along with ownership rights. It is customary to sell one-time reproduction rights, unless agreed, in writing, that images made on that assignment belong to the client. In such cases, referred to as "work for hire," you should negotiate a job rate that includes a specified number of prints or transparencies, as well as a definite fee.

Advertising photos usually bring higher prices than those used editorially. Find out what other photographers are charging for similar work, and be certain your written agreement includes all the terms and prices, so that your invoice comes as no surprise. Being specific also protects you from the shock of being told: "Sorry, but that's not what we had in mind." Successful free-lancer Fred Tonne suggests avoiding the "Never time to do it right; always time to do it over" problem by being certain at the outset that everyone concerned with a photo assignment knows what to expect from the other parties. "Get it in writing," Tonne advises, "unless you've worked before with the same client and you're sure you understand each other."

Get a Model Release

The model release is a necessary bother. Releases are such a nuisance to get signed that they're almost never obtained for routine editorial photography. Legally, a photographer or publisher is in little danger of a lawsuit, unless the subject of the photo has been ridiculed by miscaptioning, or a clear invasion of privacy is evident. You wouldn't, for example, publish a telephoto picture of someone sunbathing by a backyard pool, but almost anything occurring in a public place is fair game if the facts and circumstances are not misrepresented. It's almost impossible to get a release for travel pictures, and one is seldom expected for editorial use.

The use of pictures of recognizable people in advertising is another story. Most clients won't even consider buying a picture for use in an ad unless you can provide a signed release from any person appearing in the picture and from the owner of private property, such as a home or business. Exhibition of a photograph in a gallery or display, however, is not usually held to be advertising, unless a product is being promoted. You're usually quite safe if you exhibit non-derogatory photos of people in a public park, at a school, gallery, art fair, or camera club. If prints are sold, however, and the subject finds out about it, you might be expected to share the proceeds with your subject or remove the offending prints from display. But if prints are going to be exhibited to promote the sale of a certain brand of film or camera, for example, you should always obtain a release.

If you're on assignment for an advertiser, or if you're planning to sell stock pictures later, you'd be wise to get a signed release from anyone portrayed prominently in the pictures. Always get a routine release from anyone modeling for you, especially nudes. Without releases, picture agents' hands are tied. Many clients simply won't buy pictures without releases. Professional models who are being paid for posing expect to sign a release form as a matter of course. A few free prints often are compensation enough for most amateur models.

PERMISSION TO USE PHOTOGRAPH

Release No.______________________________

Date______________________________

I am (am not) of legal age. For good and valuable consideration, the receipt of which is hereby acknowledged, I hereby authorize______________________________

____

to take photographs of me and/or my property and authorize him/her and assigns and transferees to use and publish the same (including use and publication with my name, no name, or a fictitious name, use in the form taken or with intentional or unintentional alterations, and use for the purpose of publicity, illustration, commercial art, and in the advertising of any product or services).

Signed______________________________

Address______________________________

Witness______________________________

____

Parent or guardian (if not legal age)

Assignment: Date______________________________

For value received I assign full rights in this release to ______________________________

for the following purpose.______________________________

____

Photographer

Copyright Your Work

Placing a copyright notice on each of your photographs announces that you intend to challenge unauthorized publication of your work, but few photographers actually file the forms. Many free-lancers routinely stamp on the back of each print or the face of each slide mount a statement such as "© 1999 John Lensman," thus giving notice of intent to copyright and securing what is, in effect, a common-law copyright that takes effect when the work is "published." According to law, however, public exhibition of your images or showing them to editors without the copyright notice does not relinquish any rights you have to your work. The law defines "publication" as actual sale to the public.

You may not actually be able to recover damages from an infringer, however, unless you have followed the registration and deposit requirements, which include filling out a form, paying a fee, and depositing two copies of the work with the Library of Congress. Several photographs made in the same year and "published" together can be copyrighted as a group on the same form for a single fee. Pages of duplicate slides can be submitted, or contact sheets.

For details and forms, write to: Copyright Office, Library of Congress, Washington, DC 20559 or phone (202) 707-9100.

Always Be Ethical

Just as you don't want other people to publish — and profit from — your pictures, obviously you shouldn't rip off theirs. Besides being immoral to steal other people's work and ideas, it's also illegal. There have been enough recent court cases involving "borrowed" copyrighted images being computer-manipulated for other purposes, that a principle has been firmly established: IF IN DOUBT, DON'T!

Any image than 100 years old probably is in the public domain. Many clip-art and stock photo collections are copyright-free to the buyer for any legitimate use, but if there is any doubt in either case, it's always best to find out first.

Separate fact from fantasy

Art is one world; journalism is another. The two should never mix without clear identification for the viewer. In an exhibition or in advertising, almost any creative concept can be acceptable. On a feature page, "art" can be excellent if it is labeled clearly "photo illustration" or "digital photomontage." Editorial journalism requires an entirely different set of values.

Keith Alan Morris

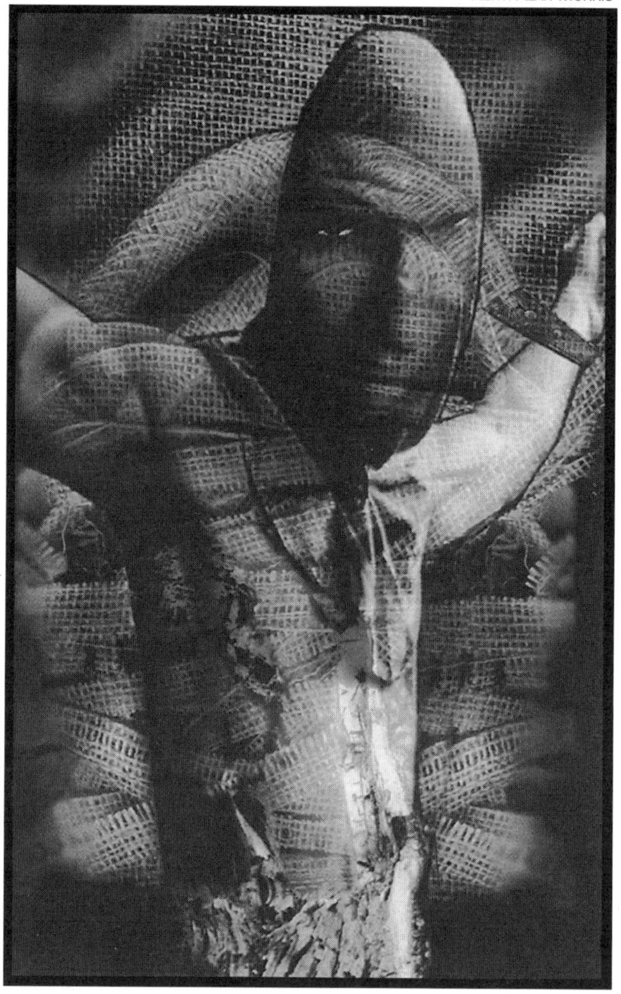

A photo-illustration from the cover of an original work of fiction — a "photo-novel" produced in Adobe Photoshop.

Because computers permit undetectable alteration, photographs presented as "true" in publications and as legal evidence must be unmanipulated. Photojournalists and editors usually are permitted to make only the kinds of changes in a picture that once were performed in a darkroom. For example: dodging or burning areas to make detail more visible, improving reproduction by enhancing overall print quality, making overall color corrections, and spotting.

Altering basic reality is a no-no. For example: removing or adding objects, cloning pixels to create a new image, or making radical alterations in color.

Here's the bottom line: People love eye-candy; but because nearly everyone still believes in the reality of photographs, there is an ethical obligation to future history. No reader should unknowingly be deceived.

"Journalism is the first rough draft of history."

— David Broder, journalist

LARRY DALY

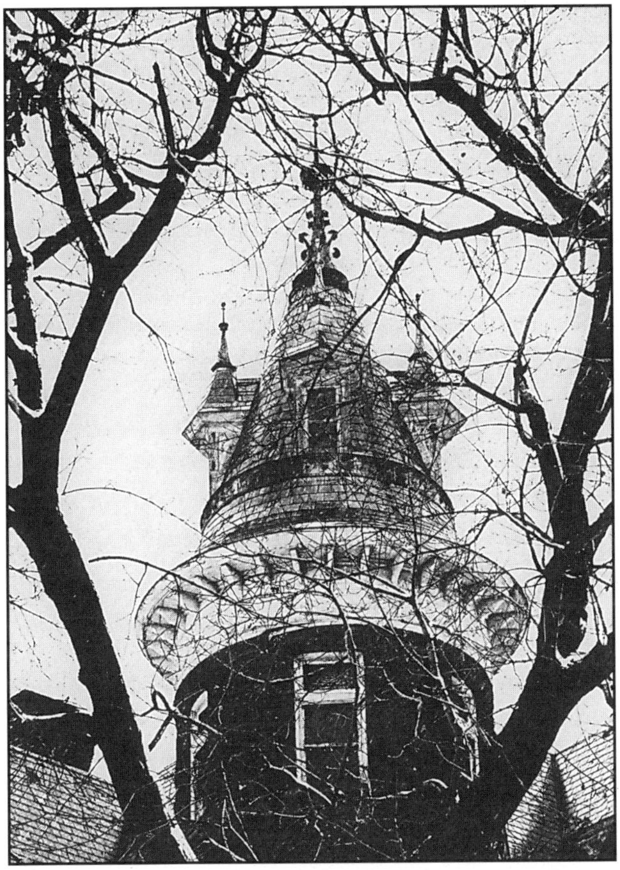

SHIRLEY BALE

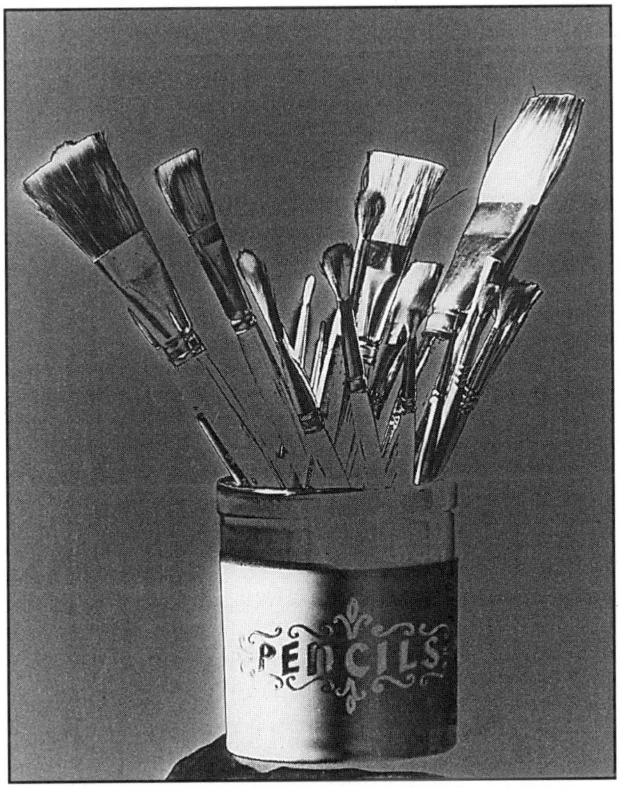

A simple and practical filing system will help you retrieve saleable images like these.

Organize Your Images

If you continue as a imagemaker, soon you'll be overwhelmed with negatives, contact sheets, prints, slides and probably computer disks. Unless you begin now with a simple filing system, you won't be able to find things when you need them. Everyone has their own way of coding and cross-referencing, but here's what I do:

1. Place all negatives in clear polypropylene or polyethylene archival filing pages. Label each page with the date and subject.

2. Punch contact sheets for a three-ring binder.

3. File each contact sheet chronologically, next to the appropriate negatives, in a three-ring binder.

4. Store slides also in archival pages. Label by date and subject.

5. Keep slide pages by date in three-ring binders, hanging files, or archival boxes.

6. Organize numbered, dated and labeled computer disks in their plastic cases, and put them in appropriate storage units. If find-file-and-retrieve software is installed on your computer, use it to catalog digital images.

7. Maintain a simple card or computer file by subject matter and/or by client. Whenever you add something to an existing category, put on the card the date (everything is filed by date). If several subjects are on the same roll and filed together, just add frame numbers or slide numbers. If several rolls are shot on the same day, number them consecutively. For example: Flowers, daffodils: 4-15-97 (3) 1-10; Birds, robins: 4-15-97 (3) 11-24. If you add a new category, start another card.

8. Slip finished, mounted prints into individual polyethylene archival bags and store them in acid-free boxes. Label the boxes by subject and/or by date.

9. Keep all image files in the driest place available, away from bright light and heat.

10. I keep some irreplaceable negatives and transparencies in my food freezer in the basement. Not only does freezing retard deterioration of the dyes in color films, but firemen have told me that they've seen the contents of the freezer intact after a house has burned to the ground. Self-locking food storage bags can be used, or special heat-sealed, negative storage envelopes.

A final word of advice: don't allow unfiled work to accumulate, or it can become a useless mess.

"Anything worth doing is worth doing now!"

— Anonymous

The Picture Story

"One picture is worth a thousand words."

— Confucius, ancient philosopher

"If a single picture is worth a thousand words, imagine the possibilities of two, three, or more photographs working together to convey more complex layers of meaning."

— Judy Dater, photographer

During the 1940s and '50s *Life, Look,* and other popular weekly magazines perfected the still-photo and text sequences that we call picture stories or photo essays to a high form of communicative art. Then television took the public's attention, along with special-interest publications. Now the Internet draws people away from the TV tube and toward the monitor. But those great word/picture formats are not dead; a few magazines continue the tradition and photographic books and now websites offer the imaginative imagemaker opportunities to communicate personal ideas while commenting on society.

"A sequence of several images can be thought of as a single statement."

— Minor White, photographer

Fine-art photographers such as Minor White have long realized that the emotional impact of a series of related images — when viewed together — can be greater than if each image is considered alone. Another storytelling method is to create a chronology in which actions occur. Perhaps the best known contemporary exponent of this approach is Duane Michals, whose hand-captioned, comic-strip-like sequences are full of whimsy, mystery, and surprise endings.

"I ... prefer those photographs that had no life until the photographer's imagination called them into being ... Photographs should ask questions, suggest dramas, reveal, rather than merely describe."

— Duane Michals, photographer

Journalistic picture stories usually follow some form of chronology or other continuity, employing words as captions or supplementary text, either to provide background for the pictures or to explain their meaning. Strong photographs, ideally, require a minimum of words to explain them, if any at all. The words and pictures should complement one another. The photo essay, a highly refined form of picture story, deals, in the literary sense, with a selected topic from an interpretive, highly personal point of view.

"After all, isn't that what life is all about, the ability to go around back and come up inside other people's heads ... and say: oh, so that's how you see it!?"

— Ray Bradbury, author

There's a strong temptation to overshoot on a picture-story assignment. Beginners often take pictures of everything that moves in the hope of later discovering great image sequences on the contact sheets. This "shotgun" approach can work if you're covering a fast-breaking news or sporting event, but it's much better to plan ahead the kinds of shots you think you'll need to tell the story.

Start with a script

The script for a picture story or photo essay may consist merely of an outline that lists each aspect of the subject to be covered. A simple checklist often is sufficient when you do your own planning.

If you prepare a detailed shooting script, each picture idea should be described in enough detail that its part in the sequence is clear and any special techniques, equipment, props, etc., are noted. Simple sketches will help you to previsualize the format and composition you'll be looking for during shooting sessions.

Whether or not you prepare a detailed script, you ought to have in mind exactly what the purpose of your story is, who the intended audience will be, and just what kind of reaction you expect from them. Do you want people to be amused, enlightened, saddened, angered, or aroused? Do you want them to *buy* something or to *do* something? Or would it be sufficient if those who view your efforts shared your very personal feelings of concern, elation, appreciation, or nostalgia? If, as a communicator, your purpose is not clearly in mind, how can you expect your viewers/readers to respond to the message as you intend?

DIANE OSBORNE (4)

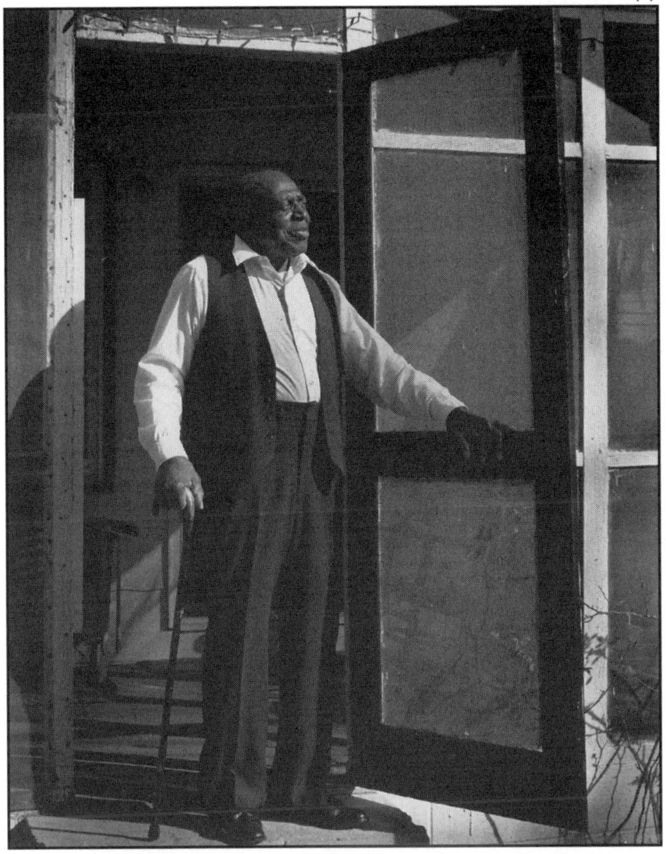

The Reverend Gadsen

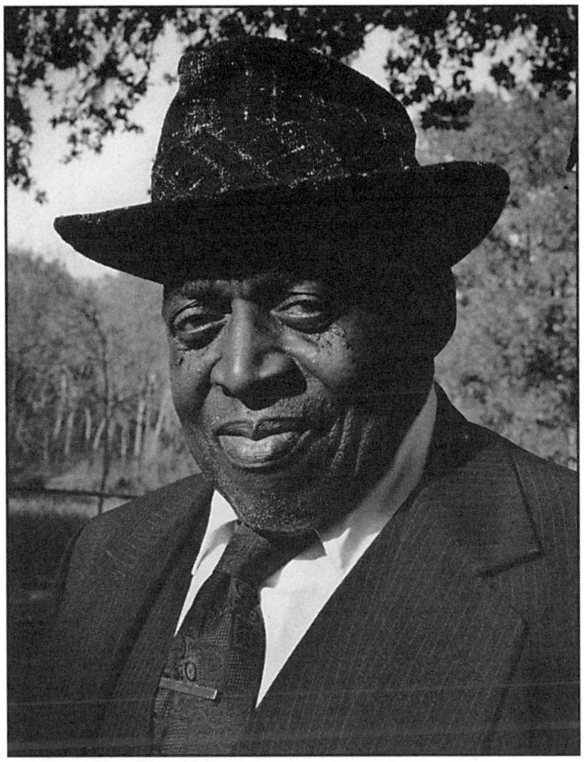

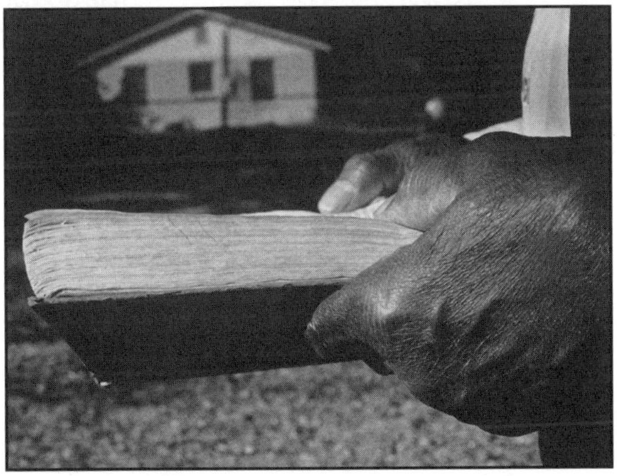

A serial portrait has been created with this photo essay, which was part of a senior independent project. Multiple images often can reveal much more than could be glimpsed from a single photograph that records only one moment in time.

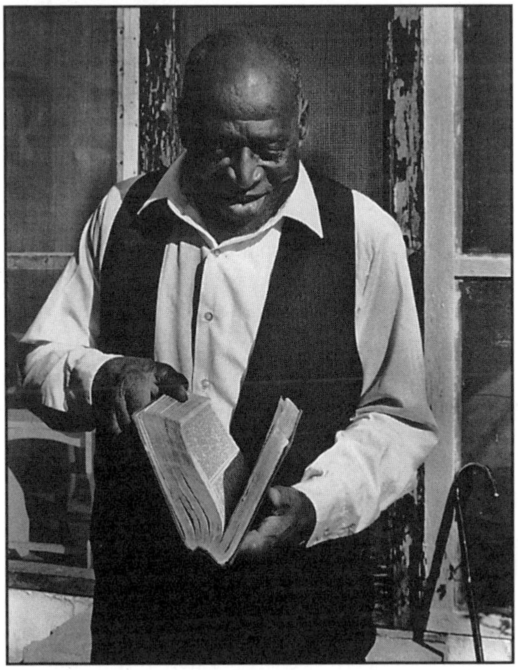

Stay flexible

Don't be a slave to the script. If what you thought you would find, or what you thought would happen, doesn't turn out as expected, stay flexible. Even while shooting, if you feel the need for a different approach, or if you encounter interesting aspects of the subject that you hadn't anticipated, don't hesitate to change. If you've thought out all aspects of the story, you can always change the script as you see fit. Without enough advance planning, however, you may discover, too late, that you have to go back and reshoot some key parts that you missed. Reshooting is seldom convenient and not always possible.

"Every story should have a beginning, middle and end — but not necessarily in that order."

—Jean-Luc Godard, filmmaker

Look for story ideas

One of the simplest types of picture story is the how-to-do-it series. These sequences are simple to produce because the continuity is already determined by the actual steps in the process. All you have to do is to write down the order of events and decide how each step can best be presented. An example of a how-to-do-it might be a story on the manufacture of a hand-tooled leather belt, or the erection of a log-cabin home. Imaginative treatment and interesting camera angles spell the difference between a mundane record of a process and an interesting and motivating experience for the viewer/reader. You can see what kinds of stories are selling by studying current issues of magazines that interest you. Or surf the Web.

"A day in the life of ..." has become a common picture-story theme. You've probably seen the cooperatively produced photo books with variations on this title. Another approach is "What it's like to be a ..." in which you present an occupation, pastime, or way of life.

A popular theme is to photograph similar subject matter, but in different locations. For example, a story on how people have restored historic houses may be told effectively by photographs made in several different towns. Or you might do an essay in depth on a singularly interesting and inviting old home in your community and about the people who are restoring it. A deeply personal essay on being alone, or daybreak, or flight, or the sea, could contain a number of evocatively related visual poems interwoven with original free verse or prose. Such personal essays can be enormously rewarding, both for the sake of doing them and for the possibility of publication.

"We see things not as they are, but as we are."

— High Museum of Art, Atlanta

Get all the information

The starting point for any picture story or photo essay is the idea. Ideas may come easily to you if you've become an expert in a specialized field, or you may need to do quite a bit of research. After the initial story idea, you should learn as much about the subject as possible, taking notes for later copy and caption writing. You should ask — and answer — the journalist's traditional questions: Who? What? Why? When? Where? and How? Get to know the people involved and become accepted by them. Virtually everyone will be friendly and cooperative if they believe you care sincerely about them and that you're genuinely interested in what interests them. Get to know your subjects. Observe how they talk and act. Listen to what they say and pay attention to their advice.

Respect everyone

Whether you represent a publication, a commercial client, or yourself as a free-lancer, you are always *taking* pictures. Try to *give* something in return, if only sincere interest, appreciation and common courtesy.

"I think photographers sometimes forget how difficult it is to stand on the other side of the camera. We forget how intrusive a camera can be."

— Lynn Johnson, photojournalist

"I try to be sensitive to people, to treat them with kindness and dignity."

— Robert Maxwell, photojournalist

"I do not believe in photography just to invade people's lives. I go into people's lives constantly, but only to make their motives, their ideas, understood."

— Cornell Capa, photojournalist

"I find no photographs superior to the decency of a man's feelings and his right to those feelings. When there is such a conflict, I ... put the camera down and take no pictures."

— W. Eugene Smith, photojournalist

Plan ahead

An experienced photojournalist, comfortable in a situation, can imagine what an image is going to look like as a finished photograph. You can train yourself to do this and to sense the exact instant when subject arrangement and action feel "right." Henri Cartier-Bresson calls this *the decisive moment.* Preplanning can help you to recognize these important instants when they occur. Self-confidence and a good relationship with your subjects can help you set up significant situations in an unobtrusive "posed-unposed" manner. Unless you plan ahead, it's easy to lose purpose and direction, and end up merely with a hodgepodge of routine pictures. Successful stories have unity and continuity.

Make a strong "lead"

Every picture story needs a strong "lead" picture to engage the viewer's curiosity and interest, and give incentive to examine the rest of the story. Most stories, even photo essays that do not have rigid continuity, require a beginning, a climax, and a conclusion. The lead picture often is an overview, or an introduction, or it may be the one most dramatic photograph, which sets the mood, introduces the main character, or establishes the environment. The lead is the picture that the editor often will run largest in the layout to catch the attention of the reader.

Consider the layout

As you study effective, published picture-story page layouts, notice that seldom are the pictures the same size and shape, nor are they usually arranged in static rows. Editors and art directors want to avoid monotony in their layouts. You'll be wise to include verticals as well as horizontals and shoot plenty of close-ups, as well as medium and long shots. Don't forget that magazine covers and book jackets usually are vertical in format. If you want to crack the lucrative cover market, your compositions have to be oriented correctly and there must be enough space allowed for the name of the magazine or title of the book, as well as other copy.

Write complete captions

Picture captions must be complete, containing all names (spelled correctly), plus all the other important data (who, what, why, when, where, and how). Captions (cutlines) should be neatly typewritten or laser-printed, and attached to the prints in such a way that they can be read while the editor is looking at the print. This is done by fastening the caption to the bottom of the reverse side of the print with nonbleeding "magic mending" or library tape, and then folding the paper up over the face of the print to save space in handling and mailing. Slides should be submitted in file pages and keyed by number to captions on a separate sheet.

Assign yourself to notice the beauty of the seasons. Look around you. See what elegant images reveal themselves.

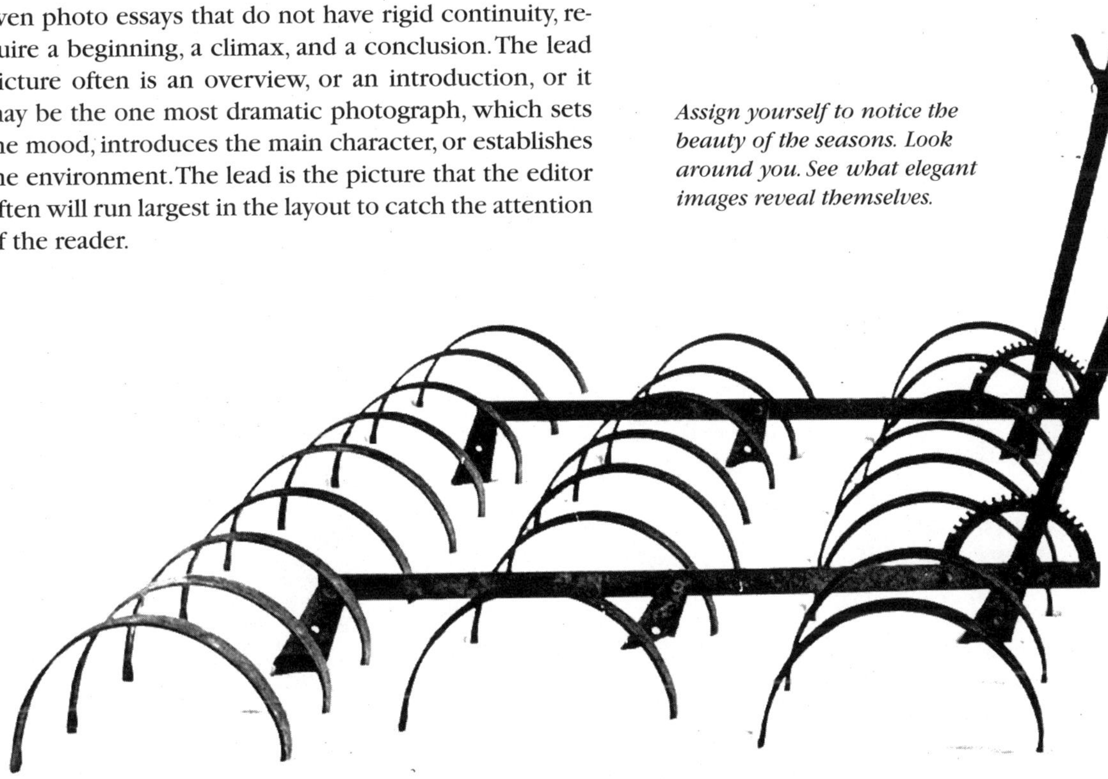

JANE HORTON

Conclusion:

Do what you love; love what you do

In this final chapter, you've read a few suggestions about how to turn your interest in imaging into income. Our occupation, even more than most professions, requires energy, talent and persistence because of the very popularity of the medium.

People who never would consider trying to be their own doctor, lawyer, accountant, plumber or farmer will believe that they can be their own photographer — until in a gentle way you educate them to see how your pictures are better then theirs. And millions of people consider themselves "experts" with a camcorder or a computer. That's one of the problems faced by imagemakers everywhere. And sadly, not all clients will appreciate the difference in quality.

But if your work is good, there's a market for it. Being successful means doing your best at all times. You will succeed if you believe in your ability to learn and to produce. Most of all, happiness can be the reward of a life spent earnestly seeking vision and humanity.

"It doesn't occur to [clients] that photography is work."

— Andrea Krause, photographer

"You can tell that you're doing the right kind of work, if: (1) you keep on doing it; (2) you love the details; (3) the process is even more important to you than the finished product."

— Lisa Palchick, painter

Blake Vulpe

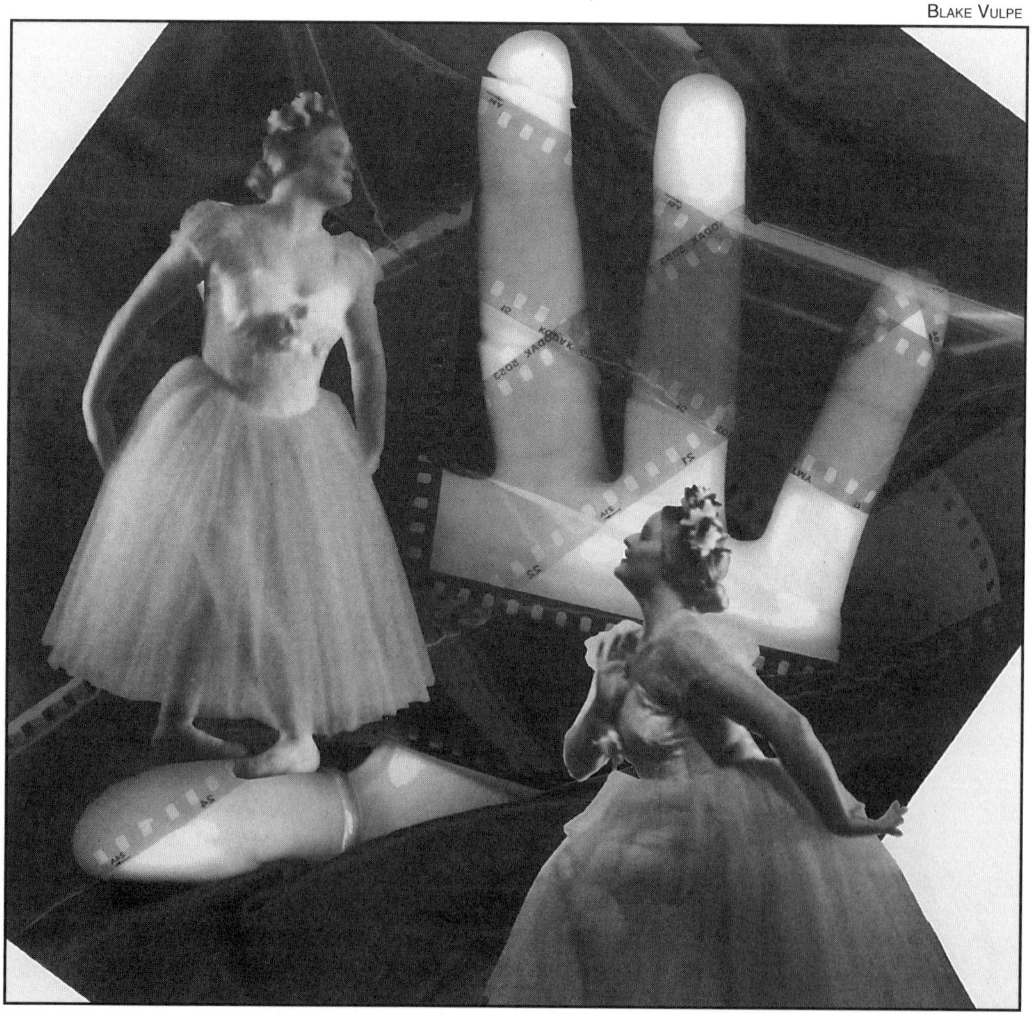

This elaborate photo-illustration, from a senior independent project exhibition, began as a scannergram. In Adobe Photoshop, each dancer was selected with the lasso tool, then pasted into the compositiion.

Independent Study Assignments

Try as many of these 30 different projects as you can. If you are enrolled in a class, your instructor may suggest several from this list, and perhaps assign some others that you can do individually and with classmates.

On each assignment, create the most interesting images you can. Print the best ones for critique and for your portfolio, and examine the others on contact sheets. If something doesn't work out, try it again. Don't be afraid to use film, paper, and chemicals. No materials are "wasted" if you have learned from the experience.

If a digital camera or scanner is available, any assignment may be done alternatively with a computer. Learning optical/chemical photography first is a good idea, because the experience will enable you to work intuitively with digital imaging software.

1. Reveal Your Feelings

Choose several images that communicate something to you. Discuss them with friends and classmates. Observe what each picture shows you, then consider how it makes you *feel.* Try to imagine the thoughts and feelings of the photographer at the moment of exposure. Do you think that your reactions to viewing each image are similar to those experienced by the photographer who was actually there? Identify any techniques that you think the imagemakers might have used, either deliberately or subconsciously, to influence the reactions of those who would later see their pictures.

2. Emulate Excellence

Study the work of several imagemakers whose work you admire. Make at least one photograph of typical subject matter as you imagine it might have been done by each of these famous artists or photojournalists. Try, for example, an "Edward Weston" vegetable or tree root, an "Ansel Adams" landscape, an "Aaron Siskind" wall, an "Arnold Newman" portrait, a "Bruce Davidson" portrait, a "Mary Ellen Mark" portrait, and a "Cartier-Bresson" street scene. Note: This work should be *emulation*, not imitation. Don't simply copy something that you've seen published, but try to react to the subject matter as you imagine that particular photographer would have reacted. Try to identify yourself with your chosen photographer, interpreting the subject matter, as well as you can, through his or her "eyes."

3. Compare Cameras

Arrange with your instructor, your friends, or a photo dealer to examine several different types of cameras. If possible, study each of the following: 35mm single-lens reflex, 35mm rangefinder, 6cm single-lens reflex, 6cm twin-lens reflex, 4x5 or larger view camera.

With help from someone familiar with each camera, practice handling them and adjusting the controls. Pretend to take pictures. Sight through the viewfinder. Focus, and operate the shutter at various speeds. Learn how to load each camera with film. Find out the following information about each camera: **(1)** name of camera, **(2)** negative size, **(3)** type(s) of film used, **(4)** focal length of standard lens, **(5)** other lenses available, **(6)** largest f/stop, **(7)** smallest f/stop, **(8)** fastest shutter speed, **(9)** slowest shutter speed, **(10)** provision for Bulb and Time exposures, **(11)** how flash is attached and synchronized, **(12)** how the camera is focused, **(13)** presence of a self-timer (delayed release), **(14)** provision for preventing accidental double exposures, **(15)** provision for *intentional* double exposures, **(16)** the kind of photography for which the camera is best suited, **(17)** any special precautions that must be exercised when using the camera, and **(18)** its greatest limitations.

4. Make a Photogram or Scannergram

Exposing with light from an enlarger or overhead lamp, arrange opaque or translucent objects on a sheet of photographic paper to create an interesting design without using a camera. Experiment with many variations of pattern and illusion. Try combining hand-drawn or photographic images with the shadows of real objects. If a flat-bed scanner or photocopy machine is available, try placing objects on the glass. Be careful not to scratch the glass or get it dirty. See what happens to colors along edges and where objects overlap.

5. Frame with Lenses

This assignment has two parts:

(A) Make a series of photographs comparing image size and perspective rendering of similar subjects photographed at the same distance from the camera with lenses of different focal lengths.

(B) With different lenses, fill the frame by varying the distance between camera and subject. Use both a wide-angle and a telephoto. For example, if you are using a 35mm camera, you should try using, in addition to the normal 50mm or 55mm lens, a 28mm or 35mm wide-angle and a 105mm to 135mm lens, or longer. If you have access to a zoom lens, try it out over its entire range.

6. Discover Depth of Field

This assignment has two parts:

(A) *With slow film, or in weak light,* photograph a subject such as a person, small sculpture, flower, etc. using selective focus. *In manual mode*, set your lens at its *widest aperture* (f/2 on many 35mm cameras) and adjust the shutter speed for correct exposure. Focus carefully on the main subject, allowing the background to remain completely out of focus.

(B) Make a series of photographs with your *normal lens*, comparing depth of field and overall sharpness at apertures (f/stops) ranging from the widest (about f/2) to the smallest (about f/16). Include an object approximately two feet (0.5 m) from the camera, something else at three or four feet (1 m), then five to six feet (2 m), 10 to 12 feet (3 m), 20 to 30 feet (7 m), and farther (infinity). Focus at about five feet (1.5 m), then notice what happens to the sharpness of objects at other distances. Mount the camera on a tripod and set it on manual mode, in relatively weak light, because your exposure settings will be like this: 1/1000 at f/2, 1/500 at f/2.8, 1/250 at f/4, 1/125 at f/5.6, 1/60 at f/8, 1/30 at f/11, and 1/15 at f/16. In bright sunlight with 100-speed film, these settings will give three stops (eight times) overexposure unless you use a dense filter that will absorb the extra light.

7. Select Shutter Speeds

This assignment has four parts:

(A) Using 400-speed film, try some shots of fast action using the fastest shutter speeds on your camera. (1/1,000 etc.). As you change from one speed to another, compensate for exposure by adjusting the lens opening.

(B) Load your camera with slow film, place it firmly on a tripod, and make a series of exposures from 1 second to 1/15 second of a subject moving past the camera. (This part of the assignment may have to be done in relatively dim light. Maintain correct exposure by adjusting the lens opening each time you change the shutter speed).

(C) Try a series with the same slow shutter speeds (in relatively dim light), but hand-hold the camera and use the *panning* technique: Follow the action with the camera, releasing the shutter while the camera is moving, and keep it moving until the shutter closes. (The image will disappear while the mirror is up, but keep following the action anyway).

(D) At night, put your camera on the tripod again, set the aperture at f/16 and the shutter at "B". Find a place where moving lights create a pattern in time (traffic at an intersection, carnival rides, fireworks), and make some exposures lasting several seconds. Try to fill the frame with a design traced by the lights. Also focus on bright neon signs or other patterns of light, and then create interesting streaks and shapes by moving the camera while the shutter is open.

8. Control Contrast with Filters

Photograph several subjects that contrast strongly in color hue with the background. Choose filters that will exaggerate or diminish the separation of each subject from its background (a red apple against green leaves, or a light-colored stone or concrete building against blue sky). Another possibility is to eliminate contrast between colors, such as in copying a stained document or old photograph, or using a filter to remove or lessen the effect of a stain. Calculate exposure using the filter factor. Compare these settings with the reading you get through the lens with the filter attached. If they differ, expose both ways and keep a record so you'll know what to do next time.

9. Light with Flash

This assignment has four parts to produce a series of photographs showing various uses of flash illumination. Compare:

(A) Direct flash on camera,

(B) Off-camera flash aimed directly at the subject, but at least at arm's length from the camera;

(C) Flash bounced from ceiling or wall; and

(D) Fill-in flash outdoors in bright sun.

If your flash unit does not automatically adjust intensity according to the distance, make practical tests to determine a guide number. To do this, place a subject 10 feet from the camera and shoot a series at different lens openings. Choose the best negative. Multiply the lens opening used for that shot by 10 to get your guide number (for example: f/8 x 10 feet = 80. To use the guide number, divide it by any subject distance to get the f/stop to use).

10. Document Architectural Forms

Photograph both the exterior and the interior of a building that interests you. Your photographs should show something of the function of the building, as well as its appearance. Experiment with a wide-angle lens and with the perspective correction of a view camera if you have one available. If you are using a 35mm or roll-film camera try to keep it as level as possible so the walls don't converge. Also try some dramatic angle shots and close-ups of details.

11. Focus on Close-ups

This assignment has three parts:

(A) Reproduce a small sculpture, household object, or natural form so that its shape and texture are clearly shown. Use either natural or artificial light, but determine exposure and development with care, compensating if necessary for light loss because of lens extension.

(B) Make a copy negative or a digital scan from a photographic print.Then make a duplicate print the same size as the original, trying to reproduce as accurately as possible (or improve) its tonal values and contrast.

(C) Make color slides from a painting using 45° lighting and polarizers.Adjust the lights for evenness. Bracket the exposures to obtain the best possible quality in the reproductions.

12. Sell a Product

Illustrate a familiar household product so that it becomes tempting to buy or to consume. A view camera, if available, may be desirable for this assignment because of its controls. But any format will do if you conceive an interesting idea, and compose and light the subject imaginatively. It's OK to emulate good published illustrations that have caught your attention.

13. Photograph Friends or Family

This assignment has four parts:

(A) Make several significant portraits of someone who is important to you. Photograph this person in various settings, under different conditions, and with both natural and studio lighting (regardless of the light source, demonstrate 45° key-light placement). Try to capture the "essence" of your subject — beyond a mere likeness — and attempt to visualize the relationship between your subject and yourself.

(B) Attempt a *nonportrait*, indicating as much as you can about the subject without showing his or her face.

(C) Photograph a person in his or her surroundings. Include as much of the background and other objects as you feel explains the subject's work, interests, or personality without cluttering the image. It's OK if this part of the assignment overlaps with (A) and (B).

(D) Create a revealing portrait of yourself.

14. Appreciate the Human Body

Find a suitable model who is willing to pose for you, either indoors or out.Try to portray the sensuous grace — the line, form, texture, and symmetry — that have made the human form a favorite subject of artists throughout history. Attempt to capture an illusion of movement flowing beyond static poses.

15. Reveal Evidence of Mankind

Without including any people, show how humans have changed their environment. Examples could range from an unmade bed or a half-eaten apple to a strip mine, a polluted stream, or a monument. Try to give viewers evidence enough to make inferences about the nature of the person or people who had been there.

16. Isolate Abstractions

Create images dominated by form, line, texture, pattern or color, in which the subject matter may not be recognizable. Also consider the relationship of *positive space* (subject) to *negative space* (background).

17. Demonstrate Light Values

This assignment has three parts to present three images in which a complete tonal range is present, but that differ in the amounts of each value:

(A) Through arrangement of objects and background, and through lighting, demonstrate the effect of *chiaroscuro* (light against dark and dark against light).

(B) Produce a *high-key* image, in which nearly all the values are light, e.g., white-on-white.

(C) Produce a *low-key* image in which nearly all values are dark, e.g., black-on-black.

18. Perceive Equivalents

Search for visual parallels or analogies:

(A) *Simile* — something that reminds you of something else (for example, a vegetable that looks like an animal).

(B) *Metaphor* — an object that symbolically represents another (for example, a lone tree symbolizing an individualistic person).

(C) *Equivalent* — a natural arrangement of forms that evokes an aesthetic sensation (for example, a pattern of leaves or clouds that elicits the feeling of having heard a musical chord).

19. Interchange Real and Surreal

Present the same subject or theme in at least two different ways:

(A) as literally and realistically as possible.

(B) in a highly unreal or *surreal* fashion.

20. Pose a Puzzle

Produce an image in which familiar subjects are juxtaposed or joined to create a new significance. In other words, make a "double-take" image, the meaning of which appears at first glance to be obvious, but which, on second examination, becomes something else, i.e., a visual *paradox* or *pun*.

21. Discover the Junkyard

Visit a junkyard or recycling center and, with permission from the owner, photograph as many abstract compositions as you can discover among the jumbled, twisted, and corroded remnants of industry. Work close-up with a single-lens reflex or view camera on a tripod, observing and recording line, form, texture, and color.

22. Explore Your Own Back Yard

Spend one or several days photographing only the subject matter you discover within the bounds of your own yard, farm, city block, or campus. Look up, down, and around. Notice how many objects, shapes, surfaces, and relationships you may have passed by hundreds of times, yet may never have "seen" before.

23. Establish a Sense of Place

Find a landmark or location that intrigues you, and explore it thoroughly with your camera, for example, an abandoned barn, a historic home, a school building, a church. Try to convey the "feel" of the place. See whether you can invoke in your final images the "presence" of the occupants without showing them.

24. Continue a Common Theme

Decide on a motif such as rocking chairs, custom vans, windows, doors, satellite dishes, the number "3," the color yellow, or (more difficult!) an emotional state such as love, joy, solitude, despair, or death. Produce a group of images (a visual essay) that, when viewed together, illustrate your choice of theme.

25. Present a Picture Sequence

Produce a series of images that depend upon continuity for their meaning. Each individual image should be a strong one, but the sequence should have a beginning and an end — a linear relationship that leads to a definite conclusion.

26. Make a Mosaic

Take several pictures of the same subject. Assemble the images to construct either a two- or a three-dimensional representation.

27. Assemble a Montage

Combine several images to create a "seamless" composite photomontage.

28. Document an Event

Document an actual or imagined event or happening, so that essentials of the participants and the occurrence can be understood and shared by viewers.

29. Create Image Magic

Experiment in-depth with one or more special effects techniques in black-and-white or color. Subject matter can be from another assignment, but emphasize the technique. Work with a computer if available.

30. Interview Professionals

Identify several successful imagemakers and interview them. Study examples of their work. Find out how they feel about the field of visual communications as a profession and as an avocation. Find out whether they received formal education or were self-taught. See whether you can learn some valuable "tricks of the trade" from these experts.

JORG JASPER

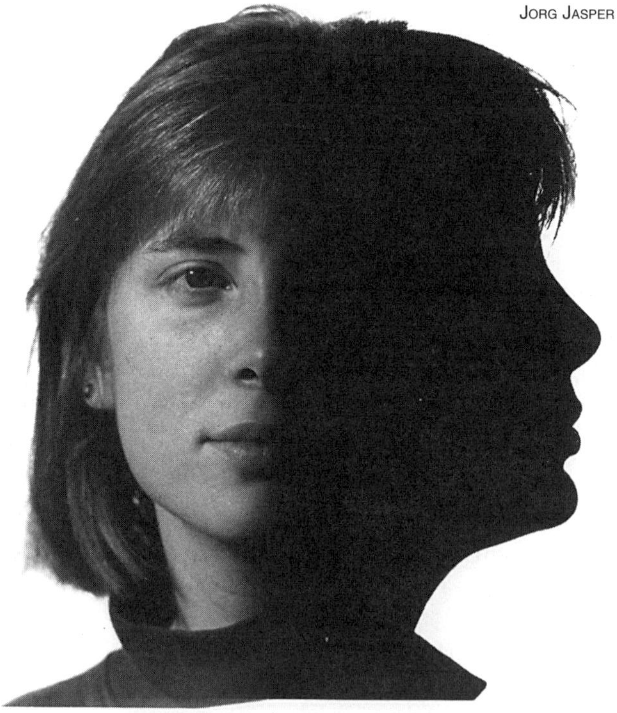

This provocative double-image portrait was created by exposing both negatives against a white background, while the height of the head was kept the same. The two images registered perfectly and were printed as a negative sandwich.

Glossary

aberations Inherent defects in a lens that cause the image to be unsharp, particularly around the edges.

AC Alternating Current. Electricity from wall sockets.

accent light Light directed at a subject from the side or back to add highlights and to separate the subject from the background. Sometimes referred to as a backlight or kicker.

acetic acid Used in diluted form to make stop bath and fixer. Commonly available in 28 percent dilution. Concentrated (glacial) acetic acid is corrosive and must handled very carefully.

achromatic Color corrected. A lens designed to eliminate most chromatic aberrations.

activator Alkaline processing solution that energizes emulsion-incorporated developer. Generally used in a stabilization processor.

acutance Sharpness. The inherent capability of a photographic emulsion to reproduce fine detail.

adapter ring A narrow, threaded ring for attaching accessories such as filters to a lens.

additive colors The red, green, and blue wave lengths that theoretically add up to make white light.

AE Automatic Exposure.

aesthetics Study of the perception of beauty.

AF Automatic Focus.

agitation Movement of the film or paper as it is processed, or movement of the processing solutions, to ensure uniformity.

air bells Bubbles of air causing transparent spots on negatives, resulting from insufficient agitation of film when first immersed in the developer.

airbrush A small compressor-powered paint sprayer used to drop out backgrounds and retouch areas of prints that require an even tone, and to add highlights or outlines. Also a software tool for "painting" on digital images.

aliasing The jagged, stair-step effect along the edges of computer graphics; also called "jaggies."

amateur One who engages in photography or other art primarily for pleasure rather than for profit.

ambient light Light existing naturally at a location (available light).

analyzer An electronic device used to determine filtration and exposure for color printing.

analog Representational or similar in appearance. The opposite of digital.

anastigmat A lens corrected for astigmatism.

ANSI American National Standards Institute. Formerly ASA.

anti-halation backing The colored layer on the back of most films.

aperture Lens opening, controlled by an iris diaphragm and expressed as an f/number or f/stop.

aperture priority On automatic cameras, a mode in which the user selects the aperture, and the camera automatically adjusts the shutter speed.

apochromat A highly corrected lens with an extremely flat field.

application A computer program; specific software.

APS Advanced Photo System. Cameras and processing equipment linked by digital exposure data encoded on special film.

archival An image processed to remove chemicals that may cause fading, staining, or disintegration. Storage methods and containers that prevent chemical deterioration.

artificial light Light brought to the scene by the photographer.

ASA Acronym for American Standards Association. A system for comparing light sensitivity of photographic emulsions now replaced by ISO.

ASMP The American Society of Media Photographers. A professional organization primarily for the benefit of free-lance imagemakers whose work is for publication.

astigmatism A lens aberration that prevents points of light in the image from being brought to a sharp focus.

automatic exposure A mode in which aperture, shutter speed, or both are adjusted by the camera instead of by the photographer.

automatic flash A flash unit containing a light-sensitive cell that shuts itself off when exposure is correct.

automatic focus A system by which a camera adjusts its lens to the distance of whatever is in the center of the viewfinder.

available light Ambient or existing light. Normal illumination found by the photographer in a place where pictures are to be made.

B "Bulb" setting on a shutter. A shutter set on B will remain open as long as the release is held down.

back The part of a camera that holds the film.

backdrop A roll of seamless paper, piece of cloth, or other material used as background for a subject to be photographed.

background The part of a scene visible beyond the principal subject, or a backdrop or wall covering behind the subject. Also negative space — the area surrounding the subject.

background light Light aimed at the background to silhouette the subject or to prevent the subject from visually merging with the background.

backlighting When the main source of illumination comes from behind the subject, toward the camera.
back projection (see rear projection)
backup To copy electronic files to another medium for safe storage.
barn doors Adjustable flaps on a studio light, used to shade parts of the subject or background or to prevent the light from shining into the camera lens.
base Material on which light-sensitive emulsions are coated. Modern films usually are on transparent acetate or polyester base, although paper, glass, metal, and cloth have been used.
baseboard Work surface beneath an enlarger, to which the enlarger column is attached and on which the easel is placed; also the base of a copy stand.
base-plus-fog Density of an unexposed area of a developed film.
bas-relief Low-relief effect created by printing positive and negative images slightly out of register.
bed The base of a view or press camera.
beefcake Slang for sexy photos of attractive men.
bellows A flexible, light-tight connection between a camera lens and the body of the camera.
bellows factor Increase in exposure required when a lens is focused on a very close subject.
between-the-lens shutter A type of camera shutter in which the leaves that open and close are located in the space between lens elements.
bit A single binary digit; the smallest unit of computer information (1 or 0).
bit map The grid of pixels forming an image on a video display terminal (monitor). The intensity and color of each pixel is controlled by bits.
bleach (see also reducer) A chemical treatment that lightens or removes the visible silver image.
bleed An image printed or trimmed without a border; also, when an image flares out and loses sharpness, usually from overexposure.
blend To create a smooth, "seamless" composite image.
block out To paint over parts of an image, such as background, to eliminate unwanted detail.
blocked-up Describes a very dense area in a negative that should have detail, but prints white without texture; usually the result of overexposure and/or overdevelopment.
blotter roll A strip of lintless blotter paper and cloth in which fiber-base prints may be rolled up to be dried.
blowup An enlargement.
boom A stand with adjustable arm, generally used to hold a light, a gobo, or a microphone.
boot To startup a computer.
bounce light Light reaching the subject indirectly because it was aimed at a ceiling, wall, or some other reflecting surface.
box-camera A simple, inexpensive camera with few or no adjustments.
bracketing Making exposures both over and under what "normal" exposure has been determined to be.
brightness Lightness or intensity of a color.
brightness range The extent of the scale of values present in a subject, ranging from the deepest shadows to the most reflective highlights.
broad lighting In portraiture, when the main or key light fully illuminates the side of the subject's face closest to the camera. The effect tends to broaden a thin or narrow face.
bulb The B setting that allows the shutter to remain open as long as the release lever is depressed. (Photographers used to release their shutters by squeezing a rubber bulb on the end of an air hose.)
bulk film 35mm film purchased in long rolls that must be cut into shorter lengths and loaded into cassettes for exposure in a camera.
burned-out The result, in the print, of blocked-up highlights in the negative.
burning-in Giving additional exposure to darken relatively small areas, while shielding the rest of the print from light.
butterfly lighting Portrait lighting technique sometimes employed for glamour portraits of women. The main or key light is placed above and directly in front of the face, casting a symmetrical shadow directly beneath the nose.
byte A group of eight bits, composing each character or pixel displayed on a video screen.
C Abbreviation for Celsius temperature scale.
cable release A flexible attachment that allows the shutter release to be depressed smoothly from a short distance from the camera, and without moving the camera.
camel's-hair brush High-quality soft brush used for spotting prints and removing dust from negatives and lenses.
camera A light-tight box fitted with an image-forming lens or pinhole that focuses onto a light-sensitive surface.
candid Unposed pictures made with or without the subjects' knowledge.
carrier The negative holder in an enlarger or film scanner.
cartridge (see also magazine) A light-tight metal or plastic container for 35mm films.
cassette (see cartridge)
catchlights Tiny reflections of light in a subject's eyes.
CCD Charge Coupled Device. A light sensor that records part of the image in a digital camera or scanner.

CC filters Color Compensating filters that are used to balance the color of the light used to expose color films and papers. CC filters are available in six colors: additive primaries of red, green, and blue; subtractive primaries of cyan, magenta, and yellow; and in various densities.

CD, CD-ROM A compact disc storage medium for digital images, usually containing files that can be "read only" and not "written" to.

center of interest The part of a scene or image that has greatest attraction to the eye of a viewer.

center-weighted A through-the-lens metering system that, in calculating exposure settings, automatically bases the exposure more on light reaching the center of the viewfinder area than on light at the edges of the frame.

changing bag A light-tight cloth bag with elastic openings for the photographer's arms, that can be used for loading or processing film when a darkroom is not available.

characteristic curve A graph depicting the response of a particular emulsion to exposure and development. Also referred to as a D Log E curve because silver density is plotted against the logarithm of the exposure.

cheesecake Slang for sexy photos of attractive women.

chiaroscuro Compositional arrangement of light against dark, and dark against light.

chroma Color saturation or intensity.

chromatic aberration Inability of a lens to focus all colors of light in a common plane. The result is a blurred image in black-and-white, or color fringing with color materials.

chrome A color transparency.

chromogenic Emulsion in which the image is composed of dyes instead of silver.

cinch marks Scratches on roll film, caused by pulling on the free end of the roll.

circle of confusion A tiny cluster of light rays that are slightly out of focus at the image plane. The size of acceptable circles of confusion determines the limits of depth of field.

circular polarizer A special polarizing filter for use on automatic and autofocus cameras.

clearing agent (see also hypo clearing agent) A chemical solution used after fixer to shorten washing time.

clearing time The length of time required by the fixer to remove all visible traces of undeveloped silver halides from film emulsion.

click stops Slight indentations that give positive indication of f/stop or shutter-speed settings. Some lenses have click stops between the marked f/stops; these half-stops should not be confused with whole f/stops when calculating exposure.

close-up A photograph made nearer to the subject than the normal focusing range of the camera; may require use of a close-up lens, supplementary bellows, or other attachments.

CMYK Cyan, Magenta, Yellow and blacK — the subtractive primaries, or process colors used in color printing.

coating A chemical layer applied to lens surfaces to reduce flare caused by reflections within the lens.

cocking Tensioning the shutter mechanism before making an exposure.

cold light Fluorescent light source for a diffusion-type enlarger.

cold mounting Attaching prints to a backing with peel-off adhesive sheets, spray adhesive, or cement.

cold tones Bluish or blue-black overall tinting in a monochrome photograph; in color, the green-blue-violet portion of the spectrum.

collage A composite "paste-up" image assembled from photographs combined with other media.

color analyzer A device for determining filtration and exposure when making color prints.

color balance Apparent accuracy or naturalness of colors as reproduced in a color photograph.

color cast An overall tint of one color in a color photograph.

color head An enlarger lamphouse equipped with a system of adjustable dichroic filters for changing the color of the light source.

color sensitivity The effective response of an emulsion to different wavelengths of light. Panchromatic emulsions are sensitive to all visible colors; orthochromatic materials are not sensitive to red; some special copy films are sensitive only to blue.

color separation The process of photographing or electronically scanning an image through three primary color filters (red, green, and blue) to produce black-and-white separation negatives used for color reproduction.

color temperature A system for measuring the color of light sources in terms of relative warmth in degrees Kelvin (°K). Daylight and flash are relatively cool or bluish white, whereas incandescent lamps are warm or yellowish by comparison.

coma A lens aberration that causes unsharpness around the edges of the image.

compensating developer A self-limiting formula that tends to develop shadow areas (low zones) fully, without overdeveloping or blocking up the higher values.

complementary colors Any two hues of light that combine, in the additive system, to reflect white; or, in the subtractive system, to absorb all wave lengths, resulting in black or gray.

composition Consciously assembling and arranging the visual elements within an image.

composite An image consisting of more than one layer.

condenser enlarger An enlarger in which a system of large lenses collects light from the lamp and directs it uniformly through the negative.

contact print A same-size print made by placing the emulsion sides of the negative and the printing paper together under pressure and exposing the paper to light passing through the negative.

contact screen A film screen containing halftone dots. When placed into contact with photosensitive material during exposure, the resulting screened image may be reproduced by offset or screen-process printing.

contact sheet A contact print made from several negatives at the same time on one sheet of paper. Also referred to as a proof sheet.

continuous tone An image consisting of continuous gradations of gray values.

contraction Shortened development, resulting in a negative with reduced contrast.

contrast The range of difference in density between dark and light areas of the same image.

contrast filter (1) A filter used on the camera lens in black-and-white photography to lighten or darken one color to separate it from another. (2) A filter used on the enlarger to adjust print contrast on variable-contrast paper.

contrast grade A system of numbering relative contrast of printing paper (usually 0-5). Paper that is not variable-contrast must be purchased by grade, and is not affected by filters.

contrasty An image with a wide range of difference in brightness between dark and light areas.

convergence Parallel lines that do not appear parallel in a photograph.

conversion filters Colored filters enabling color film balanced either for daylight or for tungsten light to be exposed satisfactorily in the other kind of light.

converter A supplementary lens attachment that changes the effective focal length.

convertible lens A lens that can be taken apart and the two major components used either together or separately at longer focal lengths.

cool colors The green-blue end of the color spectrum.

copyright Exclusive legal right to the marketing and distribution of published copies of photographs, films, videos, and other works of art and literature.

copy stand A camera support with baseboard used for copying documents and photographing small objects.

correction filters Warm or cool colored filters used to improve color rendition when illumination differs from the color temperature for which the film was balanced.

covering power The ability of a lens to produce a sharp image large enough to fill the format for which it was designed.

CP filters Color Printing filters usually placed inside an enlarger lamphouse.

CPU Central Processing Unit. The body of a computer that houses the hard drive, memory chips, and main circuitry.

critique Authoritative evaluation and constructive criticism.

cropping Trimming or masking the borders of an image to improve the composition.

cross lighting More than one main light source appearing to come from opposite sides of the subject.

curvature of field An aberration causing the center of a lens to focus on a different plane than the edges.

cut film Sheet film.

cutter (see gobo)

darkroom A light-tight room for carrying out photographic processing.

dark slide The light-tight cover of a film holder that must be removed before making an exposure.

DAT Digital Audio Tape. A backup system for computer files that uses tape cartridges similar to audio cassettes.

daylight film Color film balanced for use with light of about 5500°K, such as midday sunlight or electronic flash.

day rate A pricing arrangement whereby a photographer agrees to make as many photographs during a working day as the client requests, for a fixed price plus expenses.

dedicated flash A flash unit that sets the camera shutter speed and aperture automatically, and shows in the viewfinder when the flash is ready to fire.

definition Sharpness; clarity of detail.

densitometer An instrument for measuring the darkness or density of a negative or print.

density The opacity or light-stopping power of a negative. A dense negative appears quite dark or opaque, compared to a thin negative.

depth of field The distance between the nearest and farthest objects that appear to be in acceptable focus in a photograph.

depth of focus the shallow zone inside the camera within which the plane of focus (the film) can be moved toward or away from a focused lens without a significant change in the sharpness of the image.

derivation An abstract special effect created from a photographic image.

design Intentional arrangement of visual elements such as line, form, texture, color, etc., within an image.

developer A chemical solution that makes visible an exposed latent image.

developing tank A container, usually light-tight, into which film is placed for processing.

diaphragm An adjustable device, ordinarily located between lens elements, that controls the size of the aperture that allows light into the camera.

dichroic filters Specially-coated adjustable glass filters in the head of an enlarger designed for color printing.

diffraction The tendency for light waves to bend and scatter as they pass around the edge of an obstruction.

diffusion The scattering of light waves in random directions as they are reflected from a rough surface or transmitted through a translucent filter.

diffusion enlarger An enlarger that uses translucent glass or plastic instead of condenser lenses to even out the light that passes through the negative.

digital An image that has been recorded as binary digits (bits).

digital camera An instrument that records light impulses as binary digits instead of analog images.

digitizing Converting an analog (visual) image to electronic data that can be enhanced, manipulated and stored by a computer.

DIN Deutsch Industrie Norm. A film-speed comparison system used in Europe.

diopter A measure of the relative magnification of a supplementary close-up lens. Such lenses are commonly provided in +1, +2, +3 and +4 diopters. The higher the number, the "stronger" the effect.

disc A digital storage medium that can be "read" only (as CD-ROM).

disk A digital storage medium that can be "written" to (as hard disk).

dissolve A smooth visual transition in which one projected or video image fades out on the screen while another fades in; a cross fade.

dithering Apparent softening of the edges of a digital image.

Dmax The maximum density possible in high-contrast film or in a transparency.

dodging Shading part of the image from light during printing to make it appear lighter.

DOS Disk Operating System. A type of system software used in many personal computers.

double exposure Two or more exposures made on the same frame of film, either intentionally or accidentally.

double-weight Photographic paper thicker than single-weight.

drive, disk drive Large capacity storage device either built into a computer or attached to it.

dropout A high-contrast image from which the intermediate gray tones have been eliminated, leaving only black and white; also describes eliminating the background from around an object in a photograph by masking.

drum A cylindrical plastic container generally used for processing color prints.

dry down To become darker when dry. Most prints appear slightly darker and less contrasty when dry then during processing.

dry mounting A permanent bonding process in which a sheet of thermoplastic material is placed between a print and a sheet of mounting board and then subjected to heat and pressure.

dulling spray A removable aerosol compound that reduces glare in highly reflective surfaces.

duotone A monochrome image reproduced with an additional color separation. Usually the first tone is black.

DX coding Checkered markings on 35mm film magazines that automatically set the film speed in automatic cameras.

dye sublimation (thermal dye transfer) A color printing process that vaporizes dyes and then condenses them on paper to form an image.

dye transfer A color printing process in which full-sized black-and-white separation matrices are dyed yellow, magenta and cyan; the dye images are transferred in register onto a single sheet of prepared paper.

easel The paper holder, usually with adjustable masking strips, for use on an enlarger baseboard.

EI (Exposure Index) Film speed.

electronic flash A repeatable light source, producing a brilliant flash of light usually less than 1/500 second in duration. Sometimes referred to as strobe.

element One of the glass components of a lens.

electrostatic A reproduction process that forms an image by distributing toner particles on a magnetized drum, and then fuses them with heat.

emulsion The gelatin coating on photographic films and papers in which are suspended light-sensitive image-forming chemicals.

enlargement A photographic image, made by projection, that is larger than the original negative or transparency.

enlarger A projection printer for making enlarged (or reduced) reproductions of negatives or transparencies.

EPS Encapsulated Post Script. A commonly used format for storing digital text and image files.

esthetics (see aesthetics)

etching Removing small areas of unwanted density from a photographic image by shaving away the emulsion with a very sharp blade.

existing light Ambient or available light naturally occurring in a scene to be photographed.

expansion Extended development, resulting in an effective increase in negative contrast.

exposure The total amount of light allowed to reach photosensitive material. Exposure is the product of light intensity, as controlled by the aperture, and the length of time the shutter is permitted to remain open.

exposure factor The amount exposure must be increased when extending the lens for extreme close-up photography.

exposure index Film speed. Usually the same as ISO rating.

exposure latitude (see latitude)

exposure meter An instrument for measuring the intensity of light either falling on or reflected from a subject, for determining exposure settings.

extender A supplementary lens that increases effective focal length.

extension tubes Light-tight rings or tubes placed between the lens and the camera body to enable focusing on very close objects.

f The symbol engraved on some lenses to indicate focal length — for example, f=13.5cm.

F Fahrenheit temperature scale.

fade-in Gradual appearance of a projected or video image from black.

fade-out Gradual disappearance of a projected or video image to black.

Farmer's reducer A bleaching solution of potassium ferricyanide and sodium thiosulfate (fixer).

fast Film or paper that is very sensitive to light (high ISO number); also a lens with a relatively large maximum aperture, e.g., f/1.2 or f/1.4.

FB Fiber Base. Fiber-based paper.

feathering Evening out intensity of illumination by tilting a light source so that the brightest part of the beam is directed toward the more distant parts of the subject. Also softening the edge of a digital selection.

fiber-base paper "Conventional" paper that requires longer processing time than resin-coated (RC) papers.

field camera A lightweight, folding view camera.

fill light A light source or reflector directed into the shadow areas of the subject to reduce the brightness range or lower the lighting ratio (contrast) of the subject.

film Material on which the image is recorded in a camera. Usually consists of a light-sensitive emulsion coated on a flexible acetate or plastic base.

film back Removable device for holding roll film used on a medium- or large-format camera.

film clip A toothed clamp or a spring-type clothespin used to suspend processed film during drying.

film holder Removable device for holding two sheets of film, one on each side, for exposure in a view or press camera.

film magazine (see also cartridge) The metal or plastic container that 35mm films are packaged in.

film pack A metal or plastic container holding several individual sheets of film. Each sheet is moved into position for exposure by pulling a paper tab.

film plane The place inside a camera where the lens focuses the image.

film speed (see exposure index or ISO) The relative sensitivity of film to light.

filter A piece of transparent gelatin, glass, or plastic, usually colored, that will absorb selected wave lengths of light while transmitting others. Also a software program for modifying the appearance of a digital image.

filter factor The number of times basic exposure must be multiplied (for example, 4X=four times, or two stops) to compensate for light absorbed by a filter.

filter pack The combined filtration required in color printing.

fisheye lens An extremely wide-angle lens (as much as 180°) that usually gives noticeable curved distortion around the edges of the picture.

fixer The processing solution that dissolves unexposed and undeveloped silver halides from the emulsion, making the film or paper no longer sensitive to light; also called hypo or fixing bath.

flag (see gobo)

flare Non image-forming light reflected from within the lens and/or camera and resulting in overall fog density, halo effects, or repeated patterns of density that often take the shape of the lens diaphragm. Flare is most noticeable when photographing subjects that are strongly backlighted or when light sources appear in the picture.

flash A brief, intense discharge of light from a flash unit.

flashing Selective darkening of part of an enlargement by (1) exposure to raw light from the enlarger lamp with the negative removed, (2) local use of a small flashlight, or (3) brief, uniform exposure of film to light for the purpose of reducing contrast.

flash meter An exposure meter that determines exposure for photography by flash lighting.

flash synchronization Adjustment of camera timing so that the flash unit fires when the shutter is fully open.

flat A photographic negative or print that is low in contrast; also a large panel or screen used as a studio background, space divider, or reflector.

flood A light source designed to illuminate a relatively large area uniformly.

floppy disk Removable magnetic device for storing relatively small amounts of digital data.

f/number A number obtained by dividing the focal length of a lens by the effective aperture. When marked on a lens, it is referred to as an f/stop.

focal length The distance from the center of the lens to the film when the lens is focused at infinity.

focal plane The surface inside the camera where light from the lens forms a focused image.

focal plane shutter A curtain shutter located in the camera just ahead of the film, which exposes the film through a slit of adjustable width.

focus To adjust the relationship between lens, film plane, and subject, so that a sharply defined image is formed on the film.

focusing cloth An opaque drape used to shield the ground glass of a view camera from extraneous light while composing and focusing.

fog Overall density in a negative or print, not part of the normal image, resulting from extraneous light or chemical action.

format The size and proportions of the image area produced by a particular camera. 35mm cameras are considered to be of small format; 6x6cm and 6x7cm cameras of medium format; and 4x5 and larger cameras as large format.

four-color The process generally used to print color photographs in books, magazines, posters, etc. Black-and-white separation negatives are scanned through color filters from the original image, then four separate plates are made for printing on a press with cyan, magenta, yellow and black inks.

frame To compose; also a single negative or slide from a roll, or the useful picture area on the film.

frame grabbing Converting a still video image (frame) to digital data for storage and manipulation with a computer.

free-lancer A self-employed person who produces photographs for sale, either on assignment or on speculation.

fresnel A shallow, concentric lens used to focus the illumination from a studio spotlight.

frilling Loosening and detachment of emulsion from along the edges of film or paper during processing; usually caused by high temperatures and prolonged soaking.

f/stop An aperture setting on a lens.

front projection Rephotographing a projected image or projecting a background behind a subject, using a projector located on the same side of the screen as the camera.

full-frame An image as framed in the camera; not cropped.

full-scale A photographic image with a wide range of tonal values from deep black to brilliant white, with many gray values (zones) in between.

fuzzy Not sharp; blurred or out of focus.

gamma A numerical expression of contrast.

gel A colored gelatin or acetate filter placed in front of a lens or light source.

gelatin A jellied animal protein substance used as the basic medium in which the light-sensitive silver salts in photographic emulsions are suspended.

ghost image A blurred, secondary image of a moving subject recorded on the film by ambient light when flash is used in daylight or in a brightly lighted interior. Also a second image recorded out of register, caused by slight movement of the camera or enlarger during exposure.

GIF Graphic Interchange Format. A digital file format used for on-line transfer of images.

glossy Photographic paper with a highly-reflective surface.

gobo A small opaque or translucent panel, usually mounted on a boom stand, used to shade part of the subject or to protect the camera from light that could cause flare; also called a flag or cutter.

gradation A scale of tonal values ranging from white, through gray, to black.

graduate A calibrated cylindrical container used to mix and measure liquids.

graduated background A screen-printed plastic or paper sheet that begins in one color or value and gradually changes to another.

graduated filter A filter that is partly clear with increasing density across the other part.

grain Particles or clumps of metallic silver or dyes that form a photographic image. Grain is not usually noticeable unless the image is enlarged.

grain magnifier An optical device resembling a miniature microscope that is used to aid in focusing the image from an enlarger.

graphic arts The science and technology of reproducing images, usually in the fields of art and printing.

graphics card (or board) A circuit board installed in a computer that enables it to capture and process digital images.

graphics tablet An interface surface upon which an artist draws with a stylus to create images in a computer; a mouse replacement.

gray card A standard, neutral test card of 18 percent reflectance. Representing Zone V of the Zone System, a gray card is the basis for determining average exposure and a neutral reference for determining color balance.

gray scale A standardized rendition of tonal values, frequently shown in nine steps (Zones I through IX) arranged one stop apart in a sequence of increasing density. Computer imaging programs divide continuous-tone grayscale images into up to 256 levels of gray.

ground glass The focusing surface in view and reflex cameras.

guide number Number used with non-automatic flash units to determine f/stop setting at any given distance. Divide the guide number by the distance to get the f/stop.

halation Blurred density surrounding extremely overexposed areas of a negative, such as light sources in the picture.

halftone Printer's term for a continuous-tone image that has been broken up into a dot pattern for reproduction.

halides Silver compounds that provide the light-sensitive component of photographic emulsions.

halogen lamp A compact and highly efficient tungsten light source with a quartz envelope instead of glass.

hanger A frame, usually stainless steel, for tank processing of sheet films.

hard High contrast

hard copy A paper or film printout from a computer printer or microfilm reader.

hard disk (hard drive) A device for storing and accessing large amounts of digital data. Usually installed permanently inside a computer.

hardener A chemical solution, usually incorporated in the fixing bath, that toughens the emulsion and increases its resistance to scratching, frilling and reticulation.

hardware A term describing computer equipment, as distinguished from programs or applications (software).

haze filter (see UV filter) A colorless glass filter often used as a protective lens cover.

high contrast Predominantly black-and-white with few, if any, intermediate values of gray; a scene or image with an extended brightness range.

high-key An image predominantly light or white in overall tone, dark areas or bright color accents being very small, if present.

highlights The brightest areas, or highest values, in a scene or image; the corresponding dense areas of a negative.

holder A film holder.

hot shoe A clip on top of a camera for mounting a flash unit that has an electrical connection in its base.

hot-spot An unwanted concentration of light, usually toward the center of the beam of a studio light, enlarger, or projector.

hue Color identification such as red, green, or blue.

hydroquinone A vigorous developing agent; a chemical component of many developer formulas.

hyperfocal distance The distance from the lens to the near limit of depth of field when the lens is focused at infinity.

hypo (see fixer)

hypo clearing agent Washing aid. A bath used between fixing and washing to shorten washing time and increase permanence of the image.

image Photographic representation of a subject; a visible picture, whether reproduced optically or digitally.

image capture Recording of a visual (analog) image to later be digitized and computer-enhanced.

image enhancement Improving or modifying an image; usually refers to computer-manipulated digitized images.

imaging The broad field of visual communications technology and allied arts. Including but not limited to photography, film making, videography, graphic arts and computer graphics.

incandescent light Light from a tungsten filament bulb as distinguished in color temperature from fluorescent tubes, vapor arcs, electronic flash, and daylight.

incident light Light reaching, or falling on, the subject, as distinguished from light reflected by the subject.

incident meter An exposure meter designed or adapted for measuring the intensity of light falling on the subject.

infinity The distance, usually 50 to 100 feet from the camera, beyond which distant subjects will be in focus without further adjustment of the lens. Indicated by the symbol ∞.

infrared Invisible, long wavelengths of electromagnetic radiation. May be used to record images on specially sensitized film exposed through a deep red filter that blocks all or most visible light.

inkjet A printer that sprays tiny dots of colored dye on paper in patterns that recreate a digital image.

intensifier A chemical solution for increasing image density and/or contrast; usually for making printable an underdeveloped negative.

intensity Brightness or value of a color.

interchangeable lens A lens that can be completely removed from the camera body and replaced by another.

internegative A copy negative made from a positive transparency for the purpose of making prints.

inverse square law A principle of physics that intensity of illumination varies inversely with the square of the distance from the light source. This means that doubling the distance between the light source and the subject allows only one-fourth as much light to reach the subject. Open up the lens two stops to compensate.

iris The adjustable part of the diaphragm, controlling the size of the aperture admitting light through the lens.

ISO International Standards Organization. Formerly ASA. A system for comparing light sensitivity of emulsions.

JPEG Joint Photographic Experts Group. A digital image file compression format used to save disk space.

Kelvin temperature A system for comparing visual warmth or coolness of light sources. Daylight and electronic flash average about 5500°K (bluish) and most professional incandescent studio lamps operate at 3200°K (yellowish).

key light The principal source of directional illumination and shadows.

kicker (see accent light)

Kodalith™ (see litho film)

Kodalk™ Kodak trade name for balanced alkali used in developers and toners.

lamp A light bulb or light source.

lamphouse The part of an enlarger or projector that contains the light source.

lasso A software tool used to select a portion of a digital image.

latent image The invisible image produced by exposure of photosensitive material to light. The latent image must be developed to become visible.

latitude The amount of over- or underexposure possible without the result being an unprintable negative or unacceptable transparency.

layer One level in a composite digital image.

LCD Liquid Crystal Display. A type of screen on a camera or exposure meter that displays digital data.

leader A strip of film or paper provided at the beginning of a roll to aid in threading the material into a camera, processing machine, or projector.

leaf shutter An iris-like series of overlapping metal leaves, usually placed between elements of the lens, that opens and closes to allow a predetermined amount of light to enter the camera.

LED Light-Emitting Diode. An illuminated display or indicator light, usually colored, used in cameras and exposure meters.

lens The image-forming part of a camera, usually glass, the varying thickness of which causes light rays to be bent predictably as they pass through the denser medium, forming an image in a single plane.

lens barrel A metal or polycarbonate tube in which lens elements are mounted, usually containing an iris diaphragm, but often without a shutter.

lensboard A metal or wooden panel on which an interchangeable lens is mounted for use on enlargers and large-format cameras.

lens cap An opaque protective cover placed over either the front or rear element of a lens. Many photographers keep UV filters on each of their lenses for this purpose.

lens cleaner A special solvent that is effective in removing fingerprints, smudges, salt water, hard water, and wetting agent smears from lens and film surfaces.

lens hood A tubular or rectangular attachment for shielding the front of a lens from extraneous light that might cause flare in the image.

lens mount Both the part of the camera body that supports the lens, and especially in 35mm cameras, the metal barrel that contains the lens elements, diaphragm, and focusing mechanism.

lens shade (see lens hood).

lens tissue A special nonabrasive, lintless paper recommended for cleaning optical glass surfaces.

light Visible electromagnetic radiation; illumination.

lighting ratio A measure of the relative brightness of highlights and shadows; for example, a ratio of 4:1 means two stops difference.

light meter An exposure meter.

light-tight Capable of excluding all light, such as a camera, darkroom, or changing bag.

light trap A maze-like arrangement that excludes light, yet permits people to enter or leave a darkroom, or allows processing solutions to be poured into and out of a tank.

limbo A scene or image in which the subject is brightly lighted against a very dark background.

limn effect A scene or image in which the subject is very flatly lighted against a light background; a dark line (limn) appears around the subject.

line copy A high-contrast image consisting only of black and white, without middle tones.

litho film An extremely high-contrast film intended primarily for line and halftone reproduction in graphic arts processes; referred to by manufacturer's trade names, such as Kodalith.

long lens A lens of greater than normal focal length for a particular format camera.

loupe A magnifying glass of high quality used to examine fine image details.

low-key An image predominantly dark or black in overall tone, usually with only relatively small white or brightly colored accents.

LZW A digital image file-compression format used to save disk space.

M Flash synchronization mark on some older camera shutters to indicate the setting for flashbulbs.

Mackie lines (see also Sabattier effect) Thin outlines that appear around areas within a solarized image.

macro lens A lens especially corrected for close-up work. An extended focusing range allows very close camera-to-subject distances without accessory attachments. Sometimes the term micro appears in the name of a macro lens.

magneto optical A type of removable-disk storage system.

main light (see key light)

magazine Light-tight film container that fits into or attaches to a camera.

manual mode When the photographer adjusts the aperture, shutter speed, and focus.

marquee A software tool used to select a portion of a digital image.

masking Blocking out portions of the image area, such as the background or edge, with an opaque medium such as paint, tape, paper or film. Also, the use of a low-contrast film positive in register with a negative, or a low-contrast black-and-white negative in register with a color transparency to reduce contrast in printing or duplicating.

master An original reserved for printing or duplicating.

mat A cut-out cardboard frame placed around a print or transparency for presentation and display.

matrix A positive gelatin relief image used in dye-transfer color printing.

matrix metering A system whereby an exposure meter samples portions of the entire scene, using a microprocessor to calculate which portions represent the subject and which are background.

matte Dull, nonreflective surface.

matte box A large lens hood, into which are inserted gelatin filters or cutouts for making multiple - exposure photographs.

MB Abbreviation for megabyte.

megabyte (MB) One million bytes. A basic measure of digital image size.

memory Computer image-storage space. Measured in megabytes of RAM.

menu A list of user options presented on a computer screen.

metol A relatively soft-working developing agent that is a chemical component of many developer formulas.

microprism The structure of the focusing circle in the center of the viewing area in some single-lens reflex cameras.

middle gray Zone V; the standard 18-percent reflectance to which exposure meters are calibrated.

middle tones Gray values falling between black and white.

model A person posing for photographs.

model release A document signed by the subject of a photograph, or parent if the model is underage, or owner of a pet or property, giving permission for editorial or commercial publication.

modeling light A small incandescent lamp placed within a studio flash unit to allow visual placement of the light.

modem A device for connecting a personal computer to outside sources of output and input.

monitor The video-display unit attached to a computer.

monochrome An image or process employing a range of tones of a single hue, or grays if black-and-white.

monopod A camera support with only one leg.

montage (see photomontage)

mosaic (see photomosaic)

mottling Uneven or splotchy tones caused by underdevelopment with insufficient agitation.

mouse A hand-held device for interfacing with computer software.

muddy An image that appears flat, gray, or mottled.

multi-image A slide presentation that uses two or more projectors programmed together.

multi-media An audiovisual event that incorporates various presentation modes, e.g., slides, film, video, lasers, musicians, live performers. Also applies to digital entertainment and educational recordings combining text, sound, still pictures, and motion sequences.

narrow lighting (see short lighting)

ND filter Neutral-density filter.

negative A photographic image in which the tones are reversed from the original subject — that is, shadows appear light or transparent while light areas in the subject appear dark or dense; opposite of a positive image.

negative carrier A frame for holding negatives in position for printing in an enlarger or for scanning.

negative space The background of an image that surrounds the main subject.

neutral-density filter A gray filter intended to reduce the intensity of light without changing its color. Available in increments of .30 density which equals one stop.

NFS Not For Sale.

nonsilver processes Techniques used by printmakers to reproduce photographic images with dyes and other chemicals instead of silver compounds.

normal lens A lens with a focal length approximately equal to the diagonal of the film format the lens is designed to cover; the standard lens normally supplied with a camera.

notching code A system of notches cut into one edge of most sheet films to identify the type of film and to indicate the emulsion side when loading film holders in the dark.

NPPA National Press Photographers Association; a professional group for photojournalists.

object An inanimate subject in a photograph.

one-shot developer A developer that is stored in concentrated stock solution, diluted for one-time use, and then discarded.

opaque Incapable of transmitting light; also, a red or black paint used for blocking out or masking areas of a negative that are not to be printed.

opaqueing Painting out small imperfections in a high-contrast negative or positive.

open flash Method for taking flash pictures in which the camera is placed on a tripod, the shutter is set to B or T and opened, the flash is fired manually, and the shutter is closed.

opening up Increasing the size of the aperture of a lens. Using a smaller f/stop number — for example, opening up from f/8 to f/5.6.

ortho film (orthochromatic) An emulsion sensitive to blue and green wave lengths of light, but not sensitive to red.

outdated Film or paper that has not been used before its expiration date.

overdevelop To give more than the normal amount of development. With film, overdevelopment increases contrast.

overexpose To give more than normal exposure to light, resulting in an excessively dense negative, an unacceptably dark print, or a color transparency or slide that is lacking in density and color saturation..

oxidation Deterioration of chemicals from contact with oxygen in the air.

page rate A pricing arrangement by which a publication agrees to pay a fixed rate for photographs and text based on the amount of space they occupy in the publication.

painting with light A technique for moving a single light around a darkened interior or back and forth across a stationary subject while the camera shutter is kept open. The effect is soft, diffuse lighting.

palette The selection of colors available in a computer graphics system; also a dialog box for accessing software tools and features.

panchromatic An emulsion sensitive to all colors of visible light.

panning Following a moving subject with the camera during exposure.

panorama camera A special instrument that uses either a very wide-angle lens or a pivoting lens to record a wide horizontal view.

paper The sensitized paper used in making photographic prints.

paper grade Numbers that refer to relative contrast from 0 (very soft), 1 (soft), through 2 (normal), to 3, 4, and 5 (hard and very hard). Papers are available graded in this way or as variable-contrast.

paper negative A negative image on photographic paper, either exposed directly in the camera or printed from a positive transparency. Usually the paper negative is printed again, resulting in a positive print. If the paper negative is a final product, it properly would be referred to as a negative print.

parallax The difference in framing between what is seen through a camera viewfinder and what is actually recorded by the lens.

PC Abbreviation for Personal Computer.

PC cord An electrical cord that connects the flash contact stud on a camera with a flash unit.

peripherals External devices attached to a computer, such as modems, scanners, printers, and disk drives.

perspective Two-dimensional representation of three-dimensional space; refers to relative size of objects, convergence of parallel lines, variations of tone with distance, and camera viewpoint.

pH Measure of acidity or alkalinity of a chemical solution.

photo CD Laser-optical storage medium for digitized images.

photocomposition Setting printer's type photographically.

Photo-Flo™ Kodak trade name for a wetting agent commonly used as a final bath to aid in rapid and even drying of film.

photo essay A group of pictures that collectively describe subject matter or create a mood or feeling.

photoflood An incandescent lamp bulb of high intensity, but limited life, with a color temperature of 3400°K.

photogenic Someone or something that looks good in pictures.

photogram A shadow picture made by placing objects on the sensitized surface of a sheet of photographic paper or film and exposing to light.

photogrammetry The technology of creating maps from aerial photographs; also uses of photography in scientific measurement.

photojournalism Editorial use of imaging as distinguished from commercial and advertising.

photolithography Offset printing process.

photomacrography The making of extreme close-up photographs of small objects without using a microscope.

photomicrography The making of photographs through a microscope.

photomontage A composite image consisting of several photographs assembled together.

photomosaic A single image assembled from smaller photographs of segments of a subject or scene.

photomural A very big enlargement, usually for wall decoration.

photosensitive Capable of chemical change from the effects of exposure to light.

Photoshop™ Adobe trade name for widely used imaging software.

pictorialism "Romantic" or "pleasing" pictures, as contrasted with realistic representation.

picture story A series of photographs with an intended sequence.

pinhole A tiny, clear spot in an image resulting either from a speck of dust on the film during exposure or from an air bell during development; also, the image-forming aperture in a pinhole camera.

pinhole camera A simple camera that focuses light through a tiny pinhole aperture instead of a lens.

pinup Slang for a sexy glamour photo.

pix Abbreviation for "pictures."

pixel Picture Element. A one-byte unit of digital information used to form an image that can be stored and manipulated in a computer.

plate Photosensitive emulsion coated onto a glass support. Metal or plastic master for offset printing.

place In the Zone System, to match an actual light value in the subject with a desired gray value in the print.

polarizing filter A neutral gray filter that, because of its optical structure, can reduce or eliminate glare reflected from some surfaces.

Polaroid® Trade mark of Polaroid Corporation; used generically to mean "instant" photograph.

POR Price On Request.

portfolio A group of photographs assembled to show when applying for a job or soliciting work from a client; also a limited edition selection of prints offered for sale.

portrait Image of a person or animal.

positive A photographic image in which the tones or colors are similar to those in the original subject; opposite of a negative.

positive space The subject matter in a picture; background is referred to as negative space.

posterization A high-contrast process in which some detail is eliminated and the tonal scale usually is limited to three or four values or colors.

postvisualization Creating images, especially composites, in the darkroom or at a computer terminal, that were not fully conceived when the original photographs were taken.

power pack Case containing capacitors and batteries or AC connection for powering electronic flash.

PP of A Professional Photographers of America, Inc. A major trade association principally for studio owners and corporate imagemakers.

presoak To soak film briefly in water before development.

preset diaphragm An adjustment on some lenses to allow focusing at maximum aperture and then manual stopping down to a predetermined f/stop for exposure; accomplished automatically on most modern single-lens reflex cameras.

press camera An obsolete type of large-format camera with many features of a view camera but designed for hand use.

press-focus A button or lever on some shutters that allows the image to be seen on the ground glass without setting the shutter to B or T.

previsualization Anticipation of the forms, relationships, and tonal values of a scene or subject as they will appear in a finished print.

primary colors The basic hues, or colors, of light or pigment from which other colors may be blended.

print A final photographic image, usually a positive representation on paper.

printing frame A frame with glass and a removable pressure back used for holding negative and paper together when making contact prints.

printing-out A process of printing in which a visible image is produced by direct exposure to light, without development.

prism A solid, transparent optical form that bends light. Most single-lens reflex cameras use a prism to provide a large, bright viewfinder image that is right side up and laterally correct.

process camera A large-format sheet-film camera, usually fitted with a highly-corrected apochromatic lens, designed for line and halftone copying.

processing Subjecting photographic materials to chemical treatment in sequence, such as develop, stop, fix, and wash.

processor A machine that automatic processes film or prints.

professional One who earns a significant portion of personal income from a trade or profession; also work meeting a high standard of quality.

program Digitally coded instructions stored in a computer, camera, or processor that enable it to perform specific tasks. Programs are referred to as "software" to differentiate from equipment which is "hardware."

programmed An exposure mode that can be set into the camera so that both aperture and shutter will be set automatically.

projection printing Enlarging.

projector A camera in reverse; a machine with a lens and light source that projects an image, usually greatly enlarged, from a small transparency, negative, print, or video image.

proof A test print or sample.

proof sheet A contact print made from several negatives simultaneously on one sheet of paper; a contact sheet.

props Properties. Accessories used in setting up a studio photograph.

pull To decrease film development in an attempt to compensate for known overexposure.

push To increase film development in an attempt to compensate for known underexposure.

quartz lights (see also halogen lamps) Compact, highly efficient incandescent light sources characterized by relatively long life, consistent light intensity, and uniform 3200°K color temperature.

RAM Random Access Memory. The memory or working space used by a computer to process data. Large amounts of RAM (many megabytes) are required to manipulate high-resolution digital images .

rangefinder A system of prisms and lenses that aids focusing by presenting two images simultaneously. When the two images are brought together, the camera is in focus.

RC paper Resin-Coated paper. Printing paper with a water-resistant base that allows for rapid processing, short washing time, and quick drying.

ready light An indicator that an electronic flash unit has charged sufficiently to make an exposure.

rear projection Projecting from the back of a translucent screen (the side away from the audience or a camera using the projected image as a background).

reciprocity The principle that the amount of exposure varies directly in proportion to changes in light intensity or time. Reciprocity departure occurs at very long exposure times or with extremely short exposures with high-intensity flash.

recycling time The time required for a flash unit to recharge sufficiently for another exposure.

red-eye The effect of light near the camera reflecting back from the retinas of the subject's eyes. Often a problem with flash mounted on the camera.

reducer A chemical solution that reduces the density of a negative or print by dissolving some of the silver that forms the image.

reducing agent Chemical term for a developing agent such as metol or hydroquinone.

reel A metal or plastic spiral-flanged spool on which roll film is wound for processing.

reflected-light meter The type of exposure meter that reads light reflected or emitted by the subject.

reflection The rebounding or redirection of light from a surface; also, an image that appears to be beyond or within a shiny surface such as water, a window, or a mirror.

reflector A surface such as cardboard, fabric, or foil, used to redirect light onto a subject.

reflex camera A camera in which the image formed by the lens is reflected by a mirror to a ground-glass surface for focusing.

refraction The bending of light rays as they pass from one transparent medium into another of different density, as through a lens.

register To superimpose one image over another so that their outlines coincide.

Rembrandt lighting (see also short lighting) Portrait lighting in which the shadow side of the face is toward the camera.

replenisher A concentrated additive placed into a used developer or other processing solution to maintain constant strength and to prolong its useful life.

resolution Sharpness of the image. Resolution depends primarily on the resolving power of the lens and the acutance of the sensitized material used. Also the number of pixels comprising a digital image.

resolving power The ability of a lens to reproduce fine detail.

restoration Repairing or improving the appearance of faded, stained, or damaged images.

reticulation A wrinkled emulsion surface usually caused by subjecting film to extreme temperature changes during processing.

retouching Hand or computer alteration or enhancement of an image.

reversal Transformation of a negative image into a positive, or vice versa.

reversal film Transparency film intended to produce a positive image from first processing (direct positive). Actually, reversal film is first developed to a negative, which is bleached away during processing; a positive image is then formed from the silver not previously used to form the negative.

revolving back Camera back that permits changing between horizontal and vertical formats without tilting the camera or removing the film back.

RGB Red, Green, and Blue. The three additive colors of light used to produce video and computer images.

rim light Light coming from behind the subject that produces a bright outline, such as on a portrait profile.

ring light A circular flashtube that surrounds the lens.

rise and shift View-camera adjustments that allow some control over framing and perspective; generally used in conjunction with swings and tilts.

roll film Usually refers to rolls of film (for example, 120 or 220 size) that are supplied on a spool with paper backing and/or leader instead of in a metal or plastic magazine such as 35mm.

ROM Read Only Memory. Computer space reserved for the operating system.

rule of thirds The principle of placing the horizon or main subject away from the center of the image.

Sabattier effect Partial reversal of image tones caused by exposure of an emulsion to light during development; commonly referred to as solarization.

safelight Darkroom illumination of a color that will not fog or expose certain sensitized materials during normal handling and processing.

saturation The intensity or relative brilliance of a color.

scale Range of values that make up an image.

scaling Adjusting image size.

scanner Electronic device resembling a copy machine, that converts an image or object into digital data so that it can be stored, enhanced, and manipulated by a computer.

scannergram An image created by scanning objects into a computer.

screen A surface on which images are projected for viewing or rephotographing. Also, a sheet of glass or film containing a closely spaced pattern of dots or lines to produce a halftone image for reproduction or an overall texture effect in a print.

scrim Translucent material placed between a light source and the subject to partially shade the subject or lessen the intensity of the light.

SCSI Small Computer Systems Interface. A cabling system used to connect peripherals such as scanners and disk drives to a computer.

seamless A long roll of background paper; also describes "perfect" blending of composite images.

secondary colors Complementary colors; for example, cyan, magenta, and yellow each contain equal amounts of two of the primary colors of light.

selective focus Shallow depth of field, concentrating attention on one plane of the scene and throwing other objects out of focus.

selenium toner A chemical solution used between fixing and washing to give a slightly brownish tint and deeper blacks to a black-and-white print and/or to increase archival permanence.

self-timer A device on some cameras that can be set to delay release of the shutter for several seconds, usually so the photographer can get into the picture.

semi-matte Printing paper surface between glossy and matte.

sensitometry Measurement of the light sensitivity of photographic materials.

separations A set of master images of each color (usually cyan, magenta, yellow, and black) from which printing plates are made.

sepia A yellowish-brown color associated with antique photos. Can be achieved by bathing a black-and-white print in sepia toner, exposing color film through a sepia filter, or applying a blend of red or magenta and yellow to a digital image.

service bureau A business that provides digital-imaging services.

set An arrangement of background, furniture, etc., constructed for photography.

shadows Dark parts of a scene; corresponding light parts of a negative.

sharpness Apparent clarity and crispness of definition in a photographic image.

shelf life Length of time chemicals and sensitive materials may be stored without deterioration.

sheet film Film supplied in individual sheets instead of rolls; also referred to as cut film.

shoot Slang for taking a picture; a photo session.

short lens A lens of shorter than normal focal length; usually a wide-angle lens.

short lighting In portraiture, when the main or key light fully illuminates the side of the subject's face that is turned away from the camera. The effect is to narrow a broad face, emphasize facial contours, and conceal blemishes on the face and neck.

shortstop (see stop bath)

shutter A mechanical device, sometimes electronically controlled, that determines the length of time light is allowed to enter the camera.

shutter priority A mode of automatic camera operation in which the photographer selects the shutter speed and the aperture is adjusted automatically.

shutter speed The duration of exposure; usually indicated on the camera as the denominator of a fraction of a second — for example, 250=1/250 second.

sidelight Light shining on the subject from one side.

silhouette A scene or image in which the subject is dark against a brightly lighted background.

silica gel A moisture-absorbing material used in packing and storing photographic equipment.

silver halides Light-sensitive chemical compounds in photographic emulsions.

silver recovery Chemical processes for reclaiming silver from used processing solutions and discarded emulsions.

single-lens reflex A camera in which the image formed by the lens is reflected by a mirror, usually through a prism, onto the ground glass of the viewfinder. The mirror swings out of the way during exposure.

single-weight Relatively thin photographic paper.

skin tone Usually the most important value in pictures of people; Zone VI for Caucasians, Zone V for darker complexions.

skylight filter A pale pinkish filter intended to absorb ultraviolet and some visible blue light, giving a warmer hued color image under hazy or overcast conditions.

slave A flash unit that is not wired to the master unit, but is triggered by its flash or by a radio signal.

slide A transparency mounted in a cardboard, plastic, metal, or glass frame and viewed by projection on a screen; also the opaque cover of a film holder.

slow An emulsion that has relatively low sensitivity to light; a lens with a small maximum aperture; a long shutter speed.

SLR Abbreviation for Single-Lens Reflex camera.

snappy Slang for contrasty.

snapshot A casual photograph made with a hand held camera; a personal picture that may not appeal to other people.

snoot An opaque tube placed over the front of a studio light to narrow its beam.

sodium thiosulfate A main ingredient in most fixers.

soft Low in contrast; also, lacking in sharpness.

softbox A large, tent-like diffuser placed around a light source.

soft focus Blurred, diffused, or slightly out of focus.

software Programs stored on magnetic or optical disks or other media that enable a computer to process digital information.

solarization Partial reversal of tones caused by extreme overexposure; often used to describe the Sabattier effect.

solutions Processing chemicals dissolved in water for use.

soup Slang for developer.

SPE Society for Photographic Education. An association primarily for educators and students interested in fine-art photography.

spectrum The systematic arrangement of electromagnetic energy according to wavelength. Visible light makes up a portion of the electromagnetic spectrum, which can be observed in the rainbow effect of a prism.

specular highlights Very bright, mirrorlike reflections without detail.

speed (see also fast and slow) Sensitivity to light; also a shutter setting.

spherical aberration A lens defect that permits light rays to form the image in a curved, rather than in a flat plane.

spill Stray, unwanted light from a source improperly aimed or masked.

split-image Rangefinder in which two halves of an image must be brought together to focus the camera.

split toning Partially toning an image to vary the color effect.

spotlight A studio light using a lens or reflector to concentrate the light to a narrow beam.

spot meter An exposure meter especially suited for use with the Zone System because it enables measurement of the reflected brightnesses of very small areas.

SpoTone® Trade mark of a spotting dye used for retouching prints.

spotting Retouching small image defects.

squeegee A sponge or rubber blade for removing excess surface water from films and prints.

stabilization A rapid processing technique that yields prints of good quality but limited permanence.

stain A unwanted darkened or colored area within a photographic image, usually caused either by incomplete processing or by oxidation or chemical contamination.

static eliminator A device or substance for reducing the accumulation of dust on films.

step wedge A transparent gray scale used either for calculating print exposure or for calibrating a densitometer.

stereo camera A camera for making 3D pictures. Usually equipped with two lenses separated by the distance between human eyes.

stippling In spotting a print, making small adjacent dots that blend together when viewed from a distance.

stock photo A file image for resale.

stock solution A chemical solution stored in concentrated form, but intended to be diluted into a working solution for use.

stop An f/stop or aperture setting; also any change in exposure that doubles or halves the previous setting; also stop bath or shortstop, the acid rinse bath between developer and fixer.

stop bath A dilute solution of acetic acid used between developer and fixer to neutralize the alkalinity of the developer and prolong the life of the fixer; also called shortstop or simply stop.

stopping down Decreasing the size of the lens aperture; using a larger f/number — for example, stopping down from f/8 to f/11.

straight print Unmanipulated; with no dodging or burning-in.

stringer Slang for a free-lancer employed occasionally by a publication or agency.

strobe An electronic flash unit capable of flashing several times per second; the term often is applied inaccurately to describe any electronic flash unit.

studio A room for making photographs; also, a photographic business.

study A carefully composed still photograph.

stylus A pen-like device for creating computer images on a graphics tablet.

subject A person, object, or view photographed. The term object generally refers to an inanimate subject, although the terms are considered interchangeable.

subminiature A still camera that uses film smaller than 35mm.

subtractive colors The secondary hues (cyan, magenta and yellow) that are complementary to the red, green, and blue light primaries. Cyan, magenta, and yellow are the basic colors used in color emulsions and graphic reproduction because each of the three colors subtracts from white light all wave lengths except that of the desired primary.

superimpose To place one image over another.

supplementary lens A simple lens or lens system attached to a camera lens to effectively shorten or lengthen its focal length.

swing and tilt View-camera adjustments that allow control over framing and perspective and maximum depth of field; generally used in conjunction with rise and shift adjustments.

sync cord An electrical wire connecting a flash unit to a shutter.

synchronization (see flash synchronization)

Syquest A type of removable-disk storage system.

T Time. A marked speed on some shutters; similar to B (Bulb), except that a shutter set on T will remain open until the shutter release is depressed again or the shutter is recocked.

tabletop photography Still-life photography of small objects or miniature models.

tacking iron A small electrically-heated tool used to attach dry-mounting tissue to the back of a print and to the mounting board before insertion into a dry-mounting press.

take-up spool The spool or core upon which film is wound in a camera or processor.

taking lens The lower lens of a twin-lens reflex camera; the lens that forms the image reaching the film.

tank (see developing tank)

tear sheet A page (or copy of a page) showing published work to be filed or included in a display or portfolio.

telephoto A compact lens of long focal length. A telephoto lens is designed to form an enlarged image of a distant subject.

tenting Surrounding an object with white or translucent material that will permit control of highlights and reflections.

test strip A small test print made from a representative area of the negative. Usually exposed in segments at progressively increasing times, the developed test strip provides a range from which to estimate the exposure and contrast required for the final print.

texture screen A pattern of lines, dots or designs printed on film; the pattern is superimposed on a print from any negative printed through it.

thermal dye transfer (see dye sublimation)

thin A transparent image, usually a negative, of very low overall density.

three-quarter view A viewpoint intermediate between front and side, or between full face and profile; a portrait that includes head and torso.

through-the-lens meter An exposure meter with sensors placed inside the camera, often on the mirror of an SLR or on the ground glass of a view camera, so that reflected light readings are made of the light transmitted through the lens. A TTL meter usually eliminates the need for compensating for lens extension and filter factors.

thumb spot A mark placed on the lower left front corner of a slide mount to show how the slide should be held for viewing and projection.

TIFF Tagged Image File Format. Commonly used format for storage and retrieval of digital images.

tight framing Filling the viewfinder with the subject so that no later cropping will be required.

time and temperature The method for controlling film development by strict adherence to a predetermined development time at a carefully maintained temperature.

time exposure An exposure usually ranging from more than one second to as long as several minutes, the shutter generally being set either to T or B.

TLR Abbreviation for Twin-Lens Reflex camera.

tonality The range of gray values in a black-and-white photograph, or the quality of color.

tone A value of gray or color intensity; also to impart an overall color to an image by soaking in a chemical toner solution.

tone-line process A method for producing a high-contrast photographic image from a negative combined with a positive transparency.

toner A chemical solution used for overall coloring of an image or for improving archival permanence.

toning Changing the color of a photographic image, usually a print, by immersing it in a chemical solution following the fixing bath. Special toners are used also to increase archival permanence.

translucent Describes material that diffuses light passing through it, but does not allow objects to be seen clearly.

transparency A photographic image, usually a positive, that is intended to be viewed either directly by transmitted light or by projection.

transparent Clear; capable of transmitting light without diffusing it.

tray A shallow, open, rectangular dish in which prints, and sometimes films, are processed.

tripod An adjustable three-legged camera support.

TTL Abbreviation for Through-The-Lens exposure meter.

tungsten film Color film intended to be exposed by tungsten or incandescent light, usually of 3200°K.

tungsten light Incandescent illumination at the warm (yellowish) end of the Kelvin color temperature scale.

twin-lens reflex A type of camera that employs two similar but separate lenses: one for viewing and focusing and the other taking the picture.

ultraviolet A band of short, invisible electromagnetic wavelengths adjacent to the visible blue-violet, to which most photographic materials are highly sensitive.

umbrella A reflective, umbrella-shaped reflector attached to a light source; a black non-reflective umbrella-shaped shading device.

underdevelopment Given less development than normal; caused by shorter time, cooler temperature, insufficient agitation, or diluted, exhausted, or contaminated developer. Resulting in less density and lower contrast.

underexposure Too little light reaching photosensitive material. Resulting either in a thin negative, an unacceptably light print, or a reversal transparency with excessive density.

unipod (see monopod)

UV filter A clear glass or very pale yellowish filter intended to absorb some of the invisible ultraviolet wavelengths that may cause hazy effects and overall bluishness in photographs of distant scenes. Often referred to as a haze filter, a UV filter is used by many photographers as a protective lens cover.

values The relative intensities or brightnesses of gray or color comprising a photographic image.

vapor lamps Common ambient light sources such as sodium and mercury lamps that give light of a color temperature that must be corrected with filters to balance with color films.

variable-contrast paper Printing paper that permits varying the contrast of the image with filters or by adjusting the amounts of yellow or magenta light transmitted through the negative.

videographer Operator of a video camera and recording equipment.

videography Electronic video imaging.

view camera A large-format, tripod-mounted sheet-film camera used mostly for photography of the natural landscape and for architectural and commercial illustration. The inverted image must be focused on a ground-glass screen at the back of the camera. In addition to a long bellows for close-up work, most view cameras provide extensive adjustments, called swing, tilt, rise and shift that allow considerable control over image perspective and depth of field.

viewfinder A device for aiming a camera and framing the image.

vignetting Isolating part of an image from the background or blending the image into the background. May be done at the camera, during enlargement of the negative, or in a computer; also unintentional cutting off of the corners of a picture by a lens shade, filters, etc. Pronounced vin-yet-ting.

warm tones Brownish or reddish overall tinting in a black-and-white image, particularly in the darker areas; in color, the red-orange-yellow portion of the spectrum as well as the brown or "earth" hues.

washed-out A weak, pale, unsaturated image such as results from underexposure of a print from a negative or overexposure of a reversal transparency.

washing aid A chemical bath used to remove fixer from film or prints, shorten washing time, and increase permanence.

water-bath development A technique of soaking film alternately in water and developer. The purpose is to obtain maximum shadow detail in the negative without overdeveloping the highest values.

watt-seconds A relative measure of the power output of electronic flash units.

wavelength The distinguishing characteristic of each portion of the visible electromagnetic spectrum that causes it to be perceived as a distinct color.

weight Thickness of photographic paper base or mounting board.

wet mounting Attaching a print to a surface with a liquid adhesive.

wetting agent A final rinse for film that reduces surface tension so the film dries faster and with fewer water spots.

white light Illumination, usually consisting of a mixture of all wavelengths, to which photographic materials are normally exposed. The proportion of each wavelength present determines the color temperature of the light.

wide-angle A short-focal-length lens with an angular coverage greater than that of a normal lens of the same focal length.

Windows™ A Microsoft computer operating system; also interactive menus and dialog boxes.

wipe A transition in which one projected or video image replaces another along a border that moves across the screen.

working solution Photographic chemicals properly mixed, diluted, and ready for use in processing.

X Flash-synchronization marking on some shutters and cameras to indicate the setting or contact point for electronic flash.

Zip drive A type of removable-disk storage system.

zone A value or tone of gray corresponding to one step in the nine-step gray scale that is the basis for the Zone System of exposure and development control.

zone focus To preset the focus of a lens in anticipation of action to take place within the expected depth of field.

Zone System A systematic exposure and development method for controlling the relationship between subject brightness range, negative density and contrast, and print values.

zoom lens A lens adjustable within a specified range of focal lengths.

"As you learn and grow as a human being, that becomes what you bring to your art."

— Victoria Littna, painter

"It is not half so important to know as to feel."

— Rachel Carson, author-naturalist

"There are ... pictures that have what I call 'magic' in them where you can look at the photograph and have some delight that is beyond just a reproduction of the real thing."

—Barbara Crane, educator

JENNIFER HARRIS

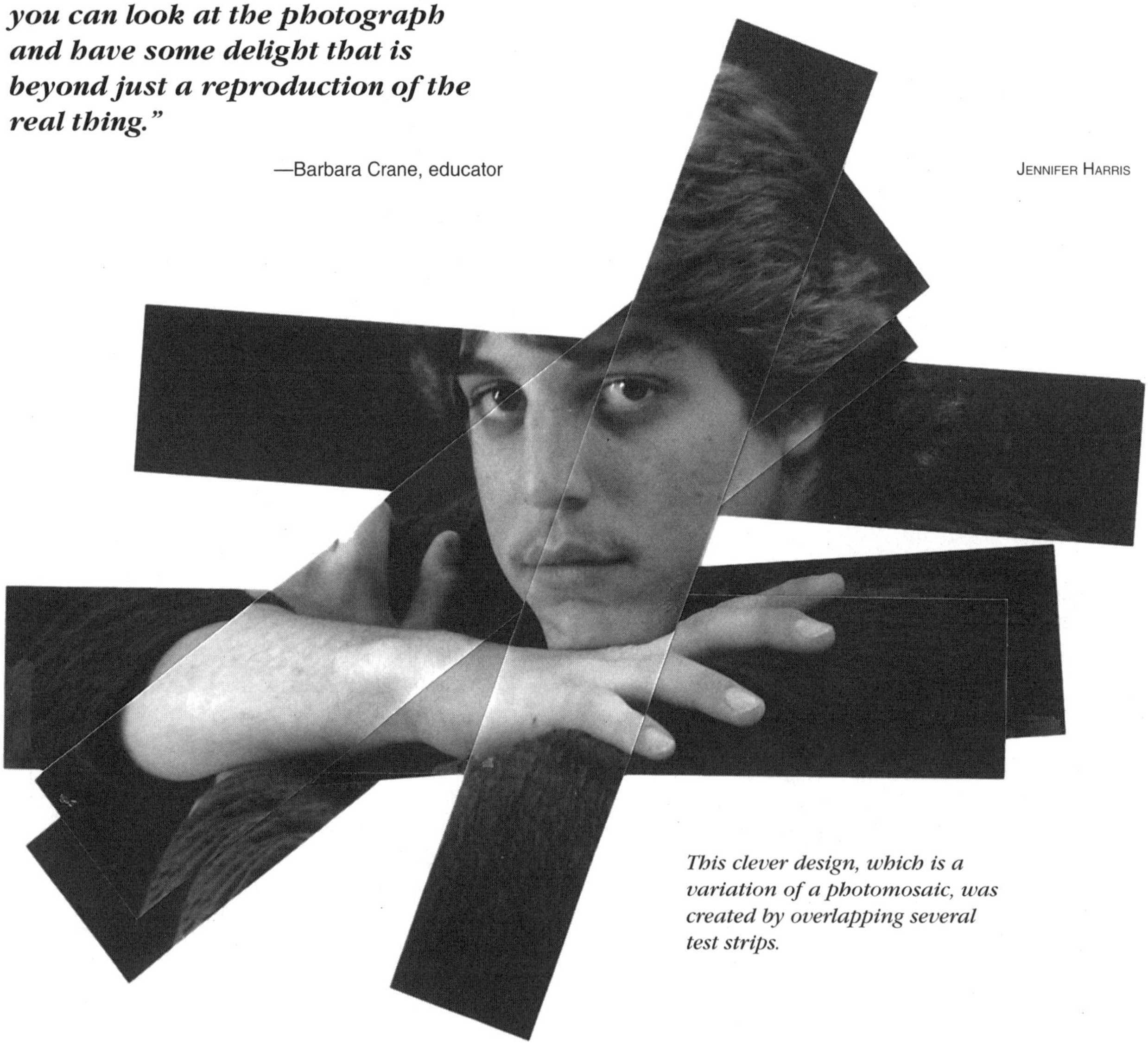

This clever design, which is a variation of a photomosaic, was created by overlapping several test strips.

References

Books about Imaging

Hundreds of fine books of photographs and books about photography and digital imaging are available for every level of interest and taste. Some are monographs featuring the work of one photographer; others reproduce collections of photographs on a theme or catalog an exhibition representing the work of several photographers. Many books are how-to-do-its on specific aspects of the craft. Some of these publications can be found in local libraries, bookstores, museum stores, and photographic dealers. Among firms publishing catalogs of books for sale by mail are the following, which specialize in imaging:

A Photographer's Place, 133 Mercer St., New York NY 10012. (212-431-9358)

Aperture, 20 East 23rd St., New York, NY 10010. (212-505-5555).

Calumet, 890 Supreme Drive, Bensenville IL 60106. (800-225-8638).

The Maine Photographic Resource, 2 Central Street, Rockport, ME 04856. (800-227-1541).

Photo-Eye, 376 Garcia St., Santa Fe NM 87501. (505-988-5152). www.photoeye.com

A few favorite titles

Adobe Systems, Inc., *Adobe Photoshop* and *Advanced Photoshop.* Macmillan Computer Publishing, Indianapolis, 1997. (Classroom in a Book) 1-800-428-5331. Very practical tutorials for building imaging software skills. Each volume includes a CD-ROM.

Adams, Ansel. *The Camera.* New York Graphic Society, Boston, 1980. A survey of equipment in all formats, with Adams' own point of view of the effects of cameras and lens on visualization. Excellent brief summary of view camera adjustments.

Adams, Ansel. *The Negative,* New York Graphic Society, Boston, 1981. Explains the Zone System and reveals technical procedures recommended and followed by this master of large-format photography.

Adams, Ansel. *The Print,* New York Graphic Society, Boston, 1983. Describes Adams' procedures for making and finishing his own extraordinarily fine prints.

Adams, Ansel. *Examples — The Making of 40 Photographs.* New York Graphic Society, Boston, 1983. Adams describes here some of the circumstances and technical considerations involved in the making of several of his favorite photographs.

Kodak Index to Photographic Information, revised periodically. Eastman Kodak Company, Rochester NY 14650. (Publication No. L-1) 1-800-242-2424. Lists hundreds of books and pamphlets sold or distributed by Kodak on nearly every photographic topic. http://www.kodak.com/cihome/products/L1

Newhall, Beaumont. *The History of Photography,* 5th ed. The Museum of Modern Art, 11 West 53rd St., New York, NY 10019, 1982. A classic history of photographic art and technology.

Photographer's Market, revised periodically. Writer's Digest Books, 1507 Dana Ave., Cincinnati, OH 45207. A directory of buyers of photographs, including agencies and galleries. Advice to the free-lancer about exhibiting and selling.

Szarkowski, John. *Looking at Photographs.* The Museum of Modern Art, 11 West 53rd St., New York, NY 10019, 1973. Penetrating essays commenting on one hundred significant photographs selected from the Museum's collection.

Szarkowski, John. *Photography Until Now.* The Museum of Modern Art, 11 West 53rd St., New York, NY 10019, 1989. A selectively illustrated and well-written history.

Weston, Edward. *The Daybooks of Edward Weston: Volume I — Mexico; Volume II — California.* Horizon Press, New York, 1966. Through his personal journals, Weston gives us extraordinary insight into the creative process.

Uelsmann, Jerry N. *Process and Perception.* University of Florida Press, 15 NW 15th Street, Gainsesville, FL 32603, 1985. A collection of several of Uelsmann's provocative composite images, with explanations of how some of them were created in the darkroom.

Workshops

"When everyone works together a workshop can be a truly inspirational event, one that can start you on a career or open your eyes to a new way of thinking, seeing and photographing."

— George Schaub, photographer

Workshops are everywhere. Most of them are expensive, many are held in scenic resort areas, but workshops are the best way to meet and learn from men and women who are tops in their field. Some offer college or adult-education credits. Whatever your interest, there's a workshop. Most attendees find the change of scene relaxing and the experience worthwhile. The following contacts are among many helpful sources of catalogs, schedules, and other information:

Brooks Institute of Photography
801 Alston Road
Santa Barbara, CA 93108
(805) 966-3888
www.brooks.edu

The Maine Photographic Workshops
Box 200
Rockport, ME 04856
(207) 236-8581
www.MEWorkshops.com

Palm Beach Photographic Centre
55 Northeast Second Avenue
Delray Beach, FL 33444
(561) 276-9797

Rochester Institute of Technology
One Lomb Memorial Drive
Rochester, NY 14623
(800) 724-2536
www.rit.edu/RIT/AA/CCE/TPD

Santa Fe Photography and Digital Workshops
PO Box 9916
Santa Fe, NM 87504
(505) 983-1400
www.sfworkshop.com

Winona International School of Professional Photography
57 Forsyth St. NW, Suite 1500
Atlanta, GA 30303
1-800-742-7468
www.ppa—world.org

Professional Associations

Most people join associations so they can interact with others, find job placement opportunities, and qualify for group insurance. There are many specialized and local affiliations, but these three organizations form the foundation of professional imaging groups in the U.S.A.

ASMP (American Society of Media Photographers, Inc.)
14 Washington Road, Suite 502
Princeton Junction, NJ 08550-1033
(609) 799-8300
www.asmp.org

NPPA (National Press Photographers Association, Inc.)
3200 Croasdaile Drive, Suite 306
Durham, NC 27705
(800) 289-6772
http://sunsite.unc.edu.nppa

PP of A (Professional Photographers of America, Inc.)
57 Forsythe Street NW, Suite 1600
Atlanta, GA 30303
(800) 786-6277
www.ppa—world.org

"Art is a means of communicating with people; not an aim in itself."

—Modest Moussorgsky, composer

Photo Credits

Parenthetical *italics* following a page number show the number of images on that page by the person named.

Chris Adamo (3)

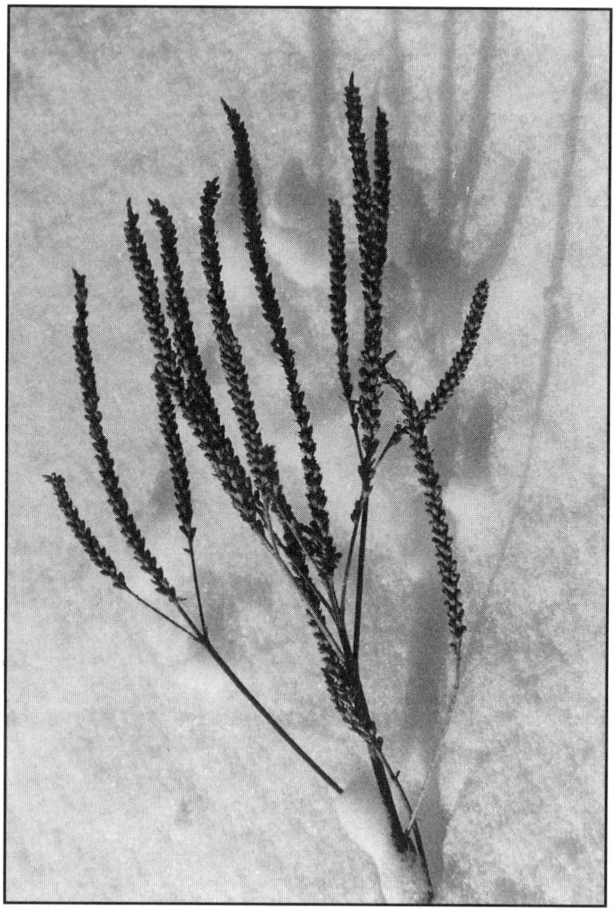

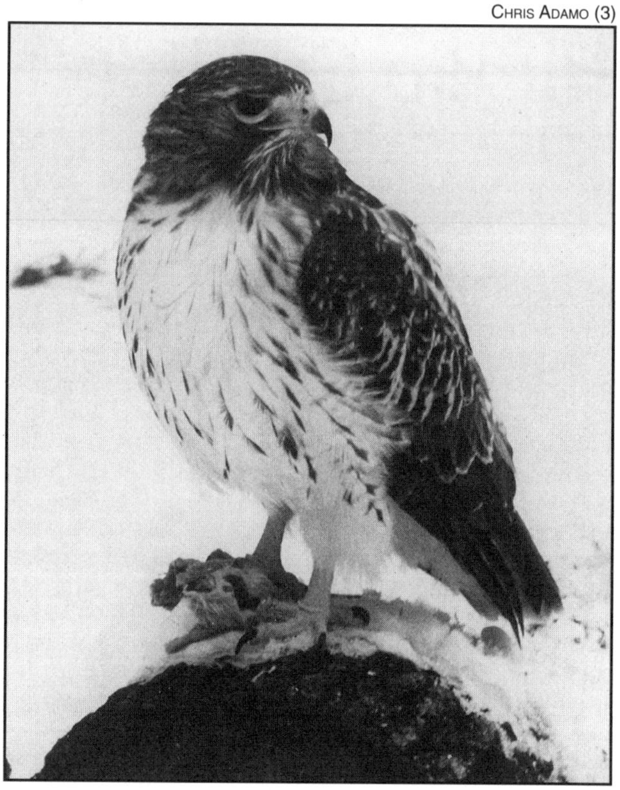

Don't let weather keep you from making pictures. On this winter day, one observant photographer found lots of interesting subject matter.

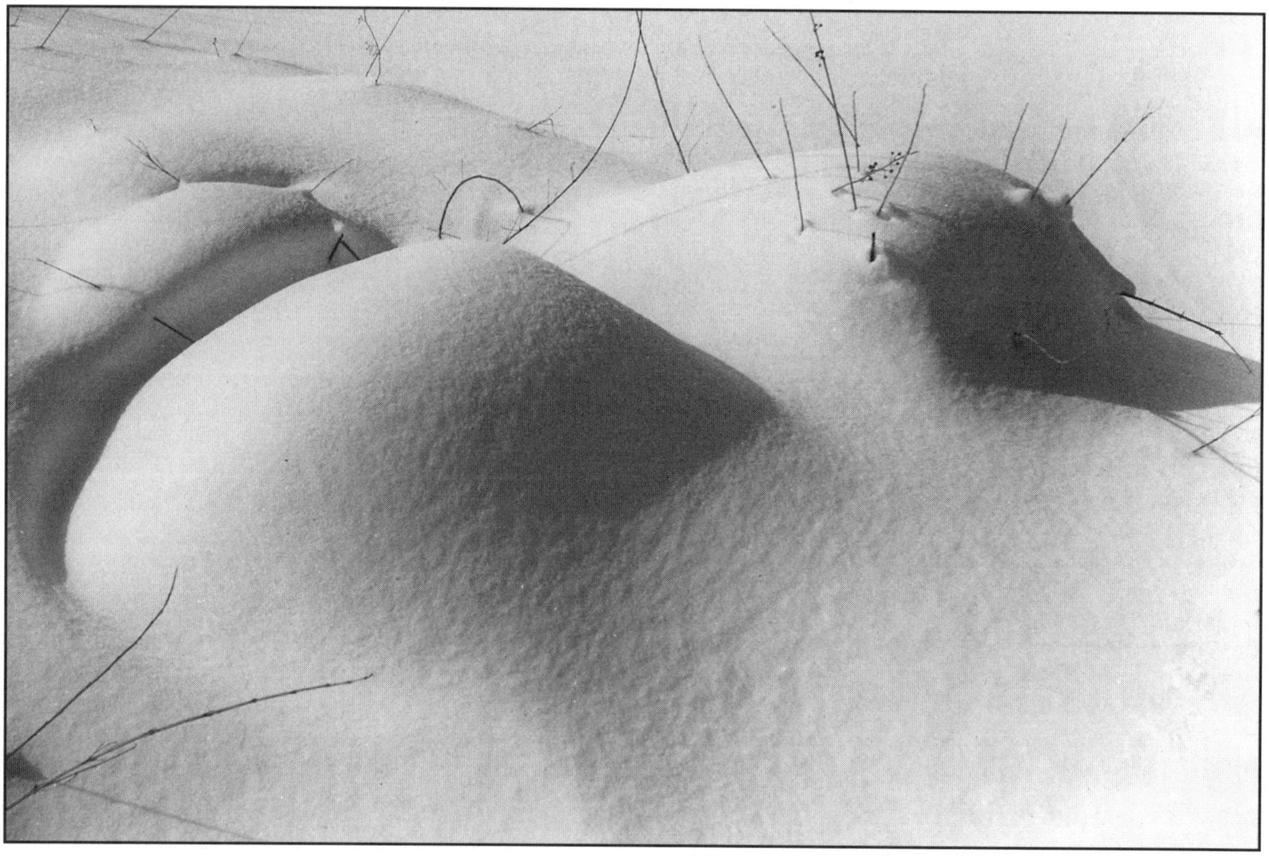

Subject Index

Page numbers in *italics* refer to quotations by the person named.

ERICA SIEGL

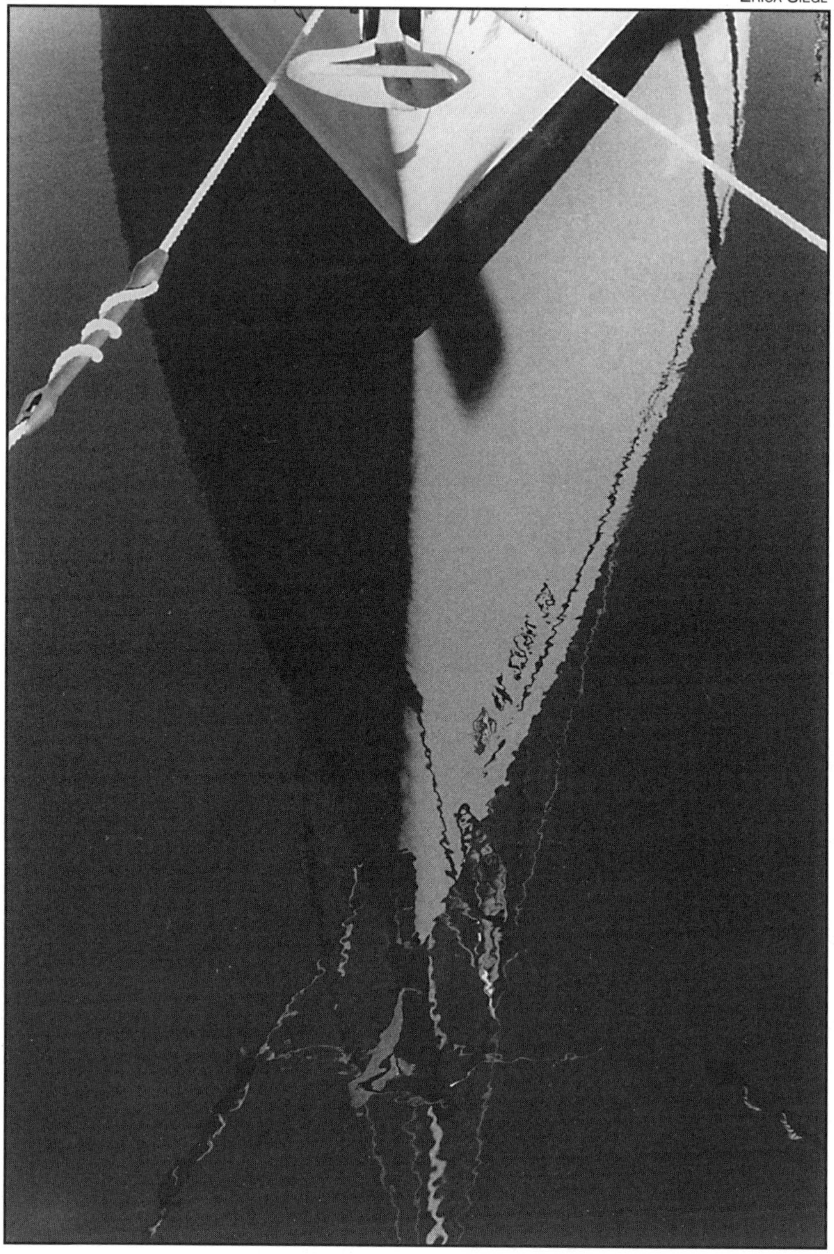

This page is approximately the same value as an 18-percent gray card (Zone V)

This page is approximately the same value as an 18-percent gray card (Zone V)